Just Call Me Coach

by Coach Dick Strahm

Printed in the U.S.A. by Kennedy Printing Company © 2008

To my wife, Ginger, who has been so supportive throughout my coaching career and my health problems. You will always be my best friend.

To my children Doug, Gina, and Steve, thank you for your loving support. You are all number one in my heart.

To three very special people: my mother and father, Mildred and Mentzer Strahm, who are now with God, and to my brother, Dale.

In loving memory of Gil Hyland, who was the first person to convince me this story needed to be told.

To every person who has faced catastrophic illness with courage and grace.

The University of Findlay's 1997 coaching staff. The 1997 team won the NAIA National Championship and was the first staff and team to have a 14-0 season.

Contents

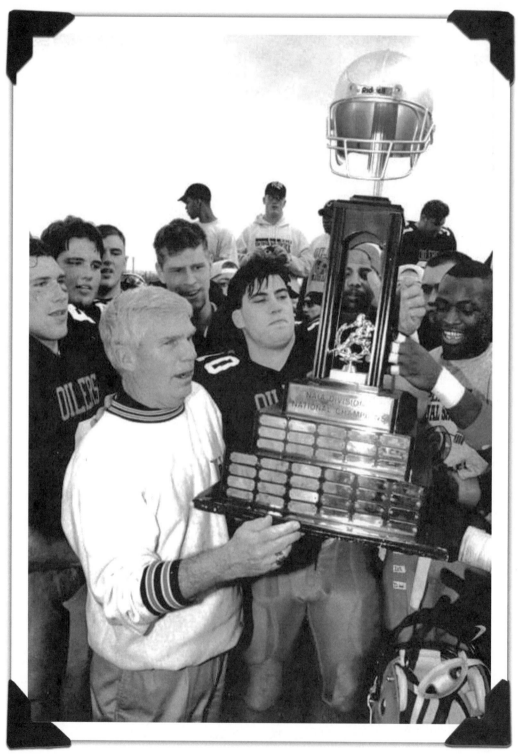

1997 Oilers celebrating their National Championship.

The Coach's Introduction

The idea for this book was hatched during a three-hour lunch with a friend of mine, Gil Hyland, the owner of Warehouse Carpet One, back in the spring of 2003. During our lengthy conversation, I told a lot of my "war" stories, and, believe me, when you coach football for more than four decades, you accumulate a lot of stories! Along the way, I've also had more than my share of health issues, and Gil and I talked a lot about health as well.

I met Gil for the first time when I was asked to speak at a father-son banquet at St. Gerard's Elementary School a couple of years earlier. Both Gil and I had battled prostate cancer, and I think it was that and a shared love of football that helped to form our friendship. Gil had been a defensive lineman back in his collegiate days at Xavier University.

During our lunch conversation, it was Gil who said, "Coach, you ought to write a book." When I asked him if he was kidding, he said that he was very serious. I took that thought with me when I drove back to my home in Findlay in the late afternoon.

So, I talked to my lunch gang about it, which consists of longtime friends Dave Kuenzli, Tom Buis, Jim Houdeshell, and Jim Dysinger. These guys, along with me, are the original members of the group that has been meeting every Friday for lunch for a number of years. We'd like to think we've solved most of the world's problems during our lunches. When I brought the subject up about a book, they were all very supportive of the idea.

I also talked to my family, and they all thought it was a good idea, too. My wife, Ginger, has always been so supportive of my coaching career, as have been Gina, my daughter, and my sons, Doug and Steve.

It was then I called Gerry Faust, the former head football coach at the University of Notre Dame, someone I've known through coaching circles for a number of years. He'd recently had a book done entitled The Golden Dream and gave me some ideas on how to get started. Gerry said to start by writing down some memories, then get a tape recorder, and start talking.

After making a number of tapes on my career from coaching high school and then moving on into college, my daughter Gina said that one of her friends could type the content of the tapes. So, Lisa Wojtkowiak spent many hours doing just that.

When she was done, she gave the transcriptions of the tapes to Gina to give to me. I read the pages over and thought they were a nice recollection of many of the people and games so memorable to me. However, I knew that what I had was pretty rough. I felt there were some good stories there, but a lot of them were not in the right sequence, and I certainly knew there were probably many problems with grammar and writing style, elements a little out of my areas of expertise.

After I was done, I decided that what I had could never be made into a book, certainly not by me, so I put the script in a drawer and thought, if nothing else, what I had would be something nice for my grandson, Hunter, to read over someday after I'm gone, and it would give him a good idea of what his grandpa was all about.

I was working as the vice president for institutional advancement after I retired from coaching football at The University of Findlay and just didn't have the time to think much more about Gil's whole book idea.

After I left that particular job and took a part-time position at the university, I got another call in August of 2006 from Gil, and he told me he wanted me to meet him and another friend,

Jerry O'Connor, a retired businessman from Lima, for lunch. He said he had a friend who was a retired high school English teacher and was now a freelance writer named John Grindrod who would also be there.

Gil told me he'd talked to John about the possibility of writing my life story, and he seemed interested. Gil said John was a newspaper columnist for the Lima News and also wrote monthly features for one of the local magazines in Lima. Gil also told me John had already written a book that was a biography, so he'd had some experience with the type of writing needed for my book. I figured I didn't have much to lose by talking about resurrecting the idea of getting a book done, so I agreed to drive down to Lima and meet for lunch.

At lunch, John told me he thought he could write my book and gave me some direction in making more tapes, this time, putting my stories in the right time sequence. I decided then to hire John. So, I went back to work and made more tapes, and this time, a young lady by the name of Kathy Launder, who worked at the mayor's office in Findlay, typed them for me so that I could give them to John.

And, that's how it all started. Obviously, there was so much work that needed to be done, but John and I worked together, and a couple of years later, the book is completed. My thanks to John for his talent and perseverance in putting my story on paper, and also to Charlene Hankinson, a friend who worked with me at The University of Findlay, particularly during the time that I served as vice president of institutional advancement. She agreed to edit the book for us.

I also want to thank Pat Gibson, who proved to be as good helping with the photo layout of this book as he was clearing a path for Oilers running backs as a two-time NAIA All-American offensive lineman in 1978, and again in 1979.

I must thank Stan Kujawa, who provided Joy Yeater from Monkey Media Productions for the design of the book jacket.

Dr. James Houdeshell, colleague and former athletic director, was a silent partner, assisting me with gathering some of the information used in this book, and whose phenomenal memory of people and events related to The University of Findlay's sports programs was very helpful.

Larry Alter, sports editor and a longtime friend, who wrote almost every game story during my 24 years as head football coach for The University of Findlay, created an invaluable record chronicling the plays and the players. John and I relied on his records for accuracy in recreating games past. He also was generous in supplying any additional information we requested.

Sadly, the man whose idea it was that I pursue the notion of a book passed away just a couple of months after the lunch he arranged when I first met John, and that will always be my regret, that cancer took Gil Hyland before he could see what his idea eventually produced.

As far the book, as I used to say before each season's opener to my assistant coaches, "Let the games begin!"

Dick Strahm

Prologue

As I sat before Dick Strahm during my initial meeting to hear of his desire to assist someone in creating a book detailing his life, I had no idea how badly I would eventually yearn to be that someone. With pocket tape recorder in hand, I came at the behest of a mutual friend, Gil Hyland, to meet someone whom I had long known about by reputation but had never met face to face. Another of Dick Strahm's longtime admirers and friends, Jerry O'Connor, made the table a foursome.

I came originally intending to listen to Dick's book idea but also had more of a personal agenda. I wanted to mine enough nuggets from our conversation to create a feature magazine piece on the man who guided The University of Findlay (Ohio) Oilers to four National Association of Intercollegiate Athletics (NAIA) football national championships.

As a freelance journalist, I realized my forté was writing shorter pieces for newspapers and magazines rather than writing books. As far as writing a book, well, you might say I had limited experience. I had written one other, that a short biography of an Ohio businessman, a graduate of The University of Findlay by the name of Harold Breidenbach, who commissioned me to write the book as a legacy for his children and grandchildren, sort of a testimony of where he had been and what he had experienced.

However, the more I listened to Coach Strahm talk about his remarkable life, the more I wanted to create more than the standard couple thousand words for the local magazine for which I contribute two pieces a month.

As I watched Dick closely while the small tape recorder whirred at a restaurant called Burgundy's in Lima, an Ohio town a couple dozen miles south on Interstate 75 from Strahm's Findlay, I jotted down some additional observations and insights as we awaited soups and salads.

I was struck by the fact that often the most impressive of men come in rather small packages. Dick Strahm is substantially less than six feet tall but retains the powerful upper body of a former athlete.

He's also a man who relishes every moment of his current status, that of a retired small-college football coach. He is a husband, a father, and a grandfather and a man approaching his mid-70s. He's also a man three different doctors felt would surely not be here discussing a book idea in August of 2006.

Strahm has that central-casting look about him. If a Hollywood producer were looking for someone to play a tough old-school football coach whose softer side resides under the veneer of several decades of being a tough mentor in the toughest of sports, he would look for someone exactly like the former Findlay Oilers football coach. There is the full head of silver hair and the strong gaze that demands the attention of all he addresses.

If you look hard enough at Dick Strahm, you may just see what I saw, a survivor. Dick achieved remarkable success as a football coach on both the high-school level, and especially the collegiate level, in a career that started during the Eisenhower presidency and didn't end until Bill Clinton was halfway through his second term. Despite these significant accomplishments, he achieved his greatest victories far from the football field.

He has faced daunting health issues, including two bouts of cancer, five heart attacks, quadruple bypass open-heart surgery, and a stroke. He also has faced the dire prognostications from three doctors who told him in 1998 that, if all went well, he would have three more years of life.

Yet, Dick continues to embrace life. He currently still resides in his adopted hometown of Findlay. It was a niche he realized and one he has never left from the time of his arrival in 1975 to revive a flagging Findlay Oilers football program.

Since his retirement from the gridiron sideline in 1998, Strahm was named special assistant to the president, and then was asked by President Ken Zirkle to become vice president for institutional advancement. After serving two and a half years and enduring a severe case of shingles, Strahm stepped down as vice president. As of this writing, he is now special assistant to the vice president of development.

He has received a multitude of personal awards, ones that inevitably follow a career that saw him win 80 percent of more than 300 high school and college games over 40-plus years. As a matter of fact, it might take the considerable efforts of mystery novelist Agatha Christie's Hercule Poirot to determine with certainty just exactly how many halls of fame into which Dick Strahm has been inducted.

One thing is for certain, though, and that is the stories that comprise the life of Dick Strahm are as diverse as they are compelling.

No doubt, the most prestigious shrine into which Strahm has been elected is the National Football Foundation and College Hall of Fame in South Bend, Indiana. It is here, ironically, five years after he stepped down from his post as the Oilers football coach that his story begins. For it is only when we can see the crowning achievement of a decades-long pursuit to touch the lives of thousands of young players and truly make a difference that we can see the significance of where Dick Strahm has been and the obstacles he has surmounted.

Many words come to mind when describing Dick Strahm – master motivator, football tactician, charismatic leader, and fighter of indomitable spirit both on the field and in the many doctors' offices and hospitals that have become as much a part of his life as the August two-a-days that were the harbingers to each new season. But, perhaps, the most apt word to describe Dick Strahm is the simplest, winner.

John Grindrod

Chapter 1

Dick and Guys Like Barry and Joe

For Dick Strahm, it was a wonderful moment, a bonding opportunity with his 5-year-old granddaughter, Danielle, as they played in the backyard of Strahm's Findlay, Ohio, home. It was a beautiful Sunday afternoon in May of 2004, and this was the kind of moment Strahm envisioned when he stepped down as the head football coach of The University of Findlay Oilers after the 1998 season. Although his tenure was illustrious, wildly successful by any measuring stick, it was time to concentrate on the business of being the best grandfather in anyone's league to his son-in-law Matt and his daughter Gina's kids, Hunter and the twins, Dalton and Danielle.

Suddenly, Dick's wife, Ginger, appeared at the back door and came into the backyard with a UPS package in hand. Dick recalls the moment. "Heck, I thought it was one of those time-share vacation offers or an offer to buy sunglasses to get a free set of steak knives, that sort of thing. I just told Ginger to throw it on the swing, and I'd look at it later."

As Dick and little Danielle continued to play, the package became a focal point for a certain 5-year-old girl. Finally, she said, "Hey, Poppy. Let's open this up!" Now, everyone knows when a grandpa plays with a grandchild, it's the grandchild who makes all the rules, so it was off to the swing to sit and open the package.

The first line of the letter accompanying the rest of the correspondence that the package contained just about knocked the former Oilers coach right off the swing. "As chairman of the board of directors of the National Football Foundation and College Hall of Fame, I have the honor of notifying you of your election into the College Football Hall of Fame. Congratulations."

Following some additional sentences that Dick's eyes looked at, sentences that never really registered with a mind that was racing in every direction, the name in the complimentary closing was Jon F. Hanson.

By the time Dick got to the full list of the 2004 class of enshrinees, he was truly in awe. He was yelling to anyone within earshot – Ginger; his son Steve, who at that time lived with Dick and Ginger; or even a stray neighbor who might be nearby. He wanted to share this good news

Family and friends gathered at Coach Strahm's August 2004 induction at the College Football Hall of Fame in South Bend, Indiana.

that he would be spending a three-day weekend in August with seventeen former players and four other coaches for the enshrinement festivities.

Suddenly, four were in the backyard when Ginger and Steve arrived on the scene. Dick remembers vividly Ginger and Steve excitedly shuffling through the literature. "Every once in a while I'd hear Steve shout a name. 'Barry Sanders?' 'Darrell Green?' We were all excited."

Of course, Dick remembered virtually every name he read. He remembered Dan Ross, who played for Northeastern University before playing ten years in the NFL. Dick recalled the Super Bowl record Ross set when the Bengals tight end caught eleven passes at the Pontiac Silver Dome against the 49ers back in 1982.

He remembered Joe Theismann, both as the Fighting Irish quarterback of Notre Dame and as a Super Bowl-winning quarterback for the NFL's Washington Redskins.

He remembered Roger Wehrli, the great All-American defensive back for the Missouri Tigers and later an All-Pro in the NFL.

The other names were equally as impressive, names like Billy Neighbors, the big All-American defensive tackle from Alabama's Crimson Tide; Jerry LeVias, the All-American wide receiver for Southern Methodist and the first African-American player in the history of the Southwest Conference; and the late Ricky Bell, the unanimous All-American tailback for Southern Cal and then Tampa Bay Buccaneer running back.

There was big Jimbo Covert, the mammoth offensive tackle of the Pitt Panthers; Tom Brown, the interior lineman who played both offense and defense for the Minnesota Golden Gophers in the early 1960s; and John Rauch, the Georgia Bulldogs quarterback of the late 1940s. In addition, there was Jackie Hunt, the halfback of the late 1930s from Marshall University in West Virginia; Bill Stromberg, the great NCAA Division III wide receiver; and Ron Pritchard, the linebacker from Arizona State. There also was Garney Henley, the halfback from Huron University, North Dakota, and a player who went on to play an incredible sixteen seasons in the Canadian Football League.

Among the coaches who would be joining Strahm were Hayden Fry, who achieved his greatest success coaching the Big Ten's Iowa Hawkeyes; Doug Dickey, who found coaching success at both the University of Tennessee and the University of Florida; Tom Beck, who guided three NCAA Division II and III schools to new heights; and National Association of Intercollegiate Athletics (NAIA) former coaching colleague Charlie Richard, who built the Baker Wildcats in Kansas into one of the top small-college programs in the country before his sudden passing, succumbing to a heart attack while in a coaches' meeting preparing for the 1995 season.

Despite the impressive individual achievements of so many of those Dick would join in the 2004 class, certainly he belonged. In 24 seasons as the head coach of the Findlay Oilers, Strahm guided his teams to 22 winning seasons, 13 conference championships, and 12 NAIA playoff appearances. The crown jewels in his career numbered five – the 1978 national championship runner-up and the four national championships in 1979, 1992, 1995, and 1997. Strahm's cumulative won-loss record was an eye-popping 183-64-5.

However, despite his accomplishments, the very thought of sharing an induction platform with the likes of Theismann, Green, Sanders, and Wehrli and the other big-timers was indeed a humbling feeling. One thing he told both Ginger and Steve between their excited rants was a certainty. "We'll show up!"

Then, of course, it was off to the phone to call his daughter, Gina, and her husband, Matt Kagy, and their two youngsters who called him Poppy, his grandsons Hunter and Dalton. It was, of course, also time to call his son Doug and his wife, Lisa.

It was Doug who had seen about every facet of Dick Strahm there is. Besides growing up under his father's roof, Doug also played two years for his father and later coached on his father's Oilers staff.

Dick also called his brother, Dale, who was nine years younger and a lifelong football coach who, at that time was not only a 29-year veteran of collegiate coaching but also the southwest regional director of college scouting for the NFL's Denver Broncos.

The following week, Strahm received a call from South Bend, where the College Hall of Fame is located. It was a call confirming that all the literature that had arrived UPS was indeed legitimate. It was also a call that gave Dick more details regarding the ceremonies and festivities which would begin Thursday evening, August 12, and extend throughout that weekend. The induction banquet itself would be on Saturday evening.

Dick, of course, was the talk of Findlay, the beautiful and thriving city of around 40,000 in northwest Ohio, located just off Interstate 75 and 47 miles south of the 70-year-old soon-to-be College Football Hall of Famer's birth town of Toledo. It was in Findlay that Strahm first drove in the tent stakes he would not pull up to seek the next big job, which ambitious, aspiring coaches often do. When he finally did retire after the 1998 season, there was never a doubt that he would stay. He felt he was home. He loved Findlay, and Findlay loved the man many simply refer to as "Coach" right back.

Strahm, even in retirement, had maintained his affiliation with the university that he had rewarded with those four NAIA national championships and its well-deserved reputation as one of the most formidable small-college football programs in the country. Upon his retirement, he was offered and accepted a position as special assistant to the president.

It was at Findlay that Dick had made his most lasting professional and personal friendships. Despite the fact that some had moved on, like the former president of The University of Findlay, Dr. Kenneth Zirkle, who served as Findlay's president from 1983 to 2003, there were those whom Strahm grew quickly to respect and admire, like Zirkle's successor, Dr. DeBow Freed. It was Freed, who, upon hearing of the honor Dick was being accorded, immediately cleared his calendar for that mid-August weekend.

There were also The University of Findlay colleagues who had remained. Perhaps none was a more respected colleague and a better friend than Dr. James Houdeshell, the Findlay graduate who returned just two years after his undergraduate years to teach and coach and never left. Known for the myriad of roles he has filled, from coach to athletic director to dean to his current position as special assistant to the president, Houdeshell has demonstrated a love for Findlay that has lasted for more than a half century.

It is Houdeshell who deserves special mention, for it was his decision as athletic director to hire Strahm in 1975. It was also Houdeshell, along with a former player, Kevin Cassidy, who submitted Dick's nomination to the National Football Foundation.

Recalls Houdeshell, "Kevin and I wrote to the College Football Foundation to tell them of the record Dick had amassed. From that point, every time they requested information, I made sure I got it to them, including soliciting some additional letters on Dick's behalf. That was really the easy part because Dick had touched so many lives during his 24 years at Findlay.

Each year, I paid attention to the individuals who were being enshrined. When I started seeing the names of some of the NAIA coaches whose records, although impressive, weren't quite on the same level as Dick's, that's when I decided to get serious about getting something done."

Kevin Cassidy was one of Strahm's first recruits when Dick hit the recruiting trail to put his first Oilers team on the field for 1975. Cassidy, out of Toledo St. John's High School, remembers a promise Strahm made. "When Coach Strahm was recruiting me, he told me, 'Kevin, if you come to Findlay, we'll win a national championship. If you don't come, we'll win a national championship.' I guess I just wanted to play for someone who exuded that kind of confidence."

After that first year in 1975, the linebacker wondered whether Strahm could actually deliver on the promise. "We went 2 and 8 that first year, but by the time I was a senior, we registered the first undefeated regular season in school history and played for a national title. Although we lost to Concordia [Minnesota] 7-0, we had come so close. I stayed in 1979 as a graduate assistant on Coach Strahm's staff, and we won that national championship he promised, beating Northwestern [Iowa], 51-6, so I guess Coach told me the truth."

To Strahm, Cassidy, who has remained a staunch supporter of the Findlay football program, is more like a son than just a former player. "While by no means was Kevin the best player who ever played for me, he was a very solid player. What makes him so special to me? I suppose it's because he was there at the beginning when I first put a team on the field for what was then called Findlay College. He felt the sting of going 2 and 8 that first season and then saw what can happen with hard work and with cultivating that special bond that some teams develop. Kevin, to me, is the embodiment of the privilege that a profession like coaching affords."

In late May, Strahm received a congratulatory phone call from a former coaching colleague, Fred Martinelli, a very successful high-school coach at Bryan (Ohio), where Dick also had coached after Martinelli left, and an even more successful collegiate coach at Ashland (Ohio) College. Martinelli had himself been inducted into the College Hall of Fame a few years earlier and wanted to prepare Dick for what he would experience. Recalls Strahm, "Fred told me that every induction I've experienced would pale in comparison. He said the experience would be mind boggling. While I'm certainly proud of every organization which has ever deemed me worthy of inclusion into its hall, Fred's prediction really piqued my curiosity."

The summer days rolled by, and while there would be the usual cookouts and fun with family and friends, Dick, and many in Findlay for that matter, eagerly anticipated the experience that lay ahead in South Bend, Indiana.

When asked by the press what it meant to be selected for inclusion in such an honored institution, especially by those like the sports editor of Findlay's *The Courier* and long-time friend, Larry Alter, a man with such respect for Strahm that he is one of those in Findlay who will only address him as "Coach," Strahm spoke without a hint of false humility. "This is not an 'I' award. This is a 'We' award. Although I will be the one to get my name in the College Hall of Fame, I hope that every coach who ever coached with me and every player whoever played for me realizes he will be with me. It might sound corny, I know, but every one of them is a part of this award."

Alter remembers his relationship with Strahm during his coaching tenure was vastly different than what exists between many coaches and writers. "Often, the relationship between a writer and a coach is an uneasy one, but Coach and I have always had a unique relationship.

I think what helped us become such great personal friends is that when I was covering Dick's program, I never told him how to coach, and he never told me what to write. I think from the mutual professional respect has grown a great personal friendship."

Alter searched for what Strahm's greatest strength was. "Well, I'll say this. He could absolutely X and O with the best of them. Anyone who was as successful as he was had to have an excellent grasp of the technical aspects of the game, but I don't think it was his greatest strength. Rather, it was his ability to both recruit and garner support from anyone and everyone for his program that, I believe, set him apart. He could absolutely befriend anyone. Heck, I think he even could have befriended a dog if he thought it could help his program."

When one is welcomed into a respected organization, it is customary to do some fact finding on what he is joining, which is precisely what Strahm did. Despite not being what the old coach might say, "Mr. Technology," he was able to find some websites and did some reading about the National Football Foundation and its College Hall of Fame.

At that time, more than 900 legendary players and coaches from NCAA Division I, I-AA, II, and III, and the NAIA were enshrined in the Hall. Dick found out he'd be joining some coaching legends – men like Woody Hayes and Ara Parseghian and Vince Dooley.

To be eligible for inclusion into the Hall as a coach, an individual must have been a head coach for at least ten years, coached at least 100 games, and won at least 60 percent of those games. Strahm easily qualified using those criteria, having coached 234 games over 24 years and winning not 60 percent but 80 percent of those contests.

The College Hall of Fame was first established in 1951 by the National Football Foundation and, for years, was located in King's Mill, Ohio, just outside of Cincinnati. The current building was constructed in football-and-Notre Dame-crazy South Bend in 1995.

There, visitors to the Hall see the rich history of college football, recapturing the thrills and pageantry in films and photos. Throughout the museum, there are busts of the coaches and players enshrined. Dick felt honored to be joining such an institution.

Although he was grateful to have been voted into the NAIA Hall of Fame in 1999 in Nashville and, before that, The University of Findlay Athletic Hall of Fame, Toledo Libbey High School Hall of Fame, the Toledo City League Hall of Fame, the Hancock Sports Hall of Fame, and the National Football Foundation Toledo Chapter Hall of Fame, Strahm sensed this would be the ultimate enshrinement, the exclamation point to a career 40-plus years in the making.

The Strahms left on Thursday, August 12, for South Bend. As Dick recalls, "After we all checked in at the Marriott, there was a welcome reception where the inductees were fitted for their Hall of Fame blazers. That was my first indication that this was going to be no ordinary ceremony. Each of us also had an interview tape made that would be shown on two giant screens on either side of the tables where we would sit on Saturday night at the induction banquet as a means to introduce each of us and establish our credentials."

After a night of restful sleep back at the Marriott, Dick and Ginger and the rest of the family attended the Mayor's Breakfast on Friday morning at the Century Center. The affair featured the inductees in their blazers for the first time.

The event began with an entrance that was a source of great consternation for the family. Recalls Dick's son Doug, "One of our biggest concerns was Dad had to walk down a long flight of marble stairs, kind of a procession of the new inductees. We were afraid he might slip because of his bad leg [a drop foot, the residual effect of the stroke Dick suffered in 1997] and fall down the stairs."

Nonetheless, Dick would not miss being a part of this grand entrance. He had worked too hard and overcome too much to let a flight of marble steps become an opponent he couldn't defeat. In addition to the stroke in 1997, Strahm had also suffered multiple heart attacks, open-heart surgery, and not one but two bouts of cancer. Each time one of these catastrophic medical crises occurred, Dick had narrowed his eyes, made his jaw like granite, and summoned the indomitable will that the courageous somehow manage to find from deep within to endure. No set of stairs was going to whip him.

He also had a new friend, who, as they say, "had his back." Roger Wehrli, a player so good he is now a member of both the College and Pro Football Halls of Fame, had noticed Strahm's gait at the Thursday night reception. Recalls Dick, "Before we were ready to make the descent, Roger came up to me and said, 'Dick, let me walk with you. If you feel a bit unsteady, just grab a hold of my arm.' What a class guy Roger was to notice something like that and offer support!"

After the entrance, the honorees were seated in front of the stage. Four of the inductees had been asked to speak at the function. Tom Beck, the former Illinois Benedictine, Elmhurst, and Grand Valley State coach; Jimbo Covert, the big-as-a-house former Pitt Panther lineman; Jerry LeVias, the former Southwest Conference pioneer; and Dick Strahm.

"Well, was I ever honored to be asked to speak! Sure, I talked about football, but I also talked about my sincere belief that, with God's help, you can overcome just about any obstacle. I'd had all three of the leading causes of death over the last twenty years, and I have God to thank for allowing me to overcome these obstacles. He made available to me all the wonderful doctors and nurses and physical therapists.

"As far as my stroke back in 1997, I told that room full of friends, supporters, and football fans that I wouldn't have been walking today if it weren't for the nurses in the rehab center. Although I don't have any feeling in my right arm, there was a time when I couldn't even flick a cotton ball with my finger. Those nurses made it their passion to motivate me to use my arms again and then my legs. They not only supported my goals to regain control physically but they embraced them to the point where my goals truly became their goals."

When Strahm finished his speech, a speech greeted by waves of applause, he returned to his table. It was a table comprised of him and no fewer than seven men who were not only college-football immortals but also former NFL players. Despite such friends in high places, it was at that moment when he felt as if he really belonged in such lofty company. "All of them leaned over and shook my hand and congratulated me on my speech. Now, that was really a special feeling."

In the afternoon, there was a golf scramble, which Dick opted out of, and a tour of perhaps the most famous football campus in the entire country, Notre Dame. Dick took the tour and enjoyed it immensely. While walking around, he wondered what it would have been like to have coached at such an institution. He reached the conclusion that his time at Findlay, while smaller in scale, certainly couldn't have been more rewarding than what he had experienced.

At 5:00 p.m. on that Friday evening, it was time for the next activity, called The Gathering at the Gridiron. Right outside the Hall of Fame doors, there's an Astroturf football field about 50 yards long. It was here that the general public could come and meet the inductees. The reunion class, men who were invited back to represent each of the ten years the Hall had been in South Bend, also had an autograph session. From 1995 to 2003 respectively, they were Jim Grabowski, Billy "White Shoes" Johnson, Hugh Green, Dave Rimington, Bill Fralic, Willie Lanier, Gordie Lockbaum, Kevin Butler and Napoleon McCallum. Again, they were some of the biggest names in college football history.

There was food, live music, and plenty of memories for Dick and Ginger and the rest of the family. They mingled among some of the greatest in the annuls of college football. All seemed to enjoy the music, provided by a group called Art and the Artichokes.

The next day, Saturday, August 14, dawned. It was enshrinement day for Dick and his new famous friends. The day began with, of course, breakfast, followed by the inductees' signing of footballs. Dick recalls, "Some of the balls would be auctioned off, with the money going to charity, but each of us also would receive one as a memento."

Then, a news conference followed as each inductee provided the large contingent of the press covering the event with their thoughts and reactions to the honor.

After the news conference, it was outside to put on an hour-long youth football clinic. It was here that excited youngsters like Dick's own grandson, Hunter, got some tips from some of the best. The inductees, like Dick, worked with the young gridiron aspirants on their stances, just as he had done with thousands of players in more than forty years of coaching. Barry Sanders worked with wanna-be running backs while Joe Theismann provided tips on playing quarterback, a position he had played so successfully in this, his college town.

For Dick's group of friends and family, there was one in particular who will remain a Joe Theismann fan forever. Lewis and Linda Jones were former Findlay neighbors of Dick's and great friends not only of Dick's but also of the Oilers football program during Dick's tenure. They had driven all the way from Broken Arrow, Oklahoma, to share this special moment with their dear friend. They also brought Linda's mother, a great Theismann admirer going all the way back to Joe's glory days under Notre Dame's Golden Dome from 1968 through 1970. For Linda's mom, Joe had a big hug and a kiss on the cheek, a cheek she vowed to leave unwashed for at least a week.

Dale, Dick's brother, had flown in from Charlotte to help his big brother celebrate. Dale, like Dick, had devoted his life to football, perhaps in an attempt to emulate a big brother he had idolized from those days back in south Toledo where the two grew up. It was during those days that Dick, despite the nine years' age difference, always seemed to have time for Dale.
Dale coached at schools like Bowling Green, Navy, Georgia, Duke, Western Carolina, and Temple. By 2004, he was in his fifth season on the Denver Broncos' scouting staff.

Recalls Dale, now the director of college scouting for the NFL's Houston Texans, "I just wasn't going to miss my only brother's big day. On a smaller scale, I knew how special it was to be inducted into a hall of fame [Dale's four years of running track and playing football at Ohio Northern University earned him entry into Northern's Hall of Fame], so I decided I was going to make it a point to be there. I just don't think there have ever been two brothers with a nine-year age difference that have been closer than we have been. He was my best man in my wedding. I have coached with him. I have coached against him. Not only am I Dick's brother but a great admirer of him as well."

It was Larry Cook who picked Dale up at the South Bend, Indiana, airport. Larry was another very special link that completed the chain that stretched from the early events in Dick's life to this glorious weekend could be there for Dick. Larry Cook was like a brother to Dale, having graduated with him from both Arlington Elementary and Libbey High School back in Toledo, Ohio.

During Dick's first experience coaching, when the sport was seventh- and eighth-grade basketball while he was an undergrad at the University of Toledo, two of those boys standing in lay-up lines during practice and pre-games were Dale and his best pal Larry Cook.

Like both the Strahms, Larry Cook chose a career in football. After playing four years at nearby Bowling Green State University, Cook became head coach at Willard, Centerville, and eventually Sandusky Senior High schools.

The only thing that could have made the weekend more perfect would have been if Dale and Dick's mom and dad been there. It was a thought that has occurred to so many who are accorded great honors later in their lives after parents have passed away. Mentzer and Mildred would have been so proud of both their sons. They both fervently supported the role that athletics played in the lives of their boys.

After the clinic, it was time for some fun and the celebrity flag-football game. Played purely for fun on the 50 yards of Astroturf in front of the Hall of Fame, the event was a great fan favorite. While the game was meaningless relative to winner and loser, the ultra-competitive Strahm is still quick to point out that the team that he and Odessa, Texas, native and well-known coach Hayden Fry coached won, although he takes no real credit for this happening.

"Heck, the extent of Hayden's and my coaching was standing around talking to one another. The game was five-on-five, and we were fortunate to have Darrell Green on our side. He was just 44 at the time and just two years earlier was covering the NFL's best wide receivers one-on-one. What a remarkable athlete Green is to have played such a demanding position as cornerback in the NFL for 20 seasons!"

Most of what Dick and Hayden talked about wasn't football. It was about the battles that supersede any that occur on the field. Both Fry and Strahm were prostate- cancer survivors, and this was as much a common ground as anything they did as coaches. For Dick, there was not only the original cancer discovery in 1995 but also the recurrence of it three years later.

For the extremely private Fry, prostate cancer was the primary reason for his retiring from coaching the Iowa Hawkeyes after the 1998 season, the same season that Dick Strahm called his last. However, there was no mention of the disease all season as Fry insisted. Fry took extraordinary measures to keep the treatment at the IU Health Care facility a secret as well. Fry told Dick, "I underwent radiation during my last season in 1998. I came at 5:00 a.m. each day before any other patients arrived at IU Health Care."

Long known for his quips to the press over the years, Fry laughed when he told Dick how he started each day. "Well, Dick, the first thing I do when I open my eyes is to get out of bed, look up above and thank the Lord I'm still on the right side of the grass. Then, I reach over to the night stand and grab a quart of 10-W-30 and chug it just to make sure the motor runs smooth."

Fry also told Dick a quick story that became one of legendary broadcaster Keith Jackson's favorites. "When I was the coach of SMU in the early sixties, we opened with Ohio State in Columbus each year. A cub reporter came up to me while I was walking in the end zone during pre-game warm ups. He said to me, 'Coach Fry, why are you walking around in the end zone while your team is warming up instead of walking among your players?' I said, 'Well, son, no one from SMU has ever been in the end zone here in The Horseshoe, and I just thought I'd like to see what it felt like.'"

Needless to say, Dick enjoyed both the serious and private Hayden Fry and also the quipster Hayden Fry. "I didn't know Coach Fry before that weekend but sure felt we hit it off and was honored he later indicated a desire to help in any way with the book project."

Recalls Fry, "Life is about helping nice and deserving people, and when it comes to that roll call, Dick's name appears. I remember him as a wonderful gentleman and am so glad he is still in remission and enjoying his retirement."

Like Strahm, Fry remains in remission in his fight against the second most common type of cancer (with lung cancer being first) that afflicts men. The former Marine threw himself into the fight against the disease that afflicted him. He helped to spearhead a $10 million campaign to fund the J. (for John) Hayden Fry Center for Prostate Cancer Research. It is a facility Fry has expressed great pride in having his name associated.

Tom Beck also joined the conversation, as he was in the midst of his own battle with prostate cancer. All three of the men agreed that with cancer, the fight is ongoing. You just have to be very vigilant in maintaining a healthy lifestyle and staying right on top of all the doctors' visits so that you know what's happening inside your body. "When you're facing cancer issues, it really helps to be able to talk to others who know what you're going through," recalls Strahm.

A pretty strong bond formed between the three men by the end of the weekend. Dick told Beck that there were three different doctors who told him back in 1998 that he had no more than three years to live. Beck told Fry and Strahm how living with the thought of his own mortality changed the way he lived his life. "I have learned to live each day one at a time. Every day is a little more important and the people I interact with also have become more important, too. That's especially true when it comes to family."

After the celebrity game, there was an autograph session. A maximum of three hundred fans were allowed in, and each paid a $75.00 entry fee. The sold-out event was another that Dick will long remember. "We sat at these long tables. Many who paid the entry fee had a poster of the inductee or a football to sign. I sat right beside Joe Theismann and Darrell Green, and it was really funny to watch fans' reactions. They'd get Darrell's autograph and then Joe's, and then they'd get to me. I could tell by the looks on their faces they didn't know me from a hill of beans, but they were very nice and asked me to sign some things."

Then, right at the end of the line of autograph seekers, a familiar face came into view. It belonged to Dr. Jack Winters, who was a great friend of both Dick and Ginger and also a great Oilers supporter. Winters is a dentist who had made mouth guards for hundreds of Findlay football players over the years. He also was a football official in the Mid American Conference. Winters had come to celebrate Dick's special moment. He looked at Dick, grinned, held out a photo for Dick to sign, and said, "I thought it'd be nice if you had a familiar face at this shindig today."

Dick was glad to see him. "I knew Jack wasn't really into autograph collecting or meeting celebrities. The fact that he plunked down the seventy-five bucks just to share this moment with me just shows you what a true friend is."

After the autograph session, it was back to the hotel to get ready for the induction banquet. Despite the variety and pomp and circumstance of what had transpired up to this point in the weekend, this would be the highlight of the weekend.

Class photos of the inductees, each wearing his Hall of Fame blazer, took place at 5:30 p.m. Then it was back to the Convention Hall in the Century Center for the night's festivities. Of course, coat and tie were required of all gentlemen in attendance.

The master of ceremonies was Joe McConnell, the longtime voice of Purdue football. The pre-meal rituals included not only the invocation but also the singing of the national anthem. It was certainly suitable, given the number of times all of these men stood respectfully with teams made up of their comrades and coaches to achieve this moment of supreme recognition. Recalls Strahm, "It would have almost seemed sacrilegious not to have the anthem sung."

Next, there were some recognition awards given to those who had promoted amateur football in a positive way. Then it was time to really get into the heart of the program.

The featured speakers that evening were Doug Dickey, Darrell Green, Barry Sanders, and Joe Theismann. They spoke of what it takes to be a football player and seasons and games gone by, and, of course, their gratitude for being accorded such an honor of being admitted into the Hall they were about to enter.

Green was a graduate of a small Division II college, Texas A & I. He was an All-American in both track and football and the Most Valuable Player of the Lone Star Conference in his final year. That was the precursor to the astonishing twenty years in the NFL, all with the Washington Redskins. Green's forté was always speed. He was the four-time winner of the NFL's Fastest Man competition. As a rookie, he ran an unheard-of 4.09 seconds in the 40-yard dash. When he was 40 years old, he ran a more astonishing 4.2 seconds.

For Barry Sanders, he learned patience during his first two years at Oklahoma State, when he was a backup to future NFL Hall of Fame running back Thurman Thomas. Once Thomas moved on to the Buffalo Bills, it was time for Barry to show what he could do. He had the greatest year a running back ever had in NCAA history. Sanders shattered 34 NCAA records as he ran for 2,628 yards from scrimmage. He accumulated 3,250 all-purpose yards and scored 234 points, both all-time NCAA marks. The end of the year saw Sanders receive all three awards given to the nation's outstanding collegiate player – the Heisman Trophy and both the Camp and the Maxwell Awards.

After the speakers came the presentation of the ring and the playing of each inductee's tape, made on Thursday evening, on the giant screens placed on either side of the long table. The ornately carved chairs upon which the inductees sat would later be shipped to each of them, another special memory to accompany the ring, the blazer, and the autographed football signed by the entire class.

Dick recalls the food was spectacular, but there was something even more spectacular than the filet mignon with bordelaise sauce or spring greens with gorgonzola and toasted pine nuts, and the rest of the delicacies which comprised the sumptuous feast. "What really made the evening so special for me was to have all my family and friends there. To have Ginger and my son Doug and daughter-in-law Lisa and my daughter Gina and son-in-law Matt and my son Steve and my grandson Hunter and my brother Dale was absolutely wonderful. Also wonderful was so many others were there, friends like John and Noreen Zito, Ray and Judy Kwaitkowski, and all the way from Florida, Jerry and Sue Biggs, along with former players like

Kevin Cassidy, Jerome Gray and Gene Fernandez, and men I've stood beside in the coaching trenches and the great administrators of The University of Findlay like Dr. DeBow Freed and Dr. Jim Houdeshell and many, many other supporters of Ginger and me. Well, it was just overwhelming, and, frankly, still is today as I look back on it.

"I was being totally sincere when I said to the writers who were there covering the event, men like *The Courier* sports editor and wonderful friend Larry Alter, a man who covered our program with fairness and a man who never took a cheap shot just to be controversial or to sell more newspapers, that I owed so very much of my success not to my efforts but the efforts of others.

"If you're going to coach at one place for 24 years and have success, you have to have very good players, many of whom played high school right in northwestern Ohio, players I didn't think Findlay College was getting enough of when I arrived in 1975. Oh, and by the way, that included some of those Findlay High School Trojans, who decided to stay home and take a chance on my program.

"You also need to have consistency within your staff. You need assistant coaches who will stay with you, work with you, and believe in what you are trying to accomplish. Jim McIntosh was with me 23 of my 24 years. Curtis Davidson was an All-American here as a player and then stayed and coached with me 16 years. My son Doug played for me and then stayed on as a coach for several years. Then there were men like Dean Pees, who's now one of the top defensive coordinators in the NFL with the New England Patriots; Doug Coate, a former quarterback of mine and a fine assistant coach for many years; Ray Kwiatkowski, who taught high school in Michigan and drove two hours every day to help us win and kept on making the long back-and-forth commute for over a decade; and Steve Mohr, who has gone on to become a great head coach himself in college. That's what I mean when I say that this is not an 'I' award. It's a 'We' award."

Steve Mohr has been the head coach at Trinity University in San Antonio, Texas, since 1990. During his time there, he has become one of the most successful NCAA Division III coaches in the nation. Not only does he boast a winning percentage of over .700 but he also has been named Division III's National Coach of the Year twice.

Recalls the eminently successful Mohr, "Coach Strahm was the first coach to give me a start in this wonderful business. After graduating from Denison University, I received a graduate assistantship at Bowling Green in 1976. That was the year Dick took a chance on a kid just out of college by allowing him to become a part-time offensive line coach at Findlay. The next year, a full-time assistant's position opened, and he hired me. I stayed nine years, and they were wonderful. I know it sounds clichéd, but Coach Strahm truly was like a father to me. Much of the success I've had in coaching after I left in the spring of 1985, I owe to him."

From purely a football perspective, Dick was thrilled to sit on the dais side by side with the man many believe to be the greatest running back in the history of professional football, Barry Sanders. Sanders not only had that season for the ages at Oklahoma State but he also was a lead-pipe cinch to become the all-time career rushing leader in the NFL until he suddenly walked away from the professional game at the age of 31 while still in his prime after ten seasons with the Detroit Lions.

The common ground the two shared was an offensive philosophy. Dick Strahm had made a living out of using an eminently successful wishbone offense while at Findlay, an offense he used to catapult his Oilers to four NAIA national titles. The wishbone is basically a run-first-and-run-often offensive set.

Recollects Strahm, "When Barry asked me what I ran in college, it really opened that conversational door, and I told him all about the way we ran the 'bone at Findlay. Imagine how I felt when one of the two or three greatest running backs of all time smiled and said to me, 'Coach, I think I could have played for you.'"

Son Doug remembers, "It really didn't hit me how special all of this was until the moment at the dinner and induction when I saw my dad sitting right next to Barry Sanders on one side and Joe Theismann on the other, and Darrell Green a bit further down. All these players, I'd grown up watching on TV. Then it struck me that my father's accomplishments didn't need to take a back seat to theirs. Although he may not have had the press coverage or the trappings of fame like the shoe contracts and other commercial endorsements, for that one moment on the dais, he was their equal and what an incredible feeling that was."

For Strahm and the other men Larry Alter referred to in his column that ran on August 17, 2004, "Strahm got to make 24 new friends," the evening was one that was over far too soon.

However, for Dick, there would be more. The next morning in one of the conference rooms at the Marriott, it was The University of Findlay's turn to honor him. It was called The University of Findlay Alumni and Friends Breakfast, and it lasted from 9:00 to 11:00 a.m.

While the room didn't have anywhere near the 600 people that attended the previous evening's induction banquet, this gathering was very special because everyone in that room had meant so much to Dick.

The University's elite all spoke, men with incredible credentials of their own like President DeBow Freed and Dr. James Houdeshell and Dr. C. Richard Beckett, the chairman of the University's Board of Trustees.

"Ginger and I and our whole family were so proud to be surrounded by such loyal friends and supporters. I'd look in one direction, and there stood Tom Smith, the captain of my first national-championship team in 1979. He and his wife drove all the way from Louisiana to be with me. I'd look in another direction, and there stood dear friends from Lima, just down the road from Findlay, Gil Hyland and Jerry O'Connor. It was another incredible moment for the Strahm family."

At the breakfast, Strahm also found out that the tribute he'd experienced over that glorious three-day weekend wasn't likely to end soon. He recalls, "Just when I'm thinking that enough is enough already, Jim Houdeshell reminded me that there would be an on-campus salute that coming fall on Homecoming, Saturday, September 25. Letters would be sent out to my former players and my assistant coaches and the supporters of Findlay football. Five tents would be erected, each representing a five-year period of time during my tenure. The tents would be a gathering place for reunions. Needless to say, the event also turned out to be such a wonderful experience."

For Dick Strahm's family, the memories of the weekend are indelibly etched in their minds.

Recalls Dick's co-head coach at home since the day they were married on April 7, 1962, Ginger, "The induction gave, I guess, some public validation of Dick's career, but it was an endorsement I don't really think his family needed. We all knew what type of man he was, how hard he'd worked, and what he'd done for his players, not just on the field but also off."

Doug remembers someone asking him if the bust of his father in the Hall looked like him. "My response was 'Yea, because we wanted it to look like him.' Perhaps to someone else, he would need to look for his name to find out which bust is Dick Strahm's...but we knew."

Daughter Gina recalls, "You know, the whole experience flashed by so quickly. I wish I could go back and relive the weekend just to pay attention to the details I know I missed. I was almost in a daze watching my father achieve the pinnacle of his profession. People who know football know Dick Strahm was a great football coach. What they may not know is that he has been an even better father. The bust of him in the Hall is a legacy really, a gift to his children and his children's children. Hunter, my dad's first grandchild, can always go there after he grows up and say, 'That's my Poppy.'"

For Dick's youngest son, Steve, his remembrance spoke of the pride he felt for all of his father's accomplishments and the difficulty in choosing a favorite one. "By this time, we'd been to so many of these hall-of-fame inductions for Dad, but this one was so well organized. While I remember Dad's speech at the Mayor's breakfast as being good, I think the best speech I ever heard him or anyone else give, for that matter, was the one I heard in January of 1999 in Nashville when he was inducted into the NAIA Hall of Fame. But, really, every one of my dad's accomplishments, including this one, is so very special to me because, well, he's my dad."

And, for Dick Strahm, himself, as he surveyed the Marriott Ballroom, Salon A, at the end of the brunch, he thought of many things, but, first and foremost, he felt blessed. He was surrounded by those who mattered the most to him.

For Dick, it was a time of reflection as he broke away from those who couldn't pat him on the back or shake his hand or hug him often enough. He needed a moment of quiet reflection in the hallway outside the room. His mind turned away from guys named Barry and Joe. Those thoughts and memories could be summoned another time.

Walking with some difficulty, *yet walking*, he remembered the rehab nurses in what he called the "Blue Gown Ward," those who simply wouldn't rest until he could walk. He remembered each and every wonderful doctor who brought him back from catastrophic health issues so that he could continue to love his family and his players and assistant coaches. And, of course, he remembered the Master Architect of the blueprint that was his life, God, and His guiding hand in all he'd done.

And he also remembered his mother, Mildred, and his father, Mentzer, and, inevitably, he remembered how far he had come and where it all began.

Chapter 2

Growing Up in the Glass City

The year was 1934, and it was, as all years, defined by a wide array of events and the people who made them happen.

In the world of football, a university that years later would set an NCAA record for consecutive losses, Columbia, was king, defeating Stanford in the Rose Bowl, 7-0. Professionally, George Halas' Bears lost in the fledgling National Football League's championship to the New York Giants, 30-13.

Horton Smith won the first Masters golf tournament in Augusta, Georgia, defeating Craig Wood by a stroke, and Bill Cummings won the Indianapolis 500 with an unheard-of average speed of 104.86 mph.

The big books released were James Hilton's *Goodbye, Mr. Chips* and F. Scott Fitzgerald's *Tender Is the Night.*

Talking pictures were still in their infancy, and the one everyone seemed to be talking about was *It Happened One Night,* starring Clark Gable and Claudette Colbert, which opened at the Radio City Music Hall in New York City.

Crime and punishment dominated the headlines as well. Bruno Hauptmann was arrested, tried, and eventually found guilty of the kidnapping and murder of the Lindbergh baby. He would later be executed for the crime. Both Charles "Pretty Boy" Floyd and John Dillinger had their gangster careers permanently interrupted when they were shot to death by federal agents in East Liverpool, Ohio, and Chicago, Illinois, respectively. That same year Bonnie and Clyde died in a hail of gunfire by law enforcement as well.

Toledo, known as the Glass City because it boasts such a long history of innovations in the glass industry and also is home to several glass companies like Owens Corning and Libbey Glass, certainly had something to shout about as well.

A couple of babies who were born in 1934, television actor Jamie Farr and feminist author Gloria Steinem, arrived on the scene in Toledo. However, there also was another born that year in the Glass City, one destined to become a small-college coaching institution.

After seeing this senior high school photo you might guess why the young Dick Strahm was not invited to a college that liked to throw the ball.

Dick Strahm was born on February 23, 1934, to Mildred and Mentzer Strahm on the day after Clark and Colbert's *It Happened One Night* made its debut. Perhaps for someone who would one day become a man of the gridiron, a forty-plus-year coach, an autumnal birth would have been more suitable than a basketball-season arrival, but when one arrives into this world is generally left to a Greater Power.

As Dick grew from infancy into childhood, he learned that activity can be a boy's best friend. He was seemingly always on the move, always playing at something in a house and a neighborhood that remains etched in his memory. "We lived at 848 Toronto Avenue in south Toledo, about a half block from the elementary school I attended, Arlington. It was a modest workingman's neighborhood with houses that had shared driveways that eventually split to one-car garages. In an age now where two-car garages are the norm, it might be hard for younger people to think of all those one-car garages, but the idea that any family would actually have more than one car, well, that just wasn't a part of our world."

The house on Toronto was a small two-story complex. It had two bedrooms upstairs and on the main floor a living room, a dining room and a small kitchen. There was also a cellar, which contained a bin for coal, which heated the home.

Recalls Dick, "Oh the dust that kicked up when the coal man backed his truck up outside to deliver the coal down the chute! But that dust was a necessary by-product of what kept us warm in the winter, or at least reasonably warm. You see, there was only one floor heat grate in the whole house. It was between the dining room and the living room on the main floor. Even though it was big, it was the only one! That meant some pretty frigid nights on the second floor, which happened to be where the bedrooms were.

It was that solitary heat vent that would bring Mildred Strahm a little newspaper notoriety, as Dick recalls. "The heat vent was huge, and this led to an unexpected problem one day when my mom took the grate off because there were men there to install some new carpeting. Well, we had a dog named Spot and, I guess, he wasn't real good at paying attention to the details around him. I'll be damned if that pooch didn't walk right towards the opening and fell right in!

"An angle in the pipe stopped the dog from sliding all the way down to the furnace dome, but the dog was stuck. Mom decided it would be her to get Spot out, so she poked her body into the pipe headfirst as the carpet layers held onto her ankles. So here was my mom stretched out on the floor barely holding onto the dog to keep from falling all the way down the pipe and these workers holding onto my mom's ankles trying to pull the both of them up! Mom finally got a hold of the dog, and the carpet layers tugged, and both Mom and Spot were extracted from the pipe."

Everyone was OK, and someone in the neighborhood eventually thought it was worth reporting to the local paper, *The Blade*, because it ran a column by Fred L. Mollenkopf called "Among the Folks," which included human-interest stories of a rather unique nature. The story ran, and Mom and Spot were kind of the stars of Toronto Avenue for a while."

Dick's memories of his childhood are rife with moments of play, which took place in the small back yards and the alley that ran behind them. It was back there that many a spirited game of kick the can, kind of a hybrid game comprised of tag and hide-and-seek, took place. "Jeez, we'd play that game for hours at a time. First, we'd find a large can and place it in the middle of the alley. Someone would be designated "it" and put his foot on the can. He'd close his eyes and count to ten.

"Then it would be time to find those hiding and hightail it back to the can when someone was spotted to yell, '1-2-3 on Johnny hiding behind the Smith bushes' before he could run to the can to kick it, which would set free everyone who'd already been caught.

"While a lot of our biggest fights involved who had to be 'it' to start the game, I didn't really mind at all. As a matter of fact, I really liked it. I guess you might say I was more defensive oriented back then because I liked to pursue my opponents."

Those games of kick the can reflected the close-knit nature of the neighborhood. Recalls Dick, "Nowadays, in some neighborhoods, there are so many interests that take people away from the home and, with so many people moving after very short periods of time, it sometimes isn't all that unusual for people to not know neighbors more than a house or two on either side of them. But, in the neighborhoods of the late 1930s and the 1940s, everybody knew everybody. Every house all the way down the alley could be identified by the family who lived within. So, it was easy for us kids to identify someone hiding specifically, like behind the Smiths' bushes or the Haverman's apple tree."

For Dick it was also in the back yards and alley that he first expressed a real interest in athletics. "My father put a basketball hoop up, and we played for hours, anything from one-on-one to five-on-five, depending on who was available. No fouls were called, and I recall the games got very physical at times. I remember one game where a kid who lived behind us got his nose broken and had to have it set at the hospital."

One Libbey High School football player, Charles Meyer, lived in the house directly across the alley behind 848 Toronto Avenue, and he was eight years older than Dick. Despite the age difference, he would often take the time to play with Dick, often picking him up and holding him high above his head for a better view of the world. This was an easy feat for Meyer, since, as one of Libbey's best lineman, he was well over 6' 3" and weighed more than 200 pounds.

Meyer went on to graduate in 1944 after playing on two teams that won the coveted Toledo City Championship. He was named to the United Press International All-Ohio Team in 1942 and was co-captain of the 1943 team.

After graduation, Charles Meyer, the boy that went out of his way to make time for Dick despite being much older, joined the Marine Corps to fight in World War II. He was wounded in action at Iwo Jima in 1945 and received the Purple Heart.

After getting out of the service, Meyer enjoyed a long career working for the U.S. Postal Service and remained active in many church and YMCA activities. Meyer would one day be a nominee for the Toledo City League Hall of Fame, thereby joining the little boy he would lift up way over his head who also was destined to be accorded that honor.

The back yard was also a source of sustenance for Dick and his family. "There was a cherry tree, actually the only tree in the yard. I remember the annual tradition in early summer was picking the cherries so that Mom could can them.

"Mom, as many moms did in the '40s, did a lot of canning. We also would make a summer day trip to Port Clinton to pick peaches.

"We'd also buy some other fruits when they were in season and reasonably priced, and then Mom would start canning and putting the jars down in the fruit cellar in our basement. I can remember how row after row of those Ball jars with the burnt orange rubber seals would lengthen as the summer days went by."

While those jars of fruit didn't hold a great deal of fascination to Dick in the summer when fresh fruit was abundant in groceries, the jars yielded a vastly different reaction during the winter months. Remembers Dick, "Boy, did that fruit ever taste good when those winter winds were howling."

Dick's parents, Mentzer and Mildred, were, as Dick recalls, very supportive of athletics. "They were really involved in my athletic pursuits as well as my younger brother Dale when he came on the scene nine years after I did. Sometimes, you hear stories of parents in the 1930s and 1940s who were resistant to the notion their children get too involved in sports, especially if it took them away from the family business or chores."

During this age, there were no millionaire athletes, and there was a mindset adopted by many parents that sports were somehow frivolous and that they wanted something better for their kids than a life in sports. Although athletes were often idolized for their achievements, many parents really didn't think it was a worthy career path.

Dick recalls, "One moment kind of forever etched in my memory might give a pretty good indication of how my parents felt about sports. In 1946, when I was about 12, my mom and dad took me to one of Toledo's biggest high-school rivalry games, which pitted the school I and Dale would eventually attend, Libbey, and Waite High School. The game was played at Waite Stadium on Toledo's east side. It was one of those fierce big-city regional affairs, and both teams were fighting for first place in the Toledo City League. What added even more spice to this annual contest was that Dad was a Libbey graduate, and Mom was a graduate of Waite.

"When we first got there, I looked around and outside the stadium I could see dozens of people who had climbed trees to get a vantage point. The game was a sell-out, and this was the only way they could get a look.

"Anyway, about halfway through the first half, it began to rain, and I mean hard. Mom and Dad and I were soaked. Many people left the game, and we did too at halftime.

"But when we got in the car, I realized what my mom and dad were going to do. We drove all the way back home and all changed into foul-weather gear and returned to Waite Stadium for the second half!

"Now, I've seen many a fan leave football games played in driving rain early but never one who went home to change and then return."

Mentzer was raised to be a strong Presbyterian by his parents Charles and Edith. They were members of the Westminster Presbyterian Church. When Mentzer grew up and began looking after his own family, he also became actively involved in the church, eventually becoming an elder as his father did before him.

When it was time to go to work, Mentzer punched his timecard at Champion Spark Plug. He worked on the line and eventually served as a committee man, a union steward, for his final ten years. To supplement his income from Champion, Mentzer also painted houses.

Dick's maternal grandparents were Harry and Frances Nichols, and they raised three daughters. Mildred's sisters were May and Gertrude. As a primary occupation, Harry and Frances ran a rooming house, but there was also a farm outside of Lambertville, Michigan, a farm that Dick remembers with fondness. "It wasn't very big, probably around thirty-five acres. Grandpa's brother Don lived on the farm and tended to much of the day-to-day operation. He and Grandpa had about twenty-five acres in corn, which helped to feed the cows, pigs, and chickens that they raised. I can remember going out there in Grandpa's Model A Ford."

Dick's primary job when he visited the farm was to go around to the chicken coops and collect the eggs. This was indeed a world very different from the one he knew back in south Toledo. "I think it was the lifestyle of my great-uncle Don that fascinated me the most about that farm. He had converted the middle of what used to be a three-car garage into a one-room apartment. The room on one side was full of tools, and the room on the other side was where the chickens were hatched. Looking back, I marvel at some of the noise from those birds he had to acclimate himself to."

The eggs gathered were sold to some of the many mom-and-pop groceries that were so prevalent at the time, and during the loading of the eggs into crates, Dick learned his first lessons in due diligence. "Boy, was I ever nervous putting those eggs into the crates with my grandfather constantly telling me to be careful because every broken egg costs money."

Dick remembers the very first time his grandfather told him to gather the eggs. "I suppose I was around eight, and Grandpa told me that I had nothing to worry about. The chickens wouldn't bother me as I went around and carefully removed the eggs. I was only supposed to fill the basket halfway. Then I was to get another basket and continue. After I got done, I thought I had done so well. Not one egg had broken. Well, it turns out some wouldn't have broken had I thrown them up against the wall because they were the wooden eggs intended to stimulate the laying of eggs. My grandfather made it clear it wasn't my fault because he had neglected to tell me about them, but he did have me return the wooden eggs to their proper places."

Sometimes as a special treat, when Dick was in the fifth and sixth grades, he would get to ride the old tractor the brothers had for farming. While Dick was not much of a farm boy, he did enjoy spending time with his grandfather.

Grandma Nichols was called Mommy Nichols, and she had little time for trips to the farm. It was her responsibility to manage the rooming house. It was comprised of two two-room apartments and three single apartments, and it was incumbent on Mommy Nichols to do all the cleaning and laundry for the tenants in addition to cleaning for herself and Harry. Recalls Dick, "I do remember I'd stay overnight many times, especially when I was very young and my grandparents would baby sit, since there was a time both my mother and father worked."

Grandma and Grandpa Nichols managed the rooming house until 1947, when Mommy Nichols passed away. Unable to run the operation by himself, Grandpa Harry moved in with the Strahms. It was then Dick remembers a very crowded scene in one of the two bedrooms upstairs. "Since one bedroom obviously was for Mom and Dad, that meant the other bedroom was where my brother Dale and I and Grandpa Nichols slept. Dale and I slept in a double bed, and Grandpa slept in a single a scant four feet away. In those years just after World War II, families just took care of their own with very few exceptions. Dale and I never complained about it. Grandpa Nichols lived with us for seven years before he succumbed to a heart attack."

Dick's paternal grandfather and grandmother were Charles and Edith Strahm. Charlie, as most called him, worked at The Community Traction Company, where he was the supervisor of the Utility Department. Remembers Dick, "As I recall, Grandpa Strahm's department maintained the city buses and trolleys and the routes as well. In the 1940s so many people relied on public transportation, so his was a very important job. As far as my Grandma Strahm, she never worked outside the home but was very active in the church, Westminster Presbyterian, doing a good deal of committee work.

For Dick, his first involvement with sports came through his church. Westminster Presbyterian had a congregation of 400-plus members, large enough for there to be a need for someone to coach the church basketball teams. Ever the advocate of athletics, Dick's father stepped forward and assumed the position. No doubt, he was simply following what he'd been shown by his own father, Charles. It was Charles Strahm who coached Mentzer at Westminster Presbyterian in the 1920s. Mentzer not only coached the church teams but also was in charge of all the tournaments as well, tournaments that involved many of the churches in the south end of Toledo.

Recalls Dick, "I really got involved in athletics because of my father. Besides his coaching the church teams, he also was very active in the YMCA."

As far as little brother Dale, well, his opinion of his big brother was clear. He idolized him. Recalls Dale, "As kids in an age when the bikes had baskets, my brother Dick would stick me in the basket and off we'd go to the playground or to my Grandma and Grandpa Strahm's house. They lived all the way across Anthony Wayne Trail, about seven miles away. At the time I probably wasn't more than four years old. Many other brothers nine years older wouldn't have been too willing to carry me around like that, but Dick did it all the time. Is it any wonder I worshipped him? As far as I was concerned, he could do no wrong."

Dick attended Arlington Grade School, and, since there was no organized football, he first joined his buddies on the playground for sandlot games of football and especially softball. Recalls one of Dick's close friends in elementary school, high school, and later at the University of Toledo, Bob Zedlitz, "The playground was sort of our field of dreams, a place where we could not only develop our sports skills naturally without much in the way of adult intervention but also our social skills. We argued often but found our way to compromises without being told how to solve our problems. That's why I like to call that playground our field of dreams. Just like the players had their own field in the movie *Field of Dreams*, the field on that playground was ours and ours alone. We supervised ourselves. We settled our own disputes. In many ways, I thought those experiences were just as important as the ones once we got older and entered organized sports."

To some, Dick's involvement in fast-pitch softball might seem a bit surprising, but the era in which he grew up was much different than today. The sport was quite popular in the 1940s and '50s in the Midwest. Strahm's involvement with softball would recommence during his collegiate years.

Bob Zedlitz was a fellow softball enthusiast, and during his and Dick's seventh- and eight-grade years, they both became involved in fast-pitch through a YMCA program. They competed against other schools involved in the program, and it gave both of them a deeper appreciation for the thrill of athletic competition.

On the days Bob, the number-one hurler, would pitch, Dick would play third, and when it was Dick's turn to pitch, Bob would play third. Recalls Zedlitz, who now resides in Pleasanton, California, since his retirement from education, "When Dick and I were going to Arlington Elementary together there was just something different about him. At a young age, he had an awareness of other kids around him. This stuck out because most kids at that age are really only concerned about themselves. I could just tell Dick was going to be a leader. Kids just naturally gravitated toward him."

By the time he was an eighth grader, Dick had developed into a pretty fair hurler, and his mother was perhaps more instrumental than one might think. Dick remembers one day in particular.

"I will never forget one afternoon. Bob had just pitched in an eighth-grade tournament the day before. Since I was the number-two pitcher, I would be the starter for that day's game.

"Throughout the morning, it was hard to keep my mind on my school work. I always got really geared up whenever I was about to compete in anything athletic, and pitching was no exception. I came home for lunch. It was easy for me to do that each day, since we lived so close to the school. After a quick sandwich, I wanted to get warmed up in the backyard. My mom grabbed the catcher's mitt, and she warmed me up.

"Mom caught me until my arm was ready. As fast as I could get it up there, she could catch it. Then I returned to school, got through the afternoon, and pitched the game after school."

Dick was the winning pitcher that day, and, of course, his noon-time battery mate was in the stands cheering him on. "As I said, Mom and Dad were both great supporters of anything I wanted to try athletically."

It was Dick's Aunt May's husband, Rudy, who gave Dick one of his real thrills of his childhood. Uncle Rudy had obtained two tickets to the biggest rivalry game in the Midwest, the Ohio State Buckeyes versus the Michigan Wolverines. The year was 1944, and the game was played at Ohio State. Recalls Dick, "We took a train from Toledo to Columbus, the first time I ever had ridden a train, and then bussed to the Horseshoe to join some of the most vocal fans imaginable. The Buckeyes won in front of 71,000 mostly Buckeye fans, 18-14. Michigan was 8-1 and ranked sixth in the nation, and the Bucks were led by the great quarterback, Les Horvath, one of my heroes. Probably, about ten thousand other 10-year-old football sandlotters in the state could say the same about Horvath. What a November 25 that was!"

During those elementary days, it wasn't unusual to find Dick and his buddy Bob at Toledo Beach, where Uncle Rudy and Aunt May had a cottage. Toledo Beach looked out over Lake Erie. The boys swam and also grabbed their fishing poles during the warm summer days of their tranquil Ohio upbringing, and Aunt May kept an eye out to be sure the boys didn't get in too much trouble.

After Strahm finished at Arlington, he moved on to Libbey High School, a school with a rich tradition in a game Dick had yet to play in organized fashion, football. Along with Scott and Waite high schools, Libbey, Central Catholic and DeVilbiss high schools rounded out the five Toledo football powerhouses in the 1940s and 1950s.

Recalls Dick, "I couldn't wait to get to Libbey. The school had such a rich tradition in football, and I wanted to be a part of that. I'd followed the careers as a hero-worshipping young fan of so many Libbey football players.

The first one I remember well was a quarterback. His name was Bob Snyder, and he played for Libbey in the 1930s. He went on to Ohio University and made All-American. Later, he played in the NFL for the Chicago Bears. After retiring from playing, he went into coaching. He coached the Los Angeles Rams and was later the quarterback coach at Notre Dame when the great Johnny Lujack played there and won a Heisman Trophy. Snyder also returned to the city of his birth to coach the Toledo Rockets as well in the late 1940s.

Then, there was George Miley, who graduated in the mid-1940s. He was an All-City player at Libbey and went on to play at the University of Toledo, where he led the nation in punting in both his junior and senior years. After he graduated from UT, he wound up teaching and coaching back at Libbey, and I was fortunate to be coached by him my senior year, when he was an assistant coach."

Dick also remembers several other Libbey Cowboys, ones who went on to play not only in college but also in the NFL. "Jerry Krall was a running back who went on to play at Ohio State. I can remember he played in the Rose Bowl and both ran for a touchdown and threw a TD pass as well. After he graduated from Ohio State, he played for the Detroit Lions.

"Then there was Ray DePerro, another Libbey graduate. He started on the offensive line at Ohio State for three years and then played for the Green Bay Packers.

Jim Root graduated from Libbey in 1949. He was an outstanding quarterback. After playing at Miami University in Oxford, Ohio, he played for the Chicago Cardinals before they became the St. Louis Cardinals. Of course, now they're the Arizona Cardinals. You know you're getting old when you remember a team like the Cardinals in three different cities!

"Then, there was Bob Momsen, who graduated from Libbey in 1947. He achieved All-American honors at Ohio State. During his time at Ohio State, Bob played in one of the most famous OSU-Michigan games of all time, the 1950 Snow Bowl. Historians call it that because it was played in an absolute blizzard. The temperature was five above and 40-mile-an-hour winds whipped over two feet of snow into really unplayable conditions. But, both athletic directors decided too many tickets had been sold and rescheduling would have caused too many problems, so they agreed to play."

Not only did Bob Momsen play in the game, but he also blocked a Michigan punt to set up a Vic Janowicz field goal. However, another Libbey graduate of 1945, Bob's older brother Tony, trumped his younger brother's efforts. Tony not only blocked a punt but fell on it in the end zone for a touchdown right before the first half. This proved to be the difference in a 9-3 Michigan win.

The game was remarkable for some of its statistical oddities. Michigan won despite not gaining one first down and only having 27 yards in total offense. The two teams combined for an absurd forty-five punts on the worst weather day in the history of college football, with the teams often punting on first down just to see if a turnover could be forced and better field position gained.

Bob went on to play for the Lions in the NFL, while his brother Tony also played in the NFL for the Pittsburgh Steelers. Those were the famous Momsen brothers of Libbey first and then the NFL.

During his first fall at Libbey in 1948, Dick got his first taste of organized football. He played quarterback on the freshman team, and it was an initial experience he'll never forget. "I remember my buddies and I played some sandlot football when we were in grade school, but, man, was it ever different in pads! As I recall, we played four games that year. I really can't remember doing anything all that spectacular, but I sure did enjoy it! In a program as strong as Libbey's, all eyes were trained on the varsity, but that was OK by me. I knew I'd get my varsity shot eventually."

During his sophomore year, Dick played on a team those familiar with Toledo high schools called a lightweight team. Strahm was technically not a varsity player at this point but did get plenty of opportunities to improve his skills under games conditions as most area schools had a lightweight squad. Recalls Dick, "We played a regular city schedule, the same schools as the varsity played."

It was during Dick's sophomore year that the Libbey Cowboys had a wealth of talent on the varsity team. Especially noteworthy was a core group of senior linemen and one junior in particular, a junior so good he would, one day, go on to play at an All-Pro level in the National Football League.

One of the tackles that year was George Jacoby, who would receive a scholarship to play at Ohio State University and eventually be chosen captain of the Bucks.

Then, there were the Geyer brothers. Ron took off north to Ann Arbor, Michigan, to play for the Wolverines. He would eventually start both his junior and senior years as an offensive lineman. His brother Paul was also a gifted basketball player for Libbey and went north with his brother to play basketball at Michigan.

It was Paul Geyer who would eventually resurface in Dick's life many, many years later, as Dick recalls. "Paul eventually wound up in Findlay during my tenure as coach. He started working at Marathon Oil, and when he retired, he became the owner of Coldwell Banker in Findlay. My wife, Ginger, was a realtor in Paul's office, from which she eventually retired. Although I didn't know Paul very well back in my Libbey days when he was a senior and I wasn't really even a varsity player yet, it's funny how life is. He came back into my life so many years later to become such a dear friend to both Ginger and myself."

Glen Mugler also played on the formidable Libbey line. Upon graduation, he headed south as a scholarship football player. Where he wound up was Coral Gables, Florida, as a member of the Miami Hurricanes.

The junior who played center that year turned out to be the best of the lot, despite the fact that the other four were Division I scholarship athletes. He would have to wait one more year for his own scholarship offer from perennial collegiate power University of Notre Dame.

His name, Dick Syzmanski, became known throughout the football world. After a stellar career for the Fighting Irish, he went on to play more than twice as long as the average NFL player, thirteen seasons in all, and all for the same team, the Baltimore Colts. He was a three-time Pro Bowler and snapped the ball time after time to one of the best quarterbacks in the history of the league, Johnny Unitas. Syzmanski also played in one of the most famous and most important games in league history, the 1958 overtime championship game between his Colts and the New York Giants. Along with the hulking Jim Parker (a graduate of Toledo Scott High School and then Ohio State), Syzmanski cleared the way for Alan (The Horse) Ameche to dive over from the one in the extra session for the 23-17 victory. Millions watched that game on their black-and-white televisions enthralled with the first truly great pro football championship game that was seen in such large numbers.

By the time Strahm entered his junior year, all that remained of the incredible Toledo Libbey Cowboy linemen was Syzmanski. Strahm was the starting safety that year, and he recalls with a chuckle, "Syzmanski was our starting center that year and also played linebacker. Although the safety is considered the last line of defense and often piles up a ton of tackles on a typical high-school defense, with Syzmanski in front of me, there wasn't a lot of tackles for me to make.

"He was so quick, especially laterally, and had such a nose for the football, well, it was obvious to me he was special and would really make his mark. But, thirteen seasons in the NFL playing a position where he got pounded on play after play? I don't think anyone could have predicted how good he would become."

In addition to his duties as the starting safety, Strahm also returned punts. One indeed was memorable. "It came against one of our biggest rivals, Toledo Central Catholic. Late in the fourth quarter, we were losing. However, we stopped them and forced them to punt, so I dropped back.

"It was short punt that I had to sprint up to field. I caught it on the fly, took off, and ran it all the way back for the winning TD. I must have made some good moves because the write-up in the paper the next day gave me a nickname. In the account, I was referred to as Dick 'Music Legs' Strahm, I guess for the way I ran. I remember I had to make several cuts while guys missed tackles.

"Boy, after that came out in the paper, did I ever get razzed as school! I'd be walking down the hall, and I'd hear, 'Hey, Music Legs, where you goin'?' Although it was really neat being recognized for something I'd done, I guess I didn't care for the nickname too much."

It was the Thanksgiving games that really remain so special in the memory bank of Dick Strahm. "Each year, there would be two games on Thanksgiving, Libbey versus DeVilbiss and Scott versus Waite. The games would start at ten in the morning, and there wasn't a seat to be had. I can remember as many as seven, eight thousand people at the games I played. In the 1940s and '50s especially, it was just the thing to do on Thanksgiving. It almost seemed if you didn't go hunting, you went to one of those two football games."

After those games, Dick would shower and return home to Toronto Avenue to clean up and then head over with Mom and Dad and Dale to Grandma and Grandpa Strahm's for the big meal and a rehashing of what had gone on at that morning's game. Now that the high-school playoffs have taken over late November and early December in Ohio, there are no city rivalry games on Thanksgiving. Those who are old enough to remember them certainly are saddened that those magical holiday clashes have irrevocably been lost. Once upon a time, these games galvanized communities.

Dick also ran track at Libbey, and the main reason was to continue to cultivate the player-coach relationship with one of the football coaches who also happened to be the head track coach, Charles Robinson.

Dick took part in all the relays. The pinnacle of his track career came during junior year when the Cowboys qualified in 880-yard relay at the state track meet. Recalls Dick, I was the slowest of the four runners, but, then again, somebody had to be. Don't get me wrong. By no means was I slow. It's just that we had some guys who could really fly on that relay team. I really relished the opportunity to run in the state meet at the big stadium in Columbus."

Despite Dick's running track and playing some basketball, his real love continued to be football, and it was a love that resonated with his father. Mentzer Strahm finally did something to address the absence of any football beyond unsupervised sandlot games for junior-high boys while at the same time continuing to affirm that he was a strong supporter of both athletics and children.

While there was still too much resistance among school officials to sponsor sixth-, seventh-, and eighth-grade football and the cost of providing uniforms and equipment was indeed prohibitive, Mentzer Strahm went another direction to create a competitive environment involving football and an opportunity for the boys to get some coaching in the rudimentary elements of the game many would want to play once they entered high school.

The other direction was to incorporate something that had just arrived on the scene, flag football. The Youth Flag Football League of south Toledo was sponsored by the South Toledo YMCA, an organization Mentzer had supported ardently. He was not only a life-long member but also volunteered countless hours to its programs. The league was comprised of Dick's former grade school, Arlington, and three other south Toledo grade schools–Harvard, Walbridge, and Burroughs–and there were separate leagues for sixth, seventh, and eighth grades.

Dick remembers his father's involvement well. "Dad was responsible for lining up other volunteer coaches and officials, formulation of rules, even lining the fields. Basically, he ran all three leagues, kind of like the commissioner."

When football season rolled around for Dick's final year at Toledo Libbey High School, the memories of those fabulous Cowboy linemen, all of whom received full scholarships to play at some of the most prominent football schools in the country, had faded. George Jacoby, Ron and Paul Geyer, Glen Mugler, and Dick Syzmanski all had matriculated to the next level and were playing before throngs of fans in the biggest of venues.

Despite their absence, Dick remains proud of his Libbey Cowboys that took the field his senior year. For his final year, he was moved from one side of the ball to the other, from safety to starting quarterback.

"When we were seniors, we tied for the city-league championship. Obviously, our offensive line wasn't what it was a couple years earlier. We didn't have those types of players, but we did have a bunch of what coaches might refer to as hard-nosed individuals. We played very well together. It was the first time that I experienced the sum of a team being far greater than its individual components."

Players like Tom Smith, Jim McCarthy, Bill Frank, Vic Domhoff, Al Manzey, and Bill Brown replaced the likes of Jacoby, the Geyers, and Syzmanski. Although not Division I linemen, they really came together well as a unit. "We were friends on and off the field, and we were very determined to become the city league football champs," Strahm remembers.

With Strahm at the helm, the Cowboys came at opponents with two excellent running backs, Charlie Craig and Willie Russell, whose job was made easier by a bruising blocking back by the name of Jim Tucholski. How well Dick remembers the contributions of players like Barry Bigelow, Barton Bay, Jim Willey, and Ron Hilfinger.

Dick's senior year also featured a stiff defense, led by the likes of Chuck Berning, Bob Haverman, Alvin Rowe, Ron Heckart, and head coach Herman "Bus" Harding's son, John.

Strahm also remembers his football coaches, "Bus" Harding and his assistant, Charles Robinson, with a respect that, to this day, has never waned. "Coach Robinson was the master motivator of the team. When there was a need for a fiery talk, it was Robinson who would deliver it.

"Now, Coach Harding was another personality type completely. He was actually quite mild mannered, a very distinguished gentleman. He was the brains behind the offense."

"I guess the two totally different approaches the men demonstrated showed me at a young age that there was more than one coaching style, and each could be effective."

Off the field, both men also were excellent educators. Robinson taught biology, and Harding taught math. Both classrooms were run in a very efficient and orderly fashion. These indeed were professional educators in addition to top-flight football coaches.

Looking back, Dick recalls that each of the men was an excellent role model and each played a role in his ultimate decision to go into education.

With the bedrock formation of Christian values upon which to build and the full support of Dale, the 9-year-old who adored him, and both Mom and Dad, Dick certainly had prospered during his journey through childhood and adolescence.

And, with the end of a boyhood journey comes a tinge or two of sadness for parents, who wonder where on earth the time went. But those nostalgic tendencies are limited to the parents. To the young, the vital, in the best shapes of their lives, capable of running with piano legs until some distant goal line is crossed, high-school graduation was a time to chart a new course much more than to examine the path already traversed.

Dick would be the first in his family to try a new path, the collegiate path. It was a path that led all the way to the state that a certain young football coach at Ohio's state university in Columbus, Wayne Woodrow Hayes, in that year of 1952 would refer to with a certain amount of disdain as "that state up north." For Dick, the next path led all the way to Ypsilanti, Michigan, and a school called Michigan State Normal. He wanted to teach, and, especially, he wanted to coach.

His senior year at college, Dick Strahm (left) and his fraternity brother, "Duke" Garner (right), with Jack Demsey, the famous heavyweight boxing champion of the world, at his restaurant.

Chapter 3

From Toledo to Ypsi and Back Again, the College Years

For Dick Strahm, the decision to leave the state of Ohio to attend college was not made lightly. He started by seeking advice on the weighty matter of where to spend the next four years to train himself for a career, and the person from whom he sought it was one of his Libbey teachers, Ruth Allen, who taught Dick typing.

Despite the fact that Allen was an Ohio State graduate, she didn't steer him in that direction. Instead, she had in mind a school that specialized in the training of teachers, Michigan State Normal College in Ypsilanti. Since one of her teaching colleagues, William Everhart, was a graduate, she sent the soon-to-graduate Toledo Libbey High School senior to him.

Everhart was the head of Libbey's English department and one of Dick's former instructors. Strahm remembers his kindness in helping Dick make this very important decision.

"Mr. Everhart really took the time to tell me about Michigan State Normal and even brought in some literature for me to look at. He also put me in touch with one of the women's physical education teachers, Mrs. Mayer, who also went to school there, since he knew I not only had a strong interest in teaching but also in staying involved in sports.

"After school I went in to see Mr. Everhart, I saw him sitting at his desk grading papers, which was not unusual. It was well known that Mr. Everhart never left his classroom before at least an hour or so of grading papers and also making himself available for any help a student might need.

"He immediately put his grading pen down and probably spent a good hour with me talking about Normal. When I told him I didn't want to take up too much of his time, he said to me, 'Richard, the most important thing I have to do at this moment is to help you any way I can to make a difficult decision.' It was this type of teacher who got me seriously thinking about a career in education."

The school that Everhart and Mayer told Dick about would train him for the only career he ever remembers seriously considering as he came through the Toledo Public Schools. His career choice was largely a result of the strong role models he observed at Libbey, especially his football coaches Herman "Bus" Harding and Charles Robinson, men who not only led teams to victories on the football field but also were so impressive in front of their classes.

"You see, I wanted to be more than just a coach. I also wanted run a classroom like Coaches Harding and Robinson."

Certainly the two coaches weren't aware of their recruiting the young Strahm into a career in teaching and coaching. All they did was present themselves as complete professionals both in school and on the field. As they did, the seeds were planted in Mildred and Mentzer's oldest son's mind. For Dick, as was the case for many young men and women of parents who endured the Great Depression, he would be the first in his family to attend college.

The school Strahm selected was called a normal school because when "Normal" schools began to appear in America in the nineteenth century, the schools' objective was to train their students to be educators whose job it would be to teach norms, or rules, to their charges.

The first were established in Massachusetts in the 1830s. The intent was that these schools produce more qualified teachers as a young America experienced its first strong movement to educate her youth. Soon, the idea of the normal school began to take root in other parts of the country.

The first normal school west of the Appalachians was Michigan State Normal College, now Eastern Michigan University. The college opened its doors in Ypsilanti in 1849.

Ypsilanti, or Ypsi as it is sometimes called, is located about 35 miles west of Detroit and 8 miles east of Ann Arbor. In many ways, it's a typical small-college town, an environment not altogether unlike Findlay, Ohio, where Dick would one day solidify his hold on the very top rung of the small-college coaching ladder.

Dick visited Ypsi with his mom and dad just after his Libbey graduation in the spring of 1952. They found a city of around 20,000, a city filled with tree-lined neighborhoods which surrounded the campus. Ypsilanti also had a strong industrial base, encouraged by the emergence of the auto industry in Detroit. Automobiles are to Ypsi what oil is to Findlay.

However, for Dick, the city's profile was of far less importance than the school, and, also, his desire to play football.

While meeting with academic advisors, he decided on a physical education major and minors in history and English so that he would increase his job opportunities when he had completed his college years.

No doubt, the visit also had to include his meeting the football coach and seeking permission to come early for August practices. The coaches were impressed with the fact that the 5'8," 152-pound Strahm, despite his smaller stature, played Toledo city football at Libbey.

It was hard to find anyone involved in college football that didn't have great respect for the kind of high school football played in Toledo.
Strahm indeed did receive that invitation to come for those August practices, known to anyone who's ever played organized high school or college football as "two-a-days." So, in effect, Strahm was signed, sealed, and would deliver himself, via State Route 23 to Michigan State Normal College in August before the fall semester.

Money did concern the family somewhat. With Dale still at home and the cost of higher education, Mentzer Strahm would do his best. However, he was a working-class man, and his job at Champion Spark Plugs and his painting houses on the side surely wouldn't be enough to pay his oldest son's tuition, books, room, board, and incidental expenses during his stay in Michigan's second-oldest city.

So, that summer, Dick took a job at SE Johnson, working construction for a wage of $1.75 an hour. All of what he earned would go towards his education. However, there was certainly no guarantee even the combined efforts of Mentzer and Dick Strahm would be enough, but they were surely going to try.

When Strahm arrived in August for two-a-days, he became one of about seventy players who took the field. There were actually two practice fields, and the first thing Dick noticed while working to make a good first impression on one field is the other field also was being used.

"I saw these men, every one of them so much bigger than anyone I saw on our practice field, and they were going through drills. It was the Detroit Lions, one of the best, if not the best team in the NFL during the decade of the 1950s. I knew the names of so many of the players, since they had been heroes of mine growing up."

The players Strahm saw were many of the league's premier players. There was the legendary Texan quarterback, Bobby Layne. A few feet away stood former Notre Dame Heisman Trophy winner Leon Hart and the great running backs Doak Walker and Pat Harder. The coach blowing the whistle was the lucky head of all that talent, Buddy Parker.

"I remember one day Leon Hart walked by us and said, 'Hey, what are you little guys doing here?' He didn't say it in a mean way. It was more like he was surprised anyone else would be here during their pre-season camp."

The Lions were indeed the scourge of professional football at this time. Led by the playboy king Layne, who played off the field with the same passion as he competed on it, the Lions were young and talented. Averaging just 25 years of age, they would a few months later win the NFL championship by defeating the Cleveland Browns of quarterback Otto Graham 17-7 in front of 51,000 fans.

To prove their championship was no fluke, the Lions would win a second straight crown in 1953 by again defeating the Browns 17-16 when Layne hit Jim Doran for a 33-yard TD pass and Doak Walker kicked the point after touchdown.

The Lions would also make two more visits to the championship game before the '50s would expire, losing to the Browns in 1954 56-10 and then returning the favor by shellacking Cleveland in 1957, 59-14.

After weeks of toiling in the hot Michigan sun, the the teams that shared the same practice facilities felt they were ready, the Lions for teams like the Packers and the Bears and the Michigan State Normal College Hurons for opponents hailing from places like Grand Rapids, Michigan, and Valparaiso, Indiana.

Many of the citizens of Ypsilanti were football enthusiasts. The older ones who had followed the fortunes of the local team sometimes referred to them as the Normalites, or, quite simply, the Men from Ypsi.

The Hurons had a junior varsity, and, as a freshman, that's where Dick found himself assigned. "The schedule was largely made up of playing junior colleges, a couple of which were in the Chicago area."

Dick's most memorable gridiron moment during that crisp fall of 1952 came against Grand Rapids Junior College. With Mom and Dad and the 10-year-old Dale in attendance, Dick, as they say in football parlance, "broke one off."

As Dick recalls, "The game was tied in the fourth quarter, and my number was called. I remember it was an off-tackle play, and the blocking was terrific. I got through the hole and made a couple of cuts in the secondary and took it all the way."

The play covered 65 yards, and it turned out to be the winning score. Dick had captured some of that old music-legs Libbey glory. "After the game, Mom was very happy we had won and that I got the winning touchdown. I remember my dad asked me why I had waited so long to break one off. I also remember my brother just wanted to get a few more glimpses at the cheerleaders."

For the kid from Libbey, the rest of the season had its ups and downs. "In a season of football, there will almost always be peaks and valleys. I guess the key is to enjoy the peaks and learn from the valleys."

Certainly, a pleasant memory was being selected to be on the traveling squad for one of the varsity's overnight games. "We played Valparaiso over in the Hoosier state. To be honest, after all these years, I don't really recall much of the game. I know I didn't see the field during the contest. I guess I was pretty much in awe. You see, freshmen didn't dress even for home games very much and even more infrequently for road games. However, each game, the coaches got together and decided who was really working hard and who deserved it, so it was really a big deal. Well, to travel by Greyhound bus and stay in a hotel overnight was a real treat."

At that point, Dick was also making his way nicely in the classroom, juggling each day's clock as well as could be expected for a student-athlete. "Anyone who hasn't experienced what it's like to try to balance time spent on studies with trying to compete in a college sport really has no idea how hard it is. Between daily practices, games, meetings, and classes, it is sometimes so difficult to fight off the fatigue of such a hectic schedule to study at night. It was taking about every ounce of energy I had and about every spare cent my family and I mustered, but I was making it."

Dick had already dressed for a couple varsity games and had even seen his first varsity action in one of them on a kickoff-coverage team. It was a thrill so vivid, he vowed if he ever got to be a head coach, he would go to almost any length to fill his special teams with as many freshmen as he could.

"Years later, some of the more, shall we say, spirited debates I had with my assistant coaches involved my insistence that special teams be made up of the younger guys who didn't start, mainly the ones who were on our scout teams, the guys who busted their tails every day in practice to make our first team better.

"My coaches would say to me, 'We need to put our best people out there because the other team is doing that. What if we give up a return for a touchdown or get an extra point blocked because we don't have our best guys out there?'

"The way I looked at it, the young guys deserved to see that game field, so I told my coaches that if our inexperience cost us a touchdown because of a special-teams breakdown, I'd take the blame when I had to face the press. And you know what? In all the years of coaching in high school and college, I can recall very few times where the young guys let me down.

"I wanted to not only reward the young guys but I also wanted them to feel they were a part of the same team those starters were on, the ones whose names were all over the post-game write ups in the local paper. I also wanted all the Moms and Dads to see their young men coming out onto that field at least a couple times a game. As a parent myself, I know how important that is.

"Besides, when I was coaching Findlay, we had no scholarships at all until 1989, and even after that, we had a very limited number [eight, for the entire team] and parceled them out in quarters to try to provide as much help to as many players as possible. So the Moms and Dads were making a tremendous financial commitment by picking up the $20,000 and more a year to send their sons to play for me.

"It just made sense to me all around to get those young guys on the field, and I believe my commitment to this coaching philosophy traces its roots all the way back to Ypsilanti and the feeling I had running down field covering a kickoff in a college varsity game."

Late in the year, Dick was forced to face one of those valleys almost all football seasons have. Early on a Friday afternoon, Dick consulted the list of players that was always posted with the names of those dressing for the next day's game. Of course, the starters never consulted it, but the custom of checking the posting was a religious one for the young guys. "Since I had already dressed for some games, including the Valparaiso overnighter, I really didn't think I'd see my name. However, there it was, my name next to number 22. It was the last home game of the year, and I knew there would be a big crowd. I would get to dress varsity again! I called my mom and told her so that she and Dad and Dale could drive up.

"Friday practices were always light workouts, not much more than walkthroughs. I had already put on the game jersey that everyone on the list wore to the final practice before game day and was heading out to the field.

"Then, and I remember this as if it happened last week instead of over fifty years ago, a sophomore came running up to me. He said, 'Hey, Strahm. Give me your jersey. Coach said I was dressing in your place because you've already dressed for three home games.' I resisted at first until he convinced me that he really was sent to find me to get the jersey. After all, no player would ever do this on his own.

"He told me that he hadn't gotten to dress all year. Of course, this meant little to me. I was too young to ever see any fairness to any of this. All I knew was I saw the list, my name was on it, and I had already called home to tell my family to head up the next morning. Then this guy comes up and tells me this. Well, you could almost hear the air rush out of me as I slowly pulled off the jersey and tossed it to him.

"I walked back into the empty locker room, and you might say I was a little pissed off."

In that moment of despair, Dick made a decision, certainly not the wisest decision but one made purely out of anger and that feeling of helplessness tinged with a pretty fair amount of righteous indignation. He'd just had the proverbial rug pulled out from under him without even a coach talking to him directly and explaining the decision. Instead, he'd sent another player to demand the jersey, that symbol of varsity stature, that piece of evidence that made you one of the Men of Ypsi.

Dick pulled off the rest of his football uniform, dressed, and went back to the dorm. "I packed a few clothes, grabbed my shaving gear and toothbrush, and left."

Strahm got on Route 23 and stuck out his thumb, and in an era where it wasn't at all unusual to see hitchhikers, he found a passing motorist who just happened to be on his way to Toledo.

When he walked in the door of the house at 848 Toronto Avenue, no one was more surprised than Mildred Strahm. She had already called her husband at work, and there was no question the family would be heading up to Michigan for the game.

Recalls Dick, "I told Mom what had happened. Although she did sympathize with me, her maternal instincts didn't mask her feeling I had made a mistake by leaving. She told me I should have gone out to that practice and supported my teammates, and it was her feeling that certainly one of the coaches would have talked to me after practice. She asked me if I wanted Dad to drive me back when he got home from work so that I could go to the game, but I was just too disappointed and embarrassed to even consider it. And, of course, being a kid, I couldn't see the wisdom in what my mom was suggesting. Also, I will admit I had a steady girl I hadn't seen in quite some time."

For Dick, this incident was another seminal moment in formulating another coaching philosophy that he would one day employ. "I made up my mind that if I ever was fortunate enough to become a head coach that I would never handle an unexpected personnel move without first talking to the player or players involved face to face. I don't know whether that sophomore had complained to the coaches and caught them at a weak moment and was told to go get that jersey or what. But, I knew how I felt and made a promise I would never handle a situation in this manner. And in thirty-four years of being a head coach, I never did!"

After the football season, Dick could devote more time to his studies. While he continued to do well academically and his disappointment over how the season had ended had subsided, by the end of the semester, it became obvious from a financial standpoint, he would not be able to remain at Michigan State Normal. "Money just became too tight. I had already committed every penny I made at SE Johnson and knew my parents just weren't able to afford to keep me in Ypsilanti. Although I really would have rather stayed and felt I would be seeing some varsity time as a sophomore, I really didn't have a choice.

"My mom and dad and I decided that enrolling for the second semester at the University of Toledo was the only option. Then I could live at home and commute to my classes. This way, Mom and Dad would take care of the room and board, and I could save enough SE Johnson money to pay my tuition."

After enrolling, Strahm decided to remain on a course that would earn him a physical education degree as well as the two minors in English and history. He also decided since he was no longer a Huron football player in Michigan, he would try to make the Toledo Rockets team in Ohio.

Dick received permission from Rocket head coach Frosty England to come out for spring football. As Dick recalls, "Back then, spring practice was much longer than it is today, something like twenty-five or thirty practices. It was a lot different playing against Mid-American Conference players than at Ypsilanti, but I made it through without any significant injuries, that is until the last practice."

Dick knew the Rockets competed in a well-respected, what would be called today, mid-major football conference, the MidAmerican. The players were bigger, quicker, and generally stronger than where he'd been, which became a problem when Dick was tabbed to be a running back on the scout team that routinely went up against the number-one defensive unit.

In the final football practice that Strahm would ever attend as a player, the scout team was going against the number-one defense. This deep into spring practice, with no game just around the corner, it's easy for a starter to lose his edge, to coast a bit and that's what Strahm thinks may have happened with one all-conference defensive tackle.

"The play we ran was a trap, and we caught the tackle totally off guard. Our guard came across and trapped him, and when the linebacker got blocked, I broke loose. I got through the hole and went untouched all the way until I heard a whistle. At that point, I was feeling pretty good. I hadn't really done much up to that point in the spring and perhaps, I remember thinking, this might catch Coach England's eye.

"It did, all right, but not the way I wanted. I saw the coaches just jumping all over this big tackle and the rest of the defense for letting a scout team score on them like that as I trotted back to the huddle. Then, I heard those words scout teamers absolutely despise. 'Run it again!'

"Of course, the second time, the lineman is, first of all, angry and humiliated, and second, fully aware of exactly what play will be run. Imagine how ineffective a trap play is when there is no element of surprise.

"At any rate, the defensive tackle charges off the ball and is waiting on the trapping guard. He gets underneath him and drives him right back into the backfield and into me right as I was getting the ball. My helmet goes one way and the ball the other, and I got my leg pinned under the combined weight of my own guard and a very angry 250-pound defensive tackle as they fell on me.

"There I was, seeing the bees buzzing around as I look up from the ground. My nose was bleeding, and the force of the blow almost knocked me out."

Dick remembers his initial attempt to get up. "I tried to stand and fell right back down. I could feel something very wrong in my knee, and even to this day, I can feel a bone sticking out at an unusual angle.

"I was on crutches for a week and then wore a brace for another week or two. Surgeries, except for broken bones in the early 1950s were pretty rare. No doubt, had a player sustained this type of injury today, there'd have been a procedure."

Several days after the spring set of practices had ended, after the coaches had met with the first-unit players and those considered top prospects to assess their performances, Dick Strahm was summoned to Coach England's office.

Of course, the first question involved the condition of Dick's knee. Strahm told the coach that if he worked all summer reconditioning it, he probably could be ready by the fall. However, that wouldn't be possible, since he would have to work full time at SE Johnson to earn tuition money for his sophomore year.

Then Dick asked England for an honest assessment of his chances of seeing any varsity action. "I remember asking Coach England, 'Can I help you win?' He told me probably not, if it meant did he ever think that I could start. He said I could contribute as a scout player for a couple years and maybe play on some special teams as a senior, but that was about all he could envision.

"I've never forgotten what he said next because it really was a sincere way to handle my situation. He said, 'Strahm, I don't doubt your heart. I've seen enough this spring to know you've got a lot of guts, but you simply aren't big enough to play at this level.'

"There is so much that goes into the making of a coach, and, I guess, this was another lesson I was taught, how to be honest yet do so with compassion and some sensitivity. It was yet another moment I mentally filed, ready to use if I ever became a coach."

The story was one that Strahm told countless Findlay Oilers scout players, especially after those sweltering August two-a-day practices during evening meetings. After the players were cleaned up and fed, when the persistent ache of countless on-field collisions announced its intent to stay, the master motivator Dick Strahm would tell the "Run-it-again" story, just so his players realized that he had once upon a time walked in their cleats; felt exactly how they felt; felt, as a matter of fact, worse than they felt.

Through the telling of this event, Strahm not only bonded with his players, especially the non-starters, but also showed them the importance of what they do to help the team win. It was also a way to use humor to teach, since Strahm's considerable speaking skills allowed him to add the necessary tone inflections and embellishments and dramatic pauses to make the story resonate. For Coach Strahm, the story was simply known by what all scout teamers would shout in unison whenever Strahm would ask what coaches yell when a scout team play catches the first unit off guard, "Run it again!"

After another summer fending off the hot Midwestern sun while working on SE Johnson asphalt crews, Dick was anxious to leave the sweltering work for the more moderate classrooms at the University of Toledo.

He was progressing nicely toward his degree, so well, as a matter of fact that he yearned to find some athletic activity to try to fill the void that football had left.

One of those activities was a sport in which Dick had little experience. Recalls Strahm, "One day, when I was walking down the main hall at the athletic complex after working out, I was stopped by the wrestling coach, Joe Scalzo. Coach Scalzo was one of the wrestling coaches for the U.S. Olympic team in 1952. He wanted me to come out for the team. The 154-pounder had sustained an injury and would be out for a while, and he wanted me to take his place. I decided to try it.

"After several practices where I was coached aggressively to try to bring me to a level I could compete with wrestlers with much more experience, it was time for my first wrestling match, and it was against a very good wrestling squad, the University of Pittsburgh.

"At that time, there were only nine weight classes, so I had to wait for the lighter divisions to conclude. I recall being pretty nervous because the guy I would wrestle was the runner-up in the NCAA finals the previous year.

Dick's brother Dale counts the memory of the match as perhaps his favorite involving his older brother. "My brother is probably the most intense competitor I have ever met, so when he came home that one day and told us he was going to wrestle, it didn't surprise me. Dick never would let a small detail like having almost no wrestling experience stop him.

"I was around ten or eleven at the time, and I went to Dad and said, 'Dick's wrestling this Saturday. I think we ought to go.' I'll never forget the look on my dad's face when he said, 'He's what?'

"See, my father knew Dick was practicing with the wrestling team but never really thought he'd get in any matches, much less have one against one of the premier wrestling programs in the country.

"Anyway, Saturday comes, and Mom, Dad, and I go to the field house. The wrestler Dick is competing against is announced as last year's NCAA runner-up. The announcer then gives his college career record as something like 65 and 6.

"Then, the announcer introduces Dick and tells the crowd that this is Dick's first match.

"Dad and I looked at one another as if to say, 'Uh-oh, Dick may be in some trouble.' Well, the match gets under way, and Dick actually scores on an escape. Despite being behind on points, Dick is wrestling pretty competitively, but even as young as I was, I could kind of sense that the guy was just toying with Dick.

"The referee told them to break, and they both stood up facing one another. They get in attack position, and suddenly, for a reason even my brother can't explain, Dick hauls off and slaps the guy in the face!

"And, that triggered the Pitt wrestler's rage. About ten seconds later, Dick was down on his back pinned. Dad looked over and said, 'I think Dick made a mistake.' I said, 'I think you're right. Dick made him mad.'"

To this day, more than a half century later, Dick is at a loss to explain what went through his mind. "I'm sure it was accidental. All I know is my adrenaline was really pumping, a combination of excitement and fear. What I do remember is the big 'Whomp' sound when I slapped him.

"After the match, he asked me why I had slapped him, and I said I didn't mean to. He told me he was getting a good workout, but when I slapped him, that was it.

"I wrestled a few more matches and then the offended wrestler came back, and that was the end of my wrestling career."

At the end of Dick's sophomore year, the former wrestler joined a fraternity, Sigma Alpha Epsilon. "My grade-school pal Bob Zedlitz was an SAE, and that's kind of why I joined," Dick recalls. There was also another fraternity brother who would become a wonderful friend long after Dick's UT days were over and a great supporter of athletics, especially the Findlay Oilers football program, Tom Hart.

The fraternity also brought Dick back to one of his great sports loves of his youth, fast-pitch softball. Not only did he and Bob and Tom and several other brothers find great success in the fraternity league but they also played during the summer on a team sponsored by Henry Meats in the Softball Association of Toledo.

Recalls Bob, "Our love of the game kind of got a booster shot. We started playing it on the playground on our own field of dreams years ago, and now we had a wonderful opportunity as young men to again do what we so loved as children.

Remembers Dick, "Bob had developed a reputation while playing during our UT days, especially in the summer, as one of the best pitchers in Northwestern Ohio. We had so many good ballplayers on that team. There were guys like Pete Finch, Duke Garner, Paul Leinger, Dave Wojtkowiak, Tom Hart, and Bob Falter. We were a very good Division A team.

"During the summer, we played all over. I remember one game we played at the Ohio Penitentiary in Columbus. The feeling once you got behind those walls was really kind of frightening. The prison team was very good and obviously had what you might call a great home-field advantage. They were on the longest stretch of home games in the history of sports!

"In the first inning I singled sharply to center. As probably the fastest guy on the team, my teammates always looked for me to steal whenever I got on first. I must have had that "I'm-taking-off-on-the-first-pitch" look because the first baseman said to me, 'Hey, boy. You aren't thinking about stealing, are you?' When I smiled at him, he said, 'See that shortstop down there? He's in for murder, and he just hates it when guys steal because he thinks it makes him look bad.' Needless to say, I never attempted to steal a base the whole game. Every time the third-base coach flashed the steal sign, I just shook my head!"

During the summer before Dick's senior year, three activities took almost all his time. He continued earning his tuition money working for SE Johnson, he and Bob did a fair share of walleye fishing and water skiing off of Toledo Beach, and Henry Meats took on all comers on softball diamonds throughout the city.

One of those comers drew one of the biggest crowds in Toledo softball history when the nationally renowned King and His Court came to play an exhibition against Henry Meats. The King, of course, was Eddie Feigner, widely regarded as the greatest fast-pitch softball hurler to ever play the game.

Feigner, who passed away in February of 2007 at the age of 81, toured with a team comprised of just four players. Besides Feigner and his catcher, there was a shortstop and a first baseman.

Feigner pitched competitively for 55 years and won 95 percent of the time, while playing in venues from Yankee Stadium to the Great Wall of China. He struck out over 140,000 batters, including Willie Mays and Roberto Clemente when both were at the peak of their Hall of Fame careers.

While pitching from second base, which Feigner did frequently, the iconic hurler once had his fastball clocked at 104 miles an hour.

When Strahm faced the King, Eddie was in his absolute prime. He was just shy of 30 years old. Despite this, the ultra-competitive Strahm truly felt he could get a hit off Feigner. Recalls Dick, "I got a chance to meet Eddie before the game. We made a friendly wager of a dollar that I'd get a hit off him, not just hit the ball, mind you, actually get a hit! I don't know which was crazier, thinking I could win that wrestling match against the NCAA runner-up or I could get a hit off the greatest softball pitcher of all time. To make a long story short, he struck me out twice, on three pitches, from second base."

Zedlitz recalls another game when Henry Meats played in an Association tournament championship game. "It was right at the tail end of the summer, and we were playing the final game of the tournament on a lighted diamond behind Waite Stadium. I was pitching, and we had a one-run lead in the last inning. The second half of the game, it was starting to get real foggy. Well, I gave up a hit and surrendered a walk and after a double steal, the tying and winning runs are on second and third.

"All we needed was one more out. The lights illuminated the infield pretty well, but from the infield all you could see when you looked out in the outfield was a huge blanket of fog. Dick was playing centerfield although no one, including the umpire, could see him out there. I was just hoping I could somehow keep the ball in the infield.

"But because so often in sports there is a gap between desire and execution, I wasn't able to get that done. I was really about out of gas and left the ball up in the zone, and the guy whacked it into centerfield. As soon as the ball was hit, every one in the infield started screaming, 'Dick, it's coming your way!'

"Of course, no one could see anything. All of a sudden, out of the fog, we hear, 'I see it!' Then a couple seconds later, here comes Dick sprinting into the infield holding his glove up with the ball in it. Although there's no way the umpire could have seen the catch, what could he do but call the batter out?

"To this day, I suppose there are those there that night that wonder if Dick really caught that ball in the air or grabbed it on a hop, but not me. There's one thing I remember about Dick, and this traces all the way back to Arlington Elementary, and that is he had an uncompromising sense of fair play. If he says he caught it, believe me. He caught it."

Years later, when Dick was told of Zedlitz's recollection, he smiled. It was a smile that had the unmistakable traces of nostalgia, not the smile of a fox that'd just robbed the henhouse and gotten away with something. "No question," he said. "I caught it."

During Dick's final years at the University of Toledo, he not only successfully completed his degree in physical education and picked up both history and English as a double minor but he also gained his first experience doing something he yearned to do before he even took the first few steps away from Libbey High School's front steps. He got to coach.

"I coached basketball at both Harvard and Arlington grade schools. It was seventh and eighth grade, and the pay was pretty decent. Of course, I probably would have done it for free, but I sure didn't tell anyone that. Besides, my pay from SE Johnson could always stand a little supplementing.

"While I had decided years before that education would be my field, my experience coaching those teams made my choice a certainty. Teaching and coaching would be my thing. It was what I enjoyed, and, I thought, gave me the best chance to be successful. This also gave me a chance to coach my brother Dale and his pal, Larry Cook."

That pal was the same Larry Cook who would over fifty years later find his way to South Bend, Indiana, to watch his old basketball coach enter the College Football Hall of Fame as one of the most successful NAIA coaches ever.

For Dick during his UT stretch run, the lessons he learned were not confined to the classrooms and the gyms. One, in particular, was a lesson so well learned that it stuck with him long after he left his college years behind. The lesson involved moderation, or, in the case of one night, the lack thereof.

"During my time in the SAE fraterntiy, I met a lot of wonderful guys and had a lot of great experiences. But, perhaps the most memorable incident was one that really wasn't at all enjoyable. I had just turned 21 when a bunch of older frat brothers insisted I go out drinking with them.

"These guys were probably 24, 25 years old. They were veterans of the Korean War, and most had been in the fraternity before they went in the service.

"I wasn't going to go at first. To be perfectly truthful, at that point in my life, I had never even had a drink, but they kept saying, 'We've got to take the little jock with us.' Finally, I relented.

"We went barhopping, and I drank whisky, whisky, and then some more whisky. Well, needless to say, I got really intoxicated.

"Instead of taking me back to the frat house, where I sometimes stayed overnight, they felt I'd be better off at home so they deposited me at 848 Toronto.

"All I remember is I crawled up the stairs to the bathroom and filled the toilet bowl a few times. Mom came in and asked if I needed help getting to the bedroom. I told her that wouldn't be necessary, since I'd be using the bowl several more times and probably was going to die anyway.

"The next day, my dad, who had never come in the bathroom for my 2:00 a.m. show, was painting the living room. I can remember how revolting the smell of paint was as I suffered through my first and only hangover of my entire life. Then, he said to me, 'Do you want some whisky?'

"I told him I didn't even want to hear the word much less drink it. I was sick for what seemed like a week after that. At any rate, the whole experience taught me a valuable lesson. To be my best, I needed to be in control. I wanted nothing to do with anything that would impair my desire to reach my goals.

"I went through the rest of college without drinking another drop of alcohol. As a matter of fact, it would be many years later, when I was 33 years old, when I had my next drink. That one night with the Korean War vets stayed with me the rest of my life.

"Even today, I'm certain if I even smelled whisky, I'd probably get sick to my stomach. I never ever wanted to feel the way I felt that night again."

As Strahm approached graduation, Grandpa Strahm thought it prudent to give him an early graduation present, his 1948 Mercury. Recalls Dick, "Grandpa actually gave it to me at the beginning of my senior year so that I could drive to my classes. Although the car was eight years old, I don't think anyone ever forgets his first car. But even more than I cherished that car, I cherish the memory of my grandfather's generosity and his attempt to give me a boost just before I was ready to make my way out into the real world."

For Dick Strahm, it was graduation time from UT, late spring of 1956. While some might say that his educational journey had come to an end, nothing could be further from the truth. When a young person decides on a career in teaching and coaching, the lessons have no immediate end. They are learned day by day until the last lecture is given, the last piece of chalk is put on the ledge, the last whistle is blown to huddle a team up.

For Dick, it was time to spread his wings and begin his ascent. He had no idea how long he could sustain flight or what altitude he'd reach, but one thing was certain. It was time to leave the nest.

Chapter 4

Venturing Forth
to Teach and Coach

Right after his graduation from the University of Toledo, Dick was faced with the prospect of putting all that education to good use. It was time to seek his first teaching job. Call it the launching of a career, and indeed if a career can be launched as a ship can be, Strahm's career was embarking on an unusually long voyage. While studies reveal that, often, people change careers at least twice before finding satisfaction, Dick Strahm never really wavered. Once he decided four years earlier as a Libbey senior that he would teach and coach, that was it. There would be little thought of doing anything else for the next forty or so years.

During the summer of 1956, Dick continued to live at home on 848 Toronto Avenue with his mom, dad and brother Dale. At that time, Dick heard of an opening at Oakdale Grade School on the east side of Toledo. It wasn't exactly what he would have preferred, since he'd always envisioned himself as a high school teacher and coach. Nonetheless, Strahm realized life often doesn't come out exactly as planned. Sometimes, especially when establishing a starting point in a career, one has to forego what is ideal for what is available.

So, after interviewing and being granted his first teaching opportunity, Strahm was ready to answer his first bell in the classroom in early September. His teaching assignment was seventh and eighth grade science. Recalls Dick, "I had been preparing the second half of the summer by outlining the chapters in the textbook and looking for supplemental material for some lectures and devising some worksheets and tests, but I also knew that the life of a first-year teacher would be full of surprises and quick adjustments. When you're a first-year teacher, you really learn one day at a time.

"During my interview, the principal knew I didn't have a teaching minor in science, but he must have thought I could do the job because they agreed to put me on a temporary certificate and hire me anyway. Remember, this was 1956, and many schools really were interested in the job applicant, sometimes so much so that certification issues weren't deal breakers if an administrator really wanted to hire someone. And that's how I got my first foot in a school door."

Dick Strahm during his first year of teaching seventh- and eighth-grade science at Oakdale Grade School on the east side of Toledo.

Since there were no coaching opportunities available at Oakdale, Strahm returned to a place he excelled as a school-boy athlete, Libbey High School. Because school officials are always interested in volunteers who wish to help with school programs, they readily welcomed home one of their graduates to help coach the freshman football team after school. On Friday nights, Dick also became a volunteer scout for Libbey's varsity.

Looking back, Strahm remembers his experiences in the science classroom and his first forays into the world of coaching fondly. "I really enjoyed teaching seventh and eighth-grade science. It seemed as if the students were eager to learn, and they were fun to be with. No matter what the age factor, there are always valuable lessons for a young teacher to learn.

"One I learned involved a school practice very common in the 1950s, a practice I engaged in for the first and last time that first year. One of my students, an eighth-grade boy, was a real behavior problem, so one day I decided enough was enough. I sent him down to the principal's office, but he wouldn't go. So, I grabbed him by the arm and marched him right out the door, down the hall, and into the principal's office.

"At any rate, we get down there, and the principal tells me that this same boy has been brought down by several other teachers in the last few weeks. Then he says, 'Mr. Strahm, this young man was told the last time he was sent down to see me that if he wound up here again, he was going to get paddled. I'd like you to do the honors.'

"After instructions from the principal, the boy removed his wallet and bent over and grabbed his knees. Then, the principal handed me the paddle. Now, I had what you might call a mentor on staff who had earlier given me some advice about corporal punishment. His name was Mike Marko, the physical education and industrial arts teacher, who was about 6'4" and probably 250 pounds, a really imposing guy.

"He'd told me that if and when the time came when I was to paddle, to only swing once. He said to swing as hard as you can but just once and then get out of there. That's all you really have to do.

"I leaned back and swung that paddle as hard as I could. That boy literally launched himself forward, and he wound up on the floor, hands spread out in front of him, about five feet across the tile. Then I heard the sound of water. I thought that I killed him. He had wet himself.

"The principal looked at me and said, 'That was a good one.' I was afraid I had hit him too hard, but the principal assured me he'd be OK and sent me back to my classroom. He later told me he called the boy's mother. He explained the situation and, in an age when virtually all parents supported school officials, she didn't contest the punishment and took the boy home.

"Although I never had another problem with him when he returned to class, I just decided I'd never go that route again with a disciplinary matter. I learned other ways to redirect behavior without resorting to that measure again."

"Another lesson that Dick learned is as common as it is embarrassing to male teachers. Recalls Dick, "You know, I've heard it said that if you're a male teacher and this doesn't happen at least once during your career, you haven't really taught. I got it out of the way my first year.

"Anyway, I had prepared a great lecture for one particular class and was up there walking around and really giving it my best. Well, there was this little girl named Peggy, who whispered, 'Psst, Mr. Strahm.' As I continued talking, I proceeded down the aisle and arrived at her desk.

"I said, 'Peggy, what is the problem?' That's when she told me in a hushed voice that my zipper was down! I'm sure a lot of the kids noticed it, but I really don't remember any snickering to indicate a problem. That little girl had really alerted me to the problem in the most subtle way possible. Really, for someone only 13 or 14 years old, she really did a nice job.

"There were a few snickers from some of the students who knew what was going on, but, red-faced, I moved on and finished my lecture. I don't know. Maybe it taught me a little something about preparation. I always checked my appearance carefully from that point on, and, fortunately, it never happened again."

Despite Dick's being involved somewhat in coaching by helping with Libbey's freshmen and doing some scouting, he really wanted more. He wanted to be on staff, not just a volunteer, and also wanted the respect that comes with such a position.

Then, an opportunity came up. "I guess my involvement as a volunteer had been noticed. When a position opened at Libbey teaching a class called Freshman Orientation, I was offered the job and accepted. I enjoyed my year at Oakdale, but really felt that to pursue my goal of coaching I needed to be in the same building as the athletes rather than just driving over after school."

Freshman Orientation was a course that, in today's curriculum, might be called by a different title, perhaps Study Skills.

Dick remembers, "The course was kind of an introduction to high school. We had a textbook. I can remember taking classes down to the library so that the librarian and I could show them how the library was used. Also, the textbook had chapters on things like etiquette and different social skills. I thought it was really a pretty good course. Looking back, I might have a hard time explaining to today's teachers how the course content was comprehensive enough to be a full-year offering but somehow it was."

Strahm also became Libbey's youngest assistant coach under head coach Bob Momson, the same Bob Momson who graduated from Libbey in 1947 and went on to play as an All-American at Ohio State, especially as one of the Snow Bowl survivors. As a matter of fact, he played so well that he became a Detroit Lion.

The varsity assistant was George Miley, who had just returned to his alma mater during Strahm's senior year back in 1951 to teach math and coach the offensive backs. Recalls Dick, "I remember he had really helped me with some quarterbacking techniques and also leadership in the huddle my senior year. Often when a coach only arrives during a player's senior year, he doesn't have much of an impact, but that certainly wasn't the case with Coach Miley."

Now, Strahm and Miley would be colleagues, and Miley, who, as a player for the Toledo Rockets in the 1940s twice led the nation in punting, would now fill two important roles for the second-year teacher-coach.

Miley became a mentor. Recalls Dick, "I can't tell you how many times George Miley impacted me professionally. I spent many hours discussing classroom techniques with him. I could see how successful he was as a math teacher, and I wanted some of his secrets. He was happy to share anything he'd learned, both from the classroom and on the football field."

As time progressed, Miley would become more George than Coach Miley to Strahm. In other words, he became a friend, actually a lifelong friend until Miley's passing in the spring of 2005. As a matter of fact, it was Miley who would one day nominate Dick for the City of Toledo Athletic Hall of Fame.

George's mother and father had opened a resort in Bellaire, Michigan, in the 1940s. Nestled in the bosom of Antrum County's famous Chain-of-Lakes, Bellaire is a veritable recreational paradise in the northwest corner of Michigan's Lower Peninsula.

Miley's Resort featured wonderful swimming, boating, fishing, and lodging in the twenty or so cabins that dotted the shores of Lake Bellaire. The Grass River connects Lake Bellaire to the equally pristine waters of other lakes with the names of Clam, Torch, and Elk.

For Miley, helping the family operation was initially a summer pursuit. However, after George left Libbey some years later to take an administrative position at the newly opened Toledo Bowsher High School, the call of Lake Bellaire became more insistent, and when George and his brother Bill's parents passed away, George left education, and he and his wife Annabel and Bill devoted all of their energies toward making sure Miley's Resort remained open and thriving.

For years, Dick remained in touch with Miley, and after Dick married and had his own family, the Strahms would spend many enjoyable vacations on Lake Bellaire at the resort. Steve Strahm, Dick's youngest son, would eventually work at the resort while in high school during the summers.

For Dick Strahm during his embryonic stages of becoming a coach, there were other Libbey coaches who impacted him greatly. The two coaches of the sophomore squad still known by the same term as they were when Dick was a member of the squad, the lightweight team, were Ben Vaznelis and Bill Wirick. Both became mentors to Dick as well.

Recalls Dick, "I really tried not to miss any opportunities to learn from the older coaches around me. I watched their techniques and their methods of dealing with players as well as their game planning. I particularly wanted to know about game preparation, how a coach gets a team prepared to the absolute highest level to compete."

For Dick, Wirick, in particular, became a wonderful source of knowledge. Wirick was a very successful biology teacher and also a track and field coach who achieved near legendary status in the city of Toledo. Not only would Wirick one day be inducted into the City of Toledo Athletic Hall of Fame, joining Dick in those hallowed halls, but he would also be voted into the state of Ohio's Track and Field Hall of Fame.

During Strahm's time at Libbey, he was still living at home, but the address had changed. Recalls Dick, "We had finally moved from 848 Toronto. Our new address, 3250 Ravenwood Boulevard, put us in a nice brick ranch close to Bowsher High School. Bowsher opened when it became apparent that there were simply too many students at Toledo Libbey. Bill Wirick lived just a few blocks away, and, not only did we share duties driving to school but there were also many, many nights I was at Bill's house talking about teaching and coaching methods."

Now living in retirement in Perrysburg, just south of Toledo, Wirick remembers well the young teacher and coach who had not yet turned 25 years old. "Even as a young guy, Dick had the qualities that make a great teacher and coach. It was amazing how quickly he established himself in what was then an older Libbey faculty and how quickly he climbed the professional ladder. Actually, I first met Dick when he was still an undergrad at UT. He approached me and said he wanted some practical coaching experience and asked if I'd take him on as a volunteer, an apprentice, so to speak. I gladly agreed, realizing how sincere he was in becoming a good coach.

"By the time he arrived at Libbey and became a full-time coach, he still was as anxious as possible to learn everything he could about becoming a successful teacher and coach.

"As a matter of fact, besides coaching football, Dick also helped me coach the track team, for free, mind you. When there was no money in the budget to pay him as my assistant, he did it for free."

It was in that track experience that Dick saw up close such marvelous coaching. By the time Wirick left some years later to become Toledo Bowsher's first head football coach, he had a ten-year stretch when the Libbey Cowboy track team was the city champion every year, losing only one meet during that entire time. Recalls Dick, "Everyone wanted to be on Bill's track teams. Heck, he had some squads that numbered well over one hundred kids."

As Strahm eagerly plunged into his second year at Toledo Libbey during the 1959-60 school year, he felt so very fortunate. He had learned so much about the art of teaching and coaching from so many of his colleagues. These men were willing to take the time to help another who would carry the torch to another generation of students and athletes long after they would retire.

Again, Dick taught Freshman Orientation and was assistant football coach.
Anxious for as much coaching experience as he could get, Dick also agreed to become Libbey's very first wrestling coach as the Libbey athletic department initiated the new program. Perhaps drawing on what you might call his brief "slap happy" career as a Rocket wrestler, Strahm dove in and got the program up and running. He also assisted Wirick again in track in the spring, to bring his coaching involvement to three sports in three seasons, fall, winter, and spring.

During the spring of 1959, Dick received a letter from the Lucas County Draft Board that indicated he would probably be drafted. Through conversations with his parents, Wirick, and officials from the Draft Board, Strahm determined that the best course of option was to join the Air Force Reserve, the 180th Tactical Fighter Squadron in nearby Swanton.

This way, he had some control over how he would fulfill his military obligation instead of sitting around waiting to be drafted when he would be told what to do and where to go. Leaving education behind for a while would be tough, but Dick now had three years' experience and had been through the interview process twice. In other words, he had the beginnings of a résumé and knew there were a lot of schools out there.

Remembers Dick, "When I got out, I didn't know if anything at Libbey would be available, but I just felt pretty certain there would be opportunities. I also had no problem with the whole concept of defending my country. I realized even as a young man not quite 25 the blessings under which I'd flourished growing up."

As it turned out, the outfit Dick joined would create quite a legacy. In 2007, the 180th, almost fifty years later, left for its second tour in Iraq. As it was when Dick joined, the squadron is based at Toledo Express Airport. To this day, Strahm still feels somehow connected. "There is a certain feeling of unity, I think, in any branch of the military, not only with the guys with whom you served but even with the ones that came after you."

For Dick, it was off to San Antonio, Texas, for basic training, and during that July and August, he remembers it was certainly a hot time in the old town. "For anyone who's never been to San Antonio in the middle of the summer, he just wouldn't believe the heat and humidity.

"At our camp, we had a red flag that officers actually would raise on days when the heat index was simply too brutal to drill. When that flag would go up, everyone returned to the barracks. Now, mind you, there was no air conditioning, and it was probably about 95 instead of 105 degrees, but at least we were out of the sun."

Strahm remembers a lot of marching interspersed with learning the military way of doing things. "We used to call ourselves 'ground pounders' because of all that marching. We would have night marches once a week, from nine to midnight.

"The rifle was also completely new to me. In spite of never firing a rifle prior to my joining the service, I did eventually become a marksman.

"Also, about every few weeks, each squadron spent a twelve-hour shift on KP [kitchen patrol]. We arrived at three in the morning and wouldn't leave until three in the afternoon after cleaning the kitchen and peeling the potatoes and performing other tasks."

After his time in Texas, Strahm was off to various bases across the country to receive more specialized training. It was at one of those stops, Lowry Air Force Base, in Denver, Colorado, that Dick would not only find more pleasant weather but an education in munitions school. Recalls Dick, "I was trained to fire a .45 revolver. Some of my early attempts to hit the target were very unproductive. The reason was the incredible kick of the weapon. It really was a problem until I got used to it."

He also received an honor he least expected. "I received the American Spirit Honor Medal Award, which designated me as the top recruit out of 750 men. Three of us were selected to be interviewed by a selection board as finalists. I remember that one of the other two guys had five years at a military school prior to joining the Air Force, so I figured he'd get it. However, when the final selection was made, I was selected."

Strahm's parents received the following letter on December 18, 1959, certainly a wonderful Christmas present for a very proud mom and dad.

> *Dear Mr. and Mrs. Strahm,*
>
> *I wish to take this opportunity to congratulate you on the awarding of the American Spirit Honor Medal to your son, Airman Third Class Richard M. Strahm.*
>
> *The American Spirit Honor Medal, adopted by the citizens committee for the Army, Navy, and Air Force, Incorporated, is awarded to our men undergoing Basic Military Training who display outstanding qualities of leadership by best expressing the American Spirit—honor, initiative, loyalty and high example to comrades in arms.*
>
> *Your son has appeared before two selection boards which interviewed him for this award, and he was selected as the leading basic trainee from his entire class. He has demonstrated excellent self-discipline and has shown evidence of proper guidance throughout his early life, for which you can take pride.*
>
> *Airman Strahm, through diligent study in Technical School and in Basic Training, by keeping up-to-date on world affairs, and because of his mature opinions and actions, is a credit to his family and to the United States Air Force.*
>
> *Sincerely,*
> *Leland S. McCants*
> *Colonel, USAF*
> *Commander*

The medallion Strahm received is bronze, almost an inch and a half in diameter. The military mandate, "Serve with Heart, Head, and Hand," appears on the front. On the back are the words, "For High Example to Comrades in Arms."

Many would, no doubt, agree that young people who distinguish themselves in the military actually foreshadow future successes in civilian life. Certainly, for Airman Richard M. Strahm, who would remain an Air Force reservist until January of 1973, the lessons learned during his training with the 180th were valuable.

When Dick completed his training at Lowry and had filled his lungs a final time with that clean Rocky Mountain air, he returned to Swanton with a second lieutenant's commission. His reservist commitment to the Air Force was to train one weekend a month and additionally during a two-week camp each summer.

Since he was unemployed upon arriving back in late January of 1960 in the Toledo area, Strahm decided to pursue a master's degree in guidance counseling at the University of Toledo in the evenings. During the day, he was a substitute teacher at schools like Union Grade School in Maumee and Toledo Rogers High School. Strahm remembers the substitute experiences with mixed emotions. "I really enjoyed the grade school assignments much more than the high school jobs. Spring is not the best time to be a substitute teacher in high schools." At the same time, Strahm was looking for a school in need of a young teacher versatile enough to teach several subjects and also a coach who could work with young athletes.

Since nothing was available in the immediate Toledo area, Dick broadened his search for employment.

"I had heard about a teaching and coaching opportunity at a brand new school that actually hadn't even been built yet, a school that would be named Lakota, south of Toledo. I applied and received my interview with the superintendent and the board. I was offered the position of the head football coach and would teach history in one of the high schools. You see, this was a very unique situation. There were three small Class A high schools [or what would be called Division VI today] out in the middle of farm country that would consolidate as soon as a new school was built. The new school would be open for the 1961-62 school year. However, that left the 1960-61 year, and school officials wanted a consolidated football program out of those three different schools miles apart to play under the name of the school that hadn't even been built yet. They were schools which had previously been long-time rivals."

For a young coach, this would indeed be a very tall order. The schools were Risingsun, Jackson Burgoon, and Jackson Liberty. All had played each other in basketball, but only one of them had even had a football team that played a full schedule and that turned out to be disastrous. Risingsun had a combined record of 0-18 the previous two years. Jackson Burgoon played only six games, and Jackson Liberty had no football program at all. If this were a poker game, one would probably discard all five cards and ask for a re-draw.

The teaching position, American history, was at Risingsun High School, and the rest of Dick's time would be devoted to taking three different groups of young men, many of whom had little else in common besides farming and many of whom had never even picked up a football, and somehow create a team capable of attaining respectability in the San-Wood league.

Surely with the problems of working around farming chores and the logistical problems of waiting for a bus to pick up players from two separate schools to bring them to a third, this was a full plate of problems for Dick. Certainly just being respectable was all anyone could expect. Right?

Well, Strahm didn't see it that way. "I really attacked that job. I was just, what you might say, 'young and dumb enough' to think I could assemble a coaching staff and bring boys from those three different schools together and be successful on Friday nights."

Strahm had gotten to know the coach for whom Bowling Green State University would one day name its stadium, Doyt Perry, through attending his coaching clinics during the Libbey years. It was actually Coach Perry who told Dick about a young man by the name of Karl Koepfer, who had played for him at BG. He had played so well that he was an eighth-round selection in the NFL draft and, ultimately, played for a couple years for the San Diego Chargers. Koepfer, the former outstanding lineman, became Dick's offensive and defensive line coach. Strahm also was assisted by Stan Trupo and John Windnagle.

Coach Perry also gave the fledgling Lakota program a lot of equipment to get started. Recalls Dick, "I'll never forget the help Coach Perry gave us. We also had to buy new uniforms and helmets. I can remember those helmets arriving. They were all white, and my dad and I painted those helmets navy blue in our garage. I wanted the Lakota Raiders to look sharp. Our new uniforms were classy, and we wanted to look as if we knew what we were doing. But only time would tell if this would happen or not."

The first job during the summer before that inaugural season was to recruit players. "I put in a lot of miles driving those country roads that summer drumming up enthusiasm for what we were about to do. There was no place I wouldn't go if someone gave me a lead on a young man who might help us.

"I remember being told about a young man by the name of Dallas Drenning, a senior-to-be who went to Jackson Liberty. Although Drenning had never played football before, I was told he was probably the toughest guy in the whole darn town. I was told I could find him down at the pool hall.

"I drove down there and walked in, and here was this really wiry looking kid playing pool and smoking a cigarette. I walked up to him and told him, 'If you'll throw those cigarettes away for the fall, I'd like you to play football for me.' We sat down and talked, and he wound up coming out. In that one year, he really became a very good football player, really a ferocious hitter and a good person."

With a chuckle, Strahm recalls, "You know, I probably still owe him a pack of cigarettes."

Strahm also remembers a young man named Murphy, who some other recruits told him could be found, no doubt, on a tractor on the family farm. He'd never played before but certainly was big enough to be sought.

"Sure enough," recalls Dick, "after I got directions to the farm, I parked along the side of a road a whole lot more narrow than any I'd ever seen growing up in Toledo. There I saw this big redhead on a tractor out in the middle of the field.

"I waved to him, and all he did was wave back and kept on working that ground. By the time he made the turn to start another row, I'd jumped the fence and was standing right in front of the oncoming tractor. I just decided that either I was going to get me a football player or I was going to be a part of that bean field!"

Strahm, even as a young coach, demonstrated an uncanny ability to get players to do what he wanted. He got them to bust their tails, to run through proverbial brick walls, and, in Murphy's case, to climb down off a tractor and play football for the first time in his life.

Recollects Strahm, "He was a big farm kid, probably every bit of 6'2" and 220 pounds, which was certainly big for 1960, especially in a league comprised of smaller schools. He told me he had all this work to do on the farm. I told him we'd work that out, and we did. What a fine football player he turned out to be. He played just as hard as he farmed, and, when he had cows to milk or a crop to help put in, I adjusted his practice schedule. Instead of making him attend an early morning August practice, I'd have him come in afterwards when he was done with his chores, and I and the rest of the coaches would work him out and work with him on technique.

"I had another player, a big fullback named George Reinhart, who also had milking in the morning that conflicted with practice. Now, I was an ol' city boy and had a hard time understanding what all had to be done for these farm boys, so I went over to the Reinhart farm, and George showed me what he had to do in the morning. I couldn't believe all the work! I figured George was probably working harder than any player I would have at practice, so I made some special accommodations for him too. I simply wasn't going to let any inflexibility on my part interfere with putting a team together."

Another player on that 1960 Raider team was Butch Houdeshell. He was the younger brother of James Houdeshell, a coach and athletic director at Findlay College and a man who a decade and a half later would bring Dick Strahm to Findlay as the college's head football coach.

Butch, who now resides in Port Clinton, Ohio, and is retired from the insurance business, remembers his first-year head coach fondly as well as what he saw as his greatest forté. "He was just fun to play for. He was very honest and upfront with everyone, and I think we all appreciated that. And, was he ever flexible! This was a farm community, and Coach Strahm understood the importance of that. He made so many accommodations for the farm kids so as to be sure that anyone, and I just don't mean the better athletes, but ANYONE could be a part of his team."

Despite the fact that Houdeshell had grown up in football-rich Cory-Rawson before his family moved to rural Fostoria two years earlier, he was another boy who had never played organized football. Remembers Houdeshell, "It was just remarkable to see Coach Strahm take guys like me who didn't know a thing about technique or strategy and make football players so quickly.

"So much of what I saw Dick do when I played for him, I eventually tried to emulate years later when I became head football coach at Bryan High School."

As the saying goes, Coach Strahm was "in it to win it," and that is exactly what the end result was during a truly remarkable 1960 San-Wood League season. Despite facing a myriad of problems, Strahm and his staff— Koepfer, Trupo, and Windnagle—led their band of thirty-nine players onto the practice field for the first time on August 19.

Strahm first began working on not only the fundamentals of the game but he also worked equally hard in breaking down cliques. "One of my main problems was getting rid of the little groups that had formed in the three different schools. I had to get them thinking as a team. Due to rivalries in other sports, especially basketball, during the years before this plan to consolidate the schools, a lot of these kids just didn't like each other very much.

"We practiced at Burgoon and played our games at Risingsun. Of course, practice was always a problem because we had to wait on the bus to pick up the players and transport them. By the time we got everyone there and, factoring in the time it would take to get everyone back, we only got about an hour's worth of practice time once school started."

When the sports editor of the *Bowling Green Daily Tribune*, Dean Roach, interviewed Dick during the pre-season, the first-year head coach showed flashes of the same optimism he would carry throughout his career. "The players are working hard, and they are eager to learn as much about football as we can teach them. They're starting to develop good team spirit, which, we feel, can carry us a long way."

After the Raiders' first scrimmage, a 2-0 loss to Fostoria St. Wendelin, a team which was undefeated and the Seaway Conference champion the year before, Strahm was succinct in his assessment. "The boys were tackling too high, and much work is needed on offensive line play."

The line play was Coach Koepfer's department, and he really went to work. Even as a young coach, Strahm understood the key to winning in football. Success was largely dependent on a strong rushing attack, obviously predicated by strong offensive line play. Dick knew controlling the ball, keeping the clock ticking, and keeping the defense off the field as much as possible would equal wins on Friday nights.

And win on Friday nights the Raiders did! The inaugural game became the inaugural win as well for the young Raiders, 18-6 over Woodville at Risingsun Field. All three touchdowns came on the ground — a five-yard Jim Peters run; a quarterback sneak by another football newcomer, Roger Harris; and an 80-yard punt return by Joe Wirkner.

After a non-league loss to Elmore, Strahm's young charges rattled off four consecutive league wins. In their 32-0 pasting of the Black Knights of Otsego, fullback George Reinhart led a ground attack along with fellow backfield mates Dale Thaxton and Wirkner that was relentless. The Raiders rushed for just three yards shy of 300.

As the calendar moved toward Halloween, the question on the lips of most of the farmers up and down the network of narrow country roads seemed to be the same. "How could a team, quarterbacked by that Harris boy who'd never played a down of football until a few weeks ago, be one win away from winning the league championship?"

Yet that was exactly the scenario. Every San-Wood league marble was going to be had by either Lakota or Maumee Valley Country Day. The site was Risingsun, and the time was October 28, 8:00 p.m. The Mohawks of Miami Valley were heavily favored despite Lakota's successes to that point. After all, they had a combined record of 22-1 over the last two seasons and had won back-to-back league crowns. The featured back was the big fullback, Jim Birr, who would go on to play Ivy League football after his playing days were over in Maumee.

For Butch Houdeshell, it was a game that was the absolute pinnacle of his high school career. "No one thought we had a chance, but we had kind of adopted Coach Strahm's philosophy of 'Why NOT us?' It was that sense of confidence we saw all week in practice that we took onto the field that Friday night."

The final score for the victorious Lakota Raiders was 20-14, and the hero was 150-pound halfback Dale Thaxton, who rushed for 132 yards on 32 totes. His performance prompted

Maumee Valley coach Les Grace to say that Thaxton, yet another young man playing football for the very first time, was the finest back he'd seen since he'd been at Maumee, despite the fact that he'd just seen his own fine running back, Birr, score twice that evening.

Strahm, Koepfer, Trupo, and Windnagle, and a band of thirty-nine inexperienced players with names like Murphy, Drenning, Reinhart, Harris, Thaxton, Wirkner, Boatman, and many others came together at just the right moment in time. They became that little engine that could as they finished the season 6-3 overall and a perfect 5-0 in the league. The team had, as they say, brought home the hardware.

By the late spring of 1961, Dick was already well into preparation for the coming season. With the opening of the brand new Lakota High School in the fall, there would be very difficult personnel decisions to be made. After all, doing the math, where there once were three full staffs for three different schools, there now would be one school and one staff.

Seniority became an extremely important word. For Dick, he was low man on the American history totem poll, so Superintendent Vic Woods knew he had to do something to keep the school's dynamic young head coach on staff. It was determined that the school district would pay for Strahm to attend the summer session at Bowling Green State University so that he could become certified to teach driver's ed. That's exactly what the coach known for flexibility did.

However, after Dick had completed the certification, one of the two who had already been tabbed to teach American history took a position elsewhere, and Dick's teaching assignment in the new school would be the same as the first year, teaching American history.

Early in this difficult transition period, when Dick was still teaching his classes the importance of the American Civil War at Risingsun, he learned a valuable lesson about not overstepping his bounds and following the chain of command.

As Superintendent Woods wrestled with personnel decisions, it became evident that there was a real possibility that Dick's top assistant, Karl Koepfer, would not be given the physical education position at the new school because another teacher had a master's degree in it.

Dick, just a couple months beyond his twenty-sixth birthday and the San-Wood League reigning Coach of the Year, knew how instrumental his line coach was and he didn't want to lose him.

Now, a father of one of Strahm's players was on the school board, so Dick decided to pay him a visit. "I drove out to the farm to talk to him instead of going to the superintendent. Despite not having any real intent to undermine anybody's authority, I did talk to the board member about Karl's importance, especially with Lakota's going in- to a much tougher league comprised of bigger schools in the fall."

About a half hour later, as Dick and the board member were drinking coffee at the kitchen table, the screen door popped open and in walked two neighbors who also happened to be on the school board as well. They'd just come over to socialize. As the conversation ensued, Strahm kept steering the conversation back to Karl, and, eventually, all three board members agreed a teaching position would need to be made for him. Strahm was pretty happy when he left.

Recalls Dick, "The next day, there I am lecturing on American history and the principal came to the door and told me that the superintendent wanted to see me immediately. I didn't think that sounded good, and was I ever right!

"When I walked in, Superintendent Woods narrowed his eyes and said, 'I heard you had a board meeting last night.' I really didn't know what to say, and before I could come up with a response, he continued. 'Do you know I could have your job for this? Certainly, given your military experience, you should know a little something about chain of command. You DO NOT go on your own to board members to ask favors!'

"I thought it best not to make even the first excuse. I simply said, 'Yes, sir, Mr. Woods. I will never do it again.'

"Eventually, they did find a position for Karl, though."

The summer passed and the Raiders now took the field, competing in the Sandusky Bay Conference. Despite the stiffer competition, Strahm did get the Lakota out of the gate at 2-1. Thus far, besides the one loss, the only negative to the start of the season had been the fact that the lights for the new field had yet to arrive. The previous week, Lakota was forced to rent the Fostoria Memorial Stadium to play.

Just as Dick was beginning to feel at home in his new classroom, he got a call from a certain uncle who hadn't forgotten about a certain pledge to defend his country.

In this early fall of 1961, the Cold War was never hotter. Long had there been tension between the United States and the Soviet Union, and, specifically the Soviets' Premier Nikita Khrushchev and President John Kennedy.

The current site of contention was Berlin in the area separating communist East Germany and the free West Germany. The Soviets joined forces with the East Germans to stop the flow of refugees going from East to West Berlin. The resulting barricade history knows as the Berlin Wall, and America felt her presence was vital to West Berlin to show the Soviets they could push their luck no further.

Strahm recalls, "I was called to active duty with the 180th. We were held in Swanton so I was able to live with my family on Ravenwood, and I reported to the Toledo Express Airport daily. We would be sent to Europe if necessary.

"As it turned out, the situation never did get worse, and we remained stateside. We had a sister Air Force squadron over in Indiana in Fort Wayne, and they were the ones who went. I can remember being envious of some buddies I had over in that squadron because they got to travel all over Europe and never saw any combat.

"But there I was, not able to teach for the rest of the school year or coach. Karl was named as coach to replace me, and I became the recreation officer for my squadron. It was my job to organize activities—pool tournaments, basketball leagues, softball, and teams. We set up a movie theater, poker tournaments and such."

Despite not spending time as wisely as he would have liked, Dick is grateful for one occurrence during his time on active duty.

"I remember it was a Wednesday, October 4, when I first met a girl from nearby Perrysburg. Her name was Ginger Farquharson, and she and I had an arranged date, I guess what you might call a blind date, set up by one of my former fraternity brothers, Pete Finch.

"The original date was supposed to be the previous Saturday, but Ginger wasn't feeling well. We re-scheduled for Wednesday. Once I told her I had a 1958 red and white Corvette, she readily accepted."

"I remember we went over to Karl's house to look at game film from the previous Friday night's Lakota game. I suppose I was kind of sending Ginger an early message that I was a football guy. However, as we watched the film and Karl and I talked football, she really didn't at all look unhappy or bored."

Recalls Ginger, "I have four brothers (Bruce, Dick, Bob, and Joe) and two of them (Bruce and Dick) had played football, so I was already a fan, as were my two sisters, Carol Kay and Sabra. As a matter of fact, my brother Dick went on to play at the University of Toledo when Dick was the defensive coordinator there. Then, if you fast-forward to 1998, Dick's last year coaching, my brother Dick's son, Brian, came to play at The University of Findlay. So, Dick coached both his brother-in-law and his nephew in addition to our own son Doug before retiring.

"I didn't really mind at all the unusual first date. I knew Dick had felt bad about leaving the team so abruptly, and he wanted to do as much as he could for Karl. I remember the highlight of that first date, though, was stopping in Perrysburg on the way home and getting ice cream at a place that became a favorite for us, Franklin Ice Cream Store. Another highlight, of course, was riding in that shiny fancy sports car.

"When we got to my front porch, Dick asked me on another date, and, again, football was the theme. His brother, Dale, was a freshman football player at Ohio Northern University, and they were playing an away game at Findlay College in Donnell Stadium the following Saturday night. I though it sounded fun and agreed to go."

Dick chuckles at the thought of that second date on a Saturday night in Findlay at the college football stadium. "Little did I know watching the Oilers of Findlay swamp my brother's Polar Bears 22-0 that I'd be back about fourteen years later to spend many a Saturday down on the sidelines of Donnell. It's funny how often life has a tendency to circle back around."

Both Dick and Ginger knew quickly that they had found someone special. A mere six months later, on April 7, 1962, Ginger Farquharson became Ginger Strahm.

The union has survived thousands of kickoffs on both high school and college fields as well as enough medical crises of Dick's to fill a whole sideline full of coaches. Their fiftieth wedding anniversary is just over the horizon.

Dick has long been in awe of his wife and her uncompromising support of his career. "Since Ginger had four brothers, I suppose it made it easier to accept football. I think she grew to love it, and I've long marveled at her ability, as a coach's wife, to run the household and raise the kids while at the same time supporting me so strongly.

"She helped me dream up motivational tricks to use on my teams and got just as excited if not more so than I about the ballgames.

"Ginger always sat in the press box whenever possible during my coaching days, and people have told me that during very close games she was so nervous she could only manage to look at the floor. She simply couldn't bring herself to watch the last two to three minutes, especially, of the tight ones. Other people would have to tell her what was going on. She'd listen to the crowd or peek up with one eye at the scoreboard to see the score or the down and distance.

"Basically, the way I see it, she went through as much anxiety during those games as I did. She got upset when I got upset. She cried when I cried and laughed when I laughed.

"I guess if you ever wanted young wives who married coaches to really gain insight into what kind of a ride they're in for, they should probably talk to Ginger. She could tell them better than anyone what it has been like to experience the peaks and the valleys."

It was the spring of 1961, and Dick was scheduled to be released from active duty at the end of that calendar year. Anticipating this, he began looking around for a job. Karl was doing fine at Lakota, and he certainly didn't want to push him aside, so he looked elsewhere.

When Dick found out there was a teaching and head football coaching position in a town of around 8,000 up in the very northwest corner of Ohio, not very far at all from both the Indiana and Michigan state lines, he really shouldn't have been interested, at least not according to many of his coaching colleagues back in Toledo.

Recalls Strahm, "They told me Bryan High School was a coaching graveyard. The school was so far up in the upper left corner of Ohio and so close to both Indiana and Michigan that it was really treated as an afterthought by so much of the press. They said only the smallest papers covered the school, certainly not the *Toledo Blade.*

"Well, it always intrigued me whenever somebody told me a situation was impossible. I tend to be drawn closer to those types of challenges. Certainly Lakota was about as impossible a situation as there could be so how could this be that bad?"

So, in his Air Force uniform, replete with evidence of his most recent promotion to first lieutenant, Dick Strahm arrived in Bryan, Ohio, to interview for the job.

"During the interview, I explained that I was still on active duty but had already been told by the Air Force that, if I were to find a teaching job, I would be granted an early release so that I could start the school year on time.

"The superintendent's name was Howard Rogge, and much to my delight and, I'll admit, relief, my Lakota superintendent, Vic Woods, had given me a strong recommendation," remembers Strahm. "I also knew he told Mr. Rogge something else."

Rogge made it known to the first lieutenant that he wouldn't really need to spend time arranging any board meetings. Rogge used some subtle humor that carried with it a message to leave the superintending to the superintendent, and Dick certainly understood.

Rogge felt the impressive young teacher and coach was just the right man for the job, but the question was, "Just what job?" While it was obvious that Strahm would be the head football coach, the two needed to discuss which teaching assignment Dick would take. There were both a physical education assignment and an American history opening.

Strahm told Rogge that if it was just the same to him, he'd take the American history. Dick recalls, "While I didn't mind teaching some physical education, I also wanted to be in the classroom. The coaches I admired the most—from Bus Harding to Charles Robinson to George Miley to Bill Wirick—all had taken their turns behind a classroom podium. I think there's an added element of respect that comes to a coach who can also run an effective academic classroom.

"Additionally, I really felt I wanted to get to know the kids as students and have them know me not just as the faculty member who always has gym clothes on. I felt I could be more effective as a coach by kind of measuring the pulse of the school, and I think that's best done from the classroom."

Perhaps it was this type of thinking that showed Howard Rogge that Strahm was not just another dumb jock coach with a whistle around his neck who was more interested in where the weight room was than where the school library was.

Dick Strahm was both Rogge's and Bryan's man, and another chapter in the making of a successful teacher and coach was about to be written.

DICK STRAHM HONORED — Former Bryan High School head football coach Dick Strahm was honored Friday night at halftime of the Bryan-Montpelier football game at Golden Bear Stadium. Mr. Strahm was recently inducted into the National College Football Hall of Fame, being recognized as being a highly successful small college head football coach at the University of Findlay for 24 seasons. Mr. Strahm was the Golden Bears head football coach from 1962-65, when he compiled a 26-9-1 record in his coaching tenure including an NWOAL football title in 1964. Making the presentation was one of Mr. Strahm's former Golden Bear players, Larry Killgallon, who is a 1966 BHS graduate. (Staff photo by Randy Bohnlein)

Coach Strahm was honored at halftime of a Bryan High School football game in September 2004. The presentation was made by his former fullback and defensive tackle, Larry Killgallon.

Chapter 5
Professional Success and Personal Loss – The Bryan Years

Bryan, Ohio is known as the Fountain City, not because of any great fountain a visitor would see, but instead because of the underground springs beneath this town of 9,000. The town's citizens were justifiably proud of their home turf when it was listed as the thirtieth best small town in Norman Crampton's book *The Hundred Best Small Towns in America*. The sign just outside the city that Dick and Ginger Strahm passed proclaimed, "Welcome to Bryan, at the Top of Ohio."

For Dick, it was actually the third time he had passed the sign. The first time, of course, was when he arrived for his interview with Bryan superintendent Howard Rogge. The second time was in the spring of 1962 to preside over his first organizational meeting for those who wished to be a part of the next installment of the Bryan Golden Bears football team.

On that second trip, when Dick walked into that meeting, not one player knew what to expect. After all, the man who was entrusted with the job of resurrecting the Bears from the abyss of an 0-9 1961 season was not even officially a Bryan High School faculty member yet.

Recalls former player Larry Killgallon, "We had the meeting in the cafeteria. I was in the eighth grade and I and the rest of my classmates who wanted to play all trudged down there to hear what this new coach had to say. What we saw when we got down there was this military-style man with short-cropped hair. He laid out what he expected of us in no-nonsense fashion and what he wanted us to be working on in the summer before two-a-day practices were to begin in August.

"For my class, I think we immediately liked what we'd heard. While the varsity hadn't won a game the previous year, my class had not lost a football game, a basketball game, or a track meet in either the seventh or eighth grades. We wanted someone who really wanted to win, and, I think, we also wanted the same type of discipline that Coach Martinelli had instilled in the program in the 1950s."

Since Fred Martinelli's run coaching one of the perennial powers in the oldest high school conference in the entire state, the Northwest Ohio Athletic League (NWOAL), Bryan had taken on somewhat of a reputation. Martinelli departed for Ashland College, where he would win more than 200 games from 1959 to 1993 and eventually be inducted into the College Football Hall of Fame. In the few years after Martinelli left Bryan, it was said by those at other schools that football players from Bryan just didn't care very much whether they won or not. It was perceived they were rather soft.

Recalls Killgallon, "For the last couple years, people in the league from schools like Napoleon, Liberty Center, Montpelier, Wauseon, Archbold, Swanton, and Delta just knew that Bryan players just weren't fully committed to success, almost as if they really didn't take losing personally. Well, all that changed when Coach Dick Strahm came to town!"

Dick was 28 years old when he arrived in Bryan with his combined record of 16-6-1 at Toledo Libbey and Lakota. He also arrived with his new bride of just a few months, Ginger. The young couple rented the lower floor of a duplex on Cherry Street in town. Nine months later, they moved, renting a little brick home on Elm Street, just two blocks from the school and right behind Park Stadium, where Bryan played their home games.

The two largest companies in Bryan were the Spangler Candy Company, which still produces most notably Dum-Dum suckers, and The Ohio Art Company, which produces toys, best known for the Etch-a-Sketch. It didn't take Strahm very long to find out about the latter company.

Recalls Dick, "The CEO of The Ohio Art Company was Bill Killgallon Sr., Larry's dad. He was an ardent football fan and was one of Bryan's most unhappy fans, given the misfortunes of the last couple of years on Bryan's Park Stadium field. He was one of the most influential men in town, a big bear of a man that people knew simply as 'W.C.'

"Bill and I grew to be great friends during my time in Bryan, really more than just friends. He became a source of advice and eventually made me an offer I almost couldn't refuse, but more about that later."

In addition to teaching American history to every junior in school and being the head football coach, Strahm also would coach the junior varsity basketball team and the track team. Dick also would receive some supplemental pay for cutting the football stadium grass. As far as his half-completed master's degree in education and his dream of one day becoming a school superintendent, that would have to be put on the back burner for now.

The 1962 squad numbered fifteen seniors among the fifty-one team members as practice opened in August. Four of those players were brothers. No real history of Bryan football can be written without mentioning the Sanedas. There were seven boys in the family, and all seven would play football for the Golden Bears. Four would be coached by Dick Strahm in his first year at the helm, seniors Frank and Walt and sophomores John and Bobby.

Remembers Frank Saneda, "My brothers and I were all of the same opinion about our new coach even after just the first few days of practice. Coach Strahm was the greatest coach we'd ever had. He commanded respect. Although his practices were very hard, we all knew that was necessary if we were to break the cycle of losing. And, he also knew how to get the most out of us. I remember one of those early practices, he brought a cooler of pop and put it on the sidelines. We practiced over at Garver Park. During the whole practice, Coach would say,

'Whoever does the best job at practice today is going to be drinking some of that ice-cold pop after practice. Mmm, will that ever taste good on a hot day.'

"Well, you wouldn't think just a can of pop would be much of an incentive, but, boy, did we ever bust our tails to be chosen to have that pop! Coach was always coming up with ways like that to motivate us.

"Then, at the end of practice, when he was comfortable with the fact that everyone had practiced as hard as possible, Coach Strahm had Coach Stockman and the other assistants bring out a couple more coolers so everyone would get a can.

"I've had a lot of pop in my life, but I've never had a can that tasted any sweeter than the ones we drank after our final wind sprints at the end of practice under that hot sun at Garver Park."

For Dick, the memories of the Sanedas are strong to this day. "Our first year, Frank and Walt both played so well. Frank was a starter on both sides of the ball at end, and Walt was a linebacker and even played some fullback when we had some injuries. The sophomores, Bob and John, played some and then really distinguished themselves as upperclassmen the next two years after Frank and Walt had graduated.

"The second-to-last game of the 1962 season against Swanton was Parents' Night, always a big deal in high school athletics. I remember the pre-game ceremonies. While most parents had one player walk onto the field with them, Mr. and Mrs. Saneda were flanked by no less than four varsity football players!

"While all the Saneda boys were very good football players, John was really something special by the time he was a junior. He was a natural linebacker who just craved contact.

"I remember his junior year, my mom and dad drove over from Toledo to watch us play Defiance on Homecoming. After the game, Dad came in the locker room while we were celebrating a victory and said to me, 'Who is that number 62?' When I told him that it was Johnny Saneda, Dad said, 'Take me to him. I have to shake his hand. He is one tough son of a gun. He was all over that field tonight on both offense [where John played guard] and defense!'"

The first year, Strahm's biggest problem was two-fold, a lack of experience and a lack of depth. In the pre-season, the coaching staff of Strahm, George Stockman, Dave Lantz, and Bill Smithpeters was supplemented by Dick's brother, Dale, who as an undergraduate playing for the Ohio Northern Polar Bears came when his schedule permitted to help coach the freshmen.

The big bully of the NWOAL was Napoleon, coached by a man widely regarded as the finest coach in the area, Chuck Buckenmeyer, known as "Bucky" to virtually everyone. The Wildcats were seeking their third consecutive league crown and had won twenty-five of their last twenty-seven games.

During the three pre-season scrimmages, the Golden Bears showed marked improvement. Despite this, Strahm felt he had to reinforce how difficult it would be to reverse the fortunes of a winless team of the previous season. Despite Bryan's holding their own against the much bigger Toledo Bowsher in one pre-season fray, a team coached by Dick's friend and former mentor Bill Wirick, Dick sarcastically told Bob Diehl of the *Bryan Times*, "Our downfield blocking was poor, our backs were hitting the holes slow, the linemen were blocking standing up, and we missed some open field tackles. Other than that, we had a good scrimmage."

As the season opener approached with Liberty Center, Coach Strahm wanted everyone to know success was expected and failure, at least the kind that revisited with clockwork regularity the previous season, would not be tolerated.

Season tickets were selling briskly, aided more by the curiosity factor of a new coach than any grandiose expectations of success. Adults were plunking down a total of $5.00 for the five home games and another $1.50 for each of their students.

Dick's offensive philosophy was to run an unbalanced line, meaning both tackles would line up on the same side on the center with one guard. This left only a guard and a tight end lined up on the other side of the center. Recalls Killgallon, "Part of what successful coaches do so well is to pay attention to every detail to gain an advantage over opponents. Dick knew that no other team in the NWOAL ran this formation, so it would force teams to have to prepare special for us. In other words, they had to do different things defensively to stop us that they didn't have to do against any other team in the league."

The backfield formation was a single wing, consisting of a fullback and a halfback split apart and another halfback slotted to one side or the other. The formation is geared towards running the football, so much so, that Killgallon recalls with a laugh, "We ran the ball on first down. We ran on second down. Hell, if it was third and fifteen, we ran it again!"

While there may be some exaggeration in Killgallon's recollection, there was more truth than fiction to his words. The Bears' running game featured that first season Bob Voigt and Chris Gotshall, and they rushed for 103 and 87 yards respectively in Strahm's 20-6 win over Liberty Center, the first in almost a year and a half. A deeply appreciative group of Bryan players carried their victorious coach off the field on their shoulders.

Ever the psychologist, Dick told the press after the game, "It was a team effort. I can't really pinpoint any one individual who was responsible for our first win." Sensing perhaps a need to justify all those wind sprints that Frank Saneda remembers running in practices, Strahm continued by saying, "I think we out-conditioned them."

The ride Strahm got off the field placed him above the leather helmets the Bears still wore. Recalls Killgallon, "We were the absolute last team in the NWOAL to wear leather helmets. When they got wet with perspiration or it would rain, they must have weighed about fifteen pounds a piece!"

After a tough home loss to non-league rival Van Wert, 14-6, Strahm was poised to show his new community how his team would rebound against adversity. Facing a talented Delta squad, the Golden Bears earned their first shutout of the Strahm regime, 36-0, before a crowd of 2,000 at Park Stadium. It was Frank Saneda who would start the scoring by pouncing on a Delta fumble in the end zone for a touchdown.

Hal Shanahan of the *Toledo Blade*, a paper beginning to take notice of a team they'd ignored the two seasons before, wrote, "The Bears' quick backs, led by 155-pound senior fullback Larry Bigler and sophomore quarterback John Frey, riddled the Delta defense at will."
Another back who came onto the scene was just a freshman, Dave Ebersole. He was the son of Bryan High School's athletic director, Dudley, who had also been an eminently successful head basketball coach at Bryan, winning the NWOAL six times in a nine-year stretch during the 1950s.

To adequately tell Dick Strahm's Bryan story, one must mention Dave and Dudley Ebersole. Before Dave's graduation in the spring of 1966, both father and son would show Dick the real meaning of determination, the stubborn iron will it takes to defeat medical catastrophe and reach the summit of success.

As the season progressed, the wins mounted. After the only tie during his stay at Bryan, 20-20 against Swanton, and an 8-point loss to tough non-league foe Defiance, the Bruins rattled off wins against Archbold, Montpelier, and Swanton. The team that won nary a game the previous season was really showing its claws.

Heading into the season's finale versus Napoleon, the bully of the NWOAL, a win for the Bears would mean a league championship. The town was delirious in their support as game night approached.

However, the Bears were not quite ready to run with Bucky's Wildcats just yet. A 30-point second quarter followed a scoreless first for Napoleon, and, by halftime, the game was essentially over. The final was 36-0, and although maybe the bubble had burst in the opinion of some, it didn't as far as the optimistic Strahm was concerned. With the sting of the defeat still upon him, Strahm addressed the media after the game. "Our young men never quit, even when down thirty! I don't think one game makes a season, and I'm proud of the Bryan Golden Bears and the season they have given me. They played 100 percent all year as far as I'm concerned."

By anyone's standards, despite the Napoleon shellacking on that final Friday night of the year, the first campaign had been a resounding success. The Bears finished 5 and 1 in the league and 5-3-1 overall.

However, Dick had more than just football on his mind on that final Friday of his first campaign. Ginger, pregnant with their first child, had experienced some severe cramping and was in the hospital right across the street from the stadium looking on from the second floor. Recalls Ginger, "Dick's mom and dad had spent a couple of hours with me before the game, and, when nurses promised to keep a very close eye on me, they went across the street to the game.

"I remember as the game went on the stadium grew more and more quiet. Even from a distance, I could tell that things weren't going very well. About halfway through the second half, it started to snow. By the end of the game, there was a thin white coating that covered up the entire field. What started as completely green ended in total white and, of course, a loss. The next morning, I was feeling better and was released from Bryan Cameron Memorial Hospital.

Frank Saneda remembers a specific feeling and a specific conversation he had with his brother as they left the locker room for the final time in their Bryan Golden Bear career. "I remember my brother Walt and I both wishing we could come back and play another year or two for Coach Strahm. We both felt something big was about to happen to Bryan football, something we knew our brothers John and Bob would be a part of."

During that first season, Coach Strahm continued to find ways to motivate his existing players while at the same time searching the halls of the 700-student high school for potential players.

One motivational tool Strahm devised the first year involved pairs of socks. Call it what a *Bryan Times* headline did, "Sox for Knocks." Players on offense and defense were graded on game films with a point system for tackles, assisted tackles, blocks at the hole of attack, downfield blocks, runs over eight yards, pass interceptions, pass completions, caused fumbles and recovered fumbles. Four winners, two on defense and two on offense, each got a new pair of game socks, and the overall winners at the end of the year received a Bryan Golden Bear pen-and-pencil set.

Recalls Dick, "Little things like buying a couple cases of pop or some socks and a few pen-and-pencil sets didn't cost much, certainly not much in exchange for the kind of effort I believe such small items inspire."

During Strahm's first year, he became quite popular in the classroom as well as on the football field. His American history lessons were often peppered with football analogies, and few ever dreaded walking into his class. Especially big fans of Mr. Strahm were the cheerleaders and all of his junior girls.

"Ginger was pregnant with our first child and had been struggling with the pregnancy. This became a bigger and bigger concern for us, especially in the second half of the season. On November 26, Ginger began experiencing more abdominal pains and began to hemorrhage, so I immediately got her in the car and drove to the hospital.

"When we got to Bryan Memorial Hospital, Dr. Meckstroth, whose son was one of my football players, told me that the baby would need to be taken by Caesarean section despite being six weeks' premature to protect Ginger's health.

"Despite the worry, my son Daniel was born fine, and except for being so very tiny, he looked just like a normal baby. The doctors and nurses kept saying, 'Everything looks good, Coach Strahm.'

"All of my coaches were there. My mom and dad were there as were Ginger's mom and dad. There were also many of my students, especially my junior girls, there to lend us support.

"All day, we stayed at the hospital and, finally, everything appeared to be fine. The baby was in the nursery, and Ginger was sleeping after the ordeal, so I took my mom and dad home to our house to get some rest while my in-laws returned to Perrysburg.

"Then, at six the next morning, the phone rang. It was one of the nurses at the hospital telling me to get there right away. We quickly dressed and jumped in the car. When we arrived, I noticed there was not one but two nurses hovering over Danny in the nursery. When they came out, I asked them if everything was all right. They said they were just making sure everything was fine.

"I sensed, though, that something was wrong. Later, in the afternoon, Dr. Meckstroth and a couple of other doctors came to see me. They told me that Danny was having trouble breathing, but they were doing their best.

"For twelve hours, we all sat and prayed. Then, Dr. Meckstroth came out and delivered the news that hit me right in the gut. On November 27, 1962, Danny Strahm had died.

"He explained that the condition to which Danny succumbed was called Hyland Membrane Disease. In cases involving premature babies, there are times that the immature lungs lack the ability to exchange oxygen. While the baby in the womb gets oxygen from the mother's lungs, once born, the baby must produce its own oxygen. What prevents this ability is a very sticky substance that lines the air sacs, and Danny just couldn't expel the substance."

At this time, the treatment wasn't advanced enough. Nowadays, there are chemicals that can be blown into the lungs to help a baby breathe independently. Thanks to new treatments, babies born as early as fifteen weeks prior to the delivery date have survived. But, this was 1962.

Meckstroth, perhaps in an attempt to provide some comfort, told Dick that President Kennedy and Jackie lost their first child to Hyland Membrane.

Now, even in his seventies, Dick often has his thoughts drift back to that terrible day at Bryan Memorial Hospital. Danny was born on November 26 and died on November 27. Recalls Dick, The absolute toughest thing I've ever had to do in my entire life is go into that hospital room and tell Ginger that our son had died. Our parents and minister were right outside the door, but it was my job, and mine alone, to go in and tell her."

Even now, so many years later, Dick thinks of Danny. "I'd have a 45-year-old son now. Wouldn't that have been something? I often wonder how he'd have grown up and what he'd be today."

During these tragic times of 1962 and the tiny casket and the funeral, Dick remembers how much the Bryan community wrapped their collective arms around Dick and Ginger Strahm. "The people were just so sympathetic, so understanding. This included both old and young alike. It included my players, the coaches, my junior girls."

Why such things happen is a question only God can answer, but in such times comes great opportunity for people to show compassion. Among the many who did were Bill "W.C." Killgallon and his wife, Ruth, who stood by ready to do anything that could assuage the sorrow.

During the spring of 1963, Dick's thoughts finally returned somewhat to football. Although he would never fully forget the loss of Danny, he knew he had to move on with the affairs of this world and pray that he would one day see Danny in the next.

Meeting with his staff for the upcoming 1963 season, Strahm told George Stockman, Dave Lantz, and Ray Tearney, that despite Dave Ebersole's relative inexperience, with the graduation of top rushers Bob Voigt, Chris Gotshall, and Larry Bigler, Ebby, as he was known, would be, as a sophomore, the featured back. The single-wing and unbalanced line would showcase his abilities from a halfback slot.

Several weeks later, just after Independence Day, something happened that again proves what the cynics of the world believe, that if you want to hear God laugh, just tell Him your plans.

Recalls Dave Ebersole, "It was a Saturday morning on July 8, around 11:30. That summer, I was mowing lawns to earn some extra money and had several customers. While mowing under a pine tree, the blade hit what was later found to be an exposed root. A portion of the blade sheared off and shot out of the back of the mower and hit my leg. It hit with such a force, I immediately collapsed, hearing a cracking sound as I went down. A neighbor came running over and took me to the hospital.

"At the hospital, the doctors discovered the blade didn't sever the Achilles' tendon, but that was the only good news. The projectile, doctors surmised still spinning with great speed, took a swath out of my tibia about three-eighths of an inch. It was like a large cutout, and it so weakened the tibia that the fibula snapped when it could not support the weight of my body. Also, the tendon in the front of my ankle was severed."

Facing the possibility of gangrene, the doctors at Bryan Cameron Memorial told Dave Ebersole's parents that they would advise amputation just above the ankle. However, Dave recalls his father's immediate response. "My dad would absolutely have none of that option. The doctors argued that the injury was what they called a dirty wound. The six-inch piece of blade had dirt and grass and many other contaminants on it, and they felt infection was inevitable.

"But, my father was adamant that there would be no amputation. A call was made to Parkview Hospital, across the Indiana line in Fort Wayne, to alert the staff what the extent of my injury was and that I would be coming. My dad drove me there with my mom riding in the back seat.

"About six hours later, I had the surgery. The front tendon was replaced with a metal thread, and a wad of cotton was inserted in the open area to promote drainage while the bone hopefully regenerated and knitted itself together over a long period of time. It was three weeks before I was allowed to come home to Bryan."

For Dave Ebersole, the healing process was long, and for Coach Strahm, the injury meant going in a whole other direction in building his offense for the upcoming campaign. Of course, there would be no sophomore football season for Ebersole.

For his father, Dudley, there would be countless hours, hours filled with labors of love, dedicated to helping his son recover. Recalls Dave, "As athletic director, my dad was able to get me into the whirlpool as soon as the cast came off in early October. He and I would come in early before school for whirlpool treatments every day. Then, he would help by massaging my foot and offering resistance so that I could try to regain some strength and flexibility. I can't even calculate how many hours he did this. He would push on the ankle and hold it on one side, and I would push against it. He was absolutely relentless, and, for that, I will be forever grateful. Without his help and support, I would have never made it back."

Even to this day, Dave Ebersole does not have full flexibility, but, remarkably, he did play both basketball and baseball his sophomore year. Recalls Dave, "I didn't have much lateral range, but I could get up a pretty good head of steam going straight forward."

Strahm had decided on fullback Mike Phillips and halfback Keith Carpenter, Larry Killgallon's cousin, to replace the contributions Dave Ebersole was supposed to make, and August practice began in 1963 for the Golden Bears.

Strahm was in mid-season form as a psychologist when he told *Bryan Times* reporter Thomas Voigt, "This team is too darn green to be tough. We can't even hurt ourselves in a scrimmage!" Master coaches have a knack for always being able to successfully take a team's temperature and ascertain what to say to motivate. He wanted to knock any complacency out early.

Although that shouldn't have been a problem, given the loss of fifteen seniors, as well as Ebersole, kids are kids, and that means kids can be naïve enough to think that such circumstances don't matter all that much.

Ever the promoter, Strahm also thought up an interesting way to build a bridge between his football program and an untapped fan base. While such a testosterone-driven sport as football has long appealed to males, Strahm wondered what was wrong with trying to engender more support with the ladies. After all, he reasoned, wasn't Ginger an ardent football fan? Wasn't she fully supportive of his efforts to make Bryan High School a football school that also happened to play basketball instead of what many believed it to be, a basketball school that happened to play some football.

Coach Strahm's idea was to put on a for-females-only football clinic. The idea came to fruition on August 27 at 7:30 p.m. in the Bryan High School gym. Women and ladies of high-school age were invited, and no men were allowed. The cost? It was only a promise, a promise to root vociferously for the Golden Bears when they took the field.

The 90-minute program was planned as carefully by the detail-oriented coach and history teacher as the game plan for the opener on September 6 against Swanton or one of his famous lectures on the American Civil War. The objective was to give women a basic understanding of the game of football.

When the doors opened, almost every one of Mr. Strahm's junior girls walked in. In addition, there were mothers of players and other women who wanted to learn as much as they could about this game played with the funny oblong-shaped ball every autumn.

Strahm started by offering proof that there is nothing abnormally dangerous about playing football. Ever the recruiter, he knew that somewhere in the audience there could be a mother of a boy not currently playing, a boy who just might be a terrific defensive end down the road. Dick explained to the ladies that football, is actually twenty-seven times less dangerous than riding in an automobile."

The program Strahm and his coaches devised explained football lingo and rules. Among the subjects covered were sportsmanship, the physical layout of a football field, gaining possession of the ball and making first downs, the positions of a field, and offensive formations, including such concepts as balanced lines, unbalanced lines, slotbacks, and split ends.

Prior to the clinic, most of the ladies in attendance thought that split ends were nothing more than an annoying hair condition they wished to avoid. Now, they knew that they were also the players who stand up furthest away from where the ball is going to be snapped.

The clinic also covered defensive formations, the secrets that are told in the huddle, penalties and their consequences, and a demonstration of football equipment. A player would come on the stage in shorts and a t-shirt and then put on shoulder pads while Strahm explained all the safety factors, and then they proceeded to do that with each piece of equipment. Of course, included in the equipment were those new hard plastic helmets the Bears would be wearing for the first time.

During the panel discussion that concluded the program, Strahm showed his flair for public relations. He actually gave the ladies some inside information in the form of what the first offensive play would be that he would call in the opener, a run off-tackle to the left with the fullback Mike Phillips.

Recalls Dick, "I wanted to give the ladies something they could use to get one over on their husbands and boyfriends. I'm sure they had a lot of fun predicting the first play and then being right!"

Larry Killgallon laughed when he was told Dick revealed his first play to the ladies at the clinic. "Hell, in Coach Strahm's offense, you could guess an off-tackle run with the fullback about any play, and, more often than not, you'd be right. There weren't a whole lot of plays in the Strahm playbook, but the ones that were there, we ran and ran and ran again until our timing and technique were as near perfect as a bunch of teen-agers could make them." Again, Strahm looked to his hometown to scrimmage much larger schools to get his Bears battle ready. This time, it was Toledo Waite. Although losing two touchdowns to one, the Bruins didn't allow a rushing touchdown, with the new starting linebacker Johnny Saneda often leading the charge. After the scrimmage, Strahm was succinct with the press, "We're pleased, but we're not satisfied."

The opener against Swanton proved to be a see-saw affair. Halfback Denny Weaver finally scored the winning touchdown late in the last quarter, and the Bears had a 22-16 road win. To Strahm, perhaps the most pleasant surprise was the hard running of Phillips, the converted 180-pound tackle.

Following a tough 20-14 non-league loss to Van Wert, Strahm's troops survived their own mistakes in the form of fumbles and penalties to beat Delta, 16-6.

Another loss, this time in the home opener at Park Stadium, left the Bears a very average 2-2. And, average just wasn't good enough for the driven young coach. The next game was against Bryan's biggest non-league rival, the Defiance Bulldogs, and the all-time record was about as even as one could imagine, 22 wins for Defiance, 21 for Bryan, and 4 ties.

Defiance was coached by Wally Hood, who Dick would face several times in his career, not only in Bryan but also later in his career.

Looking back, Strahm remembers he had some extra help in preparing for the game that was as odd as it was valuable. "I was home on Wednesday night with the good old 16-millimeter projector looking at game film and still trying to find a way to beat a very good football team. Suddenly, I heard a knock at the door. Ginger opened the door, and, lo and behold, there was Bucky [Napoleon head coach Charles Buckenmeyer], walking in the door. 'Hey, Strahm! I'm going to help you beat that Defiance group. Rewind that film, and let's get started!'

"You see, Bucky, for some reason, just hated Defiance and believed in a familiar saying printed on a lot of t-shirts I've seen over the years to describe someone's intense dislike for a certain team. In this case, Bucky's t-shirt might have said something like, 'My favorite teams are Napoleon and Whoever Beats Defiance.'

"I'm not sure that's ever happened again where one coach of a team you'll play later that year helps you with game preparation against someone else. Before he left at the end of the evening, he said, 'Strahm, don't you tell anyone I did this.' However, I think it's okay to reveal it after 40-plus years."

Apparently, whatever help Coach Buckenmeyer was able to provide may have made some difference as Bryan did defeat Defiance by a 14-6 count. One of Dick's assistant coaches, Ray Tearney, called the game one of the greatest games he'd ever seen.

Bryan, down 6-0 late in the fourth quarter after Defiance fullback Dick Memmer scored by plunging over the right, was aided by a 30-yard return by Denny Weaver on the ensuing kickoff. Fullback Mike Phillips repeatedly assaulted the Defiance defensive line. On the 55-yard game-tying drive, Phillips ran for 49 of them, carrying the ball on 12 of the 16 plays. When the conversion failed, the game was left deadlocked.

On the kickoff, the Bears received a huge break when Defiance fumbled and Bryan took possession on Defiance's 43. After the Bulldogs stiffened and faced with a third down and very long, Strahm went to the back of his playbook for his call. He had quarterback John Frey quick kick, and Defiance was caught totally off guard. The ball was downed on the one-yard-line by sophomore speedster Jim Morrissey.

After calling a timeout and exhorting his defense to make something good happen, Dick watched as the ball fell just right for the Bears. Defensive John Stockwell delivered a bone-jarring tackle as Defiance tried to run the ball out of the shadow of its own goalposts, and the ball popped loose. Sophomore defensive tackle Larry Killgallon fell on the loose pigskin for what proved to be the winning score in the end zone.

Killgallon has several recollections about the events leading up to his first chance to shine as well as about the play itself.

"Actually, I was just awarded the starting position on Wednesday of that week. You see, Coach Strahm designated every Wednesday practice 'Challenge Day.' It was the day that any backup could challenge any starter for his position.

"Well, the player I challenged had been a second-team all-league tackle the previous year and was a year older than I. But, Coach believed, to keep the edge, any position should be up for grabs, not just at the beginning of the year but throughout the season.

"He devised a drill between two tackling dummies where two players would go nose-to-nose, man-to-man. Coach had a point system to determine who could whip whom. If you could block or tackle or run through someone, you got so many points. After three rounds, I had beaten the starter, and that's how I got to start that Defiance game.

"Now, as a sophomore, I would never really have thought of challenging. Don't ever believe Coach Strahm if he tells you the coaches never got involved in precipitating those challenges. It was Coach Strahm who told Coach Stockman to tell me to challenge.

"Actually, it was classic Dick Strahm. He could motivate you by challenging you to constantly reach higher than, at times, you even wanted to.

"During the game, I was pretty nervous as you might imagine. I played OK, I guess, for my first varsity start, but I was playing against one of the best offensive tackles in the region, Jon Zachrich. He had really kind of pushed me around most of the night. That's why it was so gratifying to beat his block down on the goal line to be in a position to be the hero.

"I can remember the referee trying to get me to give him the ball. Finally, I remembered him saying, 'That's OK, son. It's a touchdown. You can give the ball back now.' What a feeling! I'm almost 60 years old, and I can still remember it.

"Looking back, it's interesting we made the two-point conversion to make the final score, 14-6. All that past summer, the Defiance players had worn t-shirts that said, 'Defiance Desire, 14-6.' The inscription made reference to the margin they missed going undefeated the previous year. Now, we had beaten them by that exact same score. I doubt if the Defiance players thought that was kind of neat, but I sure did!"

After the game in the locker room, Dick recognized one of his players who played so well. It was his junior linebacker John Saneda, who flew all over the field that night wreaking his own form of havoc.

The next game was a 28-8 win at Park Stadium over the Archbold Blue Streaks. It has been said that the truly great coaches have a knack for putting the right personnel on the field for pivotal plays in a game. If that truly has merit, the win contains verification of this theory. About halfway through the second quarter, it was 0-0. The Bears were simply not playing very inspired football, perhaps a little letdown after last week's big win over Defiance. On a second and sixteen, Strahm sent in a backup running back by the name of Lyle Moog with a play designed for him to run the ball. Eighty yards later, Moog was standing in the end zone, and the Bears had the lead. It was his only carry of the night but the most important.

Retired *Bryan Times* sports writer Herb Lewis recalled in a column entitled "Sports Talk" that Bryan's next contest versus the Montpelier Locomotives was steeped in tradition. Of course when a league is the oldest in the state, originating in 1926, every league contest is steeped in tradition.

Lewis recollected how the game had changed over his twenty-five years of covering nearly 250 games. In Bryan's early days, games were played at three in the afternoon on fields without stands surrounding them. Tin Lizzies lined the field, and fans stood beside the new-fangled automobiles watching. There were no bands at halftime, and, to get a better view of the action, reporters often joined timekeepers on the field directly behind the team with the ball. On chilly afternoons, spectators often built a bonfire beside the field at halftime.

But, that was yesteryear. In the second year of the Strahm era, the Golden Bears won 16-0 before a crowd of 3,000. Dick was really making Bryan football a must-see show, and Park Stadium was the place to be when the Bruins played host. The Bears held perhaps the NWOAL's best quarterback, Rob Richmond, to a 6-for-20-for-47-yard evening. For Bryan, the bruising tandem of Phillips and Carpenter each scored a touchdown and a two-point conversion.

Another win over Liberty Center made it four in a row and set up quite a finale, this with Bucky's undefeated Napoleon Wildcats. This time, Charlie Buckenmeyer wouldn't be knocking on the Strahms' door to help devise a game plan.

Despite another rabid 3,000 in the stands at Park, the Bears couldn't grab a share of the league championship. The Naps' quarterback, Bob Brown, ran for five touchdowns and two two-point conversions in the 36-22 win, offsetting touchdown runs by Phillips, Carpenter, and Moog. Despite the disappointing finale on an early-November night, Strahm delivered a very respectable season to fans like W.C. Killgallon. The Bears finished 5-2 in the league and 6-3 overall.

Not only was running back Mike Phillips selected as First-Team NWOAL but he also was selected Honorable Mention All-State. Other NWOAL selections were running back Keith Carpenter, offensive guard Alvie Ames, and that linebacker who seemed to be everywhere on a football field at once, John Saneda.

In late November, the Strahms were as stunned as the rest of America when an assassin cut down President John Kennedy in Dallas. Mr. Strahm tried as best he could to explain to his American history classes the why's and the wherefore's.

Closer to home, in the Strahm house, the big concern was Ginger's second pregnancy. Again, there were difficulties, and, in late April, Ginger began to experience the same symptoms as she did just a year and a half earlier. This time, Dick told Dr. Meckstroth, "We've got to get to a major hospital."

Recalls Dick, "I think Dr. Meckstroth fully understood my wanting to get to a bigger hospital. He called the Toledo Hospital and alerted them that we would be arriving later that day. A local car dealer provided a brand-new car with a front seat that folded down. I put some blankets down, put Ginger in, and drove to Toledo.

"On April 29, 1964, Douglas Strahm was delivered by Caesarean four weeks early. Just as Danny had, he had great difficulty breathing, and I can remember my parents and Ginger's parents and me in the hospital chapel praying.

"Doug remained on the critical list for nineteen days. In the meantime, I took Ginger back to Bryan to recover. Each day, after school I drove back to Toledo. My dad, the nurses told me, was at the hospital the first thing every morning before he went to work.

"Finally, Doug was taken off the critical list, and, after another week and a half, four weeks after his birth, he was allowed to come home to Bryan.

"As anyone can see, he's come a long way from that tiny guy born four weeks early struggling to breathe. Doug, I guess you could say, certainly has made up for being born so small, as he was an offensive lineman at both Findlay High School and the University of Findlay.

"The doctors at Toledo Hospital were tremendous. I think they were used to dealing with so many different types of cases and were better equipped to handle difficulties.

"Again, the people of Bryan just couldn't do enough for Ginger and me. They sent cards of support and eventually congratulations, they offered to baby-sit, and they brought food over. It was just amazing how the community embraced us. I think that's why Bryan, Ohio, will always have such a special place in our hearts."

In the late spring and early summer, Ginger and Dick would have the junior girls out to the house for a big bonfire and cookout. They brought their sleeping bags and then turned the affair into a slumber party. There would often be as many as twenty or thirty girls.

Dick remembers, "One time one of the girls knocked on our bedroom door and woke us up. She told me they'd heard some noises outside the house. I got up and opened the door and took one step out. I stepped barefoot right into something gooey. Now, we had just gotten a puppy, so you can imagine the first thing to run through my mind.

"Then, I heard a chorus of high-pitched laughter. It turned out to be a big glob of peanut butter the girls had put on a piece of wax paper. Did they ever think that was funny!"

Another August rolled around, and it was time to see just how far the Bears could go. The team had gone from 5-3-1 the first year to 6-3 the second. Could another level be reached? Time would tell.

There was, of course, good news on several fronts. First, John and Bobby Saneda would be returning for their senior year to carry on the family tradition. Keith Carpenter would now become the featured back out of the fullback slot, replacing the graduated Mike Phillips. Carpenter's cousin, Larry Killgallon, also planned on having a strong season from his new position at linebacker. Starting safety Robin Frey, who was the brother of the Bears' starting quarterback John, intended to make sure the Frey name was doubly prominent when people spoke or wrote of Bryan football.

And perhaps the best news was that Dave Ebersole would be back playing the game that he loved. As Dave recalls, "I had made it back for basketball and baseball seasons the year before, but football was a whole different matter because of the contact involved. Although I was nervous, I just loved the sport too much to not try to come back. Also, my dad worked too hard helping me overcome the injury not to try football again. While I never again would have the same flexibility in the ankle, I felt I could contribute.

"Coming off the injury, I was probably lucky to have big Keith Carpenter as our primary ball carrier. I knew I'd have my chances to run the ball some as a second option. Then, after Keith graduated, I'd get my chance to be the number-one guy my senior year."

In addition to talented skill-position starters, including some tall, athletic ends like Rich Batdorf and Milan Grove, Bryan also would have some big men up front. None were bigger than the two offensive tackles, the Lingvai brothers, Jim at 6'8" and Ed at 6'3".

The coaching staff featured the holdovers Strahm and Stockman and a couple new faces. One was Duane Brown, a former Bryan quarterback who followed Fred Martinelli to Ashland College to play the same position there. The second newcomer was Bill Mellon, who had just spent the last nine years in the service. Strahm wanted some of Coach Mellon's hard-nosed attitude to rub off on his Bears.

The pre-season scrimmages again included Toledo Bowsher, but, this year Strahm also scheduled another warm-up with Toledo Waite, the 1963 City League champions, a team that had won nine of ten games.

Perennial NWOAL power Napoleon lost all eleven offensive starters to graduation, but the rest of the league, especially Liberty Center, Swanton, and Montpelier were improved.

During the hot August two-a-days, perhaps the most interesting thing to happen didn't involve one player challenging another to take his position or the infusion of any radical coaching changes. Instead, it had to do with a fresh-faced 21-year-old *Bryan Times* sports editor by the name of Duane Schooley. In the late summer and fall, it was Schooley who had been given the job of covering every move the Bryan Golden Bears made.

Duane Schooley was a graduate of nearby Edgerton High School. He started working for the nearby Bryan paper while still a student at Adrian College, just across the Michigan line from the Little Town at the Top of Ohio. Bob Diehl was the editor at that time and hired Schooley as a photographer for the school's athletic contests.

Schooley recalls his excitement when he was asked if he'd like to try some game write-ups. "I really had no intention of going into newspaper work at that time. At Adrian, I was an education major. Just as my mom and my brother, I wanted to teach. As far as I was concerned, I would become a social studies teacher and do some coaching. With a last name like *Schooley*, it seemed like the thing to do.

"But, I wanted to show Mr. Diehl that I could do the job. I thought it was a show of faith. When I tried it, I was hooked. I had found my career.

"In 1964, I had just graduated from college and went to work full time for the *Times*. I was 21 years old, and my main job was to cover every move the athletes at the high school made. I was also given the title of sports editor.

"Well, I know there's often some sensitivity between coaches, especially in a one- newspaper town, and writers who cover their teams. Coaches, at times, feel there's too much criticism, I think.

"At any rate, I'm really not sure after forty years or so whether Richard Strahm took exception to something I wrote, but, basically, it came down to his telling me one day after one of his pre-season practices that there was no way I could really write about football if I'd never even played it. Well, I took that as a challenge, so I said, 'Well, give me a shot!'

"The next thing I know, I'm with the equipment manger, and he's issuing me a helmet and pads and the rest of the practice uniform for the next day's practice. I decided I'd write about the incident in my column, 'Schooley's Scribblings.'

"The next day, I began my practice with the Golden Bears. First, we had a chalk talk before we boarded the bus for the trip to the Garver Park field. The coaches went over some new wrinkles in both the offense and defense that they wanted to introduce that day. 'So far, so good,' I thought.

"When we got to the practice field, we began with a long jaunt around the field to loosen up. I fell in with some of the slower players and resisted the cry of my lungs telling me to stop after about five minutes of running. Then we completed the loosening up with some stretching exercises.

"After that, there was a lot of drill work to work on technique. We worked on down-field blocking, shedding blockers, and hitting the blocking sled. I was only about 5'5" and maybe 140 pounds soaking wet, so even doing the drills was pretty taxing.

"But, that was nothing compared to the biggest part of practice, which was the full-contact scrimmaging. I was put on defense at nose-guard, lined up right on the nose of the offensive center Frank Psurny, who weighed around 175 pounds.

"Then, my old friend Richard Strahm ran isolation running plays right at me over and over. That means, besides fending off Psurny's block, there was an extra blocker sent, the likes of Jim Lingvai [6'8," 240 pounds], Rich Batdorf [185 pounds], and Larry Killgallon [195 pounds].

"Well, needless to say, I got knocked on my butt time after time and really gained an appreciation the hard way what football was all about. Essentially, I spent more time on my back than on my feet for the next 45 minutes.

"By the end of practice, I was sore, my legs ached, and my fingers were numb from getting stepped on. I think the players were as interested as their coach in defending their turf and showing an outsider how difficult the game was.

"We ended practice with 40-yard wind sprint after wind sprint. I had been told about Coach Strahm's famous wind sprints. During the season, Dick had the managers keep track of the number of sprints so he would be able to tell the team at the banquet at the end of the season that they'd broken the school record for wind sprints. Coach Strahm believed very strongly that conditioning equaled wins, so his teams ran and ran and ran some more."

Larry Killgallon remembers those wind sprints. "I recall a couple of practices, in particular, where Coach Strahm just wasn't at all satisfied with our enthusiasm and our execution, so he'd just blow the whistle and say, 'Well, if you gentlemen aren't much interested in dedicating yourself to the game of football today, I'm sure you'll be much more excited about running suicide sprints.' The players called them, 'gassers.' And, that would be it. We'd run for the rest of practice."

For Duane Schooley, he never returned to a second practice. Like author George Plimpton, who forged a career in a genre known as participatory journalism, Schooley first tried football and then wrote about his experience. For Plimpton, his experience going through training camp with the Detroit Lions produced a best seller called *Paper Lion.* For Schooley, his experiences trying to fend off the charges of players just four to five years younger and 30 to 40 pounds heavier produced the scribe's "Schooley's Scribblings."

Duane Schooley survived his adventure and continued to write about mostly high school sports for four years in Bryan and another thirty-two on staff at the *Toledo Blade.* He is now retired and living in Monroe, Michigan.

The season began after, of course, the second annual ladies-only football clinic in the school gym, a tutorial organized by a young coach that had just turned 30 years old and was becoming an old pro at knowing what had to be done to elicit support for his program.

The Bears stormed out of the gate in impressive fashion, beating Swanton 28-0 behind Keith Carpenter's three touchdowns. Schooley liked the blocking on a 67-yard punt return so well that he compared the blockers to a giant lawnmower cutting down would-be Swanton tacklers.

Defensively, the stars were end Ed Lingvai and the tenacious linebacker Johnny Saneda. After the game, Strahm did something he rarely did, single out a player for an outstanding performance. The player was John Saneda, who made considerable contributions both on defense and from his position as offensive right guard.

The second week brought the Bears crashing to earth. Against the Van Wert Cougars, their non-league rival, Bryan was out of it by halftime, losing 30-0. The score would eventually grow to 46-0 in the third quarter before a late surge by the Bruins made the final a more respectable 46-20. Strahm told Schooley after the game, "There probably wasn't a person here tonight who wanted to win any more than I did. We were humiliated, but we are still going to have practice come Monday and try to collect our senses and prepare for Delta."

Recalls Killgallon, "We didn't lose too often, but when we did, Coach Strahm really wanted you to understand the difference between winning and losing. There would be no laughing or talking in the locker room or the bus. There would be no after-game dances or connecting with your girlfriend. Heck, even the girls didn't want anything to do with us if we lost.

"Now, if we won, that was a different story. We celebrated. The highlight would come Sunday. We'd get together behind Spanglers' barn and play touch football with the girls and really have a great time. Needless to say, though, after the Van Wert game, there was no co-ed touch football that Sunday."

However, from that point on, there was much in the way of Sunday frivolity. The Bears were about to prove they were the elite team of the NWOAL.

Bryan rolled Delta 42-12 the following Friday as quarterback John Frey ran for two TDs and a two-point conversion.

Next, Bryan avenged the 24-8 loss of the previous season by beating Wauseon, 30-0. The shutout inspired Schooley to use an interesting simile in his game account, saying that the Bears' defense contained the Indian offense "like glass jars contain fruit." Carpenter (144 yards) and Ebersole (89) paced a relentless ground attack.

As a treat to his son's team, W.C. Killgallon obtained tickets for the varsity to attend the following Saturday's Michigan-Navy game up in Ann Arbor. Recalls Dick, "W.C. was always looking for ways to support our football program, and, for that, and on a deeper level, for his friendship, I will always feel the richer for having known him."

The next game was against Defiance, a team not only with a score to settle after the 14-6 loss the year before but also a team sky high after beating Napoleon the previous week, 22-6, for the first win Wally Hood ever achieved against Charles Buckenmeyer's squad.

It was Homecoming night at Park Stadium, and the game turned out to be a classic. There were five lead changes before the Bears finally vanquished the Bulldogs, 28-22. Defiance was a scant 13 yards away from the tying touchdown when time expired. Keith Carpenter ran like a man possessed that night, 161 yards and four touchdowns.

Recollects Strahm, "Keith was just a battering ram. He absolutely loved contact, and, at times, he'd frustrate me. I'd say to him, 'Keith, after you get through the hole, just run to daylight, and no one will touch you instead of running straight at the safety and trying to run him over.' He'd look at me and say, 'But, Coach, it's more fun my way.'"

Strahm's charges then rolled over Archbold the following week, 44-12. Interesting in a rather trivial fashion was the fact that Bryan had lost the coin toss for the sixth time in six games. At 5-1 and 5-0 in the NWOAL, Coach Dick Strahm was carried off the field by his appreciative players.

Montpelier fell 20-6 the following Friday. Excellent blocking by Jim and Ed Lingvai and John Saneda opened the holes for Carpenter (143 yards) and Ebersole (96 yards).

The Bruins proved one less practice only meant less wind sprints on a Thursday night game the following week when they defeated Liberty Center, 30-0. With the victory, the Bears clinched the first league championship since Fred Martinelli's team won the NWOAL in 1958.

Strahm substituted freely, starting in the third quarter. He wanted as many players as possible to be able to, twenty or thirty years later, say that they played in the league-clinching win, and maybe even embellish their accomplishments a bit. After all, isn't that part of the fun?

In the following week leading to the season finale against a team Dick had lost to both of his first two years by a combined score of 72-22, Strahm did some digging through the Bryan school record books. He found out that it had been just a year shy of a quarter century since a Bryan team had won eight football games in one season. Still, Strahm doubted he had enough in the way of instilling incentive in his players basking in the afterglow of their undisputed league championship.

So, he put together what one might call a ruse. On Sunday, probably about the same time a touch football was going on behind Spanglers' barn, the Strahms drove to a neighboring town. Ginger went into the ladies' department store and purchased twenty-two pairs of pink panties, enough to match the number of every one of the Bryan starters.

The Strahms took the underwear home, and Ginger sewed the name of each Bryan player on the back. There were, of course, the Sanedas, the Lingvais, the Freys, Killgallon, Carpenter, Davis, and so on down the line.

During Thursday night's practice, the Bryan players came onto the practice field seeing a very dispirited head coach. Remembers Killgallon, "We knew something was wrong. Ordinarily, the coach was so fired up, so enthusiastic. When I looked at him standing in front of this large box at his feet, he looked like someone who'd just lost his best hunting dog!

"Of course, we all said, 'Coach, what's wrong?' He told us he'd gotten this box in the mail that morning, and it was postmarked in Napoleon. Biting hook, line, and sinker, we said, 'What's in it?'

"He opened the lid and started pulling out these pink panties and holding each up so we could see the name sown on it. Each one he's pull out, he say, 'I don't know what to do. I must really have failed you guys to have a league opponent think so little of your toughness that they'd mail something like this to you.'

"Well, with each new pair he pulled out, we got madder and madder. I was standing close to the box and could see that it was postmarked Napoleon, and, boy, was I ever infuriated! We yelled, 'Give us those things.' We wore them not only in practice that day but also under our football pants the next night in the game.

"We beat Napoleon soundly, 22-6, and really put some big hits on them. After a lot of those hits, as we were un-piling, we'd say, 'You think we wear pink panties now?' I'm sure there were some quizzical looks in those Napoleon helmets, but we thought nothing about it. We won and finished the greatest year in Bryan football history at 8-1 and 7-0 in the league."

The only way Killgallon ever found out that the panties weren't really sent by anyone in Napoleon was a chance meeting many years later. "Coach Strahm never let on to anyone his role in the pink-panty incident. About twenty years later, I'm in my late thirties, and my wife and I are at the Toledo Country Club having dinner. And, guess who I run into? Duane Schooley, who by that time was writing for the *Blade* and was out there having dinner.

"As we got to swapping stories and laughing about memories like his tough times at practice with us that one day, I brought up the pink panties. Schooley got this look on his face, and he said, 'You don't know, do you?' I said, 'Know what?' Then, Duane said, 'I'm the one who drove the box to Napoleon and mailed them to Dick's house!'

"If I hadn't been at the country club that night, I probably still would be thinking someone in Napoleon mailed them. I guess that explains those "Huh?" looks I remember on those Napoleon players' faces.

Killgallon continues, "My, what great memories I have of my time with Coach Strahm, and I feel pretty special knowing the real story because I'm certain there are still guys on that team who think someone in Napoleon actually did mail that box."

Recalls Schooley, "Well, I guess you can reveal my role in the subterfuge now that I'm retired. I think there's a statute of limitations that expired a while back. I would have never thought of helping Dick with something like this had I been working at a paper covering several teams, but this was Bryan, Ohio, and I only covered the home team."

Strahm laughs, thinking back on the moment. "Heck, after Schooley went through that practice with us, I figured he was part of our team. This was his last opportunity to contribute to a win!"

For the year, the 8-1 Bears had made history. Not only did they win more games than any Bryan football team ever but they also lost the last three coin tosses as well, perhaps becoming the only great football team to ever lose every coin toss the entire year.

When it came to league honors, Bryan was well rewarded as the Bruins had eighteen players selected All-League. Keith Carpenter won the league scoring championship with 102 points, nearly doubling the total of his closest competitor. He was named third-team All-State and received a scholarship to play football for the Toledo Rockets.

At the football banquet, Ray Eliot, the University of Illinois retired football coach, was the guest speaker. With him, he brought a message that so resonated with Dick Strahm that he would pass the message along in countless locker rooms and also repeat that message to himself when faced with adversity.

What Strahm remembers about Coach Eliot, who took the Fighting Illini to two Rose Bowls, is the way he commanded the room when he spoke. "We were all almost sitting at attention, as if we were afraid to move. As he was finishing his speech, he said he wanted to share with us a poem by an author by the name of Walter D. Wintles, entitled 'You Can If You Think You Can.'

The poem so inspired me that I couldn't wait to get a copy of it so that I could memorize it. And, here is what Strahm found.

You Can If You Think You Can

If you think you are beaten, you are;
If you think you dare not, you won't,
If you like to win, but don't think you can,
It's almost a cinch you won't.
If you think you'll lose, you're lost;
For out in the world you'll find,
Success begins with a fellow's will;
It's all in a state of mind.
For many a game is lost
Ere ever a play is run,
And many a coward fails
Ere ever his work is begun.
Think big and your deeds will grow,
Think small and you'll fall behind;
Think that you can and you will,
It's all in a state of mind.
If you think you are out-classed, you are;
You've got to think high to rise;
You've got to be sure of yourself before,
You can ever win a prize.
Life's battles don't always go
To the stronger or faster man,
But sooner or later, the man who wins
Is the fellow who thinks he can.

The poem has been one Strahm has recited many times. "I thought so many times about Wintles' message to not be a coward, to not be afraid to get up and take the next step, to get up and try to get on that stationary bike after my stroke, to throw that cane away.

"I can remember looking around the room at the faces, especially the young faces of my players. Coach Eliot finished Wintles' poem, and I could tell the message really struck home. Then, like a thunderclap, the applause started. What an inspirational moment to be a part of."

At the conclusion of the 1964 season, the Strahms entertained two special dinner guests, W.C. and Ruth Killgallon. That's about the time W.C. gave the Strahms some advice. Recalls Dick, "We had W.C. and Ruth over for dinner one evening, and after we got done eating, W.C. and I went for a little walk. We got to talking. Actually, W.C. did most of the talking, and I did the listening. Being known for his directness, he said, 'Coach Strahm, you need to buy a house.'

"I told him that I didn't think I could afford it. Then, he asked how much I made. I told him that, including my teaching salary, coaching salaries for football and track, and cutting the grass at Park Stadium, about $7,500. He said, 'My son Bill [nine years older than Larry and working for the Bank of New York] will help us arrange the financing.'

"Now, few people ever argued with Bill Sr., but I certainly tried. I told him there was no way I could afford to buy a house on less than $8,000 a year, but he persisted. He asked me what I had in the way of savings. I told him that I had been buying a $50 savings bond each month for $37.50, so I was making a whopping $12.50 profit at maturity.

"Then, W.C., as direct as ever, said, 'For a family man, you don't have much. You need an investment, and the house makes sense. With the bonds, how much do you have in savings?' I told him that I had about $800. He told me that we were going house hunting after he got with his son Bill Jr. on the phone.

"Well, I knew W.C. well enough to know that there was no sense arguing. A couple days later he drove up and said, 'I've gotten with my son, and you can afford as much as $250 a month for a house payment.'

"On the outskirts of town, we found a nice-looking brick ranch with about an acre and a half of land. To make a long story short, we instantly liked the house, W.C. made another call to Bill Jr. and we had our loan, and, eventually our own house, thanks to W.C. Killgallon."

Of course, those junior girls, who so liked their American history teacher and football coach, came out and christened the new abode with another bonfire-cookout-slumber party.

During the last month of school, Strahm, in addition to giving a lot of thought to the new home he we was about to move into also did what he always did, which was to keep a sharp eye out for any boy roaming the halls or entering his classroom he felt would make a football player. One, in particular, that intrigued him was Gus Phillips.

Remembers Strahm, "I knew Gus was a young man who had never played sports of any kind. He was probably about 6'2," 190 pounds, and I thought if he could get himself into football shape, he could really help us his senior year."

Recalls Larry Killgallon, "You see, in the past at Bryan, no coach ever asked you to come out for a sport, but here's this super-enthusiastic football coach selling his program constantly. He was always trying to get guys to come out."

Strahm approached Phillips, who, like Dallas Drenning at Lakota, had a reputation as one of the toughest kids in Bryan and one who'd had his share of scrapes, and said, "If you want to hit someone, come out for football. I'll let you hit people all day long on the field."

"For a kid who'd never played, I knew it was a long shot, but, after thinking about it for a couple days, he came back to me and told me he would!"
Phillips wound up playing defensive end the next fall. He had kind of a following of ten or so other "shop guys," and he convinced a couple of others to come out as well.

Larry Killgallon remembers those first few August practices were pretty tough on the newcomers. "You never saw such green faces in your life. They were really sick, but I'll have to hand it to them, especially Gus. They stuck it out, and Gus, especially, became a pretty good football player.

"The one thing I can remember about Gus is he really had a habit of swearing a lot. Now, Coach Strahm wanted his players to be not only tenacious football players but gentlemen. For instance, every game day, we all dressed up, both coaches and players, in black sweater vests, black dress pants, white shirts and ties. Well, Gus was able to conform to the dress code a whole lot easier than breaking himself of the cussing habit. Did he ever run extra wind sprints after practice every time Coach heard him.

"It became quite a joke on the team during my senior year. We'd all get on the bus to take us to the practice field or to an away game, and we'd have a chant. 'Don't cuss. Call Gus. Gus will cuss for all of us!' But, as I say, we accepted Gus as part of our team, and all of the ribbing was good-natured."

For Strahm, he remembers the Bryan pep rallies as the absolute best he'd ever been around. He also remembers the shop boys who didn't play football responding to Gus's telling them that, not only would they start attending the rallies but they also would sit in the first row. When Gus motioned to them to stand, they stood. When he wanted them to cheer, they cheered. Wasn't this an amazing infusion of school spirit in individuals who'd demonstrated little to that point in their high school careers! The principal, Joseph Newell, was amazed at the transformation.

Killgallon remembers the change in Gus Phillips as time went on. "At first, Gus couldn't understand the need for some of Coach Strahm's rules. For example, during practices and games, we were never allowed to take our helmets off. Our shirt tails always had to be tucked in. Coach wanted everybody always to look ready, to look focused, and to look the way he believed football players should look. But, eventually Gus caught on, and, for a guy not used to a lot of discipline, did really well, even though he did struggle with the cursing thing."

With high hopes, the Bears began their 1965 season, ready to defend the NWOAL crown. Dave Ebersole would run out of the tailback slot in Strahm's ground-pounding offensive and be the featured back. Whether the residual effects of an injury so severe that amputation was seriously discussed would hold up to the stress of carrying the football twenty-five or thirty times or even more each and every game, only time would tell. But, Ebby was very thankful that he was given the opportunity to do so. So was his father Dudley.

There were other changes necessitated by graduation losses. For one, Strahm had finally run out of Sanedas, as both Bobby and defensive MVP of the previous year, John, had moved on. Remembers Strahm, "What a big part of our success those four brothers were."

To replace Carpenter, the new Toledo Rocket, Strahm turned to his cousin, Larry Killgallon. "I think I first started to think about Larry as a running back when I saw him run over that upperclassman on Challenge Day to win that defensive tackle position when he was a sophomore. However, I had been blessed with so many great ballcarriers that I didn't feel the need to switch Larry. This year, though, I needed him to play fullback and be the second option running the ball and also be a lead blocker on our isolation plays we would run for Ebersole. We were also going to continue to play Larry at linebacker, too."

With new quarterback Mike Robinson taking over full time now that John Frey had graduated, the Bears faced their toughest opener since Strahm arrived three years earlier. While in those three years Napoleon had always been the finale, this time Charles Buckenmeyer brought his Wildcats into Park Stadium for the first game of the year before a standing-room-only throng of 3,000 fans.

In a game that both Dick Strahm and Larry Killgallon believe to this day was there for the taking, the Naps defeated the Bears 34-26 behind a strong performance by quarterback Steve Westhoven, who threw for three touchdowns and ran for a two-point conversion.

A dejected Strahm said after the game, "I feel as though the rug has been pulled out from under me, and I have a broken back."

Remembers Killgallon, "I don't know if we were overconfident after that pink-panty finale the previous year, but we just couldn't get up over the hump that night. I will say one thing, though. I truly believe it was something Coach Buckenmeyer said in the Napoleon papers that got some colleges looking at me my senior year. He said that the game I played was the best all-round game he'd ever seen a high school player have. Because of the reputation he had as one of the best coaches in the area, I think that got me some offers. Due to a lot of injuries my senior year, I didn't really have great numbers, so it couldn't have been that."

Despite the disappointing loss, Strahm would simply not allow his team to pack it in. Recalling the inspirational poem Coach Eliot recited at the last football banquet, Strahm drove his players hard at practice and they responded.

The following game, the Bears blanked Van Wert 38-0, and a jubilant Strahm talked of new beginnings after the game. "We were starting a new season tonight, and we sure got this one off on the right foot."

Unfortunately, Killgallon sustained a knee injury and missed the entire second half. It was an injury that would flare up throughout the rest of the season and cost him substantial stretches of time on the field. When Killgallon went down, Strahm turned to Robin Frey, who came in at fullback and did so well that Strahm shouted over the din of a joyous locker room, "When we reached for the bench, they came through for us!"

Dave Ebersole had solid games the first two weeks and was beginning to prove he could take the pounding of running the ball early, often, and late.

Duane Schooley's headline after the third game said it all: "Killgallon, Ebersole Star as Bruins Garner League Win." Killgallon scored three touchdowns and Ebby, two, in the 42-21 win over Delta. Despite the win, Strahm was concerned about the mental errors, especially in the area of pass defense. His team had yielded touchdown passes of 60 and 40 yards.

Despite their coach's concern, the Bears continued to play well and win. Wauseon went down, 18-8. On the clinching drive, Strahm, by his play calling, essentially said to Dave Ebersole, "You are the horse upon which I will ride." With Killgallon's punishing lead blocks, Ebersole carried the ball on all but five plays in the second half.

A 30-14 win over always-tough Defiance earned Strahm a ride after the game on the shoulders of jubilant Bears like Frank Psurny, Dan Grant, and a player who was learning to swear less and less, Gus Phillips. Dave Ebersole got loose often, running for 189 yards.

The Bears then defeated the Archbold Blue Streaks, 32-24, behind an incredible 325 yards by Ebersole on 32 carries. The 165-pounder's performance allowed Bryan to overcome eight penalties that cost the team over 200 yards and a touchdown.

Schooley's accounts of the Bears' games were classic small-town accounts. First of all, they started on the front page of the paper, running right beside stories bearing headlines like "Ambushes Mark Another Day of Conflict in Vietnam" and "President Outlines New Pact with Panama on Canal Zone."

The game accounts were lengthy and meticulous in detail in telling of the home team's drives. The young reporter often credited the most overlooked personnel on any football team, the blockers, with sentences like, "When Ebersole was carrying the pigskin, Frank Psurny, Mike Davis, Ed Lingvai, Robin Frey, Dick Hunter, and Mike Robinson, along with either Gus Phillips or Craig Farlow, provided running room with key blocks."

In Bryan, it was time for Homecoming, and the opponent coming to town was just perfect for such an occasion. Montpelier was very young and had struggled even keeping games close each week. Larry Killgallon remembers the game vividly. "It had been raining hard all week, and the field was in very bad shape. My brother Bill had never seen me play but was flying in from New York for the game.

"Well, in the first half, we could do no wrong. Everything we tried, worked. Montpelier also fumbled several times and had a number of punts blocked. Heading into halftime, we were up, 52-0. We got into the locker room and Coach Strahm said, 'I want the starters to shower and get dressed. You can go up into the stands and sit with your families. That way, you can get under some umbrellas. We won't be needing you in the second half."

Recalls Dick, "It made perfect sense to me at the time to get them out of the weather, since I was only going to play the younger guys from that point on."

The second half proved to be another couple coats of shellac. Remembers Killgallon, "Coach Richard Strahm did everything in his power to keep the score down. We ran on fourth down deep in our own territory. Heck, we even tried a field goal on first down! It was just one of those nights."

The cubs who replaced the starting Bears scored three more touchdowns, and the final score was 70-0. It was the second-most lopsided defeat in the history of the NWOAL.

After the game, Montpelier coach Pete Dreher was furious with his coaching counterpart Strahm. Recalls Dick, "Pete felt that I'd embarrassed him by sending the starters up into the stands. I tried to explain to him why I did it, and it wasn't any intent to embarrass him, but he stormed off the field accusing me of setting his program back a couple of years.

"Looking back, I doubt I'd do the same thing again. At halftime it was still raining. There were three to four inches of mud on our sideline. At that time, I thought the best thing to do was to get the starters out of the mud and rain. Right or wrong, who knows? But I didn't really feel I'd poured it on. I did everything I could to hold the score down in the second half, but you can't just tell your young players to fall down. They practice just as hard as the starters, and they want their moments to shine as well.

"I know this comes up in sports a lot, this business about another coach feeling an opponent has poured it on. But, my feeling has always been the same, even when I've had my own teams occasionally get beaten badly. And, that feeling is that coaches can't worry about the team they're playing and how many times they're scoring. Your job as a coach is to worry about your own team and do everything you can to prevent a game from getting farther and farther out of hand."

After the game, Strahm gave Duane Schooley a quote for his write up. "I certainly didn't want this to happen. Naturally, we wanted to win, but not like this. I believe the blocked punts set up the big first half score. We didn't even dress our first 22 men in the second half, but the momentum was there, and our young players were fired up. We've always had a good relationship with Montpelier, and I hope this doesn't destroy it."

For Killgallon, he has one very clear remembrance of the game. "After Coach sent us up into the stands at half time, I realized that my brother's flight had been delayed and he'd just arrived during intermission. All of a sudden, here I come walking up into the stands and sat down beside him. He'd flown all the way in from New York and never even got to see me play a down."

The next to the last game of the season saw the Bears defeat Swanton, 32-14. It was all Ebby, all the time, as the senior workhorse set a school record, rushing for 351 yards on a jaw-dropping 41 carries. He also scored five touchdowns as the 195-pound fullback Killgallon rushed for 100 yards himself. Combined, the two backs accounted for 450 of Bryan's 474 total yards.

An unexpected Liberty Center Tigers loss to Archbold meant if Bryan could defeat the Tigers in the finale, Bryan would tie for the league championship. In this age long before there were any high school playoffs to crown a state champion, a league crown was coveted greatly.

However, on the final Friday of the season, Bryan's NWOAL-crown hopes slipped away as they went down 24-14. Recalls Dick, "You might call the 1965 season our bookend season. We lost our first and last games and won seven in a row in the middle."

It was a game both Strahm and Killgallon feel they could have won. Killgallon was injured on the first play of the game and missed the opportunity to live the bittersweet moments most senior football players get to experience, the final game of their high school career.

Both Strahm and Larry Killgallon still have questions even after more than forty years about the 1965 season. What if the Bears hadn't had two punts blocked in the opener, precipitated by bad snaps of a player trying to center the ball with a hand injury? What if Larry had been able to play the last game, to take the load off Ebersole and provide the punishing blocks he was capable of producing? Such are the incidents that separate 7-2 from 9-0, but, as every coach and every player knows, such are the harsh realities of football.

For Ebersole, it was a season of unforgettable magnitude. He broke Keith Carpenter's season rushing record, running for 1,487 yards in just nine games. Including pass receiving and running back kicks, his net yardage of 1,870 was also a school record.

He had made it all the way back from an injury that nearly cost him a limb, and, if there was anyone happier than Dave, it may very well have been his father Dudley, who was his son's physical therapist long before even such a term existed in the world of sports.

After the banquet and the awarding of end-of-the-year honors, the Strahms had more time to enjoy their first Christmas in their new house. The holidays came and went for Dick, Ginger, and Doug, who was approaching his second birthday.

In January, as Dick always did, he looked for football coaching clinics to attend so that he could gather ideas to become more proficient at his craft. He found one in Michigan and had just returned home on a Sunday afternoon when the phone rang. It was Dick's big tackle, Ed Lingvai, who had put together such a solid senior season that he had received several letters from college coaches trying to entice him to accept a scholarship.

Lingvai told his coach that he had a visitor in his home who wanted to come out to Dick's house to talk to him about the type of player he was. The coach was Woody Hayes. Strahm was disbelieving at first, that is, until Lingvai handed the phone off and Dick heard the unmistakable voice of Coach Hayes.

Recalls Dick, "Coach Hayes told me he'd like to stop out to see me. The next thing I know, with Ginger and me peering out the window, here comes this big car pulling into our drive and out steps Coach Hayes himself, perhaps the most famous football coach in the entire country.

"As it turned out, Coach stayed for dinner, telling both Ginger and me that it was the first time in months he'd sat down and relaxed.

"I remember he held Doug and even gave him all the change he had in his pockets. We eventually had a picture frame made with the change glued to it and put a picture of Doug in the middle.

"It was quite a memento, at least until my daughter Gina came along and, eight years later, pried the coins loose so she could run out and buy an ice cream cone from the Good Humor truck. Well, at least someone was in good humor because it sure wasn't Gina's mom or dad! But, she was only a child, and, as a parent, you learn understanding and tolerance."

After Hayes's departure and a night's repose, Dick returned on Monday to teaching American history. While he was at school, Ginger called him to thank him for the dozen roses just delivered. As it turned out, it was that old smoothie from Ohio State who sent them. By sending those flowers, Hayes also sent a message to a young coach in the making on recruiting techniques. Remembers Dick, "Coach Hayes knew that when you recruit, you recruit the woman of the house, first and foremost."

As spring approached Dick began to receive some calls from superintendents who had noticed the resurgence of the Bryan football program. Since Strahm's arrival the Bears had compiled a record of 26-9-1, on the heels of an 0-9 1961 season.

Recalls Dick, "The calls were coming from bigger schools in Marion and Mansfield and also from bigger cities. I later found out almost all of those schools' superintendents were Ohio State graduates." Coach Hayes had made several phone calls, telling them of a certain dynamic young coach who had quite a reputation for building and rebuilding either non-existent or badly tarnished football programs.

Despite how happy he and Ginger had become in Bryan, Strahm listened and finally there was one offer that really piqued his interest. Much like Lakota, there was a brand-new school opening in Warren, Ohio, called Warren Western Reserve. The established school, Warren G. Harding, had simply become too big and so a new school was being built on the west side of the city of more than 70,000. The school would be completed by the following fall, and the superintendent wanted a young coach to organize and have a team ready the very first year.

To many, the task would seem to be impossible. Warren's newest high school would compete against some of the biggest schools in the state, schools with names like Niles McKinley, Akron Hoban, Austintown Fitch, Warren G. Harding, and Canton McKinley.

But to Dick Strahm, it seemed like the perfect opportunity. He interviewed and was offered the position. Then, things got interesting, and it was as close as Dick would ever come to leaving the coaching profession.

Recalls Dick, "W.C. asked me one day what I thought Woody Hayes made as one of the top two or three coaches in the nation. I said I had no idea, but I figured he was at the very top of the pay scale. Mr. Killgallon then told me that he knew exactly what Hayes's salary was, $28,000 a year, which was very good for that time period. He said he wanted me to come to work for him as his number-one salesman and would pay me close to the same salary as Coach Hayes was making."

"Well, I was flabbergasted. I talked it over with Ginger, and there were long conversations over whether I should accept W.C.'s offer. Who wouldn't, at three times his current salary? People just didn't say no to Bill Killgallon Sr. often. It was perhaps the toughest decision I've ever made, but I have absolutely no regrets."

Strahm accepted the position at Warren Western Reserve and sold the ranch house that he'd just purchased a year earlier for $19,000, $3,000 more than what he paid for it. This prompted a disappointed but eventually supportive Killgallon Sr. to say, "Better than your savings bonds, wouldn't you say?"

For Strahm's former Bryan Golden Bears, they scattered in all directions.

Three of the Saneda brothers entered the military. Walt, Bob, and John all served in Vietnam. Walt joined the Army and became one of the three out of every hundred tested who aspire to become a Green Beret. He became the first, and, perhaps, the only one of Strahm's former players to be accorded such an honor. Bobby served with distinction in the Air Force. Sadly, for John, the former Bruin defensive Most Valuable Player, it was he who paid the ultimate price. He was killed in action during a firefight with the Viet Cong.

John has been remembered by his old high school. In 1968, Bryan High School began awarding the John Saneda Memorial Award. The award is presented to "the athlete who has exemplified desire and determination in football throughout his varsity career."

For Frank Saneda, the emotions of those turbulent times remain. "My brothers tried not to bring any of what they'd experienced in the military with them when they came home on leaves. But, I could tell how difficult it was. John, for example, left for the Marines weighting about 175 pounds. When he came home for his first leave, he weighed 135.

"Despite how tough it was, I really wanted to join my brothers in the military, but I flunked the physical. I tried to tell anyone who would listen that I'd played four years of high school football, but they wouldn't let me join."

For Larry Killgallon, it was off to the Ivy League and Dartmouth College to study marketing and play four years of football for Bob Blackburn, a coach who would one day distinguish himself and be inducted into the College Football Hall of Fame.

"Recalls Killgallon, "I don't know how many former players can say they played for a high school coach and a college coach who both were inducted into the College Hall of Fame.

"Coach Strahm and Coach Blackburn were remarkably similar. They both demanded excellence and had incredibly sharp eyes for details. Coach Blackburn even had the engineering department study exactly where on a football you had to kick it to bounce two times before that third big bounce considered to be the perfect on-side kick. That's something Coach Strahm would have done, had he had an engineering department to go to."

Killgallon now carries on his father's dream, as president and chief operating officer of the Ohio Art Company, located at One Toy Street in Bryan, Ohio. Bill, his brother, also has joined Larry and helps run the company. Prior to his death, that's exactly what the visionary W.C. Killgallon envisioned.

It was Larry who wrote to his old Bryan coach upon Dick's retirement in 1999, "Those who have had the privilege of playing for you learned the value of committing to lofty goals, working hard to achieve them, and the teamwork that is necessary to successfully execute them. We were taught to feel the pain of defeat but also to be humble and dignified in victory."

Dave Ebersole graduated from Ohio Northern University. He played football all four years, lettering in both his junior and senior years. After graduation, he entered education, as his father did before him, and spent a rewarding thirty-two years as teacher, coach, and school administrator before retiring to Michigan.

Ed Lingvai accepted a scholarship not from Ohio State but from Indiana University. However, tragedy sometimes visits even the young and the strong. While riding a motorcycle shortly after his Bryan High School graduation, he wrecked.

For several days, his life hung in the balance. Thankfully, he recovered but never again could play football. Indiana coach John Pont demonstrated the kind of loyalty and class the truly memorable coaches possess by honoring the scholarship. Lingvai worked as a trainer in the football program and ultimately graduated from IU.

Brother Jim Lingvai received an appointment to West Point, overlooking the Hudson River. Rich Batdorf headed for the Naval Academy in Annapolis, Maryland.

With Robin Frey, Coach Strahm found out what impact a coach can have on a young player, and, with it, he knew the rewards that come from such knowledge are far more valuable than a 1965 annual salary of $28,000.

In July of 1992, Robin Frey wrote his coach of a quarter century ago. It was in the third paragraph that Strahm read that showed him the ripple effect that the coaching profession can create.

Wrote Frey, "After I quit college, I was drafted. All during Basic Training, I kept thinking to myself, 'This isn't as bad as summer practice with Coach Strahm!' That thought got me through, and when I got sent to Vietnam and would have to go days without dry clothes or rationed clean water and walk on patrol till I thought I would drop, I always thought back to high school and what we went through in August every year. I'd say to myself, 'What would Coach say if I gave up now? And I knew there would be hell to pay if I gave up, so I never did. I saw it all, the death, the killing, the uselessness of it all, but my high school football days got me through and, for that, I will always be grateful.

"Even though I have been out of school for twenty-six years, what you instilled in me as a young man has remained and will continue to remain all my life. You taught me a lot more than just football."

Duane Schooley has a final remembrance about those days in Bryan, and it is one that is as strong as his practice on a hot August day at Garver Park way back in 1964. "Richard Strahm was extremely well liked by the Bryan community to be certain. But, I'm going to say one thing. He wasn't as well liked as his wife, Ginger. She was the greatest P.R. person a coach could have, really the quintessential football coach's wife."

The Bryan days had drawn to a close, and, while packing boxes, Dick had time to reflect on his four years in the Fountain City. He was proud of the Bears' resurgence and realized while he may have played a role in that resurrection, he also had the help of so many excellent athletes and coaches.

He remembered the cherished friendships, especially W.C. and Ruth Killgallon. He remembered how the community opened its arms and immediately made both him and Ginger welcome.

He remembered the despair of losing little Danny and also the joy of Doug's birth and his successful fight to survive. Dick also remembered watching his son take his first steps in the first home he ever bought.

He also remembered the lesson, one forged by determination and perseverance, shown to him by Dudley Ebersole and his son, Dave.

And, through the myriad reflections, somehow Dick Strahm just knew a smile would crease his lips any time he heard someone speak of Bryan, Ohio, and that would just be the way it would be…for the rest of his life.

The varsity coaching staff at Warren Western Reserve in 1967: (from left) Joe Novak, Dale Strahm, Dick Strahm, Harry Beers and Jim Hilles.

Chapter 6
An Aurora Is Sighted in Warren

Dick, Ginger, and Doug Strahm arrived in Warren, Ohio, in the middle of June of 1966. The interview with the superintendent, Dr. Sanford F. Jameson, and the principal of the high school called Warren Western Reserve, John Scharf, went well and led to an offer that Dick had already accepted once before in his career at Lakota. He wanted to be the very first football coach of a brand new school. The school nickname was the Raiders, and in just about eleven short weeks, a Western Reserve football team would run out onto the field at Mollenkopf Stadium for the first time.

For the Strahms, the transition from Bryan, the little town "at the top of Ohio," population 9,000, to the vibrant city of Warren in the northeastern county of Trumbull, a city of more than 70,000, would be challenging. Warren was really at its zenith in terms of its economic power. Huge steel foundries such as Republic Steel and Copperweld made Warren their home.

One of the first items to attend to for the Strahms was to use the profits from the sale of their home in Bryan to purchase a house they hoped to make into a home on Montgomery Street on the city's west side. Ginger Strahm remembers her initial thoughts about the new dwelling well. "It was a ranch with a full furnished basement with a fireplace. The home had three bedrooms and a bathroom. Although I would grow attached to the house during our time in Warren, I won't lie. Initially, I missed our larger brick ranch in Bryan with an acre and a half that we could call our own."

The new Strahm abode was in a residential area in the heart of working-class Warren. The line of demarcation in Warren is clearly the Mahoning River, which diagonally cuts the city in half. The original high school, Warren G. Harding, had simply grown too large and is on the east side of the river. The main thoroughfare which runs through Warren is US 422. Taking it east will bring a traveler to locations that place equal importance on the game of football, tradition-laden cities like Niles and Youngstown.

After three years of construction, Warren Western Reserve on the west side of the Mahoning would be open for business for the first day of school, September 7, 1966. The football team would play its inaugural game the following weekend against the Girard Indians.

Bill Lee, then a sophomore about to call a new school his home, remembers the city his new coach saw upon his arrival. "Warren was really in its heyday. The mills were working well, with probably about 25-30 in full operation. At night, they would open their blast furnaces and the sparks just lit up the sky. The next day, there would be all that red residue covering the cars. It was very difficult trying to keep a clean car in Warren!

"In terms of ethnicity, we had most of Eastern Europe covered. There was a Lithuanian presence. We had a lot of Italians and Greeks. We had many black families and Irish families. Because of its diversity, it really was a fascinating place to grow up. I have always maintained that growing up in Warren really prepared me to live in a bigger world and has really helped me in the business successes I've been fortunate to have had over the years since my time at Western Reserve."

Strahm's teaching assignment was American history, the same as it had been in Bryan. By this time, he had completed his M.A. at the University of Toledo. While he still wanted to keep ascending the steps of the coaching ladder, he also continued to see himself as one day being the superintendent of a school district, but that would come much later. After all, he had a team to get ready.

Strahm's first job after settling on Montgomery Street was to put together a staff. Dick recalls that it was actually easier than similar efforts at Lakota and Bryan. "Since Warren Western Reserve was a brand new school, there were many teaching positions open. While Lakota, years before, was a brand new school, there was also a fierce competition from existing faculty members at Risingsun, Jackson Liberty and Jackson Burgoon to fill those teaching positions, so not very many new teachers were being hired. Remember that none of those three schools would still be open. In Bryan, there were just the normal limited amount of teaching positions open and then, of course, the men who were already on staff to choose from.

"But, in Warren, I was given really a free reign to hire anyone I wanted and then John [Scharf] would plug them into the faculty in whatever areas they were qualified to teach. It really was a unique situation. Without John's help and support of me, there is no way we would have had the success that came to us in the next four years.

"John had been a principal at East Junior High in Warren after being an assistant principal at Harding. Basically, it was his voice that really mattered much more so than Dr. Jameson's when it came to hiring staff. He was truly a gifted administrator."

The first assistant coach Dick tabbed was one who had just two years of football coaching experience. While picking up the necessary course work to become certified to teach science during the fall semester after his graduation from Ohio Northern University, he coached the university's freshman team. The next year, while teaching at Hamler High School, he was a varsity assistant. He also happened to be someone with whom he had a history, going all the way back to childhood, when Dick used to put him in his bicycle basket and ride him down to the playground in south Toledo.

Dale Strahm, just two years removed from college, did have something going for him besides his one year in Hamler, Ohio. He had been a very good college athlete at Ohio Northern

University, both playing football and running track, and doing those so well he would one day be inducted into the university's hall of fame.

Dale echoed Dick's belief in what was so vital to putting a quality football staff together. "Actually, there were two factors that, I feel, made Warren Western Reserve so competitive immediately. First, the coaching staff was hired before the teaching staff so there were so many options to get quality coaches because they could plug into really any teaching slot. Nowadays, you'd never see that, but the administration made an early statement that athletics, especially football, was going to be very important on the west side of Warren.

"The second factor was, for a brand new school, our talent level was very, very good. Although we had almost no seniors to speak of, we had an outstanding group of underclassmen."

Dick remembers, initially, some resistance in his desire to bring Dale on board. "I remember while talking with Mr. Scharf about my intention to hire Dale. He said, 'We may have a problem getting that one approved by the Board.' I said, 'Why? He's young, enthusiastic, and qualified. Mr. Scharf then said, 'The board may be afraid of the objections that always come when nepotism is perceived.'

"I saw no nepotism in my decision to bring Dale to Warren. He had played four years of college football, had coached a year at Hamler, and was qualified to teach in fields [horticulture and health] where Western Reserve needed teachers! So, what was the problem? I felt so strongly about Dale's being hired, I told Mr. Scharf that I needed him to cover my back on this one. He went to the board and Dale became my first assistant.

Dick then turned to someone Dale knew from having worked with him in the summers during his college years. His name was Jim Hilles, and he was a former captain of the Ohio University Bobcat football team. He was, at that time, teaching back in Toledo and also playing semi-pro football for the Toledo Tornadoes. Hilles was interviewed and hired as a biology teacher. For Strahm, Hilles came aboard to coach the backs and also become the defensive coordinator of a group that, over the next four years, would become known throughout the state for its tenacity and its proficiency.

Another thing that Dick liked about the Hilles hire is that Jim was originally from Warren, having graduated from Harding. He understood what the city was all about.

Recalls Dale about what Hilles brought to the mix, "Jim was so far ahead of his time in terms of the cerebral aspects of the game of football. He could break down film to ferret out a team's tendencies, like what percent of the time a certain play would be run out of a certain formation."

Hilles was 17-3 as Western Reserve's head coach in 1970 and '71 after succeeding Strahm and then followed Dave McClain into college coaching at Ball State as McClain's defensive coordinator. When McClain was named head coach of the Badgers of Wisconsin, Hilles went with him. After McClain's sudden death, Hilles became the Badgers' head coach.

Hilles later coached five years in the Canadian Football League, three years in NFL Europe, a year in the XFL, and is currently living in Tampa and serves as a pro scout for the Denver Broncos. On a typical day, he will use the talent of analyzing football film that Dale Strahm remembers so well by watching between eight and ten hours of game tape and will grade every defensive lineman and linebacker in the NFL, information vital to Bronco head coach Mike Shanahan in putting trades together.

Just as Dick found Hilles through Dale, he found his next coach through Hilles in this football version of dominos. Rich Jeric was another member of the Toledo Tornadoes, a graduate of Western Michigan. He came aboard and brought an abundance of intensity with him. In the classroom, he would teach driver's education and health. On the football field, he would coach the ends. Recalls Dale, "Rich was a no-nonsense, demanding coach. He definitely matched my brother's intensity."

Dick then needed someone to coach his tackles, and he wound up with someone who would connect the dots between Dick's days at Lakota and the steel-manufacturing city of Warren. Bob Williams was brought aboard to teach American history and civics in addition to his duties as a football coach. The connection to Lakota was Bob's brother, Gordon, who was Dick's principal at Risingsun High School the year before Lakota's doors opened. Bob Williams was a great teacher and was a calming presence on the football staff. Recalls Dale, "Bob served as kind of a counterbalance to fiery guys like Dick and Rich. This kind of allowed him to play sort of the coaching version of 'good cop' to Dick's and Rich's 'bad cop.' There really was a remarkable balance on the staff my brother put together at Reserve."

Strahm then selected Carl Meyer, who was a 1963 graduate of Findlay College, to coach his guards and centers. Again, Meyer was interviewed and approved with great speed to teach general science and coach. Meyer proved to be an excellent teacher, very knowledgeable and methodical.

Joe Youngo was then added to assist Dale with the junior varsity in addition to his duties in the classroom as a math teacher.

Remembers Dick, "Obviously, there was some stress involved in walking into a brand new school and having just a couple months to hire coaches and motivate enough of Warren Western Reserve's new students to commit to the sacrifices it takes to be a part of a successful football program. The fact that John Scharf pretty much gave me no resistance in my choices was so very important."

By the end of June, Dick had his organizational meeting in the cafeteria at West Junior High for all interested in playing football for Western Reserve. Recalls Bill Lee, a sophomore who played center for Strahm the next three years, "Dick Strahm absolutely filled the room that day. He was engaging but also tough as nails. We all sensed that. We were drawn to him but, frankly, also were scared shitless of him as well."

Dick recalls the first group of players and the manner in which it was determined who would go to Harding and who would go to Reserve. "Basically, it came down to which side of the Mahoning River you lived on. If you lived on the east side, you stayed at Harding. If you lived on the west side, you would go to Western Reserve. The only exception was that those who would be seniors had an option of remaining at Harding. and graduating with their original class. Of course, those seniors in the football program who were going to be starters obviously had no interest in Reserve.

"I think I only wound up with seven or so seniors our first year, but I was thankful they took a chance on the new school."

The organizational meeting was attended by a few seniors, young men like Anthony Lucarelli, Joe DeMattio, Dennis Barrickman, Roger Brocious, Rosselle Burch, Eddie King, Richard Johnson, and Richard Donnell. They combined with forty-one other players to make up edition number one of the Warren Western Reserve Raiders.

Harding, on the east side, was the established school. The new kid on the block, so to speak, was Reserve. Each school would have around 1,500 students when school began in the fall and each would be comprised of grades nine through twelve, with one athletic director presiding over both schools' athletic programs. While the new school had many of its own facilities, such as a gymnasium and a natatorium, Western Reserve had to share the same football stadium as the original tenants, the Panthers of Harding. Mollenkopf Stadium was capable of housing as many as fifteen thousand spectators.

The reasoning was, why build a second stadium that, despite its newness, wouldn't be as commodious or bound in tradition as Mollenkopf. Harding was a member of the All-American Conference, a league that featured some of the biggest and best high school teams in the entire state, schools like Massillon, Canton McKinley, Niles McKinley, Steubenville and Alliance. Mollenkopf spectators had seen the exploits of many great football players over the years, players like a certain halfback with lightning feet, Paul Warfield, who went on to All-American honors at Ohio State before going on to the NFL to establish a Hall of Fame career.

As soon as Strahm saw the schedule, he knew what the pecking order would be at the stadium most everyone in past years either called Panther Stadium or Harding Stadium. The Raiders of Western Reserve would play on Saturday nights whenever the Panthers were at home on the same weekend.

As the season and the school year rapidly approached and construction workers frantically put the finishing touches on the building, Strahm was indeed busy with conditioning and trying to get a weightlifting program started as well as trying to plant the right seeds to grow a booster club. Early in Dick's coaching career, Strahm immediately recognized the importance of community support in building a successful football program.

One part of the six-building campus that would definitely not be ready was the football practice field. Nonetheless, two-a-day practices in August started on time on the field at West Junior High. Bill Lee remembers a big oak tree a hundred or so yards from the field as vividly as the rest of his teammates that first year. "If Coach Strahm didn't care for your effort or execution, he'd yell, 'Hit the tree!' and you'd sprint all the way down the field and around the tree and back. We all kind of caught on early about the value our coaches placed on giving 100 percent effort on every play and drill."

From even his earliest days in Warren, Dick sensed many in the city really weren't fully sold on the idea of this new school rising up west of the Mahoning River. "A lot of the city's old guard really didn't want to see Reserve open because they wanted to see as large a talent pool as possible for Harding. They'd been used to so many great players and teams when there was only one public school in town. The fan support was tremendous for those Panther teams. When Massillon or Canton McKinley came to town that stadium overflowed with ten, fifteen thousand fans.

"Now, these fans were saying, "Why are you reducing the size of the school we've given our heart and soul to by 50 percent?' There was definitely some resentment, especially at first, on the east side of town.

Recollects Dale, "We really were seen as somewhat of an orphan child that first year. We weren't in a league and didn't play what you might call a heavyweight schedule. Now, the second year, we got some of the bigger, more prestigious schools and the third year, the schedule got even tougher, but the first year, we weren't overscheduled.

"And, despite the fact there were some negative perceptions of us because of our schedule, heck, we were just starting out! We had only seven seniors, and I doubt if any would have seen any significant playing time at Harding. So, I guess you could say that we had to learn to crawl before we could walk."

Dick remembers the athletic meetings of the first year, and it was somewhat of a reaffirmation of what many in Warren felt about the new school. Despite the beautiful new school, complete with its greenhouses for those interested in botany and horticulture, its planetarium for those who wished to star gaze, and its Olympic-size pool, Dick felt the general feeling was Western Reserve should be seldom seen and never heard. "The meetings were held and attended by both Harding and Reserve, since the same athletic director, John Angelo, presided over both schools, so John Scharf and I would go.

"First, the football coach from Harding, Bill Shunkwiler, would talk and then other members of the athletic board. Of course, the athletic director would have some things to say. After a while, I'd say to John, 'When do we get to speak?' I remember his response as if he gave it to me last week because it was only two words, 'Next year.'"

One thing that Strahm came to appreciate quickly about Warren Western Reserve was the diversity of the people in the community and, of course, in his classroom and on his football field. "Now, understand that Warren was the closest thing to my Toledo Libbey days in terms of really getting to work with so many people who had different backgrounds.

"While my time at Lakota and in Bryan was certainly very rewarding, there wasn't a whole lot of cultural and ethnic diversity within each community. But, certainly, that wasn't the case in Warren. My kids came from all sorts of different backgrounds. I had Greeks and African-American and Italians and Irish and so many other ethnic groups and really enjoyed finding out how we were all different while at the same time finding out how we were all similar.

"What's that people say about diversity? What makes us different, makes us great? That's kind of the way Ginger and I felt about Warren."

As the season approached, Dick asked John Scharf a question. Strahm wanted some help with the name of the school. "Tell me about the name, John. How do you spell *Warren Western Reserve?*" He looked at me, paused and said, 'If you start winning, they'll remember your name. I don't care how many words are in it.'"

As far as the school's nickname, Dave Zoba, the sophomore who would start three years at quarterback for Dick, remembers that it was the students who were scheduled to attend the new school that determined the name. "At the end of the previous school year, all prospective students voted. There were probably five or six names on the list, and one was the Raiders. Well, there was a very popular band at the time called Paul Revere and the Raiders, and they had just played in Warren. I think that's what did it."

Dick Strahm knew that the first year would be tough since the Raiders would be largely dependent on underclassmen. However, he had both built and rebuilt programs before. This, in a way, made it a less daunting task. "I knew I could develop some West Side Pride, that's what we coaches began calling it, and use the natural rivalry that existed between the established school and the new school to our advantage. I also recognized there was a difference between the two sides of town. The east side was, generally, more seen as the 'Haves,' while the west side was more of a working-class population.

"Before I knew it, we had a booster club, and, once the season started, we got some pretty decent crowds at Mollenkopf. Now, certainly, Harding, with their schedule, caused a bigger buzz and played before some bigger houses, but we were still probably getting around six or seven thousand fans."

One of the defensive cogs for Strahm's Raiders during that first year was Cliff Roberts, and his is an interesting story. Roberts had played quite a bit for Harding as a sophomore the previous year, and, had he lived on the east side of the Mahoning, would, no doubt, have started for the Panthers. Realizing this, he intended to establish residence with the Turner family, who were dear friends of the Roberts family. The Turners did live east of the river.

Recollects Dick, "I'd certainly had experience knocking on doors at Lakota to find players. When I heard about Cliff, that's exactly what I did. Along with a couple of my assistants, I went over and met with Cliff and his mom and dad. Cliff was concerned that playing for a first-year program instead of the big school in terms of reputation and media coverage would hurt his chances to use football to get a college education through a scholarship.

"I told Cliff that if he maintained his current residence and attended Reserve I was certain he would not only receive a scholarship, but to a big-time school. Now, I guess I didn't have any concrete knowledge that would happen, but I did know one thing. Keeping players like Cliff Roberts on my side of the river would certainly help us win and help us build a reputation.

"And, I truly felt Cliff would be offered that scholarship. Well, he did stay and was a major impact player for us both in 1966 and '67, and you know something? He got that scholarship and to one of the premier programs at that time in the country, Michigan State. He played four years and earned his degree."

Roberts, now retired from Delphi Packard Electric, where he worked thirty-one years as the administrator for legal affairs and claims administration, is back living in Warren. He remembers both his decision to attend Reserve and his experience as a Raider. "It was Coach Strahm, Coach Williams, and Coach Youngo who came to my house. They really sold me on the idea of West Side Pride. They sold it so well, I passed up a near-certain starting job at Harding and a chance to receive the publicity that came with the high-profile schedule they played. But, I decided to go with the new school.

"Looking back, it worked out perfectly. I got the chance to attend Michigan State, a top-flight academic institution, and also play for truly great coaches like Duffy Dougherty and two assistants that became huge figures in coaching themselves, George Perles and Hank Bullough.

"I think, as a black player, the thing I most appreciated about playing for Coach Strahm was he fostered an attitude that we all, both black and white, were out there for one common goal, to win. When you can sell athletes on the overwhelming desire to achieve a common goal, they cease to see color. And, that's what Coach Strahm and his staff were able to instill in us, and, for that, I will always be grateful."

Dave Zoba, the Raiders' first quarterback, remembers the ferocity Roberts brought to the field with him. "We were just in awe of him. He wasn't a very big guy, less than six feet and probably not much more than 180 pounds or so, but, man, could he ever form tackle! He would hit each ball carrier with his neck bowed so it wasn't a spear, right between the numbers, and drive right up through his chin. Most runners wound up on their backs, pancaked so to speak. As quarterback, in practice, I absolutely knew when I ran an option that I was going to get drilled by Cliff. He really defined, I felt, the grittiness of this steel-mill town, especially the working-class mentality of the west-siders."

Bill Lee remembers the first year's two-a-days in August. "We ran constantly. I remember we practiced at West Junior High. I don't know how many times I heard the coaches yell, 'Hit the tree!'

"Later in the August practices, we had a day that coaches called 'Cut-Down Day.' This was the day Coach Strahm wanted to see who had the needed mental toughness to play well. He used a drill called 'The Gauntlet,' where about ten guys were lined up about five yards a part. The first guy would be tossed a ball, and he had to run at every one of the players and try to break his tackle, all the way down the line. By the time he'd gotten to the end, he'd gotten hit ten times and was tackled on most of them. Then, that player would be the last guy in line, and the next guy would go. We had about four lines going simultaneously, so there wasn't a lot of resting.

"There's no question that part of coach Strahm's purpose of the drill was to separate the wheat from the chaff. He knew some guys would probably not be back the next practice, but he wanted to find out whom he could count on.

"I can't tell you how many guys I knew that played at Western Reserve for Dick, who went on to, say, boot camp or college football, and returned to say that whatever supposedly tough endeavor they'd experienced was nothing compared to Dick Strahm's two-a-days."

August of 1966 wound down, and, finally, after many of the young Raiders "hit the tree" on the temporary practice field at West, the school's administrators opened the new school's doors on September 7.

With Harding always given the traditional Friday slot at Mollenkopf whenever the two schools both had home games, the Raiders' coaches used that fact as part of the motivation to urge their young players to get better really fast. The fact that Harding wanted exclusive use of the home locker room at Mollenkopf also would force Reserve to dress at their home school except for shoulder pads, bus to the stadium and then finish pre-game locker room details in the cramped, rather dank confines of the visiting locker room. This certainly was not a fact that went unnoticed or unmentioned by the coaches of Western Reserve.

While Strahm, like all successful coaches, didn't feel that winning as many as you lose was acceptable, starting from scratch, with just a little over ten weeks to launch a program, perhaps a break-even season wouldn't be all that bad.

The Raiders broke quickly from the gate, winning their inaugural contest against Girard on that first Saturday night of the 1966 school year, 24-12 at Mollenkopf.

Recalls Bill Lee, "I couldn't believe how small and uncomfortable the visiting locker room was at the stadium. The visitors probably had it better dressing in the locker room up in the gym. But, I'll tell you it was in that locker room that Coach Strahm gave me some of my best memories. His pre-game talks were, to me, almost mythical. He was simply a brilliant public speaker. I can remember his building in intensity the longer he spoke. By the end, he was almost frothing as he worked himself into a rage. While I don't remember him ever crying, I always term those speeches Dick's 'tears of rage.' You could see this glisten in his eyes as he reached a crescendo. He simply wanted us to despise the idea of losing, and that's probably what I consider his legacy to me. I've used that loathing of losing in business after my days as a student, and I truly believe, much of the success in business I've had, I owe to Coach Strahm."

Lee's classmate Dave Zoba, who would go on to graduate from Harvard and is now an attorney and chief operating officer of Steiner and Associates in Columbus, Ohio, remembers the strong sense of community that Dick Strahm helped to foster. "Coach recognized right away that we were the offspring of working-class people. Probably about forty percent of the fathers worked in the steel mills. My father was a fireman. So, Coach tried to use our blue-collar backgrounds to unify us. He preached to both us, and, even to a certain degree, to our parents, that we all needed to help take care of ourselves. He really sold us on the idea that we needed to have each other's back. And, that attitude became a part of our parents' philosophy in raising us. For example, if, say my friend Ted Teringo's parents saw me doing something I shouldn't be doing, they'd reprimand me, and my parents not only expected that but they'd do the same in Ted's case, and Ted's parents expected it."

Dale Strahm remembers his three years at Warren as a time he had more fun than any time in a lifetime of football stops at the likes of Bowling Green State University, Temple, Duke, Western Carolina, University of Georgia, Navy, and eleven more years in the NFL. "We'd have probably coached for nothing, and, with the salaries they were paying back then, come to think of it, we almost did!"

The rest of the 1966 season was indeed a rollercoaster with equal parts peaks and dips. Staying at home the next two weeks, the Raiders won twice more, 16-6 over Youngstown Woodrow Wilson and 12-6 over Delaware Hayes and stood at a seemingly implausible 3-0. They were being led offensively by the likes of sophomore signal caller Zoba and his running backs Clarence Mason, Johnny Cooks, and Eddie King. Defensively, Cliff Roberts led the way and, for the first three games of the season, so did free safety Gary Hinkson. Roberts and Hinkson were co-captains.

However, the fourth opponent of the year was much bigger and more formidable than any of the first three teams. Austintown Fitch was a large school on the outskirts of Youngstown. The Raiders traveled there for their first road test and returned to Warren on the short end of a 24-12 score. The 5'11," 184-pound Roberts remembered one play, in particular, that nearly altered his own history.

"As co-captains, Gary and I certainly were living proof of the adage that on the playing field there is no color. Despite our different races, we were very close. Well, in the Fitch game, I was involved in a play that literally made me sick with guilt. You see, I was known as a tenacious tackler. Well, Gary had stood a ball carrier up from behind, so I was coming full force to polish him off with as much force as I could bring. That's just the way I played. Well, I catapulted myself with the intention of hitting my opponent right between the numbers, and, I guess, he saw me coming and ducked, and I hit Gary flush in the facemask. The force of the blow broke his jaw in three places.

"I was so down because I knew after visiting Gary in the hospital afterwards that he wouldn't be able to play the whole rest of the season. I felt responsible as I watched him trying to suck some liquid food through a straw. It hurt me so bad that, on Monday, I tried to turn in my uniform. I was going to quit. I told Coach Strahm, 'I can't do this anymore. When I get so reckless I'm hurting my own teammates and friends, that's enough.'

"Well, the coaches wound up talking me out of it, but I was willing to walk away from the game I loved, I felt so bad."

Recalls Hinkson, now a district manager for Bristol Meyers Squibb, "Hard hits and injuries are certainly a part of the game, and I knew Cliff's hitting me was certainly an accident. The fact that he felt as bad as he did and almost quit football shows you the kind of first-class individual he is. But, I certainly didn't want him to quit! From the moment I knew I would miss the rest of my junior year, I began counting the days until he and I could team up our senior year."

The Raiders rebounded the following week at Salem, 12-6, to finish the first half of their season at 4-1. The rollercoaster was at the apex of its ascent. Recalls Dick, "We, as coaches, felt pleased, but we knew we had a long way to go. With the absence of an impacting senior class, I worried whether we could sustain momentum, especially against bigger schools like Boardman and Kent Roosevelt."

The Raiders did fall to Boardman, a school just outside of Youngstown, 14-6, before rebounding to beat Akron North, 26-6. With the record standing at 5-2, quarterback Zoba felt things were right on track. "We ran a lot of unbalanced line, single wing. In many ways, I ran so much that I was really more of a tailback than a quarterback my first year. I'd grown up idolizing quarterbacks like Joe Namath, who grew up in an area similar to the Warren area. [Namath grew up in the blue-collar environs of coal-producing Western Pennsylvania.] Namath was throwing it all over the place, which is what I wanted to do. But, Coach Strahm knew I wasn't ready for that type of game as a sophomore."

Just when Zoba was feeling pretty good, the wheels fell off the Raiders' wagon the last three weeks. They were beaten soundly by an undefeated Kent Roosevelt, a team loaded with future Division I scholarship players, by a score of 36-14.

Then, Dick's squad lost to a school that he felt marked the rollercoaster's biggest dip. Recalls Dick, "Warren JFK was the Catholic high school on the outskirts of Warren. They were a small school, a school that Harding wouldn't even scrimmage, much less have on their schedule. I'd made no secret of the fact that we at Western Reserve had set our sights on Harding. While we knew we were just beginning, I also wanted everyone to know we had every intention of going toe to toe with them, and sooner rather than later.

"We certainly weren't ready for them the first year and would not have them on the schedule the next year either. But, we knew the third year, we were going to play them, and I had every intention of running with them stride for stride by then.

"What's the old saying, 'If you can't run with the big dogs, stay on the porch'? Well, we didn't intend to stay on the porch!"

Despite such a mindset, the Raiders lost to John F. Kennedy, the small Catholic school, 8-6. Remembers Strahm, "Let there be no mistake about it. JFK had a nice team and deserved to win. Had they been from any other place than right here in Warren, I wouldn't have been so bothered by the loss, but, I just couldn't stand the thought of people picking up the *Warren Tribune Chronicle* the next morning and saying, 'Look at that Strahm's team! Does he actually think he can ever play with Harding when he can't even beat JFK?'"

Perhaps suffering the aftereffects of the previous game, Reserve finished the season by losing yet again, to Howland, 22-14, to finish an even 5-5.

Even before the equipment was stored and Warren Western Reserve prepared to hit the hardwood for the first time in their initial basketball campaign, Strahm began searching for ways to improve upon his five-up-five-down season. All of the coaches agreed that there was a need for the football Raiders to improve their strength and also their agility. And, they decided to do something about it.

Recalls Jim Hilles, who, as defensive coordinator, wanted more players to come closer to delivering the kind of hits he knew he could count on from Roberts and Hinkson, "We decided we could get one of Warren's big industries to help us out. We went out to Copperweld, and the company officials agreed to make our school some free weights and bars and racks. Before long, we had all these weights in our locker room, and our guys began a lifting program.

"To help our agility, Dick developed a conditioning program on Mondays, Wednesdays, and Thursdays that involved both running the halls and stairs and also a seven-station agility layout in the cafeteria. We ran it from January through the end of March. In the halls, we'd post students at the teachers' doors when our guys ran sprints so no one would walk out in the halls and get clocked while our players were running full bore.

"In the cafeteria, we took down tables and set up our stations. Our players had so much time to complete each station before they sprinted to the next area. Everything was quick! quick! quick! I'll be honest. Dick designed such an effective workout, I took the idea with me when I moved on to Ball State and then again when I moved on to Wisconsin."

Strahm presented the seven-station agility course at several clinics over the years. Remembers Dick, "We had about six to eight kids at each station, and they had five minutes to get their work in. One station, for example, players would be doing combinations of sit ups and push ups; another station, they'd be doing quick-feet drills with dummies and ropes spread out; another station, they'd be jumping rope; and so on. The players, on the whistle, after five minutes, had one minute to get to the next station and begin. I had all my assistant coaches there running the stations. All the coaches had stop watches, and the work-out was timed to precision. Everything was quick! Five minutes times seven stations with one minute in between – forty-two minutes, and we're done, and then players would rotate with the groups doing the running program in the halls and on the stairs."

Another thing Dick did during the off season was to have his assistant coaches critique his performance of the first year. One thing Bob Williams pointed out was that when Coach Strahm spoke about the program, he would generally use the first-person singular pronoun *I* rather than using *We*. States Dick, "I had no idea I was even doing this, but I sure made an effort to change. I realized how important it was to make my assistant coaches feel appreciated and respected for their considerable efforts. It was, indeed, a valuable observation Bob made."

Before the start of the January conditioning and agility programs, Dick suffered a great personal loss. Not since the death of Danny back in Bryan had he experienced the suddenness in which death can arrive, and, this time, it occurred over the holiday season when joy is generally the order of each day.

Recalls Dick, "Ginger and I took Doug back to see his grandparents in Perrysburg and Toledo. During Christmas, we'd spend a couple days in each place. The plan was to return to Warren the day before New Year's Eve, and my mom and dad would follow us back in their car. They'd agreed to baby-sit on New Year's Eve so that Ginger and I could go out and celebrate the end of 1966 with some friends. Well, Mom and Dad spent the night of December 30 with Dale at his apartment, about four blocks away from our home on Montgomery Street.

"On New Year's Eve morning, the phone rang, and it was Dale. He told me that Dad was suffering some severe chest pains. I called our team doctor and quickly got over to Dales' so that we could get him to Trumbull Memorial Hospital.

"About an hour later, a doctor came into the waiting area and told us that my father was gone. He had sustained a severe heart attack.

"I can remember how cheated I felt. How could this vibrant man be gone at the age of 58?

"Many thoughts of his involvement with the YMCA and his love of sports and his support of both my and Dale's athletics flooded back. I remembered that rainy night he and Mom returned home to change clothes when we were drenched and returned to watch the second half of the big city rivalry between Libbey and Waite so many years before.

"I also remember all those nights in Bryan he was there waiting for me just outside the locker room, win or lose, to show his love and support.

"Of course, I knew people died but not him, not so suddenly, not this young!"

A night of grief and quiet reflection that came between the waves of sobs superseded any celebration that had been planned. Dick thought ahead to the next day when he would have to return to Toledo to tell Charlie and Edith Strahm that their son was gone. He called the Strahms' minister and also their family doctor, instructing them to meet him at his grandparents' home. Needless to say, it was an uneasy slumber, when it finally did come, in the early hours of the morning in a town that suddenly felt as cold to him as the steel it produced.

Dale and Ginger stayed with Mom, and Dick made the difficult drive back to Toledo to his Grandma and Grandpa Strahm's. "I remember I had the minister and the doctor come with me, but they waited on the porch while I went inside. I walked into the living room, and the Rose Bowl game was on the television. My grandfather looked up and said, 'What happened to my son?' That was before I even opened my mouth! He just knew, I suppose, given the fact that here I was standing unannounced in his living room on a day I had always reserved for watching the college bowl games. He just knew."

After the funeral and the burial back in Toledo, Dick and Ginger returned to Warren. For Dick, it was a return to the American history classroom and to his running and conditioning program in the halls and the cafeteria of Western Reserve.

For Ginger, it was home to the brick ranch on Montgomery Street to watch Doug grow bigger and closer to his third birthday in late April. It was also a time to continue to monitor carefully her pregnancy. The Strahms were expecting. While the due date was June 1, given the premature births of both Danny and Doug, the Strahms had to be ready to deal with any circumstance.

Remembers Ginger, "We had just had a birthday party for Doug, who turned three on April 29. Several of the mothers brought Doug's playmates. A couple of days after that, I knew our new arrival was ready. We got to Trumbull Memorial, and the doctors took over. Our new daughter, Gina, arrived on May 1, one month ahead of schedule."

The Caesarian section went well, but, for Ginger, there were some post-birth problems. "I was in the hospital ten days, and during that time I received a blood transfusion. I guess my body didn't care for the blood too much, and I went into shock."

Recalls Dick, "I thought the doctors really did a wonderful job stabilizing Ginger, and we brought both mother and our new daughter home on May 10."

For little Gina Strahm, there would be some breathing problems. However, despite causing some anxious moments for her mother and father, given what had happened in the past, the difficulties proved to be both normal and treatable. A vaporizer was used to increase the moisture in the nursery. The congestion dissipated, and the Strahms had themselves a healthy baby girl, and, of course, little Doug had himself a sister.

The precocious newest member of the Strahm family was walking by nine months, and, as any mother will tell you, this can mean trouble. Remembers Ginger, "Gina was just so active and really was fearless. If we took our eyes off her for one moment, she was jumping off the couch or the coffee table. By the time she was two, she probably had about a dozen black eyes. Although it's nice to see your child walk, when it happens that quickly, there are many anxious moments."

With the Strahm family doing well, all things considered, on Montgomery Street, the breadwinner turned much of his attention to improving on that 5-5 record as the summer days slipped away and August two-a-days loomed on the horizon. The practice field was completed, and that meant for players like Bill Lee, there would be no more mandates to "hit the tree." Of course, for Lee and the rest of the maturing Raiders, that certainly didn't mean the running would end. Strahm believed in one principle above all others. "We will NEVER be out-conditioned, NEVER!"

For Dick, there would be one more detail in addition to planning an effective summer conditioning program and preparing for August preseason. He had to replace an assistant coach, Bob Williams, who left to take a teaching and head coaching position in Michigan.

Williams was replaced by Harry Beers, a graduate of Capital University and freshman civics teacher. Recalls Strahm, "I thought it was an excellent hire. I liked the fact that Harry was at Western Reserve the previous year and, along with Dave Strini, coached our freshmen. Both he and Dave were excellent communicators. It was logical to hire from within, if at all possible, so that you get someone familiar with the players and the philosophy of the head coach. Not only did we get an excellent coach to work with the tackles on the varsity level, we also didn't miss a beat with our freshmen in 1967. Coaches Ron Shafer and Bill Kovach wound up guiding them to an excellent 5-1 record."

August two-a-days began, and the Western Reserve Raiders' coaches were determined to put more on the left side of the won-loss ledger than on the right. Recalls the player trying to earn a college scholarship, Cliff Roberts, "My position coach was Dale Strahm, and his feeling was always, 'First on the field, last off.' Much of the success I had, I owe to him."

Recalls Dale, "Cliff Roberts played both ways for us at offensive guard and linebacker. Although we tried to two-platoon as much as we could, he was simply too good to take off the field. His forté was linebacker. Let me tell you, when he hit you, you had total body shock! Even though he wasn't much more than 185, he was an absolutely devastating hitter.

"I remember one game, in particular, against East Liverpool, in 1967. They had this great running back, Warren McVey, who probably went about 6'4" and 240. Cliff met him in the hole and stood him straight up with an absolutely concussive hit. McVey wound up going to Michigan State with Cliff. I think he must have figured it was better to have Cliff Roberts as a teammate than an opponent.

"Even beyond being a great football player, what I remember about Cliff Roberts is he was such a quality person, just a great, great young man. It just made it so much easier to start that Western Reserve program with players like Cliff and John Cooks and Dave Zoba and Gary Hinkson and Fred Pisanelli and so many others."

One of Strahm's memories from that time had to do with a pair of scrimmages he and his coaches arranged in the preseasons of 1967 and '68.

"What happened was we agreed to a home-and-home scrimmage in consecutive Augusts with Shelby High School with a pretty successful, well-established coach. Now, this took quite a bit of planning because we decided to make the experience more than just the scrimmages themselves. Since the two schools were 120 miles apart, instead of the thought of the players being on a bus for around five hours in one day, we decided to make the trips overnighters.

"The first year, we traveled to Shelby the day before the scrimmage. The Shelby coaches made the arrangements to have our players stay with the families of the their players, just as we would do the next August. Now, this took a pretty fair amount of planning, but we felt this was kind of a cultural-exchange program and worth it.

"The next day we'd have the scrimmage and then the mothers of the players would feed the teams before we left to return to Warren. Then, we'd follow suit the next August.

"To be honest, my defensive coordinator, Jim Hilles, really wasn't crazy about taking the game in the first place. Shelby ran a single wing, which was an offense we wouldn't see all year in our regular season.

"However, I thought it would be not only a challenge for our team but also an opportunity to meet members of another community on a different level than you do when you just have a scrimmage.

"Well, it turned out that Jim was right to be skeptical about taking the game. In the scrimmage, we got our hats handed to us. We simply weren't able to stop their offense and had to kind of limp back to Warren after the game. While we didn't like to lose, even a scrimmage, I think the game served to light some fires under our players and coaches, and, of course, we wound up having a very successful 9-1 season.

"The next summer, the Shelby coach and I got together over the phone and got a date for our second scrimmage. We got everything arranged as far as pairing up the players for the sleeping arrangements, and, of course, you just knew the West Side Pride Moms were really going to put on a nice post-game spread.

"Now, as we were approaching the game, Jim and I decided to hell with the fact that it was just a scrimmage! We really spent a lot of time preparing to defend the single wing.

"The night before the scrimmage, everything went well with the sleeping accommodations. Everybody reported to Mollenkopf Stadium on time. The players dressed, and we're ready to go.

"When we start playing, it was really evident the outcome was going to be far different than last August. We absolutely stuffed them defensively. And, our first-team offense scored five or six times.

"After our first teams were done, the usual scrimmage routine was to get the second teams organized so that they could go against one another. Well, I was down in the end zone talking to our starters, and my assistants were organizing our second-team offense and defense.

"All of a sudden, I heard one of my coaches yell over to me, 'Hey, Coach Strahm, they're leaving!' Sure enough, I looked down at the far end of the field, and there's the bus and their players' piling on!

"The trainers had apparently gotten all the clothes out of the locker room, and, without a word, with us getting ready for the second part of the scrimmage, there went our opponent driving away! We were just amazed!

"I guess, to the Shelby coach's credit, he did call the next day. He said, 'I was just so embarrassed over how we played that I just couldn't take it anymore!'

"In a coaching career, I think you tend to remember not only the dramatic moments but also the funny stuff that happens. While I wasn't laughing at the time, looking back, it was pretty amazing. I've never heard of any team that, without notice, just snuck away in the middle of a scrimmage."

The second-year Raiders' schedule included big school Cuyahoga Falls and retained such powers as Austintown Fitch and Kent Roosevelt, so the challenge was there to get better, get quicker, and get stronger to compete with a more difficult schedule. The year after, the schedule would strengthen again, so Dick knew he had to continue to sell the message of "West Side Pride" with as much passion as he could muster.

That passion paid as quick a dividend as one could possibly imagine. While playing to the battle cry of "Do the impossible," the Raiders, in just their second year of existence, posted a remarkable 9-1 record. Hilles' defense accounted for four shutouts, thanks in large part to the senior linebacker Cliff Roberts and free safety Gary Hinkson. The reunited linebacker-safety tandem delivered ferocious hits to ball carriers who dared to come into the middle of the field. The defense yielded a meager average of 6.4 points per contest.

Dave Zoba led an offense that included elusive and punishing runners like John Cooks, Clarence Mason, Willie Thompson, and Warren G. Harding transfer Frank Sericola. The Raiders averaged 28.6 points per contest. Zoba was able to open up the attack more as Coach Strahm knew he'd be wasting much of his talented junior's abilities if he only had him handing off all season long. On the receiving end of his aerials were a couple of outstanding receivers, Bill Fisher and Fred Benson.

The only stumble during the entire season was a gut-wrenching week-four loss to Austintown Fitch, 14-6. A mere eight points separated Coach Strahm from an undefeated season.

While most coaches will tell you that any win is a quality win, one game, in particular, stands out in Dick's mind as so very special in 1967. "Kent Roosevelt had a terrific team. They'd beaten us the year before and hadn't been beaten going into week eight in well over a year. They had several athletes who would go on to play major college football. Tom DeLeone was the center. He would go on to star at Ohio State before moving to the NFL for a remarkable thirteen years, most with the Cleveland Browns.

"Kent Roosevelt also featured an excellent running back by the name of Tom Campana, whose father was the head coach. Campana followed DeLeone to Ohio State to play for Woody Hayes," Dick recalls.

For the game, Strahm reached into his considerable bag of motivational tricks. This time, the motivation came out in the form of a special jersey for the game against the favored Rough Riders of Kent. With the full approbation of the ultra-supportive Western Reserve principal

John Scharf, the school purchased some white jerseys with a simple two-word exhortation above the numerals on the front, "Beat Kent."

On that night in Roosevelt Stadium in Kent, Ohio, against an undefeated team, the Raiders would surely give the boys down at Trina's Barber Shop, considered headquarters for all things football in Warren, something to talk about on Saturday morning.

Hilles' defense shut out the vaunted Roosevelt attack, and Dave Zoba quarterbacked the offense to two scores and a hard-fought 14-0 victory. It was a win like this that really solidified west side support and got the attention of all of Warren on both sides of the Mahoning River. This was especially true since Harding was in the midst of a disappointing season in which they would ultimately lose seven of ten games.

Dick Strahm was, if not the toast of all of Warren, at least the toast of the West side. Paul Trina Sr. recalls those glorious first years of Warren Western Reserve and the support the Raiders received.

"The downtown merchants became great supporters of Dick and his program. Of course, I threw all my support behind him and so did businesses like John Allen's Heating and Cooling, Mike Casale's Drexel Park Pharmacy, G's Golden Gate Restaurant, and the Chateau Supper Club."

Dick Strahm certainly remembers one of his businessmen supporters in particular. "Mike Casale and I became great friends. His family and my family took several vacations together, generally to Miley's Resort in Michigan. I can remember one summer Mike rented a 38-foot boat up in Toronto, and we, and the rest of our families spent a really wonderful week together seeing the sights.

"That's what's so wonderful about coaching. It gives you so many opportunities to establish friendships with those in the community. Also, it gives your fan base an identity. While I certainly appreciated everyone who supported us, Mike Casale came to mean so much more to me than just a supporter or a fan of Western Reserve."

Paul Sr., whose son Paul Jr., would one day become a starting quarterback at Western Reserve and eventually play for Dick at Findlay College, remembers the support G's Golden Gate Restaurant provided Strahm's team. "The Golden Gate provided the team their pre-game meal before each home game. Now, this was Saturday night, a night that those in the restaurant business really count on to make their money. So what do they do? They provide, for free, a big meal for sixty or so people for the first half of the usual dinner slot. They're not only tying up tables but also giving their product away!"

Recalls Dick, "The amazing thing to my coaches and me is that we would go in and be treated almost like royalty. Remember, our players were from working-class families. We'd come in, dressed in our white shirts and ties and black sweater vests, a tradition I carried with me from Bryan, and, boy, did we ever look as if we were ready for business!

"We had a school bus waiting when we came out of the restaurant. We'd walk the hundred or so feet to the bus, and on both sides of us, there was a line of boosters, students, and band members. They'd be cheering at the top of their lungs and hitting those drums and tooting their horns. The lines were three and four people deep. This happened every home game! Let me tell you that when you walked through that tunnel of support, you got chills. There was so much yelling and screaming from the five hundred or so people there. If you couldn't get motivated going through that, well, nothing could get you going. The west side really supported us in unbelievable fashion."

Trina Sr. also remembers the Chateau Supper Club because he not only was able to show his support at his barbershop but also at the Chateau. "I had a band called the Paul Trina Combo, and we played three nights a week at the Chateau on Wednesdays, Fridays, and Saturdays. Well, after the game, the Western Reserve coaches and their wives would come in.

"As soon as we spotted Coach Strahm and Ginger, we'd immediately stop playing whatever we happened to be playing and break into the Raider fight song! It didn't make any difference if we were in the middle of a soft and sentimental ballad like Errol Gardner's classic "Misty." As soon as we saw them come in, it was Raider time!"

For Trina, there was another way he showed the deep regard he had for Dick and Ginger. "Something else I did after I found out what happened to Dick and Ginger's Danny was to learn the song 'Danny Boy.' I was the drummer and lead vocalist, and we'd do that song in honor of Danny Strahm. We west-siders just loved Dick and Ginger.

"Dick gave the west end so much pride. The standard, kind of tongue-in-cheek joke on the west side was to ask another fella if he was going to go down to the Mahoning River that day. When the other guy would ask, 'Why?', you'd say, "Well, don't you want to see Dick Strahm walk across the river?' Seriously, though, he and Ginger absolutely couldn't have been thought of more highly."

Trina, now 81 and still living in Warren, also remembers the Quarterback Club, the group of around two hundred people who met with Coach Strahm on Monday evenings to watch the game film from the previous weekend's game. "Dick was just an electric public speaker. He was so enthusiastic, so positive, that he captivated us. Heck, he used to get us so fired up, we were ready to go out and play!"

After the magical 1967 season, Dick continued to look for ways to both motivate players and supporters and improve his overall program. He knew he'd have to in order to compete the following season. For one thing, his terrific defensive duo of Roberts and Hinkson received full scholarships and would be off to play for Michigan State and the University of Toledo respectively the following fall.

For another thing, the '68 schedule was beefed up for the second straight year. The new kid on the block, Western Reserve, finally would get their crack at Harding in a game at Mollenkopf that would electrify both sides of the Mahoning.

Recalls Dick, "Of course, we continued with our weightlifting. In addition to using our Copperweld weights in the locker room, a lot of players, especially the linemen, would lift weights over at Ted Terringo's garage during the summer, which he and his father had turned into a weight room.

"I had just finished the reward portion of our Fighting Raider '500' Club. You see, the coaches awarded points throughout the season for different accomplishments in the games. Anyone who accumulated five hundred points got a steak dinner at my house, prepared by Ginger and the other coaches' wives. All my coaches were there, and we all had a wonderful meal. That year, we had Dave Zoba, Cliff Roberts, Gary Hinkson, Frank Allen, Peter James, Larry Jones, and Ted Terringo over. Man, could those guys ever eat!"

Strahm's next idea was to form what Dave Zoba remembers as the 3-D Club, which stood for "Desire, Dedication and Discipline." Again, players received points for so many push-ups and sit-ups and pull-ups and the like. Recalls Zoba, "I was determined to do everything I could in the off-season before my last year, both in the classroom and on the football field, to make it the best year ever.

"I threw a hundred balls a night into a tire from one knee and also sitting on my butt to build arm strength, and I also really went after the '3-D.' I wanted to wear that sweatshirt you earned when you accumulated the needed points. Although all it had on it was the name of the school and '3-D,' to me and many other players, it was an article of clothing we coveted."

Recalls Dick, "The months after football season seemed to run downhill toward the '68 season. That's because we coaches kept our players involved in a lot of conditioning, and we also knew the kind of senior class we had."

The bottom of that hill Strahm talked about was, of course, the August two-a-days prior to the opener against Ashtabula. A new coach had been added to replace the fiery Rich Jeric, who left to become a head coach at Monroe High School in Michigan.

Joe Novak was hired, and he remembers his initial impression of the man who brought him aboard after his playing days and one year as a graduate assistant at Miami University. "I remember thinking, 'Boy, this Dick Strahm is a cocky guy.'"

Novak, now one of the most successful coaches in the Mid-American Conference at Northern Illinois University, continued. "But, then again, he had to be that way, being in charge of a brand new program in a city dominated by an established school such as Harding, which probably was in the best football conference in the state."

Novak would be responsible for the ends, and, he felt, most of the pieces were in place for a successful '68 campaign. "They'd gone 9-1 the previous year. Those first few practices in August, I could see we had a lot of talent. The quarterback, Dave Zoba, was extremely impressive, and we had a whole stable of running backs, really punishing runners like Bob Davis and also some speed guys, like Johnny Cooks. I also thought our line play would be solid. About the only unknown was we were about to play some really big tradition-laden schools. I guess, first and foremost, was Harding.

"This was the game everyone was pointing to. I realized almost as soon as I unpacked my bags that Western Reserve's being built really divided that town. It was east versus west, and most of the big money was on the east side. The west side was working class, and I really think Dick probably did more to raise the self-esteem of the west-siders than anyone else had ever done. That football team kind of galvanized them and gave them a common interest and source of immense pride."

Novak continued, "People didn't really think that we were going to be that good, but, I think we felt we knew what we had."

Fifteen lettermen were back for Reserve, off a 9-1 team, and Strahm, the coach the Warren paper the *Tribune Chronicle* called "the fiery tutor of the grid game," felt the schedule maybe arrived a bit too soon. He told local sports writer Tony Angelo just prior to the Ashtabula opener, "The '68 schedule is one year ahead of the school, without trying to give any alibis. With only one year's varsity experience for probably around 35 percent of our kids and with our JV program still in the crawling phase, so to speak, we may not be able to compete with the schools on our schedule that we must face. Our kids have lost none of their enthusiasm or desire, but we, on the coaching staff, realize what a task we have ahead."

Lou Holtz, former Notre Dame football coach, and someone Dick Strahm has come to know pretty well from years of football clinics and programs, is considered the undisputed master of downplaying his team's chances against opponents. It appears, however, the third-year Western Reserve coach had some of the same abilities in expressing such pessimism over his Raiders' chances.

The first night of the season, despite their coach's concern, the Raiders proved they would be a force with which to reckon. The final score on a night where they would accumulate a school record 495 yards in total offense was 56-0. Ashtabula was 7-1-1 the previous year and was mentored by the well-respected Tony Chiacchiero, who had amassed a record of 71-22-5 in ten years at the school.

Dave Zoba got his senior season off in Namath-like fashion, finding big targets like Fred Benson and Bill Fisher time after time. He threw three touchdown passes and totaled 197 yards through the air. Hilles' defense, in addition to the shutout, yielded a paltry three first downs. In week two, versus Akron South, Hilles's defense delivered another shutout as the Raiders, led by running backs Bob Davis and Clarence Mason, prevailed 36-0.

While the skill-position players usually grab the headlines, those who really know football know the contributions of those who anchor the lines. Fred Pisanelli, like Cliff Roberts the previous season, was just too good to take off the field. He started at both the offensive and defensive tackle positions.

Recalls Pisanelli, now the director of client management at MetLife Resources, "Quite simply, Dick Strahm was the greatest motivational speaker I have ever heard. I was fortunate to receive a full scholarship to Ohio State and lettered three years in addition to going to two Rose Bowls. During my time as a Buckeye, I heard a lot of great speakers, most notably Woody Hayes. But Dick Strahm was, without question, the best I ever heard. He was absolutely captivating. When he got done speaking before a game, I was ready to play every second of the game if need be."

Week three saw Cuyahoga Falls come to Mollenkopf, and the crowds continued to grow for each home game. Before more than 8,000 fans, Western Reserve dominated the action and won 36-10. The headline above Dick Olmstead's game account said it all, "Rambling Raiders Twist Tigers' Tails." Dave Zoba and John Cooks each scored twice in the win.

Next up was an opponent Strahm had been pointing to since his lone defeat of the '67 season. Austintown Fitch was the only team that put a blemish on the Raiders record a year ago. However, this was a new season, and, when it was all said and done, it was done in a big way for Reserve. The Falcons went back home not even knowing if their side of the scoreboard was even operable. The Raiders enjoyed their third shutout in four games, 36-0.

It had been seven years since Austintown was beaten this soundly. Zoba threw three touchdown passes, proving all that work throwing a hundred balls a day to strengthen his arm seemed to be paying dividends.

Game five was the game all of Warren had been anticipating. Finally, Western Reserve, still considered by many in town as the new kids on the block, would get a chance to punch the Harding bullies right in the chops, figuratively speaking. Harding had rebounded from their disappointing 3-7 season in '67 and stood at 3-1, losing only in week two to state power Canton McKinley.

While Dick Strahm had great respect for both the Harding tradition and the Panthers' head coach Bill Shunkwiler, he was so confident of his team's chances that he again resorted to some special jerseys to motivate his charges. The special set of jerseys had been kept under wraps the entire week and unveiled only when the Raiders charged out of the visitor's locker room in their own home stadium to take on the Panthers.

And, it was these jerseys that so many in Warren still remember, either with great fondness or with a certain amount of disdain, depending upon which side of the Mahoning they happened to reside. The jersey carried a message that was not a hope as much as it was a proclamation. Above the numerals were the words, "We Will Win."

Recalls Dick, "It was reported that the Monday the tickets went on sale, every ticket was purchased within a few short hours. It was a complete sellout."

Close to 15,000 were at Mollenkopf to witness the first game between Reserve and Harding, with a much-coveted city crown on the line. Despite some outstanding seniors, Reserve still had a lot of sophomores and juniors in starting positions while the Panthers had experienced senior starters at most positions. Many felt that the Raiders were about a two-touchdown underdog.

Remembers Dick, "The special jerseys were known only to my equipment manager and me. When we went out to the field to do our pre-game warm ups, we had on our customary home jerseys. We had black and gold jerseys, trimmed in white.

"We came back in for final instructions. When I instructed the players to take their jerseys off, you should have seen the looks not only on their faces but also the assistant coaches!"

One can imagine Joe Novak's remembrance of Dick as a cocky guy may be, in part, based upon what he witnessed in that dark and cramped locker room at Mollenkopf Stadium.

Recalls Novak, "Talk about putting a team right in the crosshairs of our opponent's attention! This was the biggest game our kids had ever played, and, in front of the largest crowd they'd ever seen in person, and here they were given a set of jerseys that stated emphatically, 'We Will Win!'

"Well, those jerseys could either do one of two things. Either they could inspire our players to play the game of their lives, or they could so incense Harding that they would play the best game of their lives."

As it turned out, perhaps neither was true, but both Novak and Dick did see somewhat of a transformation when the players pulled on those jerseys. Recalls Dick, "Once everyone had his jersey on and tucked in, I could see passion in the players' eyes. Suddenly, they started chanting louder and louder, in unison, 'We will win! We will win!' They went out and put forth an excellent effort, and we won it. Although 14-6 may not be a pretty win in some people's eyes, as far as I was concerned, it was a work of art!"

Just 56 seconds into the game, Reserve's Mark Williams hit the hole with lightning speed and, 87 yards later, was in the end zone. Johnny Cooks provided the second Raider touchdown in dramatic fashion. On a fourth and two on the Panther 10- yard line, he broke free and sprinted to pay dirt.

Hilles' defense, although not recording a shutout, was absolutely money when it really counted, stopping Harding on downs four times within 10 yards of the Raider goal line.

It was a night for the ages and one Dale Strahm remembers with great clarity to this very day. "It probably was the most electric atmosphere I've ever been a part of. My brother, and

I can honestly say this without any bias whatsoever, was a phenomenal motivator. He simply knew what buttons to push to maximize his players' effort and abilities."

Suffering perhaps a bit of a letdown the following week after such a huge win, Reserve was lucky to escape with a 24-14 win against East Liverpool. Down 14-8 midway through the final quarter, Reserve roared back on a Zoba-to-Fisher touchdown pass that covered 72 yards and a Zoba conversion run for two points and then a Mark Williams 10-yard touchdown run followed by a conversion run by Marv Logan.

Despite the close call, Strahm was ecstatic after the game, telling sportswriter Gene Hersh, "It had to be one of our greatest victories. While Zoba and Fisher did a great job, we had something going for us on defense. It's the Mighty Mites, two boys who make up the right side of the line, and what a pair! Tackle Danny Barnhart is a mere 5-7 and weighs 173. His guard is Tommy Boyd, 5-8 and 175. They were terrific. And, honestly, we are for real!"

By this point, the third-year program was receiving statewide recognition in the polls. With a big game against Niles McKinley, a traditional power, only once beaten, looming just a few days away, Reserve had climbed to sixth in the state's big-school division.

Strahm knew the only Niles loss was to state power Massillon, and that, only by a touchdown. That loss was at home for Niles, and it was the first loss at home for the Dragons in a remarkable sixty-three games.

The Raiders would travel to Niles, and most felt it highly unlikely the Red Dragons would lose twice in the same year at home. However, most didn't happen to include Dick Strahm.

Dick remembers the Niles program and its coach well. "The Niles coach was Fred Conti, and he had continued the strong tradition started by former coach Tony Mason. Under Mason, Niles McKinley won the state championship in both 1961 and '63. Mason then left to become an assistant at the University of Michigan and later became a head coach at Arizona and Cincinnati. I knew the Red Dragons would be a severe test.

"So, I had an idea. I'd already used the special jerseys twice, once last year against Kent Roosevelt and a couple weeks ago against Harding, so I needed something different.

"Here's what I did. My equipment manager, Ken Gabriel, was also a teacher at Reserve, and he and I were always discussing ways to gain a psychological edge. We went to one of the school's guidance counselors, Nick Pitini, who was also a great friend of our football program.

"Anyway, a friend of mine had a small plane. We thought we could take some brown paper bags, put flour in the bottom of them, and put little sayings on slips of paper and tie them to the bag. Pitini typed them up, and Ken and I got the bags ready. The slips of paper said things like, 'Young kids of Warren, DON'T come to Niles,' and 'Dave Zoba, you're not good enough to play at Niles,' and 'Fred Pisanelli, stay in Warren, and don't come to Niles, where all the good Italians live.'

"We really made up a wide variety of derogatory things and tied them with red ribbons, kind of as a symbol of the Red Dragons.

"Anyway, at practice the day before the game, the team was warming up. I had been telling the kids all week at practice to be careful because you never knew what Niles was going to do. That afternoon at practice, we were going through our plays, and here came this plane going over our practice field. Pitini had this hat on and a scarf over his face. The door opened, and he threw these fifteen or so brown paper bags out.

"It worked just like magic. They hit the ground and broke open. Our players ran over and saw the notes tied to the tops of the bags. The notes were nasty and directed towards Zoba, Pisanelli, Cooks, and Brian Cross, our fine defensive end, and some other starters.

"The players ran back to me and said, 'Coach, look at this stuff!' I faked disgust and said to them, 'They're saying this stuff about you? I warned you they might try something to get you to feel inferior.' Well, these kids went home and even their parents got upset!

"We went over there on Friday night. Little did I know our kids had these little notes tucked inside their pants. Well, I'm not sure this gave them that much more motivation, but I do know we played an outstanding football game. Again, the coaches didn't know anything about this. When I told them after the game how I set everything up, I think they were ready to send me to the loony farm, but I sure had fun planning some of those things. We coaches agreed not to tell anyone. We certainly didn't want our players or their parents or boosters to find out.

"You and I know you win with blocking and tackling, and a great desire to be the best you can be, each and every play. Usually after the first two or three minutes of the game, the pre-game motivation has worn off. Then it comes down to man-on-man, not t-shirts, game jerseys or messages from airplanes. But man, it was fun being a little different."

The final score was Reserve 40, Niles 6. Little did Dick realize at the time, but it was a win that would make him a candidate to fill perhaps the most desirable high school football coaching positions in the entire state.

Before 13,000 mostly shocked Red Dragon supporters on a chilly autumnal Friday in Niles, Ohio, a football-tradition-rich town just north of Warren, Western Reserve handed the home team its worst defeat in twelve years. Up to that point, Niles had yet to give up a touchdown pass. Dave Zoba took relish in throwing for one score and also scoring one via an electrifying 55-yard scamper.

A power failure had delayed the game for 30 minutes, but that only temporarily gave the Dragons a reprieve. To many, it just seemed the Raiders perhaps had some extra incentive, just maybe in the form of some little typed insulting remarks tucked in behind their belt buckles inside their pants.

The following weekend, after an eighth consecutive win over a totally overwhelmed Cleveland John Hay squad, 64-6, in a game that Dave Zoba would throw for a school-record 216 yards and four touchdowns, the Raiders had moved all the way up to third in the UPI rankings.

Reserve would be supremely tested in week nine by a road game against always tough Canton McKinley. Despite what Strahm felt was an excellent week of practice, the Raiders stumbled, losing to a fired-up bunch of Bulldogs, 27-12.

Two more touchdown passes, one to Benson and one to Fisher, weren't enough to offset two early touchdown passes by quarterbacking counterpart Mark Hontas.

For Strahm, the lesson all week in preparing for the final game of the year against visiting Cincinnati Withrow would be about resiliency. Dreams of an undefeated season had been dashed on October's final Friday in Canton in a stadium not far from the Pro Football Hall of Fame, which had celebrated its fifth anniversary earlier in the fall on September 7. But, Strahm and his staff preached, "Somebody has to pay."

And, that someone was Withrow. The Raiders ended their season by setting a new scoring record in a 75-6 lambasting. In a span of seven minutes, Reserve scored seven touchdowns in the second quarter.

Zoba set two other school passing records, but since he had been the only signal caller to start a game in the school's history, actually, he was setting his own marks. The senior in his final game before a raucous crowd of west side supporters, threw five touchdown passes, giving him 19 for the season and 32 in his three-year career. His talents and leadership would be sorely missed in '69, or so one might surmise.

The 9-1 season, their second in a row, landed Warren Western Reserve in sixth position in the final UPI rankings. Across the Mahoning on the east side, Harding never lost again after their 14-6 loss to Reserve, and they finished 8-2, earning them a final ranking of tenth in the poll. Two teams from Warren in the top ten really made a statement about the importance of high school football in this steel town and, of course, gave the boys plenty to talk about down at Trina's Barber Shop.

At the end of the year, Dale Strahm left for Bowling Green State University to pursue his M.A. With him, he took memories that would sustain him at every stop in his well-traveled football career.

Reflects Dale, "Out of all those crazy motivational things my brother did, there are two that really stick with me, one pretty simple and one, pretty elaborate.

"The simple one, I think, if memory serves, was against Austintown Fitch in 1968. Now, we had lost only once in 1967, and it was to Fitch. So, the next year, Dick wanted revenge in the worst way. Well, we're all in the locker room before the game, and Dick is just about to give one of his legendary pre-game talks. All of a sudden, there is a knock on the door. Now understand that my brother rarely let any of his assistants in on whatever he was going to do, but, this time, he told me what would happen.

"Well, I walk over and open the door, and here comes this little guy with a 20-pound bag of ice on each shoulder. He has an Austintown Fitch ball cap on. He walks right up to Dick and says, 'I was told to deliver these here,' and, with that, he drops both bags of ice on the concrete floor. *Boom! Boom!* He looks at Dick and says, 'The message I was told to give you is that the ice will come in handy after tonight's game.'

"With that, he turns and walks out. Dick looks at our team with this shocked look and asks, 'Are we going to be needing this ice after the game or are they?' I'm telling you, I'm looking at these kids, and they are absolutely climbing the walls. They couldn't wait to get through that door. We just pummeled Fitch that night [36-0]. Would we have won anyway? I don't know, but Dick left little to chance.

"The more elaborate gimmick I remember was before the East Liverpool game in '67. We're at practice one day, and Dick points out that there's a guy with a raincoat and a hat standing a couple hundred yards away, writing on a tablet. He's kind of hiding behind a telephone pole. Well, all of a sudden, Dick stops practice and points him out. He sends me over to get him, and I get over there and grab him by the arm and march him back to the practice field and up to Dick.

"Dick takes the tablet from the guy and on it is one of our plays that we'd just run. Now, unbeknownst to the kids, or us for that matter, Dick earlier gave the guy the play, actually drew it for him and told him to look as if he was spying and trying to get our plays! Dick grabs the notebook, holds it up to our kids, and says, 'Look at this, guys. He's copying our plays!'

"Well, our kids are ready to go after this guy. Dick gives the tablet back to him, pushes him, and yells, 'I don't care! Keep the play. Go on back to East Liverpool, and tell your coaches that we are going to run that play over and over and over, right down your throats!'

"I think someone let the cat out of the bag on that one. Someone followed the guy when he left and saw him walk right downtown and right into one of the bars down by the river."

Joe Novak recalls essentially the same thing as Dale about Dick Strahm. "He was a brilliant psychologist, really about the best I've ever seen in all my years in football. Strahm had some pink panties dropped on the practice field from an airplane another time. He had boxes of diapers delivered to our pep rally another time, supposedly by our opponent. He had something almost every week. Perhaps today, kids maybe wouldn't buy into that kind of stuff, but back then in the sixties, they did. He was just a master at it."

After that second memorable 9-1 season, the Raider Booster Club showed just how much they appreciated their coach and his top assistant on the home front, Ginger, who never missed one game during the Strahms' Warren years.

Recalls Dick, "The president of the Boosters knew it would be very inappropriate to give us money, so he called Ginger and asked for any suggestions on what the club could do to show their appreciation for the past couple of 9-1 seasons. Ginger suggested to him that one of my dreams was to go to the Rose Bowl.

"Well, at the final Raider Booster Club meeting at the end of the season, the president called Ginger and me up front. He said he had a little surprise. At first, I thought it might be a Christmas tree.

"Boy, was I ever wrong! The president said that Ginger and I would be going to Pasadena to watch Ohio State play O.J. Simpson's Southern Cal Trojans in the Rose Bowl on New Year's. The club paid for our flight and hotel and game tickets and even tickets to the Rose Bowl Parade.

"What a trip it turned out to be. The Bucks beat Southern Cal 27-16 to win the national championship. What a gesture of support by Warren's west-siders. It's something neither Ginger nor I will ever forget."

In late winter, the coach of the newly crowned Buckeyes, Woody Hayes, would again visit Dick Strahm. This time school was in session rather than it being on a Sunday, as it was back in Bryan. Hayes was on a recruiting mission and came to Western Reserve to see Fred Pisanelli and Brian Cross, who, although just a junior, had caught Hayes's eye. Coach Hayes simply wanted to meet the young men while he was passing through that part of the state.

Remembers Dick, "I was on the second floor teaching American history, and the word got around that Coach Hayes was in the school building. Now, to my generation, that was kind of like saying that General MacArthur had just walked in.

"All of a sudden, I looked out into the hallway, and almost every teacher was outside the door just wanting to shake Woody's hand or say hello. My classroom was all the way at the end of the hall. Coach Hayes walked all the way down the hall and walked right into my classroom.

"We stepped out into the hall, and we had a conversation. He asked how Ginger and Doug were getting along and how I was enjoying Warren. He also asked several questions about Fred and Brian, both of whom he'd already talked to.

"He said he was ready to leave, so I walked him down the hall, down the steps, and out the door. We shook hands, and he got in his car as I walked back into the school building. I saw everyone at the windows watching as I turned away from the car to walk back into the school building, and, I don't mind telling you, I felt ten feet tall. I kind of felt as if Coach Hayes and I had somewhat of a friendship."

During the early spring of 1969, as Reserve was wrapping up its third school year, Dick received a phone call that could have significantly altered his career. One of the most coveted high school football jobs in the state, if not the nation, had opened.

Massillon coach Bob Cummings, who would go on to coach the Iowa Hawkeyes, committed the terrible mistake of going 7-3 and was fired. Since one of the three losses was to Niles McKinley, the same team Reserve had dismantled 40-6, Dick's name showed up on the radar at Massillon.

Recalls Dick, "What an honor to be contacted by the school once coached by Paul Brown. Despite the fact that I was very comfortable in Warren, I felt I just had to listen to their offer. I went to Massillon, toured the facilities, and, I must say, they were very impressive. I met with the committee and went through the whole interview process.

"As it turned out, I was offered the position. I did a lot of soul searching, and, of course, talked it over with Ginger.

"Finally, I decided to turn the position down. Given the national prominence Massillon had attained, many would probably think I was crazy, but I liked what we were doing at Reserve. Our schedule was getting better every year. The support from the west-siders was absolutely terrific. I thought my staff was the best in the state, and the younger kids coming up through the system had great potential. I just wasn't ready to leave Warren, even for the Massillon Tigers. I decided that it would take a college offer to get me to leave Warren."

For Strahm, the challenge in the fall of 1969 would be how to fill so many holes created by those who graduated in the spring of that year. Zoba was off to study at Harvard. Johnny Cooks accepted a football scholarship to the Big Ten's Northwestern. Fred Pisanelli went to Ohio State on full scholarship. Clarence Mason earned a scholarship to play at Kent State. Fred Benson received his scholarship to play at Ohio University. Bill Fisher was offered a scholarship to play at Bowling Green. Needless to say, the sophomores who greeted Dick three years earlier when he arrived from Bryan indeed had great potential, and that potential was being realized, given the number who departed with scholarships to play Division I college football.

But, it sure was going to be difficult to fill the vacancies. At least Strahm had the rest of the spring and the summer to address those concerns. A more immediate concern was to fill the coaching vacancy left by Dale, who went to Bowling Green State University, where he eventually served a graduate assistant before becoming a full-fledged coaching staff member and defensive coordinator for the Falcons.

Dick was happy to bring Marty Aubry aboard to replace Dale. In addition, Dave Campbell was also brought on to work with the younger Raiders. A final coaching slot was filled by Elroy Morand, a former star quarterback at traditional black college power Florida A & M.

The summer of 1969 had arrived, and it was time for the Strahms to enjoy some rest and relaxation before Dick had to return to the business of preparing the Raiders for a schedule that again would be beefed up for the third consecutive year. While Reserve had made overtures about joining the same league as Harding and Massillon and Alliance, the established All-American Conference expressed no interest in taking on another team, especially a team the caliber of Western Reserve, some west-siders thought. Therefore Strahm's team would remain an independent.

For the Strahms, vacation meant some time in Bellaire, Michigan, at Miley's Resort. It was a time to renew the deep friendship with George Miley, one of Dick's mentors back at Toledo Libbey.

Recalls Dick, "It was right at the end of a football coach's summer, which means mid-August before the two-a-days started. While we were up there enjoying Lake Bellaire, Doug was bitten by a mosquito. No big deal, right? Well, it turned out to be a very big deal! There was an adverse reaction. We got back to Warren and got him to our family doctor, and he said that we needed to get my son to the Cleveland Clinic.

"Initially, it was suggested that our little Doug had more problems than a mosquito bite. Based on tests at the Clinic, Doug, one doctor felt, may have had a brain tumor. You can imagine the shock and worry for us. After several more tests, it was determined that Doug had contracted encephalitis."

For the Strahms, there would be many anxious moments. The residual effects of what medical textbooks refer to as *epidemic encephalitis* can include blurred vision, even blindness, and also brain damage. It would be several weeks before it could be determined if the brain had been affected.

For Dick, his walks through the ward during Doug's stay nearly broke his heart. "I saw kids in such bad shape, little guys and gals with cancer, some with severe burns who were enduring painful skin grafts."

Well, those memories stayed with Dick long after it was finally determined that Doug had no brain damage and the only aftereffects of the encephalitis would be some slight vision problems in the left eye. When Dick returned to Warren to begin preparing his Raiders for the season, he sensed after one morning session that there was too much grumbling about the heat and the intensity of the work.

"Ordinarily, a coach will tolerate some of the chirping from players during the August dog days because the practices are tough, but, given what I'd just seen in Cleveland, I just couldn't keep quiet.

"I told them to drop everything and to direct their full attention toward me. And then I told them about the little kids I'd seen with cancer and the little burn victims. I wanted them to see how truly trivial their discomfort was. I finished by asking them, 'Does anyone think he is in such bad shape that he can't practice in the afternoon session? If so, please raise your hand, and I will excuse you.' Not one person raised his hand. I think they put everything in perspective and learned something that day that had a lot less to do with football than it did about life."

As the season approached, the coaches' wives, as they often did, got together to determine what they could do to help the football cause, so to speak. Remembers Ginger, "We always tried to think of things to boost morale or promote team unity. This time, we thought designing some special dinner plates that the team could eat their pre-game meals off would be nice. We had a lot of fun designing them. After we did, we fired them to set the design so that they could be used. Then, we kept them at the Golden Gate Restaurant."

Ginger would continue her game ritual in 1969. Dick's mom would come over to Warren from Toledo and baby-sit Doug and Gina so that Ginger and the rest of the coaches' wives could sit together and watch their husbands work. After the games, they would all go to the Chateau and, then, on to a house party for friends and supporters who believed fervently in the principles of West Side Pride. Often, the house party would be at the Strahms' in the finished basement.

As the August two-a-days wound down, Strahm was beginning to find some answers for filling the graduation holes. However, he still lamented at the time to the reporters from the *Tribune Chronicle,* "We had so many of last year's seniors start all thirty games for us in the first three years, it's like starting all over again." Strahm continued, but with a trace or two of optimism. "Overall, we should be bigger, but it could be a detriment in that we may be slower. But, don't get me wrong. There will be some fine football players wearing Raider colors that take the field this fall."

The good news was Strahm felt comfortable in finding a replacement for the three-year starting quarterback Dave Zoba in John Swipas. To replace the great receiving tandem of Fred Benson and Bill Fisher, Strahm tabbed speedster Alvin Burch and tight end Brian Cross. Cross also was a terrific defensive end, and Burch would also start in a secondary that had been entirely wiped out by graduation.

Western Reserve had some running backs as well, such as Bob Davis, Marv Logan, and LeRoy Williams. The team also had depth and talent on defense. Certainly, there was a positive sign in the final scrimmage before the Ashtabula opener. It was a game-conditions contest against one of the top teams in the state, the very team that Strahm could have coached, the Massillon Tigers. In a game featuring a game clock, a game which only lacked punt and kickoff returns from being exactly like a real contest, the Raiders defeated the Tigers, 14-8.

The defense's performance in the scrimmage was indeed a harbinger of what was just around the corner.

In game one, the Raiders whitewashed Ashtabula, 38-0, before 5,000 at Mollenkopf, the fourth time in four years Coach Strahm's team had broken quickly from the gate. Swipas threw for two scores, a 20-yarder to Brian Cross and a 75-yarder to Alvin Burch.

Week two saw even more offensive firepower and another dominant defensive performance as Western Reserve rolled over Akron South, 50-0. For their outstanding play, Swipas and Cross were named week two's outstanding offensive and defensive players of the week in the region.

Week three saw yet another shutout, this one, 14-0, over a stubborn group of Potters from East Liverpool. The defense not only registered its third consecutive shutout but it also yielded a microscopic 12 yards in total offense. Both touchdowns were scored by Alvin Burch, one on a pass from Swipas and the second one on a return off an interception.

Game four was against always tough Austintown Fitch at their place. *Tribune Chronicle* sports writer Murray Newman wrote of the strong road support of Warren's west side. "Thousands of Western Reserve's faithful bedecked in 'Beat Fitch' hats and 'Raider Country' jackets toted horns and rattles as they converged on the site, slogging through mud to watch the miserly Reserve defense hold its end zone inviolate while Strahm stirred the offense into a mounting wave of destruction for the Falcons."

Reserve pounded out 291 yards on the ground, led by Bob Davis, Marv Logan, and LeRoy Williams.

But it was the week five game that inflamed Warren residents on both sides of the Mahoning. It was time to see if the Panthers of Warren G. Harding could get some revenge against a team that carried the simple message "We Will Win" on their jerseys and then put actions to those words a year ago.

Heading into the game, the teams were indeed going in opposite directions. While Reserve was a perfect 4-0 and had yet to yield a point, Harding had been beset by injuries and close losses and had won only once in four tries.

It was Harding coach Bill Shunkwiler who sounded very pessimistic when addressing the media a couple days before the game. "We can't pass against them with Stan Roberts, who outshines even Canton's Rick Brown at middle guard, end Brian Cross and tackles Waverly Franklin and Tim Nichols slamming into the enemy backfield almost in time to take the handoff themselves. There's no way to get a pass off."

But records meant little to the 15,000 who jammed Mollenkopf on that Friday night. Shunkwiler's pre-game pessimism proved to be well founded as it was Strahm who got the ride off the field on the shoulders of his jubilant players after yet another shutout victory, 30-0.

In week six, the string of both wins and shutouts continued when the Raiders handed Wintersville its first shutout in fifteen years, 28-0. Recalls Brian Cross, who, after his Reserve days played at Bowling Green State University and is currently the head football coach at Canton McKinley High School, "The six straight shutouts were remarkable. I've been coaching over twenty years, and I've never had a team come anywhere close to that. What I've taken with me in my own coaching career from Coach Strahm was an appreciation for the physical toughness of the game of football. Coach Strahm, and really all of his assistants, taught it to me, and I've, in turn, passed it on to my players."

For Strahm, he knew the chances were remote that his charges could hold a powerful Niles McKinley team scoreless at Mollenkopf in week seven's contest. He'd be happy with a one-point win against new coach Bob Shaw's Red Dragons.

It was another overflow crowd of 15,000, and most went home disappointed, not with the effort of their Raiders, but certainly with the final score.

The Raiders simply could not stop Niles' running back Rick Gales, who bulled his way for 233 yards on 35 carries in a 23-14 win over the home team. For Strahm, it was only his third opportunity in close to three years to teach a group of young men any and all the lessons that spring from a loss. Perhaps the only lesson came in the form of a succinct declaration he gave the *Tribune Chronicle* sports reporter Dick Olmstead after the game. "We're not planning on losing any more games."

The Raiders rebounded the following week with a 30-6 win over Akron Hoban. After Hoban scored the game's first touchdown, John Swipas connected with Alvin Burch on a 56-yard touchdown, and the Raiders never looked back.

Week nine saw a close-to-the-vest slugfest of a game with Cuyahoga Falls. The Black Tigers were riding an eighteen-game home winning streak when Strahm brought his team to the outskirts of Cleveland. Swipas ran for one touchdown and threw for another, an 18-yarder to Kevin Dowell, and the Raiders returned home, clenching in their fists a hard-fought 14-6 win.

In the final week of the year, Cleveland East Tech came to Mollenkopf and was totally overmatched. Hilles' defense recorded a seventh shutout, and Swipas ended his high school career by throwing four touchdown passes in the 50-0 win.

When the final UPI and AP polls came out, Warren Western Reserve, with its third consecutive 9-1 season, was the fifth-best team in the state, up a notch from its sixth ranking in '68.

After that first break-even year of 1966, Dick Strahm's Raiders, who were the embodiment of what West Side Pride was all about, went 27-3. Dick, needless to say, was proud of both his staff and his team. After turning down the Massillon job the previous spring, he felt it would take a collegiate offer, and a good one, to get him to leave Warren.

Well, when you build a high school program in a mere four years into one of the best five teams in the entire state, people tend to notice. One of those people who did was a college head coach that Dick had gotten to know over the last several years through football clinics. His name was Frank Lauterbur, who had arrived at the University of Toledo in 1963. After struggling his first four years, where his teams posted a composite record of 11-27-1, he turned around his own program, going 9-1 in 1967 and winning the school's first Mid-American Conference football crown in the process. After a slight regression in '68, the next year Lauterbur led the Rockets to an undefeated season and a Tangerine Bowl win over Davidson.

Lauterbur contacted Strahm to see if he was interested in applying for the defensive coordinator's position. Remembers Dick, "I really felt if there ever was a good time to make the jump to college coaching, which I really had a desire to do, it was then. If I passed up this opportunity, who knew if there would be another? At thirty-six years of age, if I was going to step up to the next level, I felt it was time to get going.

"So, I interviewed, was offered the position, and accepted. Not only was Toledo loaded with talent, especially at quarterback with the multi-talented Chuck Ealey, who was named the conference player of the year as a sophomore in 1969, but Dick also would get to coach for a second time Gary Hinkson, who was the starting free safety and a vital defensive cog for the Rockets after his fine senior season at Reserve.

Dick remembers it was easier to leave Reserve because he knew it was in good hands. "Jim Hilles would be my successor with Joe Novak his top assistant. As far as coaching, you can't get much better than that!"

Recalls Hilles, "The year after Dick left, we finally got into a league, the Northeast Ohio Athletic League. Then we went 9-1 and 8-2 in my two years before I handed the reigns to Joe [Novak] when I left to become the defensive coordinator at Ball State."

Remembers Novak, "My first year, 1972, … the high school playoffs were in their first year, and we won it all, beating Cincinnati Princeton, 37-6 in the Akron Rubber Bowl." In Novak's second and final year at Reserve, he guided the Raiders all the way to the state finals again before, this time, falling to Youngstown Cardinal Mooney. Novak left after his second year at the helm to go into college coaching as an assistant at his alma mater, Miami University, in Oxford, Ohio.

Indeed, it had taken just three years after Strahm's departure for the school to become state champions, and Strahm felt so fortunate to have built the foundation.

Western Reserve continued to educate Warren's west-side students, that is, until June 12, 1994, when it closed its doors for the final time after twenty-four years. The trend that spawned the school, when Warren's population was booming and one school simply couldn't accommodate the large volume of students, had reversed itself. All high-school students would again go to Warren G. Harding on the east side of the Mahoning.

What made Warren such a special place? Strahm remembers it as the perfect storm. "The three key factors that must be in place to have a successful football program were all present at just the right time. We had great young talent our first year so we weren't reliant on a lot of senior players who were going to be playing one year and then leaving. We had the support of administrators like John Scharf who allowed us to assemble what I believe was the best coaching staff in the entire state. And, third, we had unbelievable community support from the west side. When you've got all three of those in place at the same time, you're going to be successful."

Thanks largely to the efforts of former players and point men like Bill Lee, Dave Zoba, and Ted Teringo, a reunion was organized and took place back in Warren on Friday, May 4, 2007, forty-one years after Strahm's arrival to await a brand new school's opening. It was a gathering of players, coaches, and cheerleaders who had been touched by the dedication and discipline of Dick Strahm and his coaches, and it was held at the very same restaurant that hosted all those pre-game meals four decades ago, G's Golden Gate.

That night, Dave Zoba remembered Strahm's impact. "Coach Strahm created a pride in the whole west side. Remember, Western Reserve started from ground zero, and he ratcheted it up very fast. There was a lot of pride and competitiveness that he instilled in us, and, now, because of that, an awful lot of people here in this room tonight will thank him for maturing them in so many ways. Perhaps the greatest success stories with a coach aren't how many teams he beats but what kind of successes his players have years after the last ball was snapped."

That night, Fred Pisanelli remembered Dick's role in the Warren story. "Dick Strahm didn't bring the tradition of football to Warren. Warren G. Harding had already established that years before Dick arrived. What Dick did was perpetuate that tradition in a brand new school with a very eager bunch of sophomores. It was almost like a tinderbox. We sophomores who wound up experiencing those wonderful three years, from 5-5 to 9-1 and then another 9-1, well, we were the tinder. What Dick did was light the match."

Pisanelli went on to recall the coaching staff collectively. "To a man, that coaching staff was the most dedicated group of individuals I've ever been around. They were knowledgeable and absolutely passionate about what they were trying to do for us. I will never forget them. As memorable as Coach Strahm, whom I used to call 'The Bulldog,' was, the other coaches took a backseat to no one in terms of their abilities and commitment."

The defensive captain of Dick's final Warren team in 1969, Brian Cross, remembers the incredible fan support. "Besides the tunnel of supporters we'd go through leaving the restaurant after our pre-game meals, there were supporters lining the route we took back to the school to dress for the games. There were also cars, both in front and behind the bus, and everyone was honking and yelling. Those are scenes for regular-season football games I've never seen duplicated, and they are memories I will always see as special."

For Dick Strahm, to this day, the recollections that he has of those wonderful four years on the west side of Warren resonate. He was there to see the Aurora, aptly the name of the

Warren Western Reserve yearbook, and, inarguably, the best title ever selected for an inaugural annual.

For, it is Aurora, the Greek personification for the Dawn, who the Greek poet Homer represented as rising from the couch of Tithonus each morning and carrying light from her chariot to gods and men. Well, Warren Western Reserve was indeed like a dawn breaking over the west side of Warren, and Dick Strahm was there to see it all develop each day for the first four years of the school's twenty-four-year history.

Before the packed room at G's Golden Gate Restaurant on a magical May Friday night, Dick expressed the deep regard he has for the memories of Warren and cemented the bond that will never loosen between himself and those west-siders he holds so dear. "To be able to come back here and see all of you is, indeed, my special time. Through all of my bouts with cancer, with the heart attacks, and with the stroke, it took God's intervention to bring me back here today to be able to share this moment with you. And, I couldn't have done it without Him. I am proud to say to you that I am a Christian.

"I feel, as I look around this room, so very, very lucky. I see the likes of Dave Zoba, Johnny Cooks, Bill Lee, Cliff Roberts, Frankie Allen, Gary Hinkson, Fred Pisanelli, Paul Trina, both Senior and Junior, and all the other players and coaches and cheerleaders and supporters surrounding me, and I truly can sense the brotherhood we share. In 1966, we had to make our own way and do it as quickly as we could. In the process of doing that, we may have ruffled a few feathers. But I think they hired me to win football games.

"This has a deeper level of meaning to us than anyone else. While we wish Warren G. Harding well, what went on in our four years around four decades ago and what has gone on in this room tonight is ours. It was, and continues to be, my privilege and my honor to share your West Side Pride!"

Coach Strahm caught up with his former player and football captain from Warren Western Reserve High School when he took the defensive coordinator position at the University of Toledo. Gary Hinkson was also the captain of the Toledo Rockets team that went 35-0 in 1969-1970-1971.

Chapter 7

The Majesty of the Rockets' Red Glare

For Dick Strahm, leaving Warren would be difficult, despite the opportunities that awaited him back in his hometown of Toledo, Ohio. He had built a program from the ground floor, a program destined to, he felt, become a veritable skyscraper on the skyline of Ohio high school football. However, his success also made him a desirable entity to those who were part of the college football landscape, those in search of enthusiastic and knowledgeable young coaches to fill positions on staffs.

While Dick proved his commitment to Warren by passing on arguably the most prestigious high school job in the state of Ohio, Massillon, to remain at the helm of Warren Western Reserve for the 1969 season, he simply had an itch he felt must be scratched, which was to coach at the college level for a Division I school.

As Dick headed back to his hometown of Toledo, he felt satisfied with how he was leaving Warren. "Really, I wouldn't even have left Warren for a small-college offer. Ironically, at my age [36], I wanted a D-I job so much that I wouldn't even have considered the Findlay College job at that point. Now, that's ironic because I eventually had the greatest experiences I could ever have imagined in Findlay. It has been a town that showed my family and me so much love and support that there was no question we would stay after I retired from coaching in 1998.

"I realized after four years in Warren that I wanted something at the next level. For me, there would have been no reason to leave Bryan if I were going to stay at the high school level in coaching. Remember, I also saw myself eventually pursuing a superintendent's position.

"When I got to Warren, I knew that if I could build a winning program and build it so that it would last, I'd be ready to take that next step up. The timing was right after three consecutive one-loss seasons to listen to Coach Lauterbur's offer. In my mind, 27-3 over three years, playing a schedule which took a backseat to very few teams in the state during the second and third years, to me, proved the program was on solid ground. And, looking at what was coming up in terms of talent, I felt certain Western Reserve would continue to thrive.

"And, as it turned out, I think the next four years proved that. Jim Hilles, my successor, went 9-1 and 8-2 before leaving to go into college coaching at Ball State. Then, Joe Novak took over and won the big-school state championship during the first year of the computer playoffs in 1972 and then turned right around and took his '73 team all the way to the title game again against Youngstown Cardinal Mooney before losing."

Recalls Dick about his Warren-to-Toledo career move, "Frank Lauterbur was a pretty darn good salesman. Ginger and I drove to Toledo to talk to him after he called. We walked around campus, and he took us to dinner. When I saw the number of starters he showed me who would be returning, especially on defensive, coming from an undefeated, untied team and the Tangerine Bowl winner as well, I just felt it was the perfect opportunity to replace Jack Murphy.

"Jack had been an assistant at Toledo even before Frank got to campus. He was the defensive coordinator of a squad so good, his defense finished first in the nation in total defense statistically. The only reason Jack left was he had an opportunity to become the head coach at his alma mater, Heidelberg.

"With my mom and my Grandpa and Grandma Strahm still living in Toledo and Ginger's folks just down the road in Perrysburg and my brother Dale just a few miles further down Interstate 75 in Bowling Green, that made the offer even more enticing.

"Additionally, there was just something about my talk with Frank that made me feel comfortable. I felt he really believed I could help sustain the great defensive momentum that Jack had fostered in '69.

"Now, don't get me wrong. I certainly felt some pressure taking the position of defensive coordinator, given the fact that I really had a lot more to do with the offense at Warren. Jim Hilles took care of the defense. But, I was honest with Frank when he asked me if I had much input with the defense at Western Reserve. I told him that I didn't. While I'm sure he appreciated the honesty, I'm not sure that answer made him very comfortable.

"I also felt some pressure following such a successful coordinator as Jack. But, I told Frank that I was totally committed to working every waking moment if need be to learn what I needed to be successful."

Now 83 years old and still living in Toledo and enjoying retirement, Lauterbur clearly remembers the hiring of Dick Strahm. "Dick reminded me a lot of myself when I was a young coach. Many people asked me if I felt nervous about hiring Dick for such an important position with no college experience, and, really, with no experience coaching defense.

"But, heck, I had a good feeling about the hire. I had heard such good things about Dick Strahm, and I knew he was a UT graduate and was also familiar with Toledo schoolboy football, which would really help since we recruited so heavily in Toledo. I needed a good, solid man, and I just believed Dick was that person.

"The fact that he was coming straight out of high school didn't bother me at all. I thought the additional time in high school coaching was attributable to his success rather than his not moving on to college coaching sooner. Each step he took was to a bigger and more prestigious program, and he'd been successful at each program.

"Also, I mentioned that he reminded me a lot of me. Listen, I got a couple big breaks in my coaching career. Why not give Dick a chance? He was enthusiastic and extremely organized. I suppose that's why I didn't feel I was taking as big a chance as others felt I was taking."

When one moves into a new career challenge, of course, there's always a back story, one that tells what has transpired before someone like Dick Strahm arrived on the scene. For the Toledo Rockets' football program, the back story has to start with the head coach, Frank X. Lauterbur. Lauterbur came to the University of Toledo in 1963 to fill two positions, athletic director and head football coach.

In doing so, he inherited a program which had only one winning season out of the previous eight. The parade of unsuccessful seasons took its toll on coaches as four came and went during this time.

Prior to arriving in Toledo, Lauterbur had coached in high school (in the Cleveland area), in college (as an assistant at Kent State, at Army under the legendary Earl "Red" Blaik, and at the University of Pittsburg), and in the pros (as an assistant under Weeb Ewbank with the Baltimore Colts) as well.

His first four years in Toledo were rocky ones for Lauterbur, as his teams finished .500 only once and had losing seasons in the other three. One assistant coach, Jack Murphy, had been at the University of Toledo since 1960 and elected to stay and join Frank's staff.

It was Murphy who recruited a quarterback out of Toledo DeVilbiss by the name of Dan Simrell. Simrell went on to become the Rockets' captain and starting signal caller in 1963 and '64 and remembers the job Lauterbur undertook when he arrived in Toledo.

"Basically, he had to change an attitude. It was that mindset so pervasive to all programs that aren't very successful, that attitude that kind of says, 'Well, we'll try, but, if we lose, well, that's not all that bad.' To try to combat that type of complacency, Frank Lauterbur really had to be a drill instructor. He weeded out those who didn't want to work, those who didn't see losing in the same way he did, which was as an insult, as an affront.

"There was a hill next to the stadium. Coach Lauterbur referred to it as Mount Suribachi. None of the players, at first, knew what he meant when he referred to our football team going up that hill. We all found out later that the name he gave that hill was the name of the hill the Marines went up to plant that American flag on Iwo Jima. And, that's the attitude he wanted to instill in the Toledo Rockets.

"Really, I felt he was a blessing both to the university and to me personally. After I graduated and left him, I went into high school coaching. He kept in contact with me and helped me. Ultimately, I returned to UT as an assistant the year after Frank left, so I never got a chance to coach with him. That certainly would have been my honor.

"I eventually coached on the college level for what is now going on thirty-six years, and I have never forgotten what Frank Lauterbur has meant to me. He's followed my coaching career and has come to watch me coach at each of my stops. To this day, I still talk to him regularly on the phone."

While perhaps those unwilling to pay the price and who wilted under the intensity of the coach Simrell remembers as a drill instructor would not feel as grateful to Lauterbur, to the players who wanted to charge up that hill with their coach to plant the flag of a successful program, the coach was seen very differently.

As Lauterbur recalls his first few years at the school on Bancroft Street, he still remembers the biggest roadblock to the Rockets' winning. "In '63 I inherited a program that, quite frankly, wasn't very attractive to a lot of coaches. The program was really in need of better personnel.

While we certainly had some solid players, like Danny Simrell, who totally committed themselves to winning, we simply needed more.

"However, I felt Toledo had too much to offer to not go after the position. First, I didn't feel a great deal of pressure. Really, Dick Strahm had a lot more pressure than I did in '63 when he arrived to fill Jack's coordinator's position in '70. Given the lack of success over the last several years, I really felt there was nowhere to go but up.

"The positives about the Rocket job, I felt, were numerous. First, a lot of very fine high school football was played in Toledo. I figured if I could just win the recruiting war within, say, a fifty-mile radius of our campus, we had a chance to be good eventually. Sure, I knew I'd lose some to Ohio State and Michigan and Notre Dame. But what I didn't want to happen was lose a Toledo kid to another Mid-American Conference (MAC) school.

"Also, there was a widely circulated paper in town, *The Blade*, and the paper really did a great job of covering UT athletics. Jim Taylor, one of the sportswriters, was very widely read and respected. There were three television stations, too.

"I just thought the media-coverage benefits would play very well to potential recruits. They knew if they played well here, they had the opportunity to become household names in Toledo, which potentially, after they graduated would open a lot of doors for them in the job force."

By 1965, Lauterbur's Rockets were a respectable 5-5, and there was a feeling that maybe this was a school that could become an elite MAC football team. Frank felt he was on the right course. One of Lauterbur's big personnel moves paid immediate dividends.

Recalls Lauterbur, "We coaches decided to move Dan Simrell permanently from defensive to full-time starting quarterback. He wound up leading the conference in total offense in both his junior and senior years."

By 1967, Coach Frank Lauterbur finally saw his team officially turn the corner. During the fall, while Dick Strahm was delighting the Western Reserve fans with the first of three consecutive 9-1 seasons, his future boss, Frank Lauterbur, got nearly all of his pieces to fall together as well.

Lauterbur's Rockets matched Strahm's 9-1 record. Recalls Frank, "We lost our opener to Ohio University. Those who know some of the history of the MAC know the name of their longtime very successful head coach, Bill Hess. After that, we won nine in a row and beat a league power, Miami University, on the road in Oxford for the first football conference championship in the history of the university."

Continues Frank, "Now, in '68, we were breaking in a new quarterback and suffered some setbacks and finished 5-4-1. But, the good news was we had an absolutely terrific recruiting class during the spring of 1968."

The class that would be seniors in 1971 was led by someone who, ordinarily, Frank Lauterbur would not have recruited, since he played so far from his targeted area for recruiting, Toledo and its surrounding communities.

His name was Chuck Ealey, and he would, during his time at the University of Toledo, become not only the most successful quarterback in the history of the Toledo Rockets but also set a national record for consecutive wins and all-time winning percentage, records that remain to this day.

Lauterbur recalls just how Chuck Ealey became a Toledo Rocket. "We had a referee in the MAC by the name of Harold Rolf, who also happened to be the superintendent of the hospital in Portsmouth, Ohio. As a favor, he asked me if I would be a speaker at a banquet in Ironton, Ohio.

"I agreed to what I felt was a worthy cause. While at the banquet, I met a priest who happened to be the principal of St. Joseph's High School in Ironton, and he asked if I'd like to go back to his place and have a beer. Well, I did, and when I walked in the living room, there was another priest there. He introduced himself, and, while we were talking, I came to find out he also was a high school principal at Portsmouth Notre Dame High School.

"When he found out I was the head coach at UT, he told me that his school had a fine football team and wondered if I'd be recruiting any of his players.

"Well, I told him that I really didn't spend a lot of time down in this part of the state so close to the Ohio River. West Virginia colleges really hit this area hard, and I was doing well recruiting the Toledo area.

"Then, he told me he had a quarterback, Chuck Ealey, who'd just completed his senior season and had never lost a varsity game that he started during the whole time he played at Notre Dame. He'd gone 18-0. Then, he said Ealey was playing basketball over in Marion the next night. I told him that I'd send an assistant over to Marion to see him play.

"After I got back to Toledo and sent one of my assistants to see him play, I was kind of wondering what we potentially had here. Coaches will often look at a recruit in another sport just to see what his athletic instincts are. Now, if you've never seen him play football, as was the case with Ealey, it is a little bit of a gamble, but I felt you had to be curious about a kid who never quarterbacked a losing season in high school.

"The next morning, I talked to my assistant, and he told me that, while he didn't know what kind of a football player he was, Chuck was as good an athlete on the high school level as he'd ever seen. He said Chuck had extremely quick hands, had several steals, and, as a ball-handling guard, seemed to complement his teammates by getting them the ball in places they could be successful. He even threw one in from half court as time was running out at the end of a quarter.

"Well, I called Chuck and asked him if he'd had any other contacts from other schools. He said that Bill Hess from Ohio University had talked to him and so had Bo Schembechler, who was coaching at Miami University.

"We arranged a campus visit for Chuck and another player he recommended, his big offensive tackle from Notre Dame, Jim Goodman. From the first time I met Chuck, I liked him. Without seeing as much as one frame of film of either him or his tackle, I offered both scholarships. Let me tell you. I never regretted either offer!"

Chuck recalls exactly what tipped the scales toward Lauterbur and the Rockets. "Well, Coach Hess never really followed up beyond his initial contact, and Coach Schembechler offered only a 2/3 scholarship. Also, he wanted me as a defensive back. He did say maybe I could compete to be like a third-string quarterback, but he really wanted me to play in the secondary.

"Well, I didn't really want to switch positions. I'd never lost a game in high school and really felt I should get a chance to compete for the starting quarterback position. Coach Lauturbur, first, offered me a full scholarship, and, second, told me he had every intention of playing me at quarterback."

Recalls Lauterbur, "I told Chuck that he would play quarterback until such time as he decided he wasn't good enough. Then, if that day ever came, we'd find another position for him to play. While I certainly wasn't used to giving recruits guarantees, I just had a feeling about Chuck. I sensed immediately that, well, he was almost born a mature man. As things turned out, I never had to find another position for Chuck. He was an extraordinarily gifted quarterback and a natural-born leader."

For Ealey, it was a time to look back briefly to his upbringing in Portsmouth, the city of around 21,000, about 90 miles south of Columbus on the Ohio River, before heading to the campus on Bancroft Street in Toledo in 1968 for his freshman year.

Ealey had grown up in an area of Portsmouth called The Projects, which was about 95 percent black. His start in life is one that certainly presented obstacles. His father, Charles Sr. and his mother, Earline, divorced when Chuck was very small.

Recalls Ealey, "I don't even remember living with my dad. This created a very desperate situation financially, especially since my mom was relegated to some low-paying jobs. She only had an eighth-grade education.

"But, she had an endless reservoir of love and support for me. It was she who stressed education and found a way to get me into Portsmouth Notre Dame, a parochial school with a really strong academic reputation as well as a great athletic tradition.

"Besides the overwhelming power of a mother's love, there are two other things that helped me survive. First, it was the support of the North End, where I grew up. So many encouraged me and also disciplined me. Two very important mentors in my life were Larry Hisle and Al Oliver, both of whom became stars in major league baseball. The other thing that helped me overcome a difficult environment was the opportunity to play sports.

"My high school football coach, Ed Miller, was really a driving force in my life. Not only did he help me athletically but he also mentored me in so many other areas that had nothing to do with football."

In addition to Ealey, the recruiting class of 1968 also boasted a bevy of very talented players who would help on both sides of the ball and, before their final college chapter would be written, catapult the Rockets of Toledo to a run of varsity success unparalleled in the history of the Mid-American Conference.

There was no nickname bestowed upon the talented group as freshmen. The reason was, of course, that freshmen were not eligible to play varsity in 1968, and, therefore, flew very much under the radar of fans. Any nickname, either collectively or individually, would have to wait.

But, Lauterbur and his assistant coaches, especially defensive coordinator Jack Murphy, knew what they had. They had a crop of extremely talented players. In addition to Ealey and his big tackle from Portsmouth, Jim Goodman, they were Don Fair, Steve Banks, Bob Rose, Ron Roberts, Leon Campbell, Dale Benington, John Niezgoda, Scott Johnston, Al Baker, Glyn Smith, Steve Schnitkey, John Downey, Lynn Aschilman, Miles O'Mailia, and, of course, Gary Hinkson, Dick Strahm's former free safety back in Warren.

Recalls Hinkson about his freshman year, "I really wasn't heavily recruited. Remember that I had missed most of my junior year in Warren because of a broken jaw, and, while I had a solid senior season, I think a lot of schools didn't really know anything about me.

"I had to, I guess you might say, talk Frank into taking me. I actually got a track scholarship but didn't even know it at the time. I didn't find out until later when the track coach wondered why I wasn't showing up to practices and meets in the spring. Well, the reason was, I was in spring football.

"My freshman year, I established residency where all UT athletes did, in the athletic dorm, Carter Hall East."

Hinkson saw the whole experience as, largely, positive. "I have nothing but good memories of Carter Hall East. The cohesiveness we felt on the football team, I believe, was born at Carter Hall East. We all lived together for, basically, four years. It was like a fraternity house.

"What was nice about it was the fact that it was not just football players. It was the basketball team. It was the track team. It was the wrestlers. Everybody got to know everybody, and we all got to support each other.

"In my own case, I got to know really well, for instance, Greg Wojcichowski, a wrestler who happened to be the number-two grappler in the entire country and a first-team All-American. I went to a lot of his meets."

In an interesting twist of fate, that the same All-American, "Wojo," as he was known to the fans who watched him compete in the Toledo Field House, would one day have a son who would play nose guard for Coach Dick Strahm at The University of Findlay.

Another wrestler Hinkson got to know was Ron Junko, a MAC champion. Recalls Gary, "It was just neat to know that the wrestlers were coming to support us at the Glass Bowl, and we were getting to a lot of their meets."

During Hinkson's first year, he and Chuck Ealey were assigned by Coach Lauterbur to room together. Despite their different ethnicities, Lauterbur knew this was not so much an experiment as it was common sense. Recalls Lauterbur, "I really didn't think too much about it. As I recall, I think we had three or four roommate assignments where blacks and whites were paired. There was absolutely never a decision I made on the football field that had anything to do with the color of a man's skin, so, why, on earth, would it ever factor in when it came to assigning roommates?

"I certainly don't want anyone to see me as any kind of pioneer. I was just a realist, someone who knew if we ever were to do anything as a team, we'd better be as one, share the same heartbeat."

Hinkson recalls how comfortable the living arrangement was. "Despite the fact that there was a lot going on race-wise in the country at the time, it absolutely didn't bother me one bit at all to room with Chuck. We got along very well.

"Remember, I was from Warren, where we had so many people from many different origins. Western Reserve was probably about 40 percent black, and one of my closest friends on the team, Cliff Roberts, is black.

"Although I got paired after my freshman year with someone, Steve Banks, who also played defensive back after my freshman year, Chuck and I remained very close friends throughout our UT careers. We connected socially. We double-dated a lot. I have nothing but great memories of my old freshman roommate. I honestly don't ever remember having an argument with Chuck the entire year. Now, for college roommates, how unusual is that?"

Recalls Ealey, "Although it may have been an issue in some schools and to some people, it wasn't an issue in either my mind or Gary's. I knew he had a lot of experience growing up in an ethnically diverse area. As for myself, I had gone to a high school that was overwhelmingly white. There were only four blacks in the entire school. So, I guess you might say that Gary and

I were perfectly suited to room together. Some might have seen it as some sort of experiment, but, to Gary and me, we didn't see it in those terms at all."

Since freshmen were ineligible for varsity competition at this time, the talented Toledo Rocket freshmen played their own schedule against other freshmen teams. The games, obviously, were very much out of the line of vision of even the most ardent UT fans, who expended virtually all their attention on the varsity squad.

Recalls Ealey, "I'm not even sure, at that time, freshman schedules were set up more than a year in advance. I think it was more a case of one athletic director calling another a few months before the season and saying, 'We've got this date available. What about you guys?'

"The games were almost like scrimmages, designed mostly to prepare you for varsity play after your freshman year. We practiced with the varsity, and, of course, the freshmen comprised most of the scout teams, where an offense and a defense would mimic the next opponent's tendencies, so the games we played against other schools were refreshing because we had opportunities to, kind of, seek our own identity by running Coach Lauterbur's offense and defense.

"We probably had four or five games all totaled. I can remember there were very few people in the stands. Now, when I say the games were more like scrimmages, I mean in terms of their relative importance as far as the final score. I don't mean they were scrimmages in the sense that there were coaches on the field and ten-play series and such. All game conditions were in place. It's just that they weren't high profile affairs."

Despite the fact that the freshmen games were dramatically understated, perhaps in Ealey's and his teammates' cases, the schedule became more relevant because they won every game, save one. Of course, the loss became more pertinent by the end of Ealey's final season in 1971 because it was the only loss the Portsmouth native sustained in what amounted to six seasons of squatting behind centers and taking snaps on game days.

Recalls Ealey about the lone loss in the fall of 1968, "It was against the University of Michigan Wolverines. One thing I can remember is their players were very, very big, compared to us. I think what happened was, I don't think they gave us any chance to even be competitive, but, as it turned out, we almost won. I don't remember the exact score, but it was only a touchdown differential of one, something like 12-6 or 12-7.

"Both offensively and defensively, we competed on a very even plane with them. But I can remember my little offensive linemen compared to their very big defensive linemen. I took some really hard shots that day.

Certainly, the lone loss the freshmen Rockets of 1968 would ever experience in four years is not a mark of shame. That group of Wolverines would, by the time they were seniors, be one of the top teams in the country. Those freshmen of 1968 would be coached by the legendary Bo Schembechler, who would get his big coaching break in the off-season before the 1969 campaign and move from the Cradle of Coaches, Miami University in Oxford, Ohio, to Ann Arbor to coach the Wolverines.

In 1971, Michigan finished the regular season undefeated and untied and, as Big Ten champions, went on to play in the Rose Bowl. They lost by a single point to Stanford, 13-12. In other words, one field goal would probably have given the men from Ann Arbor a national championship.

After the freshmen and the varsity had completed their seasons, during the off-season prior to the much-anticipated debut of the talent-laden sophomores-to-be, the Toledo Rockets football team grew stronger.

Recalls Coach Frank Lauterbur, "Mel Long showed up in the spring of 1969, just prior to when we were about to go into spring practice. I was actually playing racquetball with three of my assistants and there was a knock on the court door.

"I went out in the hall, and it was my secretary, telling me there was someone in my office who wanted to talk to me about coming out for football. Now, this was very unusual. By this point in the year, you pretty much knew what you had as a team.

"Well, I went down to meet the young man. Mel told me that he'd played football at Toledo Macomber High School before going into the Marines for two years. He wasn't overly big but was really put together. I could just tell he was an athlete. He was probably around 6'2" and 230 pounds or so.

"Let me tell you something. We, as coaches, knew nothing about Mel Long heading into spring football in '69 besides the fact that he'd played some high school ball and had been in Vietnam for almost two years and looked pretty athletic.

"But, by the end of spring ball, we all knew one thing: Mel Long was the best defensive lineman we had."

Toledo Blade sportswriter Jim Taylor remembered a comment that Frank Lauterbur made after Toledo's 1969 spring game. "Stretching out in a tattered easy chair in the Rocket dressing room, Lauterbur said, 'I can't wait...I wish the season would start tomorrow.'"

With the addition of Mel Long, who fell right into his lap, who could blame Frank Lauterbur for his giddiness in awaiting the fall of 1969?

Simply put, behind a sophomore-dominated offense and defense, Toledo rocketed to the top of the Mid-American Conference standings at the same time Coach Dick Strahm was crafting his third consecutive 9-1 season at Warren Western Reserve.

Ealey and Mel Long became dominating forces on either side of the ball, at quarterback and defensive tackle respectively, and, while there were three close calls, the Rockets ran the rack, winning every single time they stepped out onto the field, including a season-ending win in the Tangerine Bowl.

Behind junior running back Tony Harris, a converted quarterback, and his three dazzling touchdown runs of 15, 67, and 75 yards, the Rockets began their legendary three-year winning streak with a 45-18 win over the Villanova (Pennsylvania) Wildcats, despite Villanova's spectacular wideout, Mike Siani, and his two touchdown grabs. Siani would go on to play nine NFL seasons for the Oakland Raiders and the Baltimore Colts.

Marshall University out of Huntington, West Virginia, was victim number two, 38-13, as Ealey shined with both his feet and his arm. Running the option play to perfection, Ealey gained 101 yards running and also hit 8 of 10 passes for another 93 yards, with four of those tosses going to tight end Al Baker, another of Toledo's sensational sophomores.

In week three, Lauterbur's charges belted Bill Hess's Bobcats of Ohio University, 34-9. Senior fullback Dick Seymour, providing the Mr. Inside to speed merchant Tony Harris' Mr. Outside, scored twice on short plunges, and Ealey again found Al Baker a good target. He hit the former 6'2," 205-pounder out of Toledo Scott High School twice for touchdowns, once from 66 yards out and a second time from 62 yards out.

The first close call came in week three in Toledo's big rivalry game against their MAC neighbor, Bowling Green State University, a mere 23.1 miles south of Bancroft Street and the UT campus.

At Doyt Perry Field, against Falcon coach Don Nehlen's charges, it took a 37-yard field goal into the wind, with two seconds left, to send a jubilant Rocket squad back to Bancroft a 27-26 winner.

The winning drive started with just forty-nine ticks on the clock. Ealey's magic and a key pass interference call put Toledo kicker Ken Crots in a position to kick his way into the memories of Rocket fans.

In game four, a 38-13 victory over MAC foe Western Michigan, Gary Hinkson certainly has very fond remembrances. "I didn't start at the beginning of the year, but my secondary coach, Jim Flynn, continued to talk me up and really sold Frank that I was ready to go. I played quite a bit in the thriller the week before in BG, and, that, along with Flynny's championing my cause to Frank, got me a start in the Western Michigan game.

"Well, I had two interceptions in my first varsity start, and that was it. I started every game from that moment on all the way through our last game in 1971. I really have to thank Coach Flynn for so much of the success I had. He was just so intense, so enthusiastic. You talk about a guy who could coach you up and make you believe you could do anything on the football field! That was Jim Flynn."

From there, the Rockets ripped Kent State in week six in a game that saw one of the nation's top running backs, Golden Flash tailback Don Nottingham, suffer a compound finger fracture. With Ealey battling some nagging injuries, yet another marvelous sophomore, middle guard Steve Schnitkey, had the game of his life as he picked up not one, but two, fumbles and ran them in for touchdowns of 13 and 22 yards.

Close call number two came on November 2 in Oxford, Ohio, against the Redskins of Bill Mallory. The game would decide the conference championship and a trip to the Tangerine Bowl. On a rainy, gray day before a crowd of 13,213 people, Don Fair, yet another sophomore, began to build his reputation as one of the best clutch receivers in Rocket football history. He grabbed an Ealey aerial and scampered 54 yards to pay dirt in a hard-fought 14-10 crown-clincher. For Gary Hinkson, it was his key interception, his third in just two games, which set up Toledo's first score.

Close-call number three came the very next Saturday against the Huskies of Northern Illinois. Perhaps there was somewhat of a letdown after UT had clinched the league championship in Oxford, but Toledo found itself in a dogfight with the non-conference opponent and a school that would one day join the MAC.

It took a couple of fourth-quarter touchdowns to salt the game away for Toledo, 35-21, one on a 29-yard run by junior Charlie Cole, and another on a 19-yard pass, Ealey to Baker.

The regular season ended with wins in weeks nine and ten, 20-0 over Dayton and 35-0 over Xavier. The two shutouts solidified Toledo's defense, coordinated masterfully by Jack Murphy, as a national power, as they finished the regular season as the number-one statistical defense in the nation. The defensive ends were t-e-R-R-i-f-i-c, with the capital letters representing two more talented sophomores, Rose (Bob) and Roberts (Ron). The tackles, junior Don Hotz, and that player who showed up the previous spring with speed so dramatic he could run with any back on the squad, Mel Long, were run-stuffing beasts. The middle guard was the 6'0," 194-pounder out of Archbold, Ohio, Steve Schnitkey.

Should anyone get by the front five of that vaunted 5-2 angle defense, he ran right into a linebacker out of Toledo Central Catholic, John Niezgoda. Recalls Hinkson, "Everything you need to know about John as a football player can be summed up by who his football idol was, Dick Butkus."

With solid contributors such as linebacker Tony Baltes and an emerging secondary that included the ball-hawking Hinkson, the Rocket defense was every bit as formidable as the offense.

If a bowl game can be anticlimactic, the 1969 Tangerine Bowl may have been. The Rockets and Southern Conference representative, the Davidson College Wildcats (Davidson, North Carolina), were awarded bids. Ealey and the rest of the Rocket offense shredded Davidson's defense in a 55-33 victory.

It was with great anticipation that the Strahms made their way to Toledo after Dick accepted the position as defensive coordinator, replacing Jack Murphy, who was off to coach his alma mater, the Heidelberg Student Princes in Tiffin, Ohio.

The Strahms continued to live the lesson W. C. Killgallon taught them back in Bryan, Ohio, and eschewed any notion of renting. They bought a house on the west side of Toledo on Candlestick Court, not far from the UT campus.

Recalls Dick, "In so many ways, I felt I was right where I needed to be. I knew Jim Hilles would do a great job back in Warren, and I was home! My son Doug was six, and Gina was three. It was just a wonderful time. My mom was living nearby. I was joining a staff that would have the privilege to coach what turned out to be, collectively, the best group of football players in school history. How much better can it get than that?"

The fall of 1970 seemed a bit odd for Dick, despite the fact that he had bonded well with Frank Lauterbur and his fellow assistants Dave Hardy (offensive line), Sil Cornachione (offensive backfield), Don (Ducky) Lewis (defensive backfield), Elroy Morand (end and linebacker coach), and Steve Szabo (freshman coach).

Remembers Dick, "For the first time in my education career, I would not be in the classroom, teaching American history. While I always had a tremendous desire to coach, I always prided myself on being a good classroom teacher. I never wanted to be portrayed as a dumb-jock coach.

"However, despite the fact that I wouldn't be going into a classroom, it certainly felt I'd never left the world of teaching. There was so much to learn about defensive sets and multiple combinations where our front seven coordinated with our secondary coverage. And, of course, I had to learn it before I could teach it! Obviously, I worked closely with Elroy [Morand], who I'd known since my last year back in Warren when I hired him as one of my assistants, and with Ducky [Don Lewis], who joined the staff when Jim Flynn accepted another coaching opportunity. We talked about what we, as defensive coaches, had to do to retain that number-one defensive ranking in the nation that Jack Murphy coordinated so well."

With a new defensive coordinator comes an avalanche of curiosities and questions from the members of the defense, and many of the queries fell directly at the feet of the player who knew Dick Strahm the best, Gary Hinkson.

"Well, everyone on the team knew I had played for Dick in high school, so I suppose it was natural for them to ask me what to expect.

"Actually, I had to be honest. I couldn't lie to them. I told them Dick had, basically, been an offensive coach. It was Coach Hilles who had the defense at Western Reserve. As a matter of fact, while I was happy I'd be reuniting with Coach Strahm, when I first found out he'd gotten the job as defensive coordinator, my first reaction was, 'What's he know about defense?'

"I did, however, tell everyone what we were getting in Dick Strahm. I told my teammates that they were getting a super-enthusiastic coach who would treat everyone fairly and would be very organized and very focused. But, really, that was the best endorsement I could give, since I knew Dick didn't have a strong defensive background."

One thing that Dick recalls that helped him assimilate much of what he had to learn as the new coordinator in 1970 was his familiarity with Frank Lauterbur's base defense.

"In 1966, Jim Hilles and I visited Toledo to watch spring practice. When we saw Frank's 5-2 angle defense, with five defensive linemen and two linebackers and all the variations of routes that had players angling one way or the other, Jim and I both felt that suited our personnel back at Western Reserve. So, we took it back with us and used that as our base defense for the next three years. I really think my familiarity with the 5-2 angle made Frank less anxious when it came to giving me a chance despite my lack of experience."

During the August two-a-days leading up to the season opener against East Carolina, Hinkson noticed an even softer and gentler head coach. "I had always heard stories that Frank was really almost merciless when it came to trying to weed out those who just didn't want to make the commitment to win after he arrived in '63, but that's not the Frank Lauterbur I remember."

This preseason was really not a boot camp. While it was tough the year before, it certainly wasn't overwhelming. Recalls Hinkson, "I think after our undefeated year, Frank just realized he had the perfect mix of guys who were going to give him maximum effort. So, there was no need to make the preseason overly physical. It was almost as if Coach Lauterbur said to himself, 'I know these guys have each other's back. Let's work on speed and agility.'"

Recalls Dick Strahm about his first Rocket preseason in 1970, "I realized something immediately about the way Frank prepared his team. He simply was not going to have them beat each other to a pulp. He knew how tough they were and how committed they were to the physical style of play, so he didn't feel any need whatsoever to have them prove that by beating the crap out of each other before we ever kicked the ball off for real."

Recalls Hinkson, "The practices were reflections of how Frank had transformed himself as a coach. While he would still stand up in the tower and call players out, it was not done with much frequency or a great deal of malice. They were more like teaching moments."

Practices were geared toward conditioning and agility, as Hinkson reflects. "Frank knew that we had more team speed than any team we'd face. The year before, there were huge teams like Western Michigan, who tried to maul us to death, but we were a speed team.

"Since Frank did some things with his passing game with extended receiver routes and sprint-outs and moving pockets with the linemen being forced to do a lot more than simply stand in one place and zone block, he knew how important conditioning and agility were. The work we did in these areas allowed us to execute, both offensively and defensively, and do some things that other teams would have trouble either defending or attacking."

The 1970 season began auspiciously for both the Rockets and, in particular, Dick Strahm, as Toledo swamped East Carolina, 35-2. Despite the two points yielded when Ealey was tackled in his own end zone, Strahm's defense was credited with a shutout in his first game on the sidelines as the defensive coordinator of a top-flight Division I school. It was the home opener in the Glass Bowl. Bruising senior running back Charlie Cole, who ran both out of the fullback and the tailback slots, scored three touchdowns.

The win was Toledo's twelfth straight since the Rockets lost their final game of the 1968 season.

In game two, the Rockets pummeled Buffalo, 27-6. Ealey launched 42 passes, and his overall play prompted *Blade* sportswriter Jim Taylor to liken Chuck's night as a trip "into the madcap world of Fran Tarkington [the scrambling quarterbacking superstar of the NFL]." Ealey hit 22 of those passes, three for touchdowns and nine to his favorite target, Don Fair, the beanpole-thin 160-pounder out of Canton Lehman High School.

Recalls Dick, "I was pleased with my defense. We only gave them nine first downs.

"One thing I'll never forget about Hotz was he absolutely hated offensive linemen throwing at his knees when trying to block him. Now, no defensive player likes that because so many serious knee injuries have resulted from chop blocks, but Don *really* hated it.

"Well, one day at practice, the first-team defense is going against our scout team. And, this big old freshman offensive tackle, who, I'm sure, was trying to impress the coaches, fires out and chop blocks Don. Well, ordinarily Don didn't lose his cool, but when it came to someone throwing at his knees, that was different.

"The next thing I know, he's on top of this kid and beating him on the head even though he still had his helmet on! I grabbed Don and yelled, 'What are you doing?' He said, 'Coach, he's chopping me!' I said, 'I understand that. Let me handle him, okay? But don't you hit him. You'll break your hand and be out for maybe the rest of the season. Not a good idea.'

"So, he said, 'Okay, coach. I won't do that again.'

"About two weeks later, guess what? The freshman does it again! I was over on the other side of the field. All of a sudden, before I knew it, Don was on top of him again. This time, Hotz had his helmet off, holding onto the facemask and hitting the other kid's helmet with his helmet. I yelled at Don to stop. He looked up at me with his helmet drawn back and paused, 'See, Coach? I'm not going to break my hand. I'm using my helmet!'

"I had to laugh. I really think Big Don wanted me to compliment him on his good judgment by not using his hands. While certainly football is often a serious sport, full of intense moments, there are other moments that can just crack you up!"

The third win of the season and thirteenth in the streak came against Marshall University of Huntington, West Virginia. Toledo rolled 52-3 in a game *Blade* sportswriter Taylor termed "near perfect," and, defensively, he may have been right. The opportunistic Rockets had six interceptions.

Offensively, Ealey threw four touchdown passes, and Don Fair broke a Toledo single-season reception record by hauling in eleven. Marshall coach Rick Tolley said after the game that the contest was like a (lopsided) high school game.

In week four, Toledo's challenge would be to win at Ohio University's Peden Stadium, in Athens, something it had not done since 1956. On a crisp autumn Saturday in late September, Lauterbur's Rockets rolled over the Bobcats, 42-7.

Joe Schwartz, tailback, scored a couple of touchdowns, one via the air and one on the ground; and Tony Harris proved he was fully recovered from a knee injury he sustained in August by rushing for 129 yards on 18 carries.

For Harris, an introspective young man in addition to being a gifted athlete, his life had been indeed challenging. The former Cleveland John F. Kennedy quarterback, who converted to running back in 1969 as a junior, had gained 849 yards on the way to averaging 5.3 yards per tote. This season, though, he had been bedeviled by injuries.

While he obviously enjoyed the success he had as a junior running back, he did admit he was disappointed he didn't succeed at quarterback. "I really struggled, at first, with the position switch. I just wasn't used to running into the line and having people come at me. I was used to sitting in the pocket, so the position change was difficult."

Before the 1970 season, Harris also had to overcome medical issues. In addition to the knee problems, he also had to overcome a stomach ulcer that affected his eating.

Despite being one of the few married players on the squad, Harris still felt a strong connection to his teammates. For one thing, he lived at Carter East, where room and board was covered by his athletic scholarship, while his wife, Sandra, lived with her parents. Although this certainly wasn't the ideal situation for a marriage, the economic realities dictated the arrangement as Harris counted on the patience of his wife.

As a black player, Harris felt the morale of the Rockets of 1970 was about as perfect as possible. He said at the time, "No question about it. We have great spirit on this team. I suppose you have to approach from the race perspective as usual. We look at each other on this team as men – not as black men or white men – but just men. People tend to separate each other by their language and their various likes and dislikes, but we truly understand each other.

"If people in everyday life had the type of contact with each other that we get on this team, they would learn to live together and forget their differences. We have a war on this football field every day, every game, and, in a war, you have to pull together. The only way you can make it is by helping each other."

Gary Hinkson remembers the senior tailback of 1970 well. "Tony Harris was a big-time talent. Largely because of his abilities, that's why I would have to say that the '70 team was the best of the three teams in my three varsity seasons. He had the ability to explode into the hole and then simply leave opponents in his wake.

According to Lauterbur, "It's what Tony could do with his speed in the open field that made him so special. He was truly one of college's most exciting runners."

Game five pitted the Rockets against their rivals just a few miles away, the Bowling Green Falcons. Strahm's defense again responded by shutting out the Falcons, 20-0. While the score would seem to indicate the win was another "no-sweat" proposition, the reality was anything but that. Largely through the efforts of future Oakland Raider Super Bowl winner, Phil Villapiano, the Falcon defense harassed and contained Ealey.

However, Mel Long spent almost as much time in the Falcon backfield as BG's backs. Middle guard Steve Schnitkey proved his athleticism by tipping two passes at the line of scrimmage which wound up as interceptions by John Niezgoda and Gary Hinkson.

Recalls Hinkson about Schnitkey, "Often, the middle guard is really nothing more than a guy who rarely gets up out of his four-point stance, whose sole job is just to clog up the middle.

But Schnit was not your prototypical nose guard. He was a terrific athlete. How many nose guards have you ever heard of that were high jumpers in high school?."

Remarkably, there were six players on the 1970 team from the tiny village of Archbold, Ohio, population 3,400, in the northwest corner of Ohio. In addition to Schnitkey, Archbold natives Bruce Arthur (backup quarterback), Lynn Aschilman (center), Jim Crossgrove (cornerback), Paul Pape (free safety), and Bob Rose (defensive end) certainly helped to give Lauterbur the notion that it would be unwise to ignore Ohio's small towns when it came to recruiting.

In week six, for the second consecutive week, Toledo posted a 20-0 victory, this time against Western Michigan. For three quarters, the Rockets were offensively inept, and, heading into the final frame, the score was what it was before the opening kickoff.

However, a couple of Tom Duncan field goals from 29 and 41 yards, a one-yard Charlie Cole lunge, and an Ealey-to-Fair TD toss all came in the fourth quarter. The Rockets' front four of Bob Rose, Mel Long, Don Hotz, and Ron Roberts were relentless. What they didn't take care of in Kalamazoo before an MAC-record attendance of 23,200, linebacker John Niezgoda cleaned up.

Dick Strahm was overwhelmingly pleased with his defense and especially Niezgoda. "John called all our defensive signals, so he had a lot more to think about than his own coverage. We called him our garbage man. He had an absolutely uncanny ability to always be around to pick up a loose ball carrier.

"All our linebackers at Toledo were tough, hard-nosed football players. But, John really stood out from the pack. As a sophomore the year before, he made first-team All-MAC. Then, he went on and did it again in 1970 and yet again in his senior year in '71. If that sounds impressive, it is. It's the only time in the entire history of the Mid-American Conference that a linebacker has been accorded that honor.

"John was a coach's dream because he was really like another coach on the field. He studied opponents' game films until he had their running plays down to a science. Johnny was truly a class act off the field. He was a good student and a very good person. You just didn't want him to be your enemy on the football field!"

The seventh straight win of the season and eighteenth in a row over two years, came in Kent, Ohio, against the Golden Flashes, 34-17. The lithe Don Fair set a school record with six catches to bring his total on the year to fifty-one. His most stunning grab was a 36-yarder down to Kent's eight-yard line on a big third down and eighteen.

The Rockets, dubbed by *Blade* sportswriter Taylor "the Barons of Bancroft Street," since Toledo's campus was just off Bancroft Street, didn't escape without some injuries. Linebacker Tony Baltes, the 190-pound senior from Versailles who was subbing for injured starter Charlie Burgbacker, sustained a shoulder injury that was thought to be a partial separation. The next week, a home game against the always tough Miami Redskins would decide the conference championship. This would be a most inopportune time to have to go with a third-string linebacker if Baltes couldn't play.

During the week, Tony Baltes didn't practice. Team trainers and the team physician simply couldn't envision his playing, that is, until Friday. After being examined one final time, Baltes was told he could play, if he was able to withstand an exceedingly high level of pain. While the shoulder was not separated, it was severely bruised.

Both Lauterbur and Strahm were skeptical about Baltes' playing, but Tony convinced them he was up to the challenge.

The game at the Glass Bowl turned out to be Toledo's biggest of the year. Ealey proved his nickname, "The Wizard of Oohs and Aahs," to be most appropriate. He brought the Rockets into the end zone on a last-ditch drive to overcome a 13-7 deficit, after the extra point sailed through the uprights.

The key to the 14-13 win, in addition to Ealey's supreme scrambling ability, was Strahm's defense, which stopped Miami three times after the Redskins had gotten a first and goal at the Toledo five. Miami was forced to settle for a field goal, which opened the door for Ealey's three-yard TD run and the winning extra point.

Recalls Ealey, "I was fortunate to play for coaches who trusted me enough to allow me to audible plays. I did that a couple of times during our last drive against Miami.

"People often ask me if, during our winning streak, there were ever times I thought we would lose. I hope this doesn't sound cocky, but I have to say, never, even once, did I think we were in trouble. I was just very confident about what I was able to do, and I also was aware of how many great ballplayers surrounded me.

"I think what helped me more than anything was how I was able to compartmentalize the whole streak. I didn't see it as an entire work of art. Although I know it sounds clichéd, I took each game one at a time, and, during each game, one series at a time. Against Miami, I just knew we could score on that last drive."

As for Strahm's defense, Tony Baltes not only started but played the whole game. Recalls Strahm, "Tony played, what I would have to say, was the most courageous game I've ever seen one of my players have. Miami had this big running back [Tim Fortney, out of St. Marys Memorial High School], and he must have carried the ball thirty-plus times. They ran him right at Tony on the short side of the field, where we felt we had to play Tony to allow him to use the sideline to help compensate for the bad shoulder. It was one isolation play after another, so there was always a big fullback leading through the hole and looking to put a lick on Tony.

"Baltes didn't back down an inch. He took on that block over and over and played a terrific game. He was as much responsible for that win as any player on our team.

"Sunday night, when we gathered as a team to watch game films, I looked at Tony. He had on a Rocket football t-shirt, and I could see he was black and blue from his shoulder all the way up his neck to his left ear. Although the statistics reveal Fortney gained 142 yards, it took him 35 carries. Tony took on that fullback's block again and again and again, which allowed guys like Long and Rose and Niezgoda to make the tackle."

The Toledo win was its nineteenth in a row, and it also secured a second consecutive MAC title and its third in the last four years under Lauterbur.

Week nine was an easy Rocket win, 45-7 over Northern Illinois. Tony Harris scored three times. The game didn't come without some anxious moments. The Rockets led only 14-7 at halftime, but they then blitzed the Huskies for 24 third-quarter points.

Don Fair grabbed nine more passes, extending his school record to 66 catches on the season. Kicker Tom Duncan booted his then-MAC record tenth field goal as the Rocket offense accounted for 522 yards and 29 first downs.

Perhaps it was a game like this that prompted the free safety Hinkson to call the 1970 team the most talented of that wonderful three-year run of 1969-1972. "We had such great athletes on that team who were seniors, guys like Don Hotz and Tony Harris. Combine that with the guys in my class, and that squad was very good. I really believe we could have played with a lot of big schools in the country. I'm not saying we would have beaten all of them, but we sure would have competed."

In week ten, the Rockets won their twenty-first straight, 31-7, over the University of Dayton, at Baujan Field in the Gem City. The Rockets overcame not only the Flyers but also a lot of snow and mud. Despite the poor field conditions, Toledo played error-free, no fumbles and no interceptions. The Rocket defense held Dayton to a paltry 44 yards in total offense as Long, Hotz, Rose, and the rest of the Rocket defenders seemed to fly to the ball. They stuffed Dayton's Gary Kosins, the nation's second-leading rusher, repeatedly.

Strahm noticed that his prized junior tackle, Mel Long, worked well with his teammates who were considerably younger since Long had given time to the Marines before coming back to Toledo to enroll. Recalls Dick, "Mel had the respect of everyone on that team. They knew he was battle-tested in the rice paddies of Vietnam. However, he also blended so well with them despite being older. I sensed no distance whatsoever between Mel and even the freshmen." Recalls Hinkson about Long, "He fit right in. At the time, there were lots of campus protests about the war in Vietnam, but Mel wasn't phased. He didn't get angry. His attitude was, despite his strong sense of duty to his country, everyone had a right to voice an opinion."

The final game of the regular season was a non-conference affair against Colorado State at the Glass Bowl. Chuck Ealey, despite having another full season to run the Rocket attack, set a MAC record for most career touchdown passes with his thirtieth, a 15-yarder to Jeff Calabrese. Future Los Angeles Rams' All-Pro running back Lawrence McCutcheon scored both of Colorado State's touchdowns.

Strahm's recollection of the game is isolated to one play. "I remember calling a defense and McCutcheon breaking off a run right down our sideline for about 30 yards. It's the most helpless feeling in the world when the runner is running right down your sideline with you standing within a couple feet of him as he whizzes by. You can reach out and grab him, you're so close, yet you can't!

For the 11-0 Rockets, it was off to Orlando, Florida, for a return visit to the Tangerine Bowl. Their opponent, just as it had been in 1969, was from the Southern Conference. Just as Davidson was overwhelmed by Ealey and his remarkable mates the previous year, the same thing happened to The College of William and Mary, which is located in Williamsburg, Virginia. Their young coach, Lou Holtz, would one day lead the Fighting Irish of Note Dame to a national championship and become one of the truly recognizable faces in college football history.

The final score was Toledo 40 and William and Mary 14 in what turned out to be Frank Lauterbur's final game with the Rockets.

The first half, the Boys from Bancroft hung onto a scant 7-6 lead. In the second half, the Rockets scored touchdowns on four straight possessions. Each touchdown was scored by a different player (Charlie Cole, Tony Harris, Joe Schwartz, and Don Fair). Then, Strahm's defense got in on the act as John Niezgoda returned an interception 52 yards for another TD.

Coach Holtz was awestruck after the game by one thing in particular. "I knew Toledo was a fine football team, but, never, in my wildest dreams, did I think it had the speed and the overall quickness it showed against us."

Known for one-liners, Holtz once delivered one of his most famous when he summed up what he felt was the main problem in achieving more success at William and Mary, the nation's second oldest institution of higher learning. His reply was succinct. "We had too many Marys and not enough Williams."

Certainly, Jim Taylor of the *Blade* recognized the contributions to the Rockets' success made by their new defensive coordinator. Taylor likened Strahm's following Jack Murphy in 1970 to someone trying to follow Jack Benny on a comedy hour or follow Vince Lombardi in Green Bay. When Strahm was interviewed for a story Taylor wrote, Dick chose to play down his contribution by bringing up others. "I got a lot of help from Ducky (Lewis) and Elroy Morand (another defensive coach) and, of course, from Frank (Lauterbur). Toledo always has had fine defensive teams. The only thing I've done is try to improve on it."

For Frank Lauterbur, the success of the last two years put him on a grander stage in terms of publicity. When the University of Iowa's athletic director, Bump Elliott, asked Frank to fill their head coaching vacancy, it was an opportunity for Lauterbur to both improve himself economically and also compete in one of the premier football conferences in the entire country. In other words, it was an opportunity he just couldn't pass up.

As is common practice, Lauterbur wanted several of his coaches to go with him, one of whom was Dick Strahm. Recalls Dick, "I almost had to pinch myself. In about a ten-month period of time, I went from being a high school coach to being a defensive coordinator of a MAC school, and now I had an opportunity to be coaching in the Big Ten."

"Despite how flattering it was for Frank to ask me to go with him, I talked it over with Ginger, and we decided that we would remain in Toledo for the time being. We'd just moved yet again for a third time less than a year ago, and I just felt it was time to slow the old coaching merry-go-round a bit and stay put for awhile. While I didn't rule out a move at a later time, I just felt it was best for all concerned that I remain at Toledo."

Recalls Lauterbur on his decision to leave Toledo, "It was hard to leave, especially in light of the streak and my awareness of what a wonderful group of seniors were coming back, but it was a chance to go against the Ohio States and the Michigans and the Michigan States of college football, a chance to really test myself on one of college football's grandest stages.

"As it turned out, I didn't have much success at Iowa [4-28-1, over three years] and was eventually fired with two years left on my contract when I refused to fire my defensive coordinator, Ducky Lewis, whom I had brought with me from my Toledo staff.

"I continued to keep tabs on my Toledo players even after I left the next year and was thrilled they were able to have such a great '71 season. But, even more thrilling was seeing what happened after they left Toledo. That's the most gratifying thing about athletics, watching them come to you as boys and grow into men."

Two of the players Lauterbur would most miss when he departed for his Iowa field of dreams were Chuck Ealey and Gary Hinkson. The two he put together as roommates during their freshman year were special.

"Chuck was mentally so astute, a real student of the game. Physically, he could have played anywhere. If I'd have had him at Iowa, I might still be there! He was a quiet leader, but players just gravitated toward him. He was supremely confident without being cocky.

"What absolutely baffles me is Chuck was undefeated in high school, undefeated in college, and led his Hamilton Tigercats of the Canadian Football League to a win in the Grey Cup [the equivalent of the Super Bowl in the Canadian Football League] in his very first year of professional football, and, yet, he's not in the College Hall of Fame! Why?'

"Now, Gary Hinkson was a very smart defensive back. To have held the school record for the most career interceptions [18] for as long as he has, well, that's just remarkable. He played with a combination of unbelievable instinct and intelligence. He also had this great ability to see peripherally. It seemed wherever on the field the ball was thrown, he was there. He got better every year he played."

Frank Lauterbur looked to his own time as a Marine when he coached. "I demanded a lot because I felt when I was the best I could be, I gave a lot. The Marines put you through boot camp. Maybe I did a little of that as a coach."

After leaving Iowa when he insisted he have control over who he let go and who he retained on his own staff, the man of uncompromising principles, Frank Lauterbur, spent the rest of his coaching career as an NFL assistant, coaching in Super Bowl XIV as a member of the Los Angeles Rams' staff.

He then spent ten years working for the National Scouting Service before retiring in 1993. He now lives back in Toledo, close to the Rockets that he loves so much.

During the 1970 season, the first-year defensive coordinator, Dick Strahm, was the feature for an article in the *Rocket Football Magazine*. Readers of that publication discovered quite a bit about their new defensive coordinator, especially through Ginger. Among the revelations about her husband was that (a) he snored too loudly, (b) he had a moderate temper, and (c) he couldn't stand to lose at anything.

When asked about Dick's idiosyncrasies, Ginger said, "You'll have to ask the other coaches. They see him more than I do."

Ginger also revealed the mood around the house after games. "After we win, things are great around the house. That's for one day. Then, we all start worrying about the next game. After a loss, the children know enough not to say too much to Daddy."

Fortunately, the Strahm children rarely felt compelled to remain quiet, since Dick's teams had suffered, at that time, only three losses over the last four years.

Ginger also lent the readers of *Rocket Magazine* some insight into Dick Strahm, the father. "Dick loves children. I suppose that's the main reason he became a teacher. He treats our children very fairly, but he demands respect from them and is not afraid to discipline them when they need it. He takes Doug fishing whenever he gets a chance, and you will find him bicycle riding with the children at least a couple times a week. I think Dick understands so well how important it is he maximizes his family time when there are opportunities to do so. Since coaches spend so much time at work, I think that's vital to the success of the family."

The business of who would replace Frank Lauterbur was completed quite efficiently, and the selection made a lot of the Rocket faithful very happy because it marked the return of one of their favorite sons. Jack Murphy returned to Toledo after one season of coaching Heidelberg College.

Recalls Murphy, now retired and living in Toledo, "I had been at UT for ten years before going to Heidelberg and saw us go from not being very good to being very good, so it was gratifying to come back in 1971. I considered it an honor to succeed Frank."

The exodus of several assistants who followed Lauterbur to Iowa also brought new coaching faces aboard. Men like Chet Fair (Don's father), Roger Merb, and Dan Simrell joined Murphy's staff.

It was Simrell, the former Rocket quarterback of just a few years before, who would become the third secondary coach that Gary Hinkson had in his varsity career. "I had started with Jim Flynn and then Ducky Lewis came in. Now, for my senior year, it was going to be Danny. Despite his youth [27] and the fact that he had not coached at the college level I thought he did a terrific job."

Simrell, currently the quarterback coach at Division III Tri-State University in Angola, Indiana, remembers, "When I left UT as an undergraduate, I coached a year at Toledo St. Francis DeSalles High School and then moved on to a brand new school on the west side, Toledo Start, where I stayed five years, the last two as head coach.

"Murph had recruited me out of Toledo DeVilbiss when I came as a student. I think that may have been why he offered me the job, and I accepted. It was my desire to get into college coaching."

Simrell also recalls what a special relationship developed between Dick Strahm and him. "While I knew about Dick, I didn't actually know Dick. I did know Dick's brother, Dale, whom I competed against when I was playing for DeVilbiss and Dale was at Libbey. I think Dale may have picked off a pass or two of mine. He was an excellent linebacker.

"Since Dick was nine years older, I accepted him as my mentor. Although he was a sideline coach the year before, he and I went up in the press box in 1971 and also '72.

"We sat together during games, coordinating our defensive sets. Our offices were right next to one another. We even roomed together on the road. Despite the age difference, we became pretty close.

"While I enjoyed my time under Jack Murphy, I really would have loved to have coached under Frank Lauterbur. He meant so much to me and has supported me every coaching stop I have had. You name it! He's come to games when I coached at the University of Memphis, at West Virginia University, when I later became head coach back here at Toledo, and when I coached The University of Findlay.

For Gary Hinkson, the summer of 1971 would be spent in Toledo rather than back in Warren. He had switched majors and needed to get caught up on course work. Since it was summer, he would not be allowed to stay in Carter East. Recalls Gary, "I needed a place to stay, and Coach Strahm was able to help out. His mother had some extra room and agreed to take me on as a boarder. I really got to know Mildred Strahm well, and, by doing so, I realized just why her sons, both Dick and Dale, became such successful men."

The 1971 season arrived and, with a class that the media in Toledo now referred to as the "Super Seniors," hopes were sky high for the streak that had now grown to twenty-four straight wins to continue.

The Rockets opened on the road, in Greenville, North Carolina, at Ficklen Stadium, against East Carolina. New head coach Jack Murphy proved there was no thought of ending "The Streak" anytime soon.

Statistically speaking, the Rockets of the previous year had repeated under their first-year defensive coordinator, Dick Strahm, as the nation's number-one defense. This season got off to a perfect start against Carolina, as the Rockets fired on all cylinders, both offensively and defensively, in a 45-0 whitewash. The pilfering secondary came up with four interceptions. Roommates Steve Banks and Gary Hinkson certainly would have something to talk about before lights out. Banks had three and Hinkson the other.

Strahm had every intention of defending his defense's number-one national crown. But both he and new secondary coach Simrell recognized the pressure under which they would operate in 1971.

Recalls Dick, "All of us felt there would be many who would wonder whether Frank's departure would somehow spell the end of the streak. That put a lot of strain on all of us. Since we also had lost several assistant coaches who went with Frank, this year would be even more challenging.

Simrell, the 27-year-old, first-year secondary coach, may have summed it up best, remembering the '71 season. "We coaches used to say only half in jest, 'If we win 'em all, it's still Frank's team. If we lose one, it becomes our team.'"

Game two proved to be very challenging. In the Rockets' 10-7 win over Villanova, it took a 57-yard Ealey-to-Glyn Smith connection to get the ball down to the Villanova 14-yard line so that George Keim could come on to boot the biggest field goal of his life, from 30 yards out, for the win. By doing so, he atoned for the two misses he had earlier in the contest. The kick also helped Ealey erase any unpleasant memories of his worst game ever as a Rocket, a game in which he threw four interceptions.

Game three was a road trip of major proportions. Toledo went all the way to the Lone Star State to shutout the University of Texas at Arlington, 23-0, before a sparse crowd of 8,500 at Turnpike Stadium. Strahm couldn't help but remember that his Warren Western Reserve teams routinely drew more than that at Mollenkopf Stadium.

Mel Long and John Niezgoda played big roles in holding Texas Arlington to just 23 yards rushing.

Ealey rebounded from the week before and played a key role in all of the Rockets' touchdowns. He scored on a rollout from a yard out, scrambled for fifteen and a touchdown, and also hit Don Fair for a seven-yard scoring strike. Keim added a 30-yard field goal.

During the following week's practices, Dick Strahm, tried to get to the heart of what would motivate Mel Long to raise his level of play from great to supreme. Recalls Dick, "While Mel was terrific, I just wanted to know what havoc he could create if he played at an even higher level. I asked him at practice one day what really got his competitive juices flowing.

"He told me that he just got all charged up listening to the pounding of drums. Well, my neighbor just happened to be the UT band director. I asked him, as a favor, if he could work something out that featured a lot of drums for the following Saturday's game at the Glass Bowl against Bill Hess's OU Bobcats.

"Come Saturday during warm-ups, the band was playing and marched down the field and stopped about ten feet from where Mel was stretching out. Suddenly, the first line of band members opened like a gate, and four drummers emerged and advanced even closer to where Mel was before stopping in unison. Then they proceeded to break into rhythmic drumming, which progressively got faster and faster.

"You should have seen the grin come over Mel's face. He got his own drum quartet! He looked over at me and said, 'Now, that's what I'm talking about, Coach!'

"Mel went out there and had something like a dozen solo tackles, just a huge game, and we needed every bit of his effort to win a real nail biter against OU, 31-28."

It was the fourth straight win of the season and the twenty-seventh straight overall. Halfway through the fourth quarter, Toledo had what appeared to be a fairly comfortable 31-14 lead. However, as *Blade* beat writer Jim Taylor wrote, "[The lead] proved no more durable than a soap bubble." OU scored two quick touchdowns and then intercepted an Ealey pass with 5:40 left. However, a mishandled snap on a fourth and three gave the ball back to Toledo, and Ealey and his mates ran out the clock. Ealey, "The Wizard of Oohs and Ahhs," was spectacular. He threw two TD passes of 29 and 23 yards to Fair and scrambled for key first downs on several occasions.

Reflecting back to the magical streak he helped to create, Mel Long recalls something his defensive coordinator did that made him feel very unique. "Coach Strahm got a hold of several pair of white shoes from a sporting-goods salesman. Well, this was the early 1970s, and they were very unusual. When they were worn, the backs and wide receivers generally got them. I think Ealey got a pair and a couple running backs and a couple guys in the secondary. Well, he had two pair left, so he felt the linemen should get in on some of the fun. He gave a pair to me and a pair to offensive lineman Leon Campbell. Boy, did we ever get a kick out of that! Leon and I used to tell each other all the time that we had to be the only linemen in the entire country who were stylin' in white shoes."

Game five of the season was one that forced a mid-game seating shift for Mildred Strahm. The reason for the shift was because she had a son on each of the two coaching staffs of Toledo and Bowling Green. For Dick, it would be the first time he was on the same football field with Dale, the Falcon linebacker coach, since their days together coaching back in Warren.

Recalls Dale, "I saw my brother during warm-ups walking among the Rocket players. I was on the other side of mid-field, so I motioned for Dick to come over so we could talk a minute.

"He just shook his head and motioned for me to come to him. But, I saw where this was going. I was just as stubborn as he was. I just shook my head side to side!"

Dick remembered the incident, "Neither one of us wanted to cross the fifty! It was just a little gamesmanship, but that was really as close as we ever got to talking before the game. We caught up after the game, though."

As for Mildred Strahm, she spent the first half seated among the Rocket faithful and switched to the other side of the field during intermission and sat with the Falcon backers in the second.

The game went to the Rockets, 24-7, before a then-MAC record crowd of 26,860 at BG's Doyt Perry Stadium.

For Gary Hinkson, it would be a final year of bragging rights. Recalls Hinkson, "A win against BG was always big because a lot of my friends in Warren played for Bowling Green. My former Reserve teammates Bill Fisher, Frankie Allen, and Brian Cross all played at BG, and then there was also Carl Angelo from Harding.

"We used to work out together, and there was always a lot of trash talking. There'd always be comments about how lucky we were, but all I know is we played them three times and won all three. I don't think luck had a whole lot to do with that."

For Hinkson, it was his blocked punt that was scooped up by strong safety John Saunders and returned for a touchdown that really got UT rolling. Saunders, who broke his leg during the preseason of 1970 and missed the entire season, was granted a red shirt, which allowed him to play in 1971. Saunders also was a player so good, he remains etched in Dan Simrell's mind. "John was an outstanding football player. I remember he was a fourth-round pick of the Rams, and, keep in mind, that was when they only drafted twenty rounds. He played three or four years with the Rams.

"Really, my whole secondary was so special. Gary had a natural nose for the ball. The cornerbacks were Steve Banks, Pete Alsup, and Mike Hurt. They also played great.

"You really can't have a number-one defense in the nation and have a suspect secondary. I know guys like Long, Niezgoda, and Rose got a lot of the publicity, and, don't get me wrong, they played great. But I just want everyone who remembers the glory days of Rocket football to not forget how good that secondary was."

Game six was one of the games that people most remember when it comes to when the streak was really in jeopardy.

By the latter stages of the third quarter, against the Broncos of Western Michigan, the Rockets trailed 21-7. It was homecoming at the Glass Bowl before a crowd of 18,964, and, recalls, Simrell, it was time for the defensive coordinator to say something outrageous.

"After we went down by two scores, Dick looked at two of the offensive coaches seated in the press box next to us and said, 'Listen, our defense has been carrying this team for the last two years! Don't you think it's about time you guys did something to help?'

Gray Hinkson remembers what Dick did after the Rockets fell behind by two scores. "Dick actually came down from the press box after we fell behind 21-7, and that was very unusual. During a time-out, he gathered the whole defense around him. He was so cool and collected. He simply looked around the huddle at us and said, 'If you don't allow this team to score again, we'll win, simple as that.'

"Well, don't you know that's exactly what happened! We shut out Western the last quarter, and Chuck threw three touchdown passes. We scored 24 straight points and won 35-24!"

By the time Ealey's day against Western Michigan was over, he had set two MAC records, for total passing yardage (381) and total offense (392).

The next weekend, game seven, and the thirtieth of the streak, brought rain and a positive outcome for Toledo as they defeated Dayton, 35-7. Ealey tossed three more touchdowns and showed no favoritism in the process by hitting three different receivers- 29 yards to Jeff Calabrese, 42 yards to Don Fair, and 15 yards to Joe Schwartz. The superb signal caller also ran for a 27-yard touchdown.

Practices leading up to the week-eight game were indeed challenging. Jack Murphy and his staff knew it was Miami week, and certainly the traditional MAC power, a program which has won more conference football championships than any other school, would like nothing better than to short-circuit the Rocket streak at Miami Field on Halloween of 1971. However, all that history meant absolutely nothing to Toledo.

Rocket piracy was instrumental in the very convincing 45-6 win, as Hinkson, Alsup, and Schnitkey all had interceptions. Both Hinkson and Alsup ran theirs in for TDs. Defensive end Ron Roberts made it three touchdowns for the defense by falling on a Miami fumble in the end zone.

Week nine saw Toledo win its thirty-second straight against Northern Illinois, 23-8. The site was DeKalb, Illinois, and the players were buffeted by 35-mile-per-hour wind gusts the entire game. Toledo actually trailed at halftime, 6-0, before Ealey turned to magic yet again. He bolted 72 yards for the tying touchdown. Then Leon Campbell, the proud possessor of a pair of white shoes, had a lineman's dream by covering a Joe Schwartz fumble in the end zone for a TD. Schultz later got a touchdown of his own on a four-yard win.

In the tenth week Toledo ran roughshod over Marshall, 43-0. Perhaps the most important thing in the game was that there was a Marshall team to play. This Saturday in Huntington, West Virginia, marked the one-year anniversary of the tragic plane crash that claimed the lives of the Marshall football team and its coaches.

Week eleven saw UT run its consecutive streak to thirty-four consecutive games with a convincing 41-6 win over Kent State. Schwartz, the junior tailback who had replaced the graduated Tony Harris, saved the best for the last game of the regular season. He scored five touchdowns before 20,201 at the Glass Bowl. The huge crowd was there to say "Thank you" and "Good-bye" to the nineteen Super Seniors. While some fans would make the trip to Orlando for the Tangerine Bowl, for many, this would be the last time they would see this wonderful collection of athletic talent and dedication in person.

Coach Jack Murphy took his senior starters out by ones and twos, so they could take their bows to thunderous rounds of applause. Kent State's head coach Don James, who would go on to coach the Washington Huskies to multiple Rose Bowls and a national championship, put it succinctly after the game, "Toledo can play with anybody."

The 1971 Tangerine Bowl was the third consecutive trip to Orlando for Toledo. It was a game everyone expected the Rockets to win easily, and Taylor of the *Blade*, in his pre-game coverage, likened the contest to the *Titanic* versus the Iceberg. The Rockets were favored by anywhere from 22 to 25 points over the Richmond Spiders of the Southern Conference.

While the UT athletic administration did entertain some thoughts of accepting a bid to a larger bowl, say the Fiesta Bowl, and play a more prestigious opponent, like Arizona State, the decision was ultimately made to do what was best for the conference, which was to maintain the strong relationship the MAC had developed with the Tangerine Bowl officials.

Recalls Strahm, "We discussed the possibility of looking for another bid but really felt, as a whole, that the league's affiliation with the Tangerine Bowl committee was more important than our desires were to play in a larger venue.

"You see, there weren't many bowls around then, and we felt if we rejected the Tangerine Bowl people, they very well might go in another direction in the future and the MAC champ would be sitting home with nowhere to go."

The feeling among many was that, eventually, the Tangerine Bowl would find stronger teams to pit against the winner of the MAC. That feeling came to reality soon after Toledo's wonderful run. In 1973, '74, and '75, the Miami Redskins put together an extraordinary run of their own. They won three consecutive MAC championships and won three consecutive Tangerine Bowls, versus Florida, Georgia, and South Carolina.

The 1971 game was anticlimactic in many ways. After Richmond opened the scoring with a 27-yard field goal, Mel Long went to work. He stripped quarterback Ken Nichols in the end zone and pounced on the ball. It was a lead the Rockets never relinquished.

Before just 16,750 spectators, in a stadium approximately the size of Mollenkopf Stadium in Warren, Ohio, Toledo did what it had to do. The defense didn't yield another point, and three plunges by Schwartz and one by Ealey, along with the George Keim extra points made the final a coldly efficient 28-3. Taylor wrote in his game account, "They should retire the Tangerine Bowl, wrap it in cellophane, and deliver it to the University of Toledo campus."

As for defensive coordinator Dick Strahm, he was forced to make some adjustments after Richmond came out with wider splits in their offensive line than they'd showed all year. After the game, Strahm said, "I had our defense in a 6-1[six defensive linemen and a linebacker] and a 5-2 [five defensive linemen and two linebackers]. We started in a 4-3 [four defensive linemen and three linebackers]. But, in the second half, I only called two 4-3's."

After the game, Dick returned to the hotel. He was getting cleaned up to join the other coaches for a celebratory drink after thirty-five consecutive wins over the last three years. Then, there came a knock on the door.

When Strahm opened the door, there stood Mel Long, the defensive lineman of unparalleled quickness. He was holding a bottle of Chivas Regal. Long had just come to thank Dick for coaching him the last two years and wanted to have a drink with his old coach.

Of course, Dick got a couple of glasses and sat with Mel.

During his days as a Rocket, Long had not spoken of his time as a Marine in Vietnam. Those who played with him and coached him respected him so much that no one asked him to discuss his time there.

However, over a drink, Mel finally told his defensive coordinator what had happened to earn him the Navy Cross, the second highest medal that can be awarded by the Department of the Navy.

Long told Dick that he and a group of soldiers were out in a rice paddy when, suddenly, they were pinned down by Viet Cong sniper machine-gun fire. As the bullets whizzed by inches above their heads and with their chins barely above the muddy water, it was evident something had to be done.

So, while his fellow Marines lay flat, with machine guns continuously strafing the area, it was Mel Long who crawled through the muck, nose barely above water, until he was behind the snipers' nest, where four Viet Cong were sharing two machine guns.

Then, recalled Strahm, "Long dropped his eyes to the glass of scotch in his right hand and fell silent momentarily. Then, in a voice barely above a whisper, he said, 'So, I took care of what had to be done.' I asked, 'All of them?' And, Mel just shook his head in affirmation. Now, how'd you like to coach a player like that?"

Besides the intangible qualities that Long demonstrated, Dick also remembered his gifts as a player. "Mel Long in our 52-angle defense was very difficult to block because he was always moving. Mel was timed at 4.6 seconds in the 40-yard dash time after time. There were several times at the end of practices when he ran sprints. Now, ordinarily, when this happened, players ran with their group. But, Mel ran with the backs and would stay step for step with our fastest back!

"Now, add the ingredients of quickness and tenacity and a supreme desire to win with his speed, and you have your first-team All-American defensive lineman, the only one to ever be given such an honor in the Mid-American Conference."

After the season, Long was selected to every All-American team that mattered. To this day, he remains the only consensus All-American in the history of MAC football.

In December, Long appeared on the *Bob Hope Show*, the one in which Hope introduced the All-American team one at a time and cracked a one-liner as each stood in full uniform with helmet under his arm. When Long was introduced, Hope wisecracked, "Mel Long has brought down more men than the Women's Lib Movement."

Long went on to play three years for the NFL's Cleveland Browns. Recalling the transition from college to pro ball, he mentioned that even on winless NFL teams, there was just so much talent.

To this day, he is of the opinion that his NFL career could have been longer had Forrest Gregg not replaced Nick Scorich as the Browns' head coach. "I just felt there was too much effort on Coach Gregg's part to emulate Vince Lombardi, whom he played for. He felt I just didn't fit his image of what a player ought to be, I guess. Also, I did sense that if you were from a small school, as I was, that you just had to be better, a lot better, than, say, someone who may have played at an Ohio State or a Southern Cal.

"When I was released, I got a call from LeRoy Kelly, the former Browns running back, who was on Coach Willie Wood's staff in Philadelphia in the World Football League. The team was called the Bell.

"I went there for a tryout, but when I saw how inferior the equipment was to anything I'd ever used, I decided to not go through the audition. I just thought it was time to get on with life."

And, that's exactly what Long did. He currently lives back in Toledo and works as a gasoline blender for Sunoco, having been with the company since 1981.

Gary Hinkson's path in life took a twist or two, but all has turned out well. Recalls Gary, "I spent an additional year at the University of Toledo as a student coach working with the freshmen. I had some course work to complete for my degree, since I had switched majors.

"After I left in 1972, I returned to Warren and got a job at Western Reserve teaching business education and coaching under Joe Novak.

"In '74 Joe went back to his alma mater, Miami University, to take the defensive coordinator's position for head coach Dick Crum. He asked me to come with him as a graduate assistant. I stayed four years, eventually becoming a full-time assistant, coaching the defensive ends.

"During that time Miami won those three consecutive MAC championships in seasons which culminated with those three Tangerine Bowl wins against Florida, Georgia, and South Carolina. And, as history shows, we beat all three. For me, that made six Tangerine Bowls, three as a player and three as a coach, and no losses. "I'm pretty proud of that."

Hinkson eventually would be given a chance to move with Crum to North Carolina, when he took his next step to coach the Tarheels and, in the process, future NFL Hall of Famer Lawrence Taylor. However, not wishing to accept the constant movement and uncertainty that come with collegiate coaching, he decided to pursue a path in business, far from the sidelines within which he had played so successfully and beside which he had coached with equal success.

Currently, Hinkson lives in Perrysberg and is a successful businessman for Bristol-Myers Squibb.

The red-shirt safety whose broken leg earned him another season to embrace the streak, John Saunders, and also Mel Long would be given NFL opportunities. However, Chuck Ealey would not. Recalls Ealey, "I was contacted by both the Kansas City Chiefs and the Denver Broncos, but they told me they wanted me to play either wide receiver or defensive back. Basically, I told them I wasn't interested in being drafted if I couldn't at least compete for a quarterback spot."

However, at that time, the only black quarterbacks in the NFL were James Harris and Joe Gilliam. Nonetheless, Ealey refuses to this day to play the race card when it comes to his being passed over in the NFL draft of 1972. "I will certainly not blame the NFL for not drafting me because I was black. I really didn't have the perfect NFL body. I wasn't even six feet tall.

"I do think my athleticism may have been a bigger impediment to my not being drafted. I think that many NFL people automatically thought of me as a wideout or a defensive back because, at that time in the NFL, there really wasn't any prototype that fit my skill package. I just don't see it as a racial issue.

"However, everything has worked out wonderfully in my life. I really wasn't all that upset over being passed over by the NFL even when it happened. I felt I had options and didn't really need the NFL to survive. I had my degree in business economics. And, in football, I had options in the Canadian Football League (CFL).

"What happened in the CFL was this. I was put on a negotiation list. This meant that a certain team, alone, had the opportunity to work out a deal with you, until such time as that team decided to either drop you from the list or drop you when they found a more desirable option at your position.

"In my case, the first team to do so was the Toronto Argonauts. But, then they signed Joe Theismann, who had a bigger name as a Notre Dame quarterback, and dropped me from its list. Then, the Hamilton Tigercats picked me up, and that's where I wound up.

It appears the NFL's loss was the CFL's gain. Ealey went on to win the Grey Cup in his first year. He was named the league's Rookie of the Year and also the Most Valuable Player of the championship game. Altogether, he played seven years in the CFL before injuries forced him to the sidelines.

Ealey has remained in Canada since and has dual-citizenship. He lives in Bramppon, Ontario, with his wife of 33 years, Sherri. His three adult children and three grandchildren also have remained in Canada.

Ealey is the regional director for Investor Group Financial Services, specializing in estate planning and portfolio building. In addition, he does a lot of public speaking to both educational groups and corporate groups.

In February of 1972, a few months after the Rockets had again been accorded the honor of being the number-one statistical defense in the land for the third consecutive season, the 38-year-old Dick Strahm had to assist his grandma Strahm in a very difficult decision.

Recalls Dick, "My grandfather had simply become too difficult to handle at home. Although it was tough for my brother, Dale, and me to do, we felt it best to have him put in a nursing home where he could get full-time attention and care.

"Sadly, for all of us, Grandpa passed away a few months later, and a few months after that so did my grandma. They were both so supportive of each other, really great advocates of Dale and me and everything we were able to do."

When Dick and Dale's grandparents' will was read, the grandsons discovered they had been left some money. With the windfall, they decided to do something together with the money.

They bought a 22-foot boat, a Tri-Haul, thusly named because it configured in the bow to include three benches for seating in addition to the benches further back in the boat.

Recalls Dick, "We had a lot of fun with that boat. I can remember one day, in particular, Ginger and I and Dale and his fiancée, Diane, who would one day become his wife, were boating on the Maumee River.

"We pulled up to a yacht club we liked to frequent to pick up Jerry Briggs, an old Air Guard friend of mine, and his wife, Sue. Well, I don't want to seem indelicate, but Diane removed her t-shirt with her bikini on under to get some sun. She has always been quite shapely.

"At any rate, Jerry was walking down the dock, spotted us, and waved. He must have also spotted Diane because he got so distracted, he took one step too far to the left and fell right into the water, with his drink still in his hand!"

An important incident also occurred during the off season relative to Dick's career. At the National Coaches' Convention, Strahm met Vince Gibson, the head coach at Kansas State of the Big Eight, perhaps the best conference in all of college football at the time.

Recalls Dick, "Coach Gibson and I spent a lot of time together that weekend talking football. By the end of the conference, he told me that he would love to add me to his staff but wasn't sure he would have an opening. When I told him I would certainly be interested, he said he'd call me. However, before anything concrete materialized, he called back and said that no position would be available for the coming year.

"While I wasn't actively pursuing another position, I was always willing to listen. As in any profession, it's always nice to know that people are recognizing what kind of record you're forging and thinking about you. Coach Gibson's interest told me that I was on people's radar screen.

"That became even more evident a little while later when I got a call from one of Woody Hayes' assistants who told me that Coach Hayes had me on his board to fill one of his assistant coaching vacancies.

"What Coach Hayes would do was put several names on the board when a position became available, and then his entire staff would discuss the pros and cons of each candidate and eliminate them one by one.

"It was all the way down to me and one other candidate, and I was told that Coach Hayes would call me sometime on Memorial Day.

"Well, Ginger and I always had a big cookout on Memorial Day. This year would be no different. The backyard was filled with the smell of the barbeque and the sight of Lawn Jarts flying through the air.

"While some were drinking, I certainly wasn't. I was very nervous, thinking of how my life would change if I joined such a coaching legend and renowned program.

"Around five o'clock, the phone rang, and it was Woody himself. He came right out after asking me how Ginger and the kids were and told me that he was going with the other candidate. While he said I was just as qualified, he needed someone who had a strong knowledge of high school prospects along the East Coast, so he could recruit that area. The other candidate had that type of knowledge.

"While disappointed, I thanked him for being considered, and he said something I'll never forget. "Dick Strahm, you were so close this time. The next time I call, you'll be the person

I'm looking for.' While another opportunity never presented itself with Ohio State, I was very gratified to have been that close."

The 1972 season opened with so many holes to fill on both sides of the ball that it's a wonder Jack Murphy and his staff slept at all. There seemed to be quite a bit of stress in the air even during the August two-a-days before the regular season even began. Recalls Dick, "The two years before, there really was such a businesslike approach to preseason. Since we had so many players who had started since they were sophomores, they knew their roles and they also knew what they needed to do to prepare.

"But, with the uncertainty of our upcoming season, players and coaches were on edge.

"Well, one day at practice this big sophomore defensive lineman started arguing with me after I told him about a mistake he'd made in technique. The next thing I know, Jack Murphy came flying down this hill he was standing on and literally launched himself at the player. Both the player and Jack wound up on the ground.

"Now, usually Jack was a pretty mild-mannered guy, but he just couldn't stand the thought of any player disrespecting any of his coaches. He grabbed the player by the facemask while he was on the ground and yelled, 'Don't you EVER talk to one of my coaches like that, EVER!'

Recalls Murphy, "Well, it wasn't my most gracious moment, but I just couldn't let a player do that. I just feel it's critical to have a program where the coaches are fully in charge, and players totally respect that."

The Rockets opened their season on the road against a very good University of Tampa team, a team coached by the future Buckeye coach who would replace Woody Hayes, Earle Bruce.

The quarterback for Tampa that day was Freddie Solomon, who would one day play in the NFL, not as a quarterback, but as a wide receiver.

The mountain of a man the Toledoans had such trouble blocking that day was John Matuszak, a name very familiar to football fans. Matuszak eventually became the number-one pick in the entire draft class after the season was over. He went on to play on two Oakland Raider Super Bowl winning teams. A hard life of partying, which he documented in his 1987 autobiography, *Cruisin' with the Tooz*, may have contributed to an early death. The Tooz would not see his fortieth birthday, dying a year short of that milestone of heart failure.

While this strong Tampa squad finished the '72 season with a fine 10-2 record and a 21-18 win in the Tangerine Bowl over the Kent State Golden Flashes, one of its losses was not to the Rockets. The final score that day in Florida was 21-0. And, just like that, the streak was over.

The rest of the season was a classic up-and-down affair. After a 16-0 win in week two in Ypsilanti, Michigan, against Eastern Michigan, the school Strahm had attended for one semester when the institution was still known as Michigan State Normal, and a 38-24 Glass Bowl win over the University of Texas at Arlington, the Rockets stumbled twice. They lost in Athens to Ohio University, 38-22, and at home to Bowling Green, 19-8.

The Bowling Green loss was a bitter pill for big-brother Dick to swallow, since it gave the Falcon linebacker coach, Dale, bragging rights.

Recalls Dale, "Again, Dick and I had very little to say before the game. The win really felt good because it was the only one I ever had against him. When you're as good a coach as Dick was, you really don't have many opportunities to get him, so any you can get, you savor. He bought dinner that night!"

In week six, Toledo rebounded to defeat Western Michigan on the road, 20-13.

Using the momentum of that win, the Rockets built a modest three-game winning streak by beating Dayton on the road 20-17, and Miami at the Glass Bowl, 35-21.

In week nine, Northern Illinois gave Toledo a pretty sound licking, 30-7.

A win against Marshall in week ten, 21-0, at home, assured Toledo of a winning season, but the Rockets then stumbled on the final weekend, 27-9. Coaches constantly lament a final loss, that, were it a win, would have made the sound of the season record so much more appealing. Instead of what most coaches would say was a pretty sound season, 7-4, the final tally for the Rockets of 1972 was 6-5.

Nonetheless, Dan Simrell, who was in his second season as the Toledo secondary coach, felt the record was certainly not a mark of dishonor. "When you compare it to three consecutive undefeated and untied seasons, the record seems pretty ordinary, but how realistic is that type of sustained success? Considering how many three-year starters graduated in 1971, I think Jack Murphy and all the coaches did a pretty doggone good job. On defense alone, we had to replace eight of the eleven starters. Consider that before you ever even begin to talk of Ealey's departure.

"In retrospect, 1972 may have been our best coaching job."

After the season, Dick Strahm again attended the National Coaches' Convention in January. Dick ran into Kansas State head coach Vince Gibson, who invited him to lunch. This time, there was no doubt. Gibson did have an opening on his staff for a secondary coach.

While at the convention, Strahm also found out another up-and-coming coach was looking to fill an assistant's position. Bobby Bowden, head coach of West Virginia University, needed a linebacker coach.

Recalls Dick, "I had an interview with Coach Bowden at 8:00 a.m. in his hotel room the next morning. Coach Bowden must have liked what I had to say because he offered me the position that morning.

"I was so taken aback that I really didn't know what to say. I told him that I needed to make a few calls and would get right back to him. He told me he had to have an answer by 4:00 p.m.

"Later that morning, I met with Coach Gibson and interviewed for the Kansas State opening. He also offered me the position, which I was looking forward to, given our conversations a year earlier.

"I told Vince that I wanted the position, but I also wanted to take Ginger to see Manhattan, Kansas, and the campus. I asked if his athletic department would fly us out.

"Vince said that, ordinarily, they didn't pay for flights for assistants' candidates because of the drain on the athletic department budget, but he made some phone calls and received an okay that money could be set aside for that purpose.

"I then went back to my room and called Coach Bowden. Both he and Vince were from the South and knew each other. When Bowden asked me why I chose Kansas State over West Virginia, I told him that my going to the Big Eight would give me an opportunity to coach in, what many felt, was the best college football conference in the nation at that time.

"I'll never forget what he then said to me. He laughed and said, 'Now correct me if I'm wrong, but aren't Oklahoma and Nebraska in that conference?' When I said that they certainly were, he said, 'Son, you're never going to beat them. You know that, but I guess you just need to see that for yourself up close.' At any rate, he wished me luck.

"While I felt I was making the right decision at the time, who knew then that Coach Bowden would take the Florida State job in 1976 and establish one of the best programs in college football history, and, in such a nice warm climate to boot!

"How often there are two roads to travel, and you have to choose one. Anyway, Ginger and I were excited about our move out to Kansas. Actually, I was probably a little more excited than Ginger. There's always a great deal of work involved in moving a family to a brand new place, and this was the fifth time we'd done this. I'm not sure a lot of people, besides maybe career military families, who understand the difficulty of the frequent moves coaches often make.

"Within a week, Ginger and I were on a plane to Manhattan. It was a small town [less than 50,000], much, much smaller than Toledo. But Kansas State was, as far as its conference affiliation, on a big stage by being a member of the Big Eight.

"While I would miss Toledo, I really wanted an opportunity to compete against the best, and, at that time, a strong argument could be made that the Big Eight was the best football conference in the country. Of course, the two biggest dogs on the block in that conference were Oklahoma and Nebraska. Maybe, as Coach Bowden suggested, I just had to see these two huge dogs for myself, up close and very personal. I don't know. What's that they say? 'In order to be the best, you have to beat the best.' Maybe that's why I made the decision to come to K-State.

"The life of a coach's wife, at times, isn't an easy life. I was yet asking Ginger again to leave a home, to pick up everything, and to put everything back down in yet another place. I was just so fortunate in my career to have someone who supported me as strongly and lovingly as Ginger. She just went back to Toledo with me and began packing boxes."

In the football offices on the UT campus, life would go on. Jack Murphy remained as head coach through the 1976 season when he retired from college coaching.

Murphy remembers how his time at UT opened doors for him career-wise after he stepped down. "I worked for Envirosafe Hazardous Waste Landfill. Just like football, the job gave me an opportunity to work with people. I also was given an opportunity to work in customer relations with a very successful beer distributorship. The fact that people knew me from my coaching really helped me get my foot in some doors in the Toledo community, that's for sure.

"Toledo has been so very good for the Murphys. Given my position with the university, my kids were able to attend UT tuition-free. The people have been so kind to the Murphys. I guess that's why I never left.

"I've also stayed in close touch with the football program. I've been a season ticket holder for twenty-five years and very rarely miss a game at the Glass Bowl.

"While I'm at the games, I don't feel it's my place to be down on the sidelines." Jack Murphy adds with a chuckle something that all coaches can relate to, "So, I just sit up in the stands and yell, 'Pass the ball!'"

Murphy does attend some practices, and that has as much to do with head coach Tom Amstutz as anything. "Tom was a junior on my last team in '76. He was a very gutsy player, and I think he brings that same passion to the coaching sidelines."

Dan Simrell stepped into Strahm's former shoes in 1973 as defensive coordinator. He held that position under both Jack Murphy and his successor Chuck Stobart. Then, when Stobart left to take the head coaching position at the University of Utah, Simrell became the Rocket head coach and remained from 1982 through 1989.

Simrell would then move on to coach at the University of Memphis and eventually at West Virginia University under former Bowling Green coach Don Nehlen.

As the wheel turns in college coaching, Simrell placed a call in 1999 to his old friend and mentor Dick Strahm during a time when Simrell was still the Mountaineers' offensive coordinator and quarterback coach. Recalls Dan, "I called Dick to get his assessment of a strong-armed quarterback who'd just finished up his high school career in Findlay. All of pro football would one day know the name, Ben Roethlisberger.

"I really had no intention of applying for The University of Findlay coaching job until Dick asked me if that's why I called right at the beginning of our conversation. The coach who succeeded Dick after he retired at the end of the '98 season, Doug Coate, decided to move on after one season.

"The more I thought about it, the more it appealed to me. I had been gone from northwest Ohio for quite a long time and was kind of anxious to get back. I had just helped develop the best quarterback I would ever coach in my career, Marc Bulger, who signed a multi-million dollar extension in 2007 with the St. Louis Rams.

"A lot of people have asked me why I would ever leave voluntarily such a successful program as West Virginia where our teams routinely would play before 75,000 or more. But to be honest, that never appealed to me much. I really enjoy the teaching aspect of my profession, and I'm just as comfortable doing that in stadiums filled with 7,500.

"Ultimately, I did apply and, probably with a good word from Dick, got the job. I coached the Oilers from 2000 through the 2006 season before moving on to Tri-State University."

Simrell continues to have so much admiration for Dick Strahm. "He couldn't have been more supportive of me when I started in college coaching at UT. Years later, after I had seen all the medical adversities that Dick overcame with heart, cancer, and stroke, I decided to honor him.

"In 2001, while I was coaching at the same school that he had given four NAIA national championships, I started the Dick Strahm Courage Award. I gave it to the player that best exemplified courage in duress. Dick is maybe the toughest nut I've ever met, which is one of the reasons I so admire him."

And, when it was time for the Strahms to pack yet again and head for an unfamiliar place, Ginger and Dick drew strength from each other. Of course, there were uncertainties and a myriad of challenges lay ahead.

Toledo, Ohio, and Manhattan, Kansas, are 854 miles apart. That much Dick knew. What he couldn't have imagined was how very different things would be putting a product on the field before crowds quadruple the size of those who filled Toledo's Glass Bowl. Whether Dick and Ginger would regret the move, only time would tell.

The vapors of the Rockets' red glare had long since dissipated in the skies above the Bancroft Street campus after the improbable run of 1969-1971, but the afterglow would live on in the minds of all who witnessed what had streaked across the northwest Ohio autumnal skies.

Chapter 8

Manhattan, Kansas, and a Pair of Purple Pride Years

Why Dick Strahm left his hometown to travel close to 900 miles and relocate his family yet again had less to do with his wanting to leave the familiar surroundings of Toledo, Ohio, and more to do with his wanting to find out what the Big Eight Conference and its powerhouse teams were all about. Strahm remembers well the reputation that the Big Eight Conference had in the early 1970s. "While I was very pleased with what we had accomplished at Toledo, I really wanted to see what college football looked like at its highest level.

"I got very close when I almost got a chance to join Coach Hayes at Ohio State. Well, then I got to know Coach Gibson at the National Coaches' Convention, and he offered me a chance to join his Kansas State staff in what many believed was the ultimate league in all of college football.

"Schools like Colorado, Missouri, Oklahoma State, and the two superpowers, Oklahoma and Nebraska, were programs with national reputation. In addition to Kansas State, there were also the University of Kansas and Iowa State, which kind of formed the second tier of the conference. Now, I had no delusions of grandeur heading to Manhattan, Kansas. I knew Kansas State was not an elite program, and I also knew it was not even the most successful Big Eight team in its own state, since the University of Kansas had earned that right to say it was. I also knew the enrollment at Kansas State was the smallest of any of the other Big Eight schools.

"However, I just felt comfortable with Coach Gibson. He seemed fully dedicated, and if we could just get out on the recruiting trail and really worked and prepared, well, then I felt some good things might happen.

"I guess I just thought playing Nebraska, Oklahoma, Missouri, and Colorado sounded like a great challenge and opportunity. And, I really did feel that way. Listen, if you love something as much as I have football, you want to compete against the best, and that's what I intended to do."

The 2004 College Football Hall of Fame dinner in South Bend, Indiana: (from left) Hayden Fry, Doug Dickey, Barry Sanders, Dick Strahm, Bill Stromberg, and Roger Wehrli.

So, for Dick, Ginger, 9-year-old Doug, and 6-year-old Gina, it was off to become members of what was known around Manhattan as Purple Pride, since K-State's primary uniform color was purple.

While bigger than some cities that have universities at their hubs, Manhattan is certainly much smaller than conference cities like Lincoln, Nebraska (where the Nebraska Cornhuskers play), and Norman, Oklahoma (the home city of the Oklahoma Sooners).

Historically, Manhattan, a city of around 50,000, is located in northeast Kansas, right in the middle of what the Chamber of Commerce would tout as the scenic Flint Hills. Known as the "Little Apple," the city that *Money Magazine* designated as one of the top ten best places in the country to retire, is situated just off Interstate 70 and is 120 miles west of Kansas City. The permanent military post, Fort Riley, is nearby, halfway between Manhattan and Junction City. The military installation is one of the largest and most important in the entire country.

For the Strahms, west remained their favorite compass point. Just as they had done in Warren and Toledo, Ohio, they bought a home on the west side of the Little Apple. As a matter of fact, Cedar Crest was the last street on the west side of Manhattan. Anything further west would have put the Strahms smack dab in the middle of miles and miles of Kansas farmland. Recalls Dick, "When I looked west from our new backyard, all I could see were wheat fields. Then, if I looked directly east, I could see the fairgrounds. Really, it was a wonderful place to sometimes just get away from all the problems that come with trying to play successful big-time college football. Some evenings, I'd just go out in the backyard and sit on a lawn chair and look at all that open space in the reflection of the moon."

As far as neighbors, there were some in the new housing development on the edge of town. One, in particular, was a source of endless fascination for the youngest Strahms, Doug and Gina. Recalls Dick, "Doctor Morrison and his wife, who was a registered nurse, lived just across the street and were just great people. They had adopted fourteen children. Certainly, as one might imagine, they were very giving people who loved and nurtured children who really needed someone and something they could count on.

"We spent quite a bit of time with them, especially watching the kids play. Of course, Doug and Gina were thrilled to have so many playmates. Really, they were the kind of family that enriched you by knowing them. While we were only in Kansas a short time, relatively speaking, meeting people like this was very special.

As far as Dick's chosen profession, he was ready to, one might say, jump right into the deep end. "I couldn't wait to get started. Fortunately, we were able to wrap things up in Toledo in plenty of time to get to Kansas State for spring practice. This gave me a good opportunity to meet the rest of the coaching staff and the players.

Of course, every coaching staff centers on the head coach, and, at Kansas State, there was no doubt who was in charge. Vince Gibson arrived on the K-State scene in 1967. His path to coaching in the Big Eight wound throughout the South.

After graduating from Woodlawn High School in Birmingham, Alabama, Gibson went to Florida State University in Tallahassee, where he lettered three varsity years in football. After graduating in 1955, he cut his coaching teeth at South Georgia Junior College for three years and then returned to Florida State as a defensive coach from 1959 through 1963.

Then, it was on to Knoxville, to coach at the University of Tennessee for three more years before getting the opportunity to become a head coach at Kansas State. While it was a daunting task, he embraced it. When Gibson arrived in Manhattan, the Wildcats had lost 21 straight games and 43 of its last 48.

Additionally, the stadium was antiquated and also microscopic by Big Eight standards, seating only 22,000 when filled to capacity.

Gibson, along with athletic director Ernie Barrett, led a successful push for a new stadium. Known as KSU Stadium, the brand-new facility almost doubled its capacity to 42,000. It also featured one of the conference's first artificial surfaces. At the open end of the stadium was an ultra-modern office and football complex that Barrett boasted was without equal in the conference.

Recalls Strahm, the new 39-year-old defensive backs coach, "The locker room, weight room, training room, and other workout rooms were on the ground floor. On the floor above that was a great reception room, the coaches' offices, and a large meeting room which looked out over the stadium. This room was not only used for team meetings but also for recruiting when we would have Saturday on-campus recruiting visits. I can remember thinking that if we weren't successful, we certainly couldn't blame it on poor facilities."

While Coach Gibson had only gone 3-8 the previous year, 1972, he, nonetheless, could point to some progress. In 1970, led by Osawatomie, Kansas, native and All-Big Eight quarterback Lynn Dickey, the Wildcats finished second in the conference. After that fruitful senior year, Dickey was off to a very successful NFL career that spanned a remarkable fifteen years with the Green Bay Packers and the Houston Oilers.

Gibson's teams also had beaten every team in the conference, including the powerful Cornhuskers of Nebraska and the Sooners of Oklahoma, at least once. Perhaps, his 24-39 record while at K-State may not seem like much to those not familiar with Kansas State football history at the time. However, putting everything in perspective, Gibson's win total had been the most by any coach since A.W. McMillin's 29 from 1928 to 1933.

Additionally, eleven of Gibson's recruits had made All-Conference, and several (Dickey, Clarence Scott, Ron Yankowski, Ron Dickerson, and Larry Brown) had gone on to play in the pros.

However, there was also, what some would call, a cloud hanging over Gibson's tenure in the form of a three-year NCAA probation for some recruiting improprieties. For the enthusiastic Dick Strahm and the rest of the Kansas State staff, it was just another obstacle to be surmounted.

During Strahm's first days on the job in February of 1973, the Libbey and University of Toledo graduate met his fellow assistant coaches.

First, there was the 25-year-old Ron Dickerson, who would assist Dick with the defensive backs. Dickerson was recruited by Gibson in 1967 and had a very successful collegiate career as a defensive back. Drafted by the Miami Dolphins, Dickerson saw his dream of a long NFL career explode when he suffered a badly broken leg.

One of the veterans on Gibson's staff was Bobby Jackson, the defensive coordinator and linebacker coach. The Georgia native played for Gibson at South Georgia Junior College, before going on to Big Spring, Texas, to play at Howard College, where he was named a Little All-American. Five years of coaching at Florida State and coaching stints at Iowa State and Tampa University completed his coaching training for his current role in Manhattan.

Like Jackson, Gene McDowell was also a veteran on the staff. Hailing from Waycross, Georgia, McDowell was a three-year starter at Florida State before coaching there a year. McDowell coached the Purple Pride's defensive ends.

There were also those who, like Strahm, were new on the scene. The offensive coordinator, Bob Weber, had just arrived following his stint as the head coach at the University of Arizona.

Another first-year assistant was Atlanta native Billy Cox, the receivers' coach. Cox had also played at Florida State, where Vince Gibson both played and coached.

Bob Hitch was yet another Southerner in his first year. Hitch was from Glendora, Mississippi, and had just finished a four-year stint in Hattiesburg, Mississippi, as the defensive coordinator of the University of Southern Mississippi.

Offensive line coach Ted Heath certainly had some stories with which he could regale his fellow coaches. He was a high school teammate of Joe Namath back in Beaver Falls, Pennsylvania.

Rounding out Gibson's staff was someone who brought a bit of Dick's background with him. Tom Dimitroff, the offensive backs' coach, arrived in Manhattan the previous year, from Miami of Ohio, a Mid-American Conference rival during Strahm's Rocket years. Dimitroff also played football at Miami before graduating in 1958.

For Dick Strahm, these were the men with whom he would spend more time during the football season than his own family. Such was the commitment these men of the gridiron were expected to make to foster a winning program.

By the later stages of February, most of the prized high school players had made their commitments to play for the colleges of their choice. However, in 1973, there were still two prizes, players who had yet to formally announce their intentions during Dick's first month on Vince Gibson's staff. They were players who could play for any team in all of college football, and as such, they were players also coveted by Gibson.

Recalls Dick, "Ross Browner and Gary Jeter were two of the top high school players in the nation. Both were defensive linemen who had incredible upsides. They both were around 6'4" inches and 250 pounds and were as quick as they were strong.

"Certainly, both were on the verge of signing with big-time college powers, but Coach Gibson got it in his head that, somehow, I could get them to Manhattan for a campus visit.

"You see, he knew Browner was at Warren Western Reserve and that I had coached there, and he thought that could be the 'in' little old K-State needed to grab maybe him and also his friend Jeter.

"As far as Jeter, he and Browner developed a friendship playing in a couple of all-star games after their senior seasons. So, Vince actually thought I could convince these two young men to see what Manhattan looked like in February!

"I tried to reason with Coach Gibson that it was a pretty well-known fact that it was almost a certainty that Browner would be attending Notre Dame and Jeter, Southern Cal, but my new boss was adamant that I make a phone call to Browner. As a matter of fact, Vince even added some incentive. He told me that if I could get both Browner and Jeter to come for a campus visit, he would send Ginger and me to Kansas City for a big weekend, with hotel, dinner, the works!

"So, I decided I didn't have anything to lose and called Ross back in Warren. Now, I had left Warren when Ross was just finishing up his freshman year, so he certainly remembered me. He told me he'd just turned down Ohio State and Michigan and had pretty much decided he was going to go to Notre Dame. He also told me Jeter was about to make it official with Southern Cal as well.

"Now, at that time, a high school recruit could take as many campus visits as he wanted, so I sold him on that angle. I asked that he fly in with his buddy Jeter and spend the weekend in Manhattan and let me show them around.

"I leveled with him. I told him I didn't expect either him or Jeter to have any changes of heart, but they didn't have much to lose by making a visit.

"So, he then told me he'd come and would get Jeter to visit with him. When I got off the phone, I immediately called Coach Gibson.

"The next Saturday, these two absolute specimens flew into Salina Airport, and I picked them up. I drove them all around the campus and showed them our facilities, and I really think they were impressed. I think maybe they thought Kansas Sate sat out in the middle of a farm field.

"Now, don't get me wrong. I didn't think they were going to turn down the Fighting Irish and the Trojans, but I do think they liked what they saw.

"Now like some universities, we had a group of twenty or so coeds who dressed in their purple and white outfits to meet our recruits Saturday mornings after breakfast. It was their job to show the recruits around campus and to take them to meet with certain faculty members.

"After lunch, the 'Gibson girls' would take the recruits out to Coach Gibson's house. If the girls were busy, then the coaches would take them to Gibson's house. Vince had an unbelievable basement, with pinball machines, a ping-pong table, a pool table and a couple large televisions. Our recruits had a great time. Of course, all sorts of food was available.

"That night, a couple of varsity football players took Ross and Gary to a Kansas State basketball game. K-State generally had a very good basketball team under head coach Jack Hartman. I remember the big star at that time was Lon Kruger, who has gone on to become a very successful; basketball coach as well.

"Then, Sunday morning, I picked up Ross and Gary, who had stayed with a couple of our players in the athletic dorm, and took them back over to Coach Gibson's house. While I read the paper in the living room, Vince talked to them in his office.

"They told him they'd remained sure of their decision to go to Notre Dame and Southern Cal. However, they also thanked him and, a bit later, me as well, for the opportunity to see the campus. Then, I drove them back to the airport for their return flight.

"Of course, Vince wasn't surprised they didn't change their minds, but he was positively beaming that we got them to make a visit. I think he felt it gave Kansas State some credibility and also gave him some ammunition for future recruits, letting them know that prospects like Browner and Jeter visited K-State and really enjoyed their visit, although we were a little too late getting to them. Also, Ginger and I had a great time on our weekend in Kansas City!"

For both Gibson and Strahm and the rest of the Wildcat coaches, recruiting was indeed the program's biggest challenge. Recalls Strahm, "If KSU was ever to make the jump into the top half of the conference, we needed to get the Browners and the Jeters not only to visit but to commit. They turned out to be great players. Both wound up making All-American, and both played more than ten years apiece in the NFL. All of us were aware of the fact we needed this type of athlete, but, given our size and the fact that we weren't a nationally renowned school, it was exceedingly tough to go toe-to-toe for top recruits with the superpowers like Nebraska and Oklahoma, not to mention the elite programs from other regions of the country."

During the rest of the winter and spring, Strahm concentrated on putting names to faces for all of the Wildcat players through helping to run Vince Gibson's off-season workout program. Two players who were juniors, in particular, impressed him, and they happened to be roommates. Their names were Gordon Chambliss and Steve Grogan.

Chambliss, as Dick surmised, as soon as the red-shirt junior free safety opened his mouth, spoke the same language as most of the coaching staff. He was from Birmingham, Alabama, and was recruited by Coach Gibson as a quarterback. Recalls Chambliss, "After leaving Huffman High School, I competed hard my first year to be the starter on the freshman team. At the time, freshmen weren't eligible to play varsity [and wouldn't be until a rule change was enacted in 1971], but I sure wanted to establish myself as the starter for my class, so I could hopefully become the varsity starter by the time I was a junior. That was, basically, the time frame for college players at that time.

"I was in the process of doing some pretty good things leading up to our opener against our big in-state rival, the University of Kansas, and had earned the start. Then, about two weeks before the game, I got injured in practice. I tore some ligaments in my elbow and couldn't throw.

"Come game time, I dressed, but I've got my elbow heavily taped and can't do anything more than go through pre-game warm-ups and hand the ball off in running some plays with the second-team offense before the kickoff. Even just taking snaps was painful. Needless to say, I was very disappointed that I wouldn't be playing that day.

"Well, come game time, I was standing on the sidelines watching the Kansas quarterback who would go on to become an All-American by the time he was an upperclassman and then also go on to play in the NFL, David Jaynes, throwing that old pigskin all over the field.

"We had a free safety by the name of Bruce Lester, and he was knocked out when he came up to stop a sweep and got kneed in the head. Now, understand that, besides being injured, I had never played a down of defense in my entire high school career.

"A graduate assistant coach looked around and saw me and said, 'Chambliss, do you know what a deep third is, and can you play cover three?' I said, 'Yes, sir, I can play a deep third. As a quarterback, I knew what coverages defensive backfields employed. A deep third is what is also known as a cover three. That means the two cornerbacks cover any receiver deep in their thirds of the field, and the free safety takes any receiver who runs a deep pattern in the middle third.

"Well, I went in, taped elbow and all, and on the very first play, Jaynes threw deep down the middle, you know, trying to pick on the new guy, thinking he was the weak link. But, I was, somehow, able to cross in front of the receiver and intercepted the ball.

"After the game, the defensive coach, R.C. Slocum, who has gone on to make a pretty big name for himself in college coaching, particularly as the head coach at Texas A & M, walked up to me and said, 'Son, you'll never play another down on offense as long as you're here.' And, I never did."

Chambliss' roommate was Steve Grogan. Despite being a year younger, he and Chambliss both had two years of eligibility. For Grogan, his time to start was almost upon him. He had seen some varsity action as a sophomore, and the 6'4" Ottawa, Kansas, native was penciled in as the 1973 starter.

In high school, Grogan was an All-State selection in both football and basketball and recalls his senior year at Ottawa High School. "I guess you might say I was the subject of some pretty spirited recruiting, at least from the two state universities, Kansas and Kansas State.

"While I really liked basketball better, at 6'4", I played inside in high school. But, I really was too short to play there in college and hadn't really demonstrated much of a jump-shot and ball-handling game so I wasn't offered any basketball scholarships.

"Football was my better sport anyway, but I really hated to leave basketball behind when I left high school.

"Anyway, in high school, we played in one of the best football conferences in the state, the Eastern Kansas League. The league produced three quarterbacks who would go on to play in the NFL. Besides me, there was David Jaynes, who played in Banner Spring, and Tom Owens, from Turner High School in Kansas City.

"The reason I didn't decide to head to Lawrence and play for the Jayhawks of Kansas University, is Jaynes went there the year before. I figured he'd start all the way through his senior year, and that meant the best-case scenario is I would get to start one year.

"So, I accepted Coach Gibson's scholarship and headed off to Manhattan."

Chambliss remembers the arduous nature of Vince Gibson's off-season program. "Coach Gibson was, in my opinion, a fine coach, but he was really very aggressive. By that, I mean, he ran probably the toughest off-season football program in the country. Besides the weightlifting and the running, we wrestled a lot.

"If you lost, you stayed on the mat and wrestled again. One day, I had lost like four straight times and had absolutely expended about every ounce of energy in my body. I got up and started to walk towards the door to go do my running drills, thinking surely about 20 straight minutes of what amounted to hand-to-hand combat was enough.

"One of the assistants said, 'If you go out that door, it's a long walk back to Alabama.' I got the message real fast and turned around and got back on the mat. I, somehow, dug something out from deep within, something I probably at that time didn't even know I had, and won the next match and then was allowed to go outside.

"We also did something the coaches called 'stick wrestling.' Here's how it worked. You had two players facing each other on their knees. Each would put a hand on a stick wrapped in athletic tape, which was probably about twenty-four inches long. One of the coaches blew a whistle, and it was almost mortal combat. Man-on-man, no holds barred, and no rules, you did whatever it took to get the stick away from your opponent. Let me tell you. It could get brutal!"

During such intensely physical confrontations, Dick Strahm went about his duties oblivious to the indoor training. "I really wasn't involved in the indoor program that Gordon remembers. Coach Cox and I were outside on the artificial turf in the stadium conducting the running drills.

"Now that I think about it, the players coming out from inside certainly did appear glad to be outside with us. When some emerged, they did seem pretty well spent physically."

During the summer before the 1973 opener, Coach Dick Strahm was made aware there were some perks to being part of a big-time coaching staff in a relatively small town. "Living so close to the fairgrounds allowed Ginger to see horses when the county fair or 4H shows would be there. She's always loved horses. As a matter of fact, she's always been quite an artist and has drawn and painted many horses.

"When I told Vince of Ginger's interest in horses, his eyes kind of lit up. He told me he knew a very prominent rancher who had a lot of horses on his land, just west of where we lived. Well, one day, Vince arranged for us to go out to the ranch, and we met the owner of the ranch. He loaded us into the back of a vehicle with an open viewing area. We took off, and we were driving all over his multi-acre spread. He was pointing out different things.

"Suddenly, we were coming over a rise, and there was a whole herd of horses running free on the range. It was quite a beautiful sight.

"The rancher must have seen the look of wonder and appreciation in Ginger's eyes because, the next thing I know, he said, 'Pick one out that you like. That'll be yours.'

"Well, we continued our tour, and she spotted one she really liked and instantly named it Danny Boy. It was a beautiful, large animal, probably about seventeen hands high.

"The rancher literally gave her the horse. He also allowed us to keep it in a stall in his horse barn and had his hands feed him. Ginger would go out to groom the animal and, of course, she could ride him anytime she wanted. Both she and Gina would go out to ride quite a bit.

"Both Ginger and Gina became pretty accomplished riders. One day, Ginger said, 'You need to learn how to ride. Get on Danny Boy and ride him.' Now, I was a city kid. Despite the fact that I used to go out to my grandpa's farm when I was a kid, I had never ridden a horse in my life.

"So, I agreed to take a ride. It didn't seem all that hard. I'd watched both Ginger and even little Gina do it. I got on and started riding. Well, suddenly, the saddle slid to the side, and I was riding at an angle. There were fence posts to the right, and the horse was getting closer and closer to them. I was yelling, 'Stop!' but the horse didn't respond. I was later told the horse only responded to 'Whoa.'

"Finally, one of the ranchers jumped off his horse, ran up, and grabbed the reins. He led the horse back to the barn. I don't mind telling you, I was a little shaken up, and I vowed right then and there that I was done with my equestrian career! I haven't been on a horse since."

The rest of the summer passed, and it was time to see what the K-State 'Cats could do in the 1973 football campaign. The opener was against the highly touted Florida Gators. Recalls Strahm, "We flew to Gainesville, Florida, on Friday. For all our away games, we always left the day before and stayed at a hotel on Friday nights.

"The Gator coach was Doug Dickey. Little could I have imagined, or probably Doug either for that matter, that he and I would share the dais some thirty-one years later during the induction ceremonies at the College Football Hall of Fame."

Despite the 21-10 loss, the Kansas State coaching staff had every reason to feel that perhaps '73 would be a successful season, if only they could coach their young men to avoid mistakes. On a rainy, humid Florida afternoon, the Wildcats fumbled the ball five times, had a Steve Grogan pass intercepted, and were guilty of killer 15-yard penalties on all three of the Florida touchdown drives. Especially costly was KSU running back Isaac Jackson's fumble as he was trying to dive over from the one-yard line for a score.

In week two, the Wildcats were home, and, before the Manhattan home folks, they used a strong pass rush and excellent secondary play by Gordon Chambliss and his mates to record the school's first shutout in twenty-eight games, 21-0, over the Tulsa Golden Hurricanes of the Missouri Valley Conference.

Recalls Strahm, "As a first-year defensive backfield coach, I was thrilled to get the shutout. It seemed that much of what I and Coach Dickerson had been doing with our secondary was coming together. I thought it was their second straight strong performance. Against Florida, I knew their quarterback David Bowden threw three touchdown passes, but, with all the fumbles, the offenses kept putting them on such short fields."

Week three saw a return to the state of Florida, and this time, against Tampa University. The result was much more to Coach Gibson's liking than the first trip to the Sunshine State.

For Strahm, he was again very pleased with his secondary, with a second straight 21-0 win. The game did allow Dick some measure of revenge. "I really wanted this game badly. It was Tampa, led by their fine quarterback, Freddy Solomon, that snapped our 35-game streak last year when I was at Toledo. This time, we really contained Solomon."

The following week back home in Manhattan on Band Day, Kansas State extended their record to 3-1 with a hard-fought 21-16 victory over Memphis State. The game was certainly a comeback effort as KSU trailed at one point 10-0. However, a 36-yard strike from Grogan to Henry Childs put the home team on the scoreboard. From there, Isaac Jackson went over the top for a touchdown to start the comeback. For the talented Jackson, it was the third straight game he topped the 100-yard mark rushing.

Despite the win, Strahm had to be concerned with his secondary. Memphis State's quarterback Joe Brunner riddled his secondary for 20 completions and 250 yards.

In week five, the Wildcats were home to open the conference part of their schedule on Parents' Day, against Iowa State. The parents and the rest of the Purple Pride nation were tickled with the outcome, a 21-19 win, and a fourth consecutive win. The play of the game was an unbelievable 24-yard TD run by Jackson, a play in which he broke five tackles.

For Strahm, the upcoming week would be much like the first five weeks. Sure, it was a big upcoming game with in-state rival Kansas University on the road in Lawrence, a game which many Kansans referred to as the Sunflower Showdown, but Strahm had come to realize that his typical work week never varied as far as the amount of time expended, regardless of who the Wildcats were playing.

"Monday, Tuesday, and Wednesday mornings were always the same, with a 7:30 a.m. staff meeting with the head coach. After the meeting ended, we would go into separate offensive and defensive meeting rooms, where we would spend the rest of the morning.

"The rest of Monday afternoon, we'd be watching films of our next opponent and devising a game plan. Then, of course, late afternoon, we'd practice for two hours.

"After a quick dinner, I'd go back to my office and continued to break down film. As a defensive backs' coach, I would be looking for pass routes, when teams ran certain pass plays, in terms of down and distance, and out of what formation. Now, this was very time consuming because I needed to chart every pass play. What passes were they likely to throw in the red zone [inside the opponent's 20-yard line]? What passes were they likely to throw inside their own 20-yard line or even coming out of their own end zone? I'd often times be at this around three or four hours.

"On Tuesdays, we coaches met in the morning under the direction of Coach Gibson. We would talk about player personnel and get injury updates from our trainer. We also would formulate that day's practice schedule and discuss anything else the head coach wanted done that particular day. At the conclusion of the staff meeting, the coaches would separate to the offensive or defensive meeting rooms to put the offensive and defensive game plans together. Then, we prepared the practice plan for that day.

"Before practice on Tuesday, I met with my defensive backs to show them films of our opponent's last game. I wanted my guys to know tendencies and situations as well as I knew them. I wanted them to know who the favorite receivers were, who the deep threat was, and who the possession receiver was. I also passed out a sheet of information about the opponent's quarterback and receivers and all the tendencies I could give. That written report was to be with them at all times. Then, it was time for another two hours of practice.

"On Wednesday afternoons I again would meet with my defensive backs to review games films. Wednesday evenings, you would find coaches in their offices making recruiting calls.

"On Thursday, our staff meeting would start at 8:15 a.m. Then we would again go to our offensive and defensive meeting rooms, where we continued to refine our game plan, based on what we were seeing at practice, and we also planned our final changes that we wanted to insert at practice that day, since it would be the last practice of the week if the game was away. This week, it was, with the University of Kansas in Lawrence.

"Then, at Thursday's practice, we also had to allow for extra time spent on special teams. Each practice prior to Thursday's, we would work on a couple aspects of special teams, but Thursday, we worked on all phases of it. We practiced kickoffs, kickoff receiving, field goal, field goal block, punt, and punt return.

Right after practice on Thursdays, most of the assistant coaches had to get ready to take off for their booster clubs, which always met Thursday nights. Most of the coaches had a group they were responsible for. Mine was in Kansas City, which was about a 90-minute drive. Coach Bobby Jackson and I were both responsible for the Kansas City club.

"If we had an away game after the booster club meeting, I would head back to Manhattan. I would try to take a player with me since we would be returning to Kansas State. Gordon Chambliss or Steve Grogan would often travel with me to speak to the booster clubs. Sometimes it was Coach Jackson and myself. If Jackson could not make the trip, I'd take my son Doug.

"Now, if it was a home game, after the meeting on Thursday evening I'd check into a hotel. Since Kansas City, Kansas, was one of my recruiting areas, the next morning, I would go to the local high schools and visit with the high school coaches. Then, Friday night, I'd go to one of our recruit's football games. It would be well past midnight before my head would hit the pillow Saturday morning.

"If it was an away game, the players, coaches, and support staff would arrive at the football offices at 8:00 on Friday morning. Then, we boarded buses for the airport. We wanted to arrive in our opponent's city early to check into our hotel and then get to the stadium for our light workout. For short trips, we'd take buses, but departure time was always in the morning.

"For home games, I was at the stadium Saturday mornings by 8:00 a.m. Then, of course, there were final meetings and preparations. Then, it was kickoff time and, also, time to see what all those hours of preparation were for.

"Saturday nights, I finally got to spend time with my family. Of course, for home games, I'd be home after our post-game coaches' meeting. For away games, it would generally be around 9:00 in the evening before I got home. There were times Ginger and I would go out, and, if it was with the other coaches and their wives, any talk of football was forbidden, as far as the wives were concerned. But, when you spend so much time preparing for a common goal, I will tell you that it was very difficult to not let some football talk creep into our conversations. Other times, we just stayed in, and I just enjoyed a night away from all the meetings and game film and practice.

"The break didn't last long, though. Sunday morning, our defensive staff would meet to grade film from the previous day's game. That would take up to three or four hours, since we were breaking down every play and re-running the projector over and over, grading the performance of all of our starters on each snap.

"In the afternoon, we'd meet with the defensive team to review the game film, while the offense would have a light 90-minute workout with some running and weightlifting. Then the offense and defense would switch. While the offense would be in the film room, the defense would be split between the weight room and doing their running out in the stadium. That would take us up to dinner. So, the players and coaches would go to the cafeteria in the athletic dorm to eat together. That would give us coaches a chance to talk to the players about the previous day's game and also what was ahead.

Then, the coaches would return to their offices to preview the film of our next opponent for a couple hours to make Monday morning's film study more productive.

For Strahm and the rest of the coaches, the cycle was seemingly endless, from August through late November. The amount of hours fulfilling football duties was staggering, often 80-90 hours or more a week. Not only is it a tremendous strain on coaches but also on their families.

No one is more aware of this than Dick Strahm. "I can't even calculate the number of times I've told people that whatever success I've had in football would never have happened without Ginger's and my kids' support. In my forty-plus years of coaching, I've seen a lot of cases of burnout. Sometimes, it was with the coaches, but, just as often, it was the families who suffer the stress of a husband and father not being around very much, especially during the season. Without my family's love and support, well, where would I be?"

The match-up in week six with Kansas was known throughout the state as "The Sunflower Showdown." While certainly games with superpowers Oklahoma and Nebraska generated a lot of buzz, the fact is that K-State versus Kansas was THE game every fall.

The winner of the week-six contest between KU and KSU would receive the Governor's Cup, presented by, of course, the state's top politico. More often than not, it was the Jayhawks of Kansas that received the Cup, as they held a decided advantage in the all-time series, 47-19-4 heading into the '73 contest.

In this game the Wildcats' challenge would be to stop a very explosive aerial attack. The game would match two former Eastern Kansas League (EKL) standouts, Steve Grogan and David Jaynes.

For former high school competitors, there was something to prove beyond winning the game. For Steve Grogan, the KSU signal caller, it was a chance to show everyone back home, and everyone in the EKL, that he was every bit the equal of Jaynes.

The game in Lawrence was played before a raucous crowd of 52,000 at Memorial Stadium, which listed its capacity at 500 fewer than were wedged in on that brilliant Saturday afternoon. The game was a classic. The visiting Wildcats had "it" and then lost "it" in the end.

Leading 18-17 and having the ball with just 2:46 in the contest, Coach Vince Gibson had every reason to think that it would be he who would be accepting the trophy from the governor and shaking his hand after the game. That is, until KU's Dean Zook recovered a fumble by the Wildcats' Bill Holman at the KSU 40-yard line. Jaynes demonstrated why he was on his way to being selected an All-American as he directed the Jayhawks on a five-play drive that ended with his own touchdown run and a 25-18 win. With that, the Wildcats lost their chance to go 5-1 heading into the minefield of their conference schedule. What a confidence booster that might have been.

Just as Strahm and the rest of his coaches feared, the heart-rending last-minute defeat was one that had a month's worth of residual effects.

In week seven, the Oklahoma Sooners, under first-year head coach Barry Switzer, ruined Homecoming in Manhattan. Switzer would use his first year as a springboard to national championships in both 1974 and 1975. Ten years after that, he would add a third before re-emerging years later as the coach of the Dallas Cowboys to win a Super Bowl. Switzer and Jimmy Johnson are the only coaches to claim both a collegiate national championship and a Super Bowl title.

KSU turned the ball over three times early, and the Sooners, led by the mercurial Joe Washington, who would become the Big Eight's top rusher by season's end, scored touchdowns off of all three miscues. By halftime, Oklahoma was up 35-7, and, by game's end, the physical domination of brothers Dewey and Lucious Selmon and All-American linebacker Rod Shoate sent no less than four K-State offensive linemen to the sidelines with injuries.

The following week, KSU traveled to Columbia to face the Missouri Tigers. They returned a 31-7 loser, despite trailing just 10-7 at halftime. The key play of the second half was a K-State fumble recovery that was nullified by its own off-sides penalty.

Behind a depleted offensive line, Grogan ran often out of desperation and was hauled down for losses several times. This largely accounted for the paltry nine total yards of rushing.

Week nine was another case of a team overpowering K-State physically. Oklahoma State hosted the Wildcats and certainly treated them rudely, handing them a fourth consecutive loss, 29-9, in Stillwater. A rugged Cowboy defense limited KSU to just thirteen first downs and less than a couple hundred yards in total offense.

Week ten saw the other monster with a first-year head coach visit Manhattan. The coach, Tom Osborne, was destined to be perhaps the most successful and revered football mentor in conference history. In a career that spanned a quarter of a century, his Cornhuskers would win thirteen conference championships and amass a 255-49-3 record. Along the way, Big Red would pick up three national championships to match Oklahoma's trey.

K-State wouldn't just lie down for Osborne's troops, though. They repeatedly launched mini-comebacks after falling quickly behind, 23-0. At different times, it was 23-14 and 30-21, but the Wildcats just wore down. Their last best chance came when Gordon Chambliss picked off a David Humm aerial for KSU with his team trailing just 23-14. However, K-State failed to capitalize when Grogan was intercepted. The Nebraska 50-21 win earned them a bid to the Cotton Bowl, where they would cap a 9-2-1 season with a 19-3 win over the Texas Longhorns.

The final game of the season, as all coaches and players will tell you, is so much more than just a football game for teams which have fallen on hard times after a good start. It's a chance to finish on a high note, a chance to reverse a negative trend, and a chance to wash away the bitter taste of a string of defeats and allow the program to gain some momentum for the spring practices that would ensue some five months later.

And, for Kansas State, it was a chance to finish 5-6 rather than 4-7. With Colorado hosting the wounded Wildcats at Folsom Field, the visitors' chances seemed slim. However, spirit and confidence finally emerged after five consecutive losses, and the men from Mahattan pulled off the upset, downing the Buffaloes on a dramatic Keith Brumley 30-yard field goal with just five ticks on the clock, 17-14. The boot completed a comeback from a 14-0 halftime deficit. In the final drive quarterback Grogan was masterful, completing key passes and mixing in runs by Isaac Jackson, Don Calhoun, and himself on the option series.

The game almost wasn't over, though, with Brumley's field goal. Colorado super freshman Billy Waddy, playing in just the third year since the NCAA voted to allow freshman eligibility, took the game's and the 1973 season's final kickoff and broke free for 50 yards. Only a game-saving tackle by the last Wildcat, Ron Solt, standing between Waddy and the goal line allowed KSU to return to Manhattan happy. Waddy became yet another Big Eight player to go on to NFL stardom after his time in Boulder, Colorado, was done. He earned All-Pro status as a standout receiver for the Los Angeles Rams.

Reflecting back, both Grogan and Dick Strahm agree the 1973 season wasn't nearly what it could have been had the team managed to conquer their penchant for turnovers and costly penalties.

Recalls Grogan, "I think we had around twelve guys drafted off that team by the NFL. So, it wasn't a matter of not having talent. We just weren't used to big games and really didn't know how to win, especially the close games. We just hadn't been in that position before."

Dick Strahm, who saw his first losing season ever since he began coaching in 1957 at Toledo Libbey, saw the key to the '73 season more a question of depth and the lack thereof in Manhattan.

"I really felt a lot of our starters were on a pretty level playing field with who they lined up against. When a starter went down with an injury, as happens so frequently in the violent game of football, or when a starter needed a rest, we just didn't have a player with similar abilities coming in. Certainly, that wasn't the case with teams like Oklahoma, Nebraska, and Missouri.

"And the big dogs never had to wait any appreciable amount of time when losing a big-timer to graduation. At Oklahoma, in '72, Greg Pruitt left campus a two-time All-American, for the NFL, and, BOOM, a Joe Washington showed up right on his heels and led the league in rushing.

"And, of course, it all goes back to recruiting and the disadvantages of being the smallest school in the conference in one of the most remote areas. During the winter and early spring of 1973-74, Coach Gibson really tried to intensify our recruiting efforts, so I and the rest of the assistant coaches spent a lot of time on the road.

"For me, that meant not only spending time in Kansas City but also it meant flying back to Ohio to recruit the northwest part of the state several times. While I disliked the fact that it was more time spent away from my family, which has always been what mattered to me most, I was able to touch bases with my brother Dale in Bowling Green and also get back to Toledo to see Mom.

"The recruiting itself was often very frustrating. I had some players I had spent so much time on, kids who had basically given me every assurance short of a signature that they would be coming to Kansas State. Then, I would go over to their houses with the scholarship papers, expecting them to sign and then find out they had already committed to another school. But, really, what could you do?"

In the early spring of 1974, the Strahms were quite well settled in on the western outskirts of Manhattan. Recalls Dick, "The house was new, a very nice tri-level. It had a walk-in lower level, and that was where we went when a tornado was reported to be in the area. You see, Manhattan is in the middle of Tornado Alley, and in the spring, sirens would go off from time to time and people would initiate their own tornado procedures.

"The last week of March, one tornado came within a mile of Manhattan. After the danger had subsided, I loaded up Ginger and the kids, and we drove out into the farmlands to view the damage. I saw exactly where the twister passed.

"I can remember I counted seven consecutive telephone poles sheared off half way up, almost as if someone had taken a chainsaw and cut them clean off. The wires had snapped, and the tops were just gone!

"Then, I looked over, not more than a hundred yards away, and there was a herd of cows undisturbed, just grazing. Unbelievable!"

During the off season, when Dick wasn't out on the recruiting trail or helping with the off-season training program, he and Ginger tried to spend as much time together as possible. During their "date nights," of course, they'd need a babysitter. Often, recalls Dick, the babysitter would be one of his football players. "Now, Gordon Chambliss was someone both the kids and Ginger and I really thought the world of."

Chambliss still recalls one night, in particular, when his services were called upon. "I got a call from Coach Strahm to see if I could watch the kids for a couple hours while Coach and Ginger went to a movie. I'd babysat for them a few times and really didn't mind at all.

"First, Dick paid very well, and I could always use a few extra bucks. Second, I didn't really think it was such a bad idea to help your position coach when he needed a favor. And, third, I really liked Doug and Gina.

"Anyway, I got there, and after Dick and Ginger left, the kids and I were watching TV. We were down on the lower level watching a popular television show at the time by the name of *Kung Fu*. Doug was sitting on the couch with me, and Gina, who was not quite 8, as I recall.

"Well, all of a sudden, she said, 'Hey, Gordon, let's play Kung Fu!' So, I got down on the floor on my knees, and I'm ready for what I thought was some pantomime martial arts. She was standing right in front of me, and I've got my hands up in a martial arts pose.

"All of a sudden, before I could even react, she reared back and kicked me as hard as she could right where, let's just say, it hurts the most! Man, I doubled over and rolled around on the floor. And, of course, Gina's got no idea what she'd just done and was thinking I'm play acting and she was just shrieking with delight and jumping on top of me.

"Let me tell you something. I'd rather have stick wrestled than gone through that! I think that was the last time I babysat for Dick. I don't care how much he paid. Nothing was worth that. No sense taking any chances!"

In 1974, after yet another intensive off-season conditioning program, the Purple Pride of Kansas State was again ready to be put on display.

Two assistant coaches, Tom Dimitroff and Gene McDowell, left to pursue other opportunities. They were replaced by a former University of Tennessee quarterback, Dewey Warren. Warren, nicknamed "The Swamp Rat," was the first Tennessee Volunteer quarterback to pass for more than 1,000 yards in a season. After two seasons in the NFL with the Cincinnati Bengals, Warren arrived in Manhattan after two seasons as offensive coordinator at Brigham Young University in Provo, Utah, under a coach who would become legend, LaVell Edwards.

Recalls Dick, "Dewey was a good addition to our staff and also a very interesting guy to be around."

Steve Grogan remembers that, during his senior year, very little changed with the offense of Vince Gibson. "Really, Dewey Warren's input didn't really change our offense much at all. I know he'd come from BYU, where they threw the ball around a lot in that spread offense, but I didn't see much in our offensive schemes that resembled anything like that."

Also joining the staff was Jesse Branch to help with the defense. Branch was a former All-Southwest Conference halfback who also played in the Canadian Football League. Branch was arriving from a year as an offensive coordinator at the University of Oregon. For Branch, it was a return to Kansas State. He had already served as Coach Gibson's defensive coordinator in the late 1960s.

Just as in 1973, the new campaign started auspiciously for the KSU Wildcats. As many teams in top conferences try to do, the early schedule was very favorable. The first three opponents were certainly potential wins.

Week one saw the Tulsa Golden Hurricanes come to Manhattan. Despite the 33-14 Kansas State win, there were several wild shifts in momentum. Not until KSU's Les Chaves gathered in a blocked punt and ran the ball in from 30 yards did the fans of Purple Pride exhale. A Grogan touchdown pass to Tom Winchell closed out the scoring. Strahm's secondary did a nice job containing All-American and future Pro Football Hall of Fame receiver Steve Largent for most of the afternoon.

Week two saw K-State shut out the Wichita State University Wheatshockers, 17-0, at KSU Stadium. Despite the win, there was cause for concern as the home team fumbled an astonishing nine times, losing five. However, a field goal, a one-yard run by freshman quarterback Arthur Bailey, and a big 46-yard return for a touchdown by one of Strahm's cornerbacks, Rocky Osborn, spelled the difference.

In week three, Kansas State stayed home for a third straight week and defeated the University of the Pacific, out of Stockton, California. The 38-7 win snapped a Pacific seven-game winning streak. Chambliss was instrumental in the win, running an interception back 18 yards for a touchdown. Wildcat running back David Specht keyed a 252-yard rushing effort with 87 yards on 14 carries.

In week four, KSU finally was forced to go on the road. And, the road led to Starkville, Mississippi, and a game against Mississippi State. Dick has a vivid recollection of the moments before the Wildcats took the field. "Our locker room was right underneath the student section. It seemed as if every one of the Mississippi State students had a cowbell, and 15 minutes before the opening kickoff, they started ringing those damn bells. I could hardly hear myself think much less give my players any reminders and final instructions! It certainly broke your concentration. Eventually, so many visiting coaches complained that the league eventually banned the cowbells, feeling they were giving the home team an unfair competitive advantage."

With Grogan battling an ankle injury, freshman Arthur Bailey started and showed off his speed on a nine-yard option run for a score. Grogan did manage to get on the field and connected on a beautiful 34-yard TD aerial with Stan Ross. Despite a valiant effort, though, KSU fell, 21-16.

The Mississippi State game also saw the KSU secondary lose a key member. Gordon Chambliss tore his anterior cruciate ligament (ACL) and was forced to undergo season-ending surgery.

Week five was the big one, a renewal of the Sunflower Showdown with Kansas University, with the Governor's Cup on the line.

Before the largest crowd in the short history of KSU Stadium, 45,000, the outcome wasn't certain until the absolute final play of the game. It was then that Wildcat quarterback Steve Grogan was stopped just two yards short of the goal line by safety Nolan Cromwell to avoid a tying touchdown. The final was KU-20, KSU-13.

After two years as a defensive back and another two as the Jayhawks' starting quarterback, Cromwell went on to play eleven seasons in the NFL and is widely regarded as one of the best safeties to ever play in the league. During Strahm's time at Kansas State, the Big Eight was literally teeming with players who would go on to play professionally on Sundays.

Again, as was the case the year before, the loss of the Governor's Cup sent the Wildcats' fortunes spiraling downward.

First came a tough loss in Ames, Iowa, to Iowa State, 23-18. Despite the loss, Grogan was spectacular in bringing his team back. Hitting several big passes, Steve brought his team to within five points with a touchdown pass to John Tuttle and his own two-point conversion run before time ran out on the purple-clad Wildcats.

Week three was a trip to Norman, Oklahoma, to take on a team in the process of fashioning the first of two consecutive national championships. For Dick Strahm, it also gave him a close-up look at the adoration Sooner Nation had for both their second-year coach Barry Switzer and his and their Sooners.

Recalls Dick, "As usual, we traveled the day before the game. As we were settling back into our hotel after a light workout at the stadium, I got a knock on my door. Coach Gibson came in and told me that Coach Switzer had called and asked if he and the rest of the KSU staff wanted to meet him and a couple of his assistants at the Sooner Lounge. Coach Gibson also told us that since we were in hostile territory, we wouldn't be wearing any purple that evening.

"Well, naturally, I said yes, as did a couple other assistants. We got to the lounge and were directed to a table up on a stage and cordoned off. Switzer had apparently called ahead, and we were expected.

"The Oklahoma coaches hadn't yet arrived, so we ordered a drink. I noticed the mass of dancers on the floor, and they were almost all dressed in red and white, Oklahoma's colors.

"All of a sudden, the band starts playing Oklahoma's fight song, 'Boomer Sooner,' and the dancers all stopped and all formed a line facing each other. It was as if Moses had just walked in and parted the Red Sea! The crowd was just going nuts and through the tunnel of Sooner fans walked Switzer and three of his assistants.

"Barry was dressed in an Oklahoma white V-neck sweater over a crisply starched red color of what looked to be a golf shirt. The three assistants had on the opposite color scheme, red Oklahoma sweaters and crisp white collars protruding.

"It was the most impressive entrance I've ever seen anyone make. I remember thinking, 'Wow, whoever they're playing tomorrow is in trouble,' before snapping back to reality and realizing it was us!"

The next day turned out to be as lopsided an affair as Strahm had feared. First, the Sooner regulars swamped KSU's regulars, 35-0, in the first half. Then, in the second half, the Sooner backups pasted the Wildcat subs, 28-0.

Recalls Dick, "It got so bad in the second half that the Conestoga they called the Sooner Schooner, which was used to rumble across the field to celebrate each touchdown stopped running. The horses stopped coming on the field. They were just too tired!"

After the game, when Strahm was riding down on the elevator from the press box after the 63-0 whitewashing, he overheard an Oklahoma booster bemoaning the fact that the Sooners had played so poorly, that they surely would have lost to Nebraska had they come to town!

Dick was incredulous. "That was my realization that the expectations at Oklahoma were so unbelievably high. At the highest level of college football, many fans simply will not tolerate anything less than total perfection. Here, they'd won 63-0, and this guy was lamenting the fact that they actually had to punt a couple of times in the second half."

Back in Manhattan on the eighth Saturday of the 1974 season, the story was all too familiar. The Wildcats lost for the fifth consecutive time, buried 52-15, by a strong Missouri squad. In the process, they committed the same costly mistakes and gave up the same cheap touchdowns as had plagued them for quite some time.

For the Tigers of Missouri, another future twelve-year NFL veteran, running back Tony Galbreath, threw his 225-pound frame repeatedly over the top, around, and through the KSU defense, amassing 192 yards on 32 carries. Recalls Strahm, "That was the thing about the Big Eight. Every week, when you lined up, you faced a tremendous back, an absolute hammer. It seemed without exception, that was the case. While there were some fine quarterbacks in the league, at this time, it was definitely a running conference."

The next week, Oklahoma State came to Manhattan and left with a 29-5 victory. As the losses mounted, the fan base decreased proportionally. Only 18,000 were on hand to watch despite the fact that it was Homecoming.

Week nine saw KSU on their way to Lincoln, Nebraska, to take on Tom Osborne's Cornhuskers. Playing the starters all the way, Osborne watched as his charges came away with a convincing 35-7 win, as David Humm passed for 177 yards and a couple of touchdowns.

On the season's final weekend, the Wildcats would need a home win to finish 4-7. If they were counting on the famed twelfth man in the form of strong fan support, unless those in attendance indeed had stentorian voices, they wouldn't be getting much help from the 12,000 who came to KSU Stadium.

Despite the sea of empty seats, Steve Grogan took it upon himself to end his KSU career on a high note. He was at his best as he ran the veer offense to perfection. His ball handling sprung young runners. His own quick feet enabled him to gain valuable yards. He also completed 9 of 13 for 120 yards and a TD in the 33-19 win over the Colorado Buffaloes.

Recalls Grogan about his senior season, "It was frustrating because I had several nagging injuries and had to miss quite a bit of time on the field. Also, the league was in its absolute heyday. We were simply outgunned on most Saturdays. I really don't think our lack of success was a reflection of Coach Gibson's or any of the other coaches' efforts. We just didn't have either the overall talent or the depth we needed to beat the top teams.

Despite Grogan's injury-plagued final year, the New England Patriots' head coach, Chuck Fairbanks, whose departure from Oklahoma's Sooners a couple years before brought on Barry Switzer, spoke with Vince Gibson about Grogan and his pro potential. With Gibson's strong endorsement, Fairbanks drafted Grogan in the fifth round. He went on to play a remarkable sixteen seasons in the NFL, all for the Patriots, and still holds several of the club's passing records.

Nowadays, Steve is the owner and operator of Grogan-Marciano Sporting Goods in Mansfield, Massachusetts. He also does some TV work as a color commentator for football games and gives speeches to corporate groups.

For Dick Strahm, who had just suffered his second straight losing season, he began to question some of his initial thoughts in taking the job in Manhattan. "I finally realized after the second year that a school like Kansas State had a certain competitive disadvantage. Playing Oklahoma and Nebraska was really more than the interesting challenge I envisioned. But, I was certainly going to stay the course.

"I will admit, though, that we assistants talked amongst ourselves and were somewhat concerned that, after consecutive seasons of 5-6 and 4-7 that maybe Coach Gibson might be fired. Also, we knew the last couple home games had very small crowds. And, of course, we all knew what that meant, which is that if the head coach gets fired, the assistants usually are out as well.

"However, Coach Gibson brought us all in the week after the season ended and told us that the athletic director assured him he would be given another year to show some progress. Gibson told us to get out there right after Thanksgiving and hit the recruiting trail hard.

"We all got our flights booked and our itineraries set and worked the phones. After Thanksgiving, we flew out in all directions searching for players and, hopefully, closing the deal on players we'd been in contact with.

"So, I flew to Cleveland to get to work. I had two defensive linemen I was very interested in who'd played in the strong city league.

"When I got there, I ran into a coaching buddy of mine who I had known for a number of years from being on the recruiting trail. He was a coach at Dartmouth, and his name was Johnny Curtis. He and I would meet at the Holiday Inn in downtown Cleveland in the lounge whenever we were recruiting at the same time, just to have a drink and talk about how things had gone that day.

"Well, the third day of my trip, I met him around five o'clock in the evening in the lounge. I could tell something was wrong right away. When I asked Johnny what was the matter, he said, 'Dick, have you seen the TV today?' I said, 'No.' Then he said, 'You don't know, do you? Vince Gibson resigned this afternoon at Kansas State.'

"I was in total shock. When I got back to the room, I called Ginger back in Manhattan. She said it was true, that it was all over the news in Manhattan that day. She was going to call me that evening.

"After I got off the phone with Ginger, the phone rang, and it was one of the secretaries in the football offices. She told me what I already knew and instructed me to return to Manhattan.

"I was still in disbelief when I got back to Kansas and met along with the rest of the assistants with Coach Gibson. How could so much change in such a short amount of time?

"Well, anyway, he never really explained what had changed his mind. He told us he was thankful for all our efforts and would do anything he could to help us land positions. He also said our expenses would be paid to the National Coaches' Convention in January. I remember, that year, it was in Washington, D.C.

"As far as money, depending on how long it took me to find a job, now that could get pretty dicey. You see, coaches back then were paid from January 1 to December 31. Nowadays, most assistants' contracts run from July 1 to June 30, which provides some extra paychecks in the event a coach is terminated, which kind of lessens the urgency to find immediate employment. But, for me and the rest of the assistants, that meant we only had one more paycheck before we would have to rely on whatever savings we had for living expenses.

"Added stress was the fact that Ginger was pregnant and due in mid-February. Not only were there financial concerns about soon having three little ones. I also worried about whether the pregnancy would have complications again."

When December announced its arrival with all the stores in Manhattan donning their traditional festive attire, the soon-to-be ex-secondary coach of the Kansas State Wildcats had a lot more questions than answers.

Soon, Christmas was upon the Strahms, and the plan was to return to Toledo as they had done in past years. While Ginger and Gina flew, Dick and Doug drove.

Recalls Dick, "Doug and I drove from Manhattan to Toledo on December 19, and, believe me, we ran into a winter traveler's worst nightmare. On Interstate 70, between Kansas City and St. Louis, we ran right into a winter blizzard. By 3:00 in the afternoon, the interstate was closing down, and we were stranded in the middle of Missouri. We had no luck finding a motel. So, we got back in the car and tried to continue, but it was just not possible. Just when we were trying to decide what to do next, a truck driver pulled up, got out of his rig, and tapped on the window. I rolled it down, and he told me to follow him. He knew a farmhouse where we could spend the night.

"As we pulled into the farm yard right behind the big truck, we saw another eighteen-wheeler parked there. Our truck driver went into the house, and, a few minutes later, he came to the door and waved us in. Doug and I slept in a little room with a cot and a couch. It was great. We were warm and out of the storm.

"The next morning the farm couple prepared a huge breakfast, and we had a wonderful visit. Just when it appears as if your circumstances couldn't get any worse, somehow God provides. First, there's a kind trucker and then a kind farm family. That's kind of the way I saw it, and I still do.

"After we said good-bye, Doug and I cleaned off the car and got in and followed the semi driver back to the interstate. I settled in right behind him and let him widen the one-lane path that the plows had cleared the previous evening. After about 50 miles, conditions improved, and we made it the rest of the way to Toledo without incident."

Back in Toledo, Dick spoke with his brother, Dale, and told him to keep on the lookout for anything that may come available back in his home state. By this time, Dale had risen to the defensive coordinator's position at Bowling Green State University.

Recalls Dick, "I even considered a real change career-wise. I thought about seeking a school administrator's job. There was a part of me that still hadn't given up the vision of my becoming a superintendent, but I had to face it. At 41, and just starting out in school administration, I knew there were more attractive candidates out there. I even looked at a couple of things completely outside education and coaching.

"But, the fact of the matter was, I still thought of myself as a coach and still wanted to work with young men. I still had that desire.

"I had some people ask me if I was resentful about the fact that Coach Gibson did such an about face without telling any of us on staff. Some outside of football kind of see that as pulling the rug out from under us. I don't see it that way at all. The head coach is certainly not obligated to discuss his future plans with his staff. Coach Gibson is a good person and made the choices that were best for him and his family."

The Strahms returned to Manhattan after the holidays, and Dick prepared to attend the National Coaches' Convention with the fervent hope he could land a job for the next season.

After the first two days of the three-day convention, Strahm had made just one promising contact, certainly a contrast to three years before when there seemed to be a plethora of positions and both Gibson and Bobby Bowden offered him chances to fill positions. Recalls Dick, "I don't know what it was about that year. In the past, there had always seemed to be quite a bit out there. The coaching profession has traditionally always had a lot of movement, but that didn't seem to be the case in '74.

"I did, however, speak with Coach Jerry Ippoliti of Northern Illinois University. He was looking for a defensive coordinator. We spoke in an informal interview situation, but he didn't really offer me the position. He told me that he liked my credentials and philosophies but said he also had a number of other candidates he intended to interview.

"I don't mind telling you. I was pretty depressed. I'd never been through a losing season much less two in a row. I had only one more paycheck coming at the end of the month. I had a family to support, and Ginger was soon to deliver another son or daughter. Despite the fact that there was one more day of the convention, I just knew there wasn't anything else out there, so I left.

"Ginger had been having some cramping, and I wanted to be with her to help in any way I could. While Doug, who was 10 at the time, and Gina, who was 7, were big helps, I knew my place was back in Manhattan despite all the uncertainty of where we would go next."

Fortunately, the past problems Ginger experienced did not manifest themselves again, and Steven Dale Strahm made Valentine's Day even more special when he arrived on February 14, 1975.

Despite any frustrations Dick may have experienced, watching the Purple Pride win only nine times while losing thirteen, the birth of his son made the whole K-State experience worth it for Dick, and, of course, for Ginger.

By the end of the year's shortest month, Strahm was getting increasingly anxious about where he would be working in the fall. Then, recalls Dick, the phone finally rang. "It was Jerry Ippoliti, from Northern Illinois University. He said that he still had the defensive coordinator's position open and would I want to come to the university, in DeKalb, Illinois, to meet in a formal interview with the athletic director, Dr. Robert Brigham, and him.

"Of course, I said I would and flew out there.

"After the interview concluded, the three of us took a campus tour, and, of course, I got a chance to see the facilities for football. I felt pretty good about my chances. Dr. Brigham told me there would be a decision made by the next day and would I mind staying in DeKalb for another night. Of course, I said I would. So, I went back to the hotel.

"When I got there, I called my brother Dale to tell him that I had a real good feeling about Northern Illinois. I also wanted to ask him if he'd heard of any openings in Ohio.

"Well, he told me that he was just about to call me. He said that Findlay College was looking for a new head coach. Their coach, Byron Morgan, had resigned.

"To be honest, I knew nothing about Findlay, Ohio, or the college. But, I liked the fact that it was a head job. I told Dale to call the athletic director and see if he could get me an interview. Dale said that he'd certainly try.

"The next morning, Coach Ippoliti called me and wanted me to come over to the campus.

"I met with him in Dr. Brigham's office, and the three of us, again, went to see the football stadium and locker room and weight room and football office complex. I was really quite impressed with all of what I saw, and we had already talked salary. It was at that time they offered me the position of defensive coordinator at Northern Illinois University. I also had already told them that Ginger had a horse, and Dr. Brigham told me that should I come to Northern, I could board the horse in the animal husbandry facility for free. He even said that would include feeding and grooming. There were some excellent riding trails for Ginger and Gina on the western edge on the campus.

"I told Dr. Brigham that I was very interested but that I wanted an opportunity to listen to what Findlay College had to say. He said he understood but that he would need a decision within a couple of days. Coach Ippoliti wanted his staff completely in place for spring practice.

"When I got back to the hotel, there was a message at the front desk that my brother had called. When I got to my room, I called him back, and he said I had an interview with Findlay's athletic director, a man named Dr. Jim Houdeshell, late the next day.

"I flew into Toledo, and Dale picked me up at the airport. We drove straight through to Findlay. Dale told me that the interview with Dr. Houdeshell was actually in a motel restaurant off of Interstate 75.

Dale has his own recollection of the day that Findlay College would hire a new football coach. "I was going to wait in the car and take care of some paperwork for some of my recruits. Late winter is always a very busy time in terms of recruiting.

"Dick went into the restaurant, and the next thing I know, he was back tapping on the car window. I rolled down the window, and he said, 'The athletic director doesn't mind if you sit in.' So, I got out of the car and went in.

"Well, Dr. Houdeshell was asking Dick some questions, and Dick was presenting himself. I was just sitting there listening and drinking coffee. Then Dr. Houdeshell told us he'd like to show us around campus. We toured the campus and then went to Donnell Stadium. I was familiar with Findlay College because, when I was an undergraduate at Ohio Northern, I had played at Donnell.

"Then, we went through the rest of the football facilities. To be honest, at that time, they weren't much to shout about."

Recollects Dick, "I wasn't really shocked by either the smallness of the campus or the facilities either. I had visited Dale when he was at Ohio Northern, so I knew what small colleges had to offer.

"One thing I noticed when we went through the football locker room was the game jerseys were still in a pile on the floor. The weight room also wasn't much. I started to believe we would need start from scratch and work up.

"Then, Dr. Houdeshell stopped and said, 'I've got a good feeling about you and would like you to be our new football coach here.' Well, I was very interested. Even though the salary that was mentioned would actually be less than what I would make if I accepted the job at Northern Illinois, I suppose the fact that I had already been a defensive coordinator in the Mid-American Conference made that position a bit less enticing. Besides if I were to come to Findlay, I'd be a head coach again. After the last five years as an assistant, that sounded really good.

"So, as quickly as the job was offered, I accepted. Later that day, I called Dr. Brigham and told him of my decision. He said that he understood, and, although disappointed, he wished me luck."

Recollects Houdeshell on his instantaneous decision to hire Dick, "I don't want people to get the wrong idea, that I did things very capriciously. This was not at all a snap decision. I just knew I had the right man.

"Remember, my brother, Butch, played for Dick back when Dick began coaching at Lakota and always felt such great admiration for him. Ever since that point, I followed Dick's career. While he certainly didn't know me, I knew about him.

"In my role as athletic director, I tried to keep a lot of ties with high schools so that I could keep tabs on young coaches. I knew that, perhaps, one day, there would be situations where we'd need coaches at Findlay, and I would be ahead of the game in terms of who to contact.

"Well, I followed Dick's career after Lakota when he went to Bryan. I knew what kind of impact he'd had there.

"Then, when he went to Warren, one of his assistant coaches, Carl Meyer, was a graduate of Findlay College. He played football here at Findlay College. After Carl left Warren, he went to Dartmouth and was an assistant under Bob Blackburn, and when Blackburn got the football job at the University of Illinois, Carl went as an assistant.

"Over the years, Carl would call me just to see how things were going back at his alma mater, and he would periodically bring up how much he thought of Dick and how much he learned working under him when he was at Warren.

"Of course, I knew of the success Dick's defenses had at Toledo, since he was just down the interstate from us.

"When I read of Vince Gibson's resignation at KSU, I knew the assistants would be free agents.

"At the same time, By [Byron Morgan] had resigned here as the football coach after twelve seasons. The last couple of years had been pretty tough [combined record, 4-16], and he just felt, since he was in his sixties, that maybe it was time he stepped down.

"The president of the college told me to conduct a search for a football coach, and I fully intended to do that. But, I really had Dick in mind all the way.

"Then, when Dale called and told me that Dick was interested in returning to Ohio, I told Dale that I was just about to call Dick to see if he'd be interested in applying. Funny, how it sometimes works out.

"Actually, I had lined up two other candidates to interview, but, to be honest, I never even contacted them.

"There was also a committee, comprised of about six players that I had formed. The football team wanted some input on the new coach's hiring, so I didn't release the news that Dick was coming aboard until they met with him."

Jim Maisch was one of those players on that committee. Now an engineer at Minster Machine in Minster, Ohio, Maisch remembers his first impressions of Dick Strahm. "I was going to be in the running to be the starting quarterback in the fall, so I really was happy when Dr. Houdeshell asked me to be on the committee. A quarterback and a head coach have to work so closely together, and I was very anxious to meet Coach Morgan's successor.

"As soon as he walked in the room, I could sense Coach Strahm's confidence. He seemed to just know that he possessed the ability to get us going back in the right direction. After being 1-9 my freshman year and 3-7 my sophomore year, I was ready for some success."

Dick returned to Manhattan for a final time to pack and list the house and tie up all those loose ends that come with upheaval. Certainly, there were things he would miss about Kansas, but he was invigorated by knowing that, again, he would be a head coach. "I said my good-byes to the coaches and players. I wished Steve Grogan well. I just knew he would be successful in the NFL. He was such a hard-nosed quarterback. He could throw the deep ball that the NFL wants, and he could also run. It certainly wasn't surprising that he had such a long and illustrious career with New England.

"I also wished Gordon Chambliss well. Little did I know at that moment that I wasn't quite done with my old babysitter by a long shot.

"When I spoke a final time with Coach Gibson and thanked him for the opportunity he gave me, I found out that he had just accepted the head coaching position at the University of Louisville."

By March, Dick, Ginger, Doug, Gina, and the newest Strahm, Steve, were in Findlay, Ohio. Dick and Ginger decided on a house, and it would serve them very well. "This was my fifth house I'd bought, so I really hoped I'd be staying in it more than two or three years," recalls Dick.

And, Strahm's wish, ultimately, came true. The house was on the west side of his new community, on one of the last streets before the Liberty-Benton School District. Before too very long, virtually everyone in Findlay would know their college's football coach lived in that tri-level on North Ridge Road, and that's the way it remained for the entire tenure of Coach Dick Strahm in Findlay.

Despite the fact that he hadn't returned to Toledo, in many ways, Strahm felt he'd come home. "I was very excited, re-energized, you might say. Despite the fact that I knew the job ahead of me was big, I couldn't wait to get to it. I was ready to start putting a staff together and get my off-season program going in the direction I wanted it to go."

And so began the Strahm era on the campus of the Findlay Oilers in that town that truckers on their citizen-band radios referred to as Flag City U.S.A. It was the spring of 1975, at a time when disco was becoming all the rage in the music industry, as Dick filled his lungs with the sweet draughts of Ohio air. He was back in his home state. A Buckeye he was born, and, from this point on, a Buckeye he would remain, in addition, of course, to the Oiler he would become.

Coach Strahm celebrated a special time with his staff after the first NAIA national championship game in 1979: (from left) Jim McIntosh, Charlie Thompson, Dean Pees, Dick Strahm, Kevin Cassidy, Steve Mohr, and Berly Hemminger. You can tell Coach loved holding that trophy!

Chapter 9
A Perfect Five-Year Plan

Dick Strahm was coming to work for an institution that certainly had a long and illustrious history. While Findlay College may be a mystery to some who are several states away from its location in Northwest Ohio, most everyone in this area knew of this small college.

It was on January 28, 1882, that the Churches of God in North America and the citizens of Findlay established Findlay College. Despite some early growing pains, by 1897, the college had an endowment of more than a $100,000 as well as a sixteen-member faculty. A resilient institution, over the next seventy years, the college weathered the ups and downs of enrollment and finances driven by two world wars, the Depression and a devastating fire in Old Main in 1938. By the early1970s, Findlay College was developing new programs that set it apart from other institutions, such as the Freshman Seminar Program, evening classes, community education programs, and in 1975, established the Intensive English Language Institute that taught international students the English language and American customs in preparation for college-level work.

And, in Strahm's first year at Findlay College, Watergate conspirators John Mitchell, H.R. Haldeman, and John Ehrlichman were found guilty of a cover up. President Gerald Ford survived not one but two assassination attempts just seventeen days apart. It was a moment in time when, while Red Sox Carlton Fisk may have stolen a memorable game-six homerun, the Cincinnati Reds, hailing from another Buckeye city to the south of Findlay, stole the World Series the next evening by winning game seven. It was a year that Rod Serling, an icon in the entertainment industry and creator of television's "The Twilight Zone," exited this world and a year when a future sports icon, Tiger Woods, entered it.

Certainly, for Dick Strahm there was much to do in the late spring of 1975, as, essentially, half of the off-season that coaches depend on to rethink, restock, promote, and improve their programs was already gone. There was a coaching staff to assemble, phone calls to make to try to find recruits after so many high school athletes had already made commitments to other schools, and an off-season strength-and-conditioning program to ramp up.

And, of course, there was the business of learning as much as possible about the players who would be returning to the practice fields when the searing August heat had reached its apex for the two-a-days that would precede the autumnal pastime called football.

Additionally, there was the business of meeting with the media. In a town such as Findlay, there were only one high school and one college, so, of course, the hometown paper, The Courier, had reporters who had many questions. Coaches have talked about a five-year plan when arriving at a new position almost since the beginning of organized sports, and if that is the normal time frame for finding out what type of program a coach would be overseeing after somewhat of a learning curve, that meant the year 1979 would be the time to give the new Findlay coach a grade.

But, to Strahm, the five-year plan was more of a cliché than a reliable means to assess progress. "I just felt there never was anything magical about five years whenever I heard a new coach talk about some sort of a plan. While I had no delusions of grandeur that we were going to be a nationally ranked team or even a conference champion the first year, I sure didn't want the program to be lagging behind other small colleges for too long!"

Dick also needed to do some research about his newly adopted community of approximately 36,000 to find out not only how the Strahm family could become a part of the community but also how the community could become a bigger part of what he would be trying to accomplish with his football program. Simply put, he not only needed to cultivate relationships on campus to find out about the people and programs of Findlay College but Strahm also needed to get out into the community as well.

Strahm knew how much more successful a football program can be if you sell it to a community as passionately as any successful businessman who receives a commendation for entering the Million Dollar Club at the end of a fiscal year.

But, first things first, and, for Dick, that meant assembling a staff. A holdover from the previous staff was Jerry English, who filled the role of defensive coordinator. English, who also was Findlay College's wrestling coach, revealed a fact to Dick that certainly the new head coach intended to change.

Recalls Dick, "I asked Jerry what were his recruiting duties in 1974, and he told me that, since wrestling season immediately followed football, he hadn't been required to do any recruiting, nor did the rest of the coaches, who all apparently had other directions they felt they needed to go. Well, I told Jerry that he needed to get out on the road and recruit in addition to fulfilling his wrestling duties. Jerry said he would have no problem with that. He would like the opportunity to recruit."

English, an Ohio Northern University graduate and someone Strahm remembers as a fine young coach, would be the only full-time assistant coach that the athletic budget could afford. The Oilers would run the same defense that Dick ran at Warren Western Reserve and the University of Toledo, the 5-2 angle, which meant five defensive linemen, two linebackers, two cornerbacks, and two safeties. The linemen and linebackers would do a lot of angling and stunting on their rushes to make blocking schemes more challenging for opponents.

It was a defense Strahm sensed would be a work in progress. "I knew we had to have specific types of athletes to run that defense, and probably just didn't have enough of them heading into that first year in 1975, but you've got to start somewhere. A coach just starting out in a new position has to look beyond the immediate potential results.

"I think the worst thing you can do as a coach is to scrap something you really believe in and one that has been successful because you don't have enough pieces right away to make it work. Despite the late start, I was going to recruit as hard as possible right away to see if we could find more pieces and then continue adding what we needed as each opportunity presented itself."

A second holdover from Byron Morgan's staff was a part-time coach, Don Wright. He was a full-fledged faculty member who taught psychology. Strahm remembers him as a good guy who just enjoyed coming out to the practice field after classes and coming to the games on Saturdays to help any way he could. "Once I got into that first season, I saw that Don really didn't have a lot of time to devote to football. Certainly, I believed that he did the best he could, but he wasn't available during the day for any meetings because he was in class, and he had class preparation to do right after practice, so he would leave as soon as practice was over.

"So, he really wasn't breaking down film or doing a lot of the other duties incumbent on a full-time coach, but he had some knowledge of personnel and did have something to offer. He was a good on-the-field coach who would do anything I asked, but there was no doubt his teaching career took priority over anything football-related. I can remember that first year boarding the bus for away games, and there Don would be sitting up in the front grading papers.

In addition to English and Wright, Strahm found three other part-time assistants. They were men Dick sensed had something to give, had the desire, and were willing to work for peanuts. "Larry Reigle was a graduate of Findlay College and, at one time, a head coach at nearby Arcadia High School before giving up his position to concentrate on teaching.

Recalls Dick, "Jim Houdeshell found Larry for me. He was the one who convinced him to come out and help. Since I knew Jim had been a longtime coach, not only in basketball and baseball but also in football here at the college, I knew his recommendation was solid. Without question, I took Larry."

Strahm then found Dave Smith. Smith was in sales, but he was willing to almost volunteer his time to do what he could, as Strahm remembers his first staff, most of whom were paid only a few hundred dollars. "Dave was a young guy who wanted to learn. Given how quickly many of my assistants in those first few years left after one year, Dave wound up staying on longer than several others. By his third and last year, he was much more knowledgeable.

"I still needed someone to coach the secondary and, frankly, had run out of local options. Then, I thought of Gordon!"

Gordon turned out to be Gordon Chambliss, a vital cog in the Kansas State Wildcat secondary in both of Dick's years spent in Manhattan, Kansas. He had graduated with a degree in physical education, and was somewhat unsettled as to what his next step would be. Of course, Dick wasn't aware of Gordon's uncertainty, that is, until he contacted him. "I really lost track of Gordon after I left Kansas. Now, Steve Grogan was easier to keep track of because he'd been drafted by the Patriots and would be playing in the fall in the NFL.

"However, Gordon hadn't been drafted despite being a fine player. I figured Gordon was trying to get a teaching and coaching position in secondary education. So, I called him at home in Montgomery, Alabama, and invited him to come up to Findlay for a visit. Once I got him out here, I told him I'd love to have him as an assistant and that, while I couldn't pay him much, I'd do the best I could and also get him a job in the community. I really was surprised how quickly he accepted."

Chambliss, now a vice president and senior financial advisor for Merrill Lynch in his home state, remembers his decision to come to Findlay for the 1975 season. "Well, first of all, I hadn't landed a job yet. Certainly, I couldn't live on the small stipend I would receive for Dick's football position, but he got me a job and also arranged some very reasonable housing.

"What also weighed into my decision to come to Findlay is I still had a dream of playing in the NFL. Before I injured my knee my senior year and had surgery in December of '74, I did get some feelers, one of which was from the Detroit Lions.

"While I'd gone undrafted, I still could try out as a free agent, if only I got an invitation. I figured if I kept myself in shape, I wouldn't be far at all from Detroit if I got a call.

"As it turned out, no one ever called, but I don't regret coming to Findlay one bit. First, I respected Coach Strahm so much that I knew the season would be a learning experience for me. Since I wanted to get into coaching at that point in my life if I never got an NFL tryout, I needed to start getting some experience and building a résumé. After I left at the end of the 1975 season and got back down South, I think that year on my résumé coaching college may have landed me my first job in education. I taught and coached five years before going into the financial field."

Certainly, the players were amused by the thick Southern drawl that remains as layered today as it was back in 1975. Recalls Chambliss, "I can remember having to repeat myself a little bit at the beginning, but after the first few weeks, I think they understood me a lot more. Heck, I thought they were the ones who sounded funny!"

Recalls Dick about his first staff in Findlay, "My biggest problem not just that first year but, really, the first four or five years, is I couldn't meet with my own staff to organize and plan during the day. The first year, Wright, Reigle, Smith, and Chambliss couldn't show up until they were done with their jobs. You talk about a contrast with what I had just experienced in Manhattan, where I was in meetings for hours and hours every week during season!"

Besides the assembling of a staff, Dick also needed to bring some recruits to Findlay. Not only was he starting late but Dick also could not offer any scholarship help. "The Hoosier-Buckeye Conference presidents decided that no member school, which included Findlay College, Earlham College (Richmond, Indiana), Anderson College (Anderson, Indiana), Manchester College (North Manchester, Indiana), Defiance College (Defiance, Ohio), Hanover College (Hanover, Indiana), Taylor University (Upland, Indiana), Wilmington College (Wilmington, Ohio), and Bluffton College (Bluffton, Ohio), could offer scholarship incentives."

Recalls Dick, "I did the best I could getting some players to come to Findlay. One player, really my first recruit, was Kevin Cassidy. He turned out to be one of my favorite young men who ever played for me."

Cassidy, now a sales representative for Gilman Gear, a company that sells athletic equipment, lives on Catawba Island, Ohio. To this day, he remains in contact with his former coach who means so much to him. "I am so proud to say I was Dick Strahm's first Findlay recruit. As I was finishing my senior year at Toledo St. John's High School, I got a phone call from Coach Strahm. Initially, I wondered how he got my name, but I later found out that Dick, being from Toledo, had so many sets of eyes on Toledo High School football that it was no wonder he was able to get so many of his recruits from Toledo.

"Well, anyway, he convinced me to come down to see Findlay College and talk to him about playing there. After speaking with Coach Strahm for about a half hour, I just knew this was the place I wanted to be, and this was the coach I wanted to play for.

"With no scholarship help and no weight facilities that really were very impressive, some may have wondered why I was so sure that Findlay was the right place for me. I'm not sure I can even, to this day, explain it myself. Maybe it was something Coach said to me. He told me that if I came to Findlay, the Oilers would win the national championship by my senior year, and if I didn't come to Findlay, the Oilers were going to win the national championship anyway. I don't think most coaches would have put it that way. I just sensed there was something very special about Dick Strahm."

The first year's recruiting class was, predictably, given the late start and inability to offer scholarships, small. There were some solid additions, however. Besides Cassidy, Strahm brought aboard players who would become vital pieces in the Oilers football machine, players like Brent Gordon, out of Columbus; Denny Severin, out of Niles, Ohio, just up the road from Dick's former coaching stop, Warren; Ben Finch, all the way from Orange, New Jersey; and Frank Molinaro, the linebacker who craved contact, from Maumee, just outside of Toledo. Big offensive tackle Tom Spychalski, from Toledo St. Johns High School, at 6'4", 225 pounds, had a lot of ability but left school after his second year to get married.

The summer months rolled by as the Strahms settled into their new home on Findlay's west side. Some of Ginger's and Gina's time was spent with Danny Boy, the horse that had made the trip from Manhattan, Kansas, to Ohio in a trailer,

Recalls Dick, "Larry and Carol Alter were instant and lifelong friends of ours from almost the moment we stepped foot in Findlay. Larry was, and still is, the sports editor for the local paper, The Courier. The good ones have a way of settling in and making their mark, as Larry has done in Findlay. I think small towns tend to rely on the local paper more than bigger cities.

"Anyway, Ginger and Carol drove from Findlay and met the trailer that Danny Boy was in half way, in St. Louis, with a second trailer, to cut down on the first driver's trip back to Manhattan. Those two ladies loaded Danny Boy in their trailer and brought him the rest of the way. We kept him in a barn a couple miles further west of our home. Of course, it was up to us to pay for the horse's stall fees and food and, also up to us to care for the horse. It really was a lot of work, especially for Ginger."

While all of Dick players were involved in a mandatory weight program that their new head coach had instituted, the Oilers players were going about the business of getting to know their new coach.

Dick laughs when he recalls, perhaps, taking a bit of advantage of a couple young men who wanted to please their new coach. "I can remember that one pretty hot spring day, I got a hold of a couple of my players and asked them to give me a hand with something at home. Of course, they said yes. They were anxious to make a good impression. Well, we hopped in my car and started driving. I wonder if they got a bit suspicious when I drove right past the house. I drove them to the horse barn.

"Well, I told them to grab the shovels and rakes and clean out the stall and spread fresh hay. It certainly wasn't the most pleasant work they'd ever done, hot and smelly.

"I think after that, word kind of got around to the other players that if Coach asked you to help him around the house, maybe it would be best to make up an excuse. Tell him you've got to study!"

Gene Fernandez, who, along with Jim Maisch, would play quarterback in 1975, was one of several former Oilers players who landed a job after graduation right in Findlay. Still working for Marathon Oil Company, where he is now the process improvement coordinator, Fernandez had some pretty good recollections of the mandatory weight training that Dick implemented, "Until Coach got here, we really had no weights to speak of. It was Coach who went out in the community and talked to city officials, who, in turn, instructed the street supervisor to let us have some manhole covers which weren't being used. Since they didn't all weigh the same, we had to weigh them and then mark them. That way, when we put them on the bar, at least they would be somewhat balanced.

"Really, the whole weight program was very primitive. I remember we all lifted in a loft area above the swimming pool. With all the moisture in the building from the pool and the chemicals used to treat the pool, it rusted the bars that we put the weights on. You could always tell when someone had just gotten done lifting because he'd have rust-colored hands and there'd be this big old rust mark across his chest."

During the summer, Dick also tried to improve the football locker room, a place he scrupulously learned to avoid taking recruits to see. Dick recalls, "Both Kevin Cassidy and Denny Severin will tell you to this day that I never took them to see the locker room. In 1975, the locker room was in the basement of the old gym, and some of the lockers were right next to the coal bins. There was always a layer of soot over in that area of the room.

"So, working with Jim Houdeshell, we had the maintenance guys clean that area up and build us some new lockers that weren't in that vicinity. I also had them clean out an old storage room, and I turned that into a training room. Of course, there wasn't enough money in the athletic department for a full-time trainer. That wouldn't come for another half dozen years.

"Jim Houdeshell agreed to help train, and, I guess, I became a second trainer. I took care of whatever happened on the field, and Jim was in charge of rehabbing injuries and getting players back on the field. As I recall, Jim could do wonders with an ankle and a roll of athletic tape.

"Despite the improvements we made in the summer of 1975, I knew we had a long way to go. I still wasn't all that comfortable showing recruits our locker room and training room.

"Now, recruiting is like any sales job. You've got to target your strengths and sell them. One thing I knew I could sell our recruits on was our equipment. It was the absolute best money could buy. Our shoulder pads and our helmets were the same as schools like Ohio State and the University of Michigan. Jim Houdeshell would have it no other way."

Recalls Houdeshell, "I knew there wasn't enough money to provide Dick with a whole staff of full-time assistants, and there were other things I knew we couldn't afford, but I wanted to be sure that the players on that field who were representing Findlay College were in the best gear available."

When a couple more calendar pages were turned, it was time for Coach Strahm and his staff to head the Oilers onto, first, the practice fields under the August sun, and, finally, onto the enemy turf of the Greyhounds of Indiana Central (now, the University of Indianapolis) for the opener in early September.

As soon as Strahm got a look at his opponent during pre-game warm-ups, he knew that he was facing, potentially, a very long afternoon. "At the time, Indiana Central was an NAIA Division I school, which meant it could have as many as 36 full scholarships. We had none.

"When I noticed the size of the players, I turned to Jerry English and said, 'Maybe the best thing we can do is get back on the bus and get the hell out of here and try to find some bigger guys!'

"Well, once the game started, my fears were realized. The linemen they had probably weighed on the average around 270 pounds a piece, while ours were in the 200- pound range."

In the very first game of Strahm's Findlay tenure, the Oilers were routed 56-8. Week two saw the fortunes of Strahm's team reverse as Dick enjoyed his first victory both at Findlay and in the Hoosier-Buckeye Conference, a resounding 37-0 win over Earlham.

Then, two losses came on back-to-back Saturdays. Week three saw the Anderson Ravens beat Findlay, 20-18. Week four saw the Oilers fall to non-conference Georgetown College, from Georgetown, Kentucky, 30-9.

Week five saw the Oilers record their second win, a conference win against Manchester, 38-14. Sadly, that would be the last peak during Strahm's first year. Recalls Dick, "You certainly don't want the peak of the season to come in week five. When that happens, you're in for a long second half of the season."

Week six saw Findlay drop a close-to-the-vest 6-3 battle to the Yellow Jackets of Defiance, and week seven saw perennial league power Hanover administer a convincing whipping, 26-0.

Weeks eight through ten proved to be no better as three more consecutive losses, all close, went down in the books. First, the Taylor Trojans beat the Oilers, 14-7. Then the Wilmington Quakers beat Findlay, 17-7. And, finally, the season ended when the Bluffton Beavers beat their neighbors to the north just a few miles down Interstate 75, 9-6.

In the last game, even an old motivational tool of Dick's failed to produce results. While Strahm did not outfit his whole team with the sentiment, he wore a sweatshirt on the sidelines that day that proclaimed, "We will win."

In many ways, the season was full of revelations for Dick Strahm, not the least of which was the reaction of his players to playing competitively but eventually losing close games. Five of the eight losses were by a total of just twenty-five points. "I guess what really bothered me is I noticed after those close losses that several of the players almost seemed satisfied to have been close, to have been competitive. That really bothered me, and it was something I vowed to address. Despite the two tough years in Kansas State, I still was used to winning.

"I have always felt there was a reason to play games, and it wasn't just to get some exercise and be competitive. It was to win. So, I vowed I was going to work harder than ever in the off season to change that mindset of my players and somehow convinced them that a loss, even if it was close, was still a loss and not good.

"The bottom line is always the bottom line on a football field. Coaches are not in the business of adding another column on their teams' final records called 'moral victories.' The year 1975 won't be remembered by anyone for close calls. Our football media guide simply says our final record was 2-8. While I was proud of the fact that one of my offensive linemen, Mark Newburg, was named to the Associated Press Little All-American team, there wasn't a lot more to look back on fondly."

Late in the disappointing season, after another tough loss at Donnell Stadium, the Oilers' home, Dick Strahm, the proud head coach who had either built from scratch or resurrected three different high school programs and also the former defensive coordinator of Toledo Rockets' teams that registered undefeated and untied seasons, experienced something for the first time in his coaching career. He was heckled. "I was walking off the field with my head down, when I heard this really loud voice yell, 'Hey, Strahm, sure glad you came all the way from the Big Eight to show us how to play football the right way!'

"What could I say? The record was the record, and the results were the results. The only response would have to be one my team made on the field. So, I bit my lip and kept walking."

The recollections of Kevin Cassidy certainly demonstrate the disappointment of such a season as 1975.

Recalls Cassidy, "Probably the thing I remember most about that first season was the number of away games we had where it was homecoming! It seemed we were everybody's homecoming game. I saw more queens crowned that first year than the total number I've seen crowned since. At the end of the year, after 2-8, I expected more of the same in 1976."

There was a moment that remains etched in Jim Houdeshell's memory to this day that gave the former Findlay College athletic director every reason to believe that there would be improvement in the football program, and sooner rather than later. Recalls Houdeshell, "I just knew things were going to change when I heard the first words Dick had to say when he stepped to the microphone at the football banquet at the end of the season. He dropped his head for a moment and then looked up without one trace of a smile and said, 'This will NOT happen again.'"

As Strahm reviewed both the game tapes and the memories he accumulated for every Saturday of the 1975 season, he came to a number of conclusions about what happened and what needed to happen to avoid a repeat of the season he had just endured. "First of all, I concluded that we had a lack of discipline on our football team, and that fell directly at my feet. I vowed I would completely eradicate that.

"Second, we definitely didn't have a winning attitude. We needed to learn that the difference between average and good is a little extra effort so that when a score was close and a game was there for the taking, it would be Findlay College that would be the one doing the grabbing!

"Third, we had to get more athletic. And, of course, again, that all came back to me and to recruiting. I got such a late start the year before because of when I was hired, but I vowed there would be no excuses this off season. Coach English was going to get on the phone and out on the road, and I was going to do the same!

"Fourth, we were going to win the fourth quarter. I was going to make sure we were going to out-condition every team we played. That was my responsibility, and I was going to do something about it."

During the off season, Dick Strahm also pondered the type of offense that it would take to generate more points. The offense Dick used in 1975 was the same type used by both Frank Lauterbur and Jack Murphy at UT. It was an "I" formation, a set where both the fullback and a tailback align directly behind the center. The other offensive back positions himself in a slot to either the left or the right. The interior line in the offense is generally balanced, as it was in Strahm's offense in the first year, which meant there were both a guard and a tackle on each side of the center.

Recalls Dick, "I think what I discovered as I reviewed game film over and over was that maybe I had some square pegs I was trying to fit into round holes. I just didn't have the personnel to execute the offense.

"I really had been away from any involvement with the offense for the last five years. I was the defensive coordinator at Toledo and then coached the defensive backs at Kansas State."

For Strahm, it was a long time since he had run an offense at Warren Western Reserve in 1969. "You might say that I had to rediscover my offensive identity. Now, I didn't think I could totally revert back to the offense I used in Warren, but I wanted something similar because I had a lot of success, both in Warren and, before that, in Bryan."

By the spring of 1976, after an entire winter of looking at everything his Oilers were doing, Strahm had made some decisions. While he still felt the 5-2 angle defense was the way to go, offensively, he decided to scrap the "I" formation as his base offense and run the wishbone. The wishbone would employ an up back (fullback) behind the quarterback and the two halfbacks aligned deeper than the fullback to either side of him.

Remembers Strahm, "Now, I was using a three-back offense in high school quite a bit, but we never called it a wishbone.

"During my Big Eight years, I saw the wishbone run by some very fine offensive football teams like Oklahoma and Oklahoma State. I felt if I could take some elements from those offenses and combine them with what I'd run in Warren, I could find something more suitable for our personnel here at Findlay.

"That early spring, I looked at reel after reel of film on the wishbone that several colleges were running. Now, the true wishbone that Barry Switzer used at Oklahoma gave a lot of decision making to the quarterback in terms of when to give the ball to the fullback inside and when to keep it and come down the line with the option to pitch to the halfback or run it himself.

"I saw many times on film, the tailback, even way beyond the line of scrimmage, would maintain his spacing to the outside shoulder of the quarterback and behind him if he hadn't received a pitch in the backfield. That way, the quarterback could still pitch the ball back.

"Well, I wasn't too comfortable risking fumbles with my quarterback tossing the ball all over the place because every time he would do so, he'd be tossing my paycheck around as well.

"So, I decided I'd eliminate the decision making of the quarterback except for whether to execute the pitch to the halfback behind the line of scrimmage or run it himself. When our team would break the huddle, I wanted everyone to know if the fullback was going to get the ball or if the quarterback would be coming down the line either to run or pitch, or, if he was going to drop back to pass after the fake to the fullback.

"Despite the fact that the wishbone was basically a running offense, I liked the fact that we could also use a series of pass plays that were disguised in a run-dominated offense. The passing pocket was more of a rolling pocket, meaning it wasn't directly behind the center. I believed that would give our quarterback better downfield vision to pick out a receiver.

"Another change I decided to make came from my days at Warren Western Reserve, where we ran an unbalanced line on offense. That meant I had both tackles either to one side of the center or the other. I knew this would create all sorts of favorable blocking schemes, especially on running plays. Heck, that alignment got my Reserve running back Johnny Cooks a full scholarship to Northwestern in the Big Ten! I didn't see any reason why it wouldn't help a real quick back, and I happened to have one that was just going to be a sophomore, Randy Farabee."

What Dick Strahm really was seeking was an offensive identity totally unique to the Hoosier-Buckeye Conference. Since he'd seen every conference team in 1975, Strahm knew that there were no other teams in the league that ran the wishbone with an unbalanced line.

"I just wanted to run an offensive set that teams in the league would only see once a year and have to prepare for specially. I had a percentage in mind as far as running the wishbone. I wanted 70 percent of our offensive plays to come out of that formation. Then, the other 30 percent, I could mix in some "I" and some split-back sets behind the unbalanced line."

The ever-shifting assistant-coaching picture immediately became evident to Dick after that first year. Of the five assistants on his staff in 1975, three would not be returning.

After Larry Reigle and Don Wright resigned and cited reasons which involved career and a lack of time to devote to part-time coaching, Gordon Chambliss decided to head to Oklahoma City to have reconstructive knee surgery. After the anterior-cruciate-ligament (ACL) surgery in December of the previous year, it was clear that the knee just hadn't responded very well. Additionally, the young man from Montgomery, Alabama, never did get that call from the Lions and felt that, perhaps, he had strayed a bit too far from his Southern roots.

During the winter and early spring, recruiting became a huge priority in the football offices of Dick Strahm. The first thing Dick remembers doing was sitting down with a pad and pencil to write down all of Findlay College's selling points.

"I had to find a product. What were we selling here at Findlay? I felt the main product we had was a quality education. The more I met the faculty members, the more I realized just how special they were. The classes were small, which allowed for more individual attention. We had an excellent tutoring program. Also, all our classes were taught by professors, not graduate assistants."

In addition to education, Strahm wrote three more very salable items on his pad. "I wrote down that the town of Findlay was really a beautiful, clean, well-run place with a lot of very good people.

"Additionally, I wrote that there also were a lot of big industries here, such as Marathon Oil Company, Cooper Tire and Rubber Company, Whirlpool Corporation, Findlay Industries, and Ball Metal. I realized I could talk to potential recruits about the fact that if they established themselves in this town as successful students and football players, there would be the potential for jobs after graduation.

"I knew that to be a fact because I had gotten out to so many of these industries and met a lot of Findlay College graduates who were thriving at Cooper and Marathon and other industries. Heck, one Findlay College grad, Pat Rooney, was an executive at Cooper Tire and Rubber when I got to Findlay and would eventually rise to chief executive officer and chairman of the board!

"Another selling point, I believed, was the fact that the Findlay paper, The Courier, did an excellent job of covering the football team. Really, about everyone in town read Larry Alter's accounts of our games. Certainly, any player's accomplishments were going to be noticed, which meant being noticed by potential employers after they graduated."

In the 1976 recruiting class, some outstanding players arrived, players who would have an immediate impact on the fortunes of Oilers football, players who were the very round pegs Dick Strahm needed to fit into those round holes.

On the offensive side of the ball, Strahm brought in a guard who would start all four years and, also, earn Little All-American honors during both his junior and senior seasons, Pat Gibson. Gibson, currently a software engineer and manager for Plumbline Solutions, recalls the impression Strahm made on him. "I knew, of course, Findlay had only won two games the previous year, but you'd have never guessed that if you talked to Coach Strahm. I don't know. He kind of presented this idea that it would be a privilege to play at Findlay. And, you know something? It was."

Strahm also got Wes Beamon, another offensive guard, from Springfield, Ohio, and a big offensive tackle, Mike Griffith, and a center and future starter, Dave Berger. In addition, Strahm also snagged a player destined to be perhaps the best wide receiver in Findlay College history, a player so good he would join Gibson as a two-time Little All-American, Rick Hatfield. Hatfield agreed to come to Findlay, primarily to play basketball. He had come out of Oregon (Ohio) Cardinal Stritch, where, in addition to excelling in football, he also was an excellent baseball catcher.

Looking to the future, beyond quarterback Gene Fernandez's final year in 1976, Strahm also revisited his past in convincing his old friend and ardent supporter, Paul Trina Sr., to send his namesake to Findlay to, one day, call signals as the starting Oilers quarterback. Paul Jr. would fulfill that role as a sophomore in 1977 and not relinquish it until his graduation.

Defensively, Strahm did extremely well also. He picked up two linebackers who would have excellent careers at Findlay, Tom Smith, from Warren, and Jim Ryan, from Olmsted, Ohio. Ryan would become a player so good that he would one day be inducted into The University of Findlay Athletic Hall of Fame.

Strahm also grabbed a future outstanding safety, Denny Maag, from the same small town as Dave Berger, Leipsic, Ohio, and then looked just around the corner from the campus to Findlay High School for a player who was destined to become a terrific four-year starter at defensive end, Paul Street. Street was a key performer for the Trojans of Findlay High, which had just completed an undefeated regular season in 1975.

As far as special teams, Dick secured Tom Walsh, a talented punter from Warren, and Greg Philip, a place kicker from Van Buren High School, just north of Findlay.

While Dick Strahm wasn't afraid to look anywhere for a player who could help, he also worked the hardest in the places he knew best, places like his home town of Toledo, his former coaching stop, Warren, and right in the immediate vicinity of Findlay.

Recalls Dick about recruiting the communities around Findlay, "I remembered what Coach Lauterbur always felt. He never wanted to lose a potential player from Toledo to another school, unless it was like to Ohio State or Michigan or Notre Dame. I felt the same way about the Findlay area."

Besides recruiting, Dick felt that in order for his program to succeed, he had to find a way to somehow get the Findlay community to become more fully invested in his team. Then, an idea of Dick's began to crystallize in that spring of 1976. When the idea was fully developed, Dick Strahm's Foster Parent program was born.

"I just knew if I made enough phone calls and knocked on enough doors that I could get different families in Findlay to take a special interest in my players, especially our incoming freshmen. Obviously, they wouldn't be adopting the players, but once a week, an "adopted" player would share a home-cooked meal with a family, and a relationship that often became very special would grow. I had some players who used to visit their foster family two or three times a week, just to talk. Sometimes, they would baby-sit. It just became a really neat thing."

Ron Souply was a foster parent every year the program existed, from that spring of 1976 all the way through 1991, when the program finally had run its course and was stopped. The reason for the program's termination was larger recruiting classes.

Recalls the man Dick Strahm still fondly calls 'Soup,' "Some years, we adopted two kids, while other years we had as many as four, like the year we had two freshmen and two seniors.

"I guess the primary activity was a dinner once a week, either one my wife Susan prepared or one where we'd take the boys out to dinner, often with other foster families. But, there were also so many times that we had players who just wanted to come over to talk about problems they were having, either in the classroom or on the field.

"Really, I developed some wonderful and lasting relationships with some of the players. Of course, we always went to the games to watch our 'sons' play, and, often, we sat with the players' real parents.

"Probably, the player I had the longest relationship with is someone I still talk to today, Jerry Fronzaglio. Now, Jerry is from the same area where I grew up, Western Pennsylvania, just south of Pittsburgh. As a matter of fact, he attended the high school considered to be my high school's most bitter rival.

"When I first took him on, I told him that there were two things I wouldn't do for him. I wouldn't do his laundry, and I wouldn't bail him out of jail, so he'd better behave!

"As I got to know Jerry and like him more and more, I softened a bit. While I still wouldn't do his laundry, I did tell him he could at least call me from jail!

"But, seriously, Jerry has remained like a son in many ways through the years. Whenever he's back for homecoming, he and his family and I and mine always spend a great deal of time together. Susan and I have also stayed at his house while traveling. It's been a lot more than just exchanging Christmas cards. It's a relationship that is now approaching thirty years!"

Souply, a high school teacher for 24 years before leaving education to accept a position in human resources at Cooper Tire and Rubber Company, is now retired and still living in Findlay. Looking back, he sees that the program was beneficial not just to the players and himself but to his children as well. "I have three daughters, so the foster program was kind of a bonding experience. They saw the players as siblings in a way, which, at times, led to some pretty funny moments.

"One year, my oldest daughter was in a Findlay restaurant. She was talking to a guy, and one of her 'sibs' that year who happened to be black walked by and said, 'Hi, sis.' Then another player who happened to be Hispanic who also was one of ours that year saw her and walked by and said the exact same thing, 'Hi, sis.'

"My daughter told me the look on the guy's face was priceless as he looked back and forth between her and the two players, trying to figure out the genealogy thing!"

Recalls Strahm, "There are so many couples in the community who stepped up to take a special interest in our players. I really am indebted to them for stepping forward. Our players, I know, appreciated it, and I sure did. It really helped bond our football program and the Findlay community.

"I heard stories of the foster parents sitting with a player's real parents. Then, when the player made a big tackle or a big run, both the real parents and the foster parents would be on their feet yelling, 'That's my boy!'

"Steve Grogan, who was, by that time, the starting quarterback of the New England Patriots, flew to Findlay in the spring of 1977 to spend an afternoon with my quarterbacks and receivers. That evening, at one of the foster-parents' homes, we had a get-together with Steve and many of the foster-parents. What a boost that gave the program. Steve was just super.

"I owe such a big thanks to the families who helped me launch the foster-parent program, like the Souplys; the Botts families, both Dean's and his brother Jim's; the Rooneys; the McMahons; the Manleys; the Knausses; and the Joneses. And, of course, thanks to each and every one of the more than sixty families that took part in the program."

One of those families was the Alters, Larry and Carol. Recalls Larry, "It's just a damn shame that the NCAA [now, the governing body for The University of Findlay, which is a Division II member] won't allow programs for small colleges like Coach's Foster Parent Program. What a great way to bond a young player with the small community in which he plays. Carol and I still hear from some of our former kids."

In addition to some terrific recruiting by both Dick and his defensive coordinator, Jerry English, who would be returning to Strahm's staff in 1976, Dick also pushed the players already in the program hard in the off-season weight and conditioning programs.

Recalls Jerome Gray, now a consultant for Match Point, a company that helps those interested in acquiring franchises, and a starting defensive tackle for Coach Strahm during 1975 and 1976, "We were up in the loft lifting one day, and Coach Strahm was up there. He walked up to me and said, 'Hey, Jerry Gray. What'd you make last year?' I told him that I'd made honorable-mention All-Conference. He looked at me and said, 'Oh, man, I'd never tell anyone THAT again.'

"That was just his way of challenging me. And, that's exactly what I needed. When I came back for August two-a-days, I was in the best shape of my life.

"In those August practices, I could sense that things were going to change. I just knew we weren't going to be 2-8 again.

"Every day after practice, we ran what Coach Strahm used to call 'perfect 40s.' That meant we ran 40-yard dashes and kept running them until Coach Strahm felt every single player was maxing out effort-wise. I think that sort of bonded us as a team. When we all realized we were going to keep running until everyone was putting his best effort forth, I think we decided we weren't going to be in the business of letting each other down."

As far as the coaching staff, Wright, Reigle, and Chambliss were gone. Replacing them were Jeff Bower, who Jim Houdeshell found; Mark Basilius, who was working on his master's at Bowling Green State; and Steve Mohr, a Dennison University graduate who was also working on his master's at Bowling Green. All would be part-time assistants who would get to the practice field as soon as possible.

As the August practices unfolded, followed by many perfect 40s, Strahm thought he was seeing the results of the rigorous off-season weight-training program.

"I could see the difference in so many of our young men strength-wise. Dave Danhoff, for instance, seemed a lot stronger and more agile, and I thought he earned the starting tight-end position. I needed his blocking ability.

"That August, we ran hard. We ran after every practice. If nothing else, I wanted the Findlay Oilers to be the best-conditioned team in the Hoosier-Buckeye Conference.

"We never walked between drills. I took on the role as conditioning coach. Our new unity cry at the end of practice, the last thing we'd yell in unison before hitting the showers was 'Fourth quarter!' I just wanted to instill the belief that we would own that final quarter of each game.

"Did we work harder on conditioning than any other team? Who knows? But, I was trying to establish a mindset, and I believe my coaches and I accomplished that."

The dog days of August crept along for players anxious to bid farewell to the physical exhaustion and the heat. For the coaches, who had so much to prepare for, not the least of which was the brand-new offensive scheme, it seemed like the pre-season practices afforded so little time to do so much.

And no matter how fast or slow the practice days seemed to be going, there was one certainty. Strahm was going to make sure everyone on his offense knew the play upon which the wishbone offense would be built.

It was the bedrock, and it was known quite simply by the numbers '22-2.' Recalls Dick, "I felt, after what I witnessed the year before when so many of our drives stalled because we were so inept in converting short yardage for first downs, that we needed to establish one play that we could run and get two, three, or four yards when it was imperative we keep a drive alive.

"Additionally, I wanted to shorten games by running the ball, moving the chains, and keeping the clock moving.

"Now, on 22-2, we ran what is called an isolation to the strong side of an unbalanced line. The strong side would be the side with both tackles. Our halfback, who we called our 'two-back,' would lead into the hole between the tackles to block whoever showed, generally a linebacker. With the extra blockers, our fullback, who was Randy Farabee in 1976, should be able to get those short, tough yards to keep the sticks moving.

"The play really was the most important play in our playbook, not just in 1976 but throughout my career at Findlay. We had such talented offensive line coaches who would one day join our staff, men like Jim McIntosh and Curtis Davidson, and these coaches, in addition to Steve Mohr, who was just coming aboard, studied the 22-2 from every conceivable angle. They invented more ways to block that play than one could possibly imagine!

"This one single play made us, in the minds of many opposing coaches, a nightmare to prepare for. How do I know that? Because so many told me after games and at coaching clinics when we talked.

"Just to show you the success we had with 22-2, after I retired following the 1998 season, our sports information people did some calculating and determined that that one single play accounted for over 22,000 yards in the 23 years that we ran the play."

Here's how the play looked in the Findlay Oilers playbook:

Strahm continues, "As a coach, I never really wanted to do a lot of fancy things. I guess that might be because I've never really been a very fancy guy. I wanted execution as near perfect as humanly possible and, to attain that, I lived by two rules in my coaching. First, keep it simple, and, two, what you did run, practice the hell out of it! It all boils down to two words, simplicity and execution. That's why 65 percent of our offense was going to be the nine plays in the wishbone package.

"I'm sure there were probably times I exceeded the 65 percent goal and, probably, also times I put people to sleep in the stands, but I wanted to win by not making mistakes, and, to me, winning and avoiding mistakes are almost joined at the hip!"

To accomplish what he wanted, Strahm simply didn't want to, as the saying goes, "outthink the room." He wanted a thinner offensive playbook but a playbook containing a series of plays which could be run in optimum mode.

In addition to conditioning and executing the nine wishbone plays, Strahm also stressed the importance of limiting mistakes. Recalls Dick, "I certainly know every coach believes in that, but I really wanted to stress it to the absolute max. We did a lot of classroom work to show players what the turnover ratio really meant and how it impacted the eight losses we had in 1975, especially the five we lost by a total of twenty-five points.

"I wanted them to see, almost from an academic standpoint, what roles that fumbles lost, interceptions, and penalties played in a team's success or failure. I think sometimes coaches assume their players understand this, but I really believe that you've got to go to the blackboard or the overhead projector and show them. Maybe the fact that I was a former classroom teacher made it easier for me to see this."

Mixed in with the Oilers vets were 29 freshmen. Several players, despite their youth and inexperience, would log substantial playing time. Recalls Dick, "Who'd have thought that those kids fresh out of high school would be on the field for the school's first national championship before they would graduate!"

September finally arrived, and the 1976 season was about to unfold. Gene Fernandez was the starting quarterback, and the player who would be getting the lion's share of carries in the new offense was Randy Farabee.

One thing Fernandez noticed about Farabee became abundantly clear after the first couple pre-season practices. "I couldn't believe how fast Farabee got to the hole. He was so quick, so explosive out of his stance, that I barely had time to execute the reverse pivot that the wishbone requires and still get the ball to him. The first few times we ran the 22-2 in August, I missed the handoffs because Randy was already by me and into the hole.

"Of course, I knew better than to complain or try to explain to coaches that my fullback needed to slow down coming out of his stance. I'd have sounded absolutely foolish. I knew I just needed to get quicker."

The season began with a series of alternating wins and losses for the first six weeks. In week one, it was a low-scoring slugfest, a 7-0 loss to the Defiance Yellow Jackets. Week two saw an Oilers rebound, a 28-10 win over the Bluffton Beavers. Week three saw the downward arc of the yo-yo in another close 18-14 loss to the Quakers of Wilmington, a team coached by a man Dick Strahm has such respect for, Bill Ramseyer.

And, after that tough loss in week three, with his team sitting at 1-2, Strahm seriously contemplated making a major change in the direction he would take his Oilers. It was a moment senior tight end Dave Danhoff, now the superintendent of Vanguard Career Center, remembers vividly to this day.

"After the Wilmington game, Coach Strahm had reached about the absolute end of his patience. All of us could tell. I guess you could say he didn't wear his losses well. The previous year, with the 2-8 record, and then, after a lot of retooling of what we were going to do to start by losing two of the first three, well, that just wasn't going to be acceptable.

"I remember him walking into the locker room after that 18-14 loss and saying, 'If I'm going to lose, I may as well lose with freshmen and sophomores. I'm going to think about things a lot tonight at home, and tomorrow at practice, I'll let you juniors and seniors know my decision. You upperclassmen may very well be watching the rest of the year.

"Well, when we got together for a light practice on that Sunday, Coach said he'd give the upperclassmen one more chance, that despite the loss, he saw enough effort to warrant that. I don't mind telling you that the night before, that was the only topic of conversation for the juniors and seniors. There were a lot of nervous upperclassmen who arrived at practice the next day. We decided that, if Coach would give us the opportunity, we were going to respond to the challenge he laid before us. And, we did."

Recalls Dick, "I do remember what Dave recalls. I was as frustrated after that Wilmington game as, perhaps, any time in my career to that point, and I did seriously contemplate going totally with freshmen and sophomores from that point on. However, I had seen enough effort-wise in the loss to warrant one more chance. I believe so much of life is recognizing challenges which are laid before your feet and doing something about them. I guess I wanted those juniors and seniors to have that opportunity to do something about the challenge I put before them."

In week four, the beginnings of a challenge accepted began to manifest themselves in a 34-0 shutout over Manchester. While there was a tough non-conference 17-6 loss to Waynesburg in week five, it was followed by a dominating 31-3 win over Earlham.

While the 3-3 record was certainly an improvement over 1975, Dick Strahm simply didn't want to be just average, winning one week and then giving all the momentum back the next, so he continued to push and continued to reiterate the post-Wilmington challenge to his juniors and seniors.

He wanted to capture something he hadn't tasted as a head coach since his days at Bryan High School. He wanted a conference championship, and he knew it was possible if his Oilers won the remaining three games on the nine-game schedule.

Sure, there were those three consecutive 9-1 seasons at Warren Western Reserve, but, at that time, the Raiders had no league affiliation. Sure, there were a couple of MidAmerican Conference crowns during his time at the University of Toledo, but Strahm was an assistant, not the head, coach. As head coach of the Oilers, he wanted a league championship.

Strahm's team responded well in the next two weeks, finally putting together back-to-back wins for the first time in his Findlay career, 39-15 over the Anderson College Ravens and 28-14 over the Taylor University Trojans.

That set up a showdown on the final Saturday of the 1976 season with the Hanover College Panthers, and the mission was clear. A win would bring Findlay a share of their first Hoosier-Buckeye championship since Byron Morgan's 1971 team. It was a mission Coach Strahm and his assistants stressed all week in the practices leading up to the game to be played before the Oilers hometown faithful at Donnell Stadium.

Dick recalls feeling pretty good heading into the finale. "By that point, a lot of our freshmen and sophomores were playing like upperclassmen. Players like Pat Gibson and Paul Street and Kevin Cassidy really had matured. I thought we had an excellent week of practice.

For seniors like Jerome Gray, Dave Danhoff, Bill Miller, Gene Fernandez, and Mark Niswonger, it was finally a chance to feel the exhilaration of preparing for a big late-season game, a game where a conference championship would be won or lost. Recalls Gray, "I can remember talking to Dave as we left practice one day about how great it was to not be just playing out the string by a season's final week of practice. Neither of us had ever been faced with this opportunity during our Findlay careers."

In the game that Strahm sees today as the pivot upon which his program turned, Findlay responded with a convincing 44-6 win. Strahm's players executed nearly flawlessly. Recalls the senior quarterback Fernandez, "Everything I threw up, someone seemed to catch, especially that skinny freshman who had worked his way into the starting lineup, Rick Hatfield."

Kevin Cassidy recalls another player's contributions that day, a player many would have a tendency to overlook. But, as has been said, it takes a football player to truly appreciate a football player.

"I was so happy for our seniors, especially that day. After winning just six games in three years, to win six games and grab a share of the conference championship their last year, well, that's just a great story in my mind. Sure, I was happy for guys like Jerome and Dave, but I was really pleased for a senior who would go on to become an excellent high school football coach, Jerry Buti, who has had some great success at Defiance High School. He was the captain of our special teams his last two years. He was such a hard worker and really deserved that 6-3 season as much as any starter on offense or defense.

"I think that 1976 team really set the tone with their work ethic, and I was as proud to be a part of that team as any, either athletically or in business, that I've ever been on."

Remembers the starting tight end Danhoff, "Look, I wasn't a great athlete and never deluded myself into thinking along those lines, but how proud I was to play for a coach like Dick Strahm and see the transformation that occurred from the 2-8 team in '75 to that '76 team. So much changed in such a short amount of time.

"You talk about a great life lesson and one I could take into my own career in education! With the right amount of attitude and the right work ethic, I saw up close what could happen in almost a blink of an eye."

The first-year linebacker Jim Ryan remembered Danhoff fondly years later when he was inducted into The University of Findlay Hall of Fame. "It was the seniors, players like Dave Danhoff, who took me and so many of the young guys under their wings and really showed us what it meant to be an Oiler."

The 44-6 win meant Findlay College and Hanover both finished with a 6-2 conference record. The engine that drove the Oilers against the Panthers that day was the sophomore fullback Randy Farabee. The former Elmwood (Ohio) High School star scored on runs of 2, 80, and 1 yards and added a fourth touchdown on a 12-yard pass from Fernandez. He had 180 yards rushing on that glorious day at Donnell. Senior running back Keith Smith added 119 more yards as he closed out his Oilers career with TD runs of 57 and 10 yards.

It was hard to tell which unit, the offense or the defense, had the better day on that November 14. The wishbone offense was primarily responsible for 428 yards on the ground, and this came against a team which had held its last four opponents to one touchdown in the last sixteen quarters.

The defense forced seven fumbles and recovered four of them, including key recoveries to set up Oilers touchdowns by Cassidy and Mark Philmore. Mark Niswonger and Steve Heintzelman covered the other two loose balls.

After the game, Strahm told his friend, The Courier sportswriter Larry Alter, "We were just hungry today. Anytime you hold a talented team to less than 200 yards in total offense, you're putting yourself in great position to win."

In the post-game celebration, the second-year Oilers head coach earned somewhat of a dubious prize. Recalls Strahm, "After the game, I got tossed in the pond right outside the stadium. In mid-November, you don't think that was brisk? But, I didn't mind at all."

As Dick Strahm evaluated the numbers of the 6-3 conference-winning season, he was pleased. Not only did his team close with a flourish, four consecutive wins against conference opponents (as opposed to the five consecutive losses that ended the 1975 season) but his team also more than doubled its opponents in total score, 224 to 90.

In assessing his new wishbone offense, Dick saw substantial improvement. In 1975, the Oilers averaged 170.4 yards per game rushing and 52.6 yards per contest passing, for a total offense of 223. In 1976, with Fernandez under center and Farabee running fullback contributing greatly, the increase in offensive production was dramatic. The Oilers averaged 312.8 yards rushing and 71.1 passing, for a total offensive output of 383.9 yards per game. That meant the Oilers had picked up more than 160 more yards per game, a large reason why Findlay College scored 91 more points than Strahm's first year.

On the year, Strahm's 1976 team set or tied fifteen individual or team records. The wishbone wound up accounting for more yards (2,815) and more first downs (173) than any team to that point in school history. Additionally, the Oilers had two players, Randy Farabee and defensive tackle Bill Miller, who were named to the Associated Press Little All-American team.

Defensively, the squad that Strahm called his "Blood Unit" allowed the fewest yards (870) in one season than any in school history, a history that traces itself all the way back to 1892 and a 20-0 loss to Heidelberg College.

So, with the kind of substantial improvement Dick Strahm noticed from his first year to his second, he literally couldn't wait for the 1977 season. And, while he waited, he continued to tweak and upgrade his off-season strength-and-conditioning programs.

The Strahm family had settled into the Findlay community nicely. The kids were doing well at school. Doug, approaching his thirteenth birthday, was developing a growing interest in football and soon would be donning the colors of the Findlay High School Trojans. Gina was about to turn ten and had long ago ceased taking flying leaps off the coffee table, much to the relief of Ginger Strahm. She was beginning to show some athletic prowess of her own. Steve was just beginning to walk, which meant Ginger, again, was on full alert.

When the spring of 1977 came, Strahm knew that again, he would need to replace coaches as well as throw himself headlong into recruiting.

On his coaching staff, Dick would need to replace Jerry English, Mark Basilius, and Jeff Bower. Steve Mohr stayed for his second year of what would ultimately become nine, this time as a full-time assistant. Recalls Dick, "For a young part-time coach driving over from Bowling Green in 1976, I thought Steve did a terrific job. Despite his youth, I thought he had great potential in coaching. I was so fortunate that someone as fine a coach as Steve decided to stay on my staff for nine years. He was too good to stay forever, I knew that. I was glad to keep him as long as I did.

"Now, of course, he's built a tremendous record down in San Antonio at NCAA Division III Trinity University. He's been well known in small college coaching for years, and, during the 2007 season, everyone was talking about Steve on ESPN when his team executed a fifteen-lateral last play of the game to beat Millsaps College, 28-24.

Another assistant coach who would debut in 1977 was headed for an even longer run than Steve Mohr at Findlay. As a matter of fact, Jim McIntosh came aboard and never left until Strahm himself retired after the '98 season.

Recalls Dick, "I got a knock on my front door at home one day, and it was Jim. He introduced himself. Jim was a math teacher in the Fostoria (Ohio) City School and had been an assistant football coach at the high school for twelve years. I had to be honest with him. I told Jim that, while I'd love to have him, I couldn't pay much."

McIntosh, now retired after a career, first, as a math teacher and, then, as an assistant principal in Fostoria, remembers the first conversation with the man who would become both colleague and friend, "I told Dick I didn't care all that much about money. I just wanted to coach.

"It was opportunity to do what I loved to do. There had been some changes in Fostoria in the football program that I wasn't altogether onboard with and decided to stop coaching there, and I needed an outlet. Dick provided me that. Before he and I walked into coaching retirement together, I had coached on both sides of the ball. I guess most of the former players, if you gathered them in a very big room, would remember me as an offensive line coach. That, I believe, was my strength."

The two other assistants who joined the staff were Mike Von Stein and Rick Huegli.

Von Stein replaced Jerry English, who decided to go to Colorado to become a ski instructor. Mike became the defensive coordinator. However, Von Stein's tenure at Findlay would prove to be short, as he would leave after the 1977 campaign.

For Rick Huegli, his stay in Findlay also would prove to be short. A native of Washington state, after the season, Huegli returned home and eventually became the strength and conditioning coach for Don James, who became a coaching legend for the University of Washington Huskies while leading them to a national championship.

Recalls Dick, "Rick eventually co-authored a book with Don, a highly regarded book on the how's and why's of football conditioning. I read it and certainly used some of the drills and techniques right here in Findlay.

As far as recruiting, Strahm was looking to increase his numbers from the previous year's total. He continued to sell, first, the quality education available to all at Findlay College.

One hole Dick needed to fill was one he hadn't anticipated. Randy Farabee, after a stellar 1976 season that saw him gain almost 900 yards in nine games, average 5.2 yards per carry and gain a nod as a Little All-American, decided to drop out of school for personal reasons.

For the wishbone to work at peak efficiency, a hammer was needed to run the two-back. Quite simply, Strahm needed a big, physical fullback who could run the 22-2, again and again.

To find him, Strahm again relied on an area he knew well, and an area where he still had many contacts and many sets of eyes trained on Toledo schoolboy football.

Recalls Dick, "I knew there was a big, physical fullback about to graduate from Toledo St. Francis named Nelson Bolden. Now, Nelson had sustained a pretty serious knee injury at the end of his junior year and didn't run the ball that much his senior year. He was more of a blocking back for a running back by the name of Mike Kennedy, who wound up playing at the University of Toledo.

"I knew Bolden had been on a lot of big schools' radar screens before the knee injury, but those schools backed off. This allowed us at Findlay to get a shot at recruiting him.

"I figured I'd take a chance on the knee if Nelson would take a chance on us, so I went after him hard. He had the three ingredients I always looked for in a power back, strength, speed, and, despite the injury, quickness.

"Additionally, when I first met him, I was so impressed, not only with Nelson but also with his parents. Nelson had all the personal characteristics you'd want in your own son. He was humble. He was also grateful for anything anyone did for him. And, those traits came from a great mom and dad. His mother was a teacher, and his father worked for the city of Toledo. Both had always placed a very high priority on education, which is why Nelson was about to graduate from a private high school. Nelson's mom eventually would earn her Ph.D., and his father held a master's.

"I really hammered home the educational points of Findlay College. I had all my facts on student-professor ratios and the diversity and quality of our academic programs. Finally, after I got done giving all my selling points, Mrs. Bolden paused and looked at her husband and said, 'What do you think?'

"His reply was one that made me feel good about our chances to land this 6'3", 230-pound young man. Dad said, 'It sounds to me like Findlay College is a lot like St. Francis, and we never regretted for a moment sending our son there!'"

Bolden, now a manager in the restaurant business in his hometown of Toledo, remembers what really impressed him about Dick Strahm. "As an only child, I'll admit that I was a bit spoiled as a kid. I really needed approval from people, especially the authority figures in my life. Well, my senior year, during wrestling season, I made it to State. I eventually finished third, and guess who drove over to Columbus to watch me wrestle? Coach Strahm. He was right there to support me and congratulate me. He didn't have to spend an entire Saturday doing that!

"Really, I'd never even heard of Findlay College while I was at St. Francis. I really had a much stronger interest in athletics than academics, but my mom was just the opposite.

"Personally, she couldn't have cared less if I'd even played sports. She wanted me to get my degree. Of course, I was more interested when Coach Strahm told me I would be able to start as a freshman and be the featured running back. I felt my knee had come back strong, and I was ready to show those big schools they'd made a mistake by backing off. During my junior year, I'd talked to both Woody Hayes and Bo Schembechler about coming to Ohio State and Michigan. Then, I hurt my knee, and they were nowhere to be found. When you're only seventeen, that's pretty tough to take.

"So, when Coach Strahm showed so much interest in me, I was sold, probably more on him than the school.

"Coach Strahm has been more like a second father to me, which is why I have always kept in close contact with him. He not only was there for me during my four years at Findlay but also after I graduated.

"When I was in the Pittsburgh Steelers training camp, trying to make the team as a free agent during the July after I graduated from Findlay, Coaches Strahm, Mohr, McIntosh, and

Pees [Dean Pees, who would join Strahm's staff as defensive coordinator in 1979] all drove to Latrobe in Pennsylvania to watch and encourage me. When I got cut during the last week of camp after almost making the team, it was Coach Strahm again who was there to pick me up emotionally.

"He also got me a tryout with the Pittsburgh Maulers of the United States Football League. Again, I was right on the verge of making the squad, before Mike Rozier, the former All-American running back out of Nebraska, ended his holdout and signed, and I was seen as expendable and cut. And, again, Coach Strahm was there to lend support.

"After I started my career in restaurant management, Coach continued to keep tabs on me. When my father passed away in 1987, Coach came to Toledo and was with the family every step of the way.

"In 2005, I was diagnosed with prostate cancer, and the first person I called after telling my mom was Coach Strahm. I knew Coach was a two-time prostate cancer survivor, and his advice and support were invaluable in my facing the surgery and getting through the fear that I was going to die. Thankfully, I'm now in remission.

"The reason why I showed these snapshots of my life is to show the impact a great coach can have in a player's life. My cancer scare was 25 years after I left Findlay, yet Dick Strahm was STILL there for me!

"To this very day, he's still a major force in my life and always will be. When I have a problem, the first thing my mom will say to me is, 'Call Coach Strahm, and see what he thinks!'"

For Dick Strahm, taking an interest in a player like Nelson Bolden was easy. "He is such a quality person, so why wouldn't I?

"And, as a football player, he did so much for my career and this university. Listen, it's no coincidence that Nelson's arrival on campus in August of 1977 came right before Findlay College established itself nationally in the world of NAIA football."

Before Bolden came, Findlay College made the NAIA playoffs only one time and played just one game, losing to Sam Houston State (located in Huntsville, Texas) in the first round back in 1964, by a score of 32-21. Before Bolden's eligibility expired, Findlay College played in six playoff games, winning five, and culminated those half dozen appearances with a national championship.

Bolden became the mover of piles. His runs, many on 22-2's, were not pretty to many who possessed untrained eyes in ascertaining what really mattered in the world of football. To those who were football savvy, though, the tackle-to-tackle runs, often with Bolden taking shots from five or six defenders, were masterpieces in efficiency, preludes to officials who signaled first downs.

Of course, there were other players destined to become key performers who arrived on campus in 1977, players like Ron Wright, Dave Noward, Mike Stocker, Duane Tooman, and Ken Agee.

Agee's was an interesting story. He had been a highly touted running back out of the Cleveland area, and originally accepted a scholarship to play for Coach Bill Hess at Ohio University in Athens. When Hess decided that Agee should redshirt his first year, Agee decided he didn't want to sit out the year in exchange for another year of eligibility later and told Hess he was declining the scholarship.

So, Hess called Dick Strahm. The two were acquainted through Dick's days spent as the defensive coordinator at Toledo. Hess asked Strahm if he'd be interested in Agee. Of course, a player who was good enough to be a Mid-American Conference scholarship athlete would be one Strahm would covet at Findlay College.

The plot continued to thicken because by the time Dick contacted Ken, he had already accepted a full scholarship to Youngstown (Ohio) State, a school which had originally lost out in the recruiting wars to Ohio University.

Recalls Strahm, "Well, I thought I'd lost the opportunity, that is, until Ken called me and asked me if he could still come to Findlay. I asked him what happened, and he told me that, because of an unpleasant confrontation with one of Youngstown State's assistant coaches, he decided in mid-summer to, again, opt out of his scholarship.

"Now, I told Ken that I'd get the financial-aid people seeing what type of help Ken qualified for as soon as I got all the financial-disclosure information from his parents but that I certainly wasn't in a position to offer any scholarship help. At this time, none existed for any NAIA Division II schools."

Recalls Agee, who now is a senior juvenile corrections officer in Cleveland, "I still remember to this day what happened. My mom had gotten me a very good summer job, which paid very well. Well, one of my coaches at Youngstown State had called and said he wanted me on campus for a general-information meeting with some other incoming freshmen.

"When I found out that I couldn't get off work and would be forced to quit the job if I didn't work the day the meeting was scheduled, I called the assistant back and asked if I could come and get caught up on what I would miss at the meeting, perhaps on a weekend, when I didn't have to work.

"Well, he was furious with me and started talking all about my priorities. He also told me that when August practices started he'd remember this and that he was going to run me and run me until I thought I was trying out for cross country instead of football.

"After I hung up, I just decided there were going to be real problems, so I decided to pass on the scholarship. That's when I called Coach Strahm.

Recalls Dick, "I got with our admissions people, and it turned out Ken qualified for a lot of aid, so he accepted my invitation to come to Findlay.

"Later, I called him back and told him I had gotten him a job painting silos if he wanted to come to Findlay for the rest of the summer."

Agee laughs at the memory. "I turned Coach Strahm down on that one. To be honest, I didn't know what silos were, but I was too embarrassed to ask. It just didn't sound like something I should be doing, so I decided to stay with the job my mom got me until pre-season practices began."

The rest of the summer came and went, including those pre-season practices, and it was time for the 1977 season to begin. For the second straight year, the opener was with the Yellow Jackets of Defiance College. The previous season, Defiance knocked off the Oilers in a low-scoring affair.

This season, the game was again played very close to the vest and ended without resolution. The 3-3 tie extended a recent trend. In the last five games between the two rival Hoosier-Buckeye schools, including this one, the record was dead even, at 2-2-1. The five games produced a paltry 44 points combined. The Oilers won in 1973 and 1974, 7-6 and 6-3. The Yellow Jackets won the next two rounds, 6-3 and 7-0, before the 3-3 deadlock.

Recalls Strahm, "The Defiance games featured some extremely physical football. I'd like to think of those games as ones the real football purists appreciated. I'm sure there were those who may have been bored by those contests because there wasn't a whole lot of offense, but the defenses were outstanding.

"One of the fascinating things about football is each game takes on its own personality. Some are high-scoring affairs, but, to my way of thinking, it would actually be boring if they were all like that.

"I'll tell you from a coach's perspective, those low-scoring games, because they rely so very much on field position, are like tension-filled chess matches. You just know that one mistake, one lapse in judgment, where you go on a fourth and short on your own 40-yard line and come up short, instead of punting, can cost you dearly. That's plenty exciting enough for me.

"Maybe it's the fact that I'd played so much fast-pitch softball growing up, where games are typically low scoring and every hit and every base advanced means a great deal, made me appreciate football games which weren't offensive in nature."

The new signal caller for the Oilers in 1977 was the sophomore whom Dick recruited out of football-crazy Warren, Ohio, Paul Trina Jr., and he was ready to show what he could do. Trina Jr., now the athletic director for the Warren City Schools, has a vivid recollection of what Coach Strahm did during the week after the season-opening tie in a game Trina calls his worst performance of his career.

"Coach called in all three quarterbacks for a private viewing of the game film. As we watched, he said, 'Maybe I picked the wrong starter.' He wasn't afraid to challenge your manhood. The next game, I played well, and I think Coach saw that I had recognized the challenge, accepted it, and did something about it on the football field. I wanted to be the starting quarterback at Findlay College, and it was a job I never lost.

"My life after football, as everyone's is, was full of challenges, and Coach Strahm's throwing down challenges was his way of getting us ready for those challenges. His challenge was the precursor to what successes I've had in my career since I left Findlay."

Paul Sr. was still cutting hair at his barber shop on the west side of the Mahoning River. It was a shop where, in the fall, or really regardless of what time of year it was, the conversation rarely drifted far from football. But, on Saturdays, Paul wouldn't be cutting hair. He'd be in the stands watching his son.

Paul Sr. was as enthusiastic a Dick Strahm supporter as anyone in town during Dick's 1966-1969 tenure at Warren Western Reserve. So, it was no surprise that his son would play in college for Dick if given the opportunity. It was also a given that Dad would be in the stands for every one of his son's Findlay College games, both home and away, save one game. And, it took something pretty important to miss that one game, a little procedure called open-heart surgery.

After the unresolved opener with Defiance, the third-year coach's Oilers went on a three-game winning streak, and, what made it particularly sweet was that all three wins were conference games. First the Oilers crushed the Bluffton Beavers, 41-16. Then they proved they could win a close one, 16-14 over Wilmington. Then, it was back to winning resoundingly, 41-21 over Manchester.

In week five, a non-conference game against Waynesburg University, in Waynesburg, Pennsylvania, the Oilers dropped a tight one, 20-13.

Then, the Oilers express started to roll again. First they steamrolled Earlham, the Hoosier-Buckeye school from Richmond, Indiana, 55-9.

Then it was a win over Anderson, 27-14. The game was significant because it was Nelson Bolden's first collegiate 100-yard rushing effort. During his brilliant career, Bolden would crack the century barrier seventeen more times on his way to amassing a school career rushing total of 4,009 yards, which is a mark that has yet to be broken more than 25 years after his graduation.

In week eight, the Oilers dropped Taylor University, 41-27, in a shootout. It was the fourth time the wishbone offense accounted for more than 40 points in the eight games.

Despite the season-ending tough loss, 14-7, to league power Hanover, Dick was generally pleased. The Oilers improved their record, from 6-3 to 6-2-1, and also captured a share of the conference title for the second consecutive season.

Perhaps what's important about Strahm's disposition following the 1977 season is that he was generally pleased but certainly not at all fully satisfied. For one thing, he wanted an outright conference championship. He also wanted to see the Oilers in the NAIA playoffs, something that hadn't happened in thirteen years. One coach on Strahm's staff knew a thing or two about the trip to the playoffs back in 1964. Jim McIntosh was on Coach Byron Morgan's playoff team.

As far as his coaching staff, Strahm continued to search for some stability. He had positions to fill again. While Steve Mohr remained for a third consecutive year, as did the man Findlay players simply called 'Coach Mac,' Jim McIntosh, there were again holes to fill, with the departure of Dave Smith, Mike Von Stein, and Rick Huegli.

Recalls Dick, "I got Denny Studrawa to come coach the backs. Jim McIntosh was Denny's assistant before Denny retired as head coach at Fostoria High School. Certainly, a recommendation from Mac meant a lot.

"Dave Tanner also came on as defensive coordinator. Jim Hilles, my coaching colleague at Warren Western Reserve, was now at Ball State as defensive coordinator. Dave was a graduate assistant under Jim. When you get recommendations from coaches as good as Jim Hilles, well, you take them without question.

"Dave Roberts is Steve Mohr's cousin, and, let me tell you, he was one tough guy, and I don't think that ever hurts a coaching staff, to have a guy like that. Dave had served in the military as a forward observer in Vietnam."

As Dick went through the off season, he, as all coaches do, speculated on what the 1978 team was capable of. The team was now reaping the benefits of some strong recruiting classes. Heading into the '78 season, Strahm knew there would be many sophomore and junior starters, and, despite their youth, they had quite a bit of game experience. Then, of course, there would be solid senior starters, players like strong safety Kevin Cassidy, linebacker Frank Molinaro, defensive end Ben Finch, and tight end Denny Severin, who had developed into a terrific blocker in addition to being a reliable receiver.

Strahm felt that the offense carried with it the possibility of being really outstanding. At wide receiver, Dick had Rick Hatfield, easily the best receiver in the conference and a player Strahm felt could have played in the Mid-American Conference. Recalls Dick, "I still wonder how Rick wound up at Findlay. He had a skill package that sometimes just left people shaking their heads."

Recalls Kevin Cassidy, "This might sound like an exaggeration, but I honestly don't ever remember Hatfield dropping a ball, either in practice or in a game!"

Besides Severin at tight end, the offensive line, the sled that Nelson Bolden would ride, was comprised of tackles Dave Noward, Fred Lopez, and Mike Griffith. The guards were Wes Beamon and Pat Gibson. The center was the rock from Leipsic, Dave Berger.

In the backfield, Trina returned for his junior year, and second as a starter. While Bolden would get the lion's share of the carries, there were both talent and speed from the halfback rotation of Nate Phillips, Wilson Beard, and Denny Guerra.

Of the three halfbacks, the quickest without a doubt, was the senior Guerra. As a matter of fact, he was the fastest player in the entire conference, having won the conference 100-yard dash the previous spring, at 9.4 seconds. So, wouldn't a player with such incredible raw speed be a featured back?

Strahm recalls, "A lot of people probably questioned why I had Denny playing the two-back, which was, primarily, the blocking back. It was the two-back who would lead Nelson Bolden into the hole on the 22-2. Well, I wanted someone both quick to the hole and tenacious enough to be an effective blocker on the play that was the lifeblood of our entire offense. Denny Guerra was that someone."

Recalls Guerra, now a senior vice president at Citizens Bank in Sandusky, Ohio, "I really wasn't angry at all that I would be used primarily as a blocker. I knew Nelson was a special back, and he would be the horse. Heck, there's only one ball and only so many carries in any offense.

"Besides, my senior year gave me my biggest Findlay football lesson, and it's one I carried into my career once I graduated. And, that lesson is that everyone has a role to play in any successful operation, and, if everyone, without jealousy or complaint, accepts that role and executes it to the best of his or her ability, success will inevitably follow.

"As a team, we took Coach Strahm's message, and we trusted his judgment. That's why I never complained about being the two-back. I had a job to do, and I was going to get the best block I possibly could get on the first defender who showed himself in the hole so Nelson could cut off my block, and I was going to do it every single time we ran that 22-2!"

One of Strahm's best sales jobs may not have been the one he executed in convincing a 9.4 100-yard dash man that he was a blocking back. It may, however, very well have been the one he did on Ken Agee, a player who arrived on campus with a great résumé as a high-school running back at Cleveland John F. Kennedy.

Recalls Dick, "I convinced Ken that we were loaded at the running back position and that he could best help us win if he would play our nose tackle on defense along with Pat Roncagli, who also was versatile enough to play any of our down defensive tackles."

The ability to recognize and make the proper personnel moves is what some who both coached with and played for Dick remember the most.

Kevin Cassidy recalls, "I watched Coach each year take guys who had never played a new position in their lives and not only convince them to try it but get them excited about the shift! Coach was an absolute master at that kind of motivation."

Recalls Jim McIntosh, "I feel that Dick's greatest strength as a coach was his ability to evaluate talent and put people in the right positions to achieve not always individual but team success.

"He simply was fearless when moving players position-wise. And, the best example is when Dick convinced Ken Agee to play nose tackle. Imagine, from getting all the glory that backs tend to get when he was in high school to crawling around on all fours trying to figure ways to beat the center and clog up the middle.

"And, this is a kid who ran a legit 4.5 40-yard dash! Once he became a nose tackle, he was simply unblockable! I can't even tell you the number of times he made tackles in the backfield because there wasn't a center he ever lined up against that was even half as quick as he was."

The defensive ends would be outstanding, with Ben Finch, back all the way from New Jersey for his senior year, and junior Paul Street, the former Findlay High School Trojan, who seemed to get better and better with each game he played.

The tackles were Ron Wright and two almost immovable blocks of stone, former Leipsic High School Vikings, Duane Tooman and Roger Funk. The latter, Funk, certainly has one of the more interesting stories when it comes to being recruited to a small college to play football. Strahm remembers the exact place he first laid eyes on the 6'2", 235-pounder, two years removed from high school graduation.

"The Roger Funk story is certainly one worthy of being told. Actually, the first time I saw Roger, he was sitting on a bar stool at Maag's Hotel Bar in Leipsic. It was in July of 1978 when Duane Tooman's dad, Lowell, and I stopped there for lunch. I was doing some painting for Lowell.

"Well, Lowell saw this big kid sitting on a bar stool drinking a beer and jerked his head in his direction. 'See that kid sitting over there?' I nodded. Lowell told me that he was 20 years old. He said that his senior year at Leipsic High School two years earlier, he was an All-State defensive lineman.

"So, I went over to him and struck up a conversation. I told him who I was and that I was always looking for players who could help our team and asked what his plans were. He told me he'd been working some construction and had done some welding and was about to go to work for a friend as a sheep farmer. Oh, and by the way, he was also an amateur boxer and was in training for a bout.

"Well, my sales skills must have been on that day because I piqued his interest just enough for him to agree to come over to Findlay for a look around. Before too long, I had Roger's parents over there, meeting with our admissions folks, and I had myself someone who would start as a 20-year-old freshman and play so well, you'd swear he last played two weeks ago instead of two years ago!"

At linebackers, Strahm had seasoned juniors Jim Ryan and Tom Smith and the ultra-intense senior, Frank Molinaro.

Tom Smith, from Warren Western Reserve, now living in Louisiana, is the only person to have been on the sidelines for a bird's-eye view of every one of Strahm's five national championship games. Recalls Dick, "Tom played in both the 1978 and 1979 games, and he also was on the sidelines many years later watching our championship games in 1992, 1995, and 1997. It's loyalty like that in the men who played for you that is never, ever forgotten."

Recalls Dick about Molinaro, "He just craved contact. Once, before a game, I got a call from the vice president for student affairs, who wanted me to go over to Frank's dorm room to inspect some damage that apparently Frank had done that morning.

"When I got over there and walked in, I saw a few holes in the drywall. It seems Frank was listening to the theme from the movie Rocky that morning, trying to get himself psyched up for the game. He got so fired up listening to the music that he punched a few holes in the walls. He and I had to have a little talk about peaking at the right time and saving his aggression for the field."

In the secondary, besides the senior strong safety Cassidy, the Oilers had former Leipsic Viking Denny Maag at free safety. A pair of Tim's, cornerbacks Frost and Tagliapietra, rounded out an impressive unit.

Tom Walsh and Greg Philip would handle the punting and kicking, respectively.

The cornerbacks, Frost and Tagliapietra, showed the wide range of Strahm's recruiting abilities. While Frost was plucked out of Dick's alma mater, Libbey High School in Toledo, the previous year, the player affectionately known to all as "Tags," hailed from Naples, Florida, as did another cornerback on the squad, Charlie Byrd.

There were those who wondered just how a couple young men would leave the warmth and shimmering waters just beyond the beaches of southern Florida to come, without any scholarship help, to sample the often frigid winters of northwest Ohio.

Recalls Strahm, "What initially opened the Naples area for me as far as recruiting was one of our football supporters, Larry Manley. Well, Larry was one of the very first people in town to welcome Ginger and me. He ran a nursing home in town and happened to have a brother who was the principal of a high school in Naples. That's how I got wind of players like Tags and Charlie.

"Larry's son, Don, also became a big supporter of everything we did with our football program. As a matter of fact, he and his wife, Karen, became not only great friends but also tremendous supporters of the Foster Parent Program. Don, nowadays, lives down in the Naples area, not far from his uncle's old high school, and is on the Board of Trustees for The University of Findlay.

In 1976 and 1977, there were some occasional momentum-breaking losses. What Strahm drove home to his team in the August heat of preseason two-a-days was that those momentum breakers needed to be eradicated. It was a point not only heard but understood with crystal clarity. A magical season in Findlay College football history was about to commence.

The season opened with a blowout win over Bluffton, 43-9. Both Trina and Hatfield and running backs Bolden and Beard had big days for an offense that scored over 40 points for the fifth time in the last ten games.

Next, the Oilers again proved they had exorcised the demons that were the close losses of 1975 and won a tight one over Wilmington, 14-10. Any win over Coach Bill Ramseyer's Quakers was a quality win, even by a scant margin. Ramseyer would go on to a 44-year career before retiring after the 2001 season. He coached at Wilmington from 1972 through 1990 before moving on to another NAIA school, the University of Virginia's College at Wise, Va., to establish a playoff-caliber program there.

Ramseyer has since been inducted into the NAIA Hall of Fame. He inherited a Wilmington program with only one winning season in the previous fifteen and led the Quakers to a 114-58-4 record, five NAIA playoff appearances, and an NAIA championship game berth in 1980.

Recalls Dick, "Whenever you went up against Bill's teams, you knew you were in for a dogfight. He was just a tremendous coach and always had his teams ready to play. Wins against Wilmington came from executing better because there weren't a whole lot of guys out there who were going to out-coach him!"

In week three, the Oilers knocked off Manchester College, a Church of the Brethren institution, 27-7.

Then, it was a road win in Ada (Ohio) over Dick's brother Dale's alma mater, Ohio Northern University, 28-6.

A fifth consecutive win came the easy way the following week against Earlham, 42-0.

Then, there came a week of practice preceding the Anderson game that no Oiler on that squad or coach on that staff will ever forget. Ben Finch certainly had come a long way from home to play for Dick Strahm's Oilers in Dick's inaugural year of 1975. Hailing from Orange, New Jersey, Ben was raised primarily by his mother in a single-parent home. During his career at Findlay, Finch was known by teammates as much for his quiet, serious demeanor as his considerable skills as a defensive end.

Recalls his teammate, Kevin Cassidy, a fellow 1975 recruit, "Ben was what I like to call 'a quiet assassin.' He didn't have a whole lot to say, which is, needless to say, a lot different than how I'm wired. He was just very businesslike in his preparation to play and his execution during games.

"And, man, could he ever hit! He was just a humble, quiet guy who happened to be a terrific football player."

Now, obviously Ben and his mother were very close, and, despite the fact that Finch was entering the second half of his final season and well on his way to earning Associated Press Little All-American honors for the second consecutive year, his mother had never seen him play a down of college football.

Well, when some of the foster parents in Dick's program, a program that bonded the Findlay community to Oilers footballers, found out about this unfortunate circumstance, they decided that it was certainly a situation that needed to be rectified.

Unbeknownst to Ben, some foster parents, headed by Don Manley and his wife, Karen, contacted Mrs. Finch and arranged and paid for a flight from New Jersey into the Toledo Express Airport. A couple of well-intentioned foster dads picked up Mrs. Finch at the airport and drove her straight from Toledo to the practice field on the Thursday before the home contest with the Ravens of Anderson College.

Now, Coach Strahm had met with the rest of the team without Ben being present, and everyone except the serious-minded Finch knew what was about to happen. So, everyone tried to move Ben around like a big chess piece when the car pulled up to be certain his back was to his mom when she was led onto the field.

Recalls Dick, "I called Ben over to be certain his back was fully turned. The players stood behind him to form kind of a human wall.

"Now, as I got done telling Ben he needed to do a better job turning sweeps in, or something like that, which I was totally making up, I slapped him on the shoulder and told him to rejoin his teammates.

"As he turned around, the line opened up, and his mom walked through it. She was crying. I know Ben started to tear up as he ran to her and picked her up in a big embrace. Let me tell you, I don't think that there was a dry eye anywhere on that field!"

The next two nights, Mrs. Finch stayed with one of the foster parents. Of course, there was time to visit Ben over those two days, to walk the campus, to see the life her son had made for himself as one of Findlay College's proud student-athletes.

It was another Oiler who was long on action and, often times, short on words, the quiet two-back Denny Guerra, who remembers the Friday night team meeting.

"I can remember Coach got done with his talk and asked if anyone had anything to say, which he always did. It was always the vocal guys on the team, like Cass or Tags, who would get up. But, this time was a first. Ben Finch slowly rose up out of his seat. He looked down at the floor for a moment, raised his eyes, and looked around at all of us. Then he said in that deep, rumbling voice of his, 'Tomorrow, nobody embarrasses Ben Finch!' Then, he sat down. The whole room just erupted with cheers and applause. It's certainly one of my most memorable moments at Findlay."

And, the next day, with a mother bursting with pride and some new-found Oilers spirit, not one Oiler did embarrass Ben Finch. Each played smart, disciplined football, and, when all was said and done, walked off the turf of Donnell 19-0 winners over Anderson College.

On Sunday, after a nice breakfast hosted by the Foster Parents Program, Ben and his mother embraced warmly one more time. It was a moment etched in time, not only in the hearts of mother and son, but in the collective hearts of the football team, a team whose heart beat as one.

For the 6-0 top-ranked Oilers, there would be no slipups as they drove hard down the regular-season backstretch. In their sights was the first undefeated regular season in school history, and they wanted it badly.

Recalls Tagliapietra, the cornerback out of Gulf High in Naples, "Those last three weeks, I think, Coach Strahm practiced us harder than at any other time the whole year! He continued to stress the idea that we really hadn't accomplished anything yet, that we had unfinished business that needed to be resolved to validate our season.

"Coach really had an uncanny knack of never allowing you to be mediocre, to never just settle for being good. He instilled in each one of us the desire to be great."

And, great the Oilers were during the last three regular season Saturdays. First, Findlay crushed Taylor, 44-6. Then, the Oilers routed Hanover, 30-11 in week eight. The 9-0 historical record was sealed on the ninth Saturday with Strahm's players taking care of Defiance, 20-12.

By running the rack and achieving a perfect mark, Findlay College qualified for the Division II NAIA playoffs for the first time in fourteen years. When it was determined, primarily through the final regular-season poll, which the eight qualifying teams were that would be advancing to post-season play, an interesting system came into play to determine the sites for playoff games.

Recalls Dick, "The NAIA determined home-field advantage for its playoff games by a sealed-bid process. The two schools playing each other both turned in their bids, and whichever school was willing to write the biggest check, that school got the home game.

"Our college president, Dr. Glen Rasmussen, and Dr. Jim Houdeshell, our athletic director, certainly had a lot to do with the Oilers' success as they submitted a higher bid than the Oilers' opponent, Tarleton State, an undefeated team out of Stephensville, Texas."

Recalls one of Findlay's Leipsic trove of football treasures, tackle Duane Tooman, "Tarleton State had a really outstanding linebacker, a player by the name of Tally Neal. Well, leading up to the game, all we heard about was how good Neal was and how good the team was, every time we picked up the newspapers. Every time I read those accounts, frankly, I got a bit discouraged, despite the fact that we also had gone undefeated.

"At the Friday night meeting, Coach Strahm addressed the team. He started by talking about Neal and then shook his head. He continued by saying how he felt sorry for Neal because he really didn't know about Nelson Bolden nor did he know about Wilson Beard and Paul Trina and Rick Hatfield and Pat Gibson and Dave Berger and Mike Griffith, and, on and on he went, his voice rising with each name he chanted!

"Then, he named their big offensive weapons and said how sorry he felt for Tarleton State because they really didn't know about Ken Agee and Frank Molinaro and on and on he went until he names pretty much all of us on the defensive side of the ball!

"The one thing I really remember about Dick Strahm was his pre-game speeches. I'll tell you something. In a different era, he could have convinced the Christians they had a great shot to knock off the lions!"

In a slugfest, the Oilers knocked off Tarleton State, 13-6, and it was on to the second round of the playoffs. The defense played brilliantly, and the offense was efficient.

One more win would put the Oilers in the national championship game. Again, Rasmussen and the rest of the college's administration stepped up financially and submitted the superior bid. They would host the second round and welcome a team hailing from Missouri Valley College, in Marshall, Missouri.

This time, behind the strong arm of Paul Trina, the sure hands of Rick Hatfield, and the strong legs of Nelson Bolden, the Oilers posted an impressive 27-9 win over the Vikings.

On defense, the senior strong safety, Kevin Cassidy, had the game of his life. When the clock ticked to all zeroes and the statistics were added up, it became evident how dominant his performance was. Cassidy had fifteen tackles, forced a fumble, and intercepted three passes.

The win put Findlay exactly where Dick Strahm told Kevin Cassidy he would be by the time he was a senior when Strahm recruited him in 1975. And, again, for the third consecutive time, Findlay submitted the winning bid, this time for the national championship fray, so the game would be played at Donnell Stadium.

As for the opponent, it was a team coming into the Buckeye State from the cold of Morehead, Minnesota, the Concordia College Cobbers.

That meant that the Oilers would gain no meteorological advantage from playing the game in the first week of December in Northwest Ohio. The Cobbers were certainly used to playing in very cold conditions as well.

As for the game, for all who believe in football played in its most brutal conditions and at its basest element, it was indeed one for the ages. And, sadly, for Strahm and the rest of the Oilers, it was a game which ended in a monumentally disappointing way.

The Cobbers held a slim 7-0 lead on a frigid day late in the fourth quarter. The game had been played in brutal conditions in chess-match fashion. Often, in football, when the prize is the biggest, the mindset is at its most conservative, especially when the field is treacherously frozen.

Recalls Dick, "It was about seventeen degrees, and there was also a very brisk wind, which, at times, gusted to close to thirty miles an hour. That brought the wind chill down to close to zero, as I recall.

"I know before the game a lot of the players actually put on panty hose under their football pants to try to gain some extra insulation. But, I'm telling you, the Oilers home faithful were there, probably close to 5,000 of them that day.

"We had the ball first and goal at the eight-yard line of Concordia, and the place was going crazy. On the first play, Nelson ran a 22-2 to the five-yard line. The next play, we ran a screen pass to the short side of the field. We had it blocked almost perfectly. Trina passed to Wilson Beard, and he started to turn it up the field.

"Then, just as the idea was beginning to form in my brain that we were going to score, something happened. We had a lineman slip on the frozen field, which left one man unblocked, and that young man made a tremendous play and got the tackle around the four.

"Now, it was third down, so we tried Bolden again on a 22-2, and he got it to the two. That meant it was fourth down and about six feet to go to tie it up with the extra point.

"I used my last time out and called the team over to the sidelines. The play I called was a sweep with Wilson Beard. I told Wilson to run for the flag [corner of the end zone], and, if he saw a cutback, then dive into the end zone.

"Well, once the play started, Wilson did see some daylight and cut it up inside, and Mike Griffith, our big tackle, executed a near perfect block. But, somehow, and I later had to watch the film and keep re-running it over and over to see how, his man spun off the block without slipping on the frozen field, and dropped Wilson one foot short of the goal line. How close was it? Wilson's head was actually on the goal line!"

Had the touchdown been good, Dick Strahm then would have had a real decision facing him. At the time, there was no overtime system in place in the NAIA for the national championship game. Kicking the point would have given both Concordia and Findlay a co-national championship.

Recalls Strahm, "Even to this day, people ask me what I would have done. I mean, the field conditions had really deteriorated as the day wore on, and every yard gained on that frozen field was a battle by the end. But, I never had the chance to face that decision because we came up just short of the goal line.

"But, I'd like to think I'd have gone for the outright win, but, to be honest, I really don't know. I'd have listened to my assistant coaches and then made my decision. Ah, what the hell. Let's just say I'd have gone for two!"

And so, that's where it finally ended, twelve inches and one extra point short of an undefeated, untied NAIA Division II national championship season. For the 11-1 runners up, there would be reasons to celebrate, but it would certainly take a while for the sting to subside.

After the game, an extremely disappointed Dick Strahm learned a lesson from the Findlay College graduate, dear friend, and eventual CEO of Cooper Tire and Rubber Company, Pat Rooney. Recalls Dick, "After the game, the foster-parents and team parents and a lot of our supporters were having a post-game affair at the V.F.W. I went home to change clothes. Pat and his wife, Sandy, stopped over to pick Ginger and me up. I told him I wasn't sure I wanted to go. Then, Pat asked me one question. 'Would you have gone had you won?' I said, 'Certainly.' Without a word, he then handed me my coat. You're never too old to learn valuable lessons, and Pat taught me one that day. You show up regardless."

Perhaps the quickest to get over the disappointment was the head coach. "Listen, I take losses harder than most, and we all were down emotionally, but I was just so proud of what we had accomplished in just four short years. On a team with only six seniors, we were national runners-up!

"I really couldn't wait for 1979. We had so many returning starters. Now, don't get me wrong. We were losing some excellent players. Denny Severin was a tremendous blocking tight end, and Frank Molinaro, our linebacker from Maumee, was also an excellent player.

"And, of course, Cass, our strong safety would be missed as much for his sheer grit as his ability. Let me tell you something about Kevin. He played the entire Concordia game with a broken rib that he sustained in the Missouri Valley game. You talk about one tough kid. He simply refused to come off that field! The trainers had to fashion a strap from his shoulder to his rib, and he was heavily taped just to keep him from extending his arm out too far and causing any further damage.

"Additionally, I was losing an absolutely incredible defensive end in Ben Finch and also my two-back, Denny Guerro. Also, Brent Gordon was a very valuable special team player for four years."

But, there would be another recruiting class and, of course, Strahm also had a very comforting thought. He had seventeen starters back.

Offensively, Paul Trina had a terrific junior year, completing nearly 60 percent of his passes and throwing 15 touchdowns. Many of those aerials were targeted for Rick Hatfield. He hauled in 55 of Trina's throws for 13 scores from his split end position.

When it came to the tough yards, Nelson Bolden was, quite simply, the man. He had 1,091 of them, and all between the tackles, where his knees took a pounding on virtually every play. Ten of his runs found pay dirt.

Doing the blocking for Bolden and, occasionally, second-featured running backs like Wilson Beard (597 yards gained) and Nate Phillips (332 yards gained), were the likes of Severin; tackles Lopez, Noward, and Griffith; guards Beamon and Gibson, who was a first-team Little All-American selection; center Dave Berger; and two-back Denny Guerra.

Defensively, the unit that yielded just 83 points on the entire year, less than a touchdown a game, was strong at virtually every position, the defensive ends, Finch and Street; the rotating tackles of Tooman, Funk, and Wright; the nose guards Agee and Roncagli; linebackers Molinaro, Smith, and Ryan; and deep backs Cassidy, Maag, Frost, and Tagliapietra.

Heading into the '79 season, optimism abounded in Flag City, U.S.A. Fans knew that Findlay was loaded on both sides of the ball. Despite the talent returning, Strahm was also somewhat worried. One of his returning defensive tackles, the unexpected surprise he first spotted on a bar stool in nearby Leipsic, Roger Funk, apparently would not be returning to school. Funk's grandfather had given him 400 acres to farm for him, and Roger didn't think he could both continue at Findlay and get the farming done.

Recalls Strahm, "I just knew what Roger's potential was. Remember, while he was just a sophomore, he was also twenty-one years old. I just felt to make a real run at getting back to where we wanted to be and take care of those twelve inches we left on the surface of Donnell, we needed to be as strong as possible along our defensive front.

"Well, I have two people I'd like to tip my cap to because, after we started our two-a-days and I'd really turned the corner in terms of getting used to the idea that Roger wouldn't be returning, he found his way back!

"As we practiced each day, I'd see him periodically drive by the practice field in his pick-up truck taking care of the farm business. Now, Roger's girlfriend, Janet True, was one of our equipment managers, and she was really doing a lot of lobbying for me to get him to try to work it out with his grandfather and return.

"Then, one day, he showed up on my doorstep while I was out. Ginger answered the door, and he told her that he had talked to his grandpa and found him someone who would take over the acreage. He wanted to come back! She grabbed him by the arm and said, 'Roger, get in here and sit down.'

"Ginger called all over town trying to find me. Well, she finally ran me down. I came home, and there he was sitting. I personally took him over to the equipment room and got him outfitted. That afternoon, he was out there for his first practice."

Recalls Ginger, "I knew Dick really saw something special in Roger, so I wasn't going to take a chance he'd change his mind. I just sat him at the kitchen table, got him a pop, and shut and locked the door! I told him, 'Don't move. I'm going to find your coach!'"

Strahm, looking back, sees Funk's ability in much the same way as Rick Hatfield's in the sense that they were both small-college players with big-time NCAA Division I ability. "Hatfield, I just know, would have been a top receiver in the MAC [Mid-American Conference] with those hands of his.

"And Roger, I believe, could also have played in the Mid-American Conference.

"I just don't think there were too many NAIA players that you could honestly say could have played big-time football, but, I believe those two, based on what I saw, certainly could have."

What few holes left by graduation were filled nicely for the 1979 campaign. For example, two-time Little All-American Ben Finch was gone, but Dick coaxed local product, former Findlay High School Trojan Jerry Campbell, to transfer from Ball State to fill that position. By doing so, Strahm had yet another player, to go along with Agee, Funk, and Hatfield, who had NCAA Division I ability.

Paul Street and Ben Finch quite possibly, were the finest pair of defensive ends in small college in 1978. Street, however, would most certainly welcome Campbell. He and Campbell were high school teammates on that Trojan team that went undefeated in the regular season in 1975. To call them bookends wouldn't be far off, as both were exactly the same size, 6'2", 215 pounds.

But, in terms of personalities, the former Trojans were quite different. Recalls Strahm, "Paul was very emotional, almost a wild man in his approach to contact, whereas Jerry was much more under control, even though he was just as effective. I like to think of him as 'Mr.

Consistency.' He was never out of position and always executed his defensive calls to the best of his ability. In both 1980 and 1981, Jerry made the Associated Press Little All-American squads.

Other new defensive starters in the secondary were Charlie Byrd, who, like returning cornerback Tagliapietra, hailed from Naples, Florida, and Tom Walsh, from the town and the school that will always hold a special place in Dick's heart and memory, Warren Western Reserve.

On the offensive side of the ball, Mike McHugh, a freshman out of Boyertown, Pennsylvania, replaced the very good blocking tight end, Denny Severin. McHugh is now the director of football operations at the University of California. Keith Barr, the freshman from Start High School, in Toledo, and Marty Wyzlic, the sophomore out of Detroit De La Salle High School, replaced departed speedster Guerra and Nate Phillips.

On offense, Strahm narrowly missed having a huge hole to fill, one that involved Nelson Bolden.

Recalls Bolden, "I've always said that Dick Strahm was like a second father to me, and there was actually a time when he and my real father kind of double-teamed me to keep me from making a really bad decision.

"After my sophomore year, despite all the success we'd had as a team and the 1,000-yard season I'd had and all that, I really convinced myself that I wanted to drop out of school and join the Marines.

"I wasn't doing all that well in the classroom, and, I guess, I was just looking for something more physical, more challenging, and more dangerous. When I told Coach Strahm about my intentions, he told me that it would be a big mistake, but I told him that I'd pretty much made up my mind, even though I hadn't told either of my parents.

"Well, he told me to think a lot more about what I wanted to do and to meet him in his office the next day at 4:00 in the afternoon. Now, in the meantime, I didn't now that he called my dad, and when I walked in his office the next day, there sat both Coach and my father.

"Now, despite the fact that I had grown up [to 6'2", 230 pounds], I was physically very respectful of my father. He was a very strong man and had hands much bigger than my own. While I would say he had kind of a quiet strength, I thought it was a pretty loud strength that day. The fact of the matter is, he was furious, and within minutes, you might say I had my energies redirected back to school and back to improving my classroom work.

"When I left Coach Strahm's office, I also left all thoughts of dropping out and joining the Marines right on the floor!"

The rest of the starters were the same as in 1978. Despite such a strong cast of players, Strahm remained guarded in his assessment of his team's chances to return to the title game. "So much has to go right for a team to win it all and be the only team left standing in December. What made me apprehensive about 1979 is that we had lost any element of surprise that we had the year before. While we had good years the previous two years, no one expected us to be a foot and an extra point away from being national champions!

"Now, our opponents knew about us. They knew about our All-Americans, Gibson and Hatfield. They knew about Trina, starting his third year at quarterback. They knew all about the Boldens and Griffiths and Smiths and Maags!

"Probably, if you asked any other coach of a team on our schedule, each would have told you that we were loaded. But, in my mind, that just meant that we were 'The Game' on everyone's schedule. That's what some people don't factor in when it comes to teams coming off a great year with so many starters back. You are the main target for literally every team on your schedule.

"To be honest. I would have hated to coach against Findlay College in 1979!"

Of course, the yearly coaching carousel meant there were assistant coaching positions to fill. Dave Tanner left to become a head high school football coach in Indiana. He stayed there three years before moving south to Naples, Florida, to continue his high school coaching career. It was there he would become yet another recruiting conduit Strahm would use over the next several years to bring Floridians to Findlay, players like Jamie Riles and Scotty McLaughlin and Demetrice Boykin.

To fill the vacant defensive coordinator's position, Dick consulted, as he often did on football matters, his brother, Dale, for a potential candidate. Dale told Dick that there was a young head coach at Elmwood (Ohio) High School by the name of Dean Pees, who was doing a very nice job.

Recalls Dick, "I just knew immediately after I interviewed Dean that he was the right guy for the job. I told Jim Houdeshell I needed Dean as a full-time assistant, and I got him! Strahm's instincts about Pees and his coaching ability were dead on. After his tenure at Findlay (1979-1982), Pees climbed the coaching ladder and made stops at Miami of Ohio, Navy, University of Toledo, Notre Dame, Michigan State, and Kent State. Then, it was on to the NFL and the New England Patriots, where he has now risen to assume the lofty position of defensive coordinator for one of the league's true dynasties.

Strahm now had two outstanding full-time assistants in Pees and Steve Mohr. He also had Jim McIntosh, who brought with him considerable coaching abilities after the school day was done in Fostoria.

Strahm also brought in two part-time coaches who were teachers in nearby North Baltimore, a town less than 15 miles from Findlay. One was Charlie Thompson. Charlie coached the defensive tackles and was the trainer. The other played for Dick back at Lakota High School. Beryl Hemminger helped Dick with the offensive backs.

Kevin Cassidy, one of the Oilers' captains in 1978, also joined the staff as a student assistant. He would help coach the nose tackles and linebackers and also serve as equipment manager, while completing his course work for his bachelor's degree.

Recalls Dick, "While I don't want to diminish what any of the early part-time coaches did, because they worked so hard, and they were very loyal, but they were on different paths in life and came and went each of those early years. It would be sometime later before it got to the point where most of my staff, I could count on, would be returning year after year."

Right before the opening of the 1979 season, Strahm talked to a friend who was a computer programmer. He had him calculate the odds that the Oilers could repeat the undefeated regular season of the previous year. Strahm told The Toledo Blade writer Dave Hackenberg, "It came out to 19,865 to 1."

One change that Strahm decided to make was to allow his lightning-quick nose tackle, Ken Agee, some touches in the offensive backfield when he wasn't on defense, shooting the center-guard gap and blowing up enemy ball carriers in their own backfield.

"Now, don't get me wrong! I had no intention of moving Nelson Bolden out of the fullback slot, but I wanted Ken to spell Wilson Beard at halfback to get him some reps.

"If that meant he needed some plays off defensively, that was OK because Pat Roncagli, my junior out of Cleveland Cathedral Latin, was also an excellent nose tackle, not as quick as Ken but very, very solid."

The Oilers certainly weren't going to sneak up on anyone, as they carried a number-two national ranking among Division II NAIA schools into their opener with Bluffton College.

On the strength of the almost-Marine Bolden's 112 yards on "only" 21 carries and a couple of scores, Strahm's Oilers had their first win by an impressive 40-0. The victory catapulted Findlay into an uneasy position as far as Dick was concerned, the number-one team in the national poll.

Strahm lamented to The Blade sportswriter Hackenberg at the time that it was way too early for such a lofty perch. Having articulated such a tepid response, Strahm also admitted to the sportswriter, who still writes for the same paper in the Glass City, that he was also very proud of his Oilers' ascension to the top slot.

Recalls Strahm, "I took over four years earlier, hoping to win some league championships and develop a respectable program. As the number-one ranked team in NAIA, we certainly had to have pride in the fact that we had climbed to the top of the mountain that quickly. Now, the question became, 'How long could we stay on top of that mountain?'"

Denny Maag, the senior free safety, who is currently a commercial lender for Old Fort Banking in Fostoria, remembers well the lessons learned in Findlay College's rapid rise to the top spot. "By the time I was a senior, I had come to appreciate the unity on our teams and its impact on how well we worked together on the field. We did so much together off the field. When I arrived from Leipsic, a community with almost no blacks, it was literally a seamless transition to hang out with guys like Jerome Gray and Nelson Bolden. An Oiler was an Oiler, didn't matter our surface differences, didn't matter our backgrounds. I really feel that it was this belief that we all shared which helped us to go so far in such a relatively short amount of time."

In week two, one of the conference's perennial powers was coming to town, the Wilmington Quakers, led by their own NAIA coaching icon, Bill Ramseyer. Ramseyer, a fiery competitor, immediately established somewhat of a bunker mentality for the contest, and did something which, admittedly, rankled Strahm. "Bill refused to exchange film with us, so I do remember that game preparations were somewhat more challenging than usual. However, this was the fifth time that Bill and I faced each other, and I think both of us knew pretty much what to expect. They'd won close games my first two years, and we'd won the last two years by close margins, so I just knew this would be one tough game."

As for Ramseyer, well, he doesn't recall the incident. "I really don't remember that we withheld any game film," the now-retired Ramseyer recollected. "However, I can't say that it didn't happen. Dick and I had a very intense rivalry during my time at Wilmington and his time at Findlay. It was as passionate as any I'd experienced in my 44 years of combined high school and college coaching. Certainly, we didn't hate one another and did speak at league meetings and at clinics when we'd see one another, but we weren't what you'd call friends or anything like that.

"Now, we talk on the phone all the time, and, certainly, I do consider Dick a friend. I have so much respect for the man, not only for what he did in coaching but also in how he's handled the health crises in his life. But, having said that, if you'd told me back then when we were glaring at each other from across the field that we'd ever be friends, well, I just wouldn't have believed you!"

For Dick, he returns the respect card. "Bill was just a terrific coach. While I respected all the coaches I competed against because I know how difficult the job of coaching is from personal experience, there are some coaches I just know are so well organized and knowledgeable and committed to winning that any game against their teams will be a dogfight. Certainly, Bill Ramseyer is a name on that short list."

Strahm turned out to be as good a prophet as he was a football coach. When the mid-September shafts of sunlight shortened on a glorious afternoon at Donnell, the scoreboard told the story, Oilers-28, Quakers-26. Bolden came up a scant yard of the century mark for the game, on 32 carries, and he scored twice, in an almost plow horse performance.

Wilmington coach, Bill Ramseyer, was so moved by the competitive fire of the game that he did something he had never before, and never did again, in over four decades of coaching. Recalls Ramseyer, "It was just an unbelievable battle. After the game was over, despite my disappointment, I actually went and knocked on the door of Findlay's locker room and, first, congratulated Dick, and then addressed Dick's team to tell them how well they played."

Recalls Cassidy, the young assistant, who, just a year earlier, was flying around the field making tackles out of his strong safety position in an equally physical 14-10 Oilers win against Wilmington, "Nelson Bolden was simply 'the man' that day. His yards were crucial in our converting several key short-yardage third downs. The thing about Nelson is his entire play package was tackle-to-tackle, so it wasn't unusual on any given play to have four or five guys take shots at his knees."

Cassidy recalls a pattern that developed with Bolden that initially prompted some ribbing from teammates. In 1978, when Nelson started carrying 20, 25, even 30 times a game, the coaches would often hold him out of the following week's practices, until Wednesday. Nelson generally would be in the whirlpool the first two days of the next week.

"I'll be honest," recalls Cassidy. "When it first started to happen, I heard just a little bit of grumbling. But, by this point in Nelson's career, no one was even the least bit resentful. Everyone knew the physical price he paid, game in, game out."

In week three, Findlay traveled to Manchester, Indiana, to play the Spartans of Manchester College. The result was a lopsided Oilers win, 62-0. Wilson Beard scored on three touchdown runs, each seven yards. Bolden added two scores and 106 yards. Trina had his usual efficient and businesslike afternoon, completing 9 of 14 for 116 yards and two scores, both to the senior wideout Rick Hatfield.

Recalls Hatfield, now a substitute teacher and assistant football coach at McComb (Ohio) High School, "I really wanted to play basketball when I arrived on campus in addition to baseball and football. After playing junior varsity basketball for two years, Coach Houdeshell [then, head basketball coach at Findlay College] cut me. It was, frankly, the best thing that ever happened to me. Even though I was upset at the time, I realized when I grew up a little more that I really wasn't going to be a great basketball player. And, I really wasn't going to be the best I could be in football without more time to focus on it."

When Hatfield did have more time to concentrate on football, it paid off like a slot machine, as the lanky split end out of Oregon (Ohio) Cardinal Stritch hit a double jackpot, achieving Associated Press Little All-American honors both in his junior and senior seasons.

After the week three laugher, the Oilers traveled to nearby Ada for a contest with Coach Wally Hood's Ohio Northern University Polar Bears. In a game that still surprises so many of the former players and coaches at Findlay, especially Dick Strahm, the Oilers had to mount a furious comeback just to pull even at 21-21. With ten minutes to go, the Bears were leading 21-7.

Recalls Dick, "I certainly remember that tie. ONU had two backs that we just couldn't stop that day."

The backs, Strahm remembers, were Chris Kubbs, who rushed for 175 yards that day, and Dude McGarry, who ran for 131.

At the end of the game and still down 21-14, the Oilers' defense finally stiffened and gave Paul Trina a shot. He responded with a 62-yard touchdown pass to Wilson Beard. Although there were less than three minutes on the clock, Strahm elected to kick the point for the tie in the hopes that the defense could make a big stop and give Trina one more opportunity. Recalls Dick, "Had we not entered that contest ranked number one, perhaps I'd gone for two. But, I knew we just couldn't sustain a loss. Also, I really felt we had a good shot at playing good defense and getting one more possession at the end to win it."

Trina managed to get the ball back for a final opportunity but with only ten seconds remaining. It was time for a fling and a prayer, but the prayer went unanswered, and the Oilers trudged off the field that day with their first tie since the 1977 opener with Defiance.

The tie dropped the Oilers from first to third in the rankings as they awaited impatiently Indiana's Earlham College for the big homecoming weekend. After all, when there is a bump in the road, as the surprising tie the previous Saturday was, the truly competitive teams look forward to an opportunity to atone for their previously misspent Saturday.

Intent on making the Quakers from Richmond pay, the Oilers couldn't wait for the 2:00 p.m. kickoff.

Recalls assistant coach Jim McIntosh, "Dick really worked those guys hard that week. Heck, he even had Nelson out of that whirlpool and on the field in full pads on Monday. I almost felt sorry for our young men that week. We hit, and we ran…and ran…and ran some more! We ended every practice with more 'perfect 40s' than I could remember, going all the way back to August two-a-days."

Recalls Dick, "I just felt I needed to send a message that we needed to be at our absolute best every weekend if we expected to be where we wanted to be on December 9, the date for the national championship game.

"Anyway, I felt we were ready for that homecoming game. We had the parade and all the hoopla, the crowning of the king and queen, and all that stuff. We had a packed stadium. All we needed was an opponent.

"And, amazingly, that was the problem. As one o'clock passed and there was still no Earlham, I knew something was wrong. Jim Houdeshell and I got to a phone and called Earlham's football offices, and one of the coaches answered the phone!

"It turned out there was a misprint on their schedule. They were under the impression that the game was a night game, so they hadn't even left yet.

"You know, they say that if you coach long enough, everything that can possibly happen to you will, at least once, and, certainly, this was a first!

"So, we had the announcement made that everyone in the stands should leave and then return for a seven o'clock kickoff. I'm sure we lost a few hundred or so who already had made evening plans, but what could we do? We had nobody to play!"

Duane Tooman, the starting defensive tackle and one of a quartet of Leipsic players, along with Funk, Berger, and Maag, has every reason to remember that homecoming besides the obvious, the misunderstanding regarding the correct game time.

"We finally arrived back at the stadium and got an opponent there to play after the longest afternoon I can ever remember. Once you get yourself psyched up to play and then are told that it won't be for several more hours, the clock just crawls by! Finally, here we were about to go! We won the toss and took the ball.

"Our offense took the ball right down the field and rammed it in for the game's first score.

"Well, I was on the extra-point team, so when our place-kicker, Greg Philip, was ready to do his thing, I ran out there for my first play of the night. After the previous week's tie and our defense giving up the 100-yard rushing games to two different backs and then the mix up and delay that day, I was really fired up to play.

"We knew Earlham couldn't stay with us, and we were really looking forward to having some fun after the week of practice we'd had.

"On the extra point, one of the Earlham players, maybe sensing he and his team were in for a long night, or, maybe mad at how easily and quickly we went down the field and scored, took a swing at me!

"So, I retaliated. And, as is often the case, the ref only saw my punch. Bam! He kicked me out of the game. So, after a week of practices from hell and waiting all day, my 1979 homecoming contribution was exactly one play!"

Years later, there was a post-script to the incident. Tooman, who now runs his own roofing and painting company, met a man while heading to a job site. "During the conversation, he asked me where I went to school. When I told him I went to Findlay College, he laughed and said that he used to officiate college football, and, the last game he ever did was in Findlay. He said he'd never forget that game because it was the only one he ever officiated where he had to eject a player. He told me some kid from Findlay took a swing at a kid from Earlham on an extra point.'

He just about fell right off the chair when I told him he was currently talking to his one and only 'ejectee'! Talk about a small world."

The game ended favorably for the Oilers, 48-14, and they appeared to be back on track, aided largely by 165 yards by Bolden and some timely aerials from Trina to the sure-handed Hatfield.

A 21-6 win over Anderson on the road was followed by somewhat of a lackluster victory over winless Taylor at home, 29-7. Strahm remembers of the pair of wins over the Indiana schools in weeks six and seven, "We did what we had to do. The Taylor game, in particular, I just didn't think we had our heads in the game. When you're dealing with young people, you never know what circumstances might cause a key player or players to be distracted and not play very well. Some games, you just hope to get out with a win."

As Findlay came down the home stretch, injuries had begun to mount. Paul Trina played sparingly in the Taylor game, as he yielded to backup Greg Brown because of a hairline fracture in his left foot. Wilson Beard, the starting halfback, also aggravated an ankle injury against Taylor, and Bolden was nursing a torn rib cartilage. Even the punter, Tom Walsh, missed the Taylor game with a sore leg.

But, Findlay was on a mission, and the coaches felt that time would cure any physical ills that they were experiencing.

The week eight contest provided a challenge of the highest order as Findlay traveled to Hanover, Indiana, to do battle with the 5-2 Panthers.

It appeared that Findlay had the game in hand, leading 27-10 in the fourth quarter.

Shockingly, Hanover came off the canvas to score 21 points in less than five minutes to win 31-27. The explosion wiped out a Bolden touchdown run and a beautiful 41-yard strike from Trina to Hatfield.

In any loss, there are pivotal plays upon which an outcome turns. Against the Panthers, those key plays were a pair of late fumbles by the Oilers that allowed Hanover quarterback Cliff Hellyer to throw his third and fourth touchdown passes of the afternoon.

The loss put Findlay in a precarious position, as the Oilers needed to retain their ranking in the top eight to assure themselves of a playoff bid.

Recalls Strahm, "It was a game I still think about from time to time to this very day because it was one that we absolutely should have won! The beginning of the week after the loss was even more unsettling because word had come down that we had fallen to ninth in the poll."

But, the system to deliver the eight playoff teams was a bit more complicated than just finishing in the top eight in the final poll. Dick received some clarification from the NAIA that if the Oilers won their final game against Defiance, they'd be in.

The Blade writer Dave Hackenberg explained the NAIA playoff system and the Oilers' assured spot with a final-week win in a mid-week column prior to the Defiance regular-season finale. "The NAIA selects its eight Division II playoff teams in the following manner: If you are the top-ranked team in your region (which the Oilers are) and rated among the top twelve in the final poll, you automatically gain one of the four regional berths. Then, of the teams not yet selected, the NAIA takes the top four-rated teams regardless of region."

So, with a win, Findlay was in, and that was the thought in every Oiler's head as the team boarded the bus for a road contest against Head Coach Gary Schaeffer's Yellow Jackets.

On November 10, the visitors notched a physical 21-7 win to clinch a playoff berth. The win secured a share of the Hoosier-Buckeye Conference crown as well.

After the game, Strahm reiterated a thought he'd had often to reporters, "It was a hell of a lot harder to make it this year than last season. Last year, we snuck up on people. This year, we started out ranked number two in the country, won our first game and moved to number one, and then everybody was really shooting for us."

The final regular season game was hardly a portrait of athletic decorum and sportsmanship, as it was dotted with several late hits, some fisticuffs, and some player ejections.

Offensively, Bolden paced a 274-yard rushing attack with 121 yards to eclipse the 1,000-yard mark in just nine games. Strahm commented about his big, bruising fullback, "That's quite an accomplishment considering the way we punish our fullback. It's tackle-to-tackle, and [Nelson] got a lot of that yardage simply by abusing himself."

The catch of the game may very well have come after the freshman from Start High School in Toledo, Keith Barr, ripped off a 10-yard run for a first down to the Defiance six. Of course, it was Hatfield who caught the Paul Trina toss for a touchdown, a pass deflected by a Defiance linebacker. Recalls Strahm, "I can still see the catch in my mind's eye. What tremendous concentration to react to the deflection and reach back across his body to haul it in.

"I've said it many times over the years. Rick Hatfield is one of the best small-college receivers I've ever seen. And, he was also as good as any receiver I saw during my time in the Mid-American Conference as well."

Nose tackle Ken Agee and the bookend defensive ends, Paul Street and Jerry Campbell, paced the staunch Oilers defense. Agee accounted for back-to-back sacks at one critical juncture, amounting to 26 yards in losses. Recalls Strahm, "Ken was just the quickest nose tackle you could ever imagine. We always angled him left or right, and he made an absolute living in the backfield tackling shocked ball carriers who'd just taken the handoff!"

Again, when it came time for the sealed bids to see which team would host Findlay's first-round playoff tilt, the college's administration stepped up. The first game of the '79 playoffs would be at Donnell against the unbeaten Jamestown College Jimmies from North Dakota.

The November 17 game started inauspiciously enough for the Oilers. On their first possession, they netted five yards in three plays before a Tom Walsh punt. Certainly, how a game starts, however, is not always a clear indication as to how it will end.

Such was the case before the Donnell faithful. The hometown squad hit pay dirt the next four times it touched the ball in cruising to a 45-15 win.

Trina hit his first six passes, and Bolden scored three of his four touchdowns of the afternoon in those four drives to highlight the 27-0 burst on the way to the win. Beard accounted for the sweeps, totaling 87 yards on 18 carries, and Bolden, as was the norm, did his damage between the tackles. As usual, the offense line was stellar. Thanks to McHugh, Noward, Griffith, Lopez, Gibson, Beamon, and Berger, Findlay gained 280 yards on the ground.

After the game Strahm pointed out about Jamestown, "They're not the type of team to come back when they fall behind that far [27-0]. They live or die on the ground, so a big key for us was to control the ball and get an early lead."

After an extra week of practice to prepare for round two because of the Thanksgiving holiday, the Oilers readied themselves, again, thanks to Findlay's winning the sealed bid, for a home semifinal contest against a legendary coach's program.

Frosty Westering was bringing his Pacific Lutheran Lutes all the way from Tacoma, Washington. The Lutes would be led on offense by Frosty's son, Brad, the quarterback. Another son, Scott, played tight end after the scholarship athlete transferred from UCLA, so strong was the call to play for his father.

Weather-wise, the game was everything one might expect from a northwest Ohio late November Saturday. As snow blanketed the Donnell turf, the Oilers defense rose to the occasion in a 9-0 win.

It was Denny Maag, the 6'1", 190-pounder, who had the game of his life. He recovered two fumbles and intercepted three passes. His teammates added three more interceptions and another fumble as the Lutes turned the ball over an eye-popping nine times.

A Perfect Five-Year Plan 219

Recalls Maag, "All of my big plays came in the second half. It was unbelievable, almost as if the ball was a magnet, and I was a piece of metal. Two of the interceptions, it was almost as if I were the intended receiver."

Even years later, players tend to remember seemingly small details of their athletic careers. Such is the case with the talented former wide receiver Hatfield. "The one thing I remember about that Pac Lutheran game is they had a free safety who must have been assigned to me because, no matter where I lined up, he was my cover guy.

"And, let me tell you something. He put some real hits on me that day! And, after almost every hit, he held out his hand to help me up, and each time, he'd say, 'God bless you.' I don't know if he was trying to get in my head or not, but I don't think so. He sounded sincere, but too, it was kind of freaky. I can remember telling Cass [Kevin Cassidy] about it on the sidelines, and Cass said, 'He's saying what?'"

Offensively, it was Bolden who gained 98 punishing yards, a Trina-to-Hatfield TD pass, and a huge field goal by Greg Phillip from 26 yards out that accounted for the difference, besides, of course, the opportunistic and stifling defense.

For Philip, the kick that sealed the Lutes' fate was sweet redemption. After a marvelous year in 1978, a season that saw him hit 11 of 12 field goals and garner NAIA District 22 kicker-of-the-year honors, the Van Buren (Ohio) native had a disastrous 1979 regular season, missing, at one point, ten straight field goals.

After the game, Philip lauded his coaches, especially Strahm, for sticking with him. "The coaches stuck with me, and the rest of the team also had faith in me."

For the kick that made it a two-score game, coaching adjustments were made by Strahm. Recalls Dick, "I remember Greg had been kicking the ball too high in the last part of the year off the kicking tee, so, despite the snowy turf, I decided to have him kick it right off the ground. It proved to be the right adjustment."

Strahm remembers the game for more than just what he had his place kicker do. "Steve Mohr, my offensive line coach, was battling a personal crisis that week. His mom suffered a massive heart attack on the Thursday before the game. It was only at her insistence that her son was at the game. I presented him the game ball after we won to give to her."

Recalls Kevin Cassidy, "You couldn't find too many dry eyes in that locker room. We all felt very deeply for each other, and, when one of us, whether a player, a coach, or a trainer, was having a tough time, we all felt it."

The entire town of Findlay was alive with anticipation, not just for Christmas, which was just over the horizon, but for what would precede it. And, remarkably, for the sixth consecutive time in the last two years, the Findlay administration submitted the highest sealed bid and would host the national championship game for the second straight year.

On December 9, Northwestern College of Iowa would walk out onto the Donnell Stadium turf to take on the team that fell a foot short of a national crown just a year ago.

The man who always seemed to be in the shadow of Bolden, the workhorse, was junior Wilson Beard. He saw the contest as a chance to reaffirm his team-first attitude. "My senior year at Rossford (Ohio) High School, I gained 1,000 yards in just five games before I sustained a leg injury. Then, I came back in the spring and established myself as one of the top sprinters in the state. So, naturally, I thought things, from a personal standpoint, would be a little different at Findlay. But, the offense ran through Nelson, so I certainly didn't want to sound greedy talking about what I hadn't achieved personally.

"I was awfully proud to be a part of this team, and I did what was best for this team."

Of all the fans who anticipated the game, none did more so than super-fan and number-one Dick Strahm booster Pat McMahon. McMahon was famous in Donnell for his leading the O-i-l-e-r-s cheer at crucial times during the contest. Replete with his trademark ten-gallon hat, McMahon never missed a Findlay College game.

McMahon told The Blade sportswriter Dave Hackenberg that there were two reasons for that. "Well, the first day Dick Strahm was in town after he'd been named football coach, he was out at the country club for a welcome lunch. I met him, and I could just sense immediately there was something special about the man. Despite the fact that I had six season tickets to Notre Dame for longer than I could remember, after Coach Strahm came to town, I haven't used them once. In my opinion, there's nothing better than small-college football when it's played well, and, I'll tell you, these kids know how to play it well!"

Strahm remembers well his super booster for reasons other than his vociferous support of all things Oilers from his customary Donnell Stadium perch. "Pat was one of the first to jump on board when I started the Foster Parent Program in the spring of 1976. He was terrific, not only to the players that he 'adopted' but also to all of the players. He was the kind of fan a coach always looks for when he lands a job in a new community. Pat would do absolutely anything to help our program within the guidelines of the NAIA."

There would be two young men on the field for the championship game who knew McMahon well, and, to this day, both still remember the influence McMahon had on them.

Recalls Kevin Cassidy, "I was Mr. McMahon's first foster son, and he was just tremendous to me and to my parents when they came to games."

Nelson Bolden remembers McMahon as well. "In 1979, I was Mr. Mac's foster son. I could just tell that he was proud as heck of anything I did. When I would go over for dinner, I just felt so comfortable in the household. No one in the family saw race. All they saw was a young man who needed support and some pushes in the right direction to stay on the right path."

One key defensive cog couldn't wait for the contest. Linebacker Jim Ryan, from Olmstead Falls (Ohio) injected a bit of nostalgia when talking to Hackenberg during the practice week preceding the contest. "When I was a kid, I'd sit and watch football and other sports on TV, and playing for something this big was all I ever dreamed of.

"Well, last year's championship game was my chance, but we lost that one. Now that we have another shot, it's a hundred times more important. We won't let it get away again. I'll guarantee you that."

Hmm, bulletin board fodder? A guarantee from the junior Associated Press Little All-American candidate? It wasn't a coach's preference that players speak to the press in such fashion, but Strahm could sense that nothing put on a bulletin board could impact the outcome of that game. "I remember Jimmy's quote, but, it was just an affirmation of everything I'd seen in those kids as they prepared for that game. They were absolutely focused and, really, the most sure-of-themselves group of players that I may have ever coached going into a big game."

One player, in particular, noticed something very different about the locker room right before the championship game was about to start. Recalls Pat Gibson, "In most locker rooms during pre-game, usually you could hear a pin drop. But that day, it was so loud. I couldn't believe it. It was almost as if we had no nerves that day. We just knew we were going to win."

There are times when youth's bravado turns out to be nothing more than fool's gold and times when it becomes the currency upon which a game's outcome is purchased. For the Oilers, the can't-be-beat attitude turned out to be right on the money.

Despite Paul Trina Jr.'s confidence, there was a part of him that would be thinking about someone just a few days removed from open-heart surgery and still in a hospital room at the Cleveland Clinic. Paul Sr. would miss his only game of his son's career on that December day.

Just days out of surgery and still in guarded condition, Senior insisted that he be allowed to listen to the game on radio. When his doctors conferred, they came to the conclusion that it would be more dangerous to deny Trina, so insistent was he to listen to the radio account.

Recalls Trina Sr., still living in Warren and still keeping an eye on his grown son, once a Western Reserve Raider but now the athletic director for the Warren City Schools, "Call that Trina-1, Doctors-0. I was just not about to be denied the chance to at least listen to that game after trying as hard as I could to get them to release me so that I could be there!"

The positive outcome of the game for Findlay was never in doubt, and the Oilers of Coach Dick Strahm had their first national championship.

As far as the details the question was, which was more impressive, the offensive explosion or the defensive dominance? Perhaps as long as there will be games played on the surface of Donnell Stadium, that will have to be debated.

It was the offense that took the opening kickoff and drove 74 yards on 14 rushing plays. The drive was a man-on-man, in-your-face, physically dominating drive capped off in the Oilers' customary way, a one-yard touchdown by Nelson Bolden.

Halfbacks Keith Barr, the Toledo freshman, and Beard, out of Rossford, Ohio, made key contributions to assist the battering ram Bolden.

Then, after two quick turnovers by Northwestern, Findlay struck for two more scores, one through the air and one on the ground. First, there was something special from the afternoon's MVP, quarterback Paul Trina Jr. dedicated his efforts to his dad, who was glued to the crackling radio at the Cleveland Clinic. Trina hit Wilson Beard for a 28-yard TD strike.

Then, it was Bolden. The big junior slammed over for the second of his three touchdowns on the day to make it 21-0. By the time all the day's affairs had been conducted, the scoreboard read, "Findlay-51, Visitors-6."

Recalls Strahm, "Northwestern was a lot like us in the sense that they liked to control both tempo and clock by running the ball, but, in order to do that, you can't fall behind by three scores in the first quarter. After we got the big lead, they started throwing it up for grabs, and, believe me, we grabbed, especially Charlie Byrd."

Byrd, along with Tim Tagliapietra, represented Naples, Florida, superbly. Charlie picked off an NAIA national championship record four passes on his way to gaining defensive MVP honors.

After the game, he told Larry Alter of the Courier that Coach Strahm had the defense totally prepared. "Coach had us studying film until we were nearly blind. We were ready for absolutely everything Northwestern threw at us."

Defensive ends deluxe, the former Findlay Trojans, Jerry Campbell and Paul Street, keyed a unit that held Northwestern to a paltry 36 yards rushing, which happened to be less than four different Oilers running backs got on their own.

The interior of the 5-2 slant defense rushed with reckless abandon. Ron Wright, Roger Funk, Duane Tooman, Ken Agee, and Pat Roncagli forced many a poor pass.

The game was especially satisfying for someone who, one might say, Dick Strahm had lied to in 1975, Kevin Cassidy. "I missed the national championship Coach said Findlay would win before my eligibility expired by one year. But, I guess it wasn't much of a fib because I was on the coaching staff that day.

"After the game, the players threw me in Donnell Pond [a small pond just outside the stadium]. Hell, a lot of the players and coaches went in voluntarily after I got thrown in.

"In many ways, that national championship was kind of unfinished business. That was my biggest reward of needing that fifth year to finish my degree."

So, Coach Dick Strahm was indeed the King of Findlay on that second Saturday in December, and, if there was a king, surely there must have been a queen. Ginger Strahm filled that position with her customary zealous support of her husband and the style and grace anyone who knows her will attest to her possessing.

Recalls Ginger, "I remember how difficult it was for Dick to go through the losing when we were in Manhattan and then that first year here in Findlay. I'm not sure a lot of fans who are really uninitiated when it comes to the amount of time college coaching takes can appreciate the effort these men put in working with young people.

"There are so many small details I recall about that day in December. I had just bought a brand new ski suit for the game. Well, by the time I finally got home, it was splattered with mud after the celebration on the field. I couldn't wait to get down from the press box to hug Dick.

"The mud? I didn't mind. Watching that team and Dick and his assistant coaches and Jim Houdeshell receive their championship watches made every splatter of mud worth it!"

To list the bounty of awards individually for the players of the 1979 NAIA Division II champions would almost be to diminish the very essence of what they collectively were, a team.

Of course, Strahm was named NAIA Division II National Coach of the Year, and players like Pat Gibson, Rick Hatfield, Nelson Bolden, Tim Tagliapietra, and Dave Berger were accorded Little All-American accolades, but that's not what the first wave of Oilers footballers in the Strahm era would want people to remember.

Recalls Bolden, "It really was all about team for us. I was just fortunate to be in the right place at the right time and in the right system to be given the lion's share of the carries and a lot of the headlines that came with those carries. But, it was all of us who, collectively, accomplished the goal of going back on that field on that final Saturday to do something about that one foot of space between us and the goal line that we didn't take care of the year before."

Beyond that, the former cornerback still affectionately known as Tags in the Findlay football family, sees a deeper significance to the fifth season in Flag City for Coach Richard Strahm. "Really, all of us on the '79 national championship team can thank those who showed us the way when we first arrived on campus. While guys like Gene Fernandez, Jerome Gray, and Dave Danhoff didn't stand on that field after the clock ticked down, their presence was felt because they showed us the way that Oilers needed to do things to get where we wanted to be."

Paul Trina Jr. looks back with such reverence for his coach, the man who challenged him after a lackluster performance in his first start as a sophomore. "I see Dick Strahm as a bold prophet, a man who could instill in his players a belief that they could climb as high as they wanted to climb.

"His words pierced us. The words he spoke to us were delivered with such fervor. I can remember in practices, he would walk among us as we were doing our stretching out, and he would say, 'We will outwork every opponent on our schedule.' Then, he began to name the opponents, one after another in a chant, his voice rising with each school he mentioned.

"As a speaker, he was just captivating. He had such charisma. I don't want people to get the idea he was always serious, though. At the beginning of the week, there was always a lot of humor. But, late in the week, he got serious. By the time Saturday arrived, we were ready for business.

"Listen, not everyone can coach. So much of whether someone can is if he or she has a sense of timing. And, Dick had it. He knew when to push you and when to pull you up.

"As an athletic director for the last fifteen years here in Warren, I've interviewed a lot of people for coaching positions. I've hired some, not hired others, and, unfortunately, had to recommend others be let go. Coaching is a gift, and Dick Strahm had the gift. I truly believe God made Dick Strahm to be a coach."

And so five years were in the books. In the five years prior to Strahm's arrival in the late spring of 1975, the Findlay College Oilers posted a 15-23-1 record, a .384 winning percentage. In Strahm's first five years, the overall record was 35-15-2, a .673 percentage.

In the years that have ensued, several players from Strahm's first five years have been inducted into The University of Findlay Athletic Hall of Fame. These players are Nelson Bolden, Kevin Cassidy, Ben Finch, Pat Gibson, Denny Guerro, Denny Maag, Mark Newburg, Jim Ryan, and Paul Trina.

More impressively, discounting the transitional first year of 1975, in Strahm's four years, beginning in 1976, the winning percentage leaps to .785.

But, the real success of Dick's first five years can't be measured by statistical data or the number of NAIA Division 22 and National Coach of the Year awards accumulated along the way.

The real success was evident some 28 years after the cheers that emanated from the stands of Donnell Stadium on December 9, 1979, had long since faded to echoes and the scoreboard lights had stopped illuminating the 51-6 final score.

On a Monday night in mid-October of 2007, Coach Dick Strahm requested the presence of twelve former players, a former athletic director, a former assistant coach, and the man who wrote every game account of the Dick Strahm era for the local Findlay, Ohio paper. And, of the fifteen summoned, fifteen came.

They came not really for the glory of yesteryear, for the sports clippings have grown crinkled and have yellowed long, long ago. They came to say thanks. They came to show a mentor in whom they have immeasurable respect that the lessons taught through all those perfect 40-yard dashes were learned, and learned so well that they continue to resonate in the offices and places of business where men in their late forties and in their fifties must be to earn livings for their families.

And, there were stories and laughter and some tears and, of course, gratitude, as all remembered a perfect five-year plan.

Coach Strahm walks the sidelines during the 1997 national championship game in Savannah, Tennessee.

Captains of the 1995 NAIA national championship team (from left) Nate Arnold, Mike Powers, Troy Pearson, and Jason May.

The 1979 team celebrated Findlay College's first national championship.

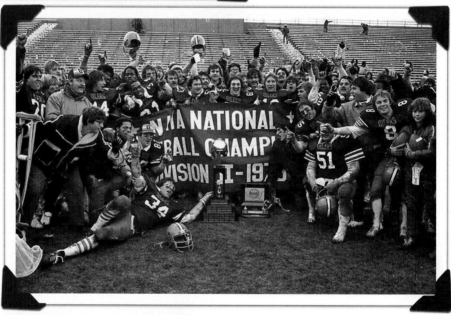

Coach Strahm gets some key ideas from Larry Alter, sports editor for Findlay's The Courier, *and Coach Dan Simrell, to use at his induction into the 2000 Toledo City Athletic League Hall of Fame.*

During the 1979 national championship season, Pat Gibson (left), confers with Coach Strahm (center) and Ken Agee (right). In back, Dave Wymer is talking to anyone who would listen.

The "Luv ya Oilers" signs were all over the stadium and around town. Findlay loves its football.

Coach Woody Hayes signed his new book, "You Win with People." Coach Strahm was a quick study.

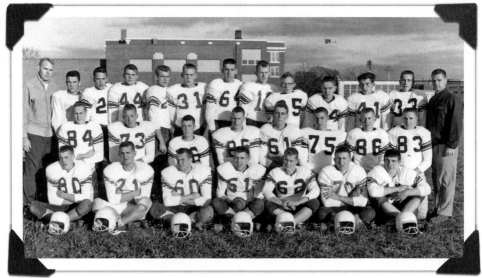

Dick Strahm (far right) at his first head coaching position at Lakota High School. The team won the 1960 league championship its first year.

Coach Strahm appreciated the presence of friends Dr. Jack Winters and his wife, Nancy Winters, and Dick's brother, Dale, at the 2004 College Football Hall of Fame induction weekend in South Bend, Indiana.

Phil D. Gardner (center), with his sons, Philip J. Gardner (left) and Michael Gardner (right). Phil Gardner made the new weight-training facility at Findlay College possible in 1989. He and his sons helped turn around the football program.

This group made the trip to Columbus, Ohio, to see the Oilers play an exhibition basketball game vs. OSU on November 6, 2007, which the Oilers won! From left: Elisabeth Zoba, Jack and Ann Ruscilli, Dr. C. Richard Beckett, Coach Strahm, Bill Lee, Herk Wolfe, Linda Lee and Dave Zoba.

Members of the 1997 national championship football team and their families gathered for a ten-year reunion Oct. 27, 2007, during The University of Findlay's Homecoming weekend. The stories keep getting better.

Winning the big one at Bryan High School. Notice the leather helmets.

Bo Hurley, senior quarterback and 1997 Rawlings Player of the Year, with Coach Strahm.

Coach Strahm with his All-American fullback Nelson Bolden in 1979. After a playoff game Nelson was named Offensive Player of the Game.

Coach Strahm is congratulated by two of his good friends, Dr. Jackson Winters (left) and Dave Kuenzli (right), after the national championship game December 20, 1997.

Strahm's coaching staff at Bryan High School included: (front row) J. Eizman, W. Mellon, R. Strahm, D. Ebersole (athletic director), G. Stockman; (back row) S. Schumm, N. Spengler, J. Reiser, R. Sumpter, D. Brown.

Dick Strahm with his first coaching staff in 1960. From left: Karl Koepfer, Stan Trupo, Coach Strahm, Gordon William (principal) and Stan Winnagle

Dr. DeBow Freed, president of The University of Findlay, with Coach Strahm at the 2004 College Football Hall of Fame induction in South Bend, Indiana.

Mel Long, first team All-American defensive tackle at the University of Toledo, went on to play with the Cleveland Browns. Coach Strahm had the privilege to coach him for two years.

While Dick and Ginger were visiting their friends Edd and Donna Groves in New Zealand, Edd found this sign and thought it was appropriate.

Dr. Kenneth E. Zirkle, president of The University of Findlay, announced Coach Strahm's retirement at a press conference in May 1999.

Coach Strahm (center) enjoys a moment with U.S. Congressman Michael Oxley (left) and Ohio Representative Michael Gilb, both from Findlay, at a dinner held in honor of Coach Strahm in October 2004.

Coach Strahm enjoys the many awards achieved by the 1995 national championship team and coaching staff.

Dick Strahm in his new office as vice president for institutional advancement at The University of Findlay.

The University of Findlay's 1997 national championship team celebrated immediately following the game.

Coach Jim Tressel and Coach Strahm at a dinner in Ada, Ohio, in May 2008 to raise funds for the Wilson Football Museum.

Dick Strahm received the "American Spirit of Honor" medal from the United States Air Force at basic training camp in Denver, Colorado.

Enjoying the Miami Orange Bowl game between Miami and Nebraska with friends: (front row) Lewis and Linda Jones, Ginger; (back row) Gwen and Dave Kuenzli, Coach Strahm.

Dick and Ginger's son, Steve, with his fiancée, Traci.

Dick Strahm's father, Mentzer, as a 3-year-old with his parents, Edith and Charles Strahm, in 1911.

Dick Strahm's grandfather, Harry Nichols, in 1881, when he was 6 years old.

Proud Grandpa and Grandma Strahm holding twins Danielle and Dalton.

The Strahm family in 2002.

The Dale Strahm family: Brian with his new son and his wife, Kimberly; Dale and his wife, Diane; Bradley, and Brett.

A happy moment for Coach and his son Doug after the 1997 national championship game. Ginger is about to join them.

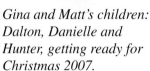

Gina and Matt's children: Dalton, Danielle and Hunter, getting ready for Christmas 2007.

Jim McIntosh, Coach Strahm with his grandson, Zachary, and Jim Houdeshell at the ten-year reunion of the 1997 national championship team.

Coaching runs in the family. Dick's grandfather, Charles Strahm, is the coach on the left, and his father, Mentzer Strahm, is holding the basketball.

The Dick Strahm family in 1983: Steve, Dick, Ginger, Doug, and Gina.

Coach Strahm beams as a proud father at his daughter Gina's wedding on November 30, 1996.

Dick's favorite three children: Doug, Steve, and Gina, in 1993.

Doug Strahm with his grandmother, Mildred Strahm, at his high school graduation.

Ginger walks up the aisle with her brother, Bruce, on her wedding day.

Ginger and Dick at their special moment at church on April 7, 1962.

Ginger (left) with her sisters, Sabra (center back) and Carol Kay (front), and her brother Bruce.

The Strahm family at Doug and Lisa's wedding, May 19, 1995: Steve, Gina, Lisa, Doug, Dick, and Ginger.

November 30, 1996, marked the wedding of the Strahm's daughter Gina, and her husband, Matt. Coach says he was really happy despite the way he looks here!

Doug and Gina on Doug's 6th birthday.

Parents Day recognition at Findlay College was extra special when Coach Strahm and Ginger walked with their son, Doug (at right), and Number 5 Brian Washington (left) who is now a member of The University of Findlay's Board of Trustees.

Chapter 10

Exploring Options, Yet Remaining an Oiler

While Dick Strahm was elated over his Oilers program, notably its rapid rise to the absolute pinnacle of the NAIA football world, he, at 46, was still young, young enough to yearn for the next rung up on the college football coaching ladder. After all, *complacency* was never an entry in Dick Strahm's football dictionary.

Recalls Dick, "The early 1980s really represented the final time in my coaching career when I still was looking a bit over the horizon to see what was out there in terms of coaching opportunities. Now, don't get me wrong. I have always loved Findlay and was so thankful that the community had embraced both my football program and my family to the extent they did.

"But, I also had enough curiosity to look around after that 1979 national championship and see if there might be some doors that would open for me."

In the late winter, after the '79 national-championship euphoria had subsided a bit, Strahm got a call from the same man who had offered him a position as defensive coordinator in 1975. The call came from the athletic director at Northern Illinois University, Dr. Robert Brigham. Brigham and Strahm had developed somewhat of a long-distance friendship after Dick declined the coordinator's position back in 1975 to take the head job in Findlay.

Dr. Brigham had a head football coaching position to fill, and he wanted to know if Dick was interested in interviewing for the position. Recalls Strahm, "I liked Dr. Brigham from the moment I met him back in 1975. Had it not been for my strong desire to become a head coach again, I would have accepted his offer five years ago.

"This time, with the head position open, I told Dr. Brigham that I would be interested in interviewing. Most coaches are looking to see how high they can climb in the profession, much like anyone in any career. It really has little to do with your level of contentment where you are. If there's a possibility of going to a bigger program with better facilities and earn a higher salary, well, you just have to listen."

Now, certainly, there reaches a point where older coaches kind of settle in, and the urges to uproot and take on a new challenge somewhat subside, but, at 46, Strahm certainly had not reached this point in his career.

So, for Dick Strahm, it was off to DeKalb, Illinois, a university town of around 35,000, for the first time since his interview in 1975. Strahm really felt that the national championship of the previous football season could very well be the ticket to a Division I head coaching job.

Nonetheless, Strahm was not oblivious to the difficulty small-college coaches historically had in advancing to big-school head positions. "I knew it was hard. After all, I had already had a couple phone calls when jobs at Army and Arizona opened during that off-season. Neither led to an interview, and I actually got pretty disheartened over something the athletic director at Army told me over the phone.

"He said that I had an excellent coaching record, but he wasn't able to consider hiring me because I was not from a major college. He told me it wasn't personal. It was just that most athletic directors felt that to satisfy the alumni, they were better off hiring assistant coaches from big programs than small-college coaches even when they'd done well."

However, Strahm was encouraged by a recent hiring in the off-season at a big school just one state further north of Findlay. "Word came down from Michigan that Michigan State gave a small-college coach a chance. The university hired Frank 'Muddy' Waters to be the next football coach. He'd previously been the head coach at Hillsdale College and Saginaw State.

"My first reaction when I heard was 'That's great!' Then, I knew it could be done. Muddy certainly had paid his dues, and he deserved the opportunity. I was hoping the tide was turning a bit, and this would help me get in at Northern Illinois. I just felt I was a damn good coach and really felt confident I could coach anywhere.

"After Dr. Brigham called to ask me if I'd like to interview, I called Coach [Woody] Hayes, who, by that time had retired. I told him about the opportunity, and he said that he knew Bob [Dr. Brigham] and would give him a call on my behalf.

"While I thought that might be somewhat helpful, I also felt Dr. Brigham was already on my side, so I asked Coach Hayes if he could call the president of Northern Illinois instead and put a word in. He said he would.

"Well, the next day, Coach Hayes called me back and said that he had just got off the phone with the president. He said he talked to him for around forty minutes and said that the he already had my name on his list of candidates. Coach Hayes said that the president promised he would give me "a real good listen" when I went for the interview. Coach Hayes told me, 'You go in there and do a good job in the interview. I think you have a really good shot at the job.'

"I told Coach Hayes that's all I could ask for and thanked him. Going back over my career, I saw yet another example of one of the greatest coaches of all time trying to help me advance. It all started back in 1965 in Bryan with Coach Hayes making several calls on my behalf. I can't tell you what a great feeling that is."

A graduate assistant picked Dick Strahm up in Chicago at O'Hare Airport and drove him to DeKalb. The interview with Dr. Brigham, Strahm felt, went very well. Then Dr. Brigham and Dick toured the campus and the football facilities. Strahm took note of what had changed since he'd taken the same tour five years earlier. "When we got to the locker rooms, I noticed they were brand new, all carpeted and very nice. I couldn't help but think of those Findlay lockers my first year that were right beside the coal bins.

After the tour, Strahm and the athletic director went to the student union, where there was a scheduled meeting with some of the football players. Recalls Dick, "I remember being very impressed with the young men who were selected to weigh in on the hiring process. They were seniors-to-be, around eight to ten of them, and were selected to help interview the last three candidates. When Dr. Brigham told me that on the way over, I felt pretty good in that I was in the final three candidates.

"The players were interested in what my offensive and defensive philosophies were and what my background was, where I'd been and what I'd accomplished. They were also interested in whether I saw myself as a coach who believed in a lot of discipline.

"I recall one player asking me what I would do if I knew a player was going out drinking a lot. I explained to them what my policy was at Findlay, and they seemed to like my answer. Really, a lot of the questions were pretty well thought out.

"I also asked them questions. I wanted to know what kind of things they expected of their head coach, what types of things bothered them in the past. I wanted to know what they thought needed to be done to win a conference championship. I thought it was a very productive meeting.

"I was also told that the total freshman football class from the previous year was red-shirted. That meant the freshman football players from 1979 had four years of eligibility left as well as the new freshman class of 1980. What a great advantage that would be for the new coach of Northern Illinois."

Later in the afternoon, Strahm also met with a group of about fifteen people. They were administrators, professors, and other coaches from different sports. There were no players at this meeting. Recalls Dick, "We first had dinner, and then after the plates were cleared, there was a group interview.

"You'd think I'd have been nervous, but I wasn't. I felt I'd always interviewed well and actually felt quite relaxed. Maybe it was the fact that I was there back in '75 when I was interviewing for the defensive coordinator's job, but I just felt very comfortable with the whole situation.

"Another reason I felt comfortable was that, unlike 1975, on this visit to DeKalb, I already had a job, and a good one. I was just coming off four very successful years at Findlay, with the last one ending in a national championship! I had some very good football players at Findlay, and I figured if I didn't get the job, it wasn't the end of the world.

"There are times when you interview, and you just know things are going well. When you're talking to people in an interview situation, and, as you're getting excited explaining something and you can see them fully engaged in what you're saying and they are nodding at all the right times, well, you get a good feeling. That's kind of the feeling I got at this interview.

"I don't know. Maybe it was my experience as a classroom teacher that gave me a sense of when interviews were going well. When I taught, there were times I just knew a lesson I'd prepared was reaching my young audience. They were involved in what I was saying and aware of where I was trying to take them. I got some of those same vibes at this group interview.

"As I was explaining something, I was standing up behind my chair. I now really had their attention and was getting excited. I even started walking around the table as I was speaking, and every head was turning with me. I felt their excitement. Listen, I have had other interviews where I just didn't get that feeling that everyone was on board with what I was saying, but this was different."

Despite the confidence Strahm remembers having, after the interview he went back to the hotel where he had checked in and slept nervously, not knowing what the result would be. Of course, people would talk after he'd left. Perhaps he'd know more in the morning.

The next morning, Dr. Brigham came over to pick Strahm up for breakfast, after which, a graduate assistant would take him back to O'Hare. Recalls Dick, "During breakfast, we talked about the previous day and also the future, relative to my possibly coming aboard as the Huskies' head coach. Dr. Brigham was confident I'd interviewed well, but he said the decision was not his alone.

"As I walked toward the car to get in for the trip to the airport, I remember the doctor shaking my hand and saying, 'Do you have your staff ready to go?' I told him that I knew who I'd be taking with me from Findlay. I knew that both Steve Mohr and Dean Pees were ready in a heartbeat.

"Dr. Brigham told me that he thought it looked good for me, and, when I heard that, I didn't even need the plane! I felt I had grown wings and could fly back myself."

When Strahm got back to Findlay that evening, he called assistant coach Steve Mohr and told him that he really felt he'd be offered the position. After he got off the phone, Steve Mohr immediately went to his office and started packing.

The next morning Brigham called Strahm. He explained that there had been a turn of events and one of the vice presidents had brought in one more candidate to be interviewed that afternoon. That other candidate was one Dick knew.

"That final candidate was Bill Mallory. He had been the coach who succeeded Bo Schembechler at Miami of Ohio in the MAC. Of course, I knew Bill from my time at Toledo. Now, I knew Bill was an outstanding coach. He had a great record at Miami before he moved on to accept the head coaching job at the University of Colorado in 1974. Now, he was back in the Midwest, ready to get back into coaching after taking the 1979 season off.

"I'll be honest. I knew Bill had a tremendous advantage in that he'd been a Division I head coach at two different schools, and one of those schools was in the Big Eight, one of the country's elite football conferences. But, still, based on my interview and the fact that I'd interviewed with Dr. Brigham in 1975, I still felt pretty good about my chances. Plus, I kept thinking about Michigan State offering its job to Muddy Waters. I was hoping that more Division I schools would be giving us small-college coaches our opportunities. At any rate, Dr. Brigham told me he'd call me back right after the interview.

"When the phone rang, I got that feeling of anticipation in the pit of my stomach. Sure enough, it was Dr. Brigham, and he said the committee had offered Bill the job. He said he was sorry and that if Mallory hadn't applied, I would have been their choice."

After Strahm dealt with the initial disappointment of missing the Northern Illinois job in the small city known as Barb City because it was the location of the first barbed wire manufacturing company in the country, he tried to remain upbeat and philosophical. Yet, he did agree to be interviewed for a story in August of 1980 to be written by Dave Hackenberg of the *Toledo Blade*. It was a story that would eventually run under the headline "Strahm Frustrated in Bid to Advance."

Strahm told the longtime *Blade* sportswriter, "I was sitting with a bunch of other coaches from the league [Hoosier-Buckeye Collegiate Conference] at a recent meeting, and the general feeling was that if I couldn't get a major college job after winning the national championship, what kind of a chance did they have?"

Strahm continued, "It's been a frustrating experience in many respects. People keep telling you the big opportunity is sure to come your way, and, sooner or later, you start believing it. All we [small-college coaches] are asking is for a few ADs [athletic directors] to have enough courage to give us a chance."

Strahm then clarified himself to Hackenberg and, perhaps, more importantly to the fans of his Findlay Oilers. He did not want to be misunderstood as ungrateful for the zealous support so many in Findlay had given his football program. "Sure, I was looking for a bigger job. But, not just for the sake of leaving Findlay. I can't worry about what didn't happen because I have a good job that I won't ignore.

"There were a couple months after the first of the year when my future as a coach here was somewhat in limbo, but now I am getting cranked up again to get the job done."

Despite the lost opportunity to become a Division I head coach, Dick did have some reasons for optimism heading into the 1980 season. For one thing, he would have, for the first time since he'd arrived in Findlay, five assistant coaches returning to his staff.

For Dean Pees, this would be his second year of college coaching. The second-year defensive coordinator who was destined to climb to truly dizzying heights in the coaching profession had come to Findlay prior to the 1979 season via Dick's brother Dale.

Dale Strahm was asked by Pees to speak at the Elmwood High School football banquet in early December of 1978, and this started a friendship between the two men. When Dean expressed an interest to Dale to get into collegiate coaching, Dale called his older brother. Since Dick had just lost his defensive coordinator, Dave Tanner, Dick agreed to interview Dean Pees for the position.

Recalls Pees about his first year, 1979, with Dick Strahm, "When I came in '79, I wanted to observe, not impose my will, so to speak, while coaching. And, I think that's a pretty good lesson for all assistant coaches coming into a new coaching experience. Look, Findlay was an established team when I arrived. In '78, the Oilers went undefeated in the regular season and won the league and were seven points away from being national champions! I wasn't about to go in there and start throwing my weight around and telling everyone what I was going to change.

"I just did my best and learned what Coach Strahm wanted me to do. I felt some pressure coming in as defensive coordinator after that 11-1 1978 season. If my defense didn't play well, I didn't want to be known as the guy who messed it up.

"Fortunately, I was able to learn from Dick's thoroughness and attention to detail, and we won the national championship."

Steve Mohr was also back for his fifth season, after, of course, taking some of the wall hangings and football-related material back out of the box he had begun to fill several months earlier when he thought a move to Barb City was imminent. He joined Jim McIntosh, the teacher in the Fostoria City Schools with the booming voice, who brought such a reservoir of knowledge about line play each time he walked onto a football field.

In addition, Charlie Thompson and Beryl Hemminger returned as part-time coaches after their teaching days were completed at North Baltimore High School, just north of Findlay.

Despite the stability of an intact staff, Strahm knew the 1980 season would be a tremendous challenge. So many terrific performers with names like Trina and Hatfield and Maag had moved on, and there were many holes to fill on both sides of the ball. Additionally, the Oilers wore the target of being the defending national champions, never an easy thing.

Recalls Dick, "I knew I had Nelson Bolden back for one more year, but the rest of the offensive backfield had very little experience. All together, sixteen starters were gone. So, the situation going into the 1979 season when we had experience up and down both lines had really flipped. While I thought we had recruited well, even on a small-college level, freshmen generally don't become impact players right away. They need time to grow."

Another challenge for the 1980 season was that Ken Agee, the fine nose tackle who also got some carries out of the fullback slot when Bolden needed a break, was going to take what amounted to a redshirt before returning for his last year of eligibility in 1981. It was a decision jointly made by Agee and his head coach for several reasons.

Recalls Agee, "During the summer before, in 1979, I had a job at Pepsi-Cola, and a tow motor tipped. I broke my wrist. Well, I played the entire national championship season with a soft protective cast and did OK. But, in the summer of 1980, I didn't feel the wrist was as strong as it should be.

"Of course, I could have played in 1980, but the wrist was only part of my decision. Listen, I'll be honest. I also felt my dream of being an elite college running back wasn't being fulfilled. I really felt I was every bit the running back that Nelson was but also understood the reality of the situation. I knew if I played, I would only get the scraps in terms of carries. Coming out of high school, I had excellent numbers as a running back, and that's the position Coach Hess at OU recruited me to play before I decided to reject the scholarship because I didn't want to redshirt my freshman year.

"It's really kind of ironic. What I wasn't willing to do as a freshman in 1977, I was volunteering to do in 1980. I just wanted to run out of that number-one fullback position to see what I could do, so I needed to wait until Nelson finished his senior season.

"Another part of my decision was I wanted to focus on my academics. Like a lot of college athletes, I needed some work in that area. College athletes make such a commitment in terms of time to their sports that sometimes the grades tend to suffer a bit. My academic advisor felt taking the year off from football was a good idea, too. As it turned out, I really improved academically in all my classes and even became a tutor. My decision to take the year off, ultimately, allowed me to leave Findlay with my degree."

Replacing Trina at quarterback was one of his backups in 1979, Greg Brown, from Youngstown South. Brown, recalls Strahm, was a vastly different quarterback than Trina. "Greg was more of a scrambler. He could throw the ball well, but Paul was really much more of a passing threat."

With so many positions to fill, the hope is for a coach to see a schedule that lines up in fortuitous fashion, meaning that the early portion of it would be soft and the more challenging games would dot the late October and the November part of the slate. Unfortunately, for Dick and his 1980 Oilers, that was not going to happen.

The opener was on the road against the Wilmington College Quakers, a top-tier Hoosier-Buckeye school. Wilmington's Bill Ramseyer and Strahm had over the last several years developed a very intense rivalry. Ramseyer recalls both the 1980 game and also the gamesmanship that surrounded it vividly. "In 1980, I found myself opening our season against the defending national champions. Now, certainly, with the rivalry Dick and I had, I didn't need to do anything special to get our fans stoked for this home opener. All you really had to do was say, 'Findlay,' and that was enough.

"But, I did think there was a possibility that my guys might be a bit in awe of playing the national champions, so I came up with something to spring on them. So, here we were warming up before the game, and we had our white jerseys on. Now, the Hoosier-Buckeye Conference always had the home team wear dark jerseys. I made sure we got out on the field before Dick brought his team out.

"Well, Dick led his team out onto the field, and he looked across the field and saw what we were wearing. He came sprinting across the field, and he had this shocked look on his face. He said, 'Bill, what's going on? *We're* the visiting team! We wear white! That's all we brought!'

"Well, I kind of faked like I forgot, you know, hit myself in the forehead. I said to him, 'Ahh, Dick. I'm sorry about that. I don't know where my head's at. We'll change when we get in the locker room.

When we got into the locker room, hanging on each hook, was a green jersey with a white patch sewn on the front. In gold letters, it said, 'Beat Findlay'!

"And, our kids, who had no idea what was going on until that very moment after our equipment manager put the jerseys on those hooks when they were out warming up, just went crazy! They started screaming and carrying on.

"And, we just tore out of that locker room after the jersey change. You talk about playing inspired football! It looked like a Civil War reenactment that day. Guys were just killing each other, and we wound up winning 28-14.

"A few years after that, college football outlawed the business of jersey add-ons, like patches that weren't sanctioned, but that 1980 opener remains such a great memory for me."

Certainly for Strahm, the jerseys reminded him of a certain ploy he used years before back in Warren, Ohio, when he festooned his Western Reserve Raiders in last-minute jerseys bearing the sentiment, "WE WILL WIN." Then, they slew a dragon in the form of the school on the east side of the Mahoning River, the Warren G. Harding Panthers.

For Strahm's Oilers, the 1980 season was certainly an uneven affair. After the season-opening loss to Wilmington, the Oilers experienced alternating highs and lows. In week two, they defeated Manchester 20-9, which preceded a tough week-three loss to non-conference NCAA Division III Frostburg State, 20-12. Recalls Strahm, "Anytime we lined up against a school like Frostburg State University in Maryland, which was a state-funded school, we knew how difficult the game would be."

Then, it was a four-game stretch of wins and losses. Findlay followed a 33-0 Earlham win with a 10-0 loss to Anderson. Then, after defeating Taylor 35-7, the Oilers lost to the Panthers of Hanover College, 23-14.

Findlay, facing the danger of following a national championship with a season in which it would lose more than it won, rallied and put together a modest two-game winning streak, 14-10 over Defiance and 49-10 over Bluffton.

So, after going 21-2-2 in 1978 and 1979 and splitting NCAA title games, the 1980 5-4 record was a bitter pill to swallow, but it wasn't totally unexpected, at least by the Oilers head coach. "We were just so young. With sixteen positions to fill, I knew 1980 would be very tough. Sure, we had Nelson Bolden back, but the offensive line that opened so many holes for him the previous couple a years had graduated."

In the fall of 1980, Strahm was looking forward to a promising young freshman recruit to help at defensive end. Unfortunately, Brian Young, out of Newark, Ohio, sustained a career-ending injury. A 1984 graduate, Young went on to a successful career as an agency field executive with State Farm Insurance. Recognized for his early achievements, the University named him for the Old Main Award in 1995, given to outstanding alumni under the age of 36. He still maintains ties with Strahm and currently serves on The University of Findlay Board of Trustees.

The 1980 season did see the emergence of some freshmen who were beginning tremendous Oilers careers. One, in particular, looks back at the 5-4 record much differently than Dick Strahm.

Defensive back Brian Washington now lives in Newark, Delaware. He is the vice president of talent acquisition for ARAMARK, an eminently successful company which provides human capital services for facility management and food services. In addition, Washington serves on The University of Findlay Board of Trustees, a position Washington feels is an honor and one he couldn't refuse when he was tabbed. "Hey, Findlay was so very good to me and really is responsible for the successes I've had in life, so when I was asked, I saw it as repaying a pretty substantial debt of gratitude."

Washington recalls both the path that led to Findlay College and his freshman year. "I was very fortunate to have played for Dick Strahm. I wasn't necessarily recruited. A defensive tackle with whom I played at Toledo Waite High School was really who Coach Strahm wanted. When he made a visit to Findlay's campus, I went with him.

"I remember Coach Strahm asking me what position I wanted to play. At Waite, I had played both running back and defensive back. Since I had such excellent coaching on defense by Coach Marvin Johnson, who really taught me how to play cornerback in a 5-2 defense, which was the same defense Coach Strahm used, I said that I wanted to be a cornerback. While that defensive tackle wound up going somewhere else, I wound up at Findlay College.

"Starting the year, I was certainly at the bottom of the depth chart. Like a lot of freshmen, I was on the scout team. I remember early in the season, on one play in practice, Bolden was coming up to block me on a sweep. You talk about a big man coming up on you with a full head of steam!

"But, I did what Coach Johnson back at Waite taught me. I dropped low and took him out at the knees.

"All of a sudden, I heard a whistle, and Coach Strahm came running over. He was pretty agitated. He said, 'Do you know who that is?' I said, 'Yes, Coach. That's Nelson Bolden.' He replied, 'No, that's our only All-American running back, and I don't want our defensive people diving at his knees. Otherwise, my young friend, that was a good effort, but save those for our opponents.' I kind of got the idea."

By the fourth game of the season, Washington had earned a starting position. He recalls a brief conversation with Strahm. "I remember Coach came up after practice before the Earlham game and said I would start. He then said, 'You know, we don't normally start freshmen.' I didn't know what kind of response he wanted, and all I could think of was, 'There's a first time for everything.'"

While Washington certainly wasn't the first freshman to start for Dick Strahm, there weren't very many. He definitely proved he belonged, making a solid contribution the second half of the season. The 5-4 record, while disappointing to many accustomed to such a high level of performance in Findlay, was actually the first winning record Washington had been a part of since his days in junior high.

Washington recalls, "I wasn't satisfied with our 5-4 record, but, to be honest, I wasn't really disappointed by it either. I finally was on a winning team and had made some contributions to several of those wins. I also feel our other cornerback, Chris Riley, from Toledo Libbey, and I had developed some pretty good chemistry out there. I was really looking forward to the 1981 season almost as soon as the '80 season ended."

Another emerging player was a freshman out of Youngstown South, the same school from which quarterback Greg Brown emerged. The player, Curtis Davidson, was an offensive lineman, one who showed so much ability after breaking into the starting lineup in week seven that he would eventually become one of the best guards in school history.

Davidson, now the senior associate director of admissions at Christopher Newport University in Newport News, Virginia, remembers the benefits of breaking into the starting lineup before his freshman year had ended. "By starting that Hanover game and also the final two, I really got some momentum heading into my sophomore season. Offensive linemen, I feel, develop a very strong, almost family-type bond, so I didn't know how quickly I'd be accepted. I was from the start, and maybe that's why even after over twenty-five years, I remember all of my teammates on that line. Kris Thacker was the tight end, and, of course, a tight end does so much more blocking than receiving in a wishbone offense that he's definitely in the linemen's fraternity. Steve Spencer from Warren Western Reserve was the other guard. Our tackles were Mike Myers and Rick Hutton."

Recalls assistant coach Jim McIntosh about that 1980 season, "We just lost so many of our skill people from the '79 squad. Despite our national championship in 1979, we had a lot of very tough games, games we felt we needed our starters in for most, if not all, of the time. So, we didn't get much of a chance to get the younger kids a lot of game experience. That hurt us in 1980."

For Nelson Bolden, the ride was over, but what a remarkable ride it was! Despite running behind a largely inexperienced line in his final season and despite wearing the target on his back that all great workhorse backs have, Bolden still managed to gain 1,079 yards. His 4.6 yards per carry was the best of his four-year career.

Bolden would leave Findlay as the most prolific back from a yards-gained perspective, than any back in school history. Even now, more than a quarter century after his final game, a 223-yard effort versus Bluffton, Bolden's 4,009 yards have yet to be equaled.

Recalls Dick, "While I hated to see Nelson go, it was very rewarding too see him receive his degree with his mother and father watching. I felt confident that Ken Agee would do very well at fullback. Ken was such an intense competitor, and I had a great deal of respect for him for changing positions and becoming primarily a nose tackle. It made us so much stronger, especially in 1979.

"Look, I know Ken wanted to run the ball more, but I felt Nelson was our best option. It wasn't that I felt Ken wouldn't be as good a back as Nelson. It was more a situation that I knew Ken was a good enough athlete that he could dominate in another position where we needed a force."

Now a member of The University of Findlay Athletic Hall of Fame, Agee certainly is a player Dick Strahm will never forget. He is memorable not only for what he did on the football field but also for a couple rather humorous incidents that happened in the late spring and early summer of 1981, just weeks away from Agee's opportunity to be the number-one running back.

Recalls Dick, "I remember in May, Ken came over to the house. I'd just had gall bladder surgery. Ginger was gone, and Ken told me that he had a date that weekend and didn't have any money.

"I told Ken, of course, that I couldn't just give him money, but if he was willing to mow the yard, I could pay him enough to take his girl out on a nice date. Well, Ken certainly was willing to work for his date money and agreed to get the mower. So, I was sitting in our family room, and Ken got to work cutting the front and back yards.

"Ginger just loves flowers and bushes and had planted these little bushes on top of a small hill in the back yard. Ken must have thought these clumps of green sticking above the grass were mutant sprouts of grass or maybe weeds, and he just mowed right over those suckers. I think his mindset was, 'If it's green, it's going down!'

"I didn't find out until later that day, long after Ken finished and I paid him and sent him on his way. Ginger had come home and went out in the back yard to water those little bushes. She came running in and asked what happened. When I told her about Ken's yard work, she said, 'Next time, just let me mow the yard!'

"Now, my theory on the whole lawn-mowing debacle is that from where Ken came from in Cleveland, there was no green stuff. It was all concrete and asphalt basketball courts, and that was it. He just figured if it was green, it must need to be mowed."

Agee, the senior juvenile corrections officer back living and working in his home city, laughs at the theory. "I've told Coach Strahm several times that I grew up in beautiful Shaker Heights and certainly had seen a lot of grass before I transferred to the Cleveland Public Schools in the ninth grade. I just didn't think those little sprigs looked like anything someone had planted!"

Dick also remembers a second time Agee came seeking dating funds for services rendered at the Strahm home on the west side of Findlay. "A few weeks later, I got a knock on the door, and it was Ken. I had already told him about the lawn-mowing problem, so I knew he wasn't looking for that type of work.

"But, he was looking for work to pay for another date. Well, let it never be said I would stand in the way of my players' social lives. I told Ken he could wash and polish Ginger's maroon Buick station wagon to earn his date money.

"So, I gave him the soap and sponges and rags and such. I also got him a buffer to use after he got done washing the car. Once he got started, I looked out the window a couple times, and, I must admit, he had that baby looking good.

"Then, I kind of lost track of him. Suddenly, there was a knock on the door, and it was Ken. He asked me to come outside and look at something. I walked out, and he and I went up to the car. He pointed, and along one side of the car was a section that had been buffed all the way down to the metal. He'd evidently pushed too hard. Now, understand that Ken was built like a Greek god. He apologized profusely about that strip of about four or five inches where there was nothing but silver.

"Well, I still paid him, but as I did so, I said to him, 'Ken, next time, if you need money, just stop by my office on campus, and we'll figure something for you to do over at the school. I just didn't think our property could sustain any more of Ken's efforts to raise date money.

"When Ginger got home and saw the car, she said, 'Please just let me give you some money.' When I asked what the money was for, she said that she was paying me to keep Ken away from the house!"

As the season approached, the Greek god that Strahm recollects was indeed ready to prove he could get off the porch and run with the big dogs. Recalls Agee, "I came into August two-a-days in the best shape of my life. The wrist that I had broken was so much stronger. I also had the fastest time on the team in both the 400-yard dash and the 40-yard dash [4.5 seconds]. During my year off, I worked out fanatically.

"You see, I had told Nelson before he graduated, I'd break his single-season school record in yards gained.

For Dick Strahm, he was again pleased that heading into the 1981 season he had no defections from his coaching staff. Pees, Mohr, McIntosh, Hemminger, and Thompson all returned. The only coaching changes were the additions of two former players who were key contributors to the 1979 national championship effort, Pat Roncagli and Ron Wright. Both came aboard as student assistant coaches as they finished their undergraduate studies, much like Kevin Cassidy did in 1979.

As far as recruiting, Dick went to Warren Western Reserve to grab Charles Dukes and Gerald Dowe. Strahm continued his pattern of recruiting hard in the areas he knew best. "I'd seen up close the kind of football played in Warren, Ohio. Charles Dukes became a terrific defensive end for me.

"I would say he was one of the very best at his position out of all the young men who ever played for me. Charles was another player we had at Findlay that I believed could have played for me at the University of Toledo.

"Gerald Dowe also became a starter for me at linebacker and had a very productive career here at Findlay."

Since Greg Brown decided to return to his hometown of Youngstown and enroll at Youngstown State to concentrate on obtaining his degree, Strahm needed a new quarterback. He selected a junior, Doug Coate. Hailing from Bellefontaine, Ohio, Coate stood about 5'8" and weighed around 175 pounds, and if you asked Dick Strahm, most of that weight was heart.

"Doug was, pure and simple, one hard-nosed football player. He was a natural leader, a tough young man who really just seized the quarterback position and held it in both '81 and '82."

For the Oilers, in a year some identified as 1981 A.B. (for After Bolden), the season would be a tremendous bounce back from the disappointment of that 5-4 1980 campaign.

Unfortunately, a 25-13 loss to Anderson College kept the Oilers out of the playoffs, despite eight wins over the likes of Wilmington, Manchester, Frostburg State, and Earlham to open the season and wins over Taylor, Hanover, Defiance, and Bluffton after the Anderson loss.

Recalls Dick, "Back in the early eighties, the NAIA sent only eight teams to the playoffs. That year, Anderson went unbeaten in the Hoosier-Buckeye, and they went instead of us. It was so very difficult to send two teams from the same league into post-season. Now, later in the eighties and into the nineties, the number of teams qualifying for post-season doubled. But, you're obviously bound by whatever the norm is for a given era, so there's no sense crying about it. The bottom line is 8-1 just wasn't good enough in that particular year."

The '81 squad outscored its opponents by more than a three-to-one margin, 283-73. The youngsters of 1980 had come of age. Additionally, a certain running back, in his only year as the starting fullback and after taking a full year off to get stronger both in the classroom and in the weight room, had a season for the ages.

Ken Agee eclipsed Nelson Bolden's school single-season rushing record by two yards with a 1,351-yard effort. He also scored 102 points on 17 touchdowns. One touchdown, in particular, was memorable. It has stood the test of time and still is the longest run from scrimmage for a score in school history.

Recalls Agee, "In the Manchester game [a 26-0 Oilers shutout], I went 96 yards for Findlay's longest TD run ever. Even though Dana Wright would break my single-season rushing record a few years later, that 96-yarder is still on the books. I'm proud of that."

Agee was named as a first-team All-American and even received an invitation to the Seattle Seahawks NFL camp in 1981, which was certainly a rare honor for any NAIA athlete.

While he eventually didn't make it as an NFL running back, Agee has no regrets about playing at Findlay, where he was locked in behind Bolden for most of his career. "Findlay College was a wonderful experience for me. I got my degree, first and foremost, which is something that Coach Strahm always stressed more than anything else. I also played in two national championship games and won one. Then I broke a couple of significant records my final year. I also met my beautiful wife there, and she and my kids have truly been the joys of my life as well. And, of course, I got to play for Dick Strahm."

As for who was the better back, Bolden or Agee, Curtis Davidson, just one year away from earning the first of two consecutive All-American selections, defers. "Their running styles were very different, but, really maybe the last person to ask who was better is a lineman who's blocking. After all, he's kind of busy and not really paying much attention what's going on behind him. Let me just say that they were both terrific, and it was a privilege to block for both of them."

The 1981 season also marked the return of a player special to Dick Strahm after he sat out in 1980. Recalls Dick, "Rusty Smith came in as a freshman quarterback in 1979. I remember he'd injured his shoulder, so, after sitting out in 1980, we brought him to the defensive side of the ball as a cornerback. I really admired him for not giving up after he injured that shoulder. He became a valuable player and also an excellent special-teams player."

Smith, currently a pharmaceutical sales representative for GlaxoSmithKline, has such fond memories of his time as an Oiler and, especially as one of Strahm's players. "The biggest thing that Coach Strahm did for me was to show me what it takes to be a national champion. While I didn't play much in 1979, I was on that team, and I saw each day the commitment that people have to make to be great.

"In business, I've led a lot of groups on leadership and have used so much of what I learned from Dick Strahm. Really, my family has ties to all of Dick's national championships. I was on the '79 team. My half-brother, Shawn Fultz, was on the next national championship team in '92. Then, I returned to coach on Dick's staff and got to experience the national championships in 1995 and '97."

Heading into 1982, there were finally some assistant coaching positions to fill after the stability of the last three years. While Pees, Mohr, and McIntosh returned, Beryl Hemminger and Charlie Thompson left, replaced by Marty Fanning and Cliff Hite. In the case of Hite, his is indeed an interesting story and a memorable one for Dick Strahm.

"Cliff was a local product. He'd gone to Findlay High School and was a fine quarterback. His father was the director of the very well-respected band there as well. Anyway, Cliff received a scholarship to play at the University of Kentucky.

"After three years at Kentucky, he still hadn't established himself as the starter, so I called him and tried to get him to transfer to Findlay College and be our starting quarterback for the '76 season.

"He told me that he would love to but had just been selected one of the team captains. Despite the fact he wouldn't be starting, he felt he would be failing to honor a commitment if he left. I told him I respected that.

"Well, Cliff graduated and took a teaching job in Danville, Kentucky, and remained there through 1980. Then, he came back to Findlay and took teaching and coaching positions at his high school alma mater in 1981. He became an assistant football coach for Findlay High School.

"Now, in small towns you tend to hear about things, and I had heard that Cliff was not very happy and was intending to only teach during the next football season in 1982. As luck would have it, he just happened to be walking by my office one day. I saw him and flagged him down.

"Then, a thought popped into my head. I asked him if he'd like to come coach my offensive backs after he got done with his teaching day at the high school. And, that's how I got him on my staff in 1982."

The 1982 season saw Doug Coate return as the starting quarterback. Joining him in the backfield as a featured runner was Lawrence (L.C.) Coleman, a talented freshman out of Warren Western Reserve. L.C. would make immediate contributions, averaging an eye-popping 6.2 yards on 120 carries. Coate also nearly doubled his touchdown passes from 6 in '81 to 12 in '82. While he didn't throw often (85 times), he threw accurately (50 completions), a 59 percent clip. Wideout Jeff Laing was on the receiving end of 29 of those tosses.

The 1982 season brought an excellent recruiting class. Besides Coleman, future big-time performers included offensive guard Steve McAdoo, punter and quarterback Kris Alge, free safety Jon Huffman, and strong safety Chris Gearhart.

Included in the 1982 class also was a player whom Dick Strahm knew better than anyone who'd ever pulled on a pair of shoulder pads for the 48-year-old coach.

Dick's son, Doug, an offensive center, was coming aboard after a solid career as a Findlay High School Trojan. Recalls Doug about his freshman year, "When I came onto the Findlay College campus, there were some good elements and some bad. I guess the good was everybody knew me. I'd been with Dad in his office. I had been on the sidelines as a ball boy on game days. I'd been on the team buses for away games. But, that also created a pretty nerve-racking situation because now, not only was I Coach Strahm's son but I was also one of his players.

"How would I be perceived by the other players? I was very nervous about that, especially at first. I didn't want any accomplishments I may achieve to be viewed as the result of being the head coach's son.

"But, I'll tell you something. I thought everyone took me as just another player. I don't think anyone had any preconceived notions or prejudices against me. I felt totally accepted."

The Oilers opened the season with a 28-0 win over Manchester. However, in week two, the Oilers were involved in what proved to be a real war.

Recalls the freshman Strahm, "Ohio Northern was always a big rivalry game for us. I remember right before the game, ONU had this really big All-American defensive tackle. He was sitting on the bench before the game with no pads, just a cut-off t-shirt. I remember he had huge arms. I mean he just looked like he could lift a house!

"When we scratched out the win, 17-14, I just knew we were going to have a great season."

For Doug Strahm, his glory moment arrived in the game against Anderson College in week four. "As a non-starter, my contributions that first year were on the special teams. I was on the kick-off return team. Anderson was a strong team. It had dealt Findlay its only loss the previous season.

"We were leading 17-3 when they scored late in the fourth quarter to make it 17-10. With just a minute or so left, everyone knew an on-side kick was coming. Well, that's what happened, and here was the ball coming off a high bounce headed right for me. I caught the ball and dropped and curled, as I was coached to do. Now, my teammates were also coached to cover up whoever caught the ball to kind of absorb the shock of the kicking team's players who'd be trying to knock the ball loose.

"For whatever reason, no one covered me, and it seemed as if eleven Anderson players took a shot at me, but I hung on. That felt awfully good.

"Dad had an award called 'The Unsung Hero Award,' which went to a non-starter who made a significant play that contributed to a win. I think it was a t-shirt. I got the award that day. While, certainly, I was never a great player, that memory is a special one."

With Coate's throwing and Coleman's running, the Oilers were coming together as an offensive force. Curtis Davidson's terrific blocking earned him the first of two consecutive All-American honors.

Defensively, cornerbacks Chris Riley and Brian Washington also were performing at such a high level that they also would be named to All-American teams at the end of the '82 season.

After Doug Strahm secured the final kickoff against Anderson, Findlay won another four in a row, with wins over Taylor, Hanover, Defiance and Bluffton. By that point, everyone in Findlay knew the hometown boys were a perfect 8-0 heading into the finale against Bill Ramseyer's Wilmington College Quakers.

Recalls Dick, "The game was at Wilmington. Coach Ramseyer had a great running back by the name of Gary Worthy, and that team was really ready to play that day. They didn't come out in any set of special jerseys that year. They just came out and beat us.

"Our quarterback, Doug Coate, was knocked out of the game in the second quarter, and that blew any chance for us. We wound up losing 27-7. Despite the fact that it was our only loss, for the second straight year, 8-1 wasn't good enough to get us into the playoffs. Wilmington went, and we stayed home."

Doug Strahm recalls the Wilmington game as memorable because of the physical nature of the play. "In addition to Doug Coate's being knocked out of the game, our running back, L.C. Coleman, also got injured and was forced to leave the game at halftime."

For Dick Strahm, it would be another off season of trying to figure a way to get back to the playoffs. In Dick's mind, you play to be the last man standing, and to be in that position, you had to make the playoffs. There was certainly a lot of frustration and some resentment as to the nature of the playoff system. How could a team win 16 of 18 games over a two-year stretch and not advance to the playoffs? Had the playoffs come down to this? That you had to go undefeated to get in?

Just a year shy of his fiftieth birthday, Strahm would grapple with one more serious temptation to leave Findlay for the perceived lushness of another school's football stadium grass. And, this time, it was a call from a friend that got Dick thinking of greener playing fields than those found at Donnell Stadium.

Recalls Dick, "In the early spring of 1983, I got a call from a friend of mine who had a friend just named president of a college in North Carolina by the name of Gardner- Webb, and he was looking for a football coach.

"Now, admittedly, I was frustrated after going 8-1 two years in a row and not even getting a sniff of the playoffs, so I told my friend that I just might be interested.

"When I did some research and found out that the university was an NAIA Division I school where 32 full scholarships could be offered, my interest grew. After all, that was 32 more than Findlay could offer.

"Then the president called, and the next thing I knew, I was on my way to Detroit, where the president was attending a meeting. He wanted to have lunch before any official interview in North Carolina took place."

The two men seemed to hit it off well at lunch, and the president asked Strahm if he'd like to come to Boiling Springs, where the Gardner-Webb campus is located, for an interview. A week later, Dick was on a plane.

"When I arrived in Boiling Springs, there wasn't anything I saw that didn't appeal to me during my tour. It was a beautiful town and campus. When we got to the football stadium, I was very impressed. It was a great complex, great locker room, an outstanding weight room, football offices, meeting rooms, a nice reception area, and even a good-looking secretary to greet us! Then I went down on the field and looked off to the west, and there were the Great Smokey Mountains. What a gorgeous setting for college football.

"I went through the interview with the search committee in a large room at the student center and found out that the athletic director's job also was open. I told the members of the committee that I would be very interested in that position in addition to the football job. Really, on the college level, that's about as close to complete control as a head coach could ask for.

"After the committee met secretly, the president came up to me and told me he was very pleased to announce that the committee was unanimous that I be the next head football coach. However, the members felt that it was in the best interest of the university to have a different individual fill the AD's role. I asked for some time to think it over and returned to Findlay to talk to Ginger.

"When I got home and talked it over, I could tell that Ginger was less than enthused. The move would mean uprooting the family, a family whose members all felt Findlay was about as fine a place to live as there was.

"Additionally, I really wanted that athletic director's job. While that wasn't on my mind when I went to interview, when I found out it was open, I just felt I had to have it. Apparently, according to the president, the last basketball coach had also been the athletic director, and there were some conflict-of-interest problems. So, the committee just felt they didn't want to go down that road again.

"So, I called the president and thanked him for the offer but declined the position."

And, with that, Dick Strahm ended any search for stadium grass that appeared to be more enticing. It was Findlay, Ohio, that embraced him, and, this, he decided, is where he would remain. At that moment, Strahm knew that he would not allow his head to be turned even for a moment by any other suitors who would come a-calling for his coaching talents. He was fully committed to making Findlay College the absolute best small-college football program in the nation.

Doug Strahm recalls how wise he felt his father's decision was and how he had seen the community support for the football Oilers since 1975. "When we first came to town, it was nearly impossible to see a Findlay College sweatshirt or hat or spirit sign anywhere in town. However, by the late seventies and from then on, they were everywhere, including those 'Love Ya, Oilers' signs.

"And, when I played for Dad, starting in 1982, I really became aware of how strong the community support was. It literally exploded.

"Of course, I was aware of the Foster Parents' Program since its inception, but when I came in as a freshman, I got an up-close look at it. All of my classmates I came in with had foster parents. It was really awesome on picture day when the foster parents and the biological parents were both there. I'd love to know how many pictures are in albums spread across the country which show the player in uniform in the middle and two sets of parents, one on each side of him."

There was one group, in particular, that Doug Strahm remembers. "They were a group of guys who all worked at Cooper Tire. They were probably the loudest and most loyal Oilers fans that the university ever had.

"These guys would show up and sit on the visitor's side in the first few rows directly behind the opponent's bench. They would just hoop and holler from kickoff all the way through to the final play. They were so loud that a lot of the visiting teams would complain and try to have them moved.

"Of course, we didn't do anything to dissuade them from their fanatical support. As a matter of fact, the coaches decided to give them all Findlay football jerseys. They wanted them to know how important and how appreciated they were.

"I guess if there's one thing after all these years that I want to say to the Findlay community, it would be a very heartfelt 'Thank you for the support you have given my father and his football program.'"

So, perhaps the knowledge of the community support the coach's son remembers so very vividly had as much to do with the Strahms staying in Findlay as any single factor. At any rate and for whatever the reason, Dick recommitted himself to Findlay College and began to plan for the 1983 season.

During the off season, the assistant coaching stability that Strahm had enjoyed since 1979 finally was showing some cracks.

First, Cliff Hite, after one year, decided he really wanted to become a head coach on the high school level. As luck would have it, a job came open that allowed Dick Strahm an opportunity to help Hite obtain. Recalls Dick, "The job opening was at Bryan High School, and I just felt Cliff would make my old Bears a fine young coach."

So, Strahm made a few phone calls, one, of course, to Larry Killgallon, a very influential Bryan High School alum and one of the many appreciative former players so inspired by Dick Strahm.

With a boost from Strahm, Cliff Hite got that Bryan job, found success, and stayed from 1983 through 1996. Hite then got a chance to return to Findlay when the high school head football coaching job opened. Again, Strahm was able to help since he was on the search committee to find the next Findlay High School Trojan head football coach. "I was in on the interview, and Cliff did a great job. I just knew from Cliff's one year with me and the record he'd established in Bryan that he would make a great head coach back in his hometown."

As it turned out, Hite got the job in 1996 and had several very successful seasons, accumulating an impressive won-loss record at Findlay High School that would place him second all-time in school history.

In 2006, Hite turned to politics. He retired from education and ran for the District 76 seat in the Ohio House of Representatives as a Republican. Using the succinct campaign slogan "Hite is right," he won the seat and now represents the Findlay area.

In addition to the departure of Hite, Strahm also was losing Dean Pees, his defensive coordinator, who was ready to take career steps almost two at a time to get to his current position as the defensive coordinator for iconic NFL head coach Bill Belichick's New England Patriots. In Pees's first year (2004) with the Patriots as their linebacker coach, the Patriots won the Super Bowl.

Recalls Pees, the former football player at Hardin Northern High School, "You might say I was pretty spoiled during my coaching career. My first year after Dick hired me, we won the national championship in 1979. Then, years later when Coach Belichick hired me to coach the linebackers, we won the Super Bowl in my very first year. You've got to feel fortunate when those things happen.

"My four years under Dick Strahm were so important to my development as a coach. Dick remains a powerful figure in my life. He was demanding of both his staff and his players, but he also knew how to have fun.

"Dick was such a thorough coach. He wanted no deviations from what he knew he wanted done. In that way, he's a lot like Bill [Belichick].

"I think a lot of young coaches who worked for Dick, like Steve Mohr and Ron Wright, would say the same thing. Dick was a lot like your father. You didn't want to disappoint him, so you gave maximum effort. You just didn't want to let him down. You coached for him out of respect. That's a lot different from coaching out of fear.

"In looking back at my time at Findlay, there is a lot I miss. Of course, there was the special bond with the other coaches on the staff. Steve Mohr and I are about the same age. Here we were, both working about 90 hours a week, which is, really, about my typical work week with the Patriots, and both of us loved every minute of it. We both had teaching assignments at Findlay College that we had to fulfill, and we both coached another sport. Steve was the baseball coach, and I coached track and field. We both also had recruiting duties. It was a lot of work but very, very rewarding.

"I also miss the effect I was able to have on young men's lives. Now, I coach men with their own homes and families. That's especially true with the Patriots because we have so many veteran players who've been in the league for years, men like Rodney Harrison [strong safety] and Mike Vrabel [linebacker] and Junior Seau [linebacker].

"But, in college coaching, you are able to get that special feeling of helping kids become successful adults. I have former players from Findlay who still call. One of those is Keith Koepke, who is now the director of Dorney Park and Wildwater Kingdom in Allentown, Pennsylvania. The wonderful thing about college coaching is you get to experience that gratitude from former players who feel that you had a lot to do with the success they've had."

Pees also misses something that can only be described as "that special feeling." The feeling Pees alludes to in such fashion is the feeling he got on those Saturdays when running out on the field with the Oilers. "The feeling I got so often is the one that told me that even if we didn't play well, we were going to win. Let me tell you, that isn't the way I've ever felt in the pros. Despite the success we've attained here in New England, it's a nerve-racking business. Every Sunday is a new challenge, and, any Sunday, if you don't prepare well and play well, you can go home a loser."

As far as Dick Strahm is concerned, it's nice to know that his former assistant has climbed to such lofty heights yet retained such a high regard to where he has been along the way. "I was just glad to have Dean on staff for four years. I very much both noticed and appreciated his dedication, work ethic, and loyalty. I knew even back then that he was destined for great things in the coaching profession."

Replacing Pees as defensive coordinator was Ray Kwiatkowski and, as Strahm recollects, his is an interesting story. "Ray was a former marine who went to Bowling Green State University and played football after he left the service. When he graduated from BG, he took a teaching and coaching position at Bedford High School in Lambertville, Michigan. After several seasons, he took the defensive coordinator's position at Adrian College in Michigan. Later, he stepped away from coaching but was still teaching health and physical education at Bedford.

"I met with Ray at a restaurant in Bowling Green. As soon as I interviewed him, I sensed he would be a good defensive coordinator. Despite the fact that he hadn't coached in a few years, he was very knowledgeable and had kept up with the changes in the game. My only concern was the fact that he was living in Michigan, about a 55-minute drive from Findlay.

"But, he said he didn't mind driving, and I guess he proved it! Ray wound up being my defensive coordinator from 1983 all the way through 1992 and never missed a practice, a game, or a Sunday meeting. That's over an hour and a half driving seven days a week during the season.

"Ray was a very demanding coach. His defensive players had better know their assignments. Like Dean Pees, he was extremely hard working and loyal to our program. He was also a master at finding an adjustment each week to cause our opponents a problem and help us game-plan more effectively."

Former player Dick Tesnow, who was a defensive back for Strahm in 1975 and 1976, returned to the Findlay campus to coach the position he used to play. Prior to replacing Hite on the Oilers staff, Tesnow was the head coach at Arcadia High School.

Ron Wright was another of Strahm's former players to join the staff in 1983. The 1981 graduate and a former starter on both the 1978 national runners-up and the 1979 national championship teams, would coach the defensive line.

Also coming onto the staff were Marty Fanning and Mark Baker. Baker had played for Strahm at Findlay from 1979 through 1982.

Says Dick of having three former players on his staff, "I continued to bring former players onto my Findlay staffs for the rest of my career. I just felt there were no drawbacks to having former players coach for me. They were used to me. They saw how we did things when they played for me. I think anytime an assistant has a deeper understanding of what the head coach is all about, I believe he's going to make a better assistant. And, let me tell you something. A head coach can't do it alone. He needs a strong support staff, guys who take charge of their position players to let the head coach work on the big picture."

Assistant coaching stalwarts Jim McIntosh and Steve Mohr returned to Strahm's staff for the 1983 campaign.

In the summer of '83, Findlay College also saw someone arrive on campus, a man Strahm would come to regard as a great advocate for both students and, especially, student-athletes. Kenneth E. Zirkle became the fifteenth president of Findlay College.

Zirkle brought with him a belief that one of the best ways a student could prepare for the real world was by participating in intercollegiate athletics. Zirkle arrived from the State University of New York at Cortland, where he had been vice president of student affairs.

As far as Strahm was concerned, Zirkle's arrival in Findlay had all the markings of perfect timing. "Dr. Zirkle came along at just the right time for Findlay College. He was a great salesman and motivator, something Findlay College needed at the time.

"Ken loved students and, fortunately for me, he also loved athletics. Financially, there were some tough times for Findlay College when Ken arrived, and he developed a number of niche programs to help keep the school moving forward. When Dr. Zirkle arrived, there was an urgent need to increase enrollment, and he certainly was instrumental in doing just that."

With the graduation of Doug Coate, Strahm turned to Ken DePriest, out of West Holmes High School in Millersburg, Ohio, to call the offensive signals. DePriest would prove to be a very efficient quarterback, as his 1,048 yards through the air were the fourth highest since 1960.

Former Spencerville (Ohio) High School Bearcat Dave Brenek and fullback Roger Darr out of Fremont (Ohio) High School were set to join the talented former Warren Western Reserve High School running back L.C. Coleman in the offensive backfield.

Doug Strahm liked what he saw heading into the 1983 season, as did the head coach who raised him. Recalls Doug, "More members of my freshman class were jumping into starting positions. I had even moved up a notch to become the number-two center. We also got the McDuffie brothers, both former standouts for the Lima [Ohio] Senior High School Spartans, through transfers. Tommy became an impact player at linebacker, and George became a good tight end. Then we also welcomed another former Lima Senior player, Todd White.

"Coming aboard that year was a terrific defensive end, Bryon Krupp, who transferred in from Central Michigan. Anytime an NAIA school gets a transfer who played Division I, it's a good thing. As a freshman Bryon was Central Michigan's swing linebacker [first linebacker to rotate into games].

"A lot of people ask me what it was like playing for my father. Well, when I got on campus, I kind of knew what to expect. I'd been to so many practices while growing up and had been on the sidelines of so many games. So, I guess you might say I knew my father's football personality.

"When I got to be a player for Dad, what was different for me than other players is that practices had a tendency to drag on at home at the dinner table at times. This was especially true my freshman year in 1982. We'd be sitting there eating, and there would be a lull in the conversation, and Dad would say something like, 'I saw you missed your block on the last 22-2 we ran today,' or 'You know, the snap count on that 46 Toss was on two, not one. You're the center, so it might be a good idea to remember the snap count.'

"In 1983, I moved on campus so that didn't happen as much. But, you know, I was old enough to know why Dad sometimes reacted that way, and I understood. Dad just didn't want anyone to say he was easier on me than the rest of the players because I was his son.

"I think in a lot of ways playing for Dad was more demanding than it was for the other players."

The 1983 season looked very similar to the 1982 season in several respects. In both seasons the Oilers ran off eight consecutive wins as they headed into the finale of the regular season against Bill Ramseyer's Wilmington Quakers. New defensive coordinator Ray Kwiatkowski's defense was especially tenacious as it recorded three shutouts and yielded just seven points in three other contests out of the eight total games.

The Wilmington game this time would be played at Donnell. Despite the packed stadium, filled with all those "Love Ya, Oilers" supporters, Ramseyer's Quakers again prevailed in a tight, defensive contest, 13-10.

Recalls backup cornerback Rusty Smith, "That last game just let the air out of us. After going 8-1 in both 1981 and 1982 and missing the playoffs both years, we thought, 'Oh, no. Here we go again. Unless you're perfect, stay home!' We gathered in the old gym as a team on the Sunday after the Wilmington game, waiting to hear if we made the playoffs. When word came down that we did, we were elated. I guess you didn't always have to be perfect."

Remembers Curtis Davidson, who would not only garner his second consecutive Little All-American honor but also, as an offensive lineman, be accorded a rare honor, that of being selected by his teammates as the team's Most Valuable Player, "It was so special. I was beginning to wonder after my junior year if making it to the playoffs just wasn't in the cards for me during my football career. What's that they say about timing being everything?

"Listen. Don't get me wrong. The individual honors are nice, the All-American selections and the MVP honors, but, unlike say golf or track and field, football is a team game. And, what is most memorable is what you accomplish as a team."

The Findlay administration, as it had in the past, stepped up and made the financial commitment to host the first-round playoff game. The opponent was Westminster College, a perennial NAIA power out of New Wilmington, Pennsylvania, 50 miles north of Pittsburgh.

The Westminster Titans were coached by a small-college legend, Joe Fusco. Fusco arrived on the campus of Westminster in 1972 and remained through 1990. During his tenure, he compiled a record of 154-34-3 and matched Strahm's total of four NAIA Division II national championships ('76, '77, '88, '89). Like the man across the field from him, Fusco would also one day be inducted into the College Football Hall of Fame.

The 1983 playoff game, for the Oilers, was largely forgettable, as Fusco's charges dominated, 28-0. Recalls Little All-American defensive back Brian Washington, "The surface at Donnell was really torn up. There had been so much rain, and there had been some high school playoff games played on it just a few days before.

"I don't want to make excuses because we were beaten, plain and simple, but our offense was based on our ability to run the ball and our backs just couldn't get any traction.

"What I most remember is after the game, it got really cold and, by nightfall, the ground had frozen, and the traction was a lot better. There was a high school playoff game that night on the field. I went and saw one of the backs run for something like 187 yards. I remember thinking, 'Why couldn't our game have been a night contest?' But, to be honest, we just didn't play very well that day, which was very unusual because we'd been so strong all year. Heck, even giving up 28 in that final game, our defense only gave up 89 points in all ten games. Going into that Westminster game, our defense had yielded only eight touchdowns in nine games.

And, for seniors like Washington and Curtis Davidson, their Oilers careers ended sadly on a muddy field. While there would be others who would come after them to carry on the Findlay tradition, their considerable talents would be sorely missed. Davidson, the former Youngstown linebacker who Dick Strahm convinced to play offensive guard, left with so many wonderful memories despite the career-ending loss. "It was just an honor to play for Dick Strahm. Despite being very demanding, he established such great rapport with his players. He believed in fundamentals. I remember he would always preach that football was really a simple game—running, blocking, and tackling. He coached toughness. He coached discipline. He coached winners. And, let me tell you, the lessons transcended the football field. His players took the things he taught and used them in their careers as well."

Davidson remained at Findlay the following year to finish his degree and served as a student assistant coach. Then, after leaving Findlay to earn a master's degree and serve as an assistant coach at Georgetown College in Kentucky, he returned in 1986 and joined the Oilers football staff. He also went to work in the college's admission's office and eventually rose to the position of director of admissions.

For Davidson, it was one of the toughest decisions he ever had to make when he left the university in August of 2002. "While my playing career was certainly rewarding in that I was named to the All-American team twice, the fact is, from a team standpoint, we only played in one playoff game in my four years. That's why I was so glad I returned to Findlay to work with Coach Strahm. That gave me the opportunity to be a part of those three national championships in the 1990s. And, let me tell you, those were more rewarding than those All-American awards."

In Dick Strahm's eyes, Curtis Davidson was a tower of strength. "Curtis was such a dominant player, truly one of the best in school history. And, then, to demonstrate such remarkable teaching skills as a coach, well, that's just special to me. The offensive lines he coached in the 1990s were some of the finest in small-college football in the entire country. You just can't write the history of Findlay Oilers football without writing about Curtis Davidson."

Recalls Doug Strahm about playing Westminster, "Playing Coach Fusco's team in the 1980s really changed how we recruited because we all realized if we were going to go anywhere in the post season, we had to beat them. So my dad and the rest of the coaches started recruiting with match-ups in mind with Westminster and its personnel who we knew would be returning for two or three years."

As 1984 approached, Doug Strahm was optimistic. "Honestly, I thought we would be a powerhouse. In preseason, Kris Alge, who backed up Ken DePriest and also did our punting, was named starting quarterback. Derek Hutchinson was really coming on as a wide receiver. Of course, L.C. Coleman was back after leading us in rushing in each of the last two years. We also had our big fullback, Roger Darr, back and a really tenacious blocking back, Dave Brenek, coming back as well. And, we also had a transfer from a Division I NCAA school, Kent State, a running back by the name of Dana Wright, who was certainly going to be in the mix.

"Defensively, I thought we would be strong. The line was anchored by a great senior tackle, Brian Vogt. Even though Brian Washington was gone, I thought our secondary would be good as well."

Dick Strahm remembers Brian Vogt well. "Brian wound up making first-team All-American in 1984. He was 6'3" and 270 pounds and could really run. Except for Mel Long, the All-American defensive tackle I coached at the University of Toledo, Brian was the fastest defensive tackle I ever coached. After Brian left Findlay, he got a tryout with the Cleveland Browns. In the preseason, he was doing very well until he injured his spine and ended his professional aspirations."

Strahm recalls something else noteworthy about Brian Vogt, his appetite. "Brian could eat like no one I've ever seen before. Guys he played with will tell you stories of large pizzas being delivered to the dorm, and Brian polishing off two all by himself.

"I recall one evening I received a call from the manager of a restaurant in Findlay that had an all-you-can-eat buffet. Brian was the only defensive lineman I coached who was asked not to return to the restaurant."

The secondary would be anchored by Jon Huffman and Chris Gearhart. Recalls Dick, "What terrific players these young men were. Huffman played his high school ball just down the road from Findlay at Liberty Benton High School. He very well just might be the best free safety to ever play for the Findlay Oilers, and was named a Little All-American after his senior season. As for Chris, my strong safety, he just wouldn't back down from anyone. He was just one tough kid. He wasn't very big but was just a perfect example of the old saying, 'It's not the size of the dog in the fight but the size of the fight in the dog.'"

The assistant coaches in 1984 were Dick Tesnow, Ron Wright, Steve Mohr, Ray Kwiatkowski, and Jim McIntosh, with Davidson starting his coaching career the same way as Ron Wright did, as a student assistant.

Kris Alge, now a teacher and head football coach at McComb (Ohio) High School, remembers what he did to train in the summer before the 1984 season. "Coach Strahm was always on me about getting faster. He felt I needed to improve my quickness if I wanted to run the wishbone. So, during the summer, my buddy and I loaded a lawnmower into the back of his car so that just the handle was sticking out.

"I grabbed the handle, and my buddy would get the car up to about 25 miles an hour while I ran behind the car. If I felt I was in danger of falling, like a water skier, I just let go. We did that ten times, three times a week, as part of my summer workouts. I really wanted to be the quarterback. Well, when August two-a-days started, I actually did improve my speed. My 40-yard dash time was a couple tenths of a second better, and I won the starting job."

Despite the optimism of Doug Strahm, who had every intention of winning the starting center position, the harsh realities of injuries sometimes intervene in the game of football. Recalls Doug, "To be honest, I wasn't a very good football player. But, I practiced hard and tried hard. The year before, I injured my back in practice. What happened was I snapped the ball and was in the process of trying to get my block when the ball carrier hit me right in the back with his helmet. The impact knocked a couple vertebrae out of place and actually twisted my pelvis, which threw my hip out of place. It got to be very difficult snapping the ball, but I made it through the rest of the season.

"Heading into my junior year, I trained as hard as I ever had in my life during the summer. Just when I was feeling pretty good about myself and thought I had a real good chance to win the position, something happened out at the Hancock County Fairgrounds.

"I was out there practicing bear crawls because Coach Mohr, our offensive line coach, used the technique in a drill a lot during the upcoming August two-a-days. It was a drill where you put your hand in the middle of a tire, spin out, and bear crawl on hands and feet to the next tire, and so on down a line of about five tires.

"Well, while practicing the technique, I put my hand in a hole and threw my back out again. I did manage to get through the August practices and even the first couple games, but, after a trip to the doctor and some X-rays, I took the doctor's advice and stopped playing.

"Although I had always dreamed of starting for my dad, the decision to stop playing was made a lot easier by two questions the doctor asked me. He first asked, 'Do you want to have kids one day?' When I said I did, he then asked, 'Do you want to be able to bend down and pick them up?' I got the message."

The 1984 season opener was on the road against Indiana University of Pennsylvania, an NCAA Division II state school. Recalls Doug Strahm, "We not only lost the game but got shut out 27-0."

Dick Strahm knew the game would be a challenge. "It was a school that offered 36 full-ride scholarships. We had none. When the numbers stack up against you like that, it is just very difficult to compete."

After a week-two win over Anderson, the Oilers had to come right back and play Coach Fusco's Westminster Titans. The team from Pennsylvania again prevailed, 27-14, and, after all the high hopes of the Findlay faithful, the Oilers had stumbled out of the gate at 1-2.

But, then fortune began to smile on the Oilers. First, Findlay nipped the perennially strong Hanover Panthers, 35-29, to even its record at 2-2. For Strahm, the next game against Defiance would carry added significance. "When you break out of the gate slowly, the game after you get to .500 is vitally important. If you slip back under .500 again, you lose momentum you may never regain the rest of the season. The good thing about our situation is we had enough games left on our schedule to have a successful season if we could win out. That was my thought going into the Defiance game."

Findlay took the first step towards Strahm's goal at Donnell on October 20. The team that, through the first four games, had little trouble gaining yardage but a good deal of trouble breaking the plane of the goal line, did both in routing the Yellow Jackets, 56-14.

In the game the Oilers broke a school record with 632 total yards. Of those, 411 were on the ground. A further look into the numbers shows 137 yards belonged to Dana Wright, who also scored three touchdowns. L.C. Coleman, the former Warren Western Reserve Raider, added 91 more yards on just 11 carries.

Kris Alge also had a terrific first half, completing 8 of 10, including a 40-yard TD toss to Derek Hutchinson. Alge wound up 9 of 11 for the game for 186 yards and an additional 51 yards rushing. Hutchinson's big day included gathering in six of Alge's tosses for 143 yards.

While Strahm was impressed by the big statistics, he also saw the bigger picture. "Those things [statistics] are nice but not really important. The main thing is our offenses got rolling, all phases of it, and we now have confidence in ourselves," Strahm told *Toledo Blade* sportswriter John Agee.

Defiance coach Gary Schaefer expressed frustration when speaking to Agee. "To be honest, after it was 28-14 [in the second quarter], our kids lost composure. After that, Findlay could pretty much do what it wanted to do on both sides of the line of scrimmage. Once we lost our confidence, it was just like we were in shock the rest of the game. When we tried to tackle their backs, they looked invisible. It was like tackling air."

Once over the .500 mark, the Oilers responded with three more wins in a row, routing Bluffton (78-10), Wilmington (35-15), and Manchester (45-15). And, with the five-game winning streak came a reward. Despite the three losses, somehow, the Oilers had made the 1984 NAIA playoffs.

Again, the team from Flag City, USA, would host the first-round game, and it was against an opponent it knew well, the Hanover College Panthers, a fellow member of the Hoosier-Buckeye Collegiate Conference. In a game that is as memorable as it was disappointing, Strahm's squad let a game it had firmly in its grasp slip away and lost on a last-second touchdown, 18-17.

Recalls Coach Strahm, "That Hanover game was such a tough loss. We really had the game won. Roger Darr, our big fullback, went out with an injury, and we had to switch our halfback Dave Brenek to fullback. Well, we're right down on the Hanover goal line. A touchdown would have given us a 24-6 lead with less than three minutes in the fourth quarter. Insurmountable, right?

"Anyway, Brenek got the handoff and tried to jump to get in the end zone. A Hanover player from behind punches the ball out, and a linebacker catches it in the air and takes a knee.

"Hanover had a great passing game, featuring a quarterback by the name of Jon Pennick, that we had really shut down all afternoon, but that changed. They marched right down the field and scored. They went for two, and we stopped them, so we still had a 17-12 lead.

"When we recovered the onside kick, I really thought we were home free. At about midfield, we ran a play called a 46 Toss with L.C. [Coleman]. He broke into the open, but one of the Hanover players made a great play and ripped the ball out on the tackle. Hanover recovered, and with just a few seconds left, scored on a throwback pass of about 35 yards. We really had good coverage, but the kid just made a heck of a catch."

So, the Oilers wound up a disappointing 6-3 and a first-round exit in the playoffs. It was an exit that was very difficult to swallow for their head coach. Recalls Dick, "It took a long time to get over that one. You know, when you get beat straight up, as we did in the opener against Indiana of Pennsylvania, that's a lot easier to get over than when you fumble twice in the last four minutes of the game and just boot one away."

Despite the painful memories of that season-ending one-point loss, Strahm was anticipating the 1985 season. Senior Kris Alge was returning to both punt and play quarterback. L.C. Coleman, after an '84 season that saw him earn Little All-American honors, was returning for his senior year. Dana Wright made all-conference in '84 and showed some serious bursts of speed at running back, and, with Coleman coming off a 1,000-yard rushing season, the Oilers seemed to have cornered the market on backfield speed.

Fullback Roger Darr and blocking back Dave Brenek were also returning to the offensive backfield. Alge would be throwing primarily to Jeff Laing and Derek Hutchinson. On the offensive line, tight end George McDuffie was a devastating blocker and a spot receiver.

Defensively, George's brother Tommy was a cat-quick linebacker who was also the emotional leader of the Oilers. In the secondary, Jon Huffman, Chris Gearhart, Todd White and Darryl Woods brought with them an abundance of experience and talent. Strahm also had a solid junior defensive back out of Berea, Tim Beckman, ready for spot duty. Strahm commented often to his coaches that Beckman had one of the best football minds on the team, certainly a prophetic statement given the fact that Beckman would years later come back to coach for Dick before moving on to coaching stops at Bowling Green, Ohio State, and Oklahoma State, where he is currently the defensive coordinator.

While two more former players, Doug Coate and Jerry Campbell, would return to Findlay to help fill out the coaching staff and son Doug would join Todd Ruppert as a student assistant, it was the departure of a longtime valued assistant, Steve Mohr, that Dick Strahm was forced to address. "It would be very difficult to replace a coach of Steve Mohr's abilities. He'd been with me since 1976 and was such a damn good offensive line coach.

"Ginger and I will always miss Steve. He is like an adopted son to us. We stood by him in the place of his parents, who had both passed away, when Steve married his wife, Jill. As a matter of fact, Jill is a Findlay College graduate, and Ginger and I both feel Steve couldn't have found a better wife.

"But, just as I had to let Dean Pees follow his dream, I had to do likewise with Steve. He accepted a position at Ithaca College in New York. Now, of course, he's built just a tremendous small-college program down in San Antonio at Trinity University."
Mohr has reached the point where, each season, he simply extends his own school record as Trinity's all-time most winning football coach. Through his first seventeen seasons at Trinity, Mohr compiled a record of 136-52, good for a .723 winning percentage.

"Joining the new assistants, Coate and Campbell, were veteran returnees McIntosh, Kwiatkowski, and Wright. Including the student assistants, five men assisting the 51-year-old Strahm had played for him as he headed into his eleventh year at Findlay.

Recalls Dick about the 1985 campaign, "I knew we had a good football team coming in. Our wide receiver, Derek Hutchinson, out of Valley Forge, Pennsylvania, was really developing into a great target for Alge. Also back was Keith Cupp, our 6'6," 305-pound offensive tackle out of Leipsic, Ohio. The other tackle was Jack Buchanon, from Sandusky. Another Leipsic product, Greg Hardy, was solid at center. Then we had Steve McAdoo, from Toledo Central Catholic High School, at one offensive guard and a transfer from Division I Northern Illinois University, Chuck Young, at the other. And, at 6'6" and 250 pounds, tight end George McDuffie was really like a third tackle playing tight end. I had a good feeling we were going to run the ball very effectively.

"I just knew Dana [Wright] especially was going to have a breakout year. He'd started in the MAC in 1983 as a freshman at Kent State after a stellar career at Kent Roosevelt High School, a school I knew pretty well from my time at Warren Western Reserve. Despite some 100-yard games at Kent State, Dana wound up leaving school after a dispute with an assistant coach over the severity of an injury when a trainer said Wright couldn't practice.

"His high school coach called me after Dana withdrew from school and asked whether I'd be interested in him as a transfer. Who wouldn't be interested? He was 6'2" and 220 pounds and ran a 4.6 40-yard dash. Additionally, he started and played well in the MAC against Division I competition! Of course, I couldn't wait to get him in uniform here. Naturally, Dana first had to meet academic entrance requirements and file the necessary paperwork with the Office of Financial Aid.

"Since I had L.C. Coleman as the featured back in 1984, that limited the number of carries I could get Dana his first year with us, which would have been his sophomore year. But, this year, I just knew we were going to get him the ball a lot more even though I still had L.C. [Coleman] for his final year."

During the 1985 regular season, the Oilers were, in a word, unstoppable. With Alge's throwing and Hutchinson's receiving, and Roger Darr's and Dana's running, and the punishing blocking provided by lead halfback Dave Brenek and a terrific offensive line, the Oilers laid waste to one opponent after another.

First, they blitzed Olivet College (Michigan), 57-3, in the opener. In week two, against Alfred University, a team out of New York that would go on to win its conference, the Oilers doubled up their opponents, 42-21. Unfortunately, Coleman injured a shoulder in the second week's win and would miss the remainder of the season. But, with Wright providing speed on the sweeps and the bruising 220-pound Darr pounding the ball inside on the 22-2, the Oilers were still capable of running teams clean off the field.

Then the Oilers overwhelmed Anderson, 62-14, in week three and followed that contest with wins over nemesis Westminster, 28-9, in week four and conference foe Hanover, 49-9, in week five.

In the Hanover game, defensive coordinator Ray Kwiatkowski yet again demonstrated his ability to make a key adjustment to help the Oilers' cause. Recalls Strahm, "Ray came to me at the beginning of our practice week before the Hanover game with an idea, which wasn't unusual.

"This time, to help shut down Hanover's very strong passing game, he wanted to take our outstanding free safety, Jon Huffman, and play him at the cornerback position to cover Hanover's best receiver. The cornerback, Darryl Woods, would then play Huffman's normal position. Ray just felt that Darryl didn't quite match up with the receiver as well as Jon could. The idea was that no matter which side the wide receiver lined up on, Jon would move to that side and cover him one on one.

"Now, normally, I gave an automatic stamp of approval to anything Ray wanted to do with the defense. I had my hands full with the offense. But, this idea, I had to think about. Huffman had always been a safety, and Woods had always been a corner. They are totally different positions that require different skill packages.

"However, Ray was very persuasive, and I gave him the OK, but with the warning that he'd better be right!

"Well, it turned out he was right. Darryl did fine at the safety position, and Huffman completely shut down his man. Jon told me after the game that once, when the receiver lined up close to Hanover's sideline, he heard one of their coaches yell out in frustration, 'Hey, 41 [Huffman's jersey number], you're not supposed to be lined up there!'

"Really, Ray was just uncanny with his ability to make practice-week adjustments before games. It got to the point where, if I didn't hear from him by Thursday, I'd go up to him and say, 'Come on, Ski. Stop holding out. What have you got for me?'"

"When Strahm was asked if the Hanover win was sweet revenge for the 18-17 playoff loss on a gray day at Donnell the previous year, he bristled. "There has never been a game won during the regular season that has ever made up for a post-season loss, ever!"

The next game is memorable because of the lopsided score that was posted on the scoreboard at the conclusion of the contest. Findlay defeated Defiance 82-3.

Recalls Strahm, "That was a very strange game. We played over at Defiance. I remember they actually drove down and kicked a field goal on their first possession and led 3-0. Then, we scored every single time we had the ball. By halftime, it was 56-3.

"We didn't even go into the locker room at halftime. The locker room was quite small, and it was a beautiful fall day, so I thought it best to just gather my team behind the visitor's stands. I know that sounds rather unorthodox, but so was the game for that matter.

"The referee called the Defiance coach and me together and suggested a continuous clock for the second half, meaning it would not stop on incomplete passes or when players went out of bounds. Of course, I agreed.

"In the second half, I only played my starters one series, and, boy, do I ever remember what happened. All week in practice, we had worked on coaching Kris Alge to call an audible if he saw the safeties cheating up into the box. The audible changed the called play to a pop pass to George McDuffie, our tight end right into the area the safeties had vacated. It was the only audible we put in that week for Kris.

"Well, at halftime, I had totally forgotten to tell Kris to not call the audible no matter what the safeties did in that first series. I guess I was too busy helping to organize subs for the entire offense and defense, the ones who would play the rest of the second half after that first series. That was always a challenge on the road, since we were only allowed a 52-man traveling squad.

"When I saw the safeties cheating up, it was such a helpless feeling. It was too late to call a timeout. Kris called the audible, which is what he'd been coached to do, and threw a perfect strike to George. He went untouched 55 yards, and that made it 63-3.

"The rest of the game, we just ran dives and quarterback sneaks with our second- and third-stringers, but we kept scoring. It's difficult to tell the substitutes who are finally getting in a game to not score.

"I've had a few games like this on both the high school and college level, and, believe me, it's not all that fun. Sure, it's always nice to win, but the closer games, I enjoyed much more. I really didn't relish beating Defiance that badly. It wasn't good for the league and wasn't really good for us."

Jim McIntosh remembers the Defiance game as perhaps the reason why Findlay decided to leave the Hoosier-Buckeye Conference after the 1985 season and play as an independent. "I and the rest of the coaches knew there was a lot of dissatisfaction over our dominance in the league since Dick arrived."

Recalls Jim Houdeshell, Findlay's athletic director, "After the season, our school administration believed that there certainly was an uneven-competition issue, so, before we were asked to withdraw, and we had a strong feeling it was reaching that point, we decided to leave voluntarily. From 1986 all the way through the 1992 season, we played as an NAIA independent. I really think that Defiance game very well may have been the game administrators at other schools would have pointed to if they voted us out."

Findlay's offensive juggernaut continued over the final three regular-season games as they rang up wins over Bluffton (49-7), Wilmington (30-0) and Manchester (34-7). At 9-0, of course, the question was not whether the Oilers would make the playoffs but who they would play and where.

Heading into the playoffs, Dick Strahm truly felt making a third visit to the national championship game was attainable. For the 9-0 Oilers awaiting the news as to whom they would face in the first round of the playoffs, life was indeed very good.

Chapter 11

More than Just a Game

What a memorable regular season it had been for Coach Dick Strahm and his Findlay College Oilers. It was mid-November of 1985, at an institution of higher learning that first opened its classroom doors in 1886, and it was time to see if Strahm's Oilers could finish the dream and capture a second national championship to conclude, this, Strahm's eleventh year at Findlay College.

Although Strahm had a couple close calls when it came to pulling up tent stakes and seeking out new environs in 1980 and, again, in 1983, he remained in the Ohio town he'd grown to love, a town just off Interstate 75, less than 50 miles from the city of his birth, Toledo.

As much as Dick Strahm loved Findlay, the town loved him right back. As the 1985 post-season approached, there was a "Love Ya, Oilers" sign in more than a few front lawns in Flag City U.S.A.

Including the 9-0 regular season that the Oilers had just completed, Dick's Findlay record was 75-25-2. This would be Findlay's fifth playoff appearance, and, among those, included a national championship runner-up in 1978 and that crowning achievement, the national championship of 1979. Sprinkle in five Hoosier-Buckeye Collegiate Conference championships, and anyone who followed small-college football could tell that the Findlay College football program was elite.

The Oilers had just come off a remarkable regular season, both offensively and defensively. Led by quarterback Kris Alge and his fifteen touchdown tosses and running back Dana Wright's 1,500-plus yards in just nine games, the offense averaged 48 points a game. Wright's total shattered the single-season rushing record set by Ken Agee just five years earlier. Defensively, led by spiritual leader and linebacker extraordinaire Tommy McDuffie, a defender so quick he had won the league track meet in the 100 meters the previous spring, the Oilers yielded just 73 points the entire nine games, an average of a miserly eight a game.

Strahm and his Oilers had every reason to look optimistically towards the '85 playoffs. Perhaps, even after an undefeated regular season, they were still stinging from a heartbreaking

The 1985 team still holds the record for average offensive score per game at 42.6 points per game. The 1997 national championship team averaged 40.5 points per game.

18-17 loss to Hanover (Indiana) in their first playoff game which ended the '84 season. After all, two fumbles inside of the game's final four minutes and watching the opponents' winning score on the game's final play is hard to completely ignore, even months after a jubilant Hanover team celebrated its improbable victory on the playing surface of Donnell Stadium. The Oilers looked to use their explosive offense and stifling defense to advance the two games necessary to get back to the national championship game.

By mid-November in Ohio, the trees had long ago divested themselves of their gold, orange, and yellow leaves. Now was a time for steel-gray skies, periodic gusts of wind that signaled the oppressive cold of winter was imminent and playoff time for Findlay College and their fans.

The first playoff game pitted Findlay against St. Ambrose, a team out of Davenport, Iowa, and the game was scheduled to be played at Donnell Stadium.

It is important to remember that in the NAIA in 1985, there were two divisions. Division I schools could grant more than twenty full scholarships and maintain that number at any given time over a four-year period. On the other hand, Division II schools were limited to less than twenty scholarships, depending on the number granted by a school's administration.

During Strahm's entire tenure at Findlay College up to this point and for several years after, it was the decision of the Hoosier-Buckeye schools' administrations to award no scholarships, which made Strahm's Oilers' accomplishments even more remarkable.

As had been the protocol for determining a game site, each school's administration submitted a figure in the form of a bid. And, as usual, the higher the figure, the more intent a school was on hosting a game. Findlay College certainly had proven its desire to play host in the past. During the 1978 and 1979 seasons, which both ended with Findlay's playing for a national championship, the college won all six bids. Donnell Stadium, an august facility in which play first began in 1928, was the site for every game.

This time, yet again, Findlay won the bid to host the Fighting Bees of St. Ambrose. However, Mother Nature had other ideas as to where the quarterfinal game would be played. It had rained for a solid week, torrential rains, some would even say, rains of Biblical proportion. That fact, along with the reality that a high-school playoff game had been played on the field the previous weekend, rendered the field unplayable.

Recalls Dick, "We felt our next best option was to ask officials at Bowling Green State University, just down the interstate a few miles, if we could use their field, Doyt L. Perry Stadium. They gave their approval, and the game was played on a Saturday at 11:30 in the morning, and what a slugfest it was."

Despite the fact that Findlay had won nine games by an average score of 48-8, a combination of the weather and a tenacious St. Ambrose defense made this game very difficult, according to Strahm. "We slipped by the Bees, 7-0, and would advance to the semifinals, but believe me, St. A's gave us every single thing they had."

Jim McIntosh, the Findlay College graduate who was a three-year letter winner as a player under By Morgan in the mid-1960s, was in his ninth year of what would become a 22-year coaching career at Findlay. He had every reason to feel special about the 1985 season. Not only did the Oilers get to 10-0 with the hard-fought St. Ambrose win, but Coach McIntosh had been inducted into the Findlay College Athletic Hall of Fame in October 1985.

Recalls the coach known with equal parts of respect and affection as Coach Mac, "That St. Ambrose game was one of the most physical games I've ever been a part of, and, as evenly matched as any I remember coaching as well. St. Ambrose was just so intent on taking away our running game, led by Dana and Darr and Brenek, that they packed the box [the area within five yards of the line of scrimmage] with eight or nine players. On most plays, there were only two in the secondary, and they just split the field with their coverage. They really wanted to take our power game, which really was our bread and butter, away.

"Well, it just wasn't a great day for passing weather-wise. We did get one great opportunity, though, early in the contest. The play was a throw back to our big tight end, George McDuffie. Now, let me preface this next reminiscence with a comment about George as a football player. He was just a terrific blocker and good enough to earn a tryout with the Dallas Cowboys in 1986. But, on this play, he got a bit too anxious, and he dropped a sure TD pass. Despite the fact that George was really a great player, the game of football can be so fickle. Bad things happen to even the best."

McIntosh remembers the game not for its offensive fireworks, which were nonexistent, but from the perspective of a coach who knew the value of strategy and field position and resisting the temptation to allow frustration to prompt a bad decision. "Listen, it was just a hard-fought win. Not every game is a game where even an extremely talented team is going to light up the scoreboard. Remember that we had averaged almost 50 points a game in 1985 through the regular season. But, this was simply not going to be that type of game.

"In this one, because of some pretty cold conditions and a very stiff wind against a quality opponent, we just had to slug it out. We punted when we should have and played great defense and looked to not waste any offensive opportunities that presented themselves.

"While we let one get away with that dropped touchdown pass earlier, we finally found a way to create a mismatch that we thought we could take advantage of pretty late in the second quarter.

"Not to get too technical, but what happened was, we broke the bone [shifted out of the standard wishbone offensive backfield set] and brought our two-back [Dave Brenek, who was primarily a blocking back in Strahm's wishbone] up in a slot off the outside shoulder of the tackle.

"Essentially, what we did was make Dave a glorified guard. It gave us an extra blocker running to strength [the side of the offensive line where Strahm aligned both tackles in his unbalanced line]. With the one-man blocking advantage, we kept hammering that side with Dana and Darr until we got ourselves in a position to do something.

"When they tried to adjust and the safeties edged even closer to the line of scrimmage, Alge hit a 21-yard pass to Derek Hutchinson for a 'touch,' and that turned out to be the game's only score!"

However, immediately after the score, there was enough time left on the first-half clock for the Bees to make things interesting…and controversial. St. Ambrose mounted its most successful drive of the entire game, and it was a drive that ended in a most disappointing fashion for St. Ambrose head coach John Furlong. Furlong remembered the critical moment for reporters after the contest. "We got the ball at about the eleven and through our quarterback Jeff Stelk and our running back Bob Jurevitz [who, at the time was leading the nation in college scoring with 27 touchdowns]. We strung together several first downs."

Then, with second and ten at the Findlay 29-yard line, Stelk hit Jeff Kimbro in the end zone for a touchdown, at least in the eyes of one official who raised his arms. Another official, however, ruled Kimbro was juggling the ball as he crossed out of bounds. After a conference by the officials, the TD was waved off, and, after two unsuccessful plays on third and fourth downs, the drive was over.

Recalled Furlong in the game's aftermath, "I thought it was a classic case of the play being a touchdown at home but a lack-of-possession call on the road."

Predictably, Strahm disagreed after the game when reporters brought up Furlong's reaction. "I didn't even think it was close. From my perspective, the player was clearly juggling the ball."

In the second half the Oilers' defense and special teams were spectacular. St. Ambrose was held to less than 100 yards in the last two quarters, and punter Kris Alge executed two terrific coffin-corner kicks, knocking one out of bounds at the 5 and another out of bounds at the 2.

The Oilers made the Alge-to-Hutchinson TD stand up, and the stubborn Bees were vanquished. While St. Ambrose had contained Dana Wright and limited him to just 57 yards, Roger Darr, the big fullback, kept the chains moving, especially in the second half, by running for 110 yards on that cold Saturday in Bowling Green, Ohio.

The misfortune of being "weathered out" of hosting the first playoff game at Donnell compounded itself during the next week. The sealed bids were submitted, and, this time, Findlay College lost the bid. The Oilers would be forced to meet the enemy on its own turf. In this case, the turf was in Tacoma, Washington, at Lakewood Stadium, and the opponent would be another perennial NAIA powerhouse, the Pacific Lutheran Lutes, coached by someone just as well known in NAIA circles as Strahm, Frosty Westering. By the time each of these men would retire, they would rank in the top five in all-time NAIA wins.

Despite the perfect 9-0 Oilers record, Pac Lutheran, with their own 9-0-1 record, had actually finished higher in the final regular-season ranking. This was indeed going to be a heavyweight bout.

Now, any coach will tell you that to have an exceptional season, a team has to have more than great talent. They also have to be fortunate. And, thus far, fate had smiled on Flag City's favorite team. During the regular-season stampede through the Hoosier-Buckeye Collegiate Conference, not one Oilers starter had suffered a major injury.

At the worst possible time, however, all that would change on the Thursday late-afternoon practice, the very day before the charter plane would depart from Toledo Express Airport. How innocuous this final practice in Ohio seemed. It was a no-contact, helmet-sweatpants affair, really just a walkthrough to polish some final details. Then, the next afternoon an excited contingent of Findlay players, coaches, faculty and administrators, alumni and other supporters would head for the West Coast.

In the most disheartening of circumstances, misfortune often walks hand in hand with irony. Such was the case when, during the very waning moments of both light and practice, the player everyone, both coaches and players alike, knew to be the heart and soul of the defense, went down.

He was Tommy McDuffie, the 6'3," 215-pound linebacker and one of the quickest lateral pursuers Strahm had ever seen on a football field. McDuffie caught a cleat in a frozen rut, and the ensuing fall broke one of the legs that had taken him to victory in the conference's 100-meter dash at the previous spring's league track meet.

Dick had not seen the play, as he was in another part of the field with the offensive unit, ironing out a few wrinkles in some new formations put in for the Pac Lutheran Lutes. However, he heard the commotion before hustling to the site.

"We took Tommy to Blanchard Valley Hospital. It was the shin bone. We made a decision as a coaching staff while Tommy was with the doctor as to whether he would go to the game if unable to play. Ordinarily, injured players wouldn't attend an away game. However, despite not being able to play, if the doctor cleared Tommy to fly, Tommy would be in Tacoma. The doctor allowed Tommy to fly with us, provided he used the crutches and the wheelchair. We, as coaches, just felt it wouldn't be right to not let him go. He had meant so much to our program, and he was a senior. Besides, his brother, George, was our 6'5," 265-pound starting tight end."

The following morning the buses loaded and departed for Toledo for the flight to the state of Washington. The job of knocking off Frosty's Lutes had just gotten a whole lot tougher. Westering, a savvy tactician, who had as recently as 1980 won his own Division II NAIA National Championship, would, no doubt, try to exploit the absence of the Oilers' quickest and surest tackler, but Strahm was enough of a realist to know that injuries and adjustments to them were as much a part of football as yard markers and goal posts.

After arriving in Tacoma and checking into their hotel, about a 35-minute bus ride to Pac Lutheran's Lakewood Stadium, the Oilers were ready for their one afternoon practice. Recalls Dick, "There's one thing I'll never forget in that beautiful little stadium. It's something I can picture in my mind even to this day, well over twenty years later. From what I was told by a stadium attendant, Mt. Rainier usually was covered by clouds, but that particular day, I looked up and there it was, standing in all its glory, with the snow caps drenched with the sun glinting off them. I blew the whistle and told my team and coaches, 'Listen, Oilers, we're here to do a job, but we're not going to miss seeing one of God's great creations.' I just stopped practice, and we all looked at it for probably a full minute. I can remember thinking that this was a moment that none of us would ever forget for the rest of our lives."

After practice, the teams followed an NAIA tradition, which was to attend a banquet together, subsidized by the host school. Ordinarily, the teams sat in separate sections of the room, but Strahm remembers the seating arrangement at this dinner to be much different. "The players who would be trying to knock each others' blocks off that next afternoon sat at the same tables directly opposite one another. This business about eating with the same team you were trying to beat, well, I'm not sure if that was such a good idea."

However, Strahm is quick to point out that both the Pac Lutheran players and his were gentlemen, not surprising given the fact that the great coaches, such as Strahm and Westering, taught as much about character as they did about football.

After the dinner, Dick always tried to follow the same routine he followed every Friday night before there was business to be taken care of, whether it was at home or on the road, regular season or playoffs.

There was a team meeting, this time back at the hotel. First, the assistant coaches would hand out what Strahm would call the "cheat sheet." Recalls Dick, "These were final reminders for different position players as to what had to be done to be successful. They were details and techniques gone over all week in practice and appeared on the sheet as more of a list using just a few words to make each point. The reminders were a lot like what a teacher might hand out on review day before a big exam over material he had gone over in depth during the teaching of a unit.

"The assistants always had the sheets pre-approved by me on Thursday. Although a successful head coach certainly delegates a lot to his assistants, he also is the one ultimately in charge of what goes on when the opening kickoff is in the air."

After that, Strahm would show a 20-minute football film. Dick recalls, "It wasn't our game film or film on our opponent. I'd have already shown our team all of that type of film. The film I would show them on Friday was a highlight film from the NFL. Each team produced one at the end of each year showing the great plays from the season just completed. Since the film was designed to promote the team being featured, the plays selected showed perfect execution on offense and also on defense, especially the big hits, which were often shown in slow motion."

After the film, two or three players spoke to their teammates. The team captains selected the players, and they were always pre-approved by Strahm. After all, recalls Dick, "I wanted to know who'd be speaking. I certainly didn't want someone to address the team who'd really not had a very good week of practice. I will say this, I never had much of a problem with the players that the captains selected. Players know during the week who is practicing well and doing the things both on and off the field that it takes to be a winner."

After the players talked for a few minutes, it was time for the ultimate man in charge to speak. While it was still hours before the game, this would be the time for the kind of Strahm emotion that used to manifest itself right before kickoffs when a younger head coach spoke to his players at Lakota, Bryan, and Warren Western Reserve high schools.

Recalls Dick, "I guess you might say I changed over the years. By the time I got to the point in my career where I was a college head coach, rarely did I give any type of Knute Rockne speech in the locker room right before the game. I tried to show a business side and wanted to as calmly as I could review a few final points before we went out on the field. I wanted my guys to be focused, and I thought a calmer side when I delivered my final pre-game comments was a better way to go.

"But, during my Friday meetings, while I wanted to do some final teaching, I also wanted to show some fire, the same fire I wanted my guys to unleash the next afternoon."

After the meeting, the players then went back to their rooms to await the inevitable bed check which would come a bit later. Although great coaches have rock-ribbed confidence in their players' decision making, they leave nothing to chance. Recalls Dick, "I never thought there was a downside to bed checks on the road. It wasn't that I thought my guys would be sneaking out and getting in trouble. It really was more that I didn't want them staying up too late talking about the game or watching television. We had to get those lights out and get them settled in to get their rest."

As Strahm returned to his room to rejoin his wife, Ginger, he was nervous. He was not as certain as he had been in the past that the Oilers were as emotionally fired up as they could be. Memories flooded back from his coaching career thus far of the tricks, the ploys if you will, that he had engineered to take teams to the edge of their emotions. Perhaps the loss of McDuffie weighed on his mind.

He also confided to his wife of 23 years that he didn't feel well. He had what he thought at the time was some pretty intense indigestion. "I remember thinking that this wasn't that odd.

After all, the winner of this game would play for the national championship, and we had to play it without an extremely gifted and vital player."

After a fitful sleep, Dick awoke. It was game day and any feelings of the discomfort he'd experienced the night before shrunk back into the shadows of his consciousness. Despite not feeling the rejuvenating effects of a full night's repose, Coach Strahm knew it was time to, as some would say, get ready to do battle.

There was a team breakfast, followed by the ritual of taping ankles as a means to increase stability and reduce the risk of sprains. Although during overnight trips during the regular season it wasn't unusual for Strahm to have his team dress at the motel, saving only shoulder pads and helmets, since many locker rooms weren't exactly commodious, this would not be the case for this game. Pac Lutheran's Lakewood Stadium was absolutely top shelf.

The Oilers arrived well in advance of the 1:30 p.m. kickoff on that December 7, 1985, so that they could acclimate themselves to the surroundings and follow the same pre-game drills as any other game. Words like *consistency* and *repetition* and *tradition* are bedrocks in the philosophy of great coaches.

Yet without McDuffie, and perhaps somewhat because of the visual of him in a wheelchair, helpless to get to the corner to blow up a sweep or cover a receiver out of the backfield going out on a circle route, Findlay played their poorest half of the entire year. Coach Jim McIntosh remembers the half far too vividly. "Pac Lutheran was really fired up and getting to our linebackers. Not to make excuses because everyone is responsible when you lose, but there is no question in my mind the Pac Lutheran coaches found out very quickly about Tommy's injury and exploited it."

Recalls Strahm, "Despite having the best NAIA punter in the nation in Chris Alge, our punt coverage was terrible. We allowed two long returns that led to two touchdowns. We also let their big running back [Mark Helm] get loose far too many times."

One of those runs by Helm was a 66-yarder, which set up a field goal to open the scoring. It snowballed from there, and the Oilers found themselves in a huge hole as they trudged to the locker room for halftime, down 26-7.

Recalls McIntosh, who spent his game days up in the booth, using headphones to communicate with Dick below, "We were just really flat in the first half and did things we hadn't done all year. We incurred costly penalties, we turned the ball over, and we had breakdowns with our special teams.

"Right at the end of the first half, it's important to play well defensively. You certainly don't want to give a team that energy boost that comes with a score right before intermission. That momentum is often carried right into the second half.

"Well, right at the end of the half, sure enough, Pac Lutheran had the ball, up 20-7, down around our 20-yard line. Well, we were down and certainly hadn't played well, but, the game was still manageable. If we make a stop and get a score the first time we get it in the second half, we're right back in it, right?

"Anyway, earlier in the game, we gave up a touchdown on a crossing pattern with the tight end and flanker, where the flanker broke to the goalpost and made a catch off our blown coverage. So, they went back to the same play. But, this time, our kids did a great job, and we got the interception in the end zone to snuff out their scoring opportunity.

"Just as we were breathing a bit easier, I looked on the far side of the field where the backside receiver had lined up, and there was a flag. This was on the complete opposite side of the field from where the play went. The Pac Lutheran quarterback never even looked in that direction. But, the referee called a hold on our guy as the decoy receiver came off the line of scrimmage.

"So, they got it back on our 10-yard line. We held them three plays, which brought on a field-goal attempt. We got a good rush off the edge [from the outside], but our guy slipped on the wet surface and slid right into the kicker.

"So, they got it again after the roughing-the-kicker penalty, first and ten, at the five-yard line. You can imagine how frustrated we were, extending their drive with stupid penalties. This time, they punched it in. Even with the missed extra point, we went in at halftime down 26-7, instead of 20-7."

McIntosh also remembers somewhat of a lesson that legendary coach Frosty Westering taught the Oilers on the slick field in Tacoma, Washington, on that December day in 1985, a lesson that involved special-teams play. "The thing I really noticed about that first half is every time the ball changed possessions, we had the ball inside our own twenty. And, every time we punted to them, they seemed to have it close to midfield.

"Their specialty teams, especially their punt-coverage team and punt team had quite a few starters whereas we'd always had a philosophy that we'd use down-the-liners on our special teams to give them a chance to contribute and also to give our starters a breather and not subject them to injuries."

However, Dick Strahm recalls a different problem, ironically one that most coaches would love to have, a punter with some thunder in his foot. "Kris [Alge] had some punts that were in the air more than 50 yards that day. He was simply out-kicking his coverage, which certainly wasn't his fault. We just couldn't get enough people down the field fast enough to cover. Their punt returner simply had too much time to field the punt, survey the running lanes and pick one. More than anything else, I think that's what swung field position so dramatically."

McIntosh got down from the press box to meet with all the coaches. This was something Dick Strahm always did before addressing his team at halftime. McIntosh noticed grave concern on his head coach's face. "I certainly wouldn't say Dick was panicky, but let's just say that Pac Lutheran really got his attention. I remember that Dick told all of us, 'Don't yell at them.' He said we all needed to remain calm and needed to calm our players down and get them to refocus so that they could go out with a plan as to how to deal with what was being thrown at them. Otherwise, the game could really get out of hand. Dick said if we, as coaches, conveyed a sense of panic to the players, we could give up sixty!

"That was the first time all year we'd been put in a situation like that. Until the St. Ambrose game, we hadn't been challenged all year, and, even in that game, there wasn't as great a sense of urgency as this because we hadn't given up any points. However, in this one, we were getting soundly beaten!"

Recalls Strahm, "Really, despite the fact we were down by 19 points, I followed the same procedure at halftime that I always did. I spoke to my assistants first and listened to their responses when I asked some questions, things like why we were having trouble blocking a certain play or why our secondary coverage was breaking down on a certain play that they were running against us. After I heard what they had to say, I gave them my thoughts, both offensively and defensively.

"Then, I spoke quickly to the team while my offensive and defensive coaches met together at the far end of the room to make their halftime adjustments. I didn't yell. I tried to get them to focus on what, from that point on, needed to be done to get back into this game. I told them that there was plenty of time on the clock. A whole half of football is an eternity. I told them we didn't even need any extraordinary breaks to win. We just needed to eliminate mistakes, execute better, and make the adjustments their coaches would speak to them about in a few minutes.

"Then, my coaches were ready for their breakdowns. The defense met in one part of the locker room, and the offense met in the other. I went with the offense because I called all the plays. Each of my coaches would ask for some input from the players in terms of what problems they were having on certain plays. Then the coaches went to the board to show the changes they had just discussed.

"While all of this was going on, the trainers checked players to make sure everything was OK. They did things like re-tape an ankle as the player was listening to the coaches.

"Then, as usual, with about four minutes left, we came together, and I spoke last. I always called it 'my final blessing.' I knew we had a lot of fight left in us and felt, despite the hole that we'd dug ourselves, that we would not give up without one hell of a fight."

As the Oilers broke out of the locker room, the coaches pursed their lips. Although hopeful, they really didn't know what to expect from their shell-shocked charges.

In the second half, the Oilers played inspired football. As a matter of fact, after the game Dick would call the effort perhaps the greatest half of football in Findlay College history.

Led by their outstanding junior running back, Dana Wright, the transfer from Kent State who would finish the season with an astonishing 1,824 yards and average 8.1 yards per carry, the Oilers roared back. Behind stellar offensive linemen like guards Steve McAdoo and Steve Young and the 6'6," 305-pound tackle Keith Cupp, Wright picked his way for 147 second-half yards. Many were on a play the Lutes had never seen Findlay run. It was a wrinkle Coach Strahm and his assistants inserted during the week prior to the game.

The play wasn't run at all in the first half and thoroughly baffled Pac Lutheran in the second. It was called a 46 Counter Trap, and Dick still remembers it well.

"Since our fullback Roger Darr was a threat when carrying the ball, we had quarterback Chris Alge execute the same reverse pivot we always had him do on isolation running plays and fake the ball to Darr. Then Wright, our left halfback in the wishbone offensive set, would take an exaggerated jab step to the left and counter back to the right to accept the handoff. Our right guard pulled and trapped the hole and our backside guard pulled and led through the hole. Since we always ran an unbalanced line with an extra lineman on one side of the center, the play ran to our strength, since we had an extra lineman blocking. Coaches Coate and Davidson did a great job with blocking assignments, and Dana did the rest."

Findlay's second-half scoring started with a safety when a snap sailed over the Pac Lutheran punter's head and out of the back of the end zone. Then the Oilers also scored quickly off the free kick.

The defense was also coming together, especially the very talented secondary, comprised of Chris Gearhart, who had led the team with seven interceptions that season; Todd White; Jon

Huffman; and Darryl Woods. According to Strahm, this was one of the best secondary units he'd coached.

Following another defensive stop, Findlay's momentum short circuited when the Lutes' Shawn Langston, who would be named the game's MVP, intercepted an Alge pass and took it in from 40 yards for a score.

Recalls *The Courier* sports editor Larry Alter, who regularly covered the Oilers and had made the to trip to Tacoma, "If Strahm's charges were going to fold, that would have been the time. Prior to the interception, they'd narrowed the gap to 26-16 and had the ball in good field position with plenty of time on the clock. Then, boom, 40 yards later, they're down again, 33-16."

However, Findlay continued its rally. They had come too far and played too well in amassing that 10-0 record to fold. An 80-yard, two-play drive, with 45 of it coming on a Wright 46 Counter Trap, culminated with an Alge 35-yard TD strike to Jeff Laing to draw the boys from Flag City to within 33-23.

Following another defensive stop, the Oilers used some deception (an Alge-to-Laing-to-Dave Brenek hook and ladder) and some good old-fashioned, hard-nosed running (by Wright, who clawed his way into the end zone from 12 yards out) to draw to 33-29 with 10 minutes remaining.

Could the miraculous comeback be completed? Signs remained positive after Oilers defender Randy Moyer broke through and sacked the Lutes' quarterback Jeff Yarnell for a nine-yard loss, forcing another punt. Field position was excellent as the Oilers huddled, ready to mount the go-ahead TD drive at Pac Lutheran's 47.

However, after the senior signal caller, Alge, kept it for seven yards, the one play occurred that coaches like Dick Strahm replay over and over in their heads for years and years. "Even now, I can see it. We ran another 46 Counter Trap with Dana. Pac Lutheran hadn't stopped it effectively the entire second half, and it broke clean again! Dana was churning inside their 30, well past the first-down stick, and, really, in the process of breaking it all the way when the last Pac Lutheran defender [Dwayne Korthuis-Smith] who had a shot at him stripped Dana of the ball. I can remember how helpless I felt watching the ball rolling free all the way down to the twenty before they recovered it."

Despite being held to only two first downs in the third quarter by the rejuvenated Oilers defense, the Lutes mustered a scoring drive of their own, their only offensive TD of the whole half, as they went 79 yards to ice the game 40-29.

And so it was over. After ten consecutive wins, Findlay would make the return flight home the following morning a loser on the scoreboard but certainly not in their head coach's mind. For some players, like Chris Gearhart and 1985 Little All-American selection Jon Huffman, the scene in the locker room in Lakewood Stadium was the last snapshot of outstanding Oilers careers.

Strahm saw a Herculean second-half effort, but he also saw the importance of the turnovers. "If we have just one less [turnover], we win the ballgame. Pick either one you want. Take one away. We win. But, that's the game of football."

For the Oilers, there were four players who would be good enough to make NFL camps. In addition to George McDuffie, an invitee to the Cowboy camp, Kris Alge received a tryout with the Browns as a punter in 1986 and then again with the Eagles in 1987. Also, Keith Cupp, the

6'7," 305-pound offensive tackle from Leipsic, was invited to the Bengals' camp. After Dana Wright's senior year in 1986, the 1985 Kodak All-American wasn't just invited to an NFL camp. He was drafted by the New York Giants.

Although a combination of injuries and the ultra-stiff competition in NFL camps took its toll on all four of Strahm's former players and none actually played in the NFL, Strahm would like to make a point. "For an NAIA school that offered no scholarships, it was extremely rare for anyone to ever get an invitation to a professional tryout. To have four on that 1985 team gives you some idea just how good the Findlay Oilers were that season."

Quarterback Kris Alge also has some vivid memories about that day in Tacoma and the team he quarterbacked. "I honestly think we had all the ingredients for a national championship in 1985. There's no question that it was the most disappointing game of my entire career, either playing or coaching for that matter.

"While we played very well in the second half, we really played poorly in the first. I don't think there's ever just one factor when you play as poorly as we did as far as why we lost. Of course, we missed Tommy on defense. I also don't think playing on the road in a different time zone helped. Heck, the flight to Tacoma was the longest I think any of us had ever taken!"

Both Coach McIntosh and Alge share the same sentiment about the post-game scene. Recalls McIntosh, "Several of the Pac Lutheran players made a real point of coming across the field and congratulating us on playing so well in the second half. Coach Westering really knew how to coach class, and his kids had it in abundance.

"They were a terrific team, but, perhaps more importantly, they were true sportsmen. I remember when we beat them in the semifinals in 1979 during our national championship season, several of their players wrote notes of congratulations on the plane back to Tacoma and mailed them when they got home. While I hated to lose to anyone, at least if you have to lose, it may as well be to a team like that."

Alge agrees with Coach Mac's assessment. "Pac Lutheran was one hard-hitting team but also very clean. They didn't cheap shot, and they didn't trash talk."

For the 22-year-old student assistant Doug Strahm, what had happened at Lakewood Stadium was more than just a game. The post-game locker room was as drained of any positive energy as it could be. "I was a senior, and I had a chance to do something so very special with my dad. It was hard enough the previous year when the back injuries forced me to give up the dream I had about starting for my father. Then, to be able to coach with him, even though I was just a student assistant helping out in a very minor way, gave me another opportunity to stand with him on the sidelines and win a national championship.

"I remember after the game, there were a lot of tears in that locker room. I was so emotional, not just because of the fact that we'd lost a football game but more because we'd lost an opportunity to give my father a second national championship."

It was Coach Mac who came over and picked Doug up and helped him compose himself. McIntosh remembers the game's aftermath. "That was really a tough one, not only in the locker room but beyond. The plane ride home wasn't until the next morning. You talk about a sleepless night. I just kept replaying the game over and over, especially that 46 Counter Trap with Dana breaking into the clear.

"You know, it really was almost eerie how similar the fumbles were in the Hanover game the year before and the Pac Lutheran game in '85. The running plays were similar in design, and we had our speed back break into the clear, only to see him have the ball punched out from behind. At that time, tackling the ball wasn't really a technique you saw very much.

"The next day, the flight home was kind of an extension of the mood in the locker room as far as how quiet it was. It definitely was the longest flight I'd ever taken, even longer than those I'd taken to Germany and Hawaii. I tried to sleep but really couldn't get that job done despite the fact that I'd probably only gotten about three or four hours' sleep the night before.

"The kids seem to bounce back quicker in losses such as these. It was both a long flight home and a very long off season. You just can't make mistakes, especially serious ones, against a quality opponent."

As a coach now himself, Kris Alge knows full well what Jim McIntosh means when he says that kids bounce back quicker from tough losses than coaches. "Sure, that Pac Lutheran game was very difficult, but I now know after coaching for several years what Mac means. When things aren't going well, as a coach, well, it just eats at you.

"And, that's when you really appreciate having played for coaches like Mac and Dick Strahm. Coach Strahm keeps tabs on how we're doing over here in McComb. Once you graduate, he doesn't forget you. Anytime we're struggling, I'll get a phone call from Dick, who'll invite me to lunch, and we'll talk.

"I just have so much respect for the man, not just for the moral support he still provides me some twenty-plus years after that last game of my Oilers career but also for all the things he's taught me, things which, I believe, have made me a better coach.

"Coach taught me you have to have a relationship with your players. Sometimes, at practice, during warm ups, he'd just come over to talk to you on a personal level. He'd say things like, 'How'd you do on that world history test?' or 'How're your folks?' You have no idea how important that is to a player when a coach shows him he's not just a position on a football team.

"The same type of feeling I got playing for Coach Strahm, I want my own players to feel for me. So much of what I do as a coach goes right back to playing for Dick Strahm. And, I'm pretty certain a lot of other former players who went into other positions of leadership in non-football fields, like business, would say the same thing."

Jim McIntosh felt his head coach and friend looked haggard after the contest. The Oilers returned to their hotel and had dinner. After dinner, Dick again didn't feel well. He had the same symptom, the upset stomach, which disrupted his sleep the night before. Again, however, Dick attributed his feeling ill to the tough loss.

He and Ginger went up to the room around 9:00 p.m., which would have been around midnight Findlay time. Recalls Dick, "I was really having what I thought was some severe heart burn."

After taking some antacid medicine, Strahm again slept restlessly. By Sunday's breakfast, he felt somewhat better.

The return flight landed the disappointed but proud Findlay College contingent back in Toledo for the bus ride back to Findlay. It was mid-afternoon when the Strahms arrived home.

With ideas already rolling through his head on what adjustments might be needed when his Oilers would strap on the pads again and what recruiting would entail, Strahm also finally turned his attention to Christmas, a little over a couple weeks away.

He wondered whether Ginger had taken care of all the details incumbent on a coach's wife while he had been busy trying to win his second national championship. While Doug, at 22, and

Gina, at 18, would be easier to please, Dick and Ginger's youngest, 10-year-old Steve, might pose more of a challenge.

Dick felt confident, though, that Ginger would come through with the same yuletide flying colors that she always seemed to, year after year.

Late in the week, Strahm decided that he wanted to take an early evening walk. It was a nice evening for winter in Ohio. A light snow was falling, just enough to heighten the anticipation of Christmas, when Dick asked his youngest son, Steve, to accompany him.

During the walk, that pesky heartburn again came back about three blocks into the walk. This time it was intense, so much so that he felt compelled to stop at a friend's house. He asked the friend to call Ginger to come and pick them up.

Recalls Dick, "Well, I've never been accused of being real smart, so I resisted Ginger's desire to go to the emergency room at nearby Blanchard Valley Hospital. I did agree, however, that something wasn't quite right, so I agreed to see Dr. Jerome Beekman, who was both a friend and a darn good Findlay cardiologist."

The next day, Dr. Beekman gave Dick a stress test and wasn't thrilled with the 51-year-old head coach's test result. So, he called a Dr. Miller in Toledo, who advised Dick come meet him at the Toledo Hospital. With Ginger at the wheel, the Strahms drove north on I-75.

Upon arrival, Dick was admitted on that Friday. For Dick, the thoughts of the events in Tacoma, Washington and of recruiting and of the necessary adjustments needed before the ball would be teed up again dissipated. There were other matters, serious ones of more immediate concern.

Findlay group Gwen Kuenzli, Coach Strahm, Ginger Strahm, Lee Kuenzli and Dave Kuenzli having dinner with the owner of the Hamburg Blue Devils, Axel Gernert.

Chapter 12

When the Game of Life Was Nearly Sudden Death

On Saturday, Strahm was visibly not well. He was flushed and had what might be described as "the sweats," a direct result of the nerves which inevitably come when there is that combination of being confined to bed, where there is nothing to do but imagine the worst-case scenarios and being fearful of what Dr. Miller would discover during the procedure called a cardiac catheterization he had scheduled for Monday morning.

By late Saturday afternoon, Dick's blood pressure had shot up dramatically. In addition, the nurses were giving him nitroglycerine. Thoughts were racing through Dick's mind, thoughts of his own father, who had died of a massive heart attack at the age of 58, just seven years older than he.

Finally, the nurses decided to call Dr. Miller at a wedding he was attending. Instead of just giving the nurses directions over the phone, Miller demonstrated the compassion that the truly great doctors have. He left the reception and came to the hospital to see his patient. For that, Dick remains grateful. "I always thought coaching was a wonderful profession to be in, but to be a doctor, well, I'm not sure anything could top that. Doctors do just unbelievable things.

"Certainly, Dr. Miller didn't have to leave that reception. He could have just told the nurses what to do. Instead, he came to me and sat down. We talked football for, I'll bet, more than an hour. I calmed down considerably, especially when he told me that, despite his almost never scheduling a procedure on Sundays, he decided to have his catheter lab team ready for the operation a day earlier."

The next morning, on a Sunday when Dick would normally have his family seated around him in a pew in the College First Church of God, on the Findlay College campus, the procedure was about to begin.

Some members of the 1948 freshman football team at Libbey High School,
where the young Dick Strahm was still hanging onto the ball.

Dick's family had gathered in the waiting room and relied on each other for support. Perhaps the fact that they were a football family would somehow make them stronger and more able to handle the stress of waiting for a cardiologist's word that all had gone well.

Of course, there was Ginger and Dick's mother Mildred. Seeking as much to support them as to be supported were Dick's three children.

The oldest, Doug, occupied a unique position in the hierarchy of Dick's life. Aside from being the firstborn, he was also a former player under Coach Strahm, an offensive center during his freshman and sophomore years before an injury ended his career. Additionally, in this, his senior year, he had been a student coach with his father. As his father did, just the weekend before, he stood on a sideline in Lakewood Stadium in Tacoma, Washington, and watched both the worst half of football the Oilers had ever played and the best half the team had ever played.

Gina was an outstanding student-athlete, very competitive in all her academic and athletic pursuits. While at Findlay High School, before matriculating to Findlay College, she had played soccer and basketball and ran track. Now in college, she had made the Oilers basketball team and would play on the tennis team in the spring. She also played indoor soccer for a club team. In addition, she also happened to be one of the Findlay Oilers' most vociferous football fans. No one could have been more disappointed than she was when her basketball involvement prevented her from traveling to the Pac Lutheran game.

Steve, the 10-year-old, was just young enough to be somewhat insulated from thoughts of the potential for disaster but also old enough to know that bad things sometimes do happen. He, too, would wait anxiously in that small waiting room.

The procedure that Dr. Miller would perform was called a heart catheterization, or more commonly, a heart cath. Miller would first insert a venous sheath so that a catheter could be inserted. After the catheter worked its way up into the coronary arteries, pictures would be taken to determine blockages. If, as Miller suspected, there was a buildup of plaque that restricted blood flow, Dick Strahm would need a small balloon which would be affixed to the end of the catheter with a small mesh tube called a stent surrounding it. The catheter would then be reinserted and the balloon inflated, thereby expanding the stent and alleviating the obstruction. Then the balloon would be deflated and the catheter removed.

While the frequency of the procedure might have led some to believe this was so routine as to not be much of a worry, they would be very wrong. A heart catheterization is an invasive act by nature, and so very much could go wrong. Also, there was the potential that more than one artery would require a stent. And, of course, there were no guarantees that blockages wouldn't reoccur. For the Strahms, there was plenty to worry about.

The Strahms had every reason to be nervous. After all, when it comes to a procedure done to a loved one, there is no such thing as a minor surgical procedure. Certainly, Dick was very nervous despite the sedation. "I just couldn't get the thought out of my mind that my dad had died of a heart attack at 58 and here I was at 51…"

One can well imagine the thoughts that raced through his head. Realizing the fears had manifested themselves into an irregular heartbeat, a deal breaker for such a procedure, Dr. Miller sent a nurse to get Ginger so that she could come in and attempt to calm her husband down.

Prior to this, Doug had been confident that his father would be OK. "To me, Dad was in good shape. He had a great doctor that we all had confidence in, and, most importantly, he was Dad! Nothing was going to happen to him."

However, when his mom was called in, Doug's confidence began to wane when he realized how nervous his father was. "As my mom followed the nurse into the operating room, I followed several steps behind. I don't know what I thought I was going to do, but I wanted to know my dad was going to be OK."

Doug remembers hiding behind a curtain trying to hear what was going on. "The next thing I remember, lights were flashing, my mom was quickly moved out of the room, and when the curtain was closed, I was discovered. A nurse politely but very loudly told me to leave."

When Gina saw her mother and Doug come back into the waiting room, she knew something was very wrong. "I looked at my mom sobbing, and Doug's face was white as a ghost. While my grandmother was holding Steve, my mom just sat down at the table, put her head down, and cried."

Dick experienced what medically is called a systole, or flat lining, which meant the heart monitor revealed his heart had stopped beating. In effect, until the heart paddles were put on his chest and the defibrillator was dialed up to around 200 joules, Dick Strahm died.

Thankfully, the machine shocked Dick's heart back into rhythm, and through the deft work of Dr. Miller's surgical team and a sedating shot, Strahm stabilized. The heart cath could then be done.

During the operation, Doug tried to remain positive. After all, he was the oldest son and felt it was incumbent upon him to keep everyone strong, to keep the family together. "I tried to think of anything I could to help everyone stay as calm as possible. We were a football family, and so we were all familiar with scenarios involving comebacks, where victories were snatched from the jaws of defeats."

Nervous energy quickly filled the room, so we went out in the hall and really began wearing out the tile, pacing and praying that Dad's heart would not stop again.

"Then, I reached an emotional point where I just needed to get away for a while because I didn't want them to see me with tears in my eyes. The one thing I had completely discounted before the flat-line incident, Dad's actually dying, started filling my head.

"As I walked the halls, I passed the hospital's chapel and wasted no time going in and sitting down. I started praying, asking God to get my father through this so that he could come home. I ran the gamut of emotions in just a few minutes' time, from fear to panic and eventually to anger at what I could not control and what I momentarily blamed God for."

Leaving the chapel, Doug found a restroom to compose himself. Then it was back to his grandmother, mom, sister, and little brother to continue to try to fill that time-honored position of being the source from which others could draw strength.

When Dr. Miller and his team had completed the procedure, one stent had been inserted to alleviate an arterial blockage. Miller had concluded that, given what the symptoms were and what the catheterization revealed, Dick had experienced two mild heart attacks, one in Tacoma and one the evening he and Steve took a walk.

Despite the seriousness of what had nearly happened, a father being taken away from his family and a beloved and respected coach away from his team forever, Dick Strahm was released from the hospital Tuesday morning, just five days before Christmas.

Gina remembers what a special moment her next home basketball game was. "There was my father, in the stands. The feeling of his presence that day just a few days before Christmas was just incredible. Of course, there's always more joy around the holidays, especially with college students getting a break from classes, but no one's joy matched mine. I had the greatest Christmas present one could ever imagine, my dad."

On Friday, it was back to the hospital to step up on a treadmill and take a stress test, to see if there would be any heart pain. While Dick's mom, Ginger, and the kids chased off the negative vibes, Dick was cleared to join the millions of others in search of that old Christmas spirit.

The next day was Christmas Eve, and the culminating event was always church services. It was yet another affirmation of Dick's strong sense of faith and an even more resounding affirmation that God can indeed do wondrous things.

As Dick sat in the pew at the College First Church of God, he felt so very fortunate and very happy. How much had happened in less than three weeks. He thought of Tommy McDuffie's run-in with a practice-field rut. He thought of the worst first half of football of the season and also the best second half of football he'd ever coached. He thought of someone telling him he'd had not one but two heart attacks. He thought of flat lining. And, he thought of the heart catheterization. And, of course, he thought about the here and now.

In this church, surrounded by the same family who drew strength from each other as they paced the halls of Toledo Hospital just days earlier, Dick had even more moments to think. It was a time to look back, to reflect on where he had been and how far he had come, and, of course, it was also a time to thank God for the role He had played in bringing him back to resume his passions in life, caring for his family, teaching, and coaching.

Although no man is afforded any guarantees in life, Dick Strahm fervently believed there would be more time for hugs, more time for laughter, and more time for truly making a difference in young people's lives.

And, with more time, maybe, just maybe, he and his assistant coaches could figure a new way to block that 46 Counter Trap so that Dana Wright could fly, untouched, through opponents' secondaries on vivid autumn Saturdays in the next calendar year.

Members of the 1995 class of inductees into The University of Findlay Athletic Hall of Fame: Jeff Shadle, accepting for his father, Homer Shadle, Larry Alter, Sharon Milligan, Dick Strahm, Fred Horstman, and Bill Feth.

Chapter 13

Tough Times Don't Last

As Dick Strahm distanced himself from the final game of the 1985 season and the angioplasty so capably performed by Dr. Roger Miller at the Toledo Hospital, the Oilers football coach turned his attention to the upcoming 1986 season. Certainly, there would be challenges, perhaps more challenges than he had faced since 1975, his inaugural year at Findlay College.

For one thing, the Orange and Black would find themselves lining up against a number of teams totally unfamiliar to them. No longer would they look across the field at Hoosier-Buckeye Collegiate Conference teams like Bluffton and Defiance and Hanover, since 1985 marked the final season in the league for Findlay.

The Oilers were independent and would remain as such until 1994. While there are some advantages to being an independent, there is most certainly another side to that coin.

Recalls Strahm of the first five years as an independent, "These were difficult years for our football team. When you coach in a league for a number of years, you get to know tendencies that your opponents' coaches have. Well, I no longer had that available to me. Basically, we started playing teams in 1986 that we knew almost nothing about. In addition, we also had no rivalry games. Over my previous ten years, we had developed a number of natural rivalries with league schools, which made getting players ready to compete that much easier. Those types of games were no longer available to us starting in 1985.

"Additionally, the teams that would fill our schedule in the second half of the 1980s often were schools that offered scholarships, and that always meant stiff competition.

"Also, when you are the school that initiates contracts to play a brand new schedule, you often have to make deals. For example, the first contract we had with Ashland was two-for-one, meaning we played two at Ashland and only one at home.

"A lot of the games we had to take were way out of our geographical region. I remember our having to travel by bus to schools in New York, Iowa, North Carolina, Michigan, Tennessee, Pennsylvania, Kentucky, and Wisconsin. Needless to say, this was a whole lot different than the Hoosier-Buckeye, where the entire league was in Ohio and Indiana."

Certainly an additional challenge for the Oilers was the fact that the nucleus of the extremely talented 10-1 team of a year ago had graduated. Findlay would go into its new schedule in 1986 having lost three of its top four running backs, its starting quarterback and punter, and most of its offensive line.

On defensive, the inspirational leader, Tommy McDuffie, some would say the player the Oilers could have least afforded to lose heading into the Pac Lutheran game the previous year, also was gone. Additionally, all four starters in the secondary graduated.

Recalls Strahm, "Offensively, I guess the good news was we did have Dana Wright returning for his final season, and we also had our fine wide receiver, Derek Hutchinson. Defensively, I thought we'd be pretty good at linebacker. We had Robert Price, an All-District player back. I also thought Alan Baumlein would be solid. On the defensive line, we also had almost everybody back. Both Randy Moyer and Bryon Krupp were All-District in '85. We also had Rick Mielcarek, Drew Hill, and Todd Smiley back. But losing my entire secondary, well, let's just say that was a real uncomfortable thought."

Strahm did feel he had a strong coaching staff returning, despite the significant losses earlier in the 1980s with the departures of Dean Pees and Steve Mohr. One of the returnees to the staff was Jim McIntosh, who would be the position coach for the strong side of Strahm's unbalanced line.

Ron Wright was returning for his fourth year as a defensive coach. Wright was his head coach's captain on the 1978 team that lost by a single touchdown in the national championship game.

Ray Kwiatkowski would begin his fourth year as defensive coordinator. In 1985, 'Ski's "Blood Unit" was the number-four ranked defense in the country. Now that the familiar opponents of the Hoosier-Buckeye were not on the schedule, certainly the new wrinkles on defense would be more difficult to come by.

Doug Coate was beginning his second year coaching the offensive backs. It would be his difficult job to help find replacements for the likes of Roger Darr, Dave Brenek, and Kris Alge.

As far as coaching newcomers, there were two, and both played for Strahm, bringing the number of assistants who played for the head coach to four. Mark Niswonger would help coach the defense. Niswonger returned to Findlay after working in the admissions office and coaching at Manchester College for two years. He was another former captain for Strahm, just as Ron Wright, and an All-Conference linebacker for four consecutive years.

The other addition to the Oilers coaching family was Curtis Davidson, the former All-American offensive guard, who'd spent the previous year working on his master's degree and coaching at Georgetown College in Kentucky before returning to Findlay to coach the backside of the offensive line and work in the admissions office.

Also new to the Findlay College campus was a first-year athletic director. After thirty years in the AD's chair, Jim Houdeshell moved over to assume a dean's position at the behest of Findlay College president, Dr. Kenneth Zirkle, the dynamic young school administrator whose forward-thinking approach to the job he would hold from 1983 through 2003 left some very deep footprints on the campus. The new athletic director whose job it would be to guide the athletic program through the difficult transition from a league-affiliated school to that of independent was Max J. Kidd. Kidd retired after 32 years in retail marketing at Marathon Oil and made the decision to pursue a new career in athletic administration. Kidd was a former football player at Purdue University. His son, John, was a punter in the NFL for fifteen years.

As the season approached, Dick Strahm got commitments from two offensive linemen who would go on to prove themselves both on the field and in the classroom.

Offensive center Ryan Sbrissa's story as to how he wound up in Findlay is certainly unique if for no other reason than he hailed from Miami, Florida. Recalls Sbrissa, now a technical expert for the Social Security Administration and a resident of Minneola, Florida, "My dad had a friend, Ralph Camiscione, who owned a tailor shop in Findlay. He told Dick about me. It turned out that Coach Strahm knew my dad from a recruiting trip that Coach took the year before.

"It was Roger Darr who hosted me for my campus tour. Although he had completed his four years of eligibility, he was still on campus finishing up his course work. I just fell in love with the campus. Both my dad and I felt Findlay was the right place for me to be."

The other offensive-line recruit came from a place just a couple hours down I-75, Dayton, Ohio. Joe Moorefield was a graduate of Dayton Patterson High School and had originally been recruited to both play football and wrestle at Wittenberg University in Springfield, Ohio.

Recalls Moorefield, who currently is a supervisor for the State of Ohio Adult Parole Authority and living in New Lebanon, just outside of Dayton, "During the summer of 1986, I played in the North-South High School All-Star Game, held in Dayton that year.

"Coach Niswonger was there, and he talked to me after the game and convinced me to come up and give Findlay a look. Since I hadn't really signed anything with Wittenberg, I decided to take him up on the offer. Well, I liked it so much I decided to forget about my plan to go to Wittenberg and enrolled at Findlay.

"By the sixth day of two-a-days, I was moving up the depth chart and felt I had a real shot at starting as a freshman. I really had a great opportunity since there were so many openings because almost the entire offensive line graduated the previous spring.

"By the third game of my freshman year, I was starting at the backside guard, which is the guard on the opposite side of the strength of the offensive line. It was the center, me, and a tight end, and that was it in, what you might call, our little club. Our position coach was Coach Davidson, and he did a terrific job not just coaching technique but also helping guys like me and Ryan Sbrissa and Chuck Hale [a fellow freshman guard out of Worthington, Ohio] and tight end Roy Haas [another freshman out of Lorain, Ohio] to bond together as a family. The fact that they were white and I was an African-American made absolutely no difference. They were, and still are, my brothers, and I was, and still am, theirs.

"And, thanks in large part to Coach Davidson, we did become like family. Not only were we close on the field and developed almost the ability to know what each other was thinking but we carried that closeness off the field. When one of us was somewhere, the others weren't far behind."

For Moorefield, the Foster Parent Program was vital in allowing him to transition smoothly from high school to college, both in the classroom and on the field. Recalls Moorefield, "I remember my foster parents were Ron and Sue Souply. They also 'adopted' Chuck Hale. They were such caring and good people that both Chuck and I just loved spending time with them.

"Man, when we'd get that phone call asking us to come over for dinner on Thursday nights, we couldn't wait. Sue was just a fantastic cook. I can remember by Wednesday, Chuck would come up to me at practice and say stuff like, 'Tomorrow night, Joe, it's chow time, baby. Twice-baked potatoes!'

"I don't think it's any great surprise I came in as a freshman at around 230, and, by the time I graduated, I was about 290. I think a lot of that had to do with Sue's cooking. Right now, I'm back to around my freshman weight. I watch what I eat and train six days a week, but, back then, we linemen had kind of an all-you-can-eat mentality."

Another interesting recruit in 1986 was well acquainted with Oilers football. His name was Bill McIntosh, and he happened to be Coach Mac's son. Recalls Strahm, "Bill came in as a center. While he wouldn't start until his final year with us, he was an instant contributor on special teams. As a matter of fact, he actually lettered all four years he played.

"The one thing I'll always remember about Bill is he had an absolute bulldog mentality. He developed into an excellent scramble blocker and, through hard work, made himself into one of the better centers I've had over the years."

Junior Ken DePriest reassumed his starting quarterback position that he held in 1983, taking over for the graduated Kris Alge. DePriest proved as a freshman starter on that 8-2 1983 team that he could scramble well and throw on the run. This year, with an inexperienced line in front him, those were good skills upon which to rely.

Recalls Strahm, "Ken was from Millersburg, Ohio, a very strong Mennonite community. I remember after he had that good freshman year, he had a personal problem and withdrew from school to go home and tend to it and missed the entire 1984 season.

"I really thought we'd seen the last of Ken, but, sure enough, he returned in 1985, accepted the backup role behind Kris [Alge], and started for us both in 1986 and the year after.

"I think it speaks very well of Ken to show that kind of perseverance to re-enroll and accept a backup role after being the starter two years before. Coaches have special and unique memories of their players, and that's the one I have about Ken DePriest. He really was a fighter."

After a season-opening 35-6 win over Valparaiso (Indiana) University, a game in which DePriest completed 16 of 21 passes for 326 yards, the Oilers had to line up against NCAA Division II power Ashland (Ohio) University, a school with the ability to offer scholarships, unlike Findlay.

In the game, the Eagles proved more than formidable. Recalls Dick, "We really got beaten soundly [30-12]. I think that was the game that kind of showed us that the teams we'd be playing over the next several seasons would certainly be quite a bit tougher than some of the teams we had been playing."

In week three, in a game dubbed "The Picnic at the Pond" because of the small body of water just outside Donnell Stadium, the Oilers rebounded with a convincing 55-14 win over the Golden Hurricanes of Geneva College (Beaver Falls, Pennsylvania). DePriest played efficiently (7 of 14 for 134 yards and a touchdown), and Dana Wright played brilliantly (16 carries, 160 yards, 3 touchdowns).

Then it was time to face a team that Strahm certainly knew something about, Coach Joe Fusco's Westminster College Titans out of New Wilmington, Pennsylvania. It was Westminster that had ended Findlay's 1982 season 28-0 in a playoff game on a very muddy Donnell Stadium surface.

In week four of the 1986 season, the Titans again proved too much, as they defeated the Oilers, 28-14.

Another loss followed in week five, 20-16, to the Flying Dutchmen of Hope College (Holland, Michigan). The loss left the Oilers at a very uncharacteristic 2-3, and some began to wonder if Strahm was looking at perhaps a losing season, something that hadn't happened since his first year at Findlay in 1975.

It was then the Oilers rallied behind their coaches and won three consecutive games. First, they beat Kentucky State (Frankfort, Kentucky), 28-8. Then Drake (Des Moines, Iowa) fell victim, 40-0. Week eight saw the Oilers defeat nearby Tiffin College, 35-3.

In the three-game winning streak, strong safety Gary Estes picked off four passes. Dana Wright scored five touchdowns in the three games and ran for a total of 371 yards. DePriest completed 36 passes, three for touchdowns. And, Derek Hutchinson grabbed 25 of DePriest's aerials.

But, in the season's finale, Strahm's hopes of a respectable 6-3 season were dashed when Findlay dropped a road contest to a strong Butler (Indiana) team, 31-12, to finish at 5-4. Recalls Strahm, "Butler was a very strong NCAA Division II school with the ability to offer twenty-five scholarships. They had a beautiful stadium called the Butler Bowl. We had to walk through that famous gym where they filmed the final game in that Gene Hackman movie *Hoosiers* to get to the runway into the football stadium. As far as the game, well, let's just say that seeing that gym was the highlight of the afternoon. They simply had bigger, faster, and better people than we did."

Despite the disappointing record, given what the Oilers had been used to, the head coach wasn't all that displeased. "Look, I knew the kind of talent we lost off the '85 team [14 starters, including nine off the offense], and I also knew we had a schedule consisting of only one team that I had ever coached against [Westminster].

"In addition, four of our opponents were scholarship schools. Drake had just recently gone from Division I to Division III, and Butler was a very highly touted NCAA Division II school. The scholarship schools were also allowed a big advantage. They could conduct spring practice, something we couldn't do at Findlay until the spring of 1994.

For the season, examining the numbers reveals how much the offensive production declined. While the '85 offense tallied 469 points, the 1986 team scored more than 200 points less.

Despite the decrease in offensive production, there were some bright spots. Quarterback Ken DePriest threw for 1,695 yards and 11 touchdowns. To put the 1,600-plus yards in perspective, the mark stands fourth on the all-time list of top Oilers quarterbacks.

Wideout Derek Hutchinson had a senior year to remember and was named an NAIA All-American. He snagged a school-record 60 balls, good for another school-record 1,018 yards, good for an average of 17 yards per catch.

Of course, Dana Wright was the leading ball carrier. Battling injuries and running behind an inexperienced line caused a dramatic decrease from his Kodak All-American 1,824 yards gained and 8.1 yards per carry in 1985. However, Wright still put together a solid season, gaining 896 yards in nine games, for an average of five yards a carry. His 14 touchdowns also made him the team's scoring leader.

For Dick Strahm, the weeks following the conclusion of the season included another medical setback. Recalls Dr. Jerome Beekman, still a full-time cardiologist and a member of the Blanchard Valley Medical Associates, "I'd been treating Dick for a couple years earlier when Dr. Phil Razor referred him to me for some high-blood pressure issues. Dick was very concerned because of the family history, what with his dad passing away while in his fifties of the heart attack.

"So, when I referred him to Dr. Roger Miller in Toledo in December of the previous year and an angioplasty had been performed to correct two arteries that were 85 percent and 90 percent blocked, I hoped that would be all that was needed.

"However, there are times when the same arteries will, again, develop some blockages, and that's what happened over the course of 1986. So, I again referred him to Dr. Miller after Dick complained of chest discomfort.

"Sure enough, a heart cath showed some blockages, and that led to a second angioplasty in early December of '86. Again, I hoped this would take care of the issue for an extended period of time.

"I will tell that Dick always has been very good at listening to his own body and has never hesitated to contact me when he doesn't feel right. Frankly, I wish everyone would have that ability. So many people convince themselves that there's nothing wrong when they experience chest discomfort, and this oftentimes has drastic, even fatal, consequences."

After the procedure, which really was in its infancy, since less than ten years had elapsed since the first angioplasty had been performed, Strahm again rebounded well and headed into 1987 optimistically. As a head coach, he also had to be so proud when one of his players was accorded a great honor.

It was in early January of 1987 that Dana Wright was given an honor that no one in school history had ever received. He was selected to play in the Senior Bowl in Mobile, Alabama. The Senior Bowl has always carried a reputation of being the top all-star game for players leaving college in the country and is administered by the National Football League to showcase the top collegiate players.

When Penn State's D.J. Dozier suffered a hip pointer in the East-West Shrine Bowl, Wright received a call inviting him to join the 35-man roster. It was indeed a crowning achievement for Wright and a great way to cap his Oilers career.

Since Wright's transfer from Kent State, he had gained 3,335 yards, second only to Nelson Bolden's total of 4,009. Wright was the only NAIA player to be invited to play in this premier event.

The rest of the winter passed with Dick trying to make the most of the family time that sometimes was rather difficult to find during the football season. Dick's son Doug had left the nest to continue his education, eventually settling into a master's program at the University of Toledo and working as a graduate assistant in Dan Simrell's football program. However, Gina, Dick's daughter, was still home as a student athlete at Findlay College.

Gina was well on her way to completing her sophomore year, achieving solid grades and also pursuing her athletic interests. Before she would graduate from Findlay, Gina would compile an athletic résumé that included a year of basketball, four years of soccer, and four years of tennis, in addition to coaching the Findlay Area Swim Team and life guarding at the Northridge Club. The summer found Gina working at Basol Maintenance handling accounts payable and receivable.

Of course, Steve, Dick's youngest, had just turned 12 on Valentine's Day and occupied a lot of his father's attention.

By mid-May, Dick discovered that the athletic director, Max Kidd, had resigned, effective at the end of the month. Recalls Dick, "I remember Ron Niekamp, who'd just finished his first year as Jim Houdeshell's replacement as men's basketball coach, and I were out in the hall talking about the resignation.

"Dr. Ken Zirkle, our president, walked up to us and asked me if I'd like the position of athletic director. When I declined, he looked at Ron and said, 'How about you?' Well, Ron said he may be interested, so off he and Dr. Zirkle went to his office.

"About 45 minutes later, Ron walked into my office, sat down, and said to me, 'Guess what? I'm your new boss!' That's how quickly that job filled.

During the early summer, Dick decided to try to combine exercise with some relaxation and was in the middle of a round of golf when he again began to sense that something was wrong. He was experiencing chest pains. Recalls Dick, "I got a really terrible burning feeling in my chest, which was the exact same sensation I had in December of 1985. I immediately got myself to a phone and called Dr. Beekman."

At Dr. Beekman's office, the news for Dick Strahm certainly could have been better. Recalls Beekman, "I again called Roger [Dr. Miller] and got Dick up to Toledo Hospital. When another heart-cath procedure was performed, I got a call from Roger, who told me that Dick's arteries kept blocking."

The previous December, Dr. Miller and Dick came to an agreement that if the arteries refused to remain open, serious consideration had to be given to his undergoing open-heart surgery.

Recalls Dick, "When I was still on the table after the heart cath, Dr. Miller came in and said, 'Coach, I have a question.' Here I am lying on the table in my birthday suit, and he asked, 'When do you start football practice?'

"I thought it was an odd question to ask immediately after the procedure, but I told him in about seven weeks. He then said, 'That will work out just great.'

"When I asked what he meant by that, he said, 'You've got four arteries mostly plugged up. If we do another angioplasty [which would have been three in the last eighteen months] that would probably get you through the season. However, if we did an open-heart surgery, I know not only will it get you through the season but well beyond.'

"Since we'd discussed the possibility of open-heart surgery some months earlier, I wasn't totally surprised by what he was proposing but just hearing the words kind of shook me somewhat. But, the way Dr. Miller put it, it seemed that open-heart surgery would be best."

Recalls Dick's daughter Gina, "Dad always said that if he had to have the big operation, he wanted it to be at the Cleveland Clinic. Dr. Miller knew that *U.S. News and World Report* had, that year, ranked the Cleveland Clinic number one in heart care for the thirteenth straight year. And, he also knew a doctor was on staff who was one of the best heart surgeons in the whole country, Dr. Toby Cosgrove.

"Well, Dr. Miller and Dad made the decision to have the operation but only after Dr. Miller assured my father that the six weeks that separated the operation and the start of football was enough time to recover so that he could coach."

On June 23, Dick Strahm was transported by ambulance from Toledo Hospital to the Cleveland Clinic. The operation would take place on June 25. That allowed time for Dick's brother Dale to fly in from Athens, Georgia, where he was the defensive coordinator for the University of Georgia Bulldogs.

The rest of the family also was at the hospital, including Dick's mom Mildred, who, recalls Gina, just couldn't get to her son's side quick enough. "I can remember that it was my responsibility to get Grandma to the hospital.

"The day before the operation, I had to go in to work at Basol to do some end-of-the-month paperwork. When I finished, I drove to Toledo to pick Grandma up. When we got on the way to Cleveland, my dear sweet little old grandma looked at me and said, 'Gina, is this all the faster this can go?'

"So, I said, 'Ok, Grandma, get ready for the pedal to the metal!'

"Once we got to the hospital, I could tell Dad was a little nervous, but he really kept a stiff upper lip. That's always been his way.

"We were all there. Doug came from Toledo and, of course, my mom and Steve were there along with my Uncle Dale. I can remember we watched a videotape of what would happen during the operation."

Strahm recollects a different mindset on the eve of the operation than the one his daughter Gina felt she sensed. "Actually, I wouldn't necessarily call it nervous. How about a little apprehensive?"

"For one thing, Dr. Miller had convinced me that the Cleveland Clinic was the number-one place in the world for this type of procedure and Dr. Cosgrove was a premier surgeon. That went a long way towards putting me at ease.

"My whole family was with me after I had been prepped for surgery. That prep involved being completely shaved from my chin on down, to reduce the chances of infection during the surgery. The nurse came in to ask if I needed a shot to calm me down, and I declined it.

"After my family left my room, I got a call from Dr. Darrell Prichard, the minister at my church back in Findlay. Dr. Prichard told me that the church had just had a prayer service, and the congregation said a long prayer for me.

"I told Dr. Prichard that I had felt the power of that prayer. I believe that's why I felt such a serenity despite the fact that early the next morning Dr. Cosgrove was going to cut me wide open. After I hung up, I fell off to sleep and slept well until I was awakened at 5:00 a.m. for the big day.

"Even though I did not actually meet Dr. Cosgrove before the surgery and really had no education on what the procedure would entail, I was calm. I felt that God would take care of everything by working through Dr. Cosgrove and his surgical team.

"I reminded myself of two of my favorite Bible passages. 'I can do all things through him [Christ] who strengthens me' is from Philippians [4:13]. The other I said to myself was 'And all things whatever you ask for in prayer, believing, you shall receive' and is from Matthew [21:22].

Gina remembers clearly the day of the actual operation. "The surgery lasted a little over five hours. I can remember Dr. Cosgrove finally coming in and telling us that everything went well but that only my mom was allowed to see Dad in the recovery room. Then, the next day, we could all visit but only one at a time.

"It's funny what you remember. I recollect my Uncle Dale deciding it would be good for all of us after the stress of that morning to find a movie theater after we all left the hospital late in the afternoon. Well, it turned out the only one he could find close to where we were staying was showing 'Predator,' which obviously has quite a bit of violence and bad language in it.

"So here we all were walking in with our popcorn and soft drinks, from my 12-year-old brother Steve all the way through my 76-year-old grandmother! I still like to kid Uncle Dale about his movie choice."

In the days immediately following what turned out to be a quadruple by-pass performed by Dr. Cosgrove, Dick Strahm's competitive spirit began to impose itself. Recalls Strahm's friend and Findlay cardiologist Jerry Beekman, "Back in the 1980s, it wasn't uncommon to be in the hospital two weeks following this type of procedure. Well, I know because I have about four inches of Dick's medical history in my files that he was discharged in ten days. By the two-week point, he was not only out of the hospital but he was walking a mile a day, which was just unheard of."

Recalls Gina, "Each day at the hospital immediately after the procedure, I witnessed Dad's competitiveness. When I'd hear the therapist say, 'I want you to lift the ball half way up,' Dad would say, 'No, I'm going to lift it all the way up.' When I'd hear the therapist say, 'Coach, I want you to walk to the end of the hall to where that wheelchair is,' Dad would say, 'No, I'm going to walk down to the end of the hall and all the way back to here.'

"It was just amazing to me. Everything was a competition to him. To me, he has an indomitable will. What he wants to happen, he makes happen. He knew the calendar was not about to slow down, and each new day brought him one day closer to the first day of practice, and that was a day he was determined to not miss."

Strahm, just 53 at the time of the open-heart procedure, remembers his time in the hospital as well as his day of discharge. "Once I got my wits about me after the surgery, I started thinking about rehab. I wanted a shot at that treadmill. The therapists in the rehab center told me that my time on the treadmill was the longest they'd witnessed after just three days following a surgery. I was trying to break records, I guess.

"On the day I was released, I was wheeled into Dr. Cosgrove's office. I just wanted to thank him. The first thing I noticed about him was that he was really a big guy, well over six feet tall. He came out from around his desk and said to me, 'So, you're the coach, huh? Well, if any of your players say you've got a black heart, you can tell them for me that they're wrong. It's red, and I held it in my hands. And, now, it's in great shape.'

"All I could think of to say in reply was, 'Doctor, I'm glad you've got a great set of hands and didn't fumble in that operating room.' He laughed, and we shook hands. And, that's the first and last time I ever spoke with him.

"It's funny, isn't it? I've been told that the type of procedure Dr. Cosgrove performed is supposed to last around ten or twelve years. Well, I've already passed the two-decade mark, so, obviously, he did a marvelous job.

"And, yet, despite the fact that he saved my life, I never talked to him again after that day I was discharged."

Perhaps there will come a day when Strahm can once again shake hands with Dr. Cosgrove yet again. Now, 67 years old, Cosgrove is still at the Cleveland Clinic and has reached remarkable heights in his career. He is currently the chief executive officer of the famous hospital and is an internationally renowned heart surgeon. Additionally, he holds eighteen patents on a variety of medical and clinical products used in surgical procedures.

Recalls Dick, "Dr. Roger Miller was absolutely right. If I was going to have an operation of that magnitude done, especially an operation that hadn't been done very many times at that point in time, why not have it done at the number-one hospital by the number-one man? Obviously, I couldn't have had better care or a better pair of hands performing that surgery."

During the six weeks Strahm needed to get ready for the August two-a-days that would ring in the 1987 season, there were so many people who stepped up to help a man so many admired and respected. Certainly, one of the most important was next-door neighbor, friend, and sports editor of Findlay's hometown paper, Larry Alter. Recalls Dick, "Larry was my rehab guy. His line every morning to me after banging on the garage door was always the same. 'Hey, coach. Time to walk. Let's go.'

"And, off we'd go. At the beginning, we were only walking around the block. Then we went three blocks, then four. By August, we were up to three miles a day, and that's the distance we maintained for ten years. We walked outside in the spring, summer, and fall. In the winter, we walked at the mall.

"I will always be indebted to Larry for helping me push myself to get healthy and stay healthy. He really is a very dear friend."

Daughter Gina, now the director of risk, liability, and safety management at Malcolm Meats, a division of Sysco, in Northwood, Ohio, recalls how her father's competitive nature manifested itself in the very early stages of the weeks that provided the scantest of buffers between the actual operation and the first day of practice. "The doctors would say things like, 'I only want you to walk three blocks down.' I'd get out there to walk with him, and he'd say, 'We're going four blocks down.' He set goals and was such an unbelievable role model for me and my brothers."

Gina also remembers how many people stepped forward to help the Strahm family. "Probably six to ten families at different times pitched in. Many of them were in the Foster Parent Program my father had started years before. People would mow the lawn, go to the store for my mom, and bring food over."

Despite the help of so many to whom Strahm is grateful, he remains firm in his belief as to how he was able to bounce back from the medical problems which had beset him. "Sure, I realize the importance of all the wonderful people with whom I came in contact, but I firmly believe it was only through God's intervention that they were sent into my life. All the wonderful doctors, nurses, technicians, and those who helped to form prayer groups and those who walked with me and pitched in to help with yard work and such, well, the list just goes on and on.

"To those who prayed for me, I have something to say, and that is, 'Thank you from the bottom of my heart' I know that prayer works because I'm living proof of that fact. And, it's because of that power of prayer that my grandkids, Hunter, Dalton, Danielle, and Zachary are able to see the joy their grandfather feels just being with them."

It was the American philosopher William James who once said, *"The greatest discovery of my generation is that human beings can alter their lives by altering their attitudes, attitudes of their minds."* And, it was with this same belief that Dick Strahm approached not only the by-pass operation but the six-week drive to recover fully before the first practice of the season.

While it was, no doubt, frustrating for the vibrant 53-year-old, at first, to measure walks by the number of houses instead of the number of miles, Strahm's friend and Findlay College president, Ken Zirkle, remembers his football coach's desire to be ready for the first day of another new season.

"Initially, I was shocked that Dick had any sort of a heart problem. Listen, I went to a lot of Dick's practices because the practice field was right across the street from where my office was, and, in my mind, I thought he was indestructible.

"Then, when I realized he had a problem when he had that angioplasty in December of 1985, I still convinced myself that the problem must have been some crazy aberration and that he would be fine from that point on.

"I really felt that Dick approached both the surgery and the recovery in textbook fashion. I told him, 'You're my coach. No other option.' I'd seen what Dick meant not just to his football program but to the college as a whole.

"Not only is Dick like a brother to me but I also saw what he meant to his players especially."

For Zirkle, the role of athletics, especially on a small college campus, is very much intertwined with academics. "Really, athletics is an adjunct to strong academics in my mind. Faculty can be skeptical of athletics as a pursuit where there is this win-at-all-cost mentality.

"But, at a small college such as Findlay, we tried to reward equally academics and athletics. When that happens, and it can only happen when you have a coach like Dick Strahm, who constantly stresses the need for his players to be good students, the faculty can become tremendous allies of athletics.

"Athletics is like a carrot to improve enrollment and enhance the college experience, and it also helps fund raising, which is so very important. So, and this is not to dehumanize Dick, I just saw him as a very valuable Findlay College asset, one I was not willing to lose.

"And, each time I checked in with Dick during that six-week period, I saw him getting stronger and more determined to prove he could come back. Attitude is a powerful thing, and Dick certainly has proven that."

Of course, Dr. Beekman also watched closely as Dick pushed himself with longer and longer walks through July. "A lot of people would have been down, but not Dick. He is one of the most positive persons I have ever encountered.

"I wish all of my patients had just half of Dick's tenacity in doing what needed to be done to get better. I think the fact that he was such an extremely well organized and successful coach had a profound impact on how he approached his recovery.

"It was like he had a game plan, and he was going to follow it. And, you know something? He didn't just follow it to get where he wanted to be by the start of the football season in 1987. He followed it way, way beyond.

"Since Dick still is my patient, I know how dedicated he is to an exercise regimen. I believe he's used as motivation that traumatic loss of his father to a heart attack when he was just in his fifties, and this has driven him to do everything in his power to extend his life as far as he possibly can.

"Not only has he been a master motivator for others, and my guess is you'll find hundreds, maybe even thousands of former players who will attest to that, he also is a master motivator in driving himself. While there are many who can do one or the other, the truly gifted positive thinker can do both, and that's Dick."

When the two-a-day practices finally arrived, the daughter who had watched her father's relentless march toward full recovery had absolutely no apprehensions that her father would push himself too much under the hot August sun.

Recalls Gina, "I really didn't worry about his being on the field. Despite his drive, my father really has always had a strong common sense when it came to listening to his own body. Also, he really had a lot of angels watching over him as practice began, both his players and a very strongly loyal coaching staff."

As far as the staff, all but Ron Wright returned from the 1986 group. Really, Dick had only himself to blame for Wright's departure. It was Strahm who contacted his brother Dale, the University of Georgia's defensive coordinator, and secured Ron a position as a graduate assistant at one of the premier football powers in the South.

Replacing Wright was Mike Ward, who would coach the linebackers and also serve as the team's strength and conditioning coach when the players would lift weights at the old Renninger building. As far as the weight facility, Strahm knew the Renninger building wasn't ideal, but it had to do, at least until he could come up with a plan to improve this part of his program.

For now, there was a football team to coach. It had been fifty-three days since Strahm was anesthetized so that Dr. Toby Cosgrove could work some coronary magic. During those fifty-three days, Coach Dick Strahm reached the point where he could walk three miles in 46 minutes.

And, after passing a stress test with flying colors just a few days before the first practice, the coach was cleared for all coaching duties. One concession Dick was compelled to make involved his using a golf cart provided by a nearby county club for the afternoon sessions.

Strahm recollects why he made the concession. "Actually, during my recuperation, I had a conversation with Nebraska football coach Tom Osborne, and by drawing on his experience of having open-heart surgery himself back in May of 1986, I made some changes in how I ordinarily did things in August two-a-days.

"During my Kansas State years, I had coached against Tom for a couple years. While I really didn't know him directly, I did get to know some of his assistants pretty well.

"So, in early July, I called the Nebraska football offices and left a message explaining who I was and asking the secretary to please ask Coach Osborne to call me back. I knew he'd had open-heart surgery and wanted to see what advice he had regarding August two-a-days.

"Well, sure enough, Coach Osborne did call back, and we had a long talk. He told me the most important thing was to not overdo it and to do the really hard work in the morning. Then, he said he always made time for an hour nap before the afternoon practices.

"So I figured that sounded like excellent advice. That's when I decided on the golf cart in the afternoon.

"Another procedure I changed after talking to Coach Osborne had to do with what I always did in the evenings during the August practices. In the past, my workday during preseason would go from 7:00 a.m. breakfast with the team all the way through to around 11:00 p.m.

"After our second practice and allowing time for showers, we had our team dinner. After dinner we would have our team meeting, and then, my offensive and defensive coaches would meet separately. I would attend each meeting for about 15 minutes apiece, just to get a feel for what was going on. Then, I'd go to my office to review practice film.

"After my coaches got done with their meetings, they'd come to my office and we'd meet together to go over what I wanted done the next day at our practices and that took us to eleven and maybe even a little later.

"But, after I spoke with Coach Osborne, I started thinking about his number-one piece of advice, which was to make time for more rest. So, I decided that I could make time in the afternoon to meet with the coaches after our practices and before dinner to go over our next-day practices. I told my coaches that even if they tried to come to my office after they met in the early evening, all they'd see was a dark office and a locked door.

"Not only did this get me home a couple hours earlier to get a full night's rest but it got all my coaches home earlier. And, that's the way I did things from that point on, not just in '87 but for the rest of my career."

And so the iron will that daughter Gina knows is a part of her father's makeup, just as surely as she knows of his sense of humor and propensity to expel a genuine hearty laugh when life presents its burlesque side, was certainly in evidence when dad submitted to an interview by *Toledo Blade* sportswriter Dave Hackenberg in August. When the long-time journalist who is still working for the same newspaper asked whether he had any apprehensions about his health heading into the 1987 season, Strahm's quote was typically chock full of optimism. "I expect I'll get tired, but I'm not going to worry about my heart. The first one lasted fifty years, so I should be OK for a while as long as I take care of myself."

Part of taking care of himself included a regimen Strahm followed between those August practices. Recalls Dick, "After the morning practice, I would go out on the field and jog from one end zone to the other end zone, which is 120 yards, walk all the way down the back line and then jog 120 yards the other way. I did four repetitions each morning.

"I also continued to see Dr. Beekman regularly, and, of course, nothing has changed in the last twenty-plus years. He is absolutely my guy. Jerry takes blood at least four times a year to check cholesterol so my medication can be changed or my diet can be reexamined.

"I owe so much to Jerry. He's been a great friend and a terrific cardiologist all these years."

As the two-a-days wound down, Strahm warily eyed the opponents he would face during the season. The Oilers mentor was anxious to return to the elite of the NAIA, but he certainly knew it would be tough sledding.

"While I had Ken DePriest back for his senior season, we'd lost his go-to guy to graduation after last season, Derek Hutchinson. Remember that Derek still is the all-time school leader for both catches in a season and yards gained for his '86 performance. So it was going to be a challenge for both Ken individually and us as a team. Dave Corley would do his best to fill the void left by Derek's departure.

"In addition, Dana Wright was gone, and that was going to be a tough position to fill as well."

The good news was Strahm had landed a top running back recruit, Jamie Horn, out of West Holmes High School in Millersburg, Ohio, thanks, in part, to some bad luck for Horn and a big assist from Ken DePriest.

Horn, as an All-State running back during his junior year at West Holmes, had received letters from several of the top NCAA schools in the nation. Recalls Horn, "I was contacted by Michigan State, Penn State, and Syracuse. However, once I sustained a rotator cuff injury, the schools lost interest.

"By the time I graduated, I decided the best fit for me was junior college. I'd gotten some letters from Oklahoma A & M Junior College, a school that had just won the junior college national championship the previous year.

"So right after my high school graduation, I enrolled and actually went to Oklahoma and went through spring practice. When spring classes were over, I returned to Millersburg, and it was then I ran into Ken DePriest. He was a senior when I was a freshman at West Holmes. Ken told me that he had one more year left as the starting quarterback, and, since Dana Wright had graduated, there was a chance I could play right away if I came to Findlay.

"Since my shoulder had completely healed, I was anxious to get on the field. After a year of junior college, I figured I could play at a Division I NCAA school, but I probably wouldn't have seen much of the field until my junior or senior year, and you know what they say about the impatience of youth.

"So, I contacted Coach Strahm and went for a visit. What sealed the deal as far as my going to Findlay was that Coach Strahm spent the whole day with me. He made it very enticing to go to Findlay.

"I knew coach was recovering from his operation, but he sure seemed strong to me. He got me with the people in the admissions office, and we got the detail work done, getting my release from A & M, and I was ready in time for August practices."

Horn began the preseason as the tenth running back out of thirteen on the depth chart. But, after the first timed 40-yard dash, he was in the running to start. That's what a 4.4-second time will do for a young man sincere in his efforts to be a starting Oiler halfback.

Recalls Horn, "I started the very first game of my freshman year and every game all the way until week eight of my senior year in 1990. I had to sit out one game because of a severe ankle injury before I got back in to play the final two games of my career with the ankle taped.

"Playing for Coach Strahm, I learned a lot about him right away. First, despite the fact that practice was anything but easy, it was fun. Coach was very witty and really didn't hesitate to crack a joke to lighten the mood. But, I'll tell you something. That usually was early in the practice week. As it got deeper in the week, he got pretty serious.

"I'll never forget my freshman year about a week into two-a-days. It was so hot, and we were really getting beat up, especially the freshmen because so many of us were on the scout teams practicing against the starters. At that time, I was running the ball for the scout team.

"Well, that was about the time when a lot of the freshmen were perhaps asking themselves whether it was all worth it. We were getting kind of homesick.

"During our post-dinner team meeting, Coach Strahm always would give a talk on how he felt practices were going. Well, this one night, he started going on and on about how he knew many of us freshmen were beat up and sore and missing the comforts of home.

"Then, all of a sudden, he said, 'How many of you have girlfriends?' Well, most of the freshmen's hands go up.

"Then, he said, 'I know you're missing them, but I don't want you to worry at all. Your best friends are doing a good job keeping them company and taking care of them. Isn't that nice? That way, you guys can concentrate on football!'

"We're all looking around the room at each other, and you can imagine what we're thinking. And, none of the upperclassmen are even cracking a smile.

"When we got back to the dorm, you have never in your life seen a longer line of freshmen out in the hall in line for the phone waiting to call their girlfriends!

"Of course, for the next three Augusts, I saw coach pull that on three more classes of freshmen, and it was hilarious. Of course, we'd wait until the freshmen left before we'd have our laugh, the same as the upperclassmen did when I was a freshman."

Recalls Strahm, "Years later, I finally had to stop doing that one. We were getting guys calling their girls and if no one picked up the phone, going AWOL and hitching rides home to see what their girlfriends were up to!"

Horn also remembers a unique way that his head coach used humor to pick up a player who was having a tough time in practice. "All of a sudden we'd hear Coach Strahm say to a player he could sense was hanging his head a bit, 'Young man, I can see you've lost your stinger.'

"Then he'd get the whole team to line up and walk down the field, looking down on the ground for it! It was just something coach would do just to lighten the mood so that the player didn't think that what he was going through was overwhelming.

"I don't know. I guess that was the combination master psychologist-comedian coming out in Coach Strahm. I remember moments like those just as vividly as I do the games I played.

"Another thing I learned about coach by the end of my freshman year was I could walk into coach's office anytime, and he always had time for me. Despite having a family of his own, he always had just as much time for his players, it seemed. Even to this day, I feel all I have to do is pick up the phone, and he'll help me if I have a problem. And, that isn't just me either. I doubt if you could find one former player who wouldn't say the same thing."

As for the 1987 season, the Oilers again faced a very challenging schedule. Findlay split its first two games, beating SUNY-Buffalo 39-13 in the opener and then losing at home to a very strong Wisconsin Whitewater team, 19-7.

Strahm remembers the Wisconsin Whitewater game not only because it was a loss but also because of something that happened unrelated to the outcome of the game. "Whitewater was a huge football team, a state school, and very talented. About half way through the last quarter, right in front of our bench, a big fight broke out among the players, and I jumped out there to help break it up. Now, remember, this was only about eight weeks after my open-heart surgery. That probably wasn't the smartest thing I ever did. The incision hadn't even fully scarred over yet!

"In all my years at Findlay, this was the first and only time that something like this had ever happened."

After Findlay rallied in Beaver Falls, Pennsylvania, against Geneva College, winning 26-20, behind 119 yards rushing by the freshman Jamie Horn, Dick Strahm was introduced to yet another first, and, again, it was not a pleasant first experience. In week four, the Oilers took to the road to play Ithaca (New York) College. Despite the extreme length of the bus trip, that was really not a first. The Oilers players had been introduced to the concept of the long bus trip the previous season, their first as an independent team after leaving the Hoosier-Buckeye Collegiate Conference.

Strahm remembers the Ithaca trip and the unpleasantness of the whole experience, including another undesirable first. "First of all, let me say that we knew from the game film that we'd need to play the best game of our lives to compete. Ithaca was a very talented and deep team.

"We boarded the bus early on Friday morning, the same as we always did for our long away trips. There simply was not enough in the athletic budget to be flying to regular-season away games.

"Well, right outside of Cleveland, we were involved in an accident, and that was a first. I'm still not sure exactly what happened. Something must have happened up ahead, and it caused a major pileup when the cars in front of us slammed on their brakes.

"At any rate, we wound up going right over the top of the car in front of us. Amazingly, the bus never turned over, and, even more amazingly, the people in the car were OK.

"Despite the fact that the bus was still drivable, the accident protocol required the driver of our charter to call back to his supervisor. He had to be replaced, so we had to wait for the new driver to be brought in, which took almost two hours.

"By the time we got to Ithaca and got checked into our hotel, it was well past one in the morning on the day of the game.

"Several hours later, we get beat soundly, 38-0. Probably out of all the games I've ever coached, and there have been hundreds, this was one of the most memorably bad, from the length of the trip to the accident to the delay and late arrival and on through the game itself."

After the drubbing just outside the town that lies on the southern shore of Cayuga Lake in Central New York State, the Oilers finally found some wind under their wings. The Black and Orange strung together three consecutive wins, against Hope College (23-14), Tiffin University (27-6), and Kentucky State (27-0). In the Kentucky State contest, quarterback Ken DePriest showed his excellent scrambling ability. He wound up as the Oilers leading ball carrier, rushing for 111 yards on 14 carries and two touchdowns.

Heading into the final two games, Strahm was still eying a possible 7-2 mark, playing a schedule both challenging and relatively new. It certainly takes time to create files on teams' tendencies and also time to develop rivalries, both important to finding that all-important comfort zone when it comes to lining up against opponents.

Recalls Dick, "Listen, no opponent is easy. Football is a game that requires mental and physical toughness and must be played at a high level, no matter which schools you play. But, having said that, after years in a league where you get a chance to develop some rivalries and emotions can run high, there really is an opportunity to be more successful. It certainly takes more than a couple years to get used to life as an independent."

Recalls Strahm, "Our eighth game was a road contest against the DePauw Tigers, an excellent Division III program over in Greencastle, Indiana. The game was really a terrifically competitive one. We battled our way to the lead, 28-22, late in the contest, and DePauw had the ball. On a long pass, we had excellent coverage, but the ball went right through our safety's hands. And, as so often happens when you fail to capitalize on a break, you pay for it. Given new life, DePauw scored at the very end, and we lost, 29-28."

If one were looking for a key reason as to why the Oilers lost in Greencastle on that long-ago Halloween Saturday, the answer just might be found in the Findlay media guide. On that day, the Oilers allowed the most completions in school history, 38.

The quarterback who torched the Oilers' secondary that day was Jeff Voris, and his name is all over his alma mater's football record book. He holds DePauw records for most career attempts, most completions, most career yards, and most career touchdowns. Recalls Strahm, "That young man was just unbelievable that day, but, when you look at his entire body of work at DePauw, I guess he was unbelievable against a lot of teams."

The final game of the season still provided a chance to finish a very respectable 6-3, but it would be against legendary coach Joe Fusco's Westminster Titans. Heading into the contest, Strahm knew the Oilers would have their work cut out. Fusco's teams were always well prepared and certainly had proven themselves to be among NAIA's elite.

In the 1987 finale, played at Donnell Stadium, Fusco's charges won a shootout, 42-38, despite the strong running performance of the freshman Jamie Horn (17 carries for 121 yards and two TDs). Strahm describes the game as hard-nosed with two very determined teams. "Whoever had the ball last was going to win. Unfortunately for us, Westminster had it last."

How many points separated 7-2 from 5-4? The answer is a measly five. The Titans made the playoffs and advanced to the second round before losing to Geneva College, the same team the Oilers defeated in week three.

Recalls Strahm, "I guess if we were going to get Westminster, it should have been that year. The next two years, they were unbelievable. They won 27 straight games and back-to-back national championships. Coach Fusco was just a terrific football coach."

While disappointed with the second consecutive 5-4 season, Strahm has taken a somewhat philosophical mindset over the years. "First of all, after the open-heart surgery, who really knew what would happen to me health-wise that year? Looking back, I certainly have to feel fortunate I had no problems. Through the brawl I found myself in the middle of, to the bus crash, to the very tough losses the last two weeks of the season – I made it!"

As far as the season's items of note, Ken DePriest remained healthy and started all nine games. While his numbers did decline a bit after his breakout junior year in 1986, that was to be somewhat expected, with the graduation of Derek Hutchinson. Still, DePriest managed to throw for almost 1,000 yards (924) and also threw seven touchdown passes.

But, perhaps more important than any set of statistics, the quarterback showed the ability to overcome obstacles and finish strong after his return to school in 1985.

The freshman Horn certainly made the most of his opportunity, leading the team in both scoring with 64 points and rushing, with 767 yards.

Defensive lineman Rick Mielcarek, the senior out of Toledo St. Francis High School, the same school that produced Nelson Bolden, was named All-American and is a player Strahm remembers fondly. "Rick wasn't a very big guy, maybe a little over six feet tall and around 220 pounds, but he had the kind of desire you almost have to be born with. He had it when he came to me as a freshman back in 1984. I certainly didn't coach that desire into him.

"He was a very quiet guy off the field, but, when you put a helmet and shoulder pads on him, was he ever intense! He could get off a block as well as anyone who ever played for me at Findlay, and that was against guys that routinely outweighed him by thirty, forty pounds."

And so, the first season was in the books for Dick Strahm after Dr. Toby Cosgrove performed a quadruple bypass on him June 25, 1987, at the Cleveland Clinic. For Strahm, it was a time to review game film, consider coaching clinics that he felt would broaden his and his assistant coaches' knowledge, and look at all aspects of his program to see what could be done to once again achieve at the highest level.

As Strahm thought about what needed to be done, he kept returning again and again to something that he had known for a long time needed an upgrade. "We certainly needed to improve our weight-training facility. You really can't overstate how important that is to a football program, not only as a means to increase strength in our players but also from a recruiting standpoint.

"To be able to show a recruit a top-shelf weightlifting program housed in a newer building really helps increase interest. At this time, our players were lifting in the old Renninger building. It wasn't really a weight room, just an open area. We also didn't have that many weights."

It was this concern that Strahm brought to the office of former athletic director Jim Houdeshell. When Dick told Houdeshell that the need for a new weight facility was important, Houdeshell vowed to help in any way he could.

Recalls Strahm, "After I told Jim what I had in mind, he suggested adding onto the west side of Croy Gymnasium. He estimated it would take around $150,000 to construct a shell for a small weight room.

"Jim gave me a list of potential donors. I felt if I could get fifteen people to donate $10,000 apiece, we could get it done. I also went to see Dr. Zirkle and told him of my development efforts."

However, when Strahm began making his contacts, he realized how difficult soliciting such an amount was. "I had a number of people who were interested in helping but not to the extent I was proposing. Some would say, 'I'll give you $500 or $1,000.'

"I realized that I couldn't find enough donors with deep enough pockets to cover the amount I needed, so I went back to see Ken Zirkle."

Recalls Zirkle, "I told Dick that one of the names on his list of potential donors that he hadn't seen yet, Phil Gardner was certainly a man worth knowing. He was the president and general manager of Findlay Industries, a company that still supplies original equipment manufacturers such as Ford, Chrysler, General Motors, and major truck manufacturers with interior trim parts.

"I actually got to know Mr. Gardner through Jim Koehler, who was a very successful builder in Findlay. It was Jim who told me I should get to know Phil."

And, so, at the urging of his college's president, Strahm made an appointment to see Gardner. However, it took some time to arrange the meeting, as Dick recalls. "I had actually met Mr. Gardner a few times at Nick and Barbara Petti's restaurant on north Main Street, so it wasn't as if I would be starting at square one with him, and I knew he enjoyed football. Mr. Gardner was a very busy man, a real hands-on businessman. He'd built Findlay Industries from the ground up and was very involved in its operation. Translated, that meant he was a very hard man to see. He just didn't allot much time for anything that didn't involve the day-to-day operation of his business.

"I remember his secretary was a wonderful woman named Annette. I got to know her pretty well when trying to set up a time to meet Mr. Gardner. I'd call, and Annette would say, 'Not today, Dick. He's got meetings all the way through five o'clock. I'll call you when I can get a time arranged for you to meet with him, but you've got to be willing to come on short notice.' I assured her I would.

"Well, one day the phone rings in my office, and it's Annette. She told me that Mr. Gardner would see me at 1:00 p.m. sharp. He had exactly 30 minutes. I dropped everything and got right over there. I knew Mr. Gardner was a very well-respected man and a great supporter of Findlay College, but he was also somewhat of a tough sell. I mean, you really had to show him his contributions were going to a very good and necessary project."

Strahm told Gardner about his desire to put an addition on Croy Gym to create a weight room. Initially, Strahm got some very negative vibes from the potential donor. "I remember he sat silent for probably about thirty seconds. Then, he began asking a lot of questions as to why, given the success our teams had enjoyed over the years, I felt a weight room was necessary.

"I did my absolute best sales job in the next five minutes or so. Finally, Gardner agreed to make a contribution of $50,000 to the project. While I was very happy when I left our meeting, I just sensed that Mr. Gardner wasn't all that happy over the location of the project."

Strahm returned to the office of Findlay College's president to tell Dr. Zirkle of the contribution pledge, and it is a moment Zirkle remembers well. "Dick was really happy that Phil Gardner was going to give so much, but he also told me that he wasn't sure he really was sold on the gift.

"I told Dick that we really couldn't take the money if Mr. Gardner wasn't completely sold on his pledge. That's one thing you learn in the fund-raising game. You absolutely need your donors, especially those who are very prominent in the community as Mr. Gardner was, not only to agree to fund a project but you really need them to be happy about it. When donors are not fully committed, they don't really become strong advocates, which means they tend not to influence others to join in the effort. This is especially important in small-college environments because there are fewer potential contributors from which to draw.

"So, Dick arranged another meeting with Phil, and he and I both went to see him.

"It turned out that Phil was somewhat dissatisfied with the idea that he was giving money to a project that was an addition onto an existing building. He said he was really more interested in exploring a project where the result would be a new building."

Naturally, both Strahm and Zirkle pursued this possibility enthusiastically. At the end of the meeting, Gardner wasn't ready to make a commitment just yet. Given the fact that the amount of money would be in the high six figures instead of the earlier amount of $50,000, he felt he should discuss the matter with his sons, Philip J. Gardner and Michael Gardner, both of whom were in the family business.

It was then that Strahm remembers a period of what one might call nervous waiting. While there was no doubt that Mr. Gardner was interested, the wildcards, so to speak, were his sons.

Recalls Dick, "I can remember calling Annette, Mr. Gardner's secretary, many times to see if she knew if any decision had been made. She'd just say, 'I'll call you when Mr. Gardner wants to see you, Dick. He's a very deliberate man. I promise the minute he wants to see you, I'll call.'"

About a week later, the phone rang in Dick's office, and it was Annette. She told Strahm that her boss wanted to meet with both him and Dr. Zirkle for lunch the next day, and he wanted to bring a friend of his, Robert Malcolm.

Recalls Strahm, "Bob Malcolm was a very successful industrialist in Findlay before his retirement as owner of Hancock Machine Company. He was also a real humanitarian, and I was thrilled when Annette told me he wanted to join us for lunch.

"The next day, I drove over to pick the men up and then out to the country club to meet Ken Zirkle. Mr. Gardner said that both his sons were supportive of the project, and he was going to commit to building a brand new fitness center."

The altruistic Robert Malcolm also agreed to make a sizable contribution as well. And it was with the combined financial support of these two friends that the building was possible. In principle, it was done. Despite the fact that the first shovelful of dirt had yet to be turned, the first phase of any major building project, the commitment, was rock-solid.

Zirkle suggested that his time at Findlay would have been considerably shorter had Phil Gardner not stepped up with a substantial gift that enabled the new fitness center to be built. "We had not had a new building constructed since Bare Residence Hall in 1970, and that's entirely too long for any college. For a college or university to thrive, it needs growth. And, that's why Phil Gardner and Bob Malcolm are both very important, both to the school and to me in terms of my career.

"And, of course, I can't ignore Dick Strahm's importance in getting the Phil Gardner Fitness Center built. It is my opinion that Mr. Gardner would never have given the money to anyone other than Dick Strahm. Mr. Gardner was a great admirer of both Dick and his football program for years."

While driving the two philanthropists back from lunch, Strahm recalls a conversation the best friends had in the back seat. "While I'm driving and obviously feeling great after our lunch, I heard both Mr. Gardner and Mr. Malcolm in the back seat asking each other, 'What are we going to name the building?' Then, Mr. Gardner said, 'Let's call it the Gardner-Malcolm Center.' But, Mr. Malcolm told his friend that only he should have his name on the building since he was giving the most money. Mr. Gardner's response was, 'But, Bob, you're my buddy!'"

As it evolved, Malcolm remained adamant that his name not appear on the building, and, reluctantly, Gardner agreed that the building would be called the Phil Gardner Fitness Center.

And so, the decision had been made to construct the building, but where it would be built was yet another matter. Recalls Strahm, "Ken and I walked all around the campus. When we got to the area right across from the Croy Gym, he stopped and asked, 'What's wrong with right here?' He was pointing to two tennis courts.

"That's where it was decided the building would go. Mr. Gardner, of course, was consulted as was Mr. Malcolm, and both agreed that the site was a good one."

Phil Gardner had his own architect in mind to build the new facility, and, of course, Ken and Dick said the same thing. "Pick whoever you want!" Both the campus president and the football coach worked with the architect to create a floor plan that would be both functional and aesthetic.

The planning of the building went on through the summer of 1988, with an eye towards an early November groundbreaking. If all went as planned the Phil Gardner Fitness Center would welcome its first users in late summer of 1989. The construction costs were calculated to be somewhere in the neighborhood of $750,000.

Others in the Findlay community stepped up and donated monies for the desks in the classrooms, furniture for the offices and weight room and other furnishings, and it was the likes of individuals such as Jim and Myra Houdeshell, Jonathan Moore and family, Dave Evans, and the Don Manley family who stepped forward.

As the season approached, all of Coach Strahm's full-time coaches returned (Doug Coate, Jim McIntosh, Ray Kwiatkowski, Mike Ward, Curtis Davidson, and Mark Niswonger). Only volunteer coach and former standout defensive end of Strahm's 1979-'80-'81 teams, Jerry Campbell, would not be returning because of his work schedule at Ball Corporation in Findlay. Arriving to fill the void was Greg Gilbert, who would help coach the defensive line after spending two years as a graduate assistant at the University of Toledo under head coach Dan Simrell, Strahm's former coaching colleague during his Rocket years.

Another former player, Tim Beckman, also joined Strahm's staff in 1988 as a part-time coach. For Beckman, it was a move strongly endorsed by his father, Dave, who was the personnel director for the Cleveland Browns from 1982 through 1988. It was Tim's father who first recommended his son make the transfer from the University of Kentucky back in 1984 to Findlay during his undergraduate years.

Dave Beckman and Dick Strahm had known and certainly respected each other for a number of years through coaching circles. So in Dave Beckman's mind, what better place could there be for a son who wanted to follow him into a career in coaching?

The coaching staff was bracing itself for a challenging season. Recalls Dick, "The schedule we would play as an independent remained very tough, and, in addition, we had lost our starting quarterback, Ken DePriest, to graduation, and, any time you have to replace your starting quarterback, there are going to be some growing pains you should expect."

Greg Steinecker, the sophomore from Wilshire, Ohio, would win the job but also experience growing pains. The running game was expected to be the team's offensive strength. Sophomore Jamie Horn was the team's leading rusher in '87, and junior Doug Brown, out of Miamisburg, returned after averaging an impressive five yards a carry the previous season.

The season opened on a positive note as the Oilers took care of always-physical Wisconsin Whitewater, 21-14, to get the season, at least initially, headed in the right direction. Doug Brown rushed for 176 yards on 25 carries, and Steinecker did well in his first start, completing 10 of 16 and throwing his first career touchdown pass.

In week two, against SUNY-Buffalo, the Oilers suffered one of those losses that a head coach remembers, even twenty years after the final score of 7-3 in Buffalo's favor had been posted.

Recalls Strahm, "I'll never forget that game. We were down 7-3 and had the ball down on Buffalo's five-yard line, about to score. We had a third down and went to two wideouts in our wishbone package. On the back side [the short side of the unbalanced line], our back came out completely uncovered. Nobody was within 10 yards of him. All of us on the sideline were screaming for our quarterback to look left, but we just couldn't get his attention. He didn't see him, and we wound up not scoring.

"Even after all these years, I still can see that wide open receiver. Maybe we all should have taken that as a sign that this was going to be a real difficult year."

The following week, Findlay dropped another close contest, this time to Joe Fusco's Westminster Titans, 23-17, despite a nice game by Greg Steinecker, who completed 14 passes for over 200 yards and two TDs.

Recalls Strahm, "Westminster was just a great team that year, and we really played them tough. Maybe with one more opportunity we could have won. Who knows? We were, at that point in the season, probably two plays away from 3-0. Instead we were 1-2."

In weeks four and five, Findlay College dropped its third and fourth consecutive games, 21-0 to strong NCAA Division II Ashland University, and 32-22 to Muskingum College (New Concord, Ohio), to fall to a very uncharacteristic 1-4 record with four games remaining.

Strahm remembers the difficulty of facing the prospects of a potentially disastrous conclusion to the season. "We just had to keep persevering. Of course, I knew we were out of the playoff picture, but I really felt we still had a shot at finishing with a winning record."

For the Oilers, two consecutive wins, 14-0 over Tiffin University, and 42-21 over Urbana (Ohio) University, provided hope. By that point in the season, Strahm felt it important to make a quarterback change. Dana Brockman quarterbacked the Oilers in both contests as well as in the final two contests. While Brockman struggled in the two wins against Tiffin and Urbana, Jamie Horn picked up the slack. The sophomore speedster averaged 134 in the two wins and scored four touchdowns. Defensively, London Rogan had an interception in each of the two contests, with the second including a 36-yard sprint to the end zone.

At 3-4, a winning record was still in the mix. It had not been since Strahm's first year in 1975 that an Oilers football team finished with a sub .500 season. But, before those final two games that would complete the history that each football season ultimately becomes, it was time for the first spade of dirt to be turned on Findlay's campus since 1970.

The architects had completed their work, and the project moved from the idea stage to the beginning of reality. Recalls Ken Zirkle about the Thursday, November 3 ceremony that was about to change the face of Findlay's campus forever, thanks to the benevolence of Phil D. Gardner and his friend Robert Malcolm, "This was just such a significant milestone in the history of Findlay College for those two men to provide one of the finest small-college fitness centers in the entire country."

And so, construction commenced on College Street, just west of Renninger Gymnasium and across from Croy Physical Education Center.

Strahm was obviously encouraged that the construction was finally officially underway. "It really was a dream come true, and that groundbreaking really couldn't have come at a better time, what with the very difficult season we were having.

"After the season, when we would get out on the recruiting trail, how great it was going to be to be able to say to a young man, 'Let me take you over and show you the progress on our new locker room and weight training center which will be open by the time you arrive for our August preseason.'"

As for the on-field proceedings, Strahm's team saw its goal of reaching .500 in week eight and nudging above that in the season's finale fall by the wayside.

In week eight, against Wayne State University, out of Detroit, Michigan, the Oilers dropped their third game of the season by a touchdown or less, 25-18.

The following week, with a season-ending 26-14 loss to former Hoosier-Buckeye Collegiate Conference foe Wilmington, Dick Strahm's most challenging and disappointing season in over a decade finally was over. The 3-6 was a mere three plays and 21 total points away from 6-3, but that is sometimes the unforgiving nature of athletic competition.

The bottom line was, to a proud coach who'd achieved so much success, the Oilers just didn't make enough plays. And, it was unacceptable. For both the first time since his first year, and, for the last time until his retirement following the 1998 season, Dick Strahm coached a team that had lost more games than it won for an entire season.

Recalls Dick, "The late 1980s were just very difficult, tough times you might say, adopting that independent's schedule with a lot of new opponents and longer travel and still no ability to offer scholarships. But, I have always been a firm believer that tough times never last, but tough people do.

"I and my coaches began looking for reasons why we would be more successful from that point on rather than reviewing the reasons why we had this drop off. I knew our fitness center and new locker room would certainly help with recruiting. The weight room was going to be huge [2,588 square feet].

"Now that alone wasn't going to get players here. I knew we were really going to have to bring our 'A' game when it came to recruiting during the winter and early spring. We just needed more good players.

"Don't get me wrong. We had some excellent players, guys like Moorefield [Joe] and Sbrissa [Ryan] and Horn [Jamie] and defensive back Andre Roberts, but we just needed more of them. I knew it. My coaches knew it. And, by golly, I intended to do something about it!"

As far as bright spots in the dismal 1988 season, Jamie Horn averaged more than 100 yards rushing per game and finished with 902 yards during a very productive sophomore season. He also led the team in scoring with eight touchdowns. Fullback Doug Brown, the 213-pound junior also ran well and finished with 793 yards.

In the trenches, Chuck Hale, who, by season's end, had started 27 consecutive games on the offensive line, was named Honorable Mention NAIA All-American. On the defensive line, Rich Ambrose, the defensive end who played a whole lot bigger than his listed height of 5'9," also played well enough to garner Honorable Mention All-American honors. Both players, through those honors, had set themselves up as preseason All-Americans heading into their senior seasons in 1989.

As the new year of 1989 arrived and the second half of the winter stepped aside for spring, the construction of the Gardner Fitness Center was progressing nicely, and this was certainly a source of great interest to Dick Strahm.

"A day didn't go by when I didn't swing over that way to check to see what had been done since the day before. One thing I wanted for the locker room was the open-air wooden lockers with the lockable compartments below. The design was the exact same as the ones in Ohio State's locker room.

"I had actually contacted one of the top carpenters in our area, the Vorst brothers, and had taken them to Ohio State University to show them the Buckeyes' locker room. I wanted them to replicate those lockers for us, and they wound up doing a fantastic job. They also did all the labor for free. Only the materials cost us money."

Someone else who rarely went a day without visiting the construction site was Findlay College president Ken Zirkle. Recalls Zirkle, "I've always enjoyed construction. Years before, my wife and I bought a farm in the hills of Pennsylvania to serve as kind of a getaway place. We had quite a bit of construction done there, and I was pretty involved in that. I guess I kind of carried that same interest into the Gardner Center.

"I just have always believed that, when a new building was being constructed on campus on my watch, if I showed a real interest in the project, then the contractors would do a better job. So, I was a frequent visitor and really got to know a lot of the workers."

And, even long after the workers had gone for the day, it wasn't unusual to see the campus president walking the beams high above the ground, checking out the work in the waning moments of a day's light.

In the spring, Ken Zirkle also made a decision that would reap immediate dividends when it came to Strahm's recruiting efforts. Recalls Strahm, "We, as coaches, were really working hard recruiting-wise, but we had never been able to offer any scholarship help. All we could ever do was work with the financial-aid aspect, depending upon how great the need was for a young man's family, the same as any other student considering Findlay College.

"Well, all that changed when Dr. Zirkle came to see me one day when I was in my office. He said that he understood how difficult it was to play scholarship-granting schools. He then said that while he knew Findlay wasn't in a position to match the total number of scholarships that many other schools could offer, he did authorize a total of eight full scholarships, which could be divided any way I would want as long as the total amount didn't exceed the total of those eight scholarships during a four-year period.

"Obviously, I was thrilled. We had never had any scholarships to this point, and, despite our overall success, it was getting increasingly difficult to compete after we'd left the league following the 1985 season, so I was very grateful.

"What we were able to do was multiply the current tuition, room, and board by eight, which gave us around $160,000. Then, I could offer any amount to a player based on need and, of course, the abilities of those we were interested in recruiting.

"Since, it wasn't an overwhelming amount, I was only interested in can't-miss individuals to award money to. I just couldn't afford to make mistakes. The young man had to be a good student as well as a good football player.

"Generally, I quartered the scholarships, which meant about five thousand dollars to a player each year. That allowed me to bring in more scholarship players. And, before I awarded any amount, I always waited for the financial-aid paperwork to come back to see what other monies the young man qualified for.

"That number of scholarships never grew any larger for the rest of my years at Findlay, but that was OK. It was what we, as an institution, could afford. Dr. Zirkle also, of course, offered some scholarship help as well to other sports."

The recruiting class of 1989 brought several young men who would turn out to be the key performers in 1992 when Findlay once again would rise to the very pinnacle of NAIA football.

Recalls Strahm, "We had an outstanding recruiting class in 1989, thanks to the ability to offer some scholarship help and, of course, thanks to the Gardner Center that would be opening in August. Todd Clark, from Lima (Ohio) Bath High School, became an excellent linebacker for us. Eric Brandstadt, from Vermillion (Ohio), became a very good defensive tackle, and so did Chris Smith from Fremont (Ohio), who also would eventually become a first-team All-American.

"Another young man, from New Breman (Ohio), would make an immediate impact and then go on to play at an All-American level as an upperclassman, Bob Heitkamp. We also got

Jeff Nagy, out of Maumee (Ohio), who started in the secondary and played at a very high level and also John Goodburn, out of Worthington (Ohio), who became a good special teamer.

"Offensively, I knew we needed quarterback help. I'd already decided to switch Greg Steinecker to the defensive secondary for the upcoming season, so I needed to address the quarterback slot.

"I was able to bring in DeMya Wimberly, all the way from Hollywood, Florida; Bob Sutyak, from Madison (Ohio); and Jason Nicolosi, from Marion (Ohio). Despite breaking in a new quarterback, I felt pretty good about choosing from those three.

"I also was able to bring in several other offensive players. Chris Cotterill, from Amherst (Ohio), become a very good offensive guard for us, and Doug Kramer, a high school teammate of Bob Heitkamp's at New Bremen, also came in and played guard. By his senior year, we had switched him to center, and he was a starter for us.

Harold Rinehart, out of New Lexington (Ohio), became a very valuable swing offensive guard, which meant he could play either our strong-side or our back-side guard in our unbalanced line. Then we got Jason Stofel, from Delaware (Ohio), who became a very intense offensive tackle.

"I can thank my son Doug for Tim Russ, a big [6'6," 250 pounds] offensive tackle. Tim went from an Illinois junior college to the University of Toledo. Well, Doug was a graduate assistant for Coach Dan Simrell, and he helped convince Tim to transfer to The University of Findlay.

"As far as running the ball, we also convinced Nathan Sprunger to commit to us. He was a halfback out of Pandora (Ohio), and I found a junior-college transfer, a fullback by the name of Balewa Walker, and his is kind of an interesting story, not just how we got him but also what happened to him once he came to Findlay.

"What happened was Doug Coate and I decided to go to the Chicago area and check out some of the junior colleges to see if any players were potential good fits for us. There are a number of jucos in and around Chicago, and what we would do is just find out where the football offices were on campuses we visited, introduce ourselves to the head coach, and ask if he had any players who might be interested in a school such as Findlay and if we could watch some game film of those players.

"By and large, the coaches were very cooperative. What we found out not just helped us in recruiting but we also enjoyed talking to other coaches and exchanging ideas.

"Well, the last school we visited before driving back to Findlay was Joliet Junior College, probably about two full hours outside of Chicago.

"We finally arrived and got some directions to the football offices, and when we got there, the place was almost deserted. We finally found a secretary who was doing some typing, and I asked if any of the coaches were around. She said they'd all gone home for the day.

"Naturally, we were disappointed that we'd driven all that way, and there was no one to talk to. Suddenly, I look up, and here comes this big, young man, probably 250, 260 pounds, with a smile as big as the set of shoulders he had.

"He came up and introduced himself as Balewa Walker and said he'd overheard us asking for the coaches. He asked if we wanted to see some game film, so we didn't feel we wasted our time, and we said we'd love to. He said he knew how to run the projector and led us down the hall into a film room.

"He selected a game, threaded the projector, and turned off the lights. As we're sitting there watching, I noticed this big fullback having a helluva game. The first time he ran the ball he ran inside and wound up carrying about three tacklers for an additional five yards after initial contact. When I said, 'Who is that?' he said, 'That's me, coach.'

"And, as the film continued, I'd hear him say things like, 'That's me delivering that crushing block' and 'There I go again, this time showing I've got enough speed to get to the corner' and 'Here I am catching a screen pass, and you'll notice how low the ball was thrown yet I still caught it.'

"It really was funny the way he was narrating his own plays. Of course, he'd selected his best game to show, no question. And, you know something? It worked! We did wind up asking him if he'd be interested in coming to Findlay for a visit, and he did.

"By late spring, we had Balewa Walker ready for Findlay. Unfortunately, after we had him enrolled, there were some questions that arose as far as credits that were transferable, and he wasn't able to play in 1989.

"Then, during the winter after the '89 season, Balewa's grandfather passed away, and Balewa returned to Illinois to be with family. Because of some family issues, he wound up not coming back for the rest of that school year and also 1990.

"But, similar to Ken DePriest's resiliency, Balewa showed that same spirit. He wound up reenrolling in 1991 and playing very well that year and having his big year in 1992.

"The one thing I'll never forget about Balewa is that big smile on his face. He was really one of the most positive people I have ever met. And, to sit out an entire year and a half and then bounce back like that not only to play well but also earn his degree, well, that's special. It's really stories like Balewa's that convince me that there was absolutely no better way for me to have earned my living than in coaching and teaching."

As spring became summer, Ken Zirkle, Findlay's dynamic, forward-thinking president, was overseeing a momentous change that had been more than a year in the making since the Board of Trustees had given its approval. Since 1882, the school had been known as Findlay College. However, on July 1, 1989, after all the paperwork had been filed, the school became known as The University of Findlay.

The institution had experienced steady growth in enrollment under Zirkle's leadership, largely a result of the many new academic programs that had been added in recent years. In addition, the school was venturing into graduate programming, with a new Master of Arts in Teaching English to Speakers of Other Languages (TESOL) and Bilingual Education, which offered its first classes beginning the previous April. Findlay also was looking to increase the population of international students attending classes on campus. Overall, the small college in northwest Ohio was reflecting the big ambitions of its president.

Recalls Zirkle, "I just felt the change from 'Findlay College' to 'The University of Findlay' kind of legitimized us. When you use the word *university*, there is kind of a different aura than when you use the word *college*.

"In higher education, you really do have to be tuned in to all of what goes into increasing enrollment, and through traveling overseas for the purpose of professional development, I realized so many of those in foreign countries looked for that 'university' designation.

"So, really, in essence, the name change was probably 99.9 percent marketing. The international population was a unique one in that the families of all these students paid cash on the barrelhead, no discounts. To increase that demographic on our campus, I felt, was important and doing so would be easier with the change in designation."

"Of course, there were those who had some trouble with our decision, those who really, for nostalgic reasons, wanted things to always stay the same, but I felt it was important for us to grow the international population."

For men like Zirkle, who always have an eye toward what is over the next rise, time eventually justifies their decisions. By the time Ken Zirkle left Findlay after twenty years in 2003 to assume the position of president of Becker College in Worcester, Massachusetts, the number of international students enrolled at The University of Findlay had burgeoned to more than four hundred.

At Becker, the same kind of dynamic thought has taken root. Prior to Zirkle's arrival, the New England school had experienced seven consecutive years of declining enrollment. By the beginning of Zirkle's fifth year in the position, enrollment had doubled.

Despite his being proud of the school's growth, Zirkle is quick to point out that his role is certainly not that of protagonist of any college, be it at the school that will always hold a special place in his heart, Findlay, or Becker.

"Listen, I am not really driving the car. I'm really just a passenger. I think I would probably best be classified as an enabler, really, more of a cheerleader.

"And, part of that role is taking a strong interest in a school's athletics, which, I think, is especially important in a small school. I've always felt that the role of athletics is as a most important adjunct to academic excellence.

"While faculties are, as a whole, often somewhat skeptical of athletics as a win-at-all-costs pursuit, in a small-college setting, we are always striving to reward equally academics and athletics. And, when a faculty senses that academics and athletics are equal partners, those on the faculty really come aboard as strong allies of sports.

"In my mind, athletics is a carrot to improve enrollment and enhance the college experience. Balance is the key. Athletics certainly helps fundraising. There is no question in my mind that without the success of Dick Strahm's football program, Phil Gardner and Bob Malcolm wouldn't have made the huge financial commitment to Findlay that they did.

"Since I believe so strongly in athletics, that's why my wife, Chris, and I are at almost every game, both home and away in all the major sports and as many other sports as my schedule will allow. I know as far as Dick's games, I missed a total of two games in twenty years. One time I was traveling on university business in China, and the other time I was in Japan for the same reason.

"My five daughters (Laura, Andrea, Bri, Dara, and Lindsay) all were involved to varying degrees in sports. Two were all-state swimmers in high school, and during our time in Findlay, they certainly became huge fans of Oilers athletics, especially Coach Strahm's teams.

"I can remember we'd all be in church, and Dick and his family would be sitting in the pew right in front of us, and one of my daughters would tap Dick on the shoulder and say, 'Coach, right at the end of the first half, why didn't you try a long pass down the sideline?'

"I am still so proud of our Academic All-Americans we had at Findlay during my tenure. They really are what I feel are the crown jewels of a university. A big part of my decision to make those eight scholarships available to Dick was to increase our chances to develop some." Coach Strahm, in fact, had sixteen NAIA scholar-athletes, many of them in the 1990s.

When the calendar clicked off another month, not only was Dick anticipating a return to the football field to erase the memories of that 3-6 campaign the previous year but he was also reveling in the opening of the Phil Gardner Fitness Center.

The new facility included $75,000 of weight training equipment. There were more than a thousand pounds of Olympic free weights, power racks, and incline benches, four lifecycle exercise bikes, and twelve machines designed to work different muscle groups to promote overall body conditioning.

The Center's main floor would include the weight room in addition to a 1,200-square-foot training room, a room equipped with treatment tables, rehabilitation equipment, and a hydrotherapy room.

On the ground floor, there would be two classrooms, capable of accommodating forty students in each. In addition, there would be shower rooms, locker rooms for both coaches and players (featuring the Vorst brothers' wooden cubicles), and the coaches' offices.

At the ribbon cutting, August 12, 1989, President Zirkle told the assembled media, "The fitness center is symbolic of the revitalization that has occurred at the college recently with the introduction of innovative new programs and increasing enrollment."

For Dick Strahm, it was hard to get the smile off his face. "I just knew how this was going to help get the young men we were trying to commit to come here. I remember when I first arrived in 1975, I did everything I could to avoid showing a recruit our locker room. Well, those days were long gone.

"I put our linebacker and strength coach Mike Ward in charge of the weight room, and he did a terrific job. I really couldn't have hired a better person to start our weight program in our brand new building. Mike Ward knew what he was doing from day one. The room was always spotless and the weights in their proper places. He made our players work extremely hard.

"We also got our first full-time trainer, a wonderful and professional lady by the name of Vi LeClaire. Together, Mike and Vi were really the backbone of the Gardner Center for a number of years.

After the building's opening, it was time for Strahm to get serious about assembling his coaches and intensifying the planning for the upcoming 1989 football season. As far as the face of the staff, it largely remained the same, with one exception. While McIntosh, Kwiatkowski, Coate, Davidson, Gilbert, and Ward returned, Tim Beckman moved south, accepting a position as a graduate assistant under head coach Pat Dye at Auburn University in Alabama.

For Beckman, who in the opinion of Dick Strahm demonstrated as fine a football mind as any player who ever suited up for him, there would be many steps on his coaching ladder. After two years at Auburn, Beckman then spent six years at Western Carolina.

Then it was on to Elon University in North Carolina to coach two years at the I-AA NCAA school before getting back to Ohio to Bowling Green State University to serve as its defensive coordinator, the same position Dale Strahm had also held years before.

Recalls Beckman, now the defensive coordinator at Oklahoma State in Stillwater, "I served first under Gary Blackney and then for someone who turned out to be a rising star in collegiate coaching, Urban Meyer.

"When Coach Meyer took the head job at the University of Utah, I went with him. However, after my father-in-law, Pat Rooney, a dear friend of Coach Strahm's and a great

Findlay supporter, passed away, my wife and I returned to Ohio, and I did something I think is pretty unique.

"I returned to Bowling Green and, again became defensive coordinator for Coach Gregg Brandon. So, in two different trips back to Bowling Green, I was a defensive coordinator under three different coaches.

"Then, in 2005, I got an opportunity to join Coach Jim Tressel's staff, coaching the secondary before moving on to Oklahoma State in 2007."

Had it not been for the opportunity to become a coordinator in a big-time football conference, Beckman probably would have remained on the Buckeye staff, but he certainly has a goal. "Listen, I really want to become a head coach. Then, I can take parts from every great head coach I have ever worked for and run my own program. Men like Dick Strahm and Gary Blackney and Urban Myer and Jim Tressel and Mike Gundy here at Oklahoma State all have the same characteristic. They have a gift for organization and a knack other coaches struggle to demonstrate for guiding young men and taking them to great heights, and I don't just mean on the field but off it as well. They're more like life coaches.

"In my mind, pure and simple, Dick Strahm's a winner. I just hope when my time comes in my career when I become a head coach that I can, one day, look back and say I impacted kids' lives to the extent Dick Strahm has."

By late August of 1989, the Oilers were in full two-a-day mode in anticipation of their September 9 home opener versus SUNY-Buffalo. The biggest question during the preseason was who would emerge from six freshmen Strahm had brought in to be the starting quarterback of the newly dubbed The University of Findlay.

While, initially, Strahm felt it would come down to a battle between Bob Sutyak and Jason Nicolosi, it became harder and harder to ignore the fleet Floridian, DeMya Wimberly. By the time the Oilers were ready to take the field for the opener, it was Wimberly who had emerged as the best match for Strahm's wishbone offense.

The strength of the attack, no doubt, would be the team's running game. Two quality backs in halfback Jamie Horn and fullback Doug Brown returned after solid campaigns the previous year. James Lover had also transferred in from the University of Akron to secure the other starting halfback position, the two back, filled so capably in years past by the likes of Denny Guerra, Dave Brenek and Doug Rode.

The freshman from Pandora-Gilboa High School, Nathan Sprunger, also would certainly see some action. The former UPI Division IV Back-of-Year ran a 4.6 40-yard dash, which put him just a step or two behind the winged feet of the junior Horn.

Of course, the strength of any running attack was the offensive line, and the Oilers were loaded in this area. Preseason All-American Chuck Hale gave the line an anchor along with senior Joe Moorefield. Ryan Sbrissa also returned at center, and Roy Hass, the tight end, rounded out the tightly knit group.

As for Coach Bill McIntosh's son, Bill, injuries forced him to the sidelines as a medical redshirt, but he had vowed to emerge as the Oilers' starting center the following year.

On the outside, the players who would, hopefully, be on the receiving end of many of Wimberly's tosses were senior Dave Corley (Carlisle, Ohio) and tight end Hass, whose releases off the line of scrimmages and catches averaged almost 13 yards the previous season.

Defensively, the line returned everybody, certainly a comforting thought to the Oilers' coaches. Preseason All-American Rich Ambrose (Granville, Ohio) returned to man one defensive end, opposite the other end, Joe Baarlaer, a graduate of prep power Cincinnati Elder High School. Paul Perrine (Cleveland, Ohio) was slated to start at one tackle and James Snipes (Huber Heights, Ohio) at the other. He would be pushed by another of the talented freshmen, Duane Ham (Upper Sandusky, Ohio). Ham was a young man with tremendous potential but unfortunately sustained a career-ending knee injury. At nose guard, it would be the 5'9," 227-pound junior out of Farmersville (Ohio), Brad Boyer.

The secondary gave all indications it would be strong. Preseason All-American Andre Roberts, the senior out of Toledo Woodward High School, picked off seven aerials as a junior and was bringing his 4.6 40-yard dash speed to a new position, free safety.

Junior London Rogan (Cable, Ohio) would occupy one cornerback, and Steve Carter, the senior out of Lima (Ohio) Senior High School, would be the strong safety.

Findlay opened the season resoundingly, with a 39-3 win over Buffalo at Donnell. Andre Roberts proved his adjustment to free safety would be smooth with two interceptions. Doug Brown gave glimpses that he would supplant Jamie Horn as the Oilers' leading ball carrier with his 19-carry, 119-yard, two-touchdown performance.

Freshman signal-caller DeMya Wimberly calmed his nerves and completed an efficient 6 of 9 passes for 84 yards and threw his first collegiate touchdown pass.

After all the positives in the opener, the Oilers encountered some adversity, and it came in back-to-back-to-back Saturdays. They lost three in a row.

The first was 35-15, to Joe Fusco's Westminster Titans, the defending D-II NAIA national champions. The Titans were destined to again march through their season undefeated and win their second consecutive national championship, Coach Fusco's fourth crown since his arrival at Westminster in 1973.

In week three, Findlay dropped an away contest in Alma, Michigan, to the Scots of Alma College, 29-20, at Bahlke Field.

Week four saw Findlay again take to the road against perennial power Ashland University at Community Stadium. When the Oilers boarded the bus after their long afternoon, they made the return to Findlay on the short side of a 33-14 tally, despite Jamie Horn's second straight 100-yard rushing game, dropping their record to the same it had been after four weeks the previous season, 1-3.

But, then something happened. Perhaps some might call it "gut check time." Strahm knew before the season started that there would be challenges, as his Oilers were home for only four out of their ten contests. "We were doing some things well. The offensive line was certainly opening some holes, and both Brown and Horn were running strong. Wimberly was making some progress, although making some typical freshman mistakes.

"I thought the next two weeks were absolutely critical because we would stay on the road for a third and fourth consecutive week, at Muskingum and at Tennessee Wesleyan. We just had to summon, what you might call, a bunker mentality, kind of an us-against-the-world mindset, to get this thing turned around."

In week five, the Oilers did bounce back, winning a tight contest against Muskingum, 16-10. Strahm had rolled the dice and went with Bob Sutyak at quarterback, and he performed capably, completing 9 of 17 for 123 yards and a touchdown.

Week six brought Strahm's troops into Athens, Tennessee, and the Oilers pounded out a convincing 41-6 victory. Wimberly returned to his starting role, and Horn averaged almost nine yards a tote in the convincing win.

After the brutal stretch of four consecutive road contests, in week seven, the Oilers proved home cooking to their liking and pounded out a 51-0 win over Tiffin University. Defensive coordinator Ray Kwiatkowski must have been pleased with his unit's first whitewash of the year.

His defense was gaining confidence and had yielded just 16 points in its last twelve quarters, after they had been torched for 97 points in the three consecutive losses to Westminster, Alma, and Ashland.

Andre Roberts intercepted a pass for the third consecutive game, and, on offense, Doug Brown had his best game of the season thus far, as he rambled for 211 yards.

In week eight, at Urbana University, both offense and defense again were dominant in a 66-7 rout. While Roberts failed to make it four straight games with a pick, London Rogan more than made up for it with his two interceptions.

Offensively, Doug Brown had his second straight dominant game, rushing for 178 yards on just 12 carries (14.8 yards per) and three touchdowns.

In week nine, in Detroit, the Oilers won a good, old-fashioned shootout, 36-30, against Wayne State University, for their fifth straight, erasing the thoughts of the 1-3 start.

Brown completed one of the most impressive three-game runs in Findlay history, running for another 222 yards to make it 611 yards in the three straight games.

Heading into week ten, Strahm knew his team's chances for a return to the playoffs were nonexistent. The three consecutive losses early in the year proved too much to overcome.

However, there was plenty of motivation for Strahm. It was not only a chance to finish 7-3 but also an opportunity to match *X's* and *O's* with long-time coaching rival, Dr. Bill Ramseyer of Wilmington College, an old Hoosier-Buckeye rival and a team like Findlay, which by that time was playing as an independent.

During the practices immediately preceding the November 11 contest, there was a moment involving the freshman quarterback out of Hollywood, Florida that Strahm remembers well. "In the later stages of a mid-week practice, we were scrimmaging, and DeMya brought his team out. When he settled under center, he slowly came back up to an erect position and took a step back and looked up into the sky. It was the first time in his life he had ever seen something. Snow!"

The University of Findlay did end its season with a win, finishing strong for a sixth straight win. In what proved to be the final contest between two giants in small-college coaching, Strahm's Oilers bested Ramseyer's Quakers, 28-20, behind a career game by the player so captivated by the mid-week snow flurry.

DeMya Wimberly completed 7 of 9 passes for 204 yards and four touchdowns. His favorite receiver was James Tyree who snagged four passes for 211 yards and three of the TD tosses.

The offense absolutely jelled in the second half of the season, averaging 41 points a game during the six-game streak. Wimberly started nine of the ten games and would return in 1990 as a seasoned sophomore.

In all, the two coaches in 1989's final contest faced each other twelve times, with Strahm's teams winning seven. Ramseyer would remain at Wilmington a final season in 1990, but his schedule would not include Strahm's team.

By the time Ramseyer would leave to begin a brand new football program at the University of Virginia's College at Wise, another NAIA school located in Norton, Virginia, he certainly had left his mark on Wilmington football. In fifteen seasons, Ramseyer's Quakers went 114-58-4, good for a .660 winning percentage.

Prior to his arrival at Wilmington in 1976, the school's football program had registered just 28 total wins in the previous fifteen years. When Ramseyer finally retired after eleven more seasons at Wise, where he carved an impressive 62-45 mark, Dr. Bill left ranked third all-time nationally in career wins and ninth in winning percentage.

Certainly, Strahm had bounced back from the 3-6 season with the 7-3 mark, a record which included that six-game winning streak. Doug Brown, thanks in large part to that monstrous three-game run, was the team's leading rusher, gaining 1,153 yards and averaging 6.4 yards per carry. Brown's fifteen touchdowns also made him, with 90 points, the team's leading scorer.

While Brown, the senior out of Miamisburg, Ohio, would be missed, Strahm was comforted in the knowledge that not only would the ultra-durable Jamie Horn be returning for his final year but sophomore-to-be Nathan Sprunger was developing fast.

With his players engaged in their off-season conditioning under the watchful eyes of strength coach Mike Ward and full-time trainer Vi LeClaire at the Gardner Fitness Center, Strahm and his coaches went about the business of breaking down film, discussing personnel, and, of course, recruiting. For college football coaches, the staff had learned long ago that there really is no off-season.

One decision Strahm had reached was to tap into both the athleticism and mental acuity of Bob Sutyak. Recalls Strahm, "Bob was simply too valuable to just serve as a backup to DeMya, our quarterback. I had already decided there would be no quarterback competition come August of 1990, and I just had to find a way to get Bobby on the field.

"I called him into my office and told him there was no question he could be a fine quarterback, but I felt our best chance to be successful was to keep Wimberly at that position.

"I told Bob that his greatest strengths were his mobility and his natural grasp of football. He was, in many ways, a lot like Tim Beckman.

"I pitched the idea that he become our starting free safety on defense, replacing the graduating Andre Roberts. Despite the fact that Roberts had intercepted thirteen passes in his last two years and had just been named an All-American for his performance his senior season, I really believed Sutyak could be just as good.

"Well, a lot of players would maybe have sulked about being asked to switch positions, especially a glamour position like quarterback, but Bob took to the idea immediately.

"He simply said to me, 'Coach, I'll be your free safety. DeMya can quarterback the offense, and I'll be your quarterback on defense.'

"And, I'll tell you something. Both of those young men were very, very smart. So, I had two leaders who would make excellent decisions, one on each side of the ball."

In early July of 1990, Dick's mother, Mildred, was making plans to fly to Athens, Georgia, to visit her son Dale and his family. The spry and strong 79-year-old still lived unassisted in her hometown of Toledo.

But, life has a way of changing quickly, especially for those who have seen many sunrises and sunsets. While her older son Dick was preparing to take care of some long overdue yard work, his phone rang.

Recalls Dick, "When I picked up the phone, I recognized the voice of one of my mom's neighbors. She told me that Mom had collapsed at home and was being transported to the hospital. Immediately, I called Dale, and he dropped everything and prepared to drive to Toledo."

Ginger and Dick drove to Toledo and got to the hospital. After seeing Mom for a few moments and squeezing her hand for reassurance, Dick and Ginger met with the doctor. He said that Mildred Strahm had sustained an aneurism. While brain surgery is always risky, it is even more so for the elderly. Nonetheless, he said it was really the only chance for survival.

And so, with her son's consent, Mildred underwent surgery. Sadly, it was unsuccessful. She was placed on life support as Dick and Ginger waited for Dale and his wife, Diane, to arrive.

Early the next day, Dale arrived, and both he and Dick agreed that their mother would not wish to be sustained by artificial means. Recalls Dick, "Of course, it was a very difficult time for us, as it is for all children who have to say good bye to a parent. Mom was such a strong woman and had handled living on her own so well for so many years after my dad died. I just knew it was best to let her join my father in heaven rather than have her linger, kept alive only by a machine. So, Dale and I said our goodbyes and made the decision to release her to the Lord."

The rest of July passed, and the sense of loss subsided a bit for Dick as another season loomed just ahead. Recalls Dick, "In a way, I was glad the season was approaching. When you're dealing with the sorrow of losing a parent, I think it helps to have work to keep your mind occupied."

In the early part of August, The University of Findlay president, Ken Zirkle, decided that he had a place to offer the Findlay football coaching staff to really concentrate on the intensive meetings to prepare for the upcoming season.

Recalls Zirkle, "I felt my farm in Pennsylvania was really a great place for Dick and his staff to have their pre-two-a-day meetings, so I made it available to them, starting that summer and from that point on each early August.

As expected, Strahm was grateful. "It was such a great place for us to meet. It gave us a chance to get completely away from all the distractions back at Findlay and just concentrate on meeting all day, each day over a long weekend. We got so much done. Then, in the evening we sat out on this big deck that came off the house, and it was so peaceful and relaxing.

"Ken's allowing us to use that farm is yet another example of what a strong advocate he was of athletics. What a terrific friend he was and still is to college athletics."

As far as the composition of the 1990 coaching staff, Coate, McIntosh, Kwiatkowski, Davidson, Gilbert, and Ward all returned. Joining the staff was part-time coach Randy Hausfeld, a key four-year performer at linebacker for Strahm's teams from 1985 through 1988.

Among the notable recruits coming in as freshmen for the season, players who would listen to Strahm's famous "your-best-friend-is-taking-care-of-your-girlfriend" speech, were Ben Cochran (Springfield, Ohio), Mike Collett (Xenia, Ohio), Andre Roach (Painesville, Ohio), and Scott Garlock, a hometown Findlay High School graduate who became the head coach at Liberty-Benton High School. Scott had great success at Liberty-Benton and is now the backfield coach at The University of Findlay.

Typical of life as an independent, the 1990 Oilers yet again would see schools for the very first time, a challenge that presented itself with regularity. Yet there were also some schools with which Strahm was beginning to gain some degree of familiarity.

The 1990 season opened with Tennessee Wesleyan College visiting Donnell Stadium. In a game similar in some respects to the 41-5 Oilers win the previous year, Findlay burst from the gate, recording a 39-0 shutout.

Emerging linebacker Bob Heitkamp certainly did his part as the sophomore out of New Bremen, Ohio, returning an interception 49 yards for a touchdown. Senior halfback Horn had a terrific game, rushing 20 times for 169 yards and four touchdowns.

In week two, the Oilers traveled to Georgetown College where the Oilers dropped a close 21-14 to even their record at a win apiece.

Week three brought the only other verdict possible after the first two games, a 23-23 tie against visiting Hope College out of Holland, Michigan. It was a game Dick Strahm still feels should have put the Oilers at 2-1, instead of 1-1-1. "We had a touchdown called back on a holding call, one I still believe was questionable. Rarely is a tie fulfilling, and this one certainly wasn't. I guess if you're looking for firsts, it was the first and only time I was ever the coach of a team that went 1-1-1 in the first three games of a season."

Bob Heitkamp kept his nose for the football, picking off passes in his second and third straight games.

After the puzzling start, the Oilers caught fire in much the same way as they had in the last six games of 1989, matching that year's six-game winning streak.

First, week four saw Findlay board the buses for Frankfort, Kentucky, to play Kentucky State University, and they returned with a thrilling 20-19 win. Cornerback Jeff Nagy got his first career Oiler interception, and Horn proved to be Findlay's workingman's hero. Many of his 25 carries and 97 yards were between the tackles and moved the chains.

Week five brought a new team to town, the Kalamazoo (Michigan) College Hornets. After the previous week's one-point win, The University of Findlay sure could have used a comfortable win, and that's exactly what happened as it cruised, 42-0. Cornerback London Rogan picked off a couple of passes, Horn rushed for 137 yards on 16 carries, and Wimberly completed 4 of 7 for two TDs.

In week six, yet another new school rolled into Findlay to take on the Oilers. Northwood University, out of Midland, Michigan, fell to Strahm's squad, 31-6, as London Rogan picked off two more passes and Horn rushed for 142 yards on 29 carries and two scores.

Week seven saw Findlay at home for the third straight Saturday against Geneva College, from Beaver Falls, Pennsylvania. The Oilers won a fourth in a row, 31-20, and Strahm saw one of his young and talented sophomores emerge. Bob Sutyak was instrumental in the win, as he picked off his first two passes of his Oilers career out of his free safety position. On the down side, Jamie Horn suffered a severe ankle injury and was doubtful for the next game. This certainly was big news, as the senior had started every game since game one of his freshman year.

Week eight had Strahm's team finally leaving the friendly confines of Donnell for a road contest against Tiffin University. Rogan grabbed another interception in the 24-3 win. But, the real man of the hour on that October 20 was DeMya Wimberly, who had his best all-round performance to date. The sophomore both threw for 100 yards (6 of 11 for 112) and ran for 100 (16 carries for 115 yards) in a convincing win.

Jamie Horn sat on the bench with a heavily taped ankle, unable to play. Sadly, the streak of consecutive starts was over.

Meanwhile, a player who had paid his dues since 1986, Coach Jim McIntosh's son Bill, continued to demonstrate a great skill package and a lot of heart as the Oilers' starting center. Recalls Strahm, "I was extremely proud of Bill and the way that he bounced back from his medical redshirt year in 1989. He took his place right along side a number of excellent Oilers centers, players like Dave Berger and Ryan Sbrissa. In the 1990s, more great centers would arrive, players like Dan Frank and Chad Ulm.

"Bill's forté was his toughness. I remember he broke a bone in his foot his senior year, and he refused to let the foot be placed in a cast.

"He told me, his dad and the doctor that he had waited too long to be a starter to let anything keep him off the field. When doctors assured us that he could play and incur no additional damage as long as he had the foot heavily taped and he did a lot of icing after games and practices, and, of course, as long as he could tolerate the pain, the decision was made.

"There were games he'd get his foot stepped on. He'd almost crawl off the field. Then after we'd gotten some ice on it for a few minutes and re-tape him, he couldn't wait to get back out there."

Week nine saw the Oilers return home and also Jamie Horn return to the field. Despite his still being severely limited by the ankle injury, the gritty senior from Millersburg, Ohio, found a way to contribute. Sophomore Nathan Sprunger stepped up, broke off several dazzling runs on an eight-carry, 105-yard effort, and the Oilers had their sixth straight, a 44-17 win over the Urbana University Blue Knights.

Recalls Strahm, "It had been a long time [1985] since we'd been in the playoffs, and, after we beat Urbana, we had that opportunity. If we won our last game, we were in.

"But, you talk about a tall mountain to climb. All we had to do was go on the road and play Coach Joe Fusco's Westminster Titans, back-to-back defending NAIA national championships and a team that had just come off a 27-game winning streak."

After a season-opening one-point loss to Northwood, the Titans were undefeated. In their last 33 games, they were 32-1. Recalls Jamie Horn, "With the ankle injury, I was probably only about 60 percent, but I also knew a win would take me someplace I'd never been, the playoffs. So, I told our trainers to tape extra tight to try to give me a bit more stability, and I was going to give it a shot."

Unfortunately, Horn's and the rest of the Oilers' best shots weren't quite good enough. On what proved to be the final game of the autumn of 1990, the Titans prevailed, 24-7.

For the Titans, their march continued as they won their season's finale the following week and then kept winning in the playoffs, winding up in the title game for an unprecedented third straight year, a game they eventually lost to finish the season at 11-2.

Recalls Horn about the last game of his wonderful Oilers career, "We had so many sophomores on the field that last Saturday, and that was the group that wound up as seniors in 1992 winning their own national championship.

"So, it really was a bittersweet day for me. While I was disappointed in losing and not getting to the post-season, I was proud of how we had rebounded after my first two years.

"I was proud to help lead the way for guys like DeMya and Todd Clark and Bob Sutyak. I knew they had the potential to go a long way. I was just sad I wouldn't be there with them when they achieved what I felt they could.

"As far as the rest of my feelings, I knew it was the last time I would play for Coach Strahm. I wished so much I hadn't hurt my ankle, so I could give him the kind of game a coach like that deserves.

"He's, no doubt, one of the biggest influences in my life. He was the type of coach who could make you play above your abilities. I think he instilled that in me. I don't know how many times I heard him challenge players by saying, 'Show me something that I don't think you can do!'

"He always was raising the bar, and, as a father, which is the most important job I'll ever have in my life, I try to do the same thing with my own kids."

Horn, after The University of Findlay graduation, finally felt the strength in his ankle return to pursue a dream of playing professionally.

In 1991, when his ankle had, he felt, recovered, Horn tried out for the Hamilton Tiger-Cats of the Canadian Football League. To show that the tentacles of the Findlay football program went in many directions, Horn, a stay-at-home dad who proudly refers to himself as "Mr. Mom," points out that his head coach in Canada was Dave Beckman, Tim's father. Horn made the team.

However, the nagging ankle injury returned, forcing Horn to finally submit to surgery in the winter of 1991. After rehab, he had tryouts with both the Steelers and the Chargers of the NFL before finally realizing football, while wonderful while it lasts, is really not a lifetime career.

To this day, not many months go by without Jamie Horn picking up the phone to talk to his old Coach, Dick Strahm. "I need to hear his voice even now, a couple decades after I last played for him. He's a fighter, and that's the thing I admire most about him. He's preached, 'Don't let little things get you down. Now, his little things, you understand, have been things like heart attacks and strokes and cancer, things that are catastrophic to others. Yet, that's the man he is. Is it any wonder I still feel the need to call him even now?"

Just as it had been with Bill Ramseyer in 1989, the 1990 finale against Westminster marked the last time Dick Strahm would coach against Joe Fusco.

While Findlay would continue to engage Westminster in the decade of the 1990s, Fusco left his coaching position at the end of the '90 season with four national championships and a career mark of 154-34-3, and a phenomenal .814 winning percentage. In 2001 he would precede Strahm into the College Football Hall of Fame. Fusco continued as Westminster's athletic director through 1999, while his long-time assistant, Gene Nicholson, assumed the coaching duties in 1991.

Following the 1990 season, offensive tackle Tim Russ was named both a Kodak and an Associated Press All-American. Sophomore linebacking sensation Bob Heitkamp also was selected as an Honorable Mention All-American and, thereby, aligning himself as a pre-season All-American for 1991.

By the end of 1990, there was a plethora of talented and seasoned juniors-to-be, ready to take the next step up in the second halves of their careers.

They were shown the Oilers way of doing things by players like Joe Moorefield and Chuck Hale and Ryan Sbrissa and Jamie Horn in much the same way as there were once players like Dave Danhoff and Gene Fernandez and Jerome Gray and Kevin Cassidy, who showed a talented group of underclassmen the Oilers way of the late 1970s.

The birth of the 1990s was an awakening in the same way each new decade gives a promise that, by its end, a legacy will have been written. Sure, there was a sense of optimism for the new decade, but could anyone have predicted that the greatest decade in the history of the Findlay football Oilers was just over the next horizon?

Oilers players Chad Mosley, Dan Franks, Todd Allen, Ray Jackson, John Ferguson, Howard Heston wait patiently for their banquet dinner in Hamburg, Germany.

Captains of the 1992 national championship team: (first row) DeMya Wimberly and Nate Sprunger; and (second row) Dave Wolfe and Bob Heitkamp.

Chapter 14

National Champions Again...

As the 1991 season approached, The University of Findlay football coach Dick Strahm liked what he saw. Not only had the terrific recruiting class of 1989 matured and would be arriving to August camp as field-tested juniors but there were also reinforcements ready to make the Oilers' picture more complete.

Balewa Walker, the 5'11," 260-pound bruiser of a fullback had returned to Findlay. The former Joliet Junior College standout had overcome the sorrow of his grandfather's passing and some other personal issues and was now ready for the first of his two years of eligibility.

Another player Strahm felt fortunate to have back for his senior year was the transfer from Urbana University, Matt Maglicic. The 6'0," 200-pound defensive end had been named Urbana's Most Valuable Player as a sophomore and then became an instant contributor in his first year as an Oiler in 1990, recording 73 tackles, including 11 resulting in losses.

Maglicic also showed the kind of versatility that defines what a collegiate student-athlete should be. In 1990, Maglicic was selected as an NAIA Academic All-American and had every intention of making the most of his final year, both on the football field and in the lecture halls on UF's campus.

As for Strahm's assistants, there were no departures from the previous year's staff. Ray Kwiatkowski was returning for his ninth season as the defensive coordinator. The Philadelphia native would continue to make the lengthy drive from Bedford High School just over the Ohio-Michigan line at the end of his teaching day.

Jim McIntosh also was returning for his fifteenth season. He and Curtis Davidson, who was entering his sixth season on Strahm's staff, would coach the offensive line.

Doug Coate was ready for his seventh season under Strahm. The former Oilers quarterback who guided his teams to back-to-back 8-1 seasons in 1982 and 1983 would coach the offensive backs.

Mike Ward was returning for his sixth season, not only coaching the linebackers but also serving as the strength coach for a team with some very serious-minded weightlifters.

Greg Gilbert was ready for his fourth season, serving as a defensive line coach. Gilbert to this day remains with the university, now serving as the assistant athletic director in charge of academics. Recalls Gilbert, "I was very blessed to have players like Erich Brandstadt [defensive tackle, from Vermilion, Ohio] and Matt Maglicic to coach. When you combine athletic ability with intensity and intelligence, as these young men did, well, you just feel blessed to be in coaching."

Sam Bello was the lone newcomer to the staff. A former Oilers player in the 1960s, he was set to coach the defensive ends. Bello, who still lives in Findlay and is a math teacher at Findlay High School, remembers well the quality of the staff he was joining. "Dick had really assembled a fine group of coaches, and I felt extremely fortunate to be joining such a group. Coaches tend to move around a lot, but the fact that there were guys on that staff who'd been with Dick for anywhere from a half dozen years all the way on up to fifteen years speaks for itself. That's a strong endorsement for both the quality of the program and to Dick as well."

As far as new personnel, several freshmen showed up in August, and by the time their Oilers careers drew to a close, they would be key performers. Some, like John Ferguson, the running back out of Yspsilanti, Michigan; Jamie Godman, the linebacker-defensive end out of Lorain, Ohio; and Kent Pelligrini, the tight end transfer out of Joliet Junior College, would play big roles almost immediately.

In the 1991 class, there also was an arrival that Dick Strahm remembers well. "Scott McLaughlin was an instant contributor and actually wound up leading our team in receptions as a freshman, in addition to returning both punts and kickoffs for us.

"I remember I took a recruiting trip to Florida in the spring of 1990. I met Scott and his dad [Bill] at a donut shop on Route 41 in Naples, Florida. I knew about Scott because he played at Barron Collier High School, where Dave Tanner, my former defensive coordinator back in 1978, was the head coach.

"Pipelines are important in college recruiting, and I was fortunate to have one open with Dave. We really did get a lot of fine players from the Naples region, and a lot of that was because of Dave's help.

"When I met with Scott and his father, Scott told me he thought he could play Mid-American Conference football. Now, understand, Scott was only about 5'9" and around 170 pounds. I figured he'd make us a great receiver, but, at his size, I had my doubts about his playing in the MAC.

"But, whenever I heard a player I was recruiting tell me he wanted to play Division I, I really didn't try to talk him out of it. I always figured if a player felt that way, why not let him go and give it a try? Scott said he wanted to try and walk on at Bowling Green.

"I wished him all the luck in the world. I also told him that if he didn't make it, remember we here at Findlay really wanted him and would love to have him transfer."

Well, Scott went to Bowling Green and, practiced with the team the entire season, but as a redshirt. He was being considered for a scholarship to play as a sophomore. Then, something happened that started the process of his eventually becoming an Oiler. Recalls McLaughlin, who now lives in Wharton, New Jersey, and works as a sales center manager for Coca-Cola, "After the season, there was a coaching change, and when that happens, basically, the whole staff changes. It became evident to me that I would not be considered for a scholarship and would have to start all over again proving myself the next season, so I wrote Coach Strahm a letter right after I finished spring ball at BG.

"He was very enthusiastic about my coming aboard. When I made a campus visit and spoke with him, I told him I expected to start as a freshman. I told him I still thought I could play in the MAC and was in line to be given a scholarship at BG until the coaching change. But, I didn't want to have to wait until I was a junior to get on the field.

"Coach looked at me and told me that I would get every opportunity to prove myself. He was not about to make any promises, at least the one I kind of wanted him to make. He made it clear to me that there'd be no handouts, that I would have to earn the position.

"Looking back, I really appreciated that. It was, what you might call, chapter one of Coach's "You-earn-what-you-get-in-life" book. So, despite no guarantees, I decided to transfer, so I would be ready in August of '91.

And, when August two-a-days arrived, it didn't take long for Coach Dick Strahm to realize what he had in McLaughlin. "Not only did he have great hands but he was also so quick. During our first 40-yard sprints, I noticed for the first 20 yards, the zone that is so important for wide-outs to get some separation from the secondary, he was running step for step with Milan Smith, the fastest guy we had."

Another newcomer who would become an instant contributor was Tony Holland. Holland, from Washington Court House, Ohio, attended Urbana University and earned two letters before coming to Findlay as a tight end. With Kent Pelligrini and Holland, Strahm felt comfortable that the tight end position, especially the blocking portion of it so vital to the back side of the wishbone unbalanced line, would be well manned.

Remembers Strahm, "When you run an unbalanced line and place both offensive tackles on one side, all you have is the center and the backside guard and the tight end opposite your overload. So, you really need a dominant blocking presence over on that back side for the offense to work."

Other key offensive linemen set for big years were back side guard Tom Forys, the huge 320-pounder out of Lockport, Illinois: junior center Doug Kramer, Bob Heitkamp's former junior high and high school teammate from New Bremen, Ohio; back-side guard Dave Wolf, a junior out of Toledo Whitmer High School; strong-side guard Chris Cotterill, a junior from Amherst, Ohio; and inside tackle Jason Stofel, from Delaware, Ohio.

Coach Strahm remembers it was Stofel who really understood the commitment it takes an offensive lineman to getting stronger. "Jason was about 6'3," 287, and was very intense in the weight room over at the Gardner Fitness Center. My strength coach, Mike Ward, kept me updated on the results of all the players' lifting. He'd told me that Jason was bench pressing close to 400 pounds, which was outstanding for a small-college lineman.

"We had so many of our players who committed totally to our weight program. Balewa Walker and DeMya Wimberly could squat 660 pounds. And, guys like Cal Dietz and Nate Arnold were absolute beasts in the weight room as well."

The Findlay head coach also thought that junior quarterback DeMya Wimberly had some nice targets in Todd Pees, the sophomore out of Dunkirk, Ohio, to go along with the freshman, Scott McLaughlin.

When it was time to hand the ball off, which is often in a wishbone offense, Strahm felt comfortable with the likes of Balewa Walker, Andre Roach, and Nathan Sprunger, and, of course, his change-of-pace speed back, Milan Smith.

As for the unsung hero in the wishbone backfield, the blocking back called the two-back, a player who would be given few carries, Strahm felt he had found a gritty one. He was Doug Rode, out of Delphos, Ohio. Recalls Rode, who now works for DR Railcar and resides in Findlay, "People ask me a lot if I had any ill feelings about not getting very many carries in our offense, and I tell them absolutely not. I was just happy to be playing. I lettered as a freshman and started my last three years and feel so very fortunate to have done so. To me, *blocking* was never a dirty word!"

Defensively, linebacker Bob Heitkamp, the team's leading tackler as a sophomore in 1990, led a tenacious group. His linebacking mate, Todd Clark, from Lima, Ohio, was also a terrific player. As a sophomore he registered 112 tackles, including 11 for losses, and is a player coach Ray Kwiatkowski remembers so fondly. "Listen, I know a lot of the headlines went to Bobby Heitkamp, and deservedly so because he was truly an outstanding linebacker. But, I don't want anyone to forget how good Todd Clark was."

In front of the linebackers were the likes of Matt Maglicic; Chris Smith, the junior out of Fremont, Ohio; Mike Collett, the sophomore from Xenia, Ohio; and junior Erich Brandstadt.

Behind the linebackers were experienced safeties and cornerbacks, led by the quarterback of the defense, free safety Bob Sutyak. Shane Dennison, another player from Naples, Florida, would start at strong safety. At the corners were Curtis Armstrong from Ohio's capital city of Columbus, and Jeff Nagy, from Maumee, Ohio.

The season opened on a positive note with a thrilling 17-14 win at Hope College, in Holland, Michigan. Nathan Sprunger ran for 123 yards, and DeMya Wimberly played very efficiently, completing 8 of 12 passes, including one for a touchdown to Scott McLaughlin in the very first game of his memorable Oilers career.

In week two, unfortunately for Strahm, the Westminster jinx continued even though the Titan head coach Joe Fusco had stepped away from the sidelines at the end of the previous season. The former defensive coordinator and new head coach Gene Nicholson, brought his squad to Donnell Stadium and ruined the Oilers' home opener, shutting out the hosts, 21-0. Quite simply, the Oilers couldn't mount any type of offensive attack. In a run-dominant offense like the wishbone, Balewa Walker's 57 yards on 13 carries was hardly the type of number that should make the beefy three-back the leading rusher.

Nonetheless, in week three Findlay rebounded nicely. The Oilers overwhelmed Lindenwood College after their lengthy bus ride to St. Charles, Missouri, 35-2. Despite a game where the junior signal caller DeMya Wimberly struggled, completing just 2 of 8 and throwing an interception, the Oilers prevailed, thanks to a stout defensive line, a key interception by Sutyak, and the fresh legs of the pride of Pandora, Ohio, Nate Sprunger, who ran for 112 yards on 17 totes.

Week four found the Oilers at home to entertain the Kentucky State Thoroughbreds. When the early October sun began to sink in the western skies, the home team was a 22-6 winner. The unsung two-back, Doug Rode, had two big catches for 53 yards, and Mike Collett fulfilled a defensive lineman's dream, returning an interception 25 yards for a touchdown.

Week five saw Findlay on the road to Midland, Michigan, for an encounter with Northwood Institute. While the offense was having its troubles, the defense dominated in a 10-0 whitewashing. Curtis Armstrong did his part with an interception. Offensively, DeMya Wimberly completed 10 of 18 for 88 yards and also ran for an additional 94 yards on 16 carries in the win. The big tight end, Tony Holland, grabbed three balls.

At 4-1, Strahm's Oilers were feeling pretty good about themselves as they boarded buses for another road game, this time to Geneva College, in Beaver Falls, Pennsylvania. Recalls Strahm, "We were a little banged up, but I can't really use that as an excuse. We just didn't play very well and lost a close one, 16-13.

In the loss, Todd Pees, the second cousin of former Strahm assistant and current defensive coordinator of the New England Patriots, Dean Pees, had a breakout game, grabbing seven Wimberly passes for 83 yards. Milan Smith also showed some electrifying moves on a 92-yard kickoff return for a touchdown, but it just wasn't enough.

Back home in week seven for a date with the Tiffin University Dragons, the Oilers rebounded with a 23-6 win, thanks in no small part to a pair of interceptions for do-everything linebacker Bob Heikamp.

Heitkamp's story is certainly inspirational. In addition to battling on the field by shedding blockers and executing bone-crushing tackles, Heitkamp also conducted an ongoing battle against a chronic disease.

Crohn's disease, a lifelong inflammatory disease that affects both the small and the large intestine and causes severe stomach pain, diarrhea, and vomiting, was Heitkamp's constant enemy.

Certainly, teammates were aware of the condition. Recalls running back Milan Smith, who now runs Mint Condition Mobile Cleaning, a car-detailing company, in addition to managing several apartment units and coaching football at Harvest Prep High School in Columbus, Ohio, "Bob Heitkamp was a phenomenal athlete. He never, ever used his medical condition as an excuse. It was like, 'No big deal. I'll just overcome it.' I just couldn't believe how hard he could hit you.

"In 1990, I wasn't eligible to play, but I did run for the scout team, so I know firsthand the type of lick Bob could put on a running back.

"When I'd go home to Columbus and get with some of my former high school teammates who were playing football at other colleges, I'd tell them that I was playing with a D-I linebacker that somehow wound up at an NAIA school. I just couldn't figure out why he wasn't playing big-time college football. I honestly believe if he didn't have Crohn's, he could have played professionally."

Heitkamp, who still is living in New Bremen and owns a farm as well as working with swine at the Farmers' Co-op, looks as if he could still step on the field and deliver a near-lethal blow to an unsuspecting running back. Recalls the two-time NAIA All-American, "I just didn't want something like Crohn's to dictate what I could do. Look, I didn't ask for it and really had little control over it, but I also wasn't about to let its impose its will on me and make me any less than the best I could be."

Week eight saw the Oilers on the road in their home state to Urbana University to play the Blue Knights at Evans Stadium. The Knights were struggling under head coach Don Akers, and the struggles continued that early November Saturday as the Oilers scored early and often and ran off with a 62-9 win.

While the defense shone, especially Jeff Nagy, Des May, and Jamie Godman, who all picked off a pass, it was Nathan Sprunger who ignited the offense with a 157-yard rushing performance and two touchdowns.

While the win was nice, it did come at a cost. The big sophomore offensive tackle out of Allen East High School, Tim Goodwin, suffered a compound fracture of his leg. He would be lost for not only the remainder of the season but also would not be medically cleared to play in 1992, either.

Recalls Goodwin, now a high school math teacher and one of the premier head football coaches in the state of Ohio at Marion Local High School, where he has won four state championships, "While I was disappointed to not be able to come back in 1992, Coach Strahm did make me a student assistant, which helped me stay connected to the team.

"That's something that Coach Strahm did extremely well, create that family atmosphere. Look, I wasn't really a star by any means, just a sophomore trying to make some sort of impression in mop-up duty. It would have been easy to forget about me, but Coach didn't. He made a place for me and much of what I picked up in that '92 season from watching him was absolutely invaluable when I began my own coaching career after I graduated from Findlay."

For the leading ball carrier that day, Nate Sprunger, the key to his success was always his work ethic. Recalls Dick Strahm, "I'll tell you something about Nate Sprunger. He worked just as hard in practice as he did in games. You hear that some about players, but, more often than not, there is somewhat of a drop off in practice for even hard-working players, but that simply was not the case with Sprunger."

Now an insurance agent at Sprunger Insurance in his hometown of Pandora, Ohio, Sprunger saw his effort on the football field as something more than just sports. "My parents taught me very early to work hard at everything I do. So, when I played, I tried to carry that same determination into the backfield. I felt every time I carried the ball, it was a tribute to my parents for what they instilled in me."

In week nine, Findlay was home to play American International College, a team of Yellow Jackets who came in all the way from Springfield, Massachusetts. Recalls Strahm, "Really, we knew very little about American International. Again, when you're a small-college independent, you sometimes have to go a long way out of your geographical comfort zone to find games. Even getting film on a team was difficult at times, but we were able to exchange films with American International.

"This was a one-year contract. I remember they were a non-scholarship NCAA Division III school, and they were very good. We really had to bring our best that day."

The Oilers' best proved to be good enough as they won a tight one, 17-14. Wimberly had his best passing game of the year, completing 12 of 19 for 149 yards and two TD strikes. The freshman Scott McLaughlin accounted for 100 yards receiving on just three catches and a touchdown. Wimberly's other TD toss was an 18-yarder to two-back Doug Rode.

Recalls Strahm, "I remember that Friday evenings, during our team meetings, DeMya was the one selected to speak to the team. Although he's only about 5'7," he had such a huge presence and commanded so much respect.

"Let me tell you something. That Friday when he got up to speak, that room got just like those old E.F. Hutton commercials. Everyone just fell silent, and the guys leaned forward.

"DeMya didn't speak much, but when he did speak, people wanted to hear what he had to say, including the coaches."

Wimberly, who remained in Ohio after his playing days at Findlay came to a conclusion, is now a supervisor at the Lucas County Youth Treatment Center outside Toledo and remembers his class of 1989 as the players became a close-knit group. "When I arrived in 1989, I could see there was some finger pointing when things went wrong between the offense and the defense.

"We were determined that wasn't what we wanted to be all about. I remember there were times when I would fumble a snap from Kramer [Doug] or throw an interception and I'd be coming off the field, and the defense would be shouting encouragement to me."

Recalls Wimberly's center, Kramer, who now lives in New Bremen and works as a plant coordinator at Hitachi Metals, "I learned about the importance of sticking together no matter what was happening out on the field early, and I just don't mean my first two years at Findlay.

"Remember, Bob Heitkamp and I had played together since we were in junior high, and he and I both knew the offense and the defense absolutely had to support one another.

The last game of the regular season saw the Oilers on a very long road trip all the way to Banner Elk, North Carolina, to play the Bobcats of Lees-McRae College.

Recalls Strahm, "This was another of those games so far out of our geographical zone that it posed all sorts of difficulties. I remember we left very early on Friday morning, around seven. We'd packed sandwiches to eat on the way, and we also stopped about 15 miles outside of Banner Elk at a cafeteria for our team meal.

"By the time we checked into the hotel, it was around 8:30 and we had to hustle to get our team meeting in and then get everyone settled in. You talk about one long day bouncing over those roads!

"The next day we did win, 20-14, but we were very fortunate because we played as if we were still on the bus! Sometimes on those long road trips by bus it is easy to lose focus."

Fortunately, for Strahm and the Oilers, Nathan Sprunger brought his "A" game as he rushed for 183 yards on 23 carries and scored twice.

Recalls Milan Smith, Sprunger's change-of-pace speed back, "As soon as I saw Nate, in 1990 when I was running with the scout team and getting my grades in order, I knew I'd have to wait my turn. I would have to settle in and play second fiddle to a player I feel is one of the best backs Findlay's ever had.

"While we weren't best friends, we respected one another totally. I think one of Coach Strahm's greatest strengths is he knew how far to push guys competition-wise so that there was respect.

"And, that's what he did with Nathan and me. Coach knew we had to come together for a common cause. I try to use the same techniques in my coaching now.

Recalls Sprunger, "Listen, Milan Smith brought the type of speed to the table I didn't possess, and he made me better in much the same way I knew I made Jamie Horn better in 1990."

The Oilers had finished the regular season at 8-2 and eagerly awaited the news that they had indeed made the playoffs. Findlay had waited a long time to wash the aftertaste from their mouths of that difficult Pac Lutheran loss in 1985.

There was cause for jubilation when word came down that Findlay had indeed made the playoffs. The fact that the opponent would be the perennially strong Westminster Titans, a team that had a fairly long history of thwarting the Oilers, only deepened Strahm's resolve to overcome this substantial obstacle.

One thing that would be working in the Oilers' favor is the school's administration submitted the winning bid and Findlay would host the first-round game on November 23 at Donnell.

When word came down that Findlay would host the contest, some of Strahm's old motivational creative juices started to flow, as he searched for a way to give his team some type of psychological edge.

This time, it wasn't something as elaborate as having his wife Ginger stitch players' names on pairs of pink panties or making plans to have hanging in each player's locker a new jersey with the proclamation, "We Will Win!" when the team came back in after pre-game warm-ups for final instructions on game day.

Instead, it was a little story Strahm told his troops early in the practice week. Recalls Des May, then a sophomore defensive back and now a mortgage loan officer for Fifth Third Bank, "I remember Coach Strahm telling us that Westminster only had bid a dollar to host the game because they were saving money to host the second-round game.

"I guess it never occurred to us how he would know the amount, since the bid process was sealed, but we believed him. We were so angry that Westminster would disrespect us like that, thinking they could just roll out of bed and beat us on our own field!"

Todd Pees, then an excellent sophomore wide receiver and now a sales representative for United Solutions, remembers Strahm's preaching something repeatedly as the practice week unfolded. "Coach must have said to us at least a dozen times that it was next to impossible to beat a good team twice in one season. Since we'd lost to them in week two, I guess that meant this battle was going to be won by the Oilers.

"I don't think we ever thought about what Coach would have said had we beaten them during the regular season."

With Thanksgiving less than a week away, the biggest game of the season was set to unfold. And, the name of that game on that afternoon was *defense* as the Oilers hung on for a 9-8 victory, the second win in nine tries against the Titans during Strahm's tenure, thus far.

Defensive coordinator Coach 'Ski (Kwiatkowski) must have been proud that day as his squad limited Westminster to just seven first downs. Additionally, the likes of Matt Maglicic, Shane Dennison, Jeff Nagy, Bob Heitkamp, and the rest of the stellar Blood Unit limited the visitors to just 49 total plays, 21 fewer times than Oilers center Doug Kramer snapped the ball.

Recalls Strahm, "During the late 1980s and early 1990s, there were some great Westminster teams. The games we had with them were always very, very physical, and this one was certainly no exception. Although I had great respect for Westminster's defense, our defense didn't have to take a backseat to anyone's!"

A key momentum shifter came at the end of the first half when Westminster, clinging to a 3-0 lead, put the ball on the ground for defensive game MVP Bob Heitkamp while trying to run out the clock. That was an opportunity the Oilers were determined not to waste.

Wimberly, who efficiently managed both the clock and the game, hit Milan Smith with a six-yard swing pass and then put one on the numbers to Todd Pees for another seven yards.

That allowed place kicker Ben Cochran just enough time to kick a 31-yard field goal to tie the game.

After Westminster regained the lead 6-3 in a game dominated by trench warfare with another 29-yard field goal in the second half on a kick by Rob Dancu, the kicker who had kicked five field goals in the week-two win by the Titans back in September, it was time for one of those famous, lengthy ball-control drives that Strahm's wishbone was capable of producing.

Findlay, behind the powerful running of Balewa Walker, moved the chains time after time in a 58-yard drive that took seven minutes off the third and fourth quarter clocks. While most of the damage was done by the runners, the key play came when Wimberly found two-back Doug Rode on a 14-yard pass to set the Oilers up with a first down on Westminster's seven.

Even after Wimberly's option keeper around left end gave Findlay its first lead of the game, the Oilers still had work to do, as nine minutes remained on the game clock.

Westminster used one of the more unusual plays of both the game and the season to tighten the contest. Right after Wimberly's TD scamper, on the ensuing extra point, there was a bobbled snap, followed by an ill-advised attempted pass, a pass first tipped and then picked by Westminster's talented speedster Aldridge Jones.

Jones raced 85 yards for what counts as a defensive safety, and those two points narrowed the lead to just 9-8.

At that point in the contest, it was time for the Blood Unit to step up. Coach Ray Kwiatkowski remembers the way his unit closed out the game. "The effort was just terrific. Bob Heitkamp was all over the field and definitely took his stellar game to an even higher level. Our nose guard, Mike Collett, really jammed the middle, and Jamie Godman and Jeff Nagy were so strong, coming up from the secondary to support the run."

For the Oilers, the game came down to a special-teams play by the defense. Earlier in the week Coach 'Ski had suggested to Coach Strahm that tight end Tony Holland be put on the field-goal defense unit.

For Kwiatkowski, it was yet another example of adding the perfect wrinkle to the game plan. Proof of that came when Holland and cornerback Jeff Nagy combined to bat down Rob Dancu's attempt at a third field goal, this one from 39 yards.

Although five minutes still remained on the clock, the block seemed to sap the Titans of their resolve. The final piece to the winning picture was locked into place on another special teams play when Mike Stucky nailed a 63-yard punt to put the Titans far out of any zone for a final-play heroic.

Offensively, the star was the unlikely two-back from Delphos, Ohio, Doug Rode. He led all ball carriers with 56 yards on 13 carries and also added four key receptions circling out of the backfield for an additional 32 yards.

Despite the win against one of the real bullies on the NAIA block, the playoff road was destined to wind through yet another very tough neighborhood. Despite again submitting the winning bid and winning the right to host the game, the opponent would be the very strong team from Kentucky, Georgetown College, which had breezed through its first-round game, defeating Eureka (Illinois) College, 42-14.

The game certainly had an interesting sidebar to it, as three coaches on Dick Strahm's staff had at one time an affiliation with both the opponent and its head coach, Kevin Donley.

Mike Ward earned NAIA All-American honors while playing for Donley some years before, and both Doug Coate and Curtis Davidson were graduate assistants at one time under Donley.

Additionally, the game would feature contrasting offensive styles. Findlay would try to control both the clock and the game, using its trademark unbalanced-line wishbone, while Georgetown would adopt more of a quick-strike run-and-shoot approach, the kind of offense that certainly would put a lot of pressure on Bob Sutyak and the rest of his Oilers secondary mates.

Certainly, Strahm's defense would have its hands full with a Georgetown offense, which averaged a staggering 568.9 yards per game in compiling a 10-1 record. While Strahm waved off such flashy numbers by telling Mark Heiman of the hometown newspaper, *The Courier*, that his defense simply views those numbers as a challenge to be met, certainly he privately expressed some concerns about Georgetown's quarterback Dane Damron, the 6'2," 205-pound sophomore, who completed 178 passes for 2,844 yards and 28 touchdowns, while throwing only nine interceptions.

But, Strahm felt that if Matt Maglicic and Chris Smith applied enough pressure from their defensive end and tackle spots and linebackers Bob Heitkamp and Lee Frank continued to play well to compensate for the loss of Todd Clark for much of the season due to injuries, and, of course, Bob Sutyak, Jeff Nagy, Shane Dennison, and Curtis Armstrong could defend capably all the multiple passing routes, his Oilers would be fine.

Strahm also knew controlling the ball for long stretches of time would be beneficial, and, to do that, Nate Sprunger and Balewa Walker needed to have big games.

Despite the positive thoughts of Strahm, it was evident by the end of the first half that the Oilers were in trouble. Despite playing good defense in the first half, the Oilers couldn't get out of their own way. They fumbled twice and lost both. The second led to a 35-yard field goal as the first-half clock expired. Despite being down only 16-7, Strahm knew his defense had been on the field for the majority of the first half. Recalls Strahm, "When you coach long enough, you learn what the game's true barometers are, and certainly one of them is time of possession. When I saw that number so heavily tilted toward Coach Donley's team, I worried about my defense wearing down in the second half. And, that's exactly what happened."

The Oilers were outscored in the third quarter 14-0, which pushed the score to 30-7 after three quarters. One of the Tiger scores was an 81-yard scamper by Ron Railey, who finished the day with 122 yards on 10 carries.

When Wimberly went out with a hand injury, Scott Garlock came in and led his offense to two scores, completing 12 of 20 for 147 yards and a TD to Scott McLaughlin, but it was not enough as Georgetown cruised to the easy 37-19 win.

Recalls Garlock, now a school teacher at Liberty Benton High School and the quarterback coach at The University of Findlay, "Although I'm not sure a letdown is what we experienced after knocking off Westminster the previous Saturday, we really made a lot of mistakes, which was pretty uncharacteristic of us. I mean, look at the turnovers alone! We lost three fumbles and threw an interception. It's very difficult to overcome four turnovers against a quality opponent."

Despite Garlock's not being willing to say for sure the Oilers experienced a letdown, there were others who have no problem voicing that sentiment.

Balewa Walker, now working in the maintenance field back in his home state of Illinois, shook his head when recalling the game. "When we beat Westminster, I felt we'd just beat up the biggest bully on the block, and we'd be playing for the national championship! And then, the next week, *boom,* that notion blows right up in my face."

Walker's quarterback, DeMya Wimberly, agrees with the ex-teammate. "Balewa is right. We just weren't ready to play. I fumbled twice in the first half alone!

"What I really remember is something happened at Donnell that day that had never happened before. I got booed. I never wanted to experience that again. The fact that Georgetown went on to win the national championship didn't make the loss any easier to accept as time went by."

Recalls Des May, the defensive back who was versatile enough to fill a variety of positions as a substitute, "When I got back to my hometown of Troy [Ohio], I was constantly reminded of that Georgetown game. You see, I had a high school friend who went to Georgetown. He kept flashing that national championship ring in my face, and I don't mind telling you, I was really envious. I wanted one of those very badly."

Recollects the then-sophomore backup quarterback Garlock, "After that Georgetown game, I felt there was a real sense of resolve that we would be on a mission in 1992. I could sense that as early as our off-season workouts that winter right after the season. A lot of the guys just attacked those weights."

For Jason Stofel, the big 6'3," 302-pound junior tackle from Delaware, Ohio, it was certainly time to look ahead with the rest of the recruiting class of 1989 to a senior year of unfinished business, and that business was to be a part of the last team standing in December 1992.

For Stofel, now a social worker at Buckeye Ranch in the Columbus area, a facility which provides therapy for families and children in need, it was time to say good-bye to a special teammate. "Matt Maglicic was such a tremendous player. I always admired the guys who could bring a high level of intensity every time they stepped onto the field, no matter whether practice or on game day, and that's what he was all about! I just loved watching him play."

The Oilers were heavily decorated as far as post-season awards. No fewer than nine players were named All-NAIA Division II, a list which included the defensive end Maglicic, who led the team with thirteen sacks; Bob Heitkamp; Bob Sutyak, a player super fan and university president Ken Zirkle to this day remembers as one of the smartest players he'd ever seen perform; Jeff Nagy; Chris Smith; DeMya Wimberly; Scott McLaughlin, in just his first year; Chris Cotterill; and Dave Wolf.

Of the above group, two were also accorded the high honor of being named NAIA All-Americans, Maglicic and Heitkamp. Heitkamp, while battling Crohn's, registered 168 total tackles. Despite the loss to Georgetown, he saved his best for that game, as he rang up fourteen tackles, five more assists, three tackles for losses, a quarterback sack, three pass break ups, and a blocked extra point.

The extraordinary performance by Heitkamp certainly did not go unnoticed by Georgetown's head coach.

Recalls Strahm, "Coach Donley told me after the game that he'd never seen anyone like Bobby. His team had just gotten done playing Eureka College the previous week, which had the number-one defense in the NAIA going into the game, and he said there wasn't a single player on the Eureka defense that was nearly as good as number 54."

For a lot of the recruiting class of 1989, their time at Findlay was made more enjoyable by their involvement in the Foster Parent Program. Recalls Todd Clark, who was set to return for a strong senior year after an injury-plagued junior campaign, "What is very unique in my situation is I went into teaching junior high science and coaching at my alma mater, Bath High School, which is in the Western Buckeye League. Well, one of the very good coaches in our league is Jerry Buti, who coaches at Defiance High School.

"When I was at Findlay as an undergrad, Jerry Buti was my foster parent and also the head coach at Findlay High School. We always had a lot to talk about because Coach Buti also played for Coach Strahm in the mid-1970s. On Thursday nights, he would have his team over for dinner, and that was the night he would also invite me. At that point, I kind of knew I wanted to go into coaching, so I was very interested in how Coach Buti addressed his team and used the evening to work on team chemistry.

"So, whenever we face each other now on the field, I never miss a chance to personally thank him for what he did for me during my time at Findlay."

During the off season, strength coach Mike Ward and trainer Vi LeClair made sure the Gardner Fitness Center ran smoothly and injuries were addressed correctly. For Ward, he still marveled at how far Findlay had come, thanks to the generosity of men like Phil Gardner and Bob Malcolm.

To anyone who would listen, as the off-season Oilers lifted three hours a day, four days a week, they would say, "Two years ago, we had nothing. Today, we have the equipment so that any athlete will be able to train year-round."

Recalls Todd Clark of those weightlifting sessions, "Really, all we talked about was winning a national championship. As a matter of fact, I still have the t-shirt all the players received."

It was a t-shirt designed by Dick Strahm, one emblazoned by a simple and emphatic statement of fact, a statement that, despite its concise nature, stretched from Findlay all the way back to Mollenkopf Stadium in Warren, Ohio. "We Will Win!"

Andre Roach, the backup fullback who was a year behind the recruits of 1989 and is now a car salesman for a Toyota dealership in Findlay, remembers Dick Strahm's philosophy about the heavy load of twelve hours of weight training a week in the off-season. "Coach used to tell us that average teams aren't in here doing extra weight training. Only the elite are. The Gardner Center still was so new that it was really much easier to make the commitment to get bigger and stronger. Simply put, we just did not want to be average."

Recalls Nate Sprunger, the featured running back in Strahm's wishbone, "Listen, in high school, I played on a team that I felt really wanted to win, but my senior year, we were 3-7.

"But, here at Findlay, you were expected to win. You learned to expect success, and when we were beaten and beaten badly in that Georgetown game on our own field, that was our wake-up call. We simply weren't going to be denied. We wanted the fourth quarter to be ours and ours alone in 1992."

Sprunger, who totaled 3,993 career rushing yards in high school on his way to earning first-team all-state honors, gained 962 yards and averaged 5.1 yards per carry in 1991, certainly a stellar season by most back's standards. However, he had every intention of eclipsing those numbers in his senior year.

For the Oilers, their off-season training had a new wrinkle, thanks to an idea Coach Dick Strahm picked up at a recent clinic. Both Des May and Todd Clark remember the new wrinkle well.

Recalls May, "We started doing aerobic workouts in the mornings three days a week. We had the music and everything, and the sessions were mandatory attendance at six o'clock! How do you get that pumped up about getting up at that hour to do aerobics?"

Before Des May could finish, the former linebacker who was determined to avoid the injuries that short-circuited his junior year in '92, answered May's rhetorical question, in effect, stealing his former teammate's punch line. "Coach Strahm added three female instructors!"

As any off-season includes, Strahm and his assistants huddled to discuss what personnel changes would be necessary to make the 9-3 team of '91 an even stronger team in 1992.

Recalls Strahm, "Of course, the strength of the wishbone was the running game. Sure, Todd Pees and Scott McLaughlin were our twin threats at wide out, and we were fortunate to have such talent and depth on the outside.

"But, with the 'bone, it all comes down to running the football, possessing the ball, and winning the time-of-possession statistic, and moving those chains. That's why we coaches spent so much time thinking about our backs and, especially, our offensive line, which is obviously where it all starts with the running game.

"One thing I knew for certain was our big tight end, Tony Holland, who'd transferred in from Urbana University, was simply too good to keep as an alternate to Kent. So, I asked Coach Mac [Jim McIntosh], 'Why don't we move Tony Holland [who played tight end for us in '91] to outside tackle on the strong side and play Kent at tight end on the back side full time?'

"I figured this would give us a potentially dominating overload with our great inside tackle, Jason Stofel, lined up between strong-side guard Chris Cotterill and Tony at the outside tackle.

"Now, I spoke with both Mac and my other line coach, Curtis [Davidson], and they had some concerns that if Pelligrini went down with an injury, we'd have no back up if Tony were moved to outside tackle. But, I figured that was something that may never happen. I knew we'd be better with Tony blocking on the strong side. As far as if Kent were to get hurt, well, I just thought that was a cross-that-bridge-when-you-come-to-it situation,"

For Jim McIntosh and Curtis Davidson, the fact that Strahm did not make unilateral decisions was important to them. Both wanted to know their opinions mattered, as did the rest of the assistant coaches, a fact that wasn't lost on Dick Strahm. "I just figured if you were going to have assistant coaches, you damn well better listen to them. Between Mac and Curtis, no one knew more about unbalanced line play, period.

"With our bread-and-butter running play, 22-2, there were multiple ways to block it, depending upon what alignment the defense presented."

To even the player who benefited most from the 22-2 in 1992, Balewa Walker, the full range of complexities relative to the blocking on the play, wasn't really understood to anywhere near the full extent.

Recalls Walker, "I was really happy when I heard Tony Holland was going to be switched to the strong side playing beside Jason Stofel. Jason was already a dominant run blocker at the inside tackle and then to be able to put Tony right on his outside shoulder, well, let's just say I wanted to ride that sled.

"I've always felt that if you could defeat our tackles in our offense, you could stop the 22-2."

Coach Jim McIntosh disagrees with Walker's stop-the-tackles-and-stop-the-22-2 theory. Now in retirement and working on his golf game as a means to continue his rehab from a procedure to insert a stent in August of 2007, Mac remembers, "Westminster thought if it stopped our tackles, that was the key. But, there was a whole lot more to 22-2 than that.

"We had eighteen different blocking schemes for 22-2, and, in four or five seconds, the line had to recognize the one that would be the most effective and yell out he right call. In our offense, that stereotype of the big, old dumb jock lineman is an absolute myth. We needed smart guys who could instantly recognize how wide the defensive line's gaps were and where players were lined up and make the right call."

Despite McIntosh's portrayal of his linemen as somewhat of a cerebral group, that's not to say that there weren't times when one of his and Curtis Davidson's former charges didn't need to be steered back on the right course in the classroom. Dick Strahm remembers one such case in the spring of 1992 involving back-side guard Dave Wolfe, the 6'1," 286-pound product of Toledo Whitmer High School.

Recalls Strahm, "I remember Dave and Todd Pees were majoring in the same course of study, one that was pretty challenging, environmental and hazardous materials management. Dave's father was a firefighter, and when I was recruiting Dave back in the spring of 1989, Dad stressed to me that education was absolutely the main reason Dave was going to college. Football was secondary.

"Now, when the weather breaks in the spring, there often is a tendency for students to kind of slack off. If you're out of school, you remember how it was. You'd been working all school year, the weather was getting nicer, and you were looking forward to summer break.

"One day, Don Collins, our student-athlete academic counselor, came to see me at the Gardner Center while I was down in my office going over some game film. He had some news that was not at all good about Dave Wolfe. He told me that he'd been skipping some classes, had a 'D' in one of his classes and was actually failing another, and both subjects were in his major to boot!"

Strahm's reaction, of course, was, "What??? This young man is going to be a senior and one of my captains next year!"

Strahm immediately called Dave's father. He told him that unless his son got the deficient grades up to "C's," he wouldn't be playing football his senior year."

Strahm didn't tell Dave he'd called his father, and it just so happened that Dave was going home for a weekend visit. After spending time on the home front, with his father having said nothing to that point about his conversation with his son's coach, it was time for Dave to return to Findlay on Sunday evening. For some reason, Dave couldn't locate his car keys to make the return trip.

Strahm remembers what transpired through what Dave eventually told him. "Dave went to his dad and asked if he'd seen his car keys. Dad's response was, 'What are you talking about, son? You don't have a car.'

"After a 'What are you talking about, Dad?' response, the meaning of his father's response began to clarify for Dave. Dad had taken Dave's car keys from the counter and put them in his pocket."

At that point, Dave knew what Dad knew, and this presented two problems, one long-term and one-short term. The long-term involved how he could somehow in a short time dramatically raise his deficient grades and the short term was how he was going to get back to school.

The second problem was solved when his tough-love father finally relented and allowed Mom to drive the suddenly car-less back-side guard back to the Findlay campus.

As for the second, well, that was going to take more time and a whole lot of rededication. It would indeed be a work in progress.

Recalls Dick, "Monday morning, Dave came to my office and knocked on my door. After he came in, he told me, 'Dad took my car away.' My response was, 'Well, gee, Dave, that's too bad. I guess that means you really won't have anywhere to go except the library and class.'

"Dave got the message. I was in almost daily contact with Don Collins, and the progress was steady."

In the last five weeks, through hard work and more than a little sense of urgency, Wolfe elevated the "D" up to a "B" and the "F" all the way to a "C." It is really a wonder what can happen when a young man used to driving around is relegated to pedestrian travel. And of course, the thought of standing apart and watching the Findlay Oilers, a team loaded with talent and gunning for nothing less than a national championship in 1992, and not being a part of that experience also had more than a little to do with the dramatic improvement.

The academic year of 1991-1992 drew to a close, and Strahm's players returned home with some words of wisdom from their coaches. Strahm recalls, "I told them while they deserved some R and R in the summer, they needed to stay in shape and return in August ready to accept a challenge. Also, each player was given an individual workout program to use over the summer."

For Dick Strahm, the summer also included some rest and relaxation. One day, in late June, he was driving down Main Street in town, listening to the radio. Recalls Dick, "I heard a public service announcement that talked about a relatively new test called a PSA [prostate specific antigen], which could detect an early-stage prostate cancer.

"The man sounded very convincing. He said that a simple blood draw had saved his life, since he, indeed, had prostate cancer. However, he had the needed surgery, and that was the only reason he was still around to make the public service announcement.

"Now, I had a physical coming up in a couple of weeks, so I had the test done, and the results came out fine. Certainly, I was relieved and vowed to have it done at my yearly physical each summer. With the heart problems I had to constantly monitor with regular visits to Dr. Beekman, I certainly didn't need any cancer worries."

Of course, the summer included the Strahms' annual family vacation to Miley's Resort up in Michigan. It was a ritual, one that connected Dick Strahm's past, his first forays into the education-and-coaching profession and, specifically one of his mentors, George Miley, and his present.

As the summer moved into the dog days of early August, it was time to gather the coaching staff for a long weekend of planning, away from distractions, at the farm in Pennsylvania owned by university president Ken Zirkle.

One thing the coaches discussed was how to use effectively the transfer running back, Jermaine Ward. Ward, who played his Ohio high school ball at Canal Winchester, had been good enough to receive a full scholarship to Miami University of the Mid-American Conference.

Despite the full ride at the Division I school, Ward was dissatisfied and wound up transferring to Findlay. He would arrive with the rest of his new teammates in a matter of a couple weeks.

Recalls Strahm, "We decided that Balewa and Jermaine would split time at fullback. Balewa would be our primary back, but Jermaine would be part of our goal-line package and also spell Walker at other times as well, since he had more speed."

The year 1992 indeed was a special one for The University of Findlay. It marked the one hundredth anniversary for the football program. Findlay's football guide that year featured on its cover eleven young men, and, apparently a coach with a very bushy nineteenth-century moustache. They were the inaugural edition of the Oilers pig skinners, a break-even squad that opened the second-shortest of possible seasons with a 20-0 loss to Heidelberg and finished on a high note with a 14-0 win over the Findlay YMCA.

The '92 coaching staff that awaited the arrival in a couple of weeks of the current squad, far greater in number than the original stout eleven who, no doubt, went both ways, certainly were expecting much more than a .500 campaign.

The staff returned basically intact, with only one defection. Additionally, there were two first-year coaches coming aboard. In addition to returnees Coate, McIntosh, Davidson, Kwiatkowski, Bello, and Gilbert, the two newcomers would bring the staff to ten, certainly a far cry from the six who comprised the Oilers coaching staff in Strahm's first year of 1975.

One new assistant was Ron Flowers, who would attempt to fill the substantial hole left by the departure of Mike Ward, the linebacker and strength coach. Despite leaving to assume the position of strength and conditioning coach at Bowling Green State University, Mike Ward would certainly have something to do with whatever success the Oilers would have in 1992.

Ward remains at Bowling Green and has risen in rank to hold his current position as the Falcon defensive coordinator.

Recalls Strahm, "Mike Ward was an absolute godsend for us at Findlay. Not only was he a fine on-field coach but he also was such an asset at the Gardner Fitness Center. He was just so organized and, thanks to him, the weight room was absolutely spotless. It was almost as if he saw it as 'his room,' and no one was going to disrespect it.

"He was always wiping down bars and equipment and making sure the players who lifted there treated the area with the same respect he did.

"I honestly believe it was Coach Ward who helped set the tempo, along with, of course my other great assistants, for our great teams of the 1990s."

Flowers would be joined by J.R. Suppes, who would head the freshman program and also fill the role of equipment manager.

On the reporting day, as the players came to check in at the Gardner Fitness Center one by one, Coach Greg Gilbert got a really good feeling. "I remember thinking how good the players looked. They were in shape and absolutely as enthusiastic as I could have hoped."

Jason Stofel, the big offensive tackle who would welcome Tony Holland to his outside shoulder on the strong side of the unbalanced line, recalls the initial mood of the players as they bounded into the building to report.

"It was absolutely incredible. Here, guys had just seen each other about ten weeks ago, and here they were high fiving and hugging one another. That's when I really got the feeling that 1992 could really be something special."

To DeMya Wimberly, 1992 would be a season of redemption, despite the fact that he had, overall, played very well the previous year. It was the Georgetown game that remained in his mind, a game in which he had fumbled twice before leaving the game with an injury when his team was far behind. "I was determined to make the '92 year our year. As the quarterback, I was expected to lead, and I was ready. We all wanted a national championship, and we saw each game as a stepping stone."

Backup QB Scott Garlock remembers how every practice that August ended. "After the final sprints of the day, when we came together as a team, our final unity chant before heading to the showers was always the same. 'Ring!' And, that was something we continued all year."

The season opened on the road for the Oilers with a trip to Frankfurt, Kentucky, to play the Thoroughbreds of Kentucky State. The game turned out to be more tightly contested than many expected. Despite having won just twice in eleven games the previous year, the Thoroughbreds gave the Oilers all they could before finally falling, 23-13.

Wimberly hit his fellow Floridian Scott McLaughlin with a 67-yard TD, and Balewa Walker paced the ground attack by running behind his twin strong-side tackles Stofel and Holland for 85 yards on just eight carries.

Recalls Stofel, "Our goal as linemen was always to get at least one of our backs a hundred yards rushing, so we were somewhat disappointed. All through August Coach Mac stressed how important it was that we hogs play well.

"We knew we had the stud defense, and we knew we had 4.4 40-yard dash running backs and an experienced quarterback, but for us to reach our goal of winning a national championship, we knew the offensive line had to gel."

Game two was the home opener against Lindenwood College, from St. Charles, Missouri. On that September 26, after back-to-back open dates the previous two Saturdays, the defensive dominated, 33-0. What Strahm worried about, the long layoff, was not an issue.

The secondary was particularly impressive. Initially, it was thought that Jeff Nagy would not play his senior year when he opted during the summer to try minor league baseball. However, just before the Oilers broke camp, he returned to assume a starting cornerback position.

Jamie Riles and Shane Dennison, both out of Naples, Florida, also played well at cornerback and strong safety, respectively. Todd Vrancken, from Galena, Ohio, had a huge day as he had an interception and also returned a punt for 76 yards and a touchdown. And, of course, the quarterback of the defense, Bob Sutyak, was stellar as usual.

The linebackers, Todd Clark and Bob Heitkamp, played with their usual intensity, and the defensive line was strong with the likes of Lee Frank (Elyria, Ohio), Jamie Godman (Lorain, Ohio), Chris Smith (Fremont, Ohio), Mike Collett (Xenia, Ohio), Erich Brandstadt (Vermillion, Ohio), and Raajih Roland (Urbana, Ohio).

Offensively, Wimberly proved that you don't have to throw often as long as you throw well. Of his seven passes that afternoon, three went for touchdowns, two to the speedster out of Dunkirk, Ohio, Todd Pees.

In week three, in what can only be described as another little twist found in small-college football, undefeated and nationally ranked Union College, out of Barbourville, Kentucky, came to Findlay for a game to be played but not at the Oilers' customary field. Recalls Strahm, "There was a conflict for another event planned for Donnell that day, a huge marching band competition. I was told in August of the conflict, and it was explained to me that the band competition could not be moved. I went out to nearby Liberty Benton High School, where my son Steve was a student-athlete, and spoke to the athletic director, Dean Butler, who was a 1969 Findlay College graduate, to ask if he'd be willing to host the game.

"I just didn't want to give up the home game by having to travel to Union, and Union didn't want to play the game at Donnell at night, which was another option. So arrangements were made, and the game was played on Liberty Benton's field. I remember we dressed at the university and bused over.

"When we got out there and started loosening up, two Union players walked by. Both of them pointed to a corn field a little ways in the distance and kind of scoffed at the fact that the game was being played in such a venue. One of them bragged about how nice their stadium was, right on campus.

"I just smiled and said, 'Young men, the field is still 100 yards long and 51 2/3 yards wide.' They just kind of smirked and jogged over to their area.

"Then, we went out and put 56 points on the Liberty Benton scoreboard!"

In Findlay's 56-28 win, Scott McLaughlin hauled in another long touchdown pass, this one good for 82 yards from the future Liberty Benton teacher and head football coach, backup quarterback Scott Garlock. Balewa Walker rushed for 101 yards, and defensively, Bob Heitkamp had a 35-yard touchdown off his interception.

Week four found the Oilers on the road, off to Kentucky and Campbellsville College. The Fighting Tigers had gone 9-2 the previous season and returned fourteen starters, so Strahm was ready for a difficult contest with an opponent that had yet to lose in 1992, that is until that day. The Oilers prevailed 28-7, as McLaughlin again snagged a touchdown pass, this one 42 yards, and Nathan Sprunger had a huge afternoon, rushing for 172 yards and two TDs on just 15 carries. His performance earned him NAIA Player-of-the-Week honors.

Defensively, Bob Sutyak also chipped in with a timely interception, and the Oilers were beginning to flex their defensive muscles, especially Lee Frank and Jamie Godman, who were applying great pressure coming from their defensive end positions.

DeMya Wimberly recalls to the fullest extent how unified the Oilers were in their quest for success. "In the second quarter we turned the ball over, and as we ran off the field, there was just a wave of overwhelming encouragement. You'd have thought we scored or something. I can remember that I actually got goose bumps."

Jason Stofel had his own favorite moment from the Campbellsville contest. "It was early in the game, and DeMya got injured and came out. So, Scott Garlock came in. He hadn't taken all that many snaps to that point during the year, so I was actually a little nervous. Scott came into the huddle and gave us the play. It was a trick play we'd put in for the Kentucky State game called the 'K-State Special' that had something like four handoffs and a double reverse.

"Then, he broke into a big grin and said, 'Just Kidding.' Then, he gave the real play. That just shows Scottie's sense of humor, and it really broke the tension. It's important for the rest of the guys to know the quarterback isn't in panic mode, especially the backup when he comes in cold.

Week five had the Oilers traveling to a place where they'd never won, Westminster College, in New Wilmington, Pennsylvania. The Titans at that time were ranked number one in the Division II NAIA national polls, and, on that October 17, they played like it.

The final score was 30-17, and the Oilers had their first loss of the year, despite Jermaine Ward's two touchdown runs. Recalls Todd Pees, "Coach Strahm always likened our schedule to running a gauntlet, where opponents were lined up on either side, taking shots at us. I guess you could say on that day, we got knocked to the ground."

When a team loses, the game-tape session is never very pleasant and such was the case for the Oilers' defense, which had given up 30 points. Bob Sutyak, currently living in the Cleveland area and working as a global EHS manager for Lincoln Electric, was often called a coach on the field, and he remembers his fiery defensive coordinator Ray Kwiatkowski's manning the remote control in breaking down one particularly offensive play by his defense.

"I remember we got to a play that was particularly distressful to Coach 'Ski, and he began to review the play multiple times. Each time he rewound the play, he forcefully pointed out a different person's mistake.

"Well, after about fifteen times reviewing the same play, he finally decided that it was time to move on, but instead of fast forwarding the tape, he actually rewound the tape to the same play he'd already shown about ten times. He started to scream something like, 'Look! They ran the same damn play again, and all you guys made the same stupid mistakes!' It was all we could do to keep from laughing out loud!

"What great memories I have of Coach 'Ski. He was such a competitor, and despite having a little trouble with the VCR, he really was a terrific coach."

Des May remembers Kwiatkowski for his pet sayings as he reviewed game tapes. "Coach 'Ski would pause the tape when he'd see me in the wrong place on coverage and a receiver would be wide open. Then, I'd hear his big booming voice, 'For crying out loud, Des! Who's going to cover number 88, God?'

The true measure of a football team's worth is what happens when it stumbles. Week six provided the answer as Findlay traveled down the short road to Tiffin University to play the Dragons of Coach Bob Wolfe. The Oilers' challenge defensively would be to find a way to stop talented running back Brian Diliberto. The workhorse racked up 243 carries on his way to his 1,076-yard season the previous year.

But, on that Saturday at Mohawk Warrior Stadium, the Findlay defense had an answer for Diliberto and the rest of the Dragons. Diliberto was held to under 100 yards on his 29 carries, and the Oilers pitched a shutout, 21-0, improving to 5-1 in the process. Balewa Walker piled up 124 yards on his 20 totes.

In week seven, it was back home for Findlay to host Urbana University on that Halloween Saturday. The result was a resounding 47-12 win for the home team. Certainly, the defensive star of the game was the player who returned from his minor league baseball experiment just in time to reassume his role as starting cornerback, Jeff Nagy. Nagy pilfered two passes that afternoon, returning one 25 yards for a touchdown.

Week eight found Findlay home again to play Northwood Institute, an NAIA Division I school out of Midland, Michigan. In a game played pretty close to the vest, the home team finally got some separation in the final quarter when Scott McLaughlin caught a Wimberly pass for a touchdown from 10 yards out, setting up a Wimberly scamper into the end zone for a two-point conversion to bring the final score to 21-6.

Nate Sprunger again had a dominant game as he rushed for 159 yards on 19 carries. First, he outraced the Northmen's secondary for a first-quarter 33-yard TD, and then, in the third quarter, he stepped inside a key block by halfback John Ferguson and bolted 14 yards right up the middle for a second score.

Another key to the win was the punting of Scott McLaughlin. While he only averaged 31.5 yards on six punts, the Oilers' special teamers, especially Des May, were all over the coverage and downed the ball on Northwood's 20-, 18-, 14-, 10-, 9-, and 3-yard lines. Recalls Strahm, "People who don't recognize the importance of field position, don't really understand football."

The final week of the regular season found the Oilers at home to play Lees-McRae College, all the way from Banner Elk, North Carolina. The result was the most lopsided win of the year, as Findlay dominated, 64-0. The visiting team's coach told Coach Strahm after the game that the trip to Findlay was just too damn long. Recalls Strahm, "I told him, 'I believe I said that to you last year after our game.' He then told me he wouldn't sign another contract to continue the series, which suited me just fine."

McLaughlin and Doug Rode both caught touchdown passes from DeMya Wimberly, Sprunger again went over 100 yards on the ground while rushing for two touchdowns, and Sutyak had an interception to fuel the rout.

Jermaine Ward tallied a pair of touchdowns on one-yard runs, fulfilling the role of short-yardage back that Strahm envisioned as he and his assistants plotted strategy in early August on the Pennsylvania farm owned by Findlay president Ken Zirkle. Even the special teams got in on the fun on that November 14 that featured high winds and light snow. Chris Rothhaar picked up a blocked punt and returned it 22 yards for a touchdown.

At 8-1 the Oilers were ranked fifth in the NAIA polls and ready for a playoff run, determined to learn from their letdown against Georgetown after the big win over Westminster the previous year.

Recalls fullback Andre Roach, "We knew how hard we'd worked to get a chance to make the post-season special. I remember Coach Strahm telling us that teams that were just average weren't out on the practice field doing the extra sprints we were running."

Jason Stofel remembers Coach Strahm for his motivational skills. "I remember we got our game grades from the Lees-McRae game, and mine was the lowest it'd been all year. Coach just ripped me. Well, I was furious, and I took that fury and turned it into the determination it took to dominate my man in the playoffs. Looking back, I'm sure my performance in that final regular season game wasn't that bad. Heck, how bad could it have been? We rushed for over 300 yards [337 yards to be exact], but Coach instinctively knew which buttons to push for his players, and he knew grading me low right before the playoffs started was the right button to push at the right time."

If the Oilers were interested in settling a score with Georgetown College, they didn't have to wait long because it was the defending national champs that Findlay drew as its opening-round opponent. The school from Flag City U.S.A. also submitted the higher sealed bid and also would host the game. While some saw that as a good omen, no one on the Oilers squad needed to be reminded that it was on the playing surface of Donnell Stadium that Georgetown had so dominated the home team to bring to an end the previous season.

But, this was a different year, and the Oilers went out on the field on November 21, the Saturday before Thanksgiving, and proved it, winning 32-14, behind player-of-the-game performers Balewa Walker on offense and Bob Heitkamp on defense. Walker rumbled for 123 yards, and Heitkamp, the ubiquitous linebacker, recorded 17 tackles, 11 of them solo.

The dominating play of the senior-laden offensive line consisting of tackles Jason Stofel and Tony Holland, guards Dave Wolfe and Chris Cotterill, center Doug Kramer, and tight end Kent Pelligrini made it possible for the Oilers to rush for over 300 yards.

Georgetown coach Kevin Donley admitted after the game that it was the line play that held the game's key. "They did an outstanding job on offense maintaining control of the ball. They were so strong up front, and the constant pounding from one side of the line all the way to the other by a big, physical football team left our kids totally exhausted."

Big defensive plays also played a major role in short circuiting Georgetown's quest for a win. Both Jeff Nagy and Bob Sutyak intercepted passes, and tackle Erich Brandstadt recovered a pair of fumbles. In '91, it was turnovers that doomed the Oilers. This year, it would Georgetown's undoing.

DeMya Wimberly instantly showed he was intent on erasing the memories of last year's two fumbles. It was his 52-yard touchdown pass to the Floridian speed merchant Scott McLaughlin that put the Oilers on the scoreboard for the first time.

Recalls running back Milan Smith, "I remember early in the game I had about a 60-yard kickoff return where I made several open-field moves and did a lot of lateral running. When I got to the sidelines, I could tell just how focused our coaching staff was. Coach Gilbert came up to me, I thought to congratulate me. He looked at me instead and said, 'If you wouldn't have danced so much, you'd have scored.' I must admit, he was probably right. There were times I probably did do a bit too much dancing instead of running more north and south."

The second week of the playoffs presented a huge challenge. The Oilers, this time, were outbid for the right to host the game, which meant they would have to travel to new Wilmington, Pennsylvania, to take on the Westminster Titans on December 5.

The Titans had run the regular-season rack, and, at 10-0, were the number-one ranked team in the NAIA. Of course, one of those ten wins was that week-two victory over the Oilers, which left Findlay with its only loss of the season.

Secretly, Strahm was somewhat concerned about the Titans' defense, a unit which featured three outstanding performers. Linebacker Matt Raich had just been selected as a Kodak first-team All-American. Defensive end Shane Newhouse was a relentless pursuer, and Aldridge Jones had scored in about every conceivable way a defensive and special-teams player could score.

Both coaches, Strahm and Gene Nicholson, agreed that the game would largely be determined by field position. The offenses were both ball-controlling units, and if the weather would become a factor, always a possibility in December in the Keystone State, controlling the ball meant controlling the game clock.

Recalls Strahm, "I remember it was the usual four-hour bus ride to get to New Wilmington. During the trip, I noticed the weather was really pretty good. And, that's the way I left the weather after we had our meal, our meeting, and settled in for some sleep.

"The next morning when Ginger and I got up, we looked out, and I bet there were five inches of snow on the ground, and it was still coming down. In addition, the wind was howling.

"It was then I knew our kerosene heaters would be needed for the sidelines. So, I asked Coach Curtis Davidson to go to the store get some kerosene. I remember one of our most rabid fans, Ken Zirkle, lent Curtis his car.

"Well, it was getting close to the time the bus was scheduled to leave for the field, and Curtis wasn't back yet. All of a sudden, there he was, running up to me with sweat dripping from him.

"He was panicky and told me that he got the kerosene, but, in his haste, after he took his purchases out of the car, he punched the lock down on the car. It was only then he realized that not only were the keys still in the car but the motor was running!"

One can only imagine how scared the young assistant was when he had to go tell the university president what had happened.

Recalls Davidson, "It was typical Dr. Zirkle. He simply said, 'Curtis, don't worry about it. Relax. Go get your offensive line ready. I'll break the window if I have to.'"

As it turned out, such drastic measures weren't needed. Zirkle called back to the dealership in Findlay where he'd gotten the car. Someone then contacted a dealership in the New Wilmington area, and help arrived and got the car open.

Strahm remembers the arrival to Memorial Field, the home of the Titans. "At that time, there probably was about seven inches of snow on the ground. The ground crew guys were trying their best, but, really, about all they could do was shovel the lines so you could tell where the sidelines and end zones were, but after about 10 minutes they were covered up with snow again. Snow blowers were in constant use throughout the game.

"Both teams warmed up on a couple practice fields nearby so that the crew could continue their work.

"Right before the game, I remember telling Coach Kwiatkowski that at least we didn't have to worry about anyone breaking a long run against us since the field conditions were so poor.

"Then, *boom!* on the second play of the game, the Westminster back [Kyle Hetrick] broke out of a scrum at the line of scrimmage and went 45 yards for a touchdown. I looked at 'Ski and said, 'So much for that theory.'"

Despite the inauspicious start, the Oilers rebounded even though they were having a difficult time keeping the All-American linebacker Matt Raich blocked. Findlay knotted the score on a two-yard plunge by goal-line specialist Jermaine Ward and a conversion kick by Ben Cochran, the place kicker out of Springfield, Ohio. A key play, an interception by Jamie Godman, prevented Westminster from taking a lead as the teams broke for the warmth of their halftime locker rooms with the score tied at 7-7.

Recalls Milan Smith, Nate Sprunger's backup, "I don't think I've ever been that cold in my life that day. Nathan wound up playing the entire first half because he was playing well. And, to be honest, that suited me just fine. I really didn't want to move too far away from those heaters!"

In the second half, after a scoreless third quarter, the 800 screaming Oilers faithful who made the trip exhorted their charges to somehow find their way through over a half a foot of snow to mount a scoring drive.

Recalls Strahm, "While we, on occasion, had beaten Westminster on our field, we'd never beaten them on their own turf. And, for a while, it looked as if we weren't going to get it done again."

What Strahm, no doubt, remembers is before the drive, his Oilers had lost a fumble to linebacker extraordinaire Raich at Findlay's 46-yard line. From there, the Titans drove all the way down to the 14 on six consecutive running plays. Then, it was Todd Clark who stepped up, the player whose previous season was almost totally wiped out by injuries.

Recalls Strahm, "I remember Todd put on a terrific rush and got his hands up on a pass play and tipped the ball. It was intercepted by Bob Sutyak in the end zone."

The Oilers took over at their own 20 on the change of possession and produced what Dick Strahm truly believes is *the greatest drive in the history of the Findlay Oilers football program* commenced with 10:57 left on the fourth-quarter clock. "I got so involved in that drive that, even right after the game, I couldn't have told you all the plays I called."

It was evident early that Findlay was intent on doing what it had tried to do all day, establish the run.

UF ran eleven consecutive times, starting with a DeMya Wimberly seven-yarder. On a crucial third and three, the tank wearing number 39, Balewa Walker, got the three yards by the nose of the football, first down. On his own 38, or as near as anyone could estimate on the snow-covered turf, Wimberly then snuck two yards on a third and two, another first down.

Later, at the Oilers' 49, it was fourth and a yard. Strahm rolled the dice and called his quarterback's number again. Two yards later, the Oilers got to keep the ball.

Finally, after eleven consecutive rushes, Wimberly attempted the second and final pass of his afternoon. And, it was the most important play of the day. With the ball resting close to the Titans' 40-yard line, Wimberly hit Nathan Sprunger on a circle route out of the backfield for eleven yards and a first down at the Westminster 30.

From there, it was back to the ground attack, as Walker carried consecutively for 5, 7, 8, 7, and 2. The play was the 22-2, and he rode that human blocking sled consisting of Doug Rode, Doug Kramer, Chris Cotterill, Jason Stofel, and Tony Holland.

It was on the twentieth play, with 9:05 minutes taken off the scoreboard clock, the offensive game MVP, Balewa Walker, came up with a facemask full of snow and six points from a yard out.

The 13-7 lead held up over the final 1:52 after Bob Sutyak ended the Titans' last scoring opportunity by way of an interception. The Memorial Field curse was a thing of the past.

For Dick Strahm, it was a mental and physical drain, this jinx-breaking business. He had to be checked by a doctor after the game when perhaps the exhilaration of the moment triggered an asthma attack. Ginger was found and brought to the locker room with an inhaler. After a couple puffs, Coach Strahm got his breathing back to normal.

Recalls Strahm, "Once I calmed down I put the team and the assistant coaches on the bus, and Ginger and I decided we'd travel back to Findlay with Charlie Spragg, a Findlay dentist and The University of Findlay trustee; his wife, Phyllis; Dave Kuenzli, a Findlay attorney and one of my best friends; and his wife, Gwen, who taught at the university and had several of my players in class.

"They'd driven over to the game in Dr. Spragg's big van, and there was room for us. Well, while we were on the way back, they decided a big meal at the fanciest restaurant we could find was in order. They found what looked like a nice place, but the only problem was that it wouldn't be open for about 45 minutes for dinner.

"So, we had some time to kill. We drove around town a bit, and the wives spied a shoe store and wanted to shop.

"Here I was, still basking in the afterglow of one of the biggest wins I'd ever been associated with, with me trying to remember all twenty plays on our drive, and I was going into a shoe store! While the women were shopping and Dave and Charlie were looking for a pair of boots, I was sitting down on a bench in the front of the store, and there was a guy sitting next to me.

"I was still so pumped up from the game, so I asked the guy if he'd been to the game. He said he wasn't aware there was a game that day! I told him we'd beaten Westminster and were going to the semifinals.

"He looked at me very calmly as if he couldn't care less, wished me luck and got up and left. Here I was at the greatest time of my life, and I couldn't find anybody besides my travel mates who even cared!

"I guess that's what small-college coaching is all about. There are very few reporters, no TV or radio interviews, just a few thousand spectators, a big win, and waiting for a restaurant to open while sitting in a shoe store. But, you know something? I was just as thrilled as if I had just won the Rose Bowl!"

Dave Kuenzli chuckles at Strahm's recollection. "The poor guy. Here, he'd just reached one of the pinnacles of his coaching career, and he wound up talking to a guy who wasn't even aware there was a game that afternoon!"

During the few days that followed the Oilers' historic win, the bids for the next game were unsealed, and Findlay indeed would host their semifinal game against Benedictine (Kansas) College, a team very similar to the Oilers. Benedictine head coach Larry Wilcox told the press that both teams were ground-oriented and focused on field position.

The Ravens entered the contest at 11-1, compared to Findlay's 10-1, and was ranked second in the nation in rushing offense, averaging 328.1 yards a game. The Oilers were just behind them, third, with an average of 306.4 yards a contest.

Benedictine would rely on the top Division II NAIA running back in the nation, Don Brown, who had rushed for 1,910 yards in the twelve games. In addition, fullback Steve Torline had found the end zone eighteen times.

Quarterback Chris Tabor, also presented somewhat of a twin problem. He'd thrown for over 1,000 yards and ran for over 500 more.

Certainly, Benedictine had some size, with 6'7," 300-pound tight end Jasper Johansson and 6'3," 300-pound tackle Michael Spoehr. One formation the Ravens relied on heavily was one they called "Beef." What concerned Strahm was the threat that Benedictine would be able to control the ball for long stretches of time.

"A team that can sit on the ball keeps its defense on the bench. Those long drives just drives the other team up the wall. Benedictine is very capable of doing that, and that's the thing that can hurt us," Strahm told Larry Alter, his friend and sports editor of Findlay's paper, *The Courier,* in the days preceding the December 12 kickoff.

Riding on the game's outcome was a trip to the national championship game on December 19 at the 25,000-seat Civic Stadium in downtown Portland.

On a day rife with crucial plays, the final one came with 39 seconds left when Benedictine College's kicker Mark Gormley lined up to attempt a 47-yard field goal. A good kick would have sent the game to overtime. Instead, when the ball, which had plenty of distance, clanked off the left upright of the goalpost, the miss sent the Oilers to Portland. Findlay had survived 27-24.

Strahm told the press after the game, "When you're on a roll, good things happen to you. We certainly know what three or four inches can mean in a game. I think everybody's familiar with the old saying, 'I'd rather be lucky than good.' Well, I knew we were lucky, but we were also good, and that's a pretty unbeatable combination."

Offensively, Wimberly hit 5 of 8, including a 24-yarder for a TD to Scott McLaughlin. While the Oilers did fail to reach their season rushing average, the wishbone still produced 273 yards, including 98 by Walker and 78 by Sprunger and 59 by Wimberly.

So, for the Oilers, it was on to a final week of preparations for the title game. Despite its 11-1 mark, Findlay was considered the underdog to a powerful opponent that favored the spread offense, the Linfield (Oregon) College Wildcats.

Running back Gary McGarvie led the Linfield ground game with 1,270 yards rushing and 14 touchdowns. The Oilers would also have to account for an outstanding quarterback, Shannon Sells, who'd thrown for 1,899 yards and 16 touchdowns. Additionally, the Wildcats had momentum. In their semifinal game they'd crushed Minot State, 47-12, with an offensive output of 662 yards.

When the Oilers contingent arrived on the Thursday before the game after the flight from the Toledo Express Airport, they checked into the Red Lion Hotel, which was very close to the Columbia River in Portland, Oregon, a very scenic location for lodging.

It didn't take long for the Oilers to feel they were being disrespected. Recalls Balewa Walker, "I remember we were walking around at a mall on Thursday night after supper, and people saw our Findlay jackets. Some of those Portlanders had no problem walking right up to us and saying, 'You're going to lose.' Linfield wasn't very far [about 50 miles] from Portland, and it was evident we were kind of going to have to play this game on hostile territory."

There were also references to Findlay as not being very far from Hicksville, Ohio, that began popping up in the pre-game press coverage. Even UF president Ken Zirkle sensed the cockiness of the team the Oilers would play. "I think Linfield kind of thought its explosive offensive would certainly overwhelm us. They'd not been beaten, and many of the Linfield supporters made sure you didn't forget that fact."

Todd Clark, the Oilers' rock-solid starting linebacker, recalls the championship banquet on the eve of the game. "When it was time for Coach Strahm to give his speech after dinner, he went into his Lou Holtz thing. You may remember whenever [former Notre Dame head coach] Holtz was asked about an opponent, no matter how weak or how good the team was, he would make them sound like the other team had invented football!"

Also at the dinner was someone who acted as the host for the game. His name was Neil Lomax, who played his football at Portland State on the very field where the national championship would be decided. Lomax also played in the NFL for nine years with the Cardinals of first St. Louis and then Phoenix.

Lomax's college coach was a noteworthy person in college football. Darryl "Mouse" Davis was the originator of the high-powered run and shoot, an offense which often featured as many as five different receivers running routes. He had coached at Portland State from 1975 through 1980 before moving on to coach in the Canadian Football League, the United States Football

League, and the National Football League. It would be Davis who would provide the color commentary for the televised coverage.

For Davis, who prepped for his TV work by attending both of the teams' practices, he just couldn't quite seem to embrace Findlay's ball-control, ground-oriented wishbone.

Strahm's offensive philosophy was as conservative as Davis' was daring. Recalls Strahm, "I spoke with Mouse some in the couple of days before the game, and he just couldn't figure out how I could win games by throwing the ball less than ten times a game.

"Hell, I never even told him about our Westminster game, when we only threw it twice! I didn't think he could handle that without fainting. I just couldn't get him to see there were a lot of ways to win football games."

Defensively, Ray Kwiatkowski had come up with one of his famous tweaks early in the week. His proposal to Dick Strahm was that two players, defensive tackle Chris Smith and the undersized redheaded bulldog of a nose guard, Mike Collett, change positions.

Recalls Strahm, "Mike was barely 200 pounds but very quick, which I've always felt is more important than bulk at the nose guard position. Well, my concern was, if he and Smitty switched, that would put Collett right over a mammoth offensive tackle that weighted over 300 pounds.

"But, 'Ski countered with the opinion that Chris Smith's being over center, and outweighing him by around 20 pounds and also being very quick himself, would allow him to defeat the blocks of Linfield's center and that Collett's quickness would make it very difficult for their big tackle to block him.

"Although I had my doubts, I remembered 'Ski had an uncommon knack for making this type of adjustment, so I said OK."

Game time finally arrived, and for university president Ken Zirkle and the former athletic director Jim Houdeshell, that meant selecting the best place from which to watch the game. And, that always seemed to be wherever Ron Souply, who filmed the game, happened to be.

Recalls Zirkle, "Ron set up in like a crow's nest on top of the press box. When I told Jim we were going to climb the metal ladder on the outside of the press box and watch from the roof, he expressed some real concerns about either my sanity or our chances for survival if a strong wind came up suddenly. The temperature was in the 30s, and there was a light rain."

For the Oilers, the game started roughly. Coach 'Ski had made some other defensive adjustments besides flip-flopping Smith and Collett, to combat the wide-open offense, and there was some confusion on the opening drive. After taking the opening kickoff, the Wildcats needed only 2:24 and six plays to cover 64 yards and find pay dirt. Quarterback Shannon Sells ran it in from five yards out.

Recalls Ray Kwiatkowski, now retired and living in Ft. Myers, Florida, "I think the thing that I'll always remember about those 1992 players is they weren't 'Me' players. After that first Linfield drive, I called them over and apologized to them for trying to make too many changes too fast. They all started to say, 'No, Coach. I didn't do this or didn't do that! They accepted responsibility when they easily could have said nothing, but, here they were, in the biggest game of their lives, concerned about me and my feelings!

"So, we basically, except for staying with the Smitty and Collett switch went back to what we'd been doing all year. What's the old saying, 'You dance with the girl who brought you'?

"Really, I have to thank Dick for all the freedom he gave me to make changes during my years with him. I remember sometimes when something didn't work, he'd come up to me on the sidelines and say, 'Coach, was that our defense or yours?' I think he did that after Linfield's first drive!"

After the ease of the Wildcats' first drive, no doubt, there was some uneasiness among the Oilers faithful. One of those, due to a work commitment, did not make the trip to Oregon. Recalls Dick, "My son Doug had moved back to the Findlay area. I got him a job in a meat-packing plant in Rossford, not far from Findlay."

Recalls Doug, "I had to work third shift, meaning from nine at night to six in the morning, so there was no way I could go to the game. I knew the game was being televised in Findlay, so I went to a sports bar to watch. So many people were asking me questions during the game, I just left. I just couldn't concentrate on the game.

"I wound up going over to mom and dad's home, went downstairs, and watched the game with no one else around to bother me."

By halftime, things had improved dramatically for the Oilers. First, they came back to tie the game on a play known in Findlay's playbook as 46 Toss, and Milan Smith had his 21-yard TD. It appeared Smith was stopped at the line of scrimmage, before popping out into the open. He bounced off three would-be tacklers on his way to the score.

Recalls Smith, "When I crossed the goal line, the ball clipped my hip and came out, but, fortunately, I had already broken the plane, so it was all good. I'd only had a handful of carries all year [58] because Nate [Sprunger] was playing so well, so that was certainly the highlight of my season."

After Linfield got the ball back, hoping to score with the same ease as on its opening drive, it was time for one of Coach Kwiatkowski's wrinkles to produce some results. Recalls Dick Strahm, "Linfield tried to run two options, and Chris Smith, who turned out to be the game's defensive MVP, shot the gap, and the center never even touched him. Smitty tackled Sells twice for losses, the second time combining with Todd Clark. That forced a punt."

It was then that Strahm saw the pivotal play of the game. After a 15-yard personal-foul penalty was tacked on to a DeMya Wimberly seven-yard keeper, the senior quarterback from Florida must have put a smile of Mouse Davis' face up in the television booth. He threw a 45-yard bullet to a streaking Scott McLaughlin, who finally was hauled down at the one. From there, Balewa Walker plunged for the go-ahead touchdown. A Ben Cochran point after touchdown put the Oilers up 14-7 at halftime.

Up in the crow's nest, Ken Zirkle watched the teams leave the field and expressed to Jim Houdeshell the hope that the Oilers could hang on in the second half. Recalls Houdeshell, "I told Ken I had no doubt we were going to win the game. I pointed to the Linfield quarterback as he left the field with his head down. Body language most generally is a pretty good indicator whether you've got an opponent beat."

The second half featured few chances offensively and more ball control by the Oilers. First, it was Wimberly taking it in from six yards out to push the lead to 20-7. It was a score set up by a well-timed interception by Bob Sutyak.

Then, it was time for another Chris Smith play. Despite a heavily taped ankle, he again shot the gap untouched and blew up a ball carrier in the backfield who was trying to convert a fourth and inches on Linfield's own 44-yard line.

"It really was the key play in the game. Linfield wasn't used to having close games. When the time came for them to play effectively from behind, they couldn't because they simply had never been in that position before. On the strength of Chris Smith's play, our offense covered 44 yards in nine plays with Walker going in from a yard out to put us up, 26-7."

A final desperation score for Linfield when Sells hit Gary McGarvie only made the score a bit more respectable. With the scoreboard showing 26 for Findlay and 13 for Linfield, there was no doubt about who the national champions were. For the 8,741 lucky enough to have been at Civic Stadium, they saw a clinic on something Mouse Davis just wouldn't have believed, had he not seen it with his own eyes.

Walker's 103 yards on the day gave him 997 on the year. For Nate Sprunger, his 65 yards made him the first Oiler since Dana Wright to crack the 1,000-yard barrier. On the day, the Oilers got their rushing average and then some, finishing with 313 yards.

Defensively, in addition to Chris Smith, it was Todd Clark who really came up big. The senior linebacker made the final Oilers game of his career a memorable one as he recorded 13 tackles, 11 of them solo. Bob Heitkamp, Clark's linebacker mate, also had a productive afternoon with nine tackles.

Linfield's head coach Ed Langdorf eschewed making any excuses after his team's first loss in thirteen games. "The Findlay team played pretty damn well today. My hat's off to them. They came a long way and played in front of a pretty hostile crowd."

And, so the Oilers who felt disrespected were indeed the last team standing. For the sophomore Milan Smith, he knew the graduations of Balewa Walker, Nate Sprunger, and DeMya Wimberly meant he would assume a much bigger role in the next two years, but despite that awareness, he remembers his thoughts as he watched his teammates during the post-game interview panel. "I remember thinking, how are we ever going to climb this high again? The seniors, guys like Heitkamp and Clark and Sutyak and DeMya and Nate and Balewa, they would all be gone.

"Certainly we could duplicate the effort but not the men. I guess I just knew immediately as I looked around at my teammates how much we were going to lose. Even in the midst of celebration, there are some sad thoughts hanging around as well."

For the season, Findlay set several team records, especially those marks that involved the running game. The team accumulated 252 first downs, 196 rushing first downs, 3,956 yards rushing, and 5,199 yards in total offense, all new school standards.

Bob Heitkamp carved his name in the Findlay record books when he became the school's first linebacker ever to earn consecutive first-team NAIA All-American honors. Recalls Dick Strahm, "The stomach pain resulting from the Crohn's disease, at times, was so obvious. A lot of players would have quit, but that's just not a word that ever was in Bobby's vocabulary."

In addition to Heitkamp's selection, Chris Smith was a second-team All-American selection, and Tony Holland, remarkably in his only year starting at offensive tackle, was accorded honorable mention All-American honors.

For Dick Strahm, the win cemented his selection as the Division II NAIA National Coach of the Year. It was an honor Strahm would humbly accept on behalf of his entire program. "Every assistant coach, our trainer, our academic advisor, our players, our cheerleaders, and all our fans certainly can feel they were a part of that award. No successful coach does it alone."

For the recruiting class of 1989, there was a sense of closure after the way the 1991 season ended. And, while youth are often not great lovers of history, the fact that this group had brought the national championship home during a year when the football program was turning 100 years old seemed fitting.

Perhaps they weren't the most gifted group of athletes ever to go through the Oiler football program, but, collectively, the players who comprised the recruiting class of 1989 had an indomitable will, one unmistakable to those administrators, coaches, and fans who traced their evolution from August of 1989 through December of 1992.

While former UF president Ken Zirkle will not dispute the group's determination, there is another quality he will always remember. "That 1992 team just had great mental discipline. They may not have been the most talented, but they simply did not make mistakes. And when you combine athleticism with the intelligence it takes to demonstrate mental discipline, well, that's just an unbeatable combination."

Despite the heavy losses to graduation that he would have to counter, Dick Strahm saw even after the harvest had been gathered that there were some reasons to smile looking ahead to 1993. He knew he had Milan Smith to assume the four-back position after Nate Sprunger's departure and Jermaine Ward to assume Balewa Walker's three-back slot. And, he knew he could count on the continued unselfish and rock-steady play of two-back Doug Rode.

As for the quarterback slot, Strahm was also thankful to be able to rely on Scott Garlock, the senior who had played so capably when called upon during DeMya's time. Backing up Garlock would be sophomore Ray Materni, from Holland, Ohio.

As far as targets for the occasional passes needed to keep a wishbone offense moving forward, both Scott McLaughlin and Todd Pees had another year of eligibility.

The biggest challenge offensively would be the primary responsibility of assistant line coaches Jim McIntosh and Curtis Davidson, whose job it would be to replace an offensive line as good as Pelligrini, Wolfe, Kramer, Cotterill, Stofel, and Holland, none of whom would be returning.

Defensively, while the Oilers obviously lost a lot with the graduation of players like Heitkamp, Clark, Smith, Nagy, and Sutyak, Strahm would have a handful of talented players returning. The head Oiler knew he could bring pressure off the edges, since both Lee Frank and Jamie Godman had another year. Additionally, Mike Collett had a senior season to play. And, in the secondary, all four players who would be back were either starters or played extensively in 1992. Todd Vrancken and Chris Rothhaar would be the corners and Shane Dennison and Des May were ready to occupy the roles of strong and free safety, respectively.

As the off-season progressed and recruiting efforts intensified and the players followed their off-season weight programs and attended their 6:00 a.m. aerobics sessions, Dick Strahm made a decision to take in another assistant coach, that is, if he could lure him away from a 38-degree meat locker in Rossford, Ohio.

Coach Strahm and the captains of the 1995 national championship team with their trophies: (first row) Cal Dietz and Ray Long; (second row) Larry Williams, Coach Strahm, and Bill Yeager.

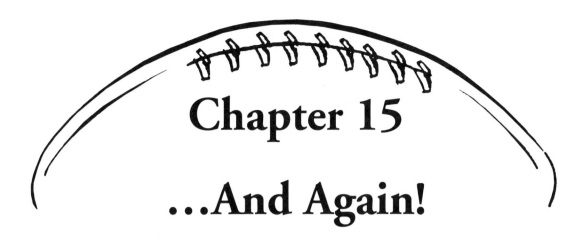

Chapter 15

...And Again!

As Dick Strahm evaluated his coaching staff, he saw stability in who would be returning. Of course, he'd be back for his nineteenth season. And, beyond that, Jim McIntosh was ready for season number seventeen as an Oilers assistant; Doug Coate, for his ninth; Curtis Davidson, for his eighth; and Greg Gilbert, for his sixth. Additionally, Sam Bello was settling in nicely and anticipating his third year on staff.

Beyond the veterans, there were also two newcomers who would join Strahm's 1993 staff. Mike Schanski would be welcomed to his post working with the defensive backs. He would also serve the athletic department at The University of Findlay as its coordinator of athletic recruitment.

Recalls Schanski, who is currently an assistant Oilers football coach, "In 1991, I went to the University of Toledo as a graduate assistant to Gary Pinkel. I remained there in '92 and worked under defensive coordinator Dean Pees.

"Well, as it turned out, Dick Strahm called Coach Pees and asked if he knew anyone who could both coach the defensive backs and also fill that new position as coordinator of athletic recruitment, and Coach Pees recommended me. I interviewed and got the job.

"In addition to coaching football, I kept people up to date with all the rules we had to follow to maintain compliance with the NAIA. As far as recruiting, I also worked pretty closely with our president, Ken Zirkle, and I was also responsible for organizing our big on-campus all-sports recruiting day."

The other newcomer to the Oilers staff one might say was the coach who came in from the cold, literally. It was Dick Strahm's son, Doug, who decided to accept his father's offer to return to coaching at the place where he had both played and coached as student assistant in 1985.

Recalls Doug, who now lives in Delaware, Ohio, with his wife, Lisa, and son, Zachary, while working for Mac Tools, "I'd really moved around a lot since I'd left what was then Findlay College after the '85-'86 school year. In '86 and '87, I taught and coached at Liberty

Benton High School. Then in '88, I went to the University of Toledo to work on my master's and became a GA [graduate assistant] to Dan Simrell.

"Then, in 1989, I went to Western Carolina University to continue work on my master's and coach on my Uncle Dale's football staff.

"Then, in 1990, I left coaching and helped run a bed and breakfast up in the Smoky Mountains after my uncle took a coaching job at Duke. The bed-and-breakfast opportunity came up because another one of the GAs had a father who owned the bed and breakfast and needed help.

"In 1991 I moved to Georgia to go back into teaching and coaching at Rockdale County High School.

"After a year, I returned to Ohio and went to work in the meat-packing plant. I worked grinding hamburger in a 38-degree cooler on third shift and really tried hard to convince myself that I was going to stay and climb the ladder of success in the meat packing business."

Recalls Dick Strahm, "Doug took me to Rossford to the plant where he worked. He was showing me around and enthusiastically, pointing out different parts of the operation, but I know my son, and I just thought he was trying to oversell me.

"So, I stopped finally and said, 'I don't know how you do this. I couldn't do it for anything in the world. Is this what you really want to do?'"

As it turned out, Dick's ability to read the underlying thoughts of his elder son was right on the money. Doug Strahm was not happy grinding hamburger in freezing conditions from nine at night until six in the morning five days a week.

Recalls Doug, "I didn't tell Dad because I just didn't want to let him down. I knew he'd gotten me the position, and I hadn't really settled in as far as staying in one place. So, I really wanted to like it."

However, Doug's career in the meat-packing industry only lasted about another week, as Dick recollects. "Right after I got back to Findlay from the tour, I started thinking long and hard about how we could bring Doug back to the university. I did some checking, and there was a position opening in the admissions office for the next school year. I also needed another assistant. As soon as I offered Doug a position on my coaching staff and told him he would also have the opportunity to apply for the position of admissions counselor on campus, he jumped at it. Once he was interviewed, he was offered the job."

So, finally after several years of being on the move, the 28-year-old had his chance to settle in. He was back working for the university he loved and working for a head coach he loved even more. Doug's return allowed him for the next five years to get an inside view of some very special seasons in Findlay Oilers history.

With Doug already set to rejoin him, Dick Strahm again settled into a summer routine in 1993. Of course, he worked on football. He also took care of a variety of appointments, especially with his cardiologist Dr. Jerome Beekman, appointments that sometimes were difficult to accomplish when school was in session full time. Summer also included the family vacation to Miley's Resort up in Michigan.

During Strahm's mid-summer physical, he again had blood drawn for his PSA test, and he was pleased that the results were fine.

The football schedule was set for the 1993 season, and there was something very interesting about it. After opening at home against Kentucky State, the Oilers would play the following week at Donnell against a team from Hamburg, Germany, in an exhibition game that would make history. Never had the word *international* been used to describe an athletic contest of any sort at Donnell Stadium.

The story as to how the semipro Hamburg Blue Devils would be making the trip to Findlay, Ohio, in the first contest ever pitting a foreign team against a U.S. collegiate team actually has its genesis in a friendship.

The friendship was one shared by a Findlay dentist, Dr. Jackson Winters, and Rusty Ekland, the player-coach of the Blue Devils. In addition to being a dentist, Dr. Winters also officiated football games for the Mid-Am Conference, and occasionally, for NCAA Division III contests.

Ekland was a former Pacific Lutheran University linebacker. Two years earlier, Pac Lutheran accepted an invitation to play a series of three exhibition games in China, games Winters had been selected to help officiate. It was at that time that the graduating senior and Dr. Winters struck up a friendship.

In the summer of 1992, Ekland had settled in Hamburg and helped to form the semipro Blue Devils. He also contacted Winters, wanting him to come to Hamburg to officiate an exhibition game with his former school, Pacific Lutheran, and his new creation, the Blue Devils.

Between Ekland and Winters, an idea evolved for the team from Germany to play two exhibition games with The University of Findlay, one in September during a bye week for the Oilers, and one in May of 1994 in Hamburg. That would give the German players a chance to experience American culture, Findlay-style, during their six-day visit and provide the Oilers a chance to experience the German culture the following spring.

Recalls Dick, "I was fully on board when Jack came to me with the idea. We had an open date anyway, and the game would give us a chance to work on a few things after our opener, which, I saw as a positive, especially since we were scheduled to play our biggest rivals, Westminster, next.

"Additionally, I liked the spring contest. To that point, we'd never been allowed to have spring football, but Dr. Zirkle had already approved it to help us get ready for the game in Hamburg. So, I really thought the whole idea was a win-win."

So, everyone agreed with the idea, Dr. Zirkle, athletic director Ron Niekamp, Dick Strahm, and his coaches. The Blue Devils would be in the Findlay area for six days and attend a variety of activities designed to show off the city of Findlay, Hancock County, and the Midwest as a whole.

Pat McMahon, Oilers super booster and staunch supporter of Strahm's Foster Parent program, also was instrumental in helping to organize the event and finding local families to host the Blue Devils' players and coaches.

One player who was really anticipating a return to the field was Tim Goodwin. Goodwin was set to graduate in mathematics education and, hopefully, would follow his father Bill, a distinguished high school football coach who would one day be inducted into the Ohio High School Football Coaches' Hall of Fame, into a teaching and coaching career. He had spent the previous year as an Oilers student assistant coach while rehabbing the serious leg fracture he sustained in 1991 and was in the best shape of his life.

Recalls Dick Strahm, "During the summer, Tim severely cut his foot while mowing a lawn. I felt badly for him because he had worked so hard to come back from the broken leg. While he still wanted to play in '93, he just could not push off his foot when he went into his stance and decided to retire from the game."

While some may have thought that football was done for Tim Goodwin, nothing could have been further from the truth. He graduated and taught and coached at Bluffton High School, where you might say he cut his coaching teeth for an excellent coach, Dennis Lee.

Continued Strahm, "For the past nine years, Tim has been at Marion Local High School and has won three Division VI titles and one Division V title. As far as the list of my former players who went into coaching, who has had that kind of success? Well, the list begins and ends with Tim Goodwin."

In August, as new starters Scott Garlock at quarterback, Milan Smith at the featured four-back, and Jermaine Ward at Balewa Walker's former three-back slot, coaches Jim McIntosh and Curtis Davidson worked feverishly to put together an offensive line. Every starter from 1992 was gone, and it would take some time to create a cohesive unit.

Among the offensive line candidates were all Ohioans except for one. Dan Varner (Cincinnati), Steve Mutersbaugh (Uniontown), Marty Simon (Olmstead Falls), Shawn Fultz (Bucyrus) Rick Reynolds (Delphos) and Loren Ragland (Santa Ana, California) worked overtime to understand the intricacies of the blocking schemes required of all who wished to play in Strahm's wishbone unbalanced line.

The 1993 schedule was a favorable one as six of the nine regular season games would be played at Donnell Stadium. In addition, the Oilers also were hosting Hamburg in the historic September 11 contest.

The opener was on September 4, a Thursday night game at 7:00 p.m., something that, no doubt, pleased much of the fan base. The orange and black opened the season on a positive note with a 27-3 win over the Kentucky State Thoroughbreds. Scott Garlock played extremely well in his first start. The senior signal caller completed 8 of 13 for 171 yards and two TDs. Jermaine Ward paced the running attack with 112 yards on 25 carries and a touchdown. Defensively, it was sophomore Larry Williams who would gather in his first Oilers interception.

Then the Blue Devils came to Northwest Ohio. The exhibition game, which Dick was thankful to have rather than an open date before the September 18 Homecoming game with the perennially powerful Westminster Titans, commenced at 4:00 p.m. In somewhat of a shock to the overflow crowd of 6,000, the Oilers could mount little in the way of an offense on its opening possession after a 46-yard kickoff return by speedster Scottie McLaughlin.

After a McLaughlin punt, the team from Hamburg took over at the ten and methodically moved the ball downfield, covering 90 yards on 13 plays for a score.

It was then the Oilers finally woke up. In the second quarter, Garlock hooked up with McLaughlin on an 80-yard catch-and-run. Then, Doug Rode scampered for 26 yards and a touchdown in the third quarter. Garlock then fired his second touchdown pass of the afternoon, a 13-yarder to Todd Pees. Finally, it was Jermaine Ward's 47-yard burst that capped the scoring.

After the first-quarter scare, the team headquartered in Hamburg couldn't seem to get out of its own way. Key fumbles prevented any further scoring, and, by day's end, the scoreboard proclaimed the Oilers a 28-7 winner.

Strahm, perhaps remembering more the 7-7 deadlock at the intermission than his team's second-half dominance, was less than excited as he spoke to the press after the game. "We didn't play with a whole lot of enthusiasm. I guess it's good to win, but we have to play with a lot more passion against Westminster if we expect to win."

During this era of Oilers football, there was always thought given to the Titans, the team from Westminster that most of the Findlay faithful would agree was the arch rival of their hometown team. The September 18 game marked the tenth consecutive year the two teams squared off.

There has long been the notion that athletic administrators look to schedule a weaker opponent for a homecoming game. That theory could be thrown right out the window in 1993. When the alumni returned to once again try to remember what made their time at the small college so special, one of the premier teams in all of the NAIA, the Westminster Titans, awaited to try to spoil the Oilers' weekend.

Many of the members of Dick Strahm's first team to play for a national championship in 1978 returned for their fifteenth anniversary, both to lend support and, also, to remember a magical run that ended just a yard short of what would have been Strahm's first national title.

In a game as evenly matched as any in the series, it was the Oilers that sent its fans home happy after a 21-15 win. Backup halfback John Ferguson had a huge game with 153 yards rushing on 20 carries and a touchdown. The workhouse was Jermaine Ward as he carried 31 times on his way to 121 yards.

Week three found Findlay on the road for the first time, traveling to Northwood University in Midland, Michigan. In a game that, no doubt, shocked many after the big win against Westminster, the Northmen, who had failed to win a game the previous year, came away with a 22-21 win when the Oilers failed to convert a 29-yard field goal that would have sent them back to Findlay a winner. The kick hit one of the uprights in the closing moments, denying Strahm's squad the win. The loss wasted a 91-yard kickoff return for a touchdown by Scott McLaughlin.

Recalls Strahm, "I think every coach fears a letdown after a big win, and I guess we were prime candidates for such a letdown. You can cry all you want about the bad luck with the kick bouncing off the uprights, but a miss is a miss. Besides, the game never should have come down to needing a field goal at the very end to pull it out."

Week four found Findlay again traveling, this time for a game with Union College in Barbourville, Kentucky. Scott Garlock turned in an excellent game, throwing for 171 yards on 10 of 13 and two touchdowns. Milan Smith led the ground game with 126 yards on 18 carries and a touchdown.

Defensively, Ray Long, the sophomore out of Clyde, Ohio, had taken over as a starting linebacker and chipped in with an interception in the Oilers' 34-7 victory.

Recalls Long, who still lives in his hometown and works for HJ Heinz, "In 1992, I was a freshman on the scout team and shadowed Bob Heitkamp in practice. I really owe a lot to Bob. A lot of times, seniors don't pay much attention to the younger guys, but he helped me immensely develop as a player.

"I think I owe the fact that I was the only sophomore starter in '93 to Bob. Since I was only around 200 pounds, Bob was the one to impress upon me the need to keep my feet moving, something I never forgot."

Week five brought a return to Donnell Stadium for the first of three straight home games. The Cambellsville Fighting Tigers made the drive from the Commonwealth with a strong squad, and, at least on paper, the game appeared to be a good match. Cambellsville had been 7-3 the previous year and returned thirteen starters.

But, what happens on turf often is not the same as what things appear to be on paper, and such was the case on that October 9. Garlock threw for 140 yards and two touchdowns, Doug Rode had a 78-yard run for a score, and Jermaine Ward ran for 148 yards on 17 carries and three scores as the home team took the bite right out of the Tigers, 70-12.

The middle contest of the three-game home stand was against St. Xavier University out of Chicago. The school, just in its first year of football, was no match for the far more experienced Oilers. The final score of 49-0 reflected the Oilers' first shutout of the year. Garlock continued to demonstrate a high degree of accuracy, hitting 7 of 9 for 119 yards and a TD, and Milan Smith ran for an even 100 yards on just 10 totes.

Week seven brought the Tiffin University Dragons to town with an outstanding running back, Brian Diliberto, who was destined to finish his career as a two-time NAIA All-American and the holder of more individual records than any player in his school's history. To this point, the Oilers had, quite frankly, dominated that week's opponent since Strahm's arrival to Findlay, winning all seven times the schools competed by a combined score of 193-18.

However, this day would prove to be different as Tiffin's coach Bob Wolfe watched his charges finally vanquish Findlay, 31-20, to hand the Oilers their second loss of the year.

For Strahm, while the game ended in a loss, it also gave him a lasting memory, one that forever would remind him of both the violent nature of the game he loves and the resiliency that the game sometimes can elicit.

"Tiffin was just having a field day running the ball against us, especially Diliberto. Well, Coach Wolfe ran a quick toss to Diliberto to our sideline, so I was no more than maybe twenty feet away when I saw our free safety, Larry Williams, come flying up and absolutely leveled Diliberto.

"The force of the blow knocked Brian out. It was the hardest hit I have ever personally witnessed.

"But, I'll tell you what a tough kid that Diliberto was. He missed the rest of the second quarter and the entire third quarter, but with Tiffin only leading 24-20, I looked across the field in the fourth quarter and here that gritty kid was, coming back in the game!

"And, he reasserted himself, *Boom,* going five yards, eight yards, six yards, carry after carry all the way down the field and into the end zone for the score that iced the game."

Despite Garlock's again having a good day throwing the football, hitting 13 of 24 for 217 yards and two touchdowns, Findlay just couldn't find its the running game.

Recalls Milan Smith, who led the Oilers with a meager 44 yards on 13 carries, "I remember Coach Strahm was basically disgusted. He came up to me early in the practice the following week and told me that if 44 yards was all he could count on from his four-back, maybe it was time he started looking for a new four-back."

With a loss under their belts, the Oilers left in week eight for their third and final road game, traveling to Urbana Ohio to face the Blue Knights. Strahm's team pounded out a convincing 44-6 win as the Oilers' Garlock went a perfect 8 for 8 for 73 yards and a touchdown to Scott McLaughlin. The bulk of the carries, 27 of them, went to Jermaine Ward, and he responded with 169 yards and a touchdown. Defensively, Des May had a memorable afternoon as he picked off not one but a pair of passes.

All that was left of the regular season was a game at Donnell versus the NAIA Division I Hilltoppers of West Liberty State from West Virginia. The home team responded with a solid effort, both offensively and defensively, and pounded out a 38-14 win. Garlock, despite only hitting an uncharacteristic 6 of 15 passes, did toss three touchdown passes, all to Scott McLaughlin. As far as running the ball, Milan Smith responded with 130 yards on 18 carries.

Defensively, Chris Rothhaar followed May's two-interception performance of the week before with two picks of his own.

While the win, was nice, even nicer was that the Oilers' 7-2 mark qualified them for the post-season. When the pairings were decided and the bids unsealed, Dick Strahm liked both the opponent and the location. "We got our chance to even the score with Tiffin. Despite the fact that Brian Diliberto was a terrific back, Tiffin was a school with whom we were familiar. I also liked the fact that we got to stay at home."

The Oilers were ranked sixth in the final NAIA poll, while the Dragons were ranked number seven. The only stumbling blocks for Tiffin had been a season-opening tie with Cincinnati's Mount St. Joseph and a 34-13 loss to the Oilers' nemesis over the years, the Westminster Titans the week after Bob Wolfe's team knocked off Findlay.

For Dick Strahm, it was a week of reminding his team of how difficult it was to ever beat a team twice in a season. Until such an occasion arose when his team would have to play a team it had already defeated for a second time, that was Coach Strahm's story, and he was sticking to it.

Perhaps what concerned Strahm the most, besides, of course, trying to stop the All-American Diliberto, who managed to gain 174 yards in the first contest despite missing almost an entire quarter and a half after the sledgehammer hit of Oiler safety Larry Williams, was the fact that his own ground attack accounted for just 63 rushing yards in the first game. It was something Oilers backs Jermaine Ward, Milan Smith, and John Ferguson were reminded of quite often as the practice week unfolded.

Strahm saw the game as a contest between two teams which mirrored one another. "We both were running teams that featured quarterbacks who could throw. And, while I'm not sure either team had any great defensive players, both had a lot of very good ones."

But, many felt it would be Brian Diliberto who the Oilers needed to at least slow down. The senior from Eastlake, Ohio, was coming off a spectacular 327-yard day against Taylor in the regular season finale. Additionally, the 5'10," 185-pounder broke the all-time NAIA marks for yards gained (2,132) and carries (340) during the '93 season.

With just 35 yards gained, Diliberto would become the most prolific back in NAIA history. While the prospect of readying a team to stop such an offensive force would certainly have given many coaches sleepless nights, Dick Strahm recalls remaining philosophically realistic.

"Listen, he [Diliberto] was really a great one. We were aware of him, of course, but I didn't have as a goal holding him under a 100 yards rushing. I knew he was going to get his yards because he was going to get over thirty carries. Certainly with that many carries, he was going to break a few.

"What I preached all week was the importance of keeping him between the tackles and keeping him from getting to the corners. I wanted Diliberto to be running where we had numbers and give guys like Ray Long, who was having a terrific sophomore season, a chance to put a hat on him."

Finally, game day, November 20, arrived, and the stands at Donnell Stadium filled with the Oilers faithful, some who had been exhorting the home team for all nineteen years that Dick Strahm had led the program.

The contest featured two huge plays by Findlay, one by the offense and one by the defense. The combination of the two paved the way for an Oilers victory, 28-14.

Offensively, Jermaine Ward, who led all rushers with 147 yards on 18 carries, exploded for 53 yards and a touchdown in the second quarter. On his way to capturing the game's MVP honors, Ward also scored two more touchdowns.

Defensively, it was defensive tackle Nate Arnold who turned in the key play when he forced a fumble at the Tiffin 27-yard line, setting up a Chad Moxley recovery to put the game on ice.

As Strahm predicted, Diliberto did get his yards, 139 of them, and he left the field having gained the most yards in NAIA history and the third-most yards in a career in the history of all divisions of college football. But, besides the records, that was all the workhorse had. Although he craved victory, as all athletes do, it was not in his possession.

In addition to the heroics of Ward and Arnold, several other Oilers stepped up. Scott Garlock completed 8 of 12 and a TD to McLaughlin, and Milan Smith shook loose for 93 yards on 17 carries.

Coach Ray Kwiatkowski's wrinkle, that of using a 4-4 alignment by dropping senior Lee Frank off his customary defensive end position as well as playing the Oiler position Jamie Godman off the defensive line as a fourth linebacker, worked extremely well.

The defensive MVP was a talented sophomore linebacker, Curtis Peoples, who combined with fellow sophomore linebacker Ray Long to remind some of the duo of Bob Heitkamp and Todd Clark.

With the win, the Oilers returned to the second round to play a familiar foe, one they'd only in the past few years learned to defeat. The Westminster Titans of head coach Gene Nicholson were set to roll into Findlay for a 1:00 p.m. kickoff on Saturday, December 4.

Westminster had earned the right to advance by knocking off the 1991 national champion Georgetown College, 20-13. Findlay, yet again, won the sealed-bid process to host the game.

During the week of preparation, not surprisingly, Dick Strahm tried to avoid talking about the near impossibility of beating a good team twice in one year, given the fact that Findlay had knocked off Westminster in week three of the season, 21-15. Combined, the two teams had won three of the last five Division II National Championships (Westminster twice and Findlay once), and both teams would enter the contest at 8-2.

Just as there was somewhat of a targeted player in Brian Diliberto in the first game, there was also a targeted Titan. However, this time the player was more difficult to game plan for because, unlike the running back Diliberto, Aldridge Jones was a defensive back and special teams player.

In a game with a run-oriented wishbone team like the Oilers, it was somewhat ironic that Jones would be such a source of concern, but he was a ball player with what old-time coaches might call a nose for the football and also for the goal line.

In addition to his considerable skills in the secondary, Jones was a premier talent as a kick and punt returner. The Youngstown East High School product had averaged more than 25 yards per kickoff and an additional 16 yards a return on punts, including one for a touchdown in the opening-round win over Georgetown. Jones's seven touchdowns on returns was a school record, and the junior looked to extend that mark and continue his season against the Oilers.

Prior to the contest, Strahm did finally acknowledge to Larry Alter of Findlay's *The Courier* that it would be difficult to knock off Westminster a second time in one season. "Westminster is an excellent football team, and it's awfully tough to beat a good football team twice in one season. I know it's never been done in the history of Westminster. You know they are going to play tougher than the first game."

Unfortunately, for Findlay, its head coach's comments to the press proved to be prophetic, as the visiting Titans stymied the Oilers in front of their home crowd, 24-0. It was Westminster's power running of Andy Blatt and Matt Buggey that kept the ball out of Scott Garlock's hands for inordinately long stretches. When Garlock did go to the air, it was Aldridge Jones who played lock-down pass defense. Additionally, he contributed a key 46-yard punt return in the contest.

Dick Strahm was understandably terse after the contest and explained the outcome succinctly. "Westminster controlled the offensive and defensive lines of scrimmage period." Sometimes, it really doesn't take long for a coach to cut to the heart of the matter.

And so, the 1993 Findlay season ended at 8-3 on a very muddy field, in part because the wishbone offense produced just 125 yards on the ground. Perhaps there was some consolation that Westminster did go on to win yet another national championship.

As far as post-season honors, Marty Simon wrote his name right along side other great Oilers centers with his selection as an NAIA All-American. Receiving honorable mention nods were fellow offensive lineman Steve Mutersbaugh, running back Jermaine Ward, defensive lineman Mike Collett, and defensive back Shane Dennison. In addition, both Simon and Mutersbaugh were Academic All-Americans.

Scott Garlock finished his Oilers career second only to Kris Alge in school history in completion percentage, with a mark of more than 55 percent from 1990 through 1993. He also threw for fourteen touchdowns in his senior season, certainly a more-than-respectable number in a ground-oriented offense.

On the receiving end of many of Garlock's darts was Scott McLaughlin, who again led the Oilers in all receiving categories.
Jermaine Ward went over 1,000 yards rushing, finishing with 1,041 and a 5.1 yards-per-carry average.

Defensively, perhaps the most pleasant surprise was Ray Long, the tough-as-rawhide linebacker out of Clyde, Ohio, who led the team in tackles.
As the Oilers moved into their off-season weight and conditioning programs, the talk began to build of their spring trip to Hamburg, Germany, to complete the two-game exhibition series with the Blue Devils, a team comprised of a mix of former American collegiate players and Europeans.

While not all the players could afford the cost of the trip, which was a necessity in the world of small-college football, there would certainly be a representative traveling squad that would make the trip. The seniors, who had just the previous fall completed their eligibility, were also given the opportunity to make the trip and play. The ball players, coaches, and trainers had to pay for their own airplane tickets. Once in Hamburg, room and board was provided by the host team, as was most of the post-game travel for sight-seeing.

Perhaps what excited Dick the most was the opportunity for the first time in his Findlay career to conduct spring practices. "I was thrilled to be able to get in some sanctioned practices, especially since we were moving into a brand-new experience in 1994. We were finally joining a league after eight years as an independent."

The name of the league was the Mid-States Football Association, and it was divided into two leagues, consisting of eleven teams total. The Mideast featured such Ohio schools as Urbana, Geneva, Tiffin, and Malone as well as the beast from Pennsylvania, the Westminster Titans. The Midwest included three schools out of Illinois – Trinity, St. Xavier University, and Olivet Nazarene; Taylor University from Indiana; Lindenwood from Missouri; and The University of Findlay Oilers.

With Jack Winters playing a major role, the contingent of Findlay Oilers players, coaches, and supporters departed for Hamburg in late May for their date with the Devils. Recalls Strahm, "While we couldn't take the whole team, we did bring a traveling squad of forty players.

"My very good friends Dave and Gwen Kuenzli and their daughter Lee also joined us. Both were great supporters of both me and the football program. Each August, I would have both of them talk to my team, Gwen about academic matters and Dave about the role that being a good citizen plays in young people's lives."

As a communications professor, Gwen Kuenzli had many of Strahm's players in class and specialized in working with those who were academically marginal. The trip to Hamburg was especially gratifying for her because she had gotten to know several of the players from a far different perspective than simply watching their performance on a football field. She saw the trip as much for its potential for great teaching moments as an opportunity to see a football game. After the game, there would be time to take tours and learn about the history of the German culture.

Recalls Gwen, "I remember we took two planes. After the first left, the other flight was delayed for almost six hours. So, there was some confusion with the planes arriving six hours apart.

"But, once we got everything synchronized, things went very well. I think the neatest part about the whole trip was so many of the kids had only been on a plane once or twice, and most had never been further than a few states away."

Dave Kuenzli recalls the genesis of his friendship with Dick Strahm as well as the trip to Germany. "It was through Dick's friendship with Gwen because she had several of his players in class that I became close to Dick. Those six days in Germany were very special. It was, in my mind, a once-in-a-lifetime opportunity for our young people, and I was so glad that Gwen and I were able to be a part of such a special memory."

Recalls Dick about the game itself, "I remember the game was played in a soccer stadium, and there was really a raucous crowd there. They were allowed to drink beer, and maybe that had something to do with the crowd cheering, basically, about everything that happened on the field.

"I'll bet there were about twenty-five cheerleaders, and they led cheers the whole game. If we fumbled, people cheered. If Hamburg fumbled, they cheered. If we scored, they cheered. If Hamburg scored, they cheered. It just didn't make any difference.

"I do recall it was a pretty physical game, and we won a pretty tight one [21-14]. But, really, beyond the game, the whole experience was much more valuable than anything that went on at the stadium.

"While I wouldn't allow our players to do any sightseeing before the game because I wanted them to take the game seriously, afterwards, we did take several tours around Germany."

Strahm has particularly strong memories of taking his team on a tour through the concentration camp Bergen-Belsen. "That was a day all of us will remember as a very serious and solemn one. What we heard and what we saw on the film was a history lesson the University could not have provided. Our walk through the camp really will remain with us always, especially when we got to the Crematoria."

Another tour that was memorable, but for its beauty rather than the solemnity of the camp experience, was one taken through the German countryside. Recalls Strahm, "We saw many churches and castles that date all the way back to the sixteenth century. Our buses would stop along the way so that we could visit some of the churches. We also stopped in a small village to have lunch at an outdoor restaurant to get some authentic German cuisine."

Strahm remains in several people's debt for helping to make the trip so special. "I do need to thank Jack Winters for all his work in arranging both games. He helped officiate both games and, were it not for him, the cultural exchange would not have been possible.

"It was Jack who really was the conduit between us and the Hamburg team. He was working with European officials, training them, and developed a close relationship with the general manager of the Blue Devils, Alex Gernert.

"When the Hamburg team was searching for an American small college to play a two-game exhibition series, Jack suggested us.

"Really, a lot of people helped us. The game over in Germany was actually given a name, the UNICEF Bowl. I remember it was Phil Gardner, Sr., who bought fifty-five beautiful black hooded nylon jackets for the players, trainers, and coaches.

"Then, Jack Winters, as if he hadn't done enough, decided to dip into his own pockets and funded very nice travel bags for us too. For an endeavor of this magnitude, it really takes a lot of people like the businessmen in our town like Pat McMahon, Pat Rooney and Phil Gardner, but Dr. Jack Winters was really the vital cog."

After the Oilers returned to the states to put the finishing touches on the school year, Strahm's goal was to take a final look for any young men he could add to his list of recruits for the upcoming '94 season.

And, wouldn't you just know it? Strahm did find one, and in the most unlikely place he could have ever imagined.

Recalls Strahm, "One day, a good friend and staunch supporter of both the University of Toledo and The University of Findlay, where he was on the board of trustees, Mike Cicak, drove down from Toledo to Findlay to see me. He said he wanted to take me to lunch.

"I really didn't have anything going for lunch that day, so I locked my office door and off we went. Now, let me tell you something. Mike is a very fast driver, so here we go speeding out of town.

"I asked him where we were going, and he said he knew a place over by Stryker, which was about 70 miles away, but it was kind of a slow-down afternoon and I figured with Mike's lead foot, it wouldn't take all that long. I believe in Mike's next life, he'll be driving in the Indy 500.

Besides, it had been some time since I visited with Mike, so even the long drive didn't bother me.

"As we're driving through the country, I'm just looking out the window and relaxing when Mike suddenly says to me, 'Dick, I've got a young man I'd like you to meet before we eat.'

"Well, I couldn't believe it when a while later, he pulled into the entry for the prison located in Stryker. He parked the car, and we went through all the procedures to get inside the gate.

"Mike told the guard we were there to see Chris Jaquillard and went into a receiving room to wait. As soon as Mike said Chris's name, I recognized it.
"I have always kept up with high school football back in my home town of Toledo, and, really, even if that weren't the case, I probably would have known the name anyway.

"Chris Jaquillard graduated from Toledo Woodward High School a couple years earlier. When I heard the name, what flashed through my mind was he was one of the top Division I running backs in the state of Ohio both his junior and senior years.

"I remember also seeing Jaquillard on a TV news broadcast being sentenced for his role in a drug sting operation after he'd graduated while he was going to the University of Toledo. He was a scholarship football player for then-Rocket head coach Gary Pinkel."

Both Strahm and his friend Mike Cicak reacted to the opening of the door of the receiving room, and the two men's eyes met a powerfully built 5'10," 210-pound 20-year-old walking across the room with an inquisitive look on his face.

Recalls Jaquillard, who now runs a successful business called TLC Health Care Services and lives in the Toledo area, "I knew Mike Cicak from Toledo. He was kind of a mentor to a lot of high school athletes coming out of Toledo and helped with college selection and such, but I really had no idea why he was coming to see me. As for the man sitting beside him, well, I didn't know him at all.

"Actually, I was a little annoyed. I was in a thirty-day lock-up situation before I started doing my community service and just wanted to get through it. I instructed my family and friends not to visit me.

"I was embarrassed and really needed some time to think about my life. Here I was, a convicted felon, a guy who had made some mistakes, not by taking drugs myself but by helping some acquaintances get some drugs. I had lost my scholarship at UT and my right to play the game I'd loved my whole life and also my chance to get the education my family really couldn't afford. Basically, I thought my life was over. All I wanted to do was be alone.

"I guess more out of curiosity than anything else, I agreed to go through the demeaning weapon and contraband search and come to the receiving room to see who had come."

As Jaquillard settled into a chair, Cicak introduced the head coach of The University of Findlay football team to the former Ohio High School Division I Back of the Year.

Strahm was obviously not fully aware of all the details as to what had happened in the relatively short life of Chris Jaquillard. The last three or four years saw Jaquillard go from the summit of potential and promise to the absolute abyss of lost opportunity. Clad in an orange jumpsuit and a convicted felon, there was only one person of the three at the table who knew every single detail from the inside out. And, at Mike Cicak's directive, it would be he who would provide the narration to explain what had happened that brought him to his present circumstance.

Remembers Jaquillard about his receiving-room explanation, "I thought it was important to back my story up for Coach Strahm all the way back to my Woodward days.

"I told him I started at Woodward as a sophomore running back. I grew up in Toledo's inner city, close to Wilson Park. While I could have gone to other high schools, Woodward was within easy walking distance of our house, and, besides, my older brother Aaron, whom I idolized, was a sophomore there on the football team.

"Well, my first year of varsity as a sophomore, I was selected as Woodward's MVP and named to the All-City Team. I just loved playing. It gave me a purpose, and I think because of football, I was also more focused in the classroom.

"By the end of my junior year, I was named the city of Toledo's back of the year, and, right after that and throughout the summer before my senior year, I started getting all sorts of letters from schools recruiting me. The letters came from about every major football power in the country, schools like Notre Dame, Ohio State, Michigan, and Tennessee.

"My senor year, I repeated as the city back of the year and was also named by one organization as the top running back in the state.

"However, I couldn't score high enough on the ACT. I took it six times during my junior and senior years, and the best I could score was a seventeen. I needed an eighteen to go to a bigger school, so that ran my self-esteem down some. I had like a 3.5 GPA, but I just wasn't a very good test taker.

"So, I ended up having to chose a Mid-American Conference school, and Toledo offered me a full scholarship, so I took it. My first year, I was what was called a Prop 48 case, meaning I had to sit out my freshman year, but as long as I maintained my grades and got at least a 2.0 GPA, I would have three years of eligibility starting as a sophomore."

In Jaquillard's first year, he easily maintained an above-2.0 GPA and was geared up to have a big sophomore year. However, much to Jaquillard's surprise and also his frustration, he wasn't as big a piece of the Rockets' puzzle as he thought he deserved to be.

"I played special teams but just never really got the chance to run the ball. In practice, I ran it on the scout team, and so many players would come up to me after practice and tell me there was no way I shouldn't be starting ahead of the two upperclassmen who were starters, but that was just the way it was. The decision was not mine.

"After the season, Chris Jaquillard settled into his off-season regime. He had lived in a dorm during the fall quarter to remain close to the team activities and the same would be the case during winter quarter.

"I had weight training at five in the morning and wasn't about to do anything that would put my scholarship in jeopardy, like oversleeping and missing a session, so I stayed on campus.

"Well, in the dorm, there were some people from Cincinnati and Akron who were doing a lot of recreational drugs. That didn't really bother me because I'd never been into drugs and certainly wasn't tempted by them. To me, they had no appeal. I saw so much drug use in high school, especially since I was raised in the inner city, but I loved football so much and had a goal of taking the sport as far as it could take me that, in a way, football became my drug.

"But, I was pretty immature and wanted to be accepted, so I did agree to introduce some of my dorm acquaintances to some of my neighborhood friends who could get drugs pretty easily."

At the end of winter quarter, Jaquillard moved home after off-season workouts had concluded. That would give him a chance to commute to class as he awaited spring football practices. Additionally, it was a great way to save some money.

"You see, I got $600 a month for a living allowance to pay for room and board, so those monthly checks, I was able to bank.

"A couple of months after I'd moved home, the kid who was my dorm roommate started showing up at my house and asking if I could get him some crack cocaine. I don't know how in the world he ever got there the first time because I never told him where I lived."

If teens had the ability to always make mature decisions, Chris Jaquillard would have sent the acquaintance packing with a stern admonishment to never ask for such a favor again. But, youthful indiscretion is as much a part of the maturation process as the physical changes that announce themselves to teens at regular intervals.

Recalls Jaquillard, "It was really stupid judgment on my part, but I did help him make his connection, ironically, not from a high school friend but from a UT football player. It was four rocks of cocaine. When I gave it to my old roommate, the guy sitting next to him who was introduced as one of the guys who lived in the dorm was really a vice detective, as I would soon find out.

"About a month later, I was home eating some ice cream and talking to my girlfriend on the phone. I hung up, and it was my former roommate again. He asked me if I could help him score some weed, and I told him I didn't want anything to do with helping him anymore. I'd just decided that the risk was far too great. But, he was so persistent, so I agreed to help him one final time to set up a buy. What I didn't know is he was in the back of a police van right down the street. It was a sting operation, and the phone was tapped.

"Less than a half hour later, law enforcement came bursting through my front door with a battering ram. My dad came running down the stairs pumping a shotgun, as police had weapons drawn yelling, 'Put the gun down!'

"They grabbed me and slammed me to the floor, cuffed me, and took me to the police station."

For Jaquillard, he had allowed peer pressure, the desire to be accepted, to cloud his judgment, and now he had trouble by the bushel. Jaquillard had been caught in the middle of a drug sting operation, and despite not actively engaging in any drug use himself, Jaquillard would pay the heaviest of prices.

Jaquillard was eventually found guilty of trafficking in drugs, and the former high school star whose exploits were splashed across newspapers throughout the region virtually every Saturday morning in the fall, would again be in the paper, but for the wrong reasons.

He was sentenced to community service, one year at the prison in Stryker, and two additional years' probation upon his release, contingent on his maintaining a spotless record. Otherwise, he would return and finish the balance of the original sentence. The only good news was that the judge agreed to shock probation for the year handed down and a release after thirty days, pending Jaquillard's good behavior.

Recalls Jaquillard, "I remember feeling somewhat betrayed by the press. The next day's *Toledo Blade* put the whole story on the front page. In a huge picture, there I was, handcuffed, standing before the judge.

"The same paper that ran my picture scoring touchdowns now seemingly couldn't wait to put me on the front page in handcuffs."

The picture and story ran right beside a story on Pablo Escobar, the Columbian drug lord who was nicknamed "The King of Coke." Escobar had been gunned down the previous December. To Jaquillard, the placement and size of his picture right beside the picture and story involving a notorious drug lord was not accidental.

"It was almost as if the press was lumping me in with Escobar!"

The University of Toledo football program wanted nothing more to do with Chris Jaquillard, and, as the sad dominos continued to fall, that's what put him on the opposite side of the table in the receiving room from Mike Cicak and Dick Strahm at the correctional facility in Stryker, Ohio. During his time there, he had a lot of time to think and had come to a conclusion that sometimes takes others in similar circumstances years to realize.

"I realized that I, and I alone, was the one to blame for what had happened. Obviously, I should have been strong enough to say no when I was asked to help someone get drugs. And, when UT and Coach Pinkel severed all ties with me, I totally understood.

"Although I couldn't have imagined at that point ever getting there, I guess they say if you're ever going to get to the top, you have to hit rock bottom. For me, this was rock bottom. I felt I had completely ruined my life. Here I was, just barely 20 years old, a convicted felon. I'd lost my scholarship. I'd lost the opportunity to experience the joy I'd always felt on the football field. I was labeled a drug dealer. Who would ever trust me again? Who would ever hire me?"

Someone who was willing to help was Dick Strahm, who was certainly moved by the narrative Chris Jaquillard laid out. "I had worked with young people long enough to know what a powerful force wanting to be accepted is. I saw before me a truly repentant young man who took full ownership of the mistakes he'd made, a young man who refused to blame anyone but himself, and a young man who needed a helping hand if at all possible."

If Chris Jaquillard could get admitted to the University, then I would certainly give him the opportunity to play football. As far as his possible admission, Strahm was also very clear there were no guarantees. "After Chris told me that the court had granted shock probation and that he would be released after he'd served thirty days, I told him to contact me, and I'd have him for a campus visit.

"However, I also told him that whether he'd be admitted to the university was completely out of my hands. It would be Dr. Zirkle's decision. I told him he'd sold me on the fact that he should get a second chance, but the person he really needed to sell was the president of The University of Findlay."

In early June, Chris Jaquillard made his campus visit after driving the 45 minutes to Findlay from his Toledo home. Strahm showed Jaquillard the football stadium, and, of course, the Gardner Fitness Center and the rest of the football facilities. After walking him around campus and arranging for Chris to have some preliminary discussions with Doug, who worked in the admissions office, Dick Strahm took the former high school football star to Dr. Zirkle's house, and it was there he left him to speak with the president alone.

Recalls Jaquillard, "I remember Dr. Zirkle's daughters were actually in the room when I walked in. I told Dr. Zirkle the whole story. He said he needed some time to deliberate and told me that he'd be in touch. That's really all I could ask for, so I thanked him and left."

For Zirkle, he had always considered the thoughts and opinions of his daughters when quandaries arose, and this was another such occasion.

"I'd always trusted my oldest daughter Laura's instincts when it came to my dealings with young people. I told her Chris's entire story just as he'd laid it out to me, and I asked her what she thought. She reminded me that I'd always been a staunch advocate for kids and a real second-chance guy. And, she was right. I just hated to give up on young people.

"My other daughters Andrea, Brianne, Dara, and Lindsay all agreed that people needed second chances. Their feeling, collectively, was that Chris had already been punished once and had to face dire consequences. He'd paid his dues. Why should he have to keep paying them over and over?

"The longer I thought about it, the more I thought my daughters' feelings had a lot of validity. And, I also thought about the last thing Chris said to me before he left the house. He told me that if he were allowed to attend Findlay, he would look me in the eye on graduation day after he'd completed the requirements to obtain his degree and thank me on the platform. I made up my mind that I was going to give Chris Jaquillard a second chance.

Dick Strahm, to this day, is appreciative of Zirkle's decision. "In my mind, it was courageous what Ken did. He knew the story of Chris Jaquillard, at least the version that was portrayed in the media, because it was so well publicized throughout Northwest Ohio. It was on TV. It was in all the papers.

"There would certainly be people, both on the faculty and in our fan base, who would immediately ask, 'Why are we taking a drug dealer into the university? Are we compromising our principles just because this young man can make for a stronger football team?' It was a legitimate question but a question that may not have been asked if Chris were not a football player. Ken knew what a slippery slope he was standing on, but he was strong enough to base his decision not just on what would benefit the football program but what would be in the best interest of Chris Jaquillard as well."

The paperwork was completed, Chris selected criminology as a major, and his academic advisor, Don Collins, helped him map out an academic strategy to fulfill the promise that Chris eventually would accept his degree from Dr. Zirkle and thank him personally for the opportunity during a future commencement exercise.

For the rest of the summer, Chris Jaquillard worked out like a young man possessed as he anticipated the August two-a-days that would be his indoctrination into the Oilers program. He was thankful beyond words for his opportunity and was determined nothing would compromise the second chance he had been given by Dick Strahm and, most of all, by Ken Zirkle.

For Strahm, the summer again was a chance to take care of much of the business he had trouble finding time to address during the school year. Some of that business ensured his continued well being physically and some involved strengthening the family bonds during vacation.

As for the well-being part, Strahm again went for his annual physical, which, since 1992, included taking a blood test to measure his PSA. Since the Findlay head coach had a history of heart problems, he certainly didn't want to add cancer to his list of health issues.

Recalls the head Oiler, "I had the blood draw needed for the test to determine if there were any prostate cancer concerns. Before I got the result, my family and I left on our vacation to Miley's Resort in Michigan.

"The trip was always just before our football staff meetings at Dr. Zirkle's farm in Pennsylvania. While we were up in Michigan, having a great time out on the water fishing and boating, I received a phone call from my doctor that my PSA number had elevated. When I returned to Findlay, I was supposed to get some biopsies to find out what was going on.

"Well, obviously, I was concerned, and we cut our vacation short and returned to Findlay.

"Those of you who've had a biopsy taken know it's not a pleasant procedure, and the results weren't very pleasant either. The sample was malignant. As Ginger and I sat in Dr. Johnson's office that Thursday afternoon, we heard the doctor get right to the point."

Johnson told Dick Strahm that he indeed did have prostate cancer. It was, however, slow growing, so there were some options as Dick recalls.

"Dr. Johnson told me that we could wait to have surgery until after the season, or we could go after the cancer as soon as possible. He said before we decided what course of action to take, he wanted me to take a bone scan to make sure the cancer had not spread.

"The doctor made arrangements at the hospital to take a test for bone cancer, and the very next day I took the test. The nurse said she would have the results sent to Dr. Johnson Monday morning."

For Dick Strahm and his family, that meant a long weekend of trying not to think about possibilities…and thinking about possibilities, trying not to worry…and worrying. But, this was also a time when dear friends also step forward, as Strahm recalls. "Dave and Gwen Kuenzli tried to help get my mind off the subject by taking Ginger and me out on their boat for the weekend to fish and relax. I don't believe I was very good company, but I tried, and, really, the weekend did help somewhat.

"Monday morning came, and I received the call I'd been waiting for. It was the nurse from Dr. Johnson's office, and she told me that the results of the bone cancer test were negative. Of course, by no means was I out of the woods, but I was so relieved. It was the first and only time I had ever cried about any of my health problems that I've had to face. Tears were rolling down my cheeks while I was thanking the nurse aloud and thanking God privately."

Dr. Johnson felt the negative results of the bone scan bought Strahm some time as to when to have the surgery.

So, it was time for Dick Strahm, despite yet another significant health issue, to begin his twentieth season as the Oilers head coach. While he thought about football, of course, he also thought a lot about the slow-growing serious problem within.

One change in Strahm's coaching staff was certainly a significant one. For the first time since 1982, there would be no more visits to Dick's office at the beginnings of practice weeks from the defensive coordinator intent on talking his head coach into allowing a new wrinkle in the base defense.

Ray Kwiatkowski had resigned his position during the off season, opting to remain in education and coaching at the high school level in Michigan.

Coach 'Ski's defenses were ranked in the top ten nationally in 1983, 1984, 1985, 1991, and 1992. He left behind in Flag City, USA, lasting memories of scores of players who admired his toughness and his dedication to making them the best they could possibly be.

Recalls Kwiatkowski, "To this day, I carry with me such strong memories of my players, young men I felt privileged to coach. Players like Todd Clark and Bobby Sutyak and Matt Maglicic and the list just goes on and on. Bob Heitkamp showed desire and intensity that was simply unmatched. Although he had the physical problems with the Crohn's, he just had the attitude that said, 'I am just not going to let that factor into my performance.' I really feel he's one of the great human beings in the world. I know that sounds pretty dramatic, but I believe it."

As for why retirement, Kwiatkowski remembers the sacrifices of a certain woman who stood strongly by her man in what he wanted to do. "My wife was so patient and so supportive all those years I was making the long drive back and forth to Findlay. So many days, I'd leave the house at 5:30 in the morning for school to work before my students came in and then, right after the final bell, I'd jump in the car and head to Findlay. Most days, I wasn't home until after 10:00 p.m. That is an awful lot to ask a wife to support."

Recalls Dick Strahm, "He and I became very close friends. While I certainly would miss Ray, I also felt very fortunate to be bringing someone on our staff that, I felt, would do a great job. Don Akers was a former head coach at Urbana University. He and I competed on opposite sidelines, and I knew the type of individual he was."

Strahm also welcomed Maurice Hall to his staff to serve as wide receivers' coach. He was a former starting quarterback at the University of Toledo.

The rest of the staff remained as constant as the overall level of excellence of Findlay's football program. Returnees included Jim McIntosh, Doug Coate, Curtis Davidson, Sam Bello, Mike Schanski, and Doug Strahm.

For Dick, he saw a relatively inexperienced team take to the practice field in August. Certainly, an unexpected hole had to be filled when Jermaine Ward, the team's leading rusher the previous season, decided not to return for his senior year. He found what he felt was too good of a job during the summer to leave to return to UF in the fall. Sadly, while driving to work less than three year later, Jermaine Ward would perish in an automobile accident.

Milan Smith was set for his senior year after a 736-yard junior season. Another back Strahm hoped would blossom was Troy Pearson, a sophomore fullback out of Detroit.

At quarterback, Strahm was set to hand the reigns of the offense to the third different player in the past three years. Junior Ray Materni (Holland, Ohio) was set to start the season. Two other signal callers were also in the mix, sophomore Mike Konopka, from nearby Elida, Ohio, and a freshman by the name of Bo Hurley, from Alger, Ohio, a young man whose route to Findlay was certainly a circuitous one.

After Hurley's breakout senior year at Upper Scioto Valley High School, a season in which the 6'3," 215-pounder threw for 2,250 yards and 18 touchdowns, Ohio State football coach John Cooper invited Hurley to walk on in Columbus. As a member of the Buckeye scout team, Hurley played most of the second half in the annual Scarlet and Gray game.

Realizing that the chances of his supplanting starter Bobby Hoying as the Buckeye signal caller, Hurley transferred to the University of Cincinnati. By NCAA rules, Hurley was required to sit out one full season before being eligible to play.

Before Hurley could settle in, UC head coach Tim Murphy took the head coaching job at Harvard, and the new coach, Rick Mentor, brought in two junior college transfer quarterbacks. Again, Hurley felt he wouldn't see playing time, so he decided to transfer again.

However, since the NCAA only allowed one transfer for a student-athlete, Hurley was forced to look elsewhere for a school, which brought him to the landscape of the NAIA. Recalls Hurley, "I wanted to go to a school with a strong tradition. And, that led me to look at Findlay. I visited the campus, worked out for the coaches, and talked to Coach Strahm. And, even though I knew Ray was slated to be the starter, I decided on Findlay."

While Hurley was known primarily as a passing quarterback, he was out to prove a passing quarterback could run the wishbone offense and, perhaps, even do a little running himself. Only time would tell.

Scott McLaughlin was set to return at wide receiver for his senior season. Recalls McLaughlin, "Looking back, the one thing I'll always remember is how Coach Strahm treated each and every one of his players, and that is with the utmost respect. He really engendered in all of us such a feeling of team-first, me-second, which is really a life attitude as much as it is a sports attitude.

"So many things he taught me while I was playing for him, I've been able to use both in my career and in raising my family.

"At work, I lead a team of 215 people, and I apply so much to what I learned from Coach Strahm when I lead them. At home, I have six children and, of course, my wife Rhonda, so, obviously, to function at a high level as a family, we have to be team-first at home."

McLaughlin also has Dick Strahm to thank for his career. It was Dick who first helped him land a part-time position with Coca-Cola during summers while McLaughlin was still a Findlay student.

To this day, Scott McLaughlin's parents, Bill and Mary, recognize what a role Dick Strahm played in their son's life and the lives of so many others. Says Bill, "Dick Strahm deserves kudos for an exceptionally successful football career. But, beyond the amazing winning percentage, he can be even prouder of the positive influence he had on the lives of literally thousands of student-athletes, including my son Scott. I absolutely couldn't have handpicked anyone better who I would have wanted Scott to play for."

Scott's wife Rhonda has her own vivid snapshot memory of Dick Strahm. But, it's also a memory she can literally rewind and see as many times as she wishes. It was after Scott had graduated, and Dick had attended Rhonda and Scott's wedding reception. Recalls Rhonda, "We had a videotape done at the reception as a keepsake where people talk for a bit and wish us luck and such. On our wedding reception tape, we've got the coach saying, 'Scott made a lot of great catches throughout his career, but Rhonda is definitely the best catch he ever made!'"

McLaughlin led the Oilers in receptions all three years he had been an Oiler and had every intention of making it a fourth his senior year. He also intended to finish his Oilers athletic career in the spring on the baseball diamond, where he also had played the last three years for one of Strahm's valued assistant coaches who also happened to be the head baseball coach, Doug Coate. Both of McLaughlin's intentions were realized by the end of the spring of 1995.

Strahm felt the offensive line would be strong, anchored by NAIA All-American candidate Cal Dietz, slated to play the inside strong tackle. The Shelby, Ohio, native would be joined by the likes of Paul Cromer (West Chester, Ohio); Loren Ragland, the native Californian; Shawn Fultz (Bucyrus, Ohio), the half brother of former Oilers player and future Oilers assistant coach, Rusty Smith; and tight end Duane Smith (Zanesville, Ohio).

Defensively, Chad Moxley (Urbana, Ohio), Brooks Pighin (Temperance, Michigan), and Nate Arnold (Lucas, Ohio) were set to provide a strong defensive presence. Strahm also had tandem linebackers he felt had the ability to be as good as the terrific duo of Heitkamp and

Clark, in the persons of Jamie Godman (Lorain, Ohio) and the team's leading tackler of the previous year from Clyde, Ohio, Ray Long.

There was a concern about the relative inexperience of the secondary. While the player who so forcefully introduced himself to Tiffin's Brian Diliberto the previous season, Larry Williams, was set at one safety, players more than a bit shy of game experience, such as Jamie Riles (Naples, Florida), John Ferguson (Ypsilanti, Michigan), and Nate Weihrauch (Liberty-Benton High School, Ohio) had to fill the other safety and two cornerback slots and learn quickly.

The Oilers opened on the road against West Liberty State, a non-Mid-States Football Association foe out of the West Virginia city of the same name. Recalls Dick Strahm, "I remember West Liberty had a lot of starters back, not exactly what you want to see in game one when you know you've got a lot of inexperience. We played pretty well but sputtered in the second half when our quarterback, Ray Materni, was injured. He broke his collarbone."

The break proved to be more costly than the 16-14 loss as Materni, doctors determined, would be lost for the remainder of the season. Strahm would have to look elsewhere for the player who would engineer the wishbone offense.

Week two provided a glimpse into just how tough The University of Findlay's new league truly would be. Trinity International University, out of Deerfield, Illinois, came to town for the Oilers' home opener and overwhelmed the home team, 40-15. It was the worst beating a Dick Strahm team had taken since week four of the 1987 season when Findlay was shut out by Ithaca College, 38-0.

Recalls Strahm, "I remember the weather was very warm. Trinity had a terrific quarterback named Todd Johnson, and he just carved us up. The secondary was still learning on the job, and they were really no match for Johnson."

Despite the loss, Strahm was pleased to see Chris Jaquillard make some nice plays from his defensive position as the strong safety, a combination defensive end-strong safety. On offense, he also gained 61 yards on 15 carries. Replacing Materni at quarterback was the freshman, Bo Hurley, who got his feet wet while completing 4 of 9 passes.

For the Oilers, week three would get no easier when they traveled to long-time rival Westminster in New Wilmington, Pennsylvania, to take on a now-league affiliate. The Titans were, as usual, strong and put a third consecutive loss on the Oilers, 17-14.

In the game, Hurley threw his first Oilers TD pass, and Jaquillard again led the ground attack with 80 yards on 23 carries and a touchdown, but it wasn't enough.

Meanwhile, in addition to figuring out what needed to be done to chase away the first 0-3 start in Strahm's Oilers coaching career, Dick also had some decisions to make about a slow-growing malignancy within. After all, prostate cancer doesn't go away on its own.

Recalls Strahm, "Dr. Johnson had given me the name of an outstanding Toledo physician, Dr. Greg Emmert. He wanted me to see him, so I took my wife and daughter Gina to Toledo to meet with him."

Dr. Emmert agreed with the options Dr. Johnson had given Dick in August. The cancer was indeed slow moving, so if Strahm wanted to wait until the season was over, that would be one option. But, it was an option that the head coach felt sounded more and more unappealing as each day passed.

"I told Dr. Emmert that I didn't want to wait. I told him I wanted the surgery as soon as possible to get that cancer out of there.

"He seemed pleased and said we could schedule the surgery for Tuesday, two weeks from tomorrow. He explained that he didn't do surgeries on Mondays."

And, that's when a goal-oriented football coach changed an experienced doctor's routine. "I told the good doctor we had to have the surgery on Monday because I had a game plan.

"I'd given some thought to this in the last few days, and I decided if we could get a couple wins in the next two weeks against Lindenwood (St. Charles, Missouri) and Olivet Nazarene (Bourbonnais, Illinois), which I felt we could, that would put the surgery on the very first day of our open date.

"Then, I figured I could listen to the next game on the radio against St. Xavier University. I thought we'd win that one because they were struggling.

"The week after that, we were scheduled to play Tiffin, and I wanted to be back at least in the booth coaching if I wasn't cleared for the sidelines because this was an important game."

While Dr. Emmert looked at Ginger and Gina Strahm, as if to say, "Is this guy serious?" they both nodded as if to say, "Yes, he's really serious. Football is that important to him." Emmert agreed to the Monday surgery on October 3. The game plan was in place.

Now, it was time to devise a more conventional type of game plan for Strahm, one that would result in UF's first win over Lindenwood College.

In week four, the Oilers released every pent-up frustration that three weeks' worth of losses had brought and swamped the Lions on their own field, 70-0. The freshman Bo Hurley played like a veteran, completing 8 of 12 for 164 yards and a TD. Scott McLaughlin caught 6 for 164 yards and a couple of TDs. Milan Smith finally was able to shake and bake in the open field for 152 yards and a touchdown on just 10 carries.

Defensively, the opportunistic Oilers picked off three passes, one each by Demetrice Boykin, Jamie Godman, and Nate Weihrauch.

The week before the home contest versus Olivet Nazarene, Dick Strahm tried to keep his mind off the cancer surgery and on the football game plan. By Friday late afternoon, perhaps there might be some time to think a little about what would take place at the Toledo Hospital on the following Monday morning.

For Strahm, late Friday afternoon always called for some introspection, some time far from all who depended on him, in a place as serene and as comforting as any he had found on Findlay's campus.

"On Friday late afternoons, I always went to the chapel at the College Church of God if we were home. It always was a great place to relax, catch my breath, and have a talk with God.

"It was also a great time to review what I wanted to say to my players at our Friday night meeting and also think about the game.

"As I was sitting in the chapel, the sun was coming through the stain-glass windows, and I dozed off. I had a dream about the aftermath of the surgery. I could see so vividly Dr. Emmert coming down a long hallway and walking into the waiting room.

"My family was there. Suddenly, Dr. Emmert broke into this big smile and told them that the surgery had gone well, and he had gotten all of the cancer. He told them the old coach was going to be just fine.

"I woke up and felt so confident after having that dream that the Monday morning surgery didn't even seem as important as the Saturday game with Olivet!"

The pre-surgery game at Donnell went well as the Oilers pounded out a 31-6 win over the visiting Tigers. Hurley was a very accurate 7 of 9 for 126 yards and another TD strike to Scott McLaughlin, and senior Milan Smith raced for 185 yards and a score.

After the cheers at Donnell subsided and the rest of the weekend expired, it was time for the business at Toledo Hospital.

Recalls Strahm, "We were all at the hospital early Monday morning. I remember as I was waiting to go into the operating room, I was surrounded by family and my pastor from College First Church of God, Dr. Darrell Prichard, who was so important from a support standpoint when I had my coronary procedures. Everyone was talking very positively, and there were a lot of smiles going around that room.

"I really believed that Friday afternoon while I was in the chapel, God showed me a picture of what was going to happen. That's why I was so relaxed on Monday morning. As a matter of fact, I don't think anyone in my family could believe how relaxed I was, but I never said a word to anyone about the dream.

"After the surgery and finally back in the recovery room, I came to. I asked my family what Dr. Emmert told them. Doug, my son, told me the doctor came walking through the door of the waiting room and broke into a huge smile. That's when everyone knew everything would be OK.

"It was only then I told them about my dream. I told them I had seen the exact smile in my dream. I also told them how very good God was to me.

"I was in a rather large room at the hospital with just my single bed. By the second day, my room looked like a flower shop. The nurses said they had never seen a room so full of flowers and plants. Even nurses from other floors came to see the flower display. The flowers came from all the wonderful supporters – the University, foster parents, football players, coaches, and friends in Toledo. To wake up every morning surrounded by flowers from the floor to the ceiling would put a smile on anyone's face. And, then to know the cancer was gone, well, I just felt so very blessed.

"Late one morning, I woke up to find one of my old friends waiting for me. It was so good to see Gary Pinkel, who was then the head coach of the Toledo Rockets. We talked football. I also told him that, since I was an alumnus, I expected a win that coming weekend. Since then, Pinkel has moved on and is now the head football coach at the University of Missouri.

"During my recovery, I had to deal with a very painful by-product of the surgery. I had bladder spasms that literally brought me to my knees from time to time. Then, of course, the catheter was in for my entire stay in the hospital and then for about twelve days after I went home."

Six days after the successful surgery, Dick Strahm was ready for his trip home. A very good friend, Edd Groves, drove up from Findlay to bring Strahm home as the family prepared the house for the homecoming.

On Saturday, Strahm remembers quite a surprise and certainly a pleasant one. "Ginger had our bedroom rearranged so I could watch TV along with family and friends, and we were all together as a family watching a national broadcast of the Ohio State game.

"During the first quarter, the announcer, Brent Musburger, made a rather startling announcement. He wished Coach Dick Strahm, head football coach of The University of Findlay Oilers, a speedy recovery from cancer surgery.

"I think one of my old friends from Toledo, Oris Tabner, who was the sports editor for WTOL-ABC somehow got a hold of Brent.

"It really made me feel good. But, I'll tell you something. The announcement on the TV wasn't nearly as important as being home, surrounded by family and knowing I was on the road to recovery from successful cancer surgery.

As far as Dick Strahm's surgical game plan, it was executed flawlessly. While he recuperated, the Oilers easily defeated St. Xavier, 34-0, aided by key interceptions by Nate Weihrauch and Jamie Riles and a 98-yard rushing day for Milan Smith.

And, week seven, did bring Dick Strahm's return for the Tiffin game. Although not cleared for sideline duty, Strahm was in the press box, calling the offensive plays and, no doubt, driving his offensive coaches crazy.

The Oilers won their fourth straight, 30-3, with Hurley hitting 6 of 7 for 126 yards and a touchdown. McLaughlin grabbed Hurley's TD toss and four others for his 132 yards receiving. Milan Smith had a monster game, carrying the ball 22 times for 206 yards and two scores. Jamie Riles and John Ferguson both recorded interceptions.

And so, after a 0-3 start, the Oilers crept back over the .500 mark at 4-3, and the playoffs were not out of the question, if they could win out against Urbana University and Taylor University.

The first part was accomplished the following week when the Oilers swamped Urbana, 62-9, on the way to their second-highest offensive output of the year. Included in the scoring spree were two more TD passes from Hurley, the talented freshman who had finally found a home after stops searching for bigger stages in Columbus and Cincinnati.

The season's regular season finale again was at Donnell Stadium against a long-time opponent, Taylor University, out of Upland, Indiana. The Oilers and Trojans had faced one another often years ago as fellow members of the Hoosier-Buckeye Collegiate Conference. They now shared the Midwest League in the Mid-States Football Association.

The game went Findlay's way, 35-6. Bo Hurley was 7 of 9, for 112 yards, and one TD, certainly a good performance. But, it was two seniors playing before their home fans for the final time that made the day their own.

For the fourteenth consecutive game, Scott McLaughlin was the Oilers' leading receiver with four catches, one for a touchdown. And, the swivel-hipped Milan Smith saved his best for last, rushing for a career-high 231 yards and a touchdown.

While Strahm had teams that finished as high as 8-1 in the regular season and missed the playoffs, in the year 1994, 6-3 was good enough to qualify.

This time, the playoff game would be on the road, as Findlay was outbid by an old rival, Westminster. That meant there would be a trip to New Wilmington, Pennsylvania.

As the two teams went about their business of preparing for the game, head coaches Dick Strahm and Gene Nicholson surely must have felt there was little in the way of secrets. Perhaps there would be a slight variation here or there, but the run-oriented packages of both teams would be largely the same as they had always been.

It was Strahm who pointed out to the sports editor of *The Courier*, Larry Alter, "This is the eighth time we've played these people. We know what they are going to do, and they know what we are going to do."

Westminster finished the regular season at 6-3 and would take a number three national ranking into the contest in this, their record fifteenth NAIA playoff appearance.

The key to the Oilers' chances appeared to be how well their defense would be able to stop the Titans' hard-charging tailback Andy Blatt, who'd rushed for almost 1,400 yards and scored 17 touchdowns in the regular season.

However, what also concerned Strahm and the rest of his coaches was that this year the Titans also had a seasoned and very talented quarterback, Sean O'Shea. He had thrown for 16 touchdowns and completed 61 percent of his throws.

Nonetheless, Bo Hurley had been improving game by game, averaging 157.8 yards per game in total offense. Westminster coach Nicholson concluded that Hurley had made a big difference in the Oilers' offense. "He is running and throwing well and adds another dimension to an already strong offense."

Finally, game day, November 19, arrived. While the regular season game was a relatively low-scoring 17-14 Westminster win, this game took on a vastly different personality. Like heavyweight boxers, the Oilers and Titans slugged and got slugged.

It was the Oilers who jumped out quickly, with Milan Smith scoring from four yards out. After Shawn O'Shea answered by tossing a touchdown pass to Bob Santangelo, the Oilers responded with a Mark Barnes' 26-yard field goal and a 26-yard TD grab by Scott McLaughlin from Hurley, and Findlay seemed to be on the verge of taking control of the contest. That was especially true after Milan Smith electrified the Oilers traveling fans with a 57-yard touchdown run to send his team to the halftime locker room up, 23-14.

A scoreless third quarter perhaps gave Findlay a false sense of security because of how the momentum turned in the final stanza. The Titans exploded for 27 points, scoring four times on Andy Blatt runs of 2, 1, 24, and 2 yards. Combined with a pass Blatt caught for a touchdown in the first half, his five TDs were simply too much for the Oilers.

O'Shea also had a big afternoon, completing 20 of 31 for 254 yards.

Recalls Strahm, "After we'd given up our 23-14 lead and fell behind 34-30, we still had an excellent opportunity. We had driven the ball down to Westminster's 12-yard line in the middle of the fourth quarter. It was second and six when they got a good pass rush on Bo. His pass was tipped and intercepted, and that turned out to be the pivotal play."

Blatt scored his final touchdown after the 35-yard interception return by Craig Villwock, making the final 41-30, Titans. The Oilers post-season was a case of one and done. As for Westminster, behind the considerable talents of O'Shea and Blatt, Westminster again captured the Division II NAIA national championship in 1994.

Despite the relatively modest 6-4 season, modest at least by Dick Strahm's lofty expectations and accomplishments, there were certainly signs that the Oilers certainly could be in for a special 1995 season.

In his first year as the starting Oilers quarterback, Bo Hurley completed more than 50 percent of his passes for 908 yards and nine touchdowns. Additionally, he averaged more than five yards a carry, gaining 502 yards and scoring ten more touchdowns.

While McLaughlin and Milan Smith would be missed when the Oilers took the field in 1995, many key offensive-skill performers were set to return. Besides Hurley, three-back Troy Pearson and four-back Chris Jaquillard were both ready. Bill Yeager had settled in nicely at Doug Rode's old two-back position as a punishing lead blocker and a reliable spot ball carrier.

But more about 1995 later. It was time to rededicate to the off-season workouts and lay the foundation for 1995. As Strahm plotted for the next season, he just couldn't wait to see Chris Jaquillard take over full time the four-back now that Milan Smith was done with his piece of Oilers history.

"Chris, I thought, had a very good first year. We played him on both sides of the ball at different times, but I'd decided to play him only at left halfback (four-back) in our wishbone and get him a lot of carries. Remember, as a senior at Woodward, many felt he was the most outstanding back in the state."

The weeks rolled by, and winter yielded to spring. In early April, The University of Findlay sponsored a golf tournament, and the school's benefactors and several administrators and coaches were given the chance to escape the April showers of Ohio for the sunny climes of Cape Coral, Florida, less than an hour from Naples.

Of course, the event was Ken Zirkle's brainchild and was part public relations and part good will to promote those whose donations to the university had been so vital.

Recalls Strahm, "Several of the school's administrators were invited to play golf and also to speak at the golf awards dinner, and I was asked to go. I thought it was a great idea. I remember it was a scramble-type tournament, where each member of the foursome hit from the same place and then took the best shot and proceeded in like manner.

"Well, after the event was over, I was headed for my car to drive back to Naples, and Bill Fitzgerald yelled for me. Bill had been a donor to the university. He'd retired in 1991 as president and chief operating officer of Cooper Tire and Rubber. At that point, another great supporter of The University of Findlay, Pat Rooney, took his position. Rooney, who eventually ascended to chief executive officer was the chairman of the Board of Cooper from 1995 through his retirement in 2000. It was indeed a sad day for all of us when Pat, one of my dearest friends, died from a heart condition in December of 2002.

"Bill Fitzgerald was just a tremendous individual, and, before his retirement, oversaw, along with Ivan Gorr and Pat Rooney, what many in the world of business believe is the best-run company in the world.

"I walked over to shake Bill's hand, and he told me that I'd been doing a good job and that he'd like to do something for the football program. He told me to think of something and get back in touch with him."

After returning to Findlay, Strahm talked to his defensive coordinator Don Akers, who also was the team's strength coach, the same position filled so capably by Mike Ward before his departure after the season. The question Strahm had for Akers involved what he felt was needed to make The University of Findlay weight facility the best in all of small college football.

Recalls Dick, "When Don asked me how much money did we have to work with, I really didn't know what to say because Bill never mentioned an amount.

"So Don promised he'd inventory what we had and do all the research on new weight-training equipment for our list of needs.

"About a week later, Don came to me with a well-organized list of the weights and weight machines and their prices for what we needed to totally equip our weight room. He had the brochures and prices for all sorts of equipment. I remember the total came to almost forty grand! I was concerned that the amount might be too high.

"But, since Bill didn't mention an amount, I figured, 'What the heck? All he can do is say no and give me a budget.'

"So, I had lunch with Bill at the Findlay Country Club and made my presentation. I can remember to this day his reaction. He looked at me, narrowed his eyes, and said, 'Hmmm, forty thousand, huh?' Then, he paused and said, 'I was thinking more along the lines of fifty thousand. Why don't you get some costs and descriptions for a few other pieces of equipment, and I'll take care of those, too?'

"I guess I shouldn't have been surprised. Bill and his wife Rita truly believe in The University of Findlay. We made our purchases and by the end of May, we had what I believe was the best-equipped weight room of any small college anywhere!

"So many of our players were geographically close to Findlay, and they came to the Gardner Center throughout the summer months leading up to our 1995 season.

"To me, it was no surprise that the 1995 defense was nationally ranked in so many statistical categories. Through Bill's generosity, our football players made such significant strength improvements that it made the years of 1995-96-97 so very special."

During the summer of 1995, Dick Strahm received a phone call that would eventually force him to change his offensive backfield plans for the next season.

Recalls Dick, "The call I got was from Chris Jaquillard. He said there'd been a fight in a bar in Toledo, and he was being accused of starting it and was going to have to face an assault charge.

"Now, I immediately knew how serious this was, despite the fact that Chris assured me he was completely innocent. Chris had told me the day I first met him that the judge at his first trial told him at his sentencing that if he were found guilty of anything, he would be sent back to prison to serve the entire three years he received before there were probationary reductions.

Chris Jaquillard remembers vividly both the events of that mid-summer night in a Toledo bar and the legal proceedings that soon followed.

"I was in the bar legally, since I'd turned 21, so I wasn't in danger of breaking any laws pertaining to underage consumption. It was me, my older brother Aaron, and a couple of my friends. We were in there, just minding our own business and shooting some pool.

"I'd already done my summer workout that day. When Coach Strahm told me I'd be starting at four-back, provided I had a good August camp, I just wanted to get in the best shape of my life, get the summer over with, and get back on the field in August.

"Well I looked across the bar, and, wouldn't you know, there were the four off-duty cops who were involved in the drug sting and my arrest. There was a lot of resentment they had for me, and I certainly recognized that from the trial and their testimony.

"I felt they knew I wasn't a drug dealer, but they went to every length to paint that picture of me. You know what I mean, don't you? It was kind of like, 'Well, here's this big football star that was in the paper every Saturday morning when he was in high school, but now, look at him!'

"When my brother saw them sitting there looking over at us and snickering and talking among themselves, he said he just had to go over there. I told Aaron not to, to just leave it alone, but he said he wasn't going to be confrontational or anything. He said he just wanted to let them know that Chris Jaquillard was no drug dealer!

"So, he went over, and the next thing I know, there was a little pushing and suddenly a fight broke out. I really don't remember even if it was Aaron who threw the first punch, to be honest.

"At that point, I thought about the second chance I was given by Dr. Zirkle, so I actually ran to the farthest corner of the bar and stayed completely clear of the fight. I wanted everyone to know I was not at all involved. Well, the fight finally gets broken up, and we left.

"The next day, I turned on the television, and the local news was on. The newsman said there was a warrant out for me! I was both shocked and scared. I had three years in prison hanging over my head if I violated my parole in any way. Then, there would be additional charges of assaulting a police officer which would be even more time!"

Not wishing to make a bad situation worse, Jaquillard immediately phoned Mike Cicak, who, in turn, contacted a top-notch Toledo attorney, John Richardson. Despite the fact that Jaquillard knew he was innocent, he knew two things. They were the police who would again testify against him, and he was a convicted felon. Who would believe him even if Aaron did take the stand as he said he would and tell everyone it was he who was involved in the fight, not Chris? Wouldn't that be seen as one brother taking the blame for the other who had much to lose if he were found guilty?

Chris remembers, "I even took a lie detector test before the trial began and passed it, but the results weren't admissible in court. My attorney thought there might be a way to get the results admissible, but the judge disallowed the request."

Of course, Dick Strahm went to Ken Zirkle and told him of the incident, Chris's vociferous claims of innocence, and the pending trial, which wouldn't come up on the docket until sometime in October.

While Zirkle told Dick that he did believe Chris was probably being set up by some police officers who let their personal feelings taint the way they went about their jobs, he felt he had no choice.

Since the case was pending, Chris Jaquillard would not be allowed to play in 1995. He could continue as a UF student, but he would have to sit out the year in football.

Recalls Jaquillard, "I was crushed. I felt I had worked so hard turning my life around, and here I was being falsely accused, and everything I'd worked so hard to achieve was being taken away from me."

Jaquillard was not considered a flight risk, and when school was scheduled to start, he would be allowed to attend classes.

As for the 1995 season, it began in August for pre-season camp without Chris Jaquillard on the field but in street clothes watching, just as he would attend every practice until such time that he could rejoin as a participant.

Robert Shelton, the sophomore who played his high school football in Westerville, just outside of Columbus, Ohio, slid into the slot that was ceded by Jaquillard.

Troy Pearson and Bill Yeager were ready to go at fullback and blocking back respectively. Bo Hurley was penciled in as the starter at quarterback.

As for the receivers Hurley would be throwing to, Walter Jackson (Columbus, Ohio) would start in Scott McLaughlin's old position, and Todd Allen (Wooster, Ohio) was slated to start at tight end. Allen was being asked to make the transition from offensive guard.

The offensive line was again led by Cal Dietz, the 270-pounder from Shelby, Ohio, who was named Honorable Mention NAIA All-American the previous year.

Dietz, now living in Hudson, Wisconsin, and working as the strength coach at the University of Minnesota, remembers Dick Strahm, the coach. "He is, quite simply, the measuring stick I use to judge coaches by, and, remember, I've coached with world-class individuals. Coach Strahm instilled such a spirit of intense competition, and that's something that is with me today."

Dietz remembers his transition from defense to offense during his Oilers career. "My freshman year, I played defensive tackle, mostly on the scout team. I used to marvel at the ability and desire of Bobby Heitkamp. Had he not had Crohn's, there is no doubt in my mind he could have played professionally. When I think of players like Bobby and so many others on that '92 national championship team, I think of a ham-and-eggs breakfast. To make one, you need a chicken and a pig. Well, the chicken is involved in the outcome. The pig is committed. Those '92 guys wanted to be the pigs!

"At the beginning of my sophomore year, Coach Strahm wanted me to switch to offense and that's when I had the privilege of having Jim McIntosh as my position coach. I couldn't imagine anyone knowing any more about blocking schemes than Coach Mac."

"I thank him for getting me to see the big picture of running an unbalanced line. At first, I was overwhelmed, but by the time I was a junior and then a senior, I could within seconds run through about fifteen different possible blocking scenarios for the 22-2 and make the right read, thanks to Coach Mac's teaching ability."

Dick Strahm certainly remembers Dietz's position change well. "When I brought Cal into my office to convince him to switch to offensive tackle, he really wasn't a very happy camper. He wanted to play next to Nate Arnold on the defensive line. They were the best of friends. But, Cal knew we needed help at inside tackle. He accepted his new assignment and eventually became an All-American."

Joining Dietz on the offensive line was center Chad Ulm, who followed in the footsteps of Doug Rode, another Delphos, Ohio, player.

Recalls Ulm, now an environmental engineer and still living in his hometown, "I remember even though we lost to Westminster in the '94 playoffs, I thought the '95 year had the potential to be special. As a lineman, I naturally always believed that the strength of any team was in its lines. I knew, heading into the new year that we had lots of returning starters on both offensive and defensive lines.

When Ulm finally assumed the starting position after Marty Simon graduated the previous spring, he remembers what Coach Strahm felt compelled to say to him during August practices. "When I screwed up, Coach would tell me that he was going to send me back to Delphos on a slow boat. But, it was never said in a mean-spirited way.

"I saw, and still do see Coach Strahm as a peerless leader. He was such a great motivator. And, you really saw that during our Friday night meetings. He kind of reminded me of an Army general. While he was small in stature, he had a personality that could just fill up an entire room."

Joining Ulm and Dietz on the offensive line would be inside tackle on the strong side, senior Paul Cromer (West Chester, Ohio), 312-pound strong-side guard Jason May (Lore City, Ohio), and backside guard Jason Berger (Leipsic, Ohio).

Defensively, the 1995 Oilers looked to be solid. Howard Heston (Elyria, Ohio) was set at defensive end. Chris Barbara (Northville, Michigan), who lost 1994 to an injury, was accorded the honor of assuming the position of Oiler, sort of a combination defensive end-linebacker.

Playing tackle would be Chris Garner (Cincinnati) and, along side him, was the undersized nose guard who knew only one speed to play, full throttle, the 5'7," 200-pounder out of Columbus, Ohio, Ray Jackson.

Jackson, still living in Columbus and working as a wealth management advisor for Merrill Lynch, remembers how Dick Strahm stood by him during troublesome times. "I actually came to Findlay in 1991 but was redshirted. Without the structure of football, I guess you might say I strayed a bit, got into some trouble, and got kicked out of school. So, I wasn't even enrolled in 1992. I worked in a warehouse.

"Now, it would have been easy for Coach Strahm to turn the corner and move on. But, he didn't. When I grew up and got my life and my priorities straight, I wanted to come back in '93. And, it was Coach Strahm who accepted me back.

"During my freshman year in '93, I played some linebacker and also some Oiler. After the season, during our game with Hamburg in May, there was an injury, and Coach Strahm asked me to play nose guard. It wasn't as if I was brand new to the position.

"Despite being small, I had played in the trenches in high school. I figured I could use my quickness to compensate for my lack of size."

Ray Long was back at linebacker to see if he could lead the team in tackles for a third consecutive year. In '94, Long was named a first-team Division II NAIA All-American after ringing up an astonishing 164 tackles, including ten for losses. Joining him after the graduation of Jamie Godman was Mike Powers, the senior from Marysville, Ohio.

Rounding out the Oilers defense in the secondary were Terrence Auster (Dayton, Ohio) and Demetrice Boykin, from Naples, Florida, at the corners. The free safety would be the hitting machine out of Cincinnati, Larry Williams, and, at strong safety, Nate Weihrauch, who went to Liberty Benton High School and played football with my son Steve.

As far as the kicking game, the punting would be handled by the senior from Morris, Illinois, Mark Barnes, and the place-kicking fell to Tom Sellers, the diminutive (5'7," 140 pounds) Tipp City, Ohio, product.

The coaching staff for the upcoming 1995 season was a nice mix of veterans and a couple of new faces. Of course, Jim McIntosh, Doug Coate, and Curtis Davidson were back. Between them, they had accumulated forty years of Oilers experience on the sidelines.

Don Akers headed into his second year coaching linebackers and serving as both defensive coordinator and strength coach.

Doug Strahm was three years removed from working the graveyard shift as a meat cutter in Rossford, Ohio. In addition to coaching the defensive line, he would also serve as equipment manager.

Also entering his third year coaching the defensive backs was Mike Schanski. Schanski, now an assistant coach at The University of Findlay, remembers his luck coming in two years before. "My first year was 1993, and I was so lucky as a young coach to have so much experience in the secondary. Shane Dennison, Chris Rothhaar, Des May, and Todd Vrancken were all seniors. Until I got more experience, I think they helped me as much as I helped them.

"Coming into the '95 season, I knew we'd gained the needed experience in the secondary the previous year to be a strong unit. I couldn't have predicted how good we would prove to be, especially intercepting the ball."

One of the two newcomers to Strahm's staff was Rusty Smith, who would work with the wide receivers and also work in the Office of Institutional Advancement. Smith, a member of the 1979 NAIA Division II national championship team, would be joined by someone who would, one day, try to fill the considerable shoes of Dick Strahm.

John Wauford would coach the defensive ends. He had played three years in the Canadian Football League after graduating from Miami of Ohio, where he was twice named team MVP. He was also a three-time All-Mid-American Conference selection at defensive end.

For Wauford, coming to Findlay meant following the road home. As a 1988 graduate of Findlay High School, he was a three-time Buckeye Central Conference selection at both tailback and linebacker.

Recalls Wauford, now the head coach at The University of Findlay, "Dick Strahm continues to be someone I learn from in my coaching career. I knew what a special opportunity it was to join his staff back in 1995, so I grabbed it."

The 1995 season would be the Oilers' second in the Mid-States Football Association, and they hoped to improve upon their second-place 4-1 league mark in the Midwest League in '94.

The season opened with an away game against the team that finished ahead of them in the Midwest League the previous season, Trinity International. The Oilers were chomping at the bit to get at the team from Deerfield, Illinois, after the previous year's embarrassing 40-15 loss.

Recalls Strahm, "Trinity was number ten in the national pre-season polls, and our second opponent, Westminster, was ranked number one, so I knew we had our hands full in the first couple weeks. I remembered last season's 0-3 start and certainly didn't want to go down a similar road."

The quarterback who made Findlay so uncomfortable the previous year, Todd Johnson, was back. But, this time the Findlay defense led by All-American linebacker Ray Long was ready. They held the offense to 26 points fewer than the previous year. Nonetheless, it was again the Oilers who would walk off the field a loser to Trinity, this time, 14-7.

Despite the loss, Coach Schanski watched the first opportunistic vestiges of his unit's pass defense. Both Nate Weihrauch and Terrance Auster picked off Johnson's aerials.

There also was some additional bad news on that September 9 in Deerfield, Illinois. Sophomore Bo Hurley separated his shoulder and would be out anywhere from two to four weeks.

Certainly, there is never good timing to lose your starting quarterback, but the fact that the defending national champions, the Westminster Titans, were up next on Findlay's September 16 home opener made the timing even worse.

With backup Mike Konopka taking the snaps, Strahm played it even more conservatively than he ordinarily would. In a defensive slugfest, the game ended in a 3-3 deadlock. Robert Shelton led the ground game with 97 yards on 23 carries.

Recalls Strahm, "At that time, the NAIA administrators and coaches voted that there be no overtimes to decide ties in any regular-season games and even in the national championship game. The only overtimes allowed were those necessary to see which of two deadlocked playoff teams were allowed to advance to the next round in post-season."

Sitting at 0-1-1, the Oilers then got angry, and the results of the next three weeks proved that.

First, Findlay celebrated their Homecoming by pasting Lindenwood, 63-9. Konopka, substituting for the rapidly recovering Hurley, looked a bit more comfortable, especially when he handed the ball off to Robert Shelton, who rushed for 101 yards and a couple scores.

Defensively, assistant coach Mike Schanski's jaw must have dropped by game's end. Not only did he watch four interceptions (Ray Long, Bill Minter, and two by Nate Weihrauch) but both of Weihrauch's were returned for touchdowns.

In week four, Findlay traveled back to Illinois, this time to Bourbonnais, to engage the Olivet Nazarene Tigers. The decisive 42-10 Oilers win was highlighted by the returning starting quarterback Bo Hurley, who threw sparingly (three times) but threw well (two completions, both for scores). Troy Pearson caught one touchdown pass from 10 yards out, and wideout Walter Jackson stretched the field and hauled in his 47-yard scoring strike.

Robert Shelton broke loose early and often, finishing with 223 yards on 24 carries and a pair of touchdowns.

Defensively, Chris Barbara picked off the team's seventh pass of the year, and then, for good measure, returned it 26 yards for a score.

Week five found Findlay home for Iowa Wesleyan, and the result was another convincing Oilers win, 49-14. Fullback Troy Pearson was beginning to assert himself and led the ground assault with132 yards and two TDs.

Defensively, Ray Long had a great day and matched Nate Weihrauch's two touchdowns off interceptions two weeks before with the exact same performance. That made it five interception-return touchdowns in the last three games.

With the Oilers really picking up momentum, Chris Jaquillard continued to attend every single class and grew more nervous as the trial approached. Finally, it arrived, and he would have his day in court. All that hung in the balance was his future as a student and athlete at The University of Findlay, his freedom, and, perhaps, the course of the rest of his life.

Recalls Jaquillard, "In early October, my trial finally came up. The prosecutor wanted me to plea to a lesser charge, but I knew any admission of guilt would spell the end for me at Findlay. Dr. Zirkle made it clear to me that the chance he provided me was contingent on my maintaining a spotless record. In essence, I felt I was fighting for my life.

"My brother Aaron took the stand and testified that it was he who was in the fight, but I know a lot of people assumed he was taking the rap for me.

"Fortunately, the judge was able to see how flimsy the prosecution's case was, and, thanks to my attorney, all the charges were dropped. It was one of the happiest days of my entire life."

For Jaquillard, there was vindication that far exceeded the four walls of a Toledo courtroom. "When I was told while the trial was pending that I couldn't play football, I was crushed. My first year, I attended every class and worked my butt off, yet I couldn't play?

"Don't get me wrong. I don't blame Dr. Zirkle. It was really the only way he could rule until everything came out at the trial.

"When Dr. Zirkle made his decision, I think a lot of people thought my not being allowed to play would signal an end for me, that the disappointment would be too great and that I'd stop going to class and drop out and show the world that I was a bad seed.

"But, I went to every class and attended every practice to support players I sure hoped would be my teammates in 1996 and 1997."

Jaquillard returned to Findlay and resumed his studies. While the playing rotations were already set and the team in place in '95, he resolved that nothing could stop him from being an Oiler in '96 and the year after, absolutely nothing!

Week six of the regular season arrived, and, on a Saturday that was part of Family Weekend, the Cougars of St. Xavier traveled from Chicago to provide the opposition at Donnell. There was little doubt which the superior team was, as the Oilers rolled, 56-0. With Hurley taking the week off to recover from some bumps and bruises, second and third-string quarterbacks Mike Konopka and Andy Booth, from McArthur, Ohio, did well. They combined to complete 5 of 9 for 105 yards, and Booth threw the first touchdown pass of his Findlay career.

Booth, who currently resides in Keller, Texas, and is a corporate account manager for Ashland Incorporated, remembers some of the doubts he had watching the Oiler talent around him. "In '94 I ran the scout team, and I really questioned if I'd ever see the field on Saturdays. I spoke with my dad a lot on the phone about my doubts, and he told me to just keep working hard and things would work out as they were supposed to.

"That's the way he put it. Look, he'd been to some games and saw Bo [Hurley] play. Obviously, he could see how talented he was, so he didn't say I should work hard and I'd eventually beat Bo out. He simply said to work hard and things would work out as they were supposed to. Pretty smart guy, my dad was, huh?"

Robert Shelton scored twice on his 125-yard afternoon as the Oilers sent their families home happy with the big win.

The defense, again, stole much of the show. Nate Weihrauch tied Harold Barnett's 1963 school record by returning an interception 100 yards for a touchdown. Then, Demetrice Boykin stepped in front of an out pattern, intercepted, and streaked 75 yards down the field for another touchdown. That made it seven interceptions returned for touchdowns over a four-game stretch.

Secondary coach Mike Schanski could not believe his eyes. "I have never seen anything like that four-game run in my whole coaching career. Listen, interceptions are hard enough to get in and of themselves, but to have seven of them returned for scores in just four games, well, that's just not reality!"

Week seven found Findlay in the friendly environment at Donnell, hosting Tiffin University. The spirited games the two schools had when Brian Diliberto was on his way to becoming the most prolific runner in NAIA history seemed a distant memory as the Oilers rolled, 42-0.

Bo Hurley had his first great passing-running combination game. He threw for 106 yards on 5 of 6 and ran for 148 yards on just 8 carries, scoring twice.

Defensively, the interceptions continued to pile up, as Brett Macy, Larry Williams, and Terrance Auster all snagged one. Schanski certainly must have been tempted to express mock disapproval when none of the three returned his pick for a touchdown.

Week eight saw the Oilers travel to Urbana University to take on the Blue Knights at the Urbana High School field. Wide receiver Ben Dils grabbed five of Hurley's passes, good for 89 yards, and Bo ran for another 127 yards as Findlay crushed another opponent, 37-3.

Of course, the defense chipped in with three more interceptions, by Weihrauch, Long, and Brooks Pighan.

In week nine, Findlay traveled to Taylor University in Upland, Indiana, in search of its seventh straight win since the 3-3 deadlock with Westminster. Another win would make the Oilers 7-1-1 and virtually assure them a playoff berth for the fifth consecutive year.

Despite deplorable weather conditions, caused by a combination of sleet, snow, mud, freezing temperatures, and fierce winds, which gusted to 40 miles an hour, Findlay scored on its first four possessions and ran away from its long-time opponent, 35-6.

Robert Shelton had two touchdowns and 124 of Findlay's 332 yards rushing. Meanwhile, the Oilers defense, statistically, the top-ranked unit in the NAIA, held the Trojans to a negative eight yards on the ground.

Of course, there were also interceptions, two of them, by Nate Weihrauch and Demetrice Boykin.

Strahm told the media after the game that he felt, given the field conditions that were bound to deteriorate as the game progressed, that it was important that his team score early. "I figured the field would be virtually unplayable in the second half, so I felt pretty comfortable by halftime. I'll tell you how cold it was. Some of our offensive linemen had t-shirts frozen to their skin. Troy Pearson had hypothermia. At halftime we had to put him in a hot shower. He never returned in the second half."

Certainly, although drenched and cold, Strahm was indeed warmed by the fact that 7-1-1, given recent NAIA bid history, almost assured the Oilers a shot at the post-season, and he really felt that he had a team that could announce its presence with authority once the playoffs began.

Findlay did earn a post-season spot and drew Frosty Westering's Pac Lutheran Lutes, the very team that derailed what many Oilers historians feel was the greatest offensive team in school history a decade before by a score of 40-29.

While Findlay traveled to Lakewood Stadium in Tacoma, Washington, for that contest, this time, The University of Findlay won the bid and would host the game. When Pac Lutheran rolled into Donnell, it came armed with a West Coast-style offense that really was the antithesis of Strahm's run-first-run-second-and-maybe-even-run-third attack.

Strahm recalls a conversation he'd had with Westminster head man Gene Nicholson about playing Westering's Pac Lutheran teams. "Gene may have said it best. He told me, 'You and I are like Neanderthal men compared to the Pac Lutheran offense. I could lay in bed for nine years and not think of the stuff they come up with.'"

The legendary Westering would bring his 236 wins, first at the time among all NAIA coaches, to Donnell. He also brought with him a terrific quarterback, Dak Jordan, a player Strahm called "The Man with the Golden Arm."

Strahm continued, "'The Golden Arm' will test our defense the best they've ever been tested. Because he throws the ball so quickly, you try to blitz him, and he'll pick you apart. He passes in a quarter what we throw in an entire game."

But, the Oilers felt they were ready. They had the top-ranked defense overall in the NAIA, yielding just 172.4 yards per contest. During the regular season the group dubbed The Lightning Unit was giving up less than seven points a game.

And, so it was on that November 18 Saturday before a packed house of mostly Oilers supporters that Findlay started down the road that they hoped would lead to a second national championship in the last four years.

When game day arrived, it was evident that field conditions would play a role in the outcome. The previous night, a high school playoff game between Woodmore and Coldwater high schools was played at Donnell.

When two-back Bill Yeager, from Castalia, Ohio, saw how muddy and torn up the field was, he smiled. "I knew I was going to love it! I was a mudder, and there's nothing that a mudder likes better than a quagmire."

Yeager, who now lives in Cumming, Georgia, and is part owner of Zip Wireless Products, remembers how such a field always seemed to benefit one team or the other. "In about every game I ever played on that type of surface, there always seemed to be a benefit to one team or the other. And, really, with our offensive philosophy, those conditions favored us more often than not because we were so ground-oriented.

"As the two-back, I was more of a guard in the backfield, but I loved it. I had a lot of experience with the wishbone. We ran it in high school, but I was the four-back and got a lot of carries. My senior year, I scored eighteen touchdowns.

"So, two-back took some getting used to, but I was happy to play. When you play for great coaches in a great program, you don't mind accepting what you might call less of a glory role. Really, the first time I saw Troy Pearson run as a freshman, I said, 'Oh my God, what skills!' I knew I wasn't going to be starting at four-back!"

The game plan that Saturday really was vintage Oilers football, or, in other words, Dick Strahm football, as Findlay dominated the clock with a relentless ground attack and then turned to its rock-ribbed defense to stonewall the Lutes' quick-strike offense.

The final score was 21-14. Oiler quarterback Bo Hurley executed the wishbone beautifully, scoring on a 13-yard run. He threw sparingly but very well, completing 7 of 9. At one key juncture in the third quarter Hurley completed five passes in a row with the key one being a 14-yard TD toss to tight end Todd Allen, amazingly his first catch of the year.

Strahm remembers Allen's catch well. "I swear, a hush came over the stadium when the ball was in the air. Todd had been an offensive guard in our program for three years prior. I think during that split-second when the ball was in the air, everyone realized who it was heading for. So, people were probably wondering if this big old lineman could even catch a ball. Well, by golly, he did!"

Although Findlay had no 100-yard rushers on that afternoon, there was good balance. Hurley called his own number 19 times for 79 yards, Troy Pearson racked up 57 yards, and even Bill Yeager, much more accustomed to blocking than running, chipped in with 37 as well as catching a couple of key passes.

Defensively, with Findlay leading by a touchdown, it took two more interceptions to preserve the win. First, it was Brett Macy who picked off a pass in the end zone, and, then, on a final Pac Lutheran possession, linebacker Mike Powers also made a diving grab.

Nate Arnold also came up huge with nine tackles, two for losses and a key pass deflection. Westering tipped his cap to the Oilers defense after the game. "Findlay applied a lot of pressure. They did a great job one-on-one with our guys. They keep pressure on you all the time. That's the strength of their team."

As for Strahm, he spoke of the difference between the two teams' approaches. "I thought the contrast between the two styles made for a great game. We talked all week about how our offense could help our defense by keeping number 13 [Dak Jordan] on the bench."

Next up on the playoff trail was the team ranked sixth in the final Division II NAIA poll, the Malone College Pioneers, out of Canton, Ohio. Again, UF administrators stepped up and submitted the higher bid, and the game would be played at Donnell Stadium.

Malone entered the game at 10-0-1, not having lost in fifteen games. They were winners of the Mid-States Football Association (MSFA) Mideast League. The Oilers, winners of the Midwest League, came in at 8-1-1. Unlike the Pac Lutheran game, this fray would feature two schools with very similar styles. First-year Malone coach Mike Gravier noted in Strahm-like fashion, "Both teams are built around their defense, and defense is always the cornerstone of a championship football team."

In terms of health, one concern for Strahm and his staff was the questionable status of all-conference safety Nate Weihrauch, who injured his knee in the Pac Lutheran game. However, even if Weihrauch, who had six interceptions and three returned for scores on the season, was not available, five other all-conference performers were locked and loaded, including tackles Nate Arnold and Chris Garner, linebackers Ray Long and Mike Powers, and cornerbacks Terrance Auster and Demetrice Boykin.

December 2, game day, arrived, and it was an incredibly physical affair. Fortunately, for Strahm's Oilers, they managed to preserve a 15-7 fourth-quarter lead, first, by holding on downs just 11 yards from the goal line after a fumble put the Pioneers in business, and, second, by stopping Malone a final time just five yards from pay dirt after a final 60-yard drive.

It was, for the Oilers, what one might call a "Whew!" game. Troy Pearson led the ground attack with 101 yards, and, defensively, Brett Macy pilfered a pair of passes, giving him three in the last two weeks.

While some may say it wasn't a pretty win, Strahm had an answer. "This was one of those games where you're not real interested in seeing the stats. You just want to see the final score. I've never played a game to be pretty. I always play a game to win."

In addition to Pearson's 101 yards, Findlay showed a balanced attack with Hurley's 69, Robert Shelton's 53, and Bill Yeager's 32 yards on eight carries, certainly high for a blocking back.

Recalls Yeager, "I really didn't expect that many carries. Once I settled into that two-back my junior year, Coach Mac [McIntosh] kind of adopted me and brought me in with his hogs."

For Yeager, there was a price to be paid for launching himself into linebackers in blocking mode time after time. "I had neck surgery in 2000. When the doctor looked at the CAT scan before the procedure, he asked me if I played football. I said, 'How did you guess?' He said, 'Your neck's a mess, that's how.' I guess that's what happens when you lead a few too many 22-2's."

The win propelled the Oilers into the semifinals, and this time they would have to travel to play, to Jackson, Tennessee. The opponent would be Lambuth University, another hot team that would enter the contest with the same record as Malone, 10-0-1. The Eagles were exceedingly comfortable at L.L. Fonvile Stadium, where they hadn't lost in the last seventeen games.

However, the 9-1-1 Oilers would not be intimidated. The defense was holding opponents to just seven points a game, a microscopic 80 points total in eleven contests. However, to win, UF would have to slow down a team that had scored 480 points in eleven games, including 49 and 63 in its two play-off wins.

Despite such strong numbers, Lambuth coach Vic Wallace chose to poormouth his team's abilities during the week leading up to the game. He told the media, "We are a very average team with an above-average quarterback [Cory Hill, who'd thrown for 2,718 yards and 25 touchdowns]."

Whether Wallace's comments played a role in the outcome of the game, who knows? But, despite the 10-0-1 mark, Lambuth was absolutely no match for the Oilers on a day marked by freezing temperatures and a strong northerly wind.

The opportunistic and stingy Oilers defense forced eight turnovers, and the offense turned five of those into touchdowns in a 63-13 cakewalk.

The offense ran roughshod over the Lambuth defense, accounting for 367 yards, including 117 and a pair of TDs from game MVP Troy Pearson. Robert Shelton added 75 yards running, and reserve running backs Contrell Johnson (Ft. Wayne, Indiana) and E'Leon Henry (Elyria, Ohio) added fourth-quarter scores in the rout.

Lambuth simply never adjusted to the frigid temperatures, conditions which the Oilers were much more accustomed. Perhaps it was more a case of Lambuth not being able to adjust to the immovable tandem tackles, Chris Garner and Nate Arnold.

Four more interceptions, by Terrance Auster, Brett Macy, Larry Williams, and Ray Long, who returned his 54 yards for a touchdown, brought the season total to 28, including a school record seven for touchdowns.

And so, it was back to the national championship game for the fourth time in Dick Strahm's Findlay tenure. The opponent would be the Central Washington University Wildcats, quarterbacked so capably by a player who would eventually become an NFL starter for both the Cincinnati Bengals and the Detroit Lions, Jon Kitna. The senior would enter the game with a jaw-dropping 4,330 yards passing and 39 touchdowns.

For the Oilers, some good news arrived by mid-week prior to the December 16 kickoff in the Tacoma Dome in Tacoma, Washington. Nate Weihrauch would start. Provided he wore a knee brace, he was cleared by doctors to receive his first action since injuring the knee against Pac Lutheran.

Central Washington head coach Jeff Zinisek spoke of both the artificial-turf surface upon which the game would be played and the impact it might have on the outcome. "The turf shows some wear and tear. There's a ridge out there, and there are a couple seams showing, but that's to be expected. With dry conditions and no wind, we'll be able to throw the ball 100 miles an hour, because we're used to throwing it 50 miles an hour in the wind. This will be advantageous for us. Also, I'd rather defend Findlay on an artificial surface than on a muddy field, because they're so big and powerful.

"It [the surface] really gives both teams an advantage. Findlay hasn't played on it, and they'll feel like they can run 100 miles an hour. It gives you that kind of confidence. It should be a fun game, I know that much."

The last time the Oilers had played on artificial turf, things worked out very well. It was 1992 in the national championship win in Portland against Linfield.

As far as the flight out, the Oilers hoped the game would go better than their travel. A winter storm blasted the East Coast during their Thursday travel day, which forced a long delay in the arrival of the Continental flight from Newark, New Jersey, into the Seattle-Tacoma International Airport.

Recalls Strahm, "It was four in the morning before we finally reached the Sheraton-Tacoma Hotel on Friday. That was something that concerned me greatly. Rhythm is so very important in preparing for big games, but what can you do? While you can predict weather reasonably well, you certainly can't control it!"

For Central Washington, there would be a decided home-field advantage. Less than a hundred Findlay parents, alumni, and fans had made the trip. Additionally, twelve Central Washington players, including Kitna, performed at area high schools.

On Friday, with the 14,410-feet Mount Rainier visible in the distance, the Findlay Oilers began their final day of preparation when they left for their walk-through practice at the Tacoma Dome.

As soon as secondary coach Mike Schanski saw the fast track, he grew apprehensive. "Central Washington had four or five receivers as good as any we'd seen. Heck, my goal going into the game was to hold Kitna somewhere under 600 yards and 10 touchdowns!"

After both teams practiced, it was time to settle in for the traditional championship dinner attended by both teams back at the hotel, which was an NAIA tradition. The dinner also gave Dick Strahm his first in-person look at the rifle-armed 6'2," 220-pound opposing quarterback, Kitna. "As soon as I saw him across the room, I remember thinking that we had linemen who weren't as big!"

One of those linemen who wasn't nearly as big was Ray Jackson, the undersized but lightning-quick Oiler nose guard who has a lasting memory of the dinner. "I was seated at a table with a few of Central's offensive linemen. There was some trash talking directed my way. One of the lineman said, 'Little boy, we're going to kick your butt tomorrow.' All I did was smile and say, 'We'll see.'"

Game day arrived too soon for coaches who wanted some additional preparation time to combat the opponent. The game would again match contrasting styles of the defense-minded, ground-oriented Findlay Oilers and the aerial circus that revolved around Jon Kitna.

Recalls Oiler nose guard Jackson, "I remember the introduction of the starting lineups. When Kitna came out, he had both arms raised triumphantly, as if he were coming into a conquered territory. I thought it was a pretty arrogant entrance, and I think that got my motor running even faster!"

For Jackson, he would make his presence known immediately. During the first play of Central Washington's first possession, he shot the gap untouched past two of the same linemen who'd denigrated him the previous night and sacked Kitna for a four-yard loss as the quarterback was attempting to roll out. Before the end of the day, Jackson would add two more sacks of the future NFL star.

Ray Long, Findlay's All-American linebacker, remembers one thing that certainly contrasted greatly with the frigid conditions of the last four games against Taylor, Pac Lutheran, Malone, and Lambuth. "It was so humid in that dome. I was doing everything I could to get my visor off my helmet. I had a lot of trouble breathing.

"Then, from the second quarter on, Central went no-huddle, which made it even more difficult to maintain stamina."

During Findlay's first possession, a potentially game-changing moment occurred. Recalls Strahm, "On our third play of the game, Bo Hurley broke loose on an option and was running free down the sidelines. He was finally knocked out of bounds and went down in a heap, and, man, did I ever get a sick feeling."

The play resulted in a severe knee injury, an injury so bad that trainer Vi LeClair had to tell Strahm that the engineer of his wishbone offense was through for the day. It was time for someone to step up.

Andy Booth, who had only at the very end of the regular season been promoted to second-string quarterback when Mike Konopka was switched to defense, was the man fate would thrust into the spotlight.

Recalls Booth, "When Bo went down, everything happened so fast. I immediately started scrambling around, looking for my mouthpiece. Coach Strahm simply came up to me and said, 'Go play.'

"My folks [Dave and Ruby] hadn't come out for the game. The airfare was very expensive, and, while they said they would come, I told them there was almost no way I'd see the field, so they stayed back in Ohio and listened on the radio.

"I could only imagine their shock when the radio announcer said I was coming into the game. My dad told me later that my mom got so nervous she made him take her to the mall to shop.

"Dad said he was listening on the car radio, and Mom would walk around the mall for a while and then would go back to the car and ask how I was doing. Then, she'd go back in and walk around some more and then return with the same question. Dad counted how many times she did that, and it was ten!"

For Booth, he recalls the overwhelming support of his offensive mates. "The guys didn't lose hope. I really sensed they had my back. We had such a great offensive line with Chad [Ulm] and Cal [Dietz] and the rest of the guys, and it sure didn't hurt to be able to hand off to Troy Pearson and Robert Shelton, so I didn't feel it was up to me to win the game."

After a scoreless first quarter, Troy Pearson, who was on his way to shredding Central's defense for 176 yards rushing, scored twice, once from a yard out and again on a 24-yard dash up the middle.

Andy Booth contributed key plays in both scoring drives with an eight-yard gain on an option run and then a nine-yard pass for a first down to the big freshman out of Cedarville, Ohio, Jason Hamby.

However, Kitna responded just before intermission with his own 26-yard strike to Kenny Russaw to narrow the score to 14-7 before the teams headed to the locker room.

In the third quarter, Kitna drew his team even when he again threw a rocket for 49 yards and a touchdown to split end E.J. Henderson. It was a throw that remains etched in Oilers' secondary coach Mike Schanski's mind. "Kitna just did some eye-popping things that day despite the fact that we really contained him pretty well. On the tying touchdown, I remember it was a play-action fake to the right, and then he bootlegged back to the left all the way to the hash mark. Then, against his body, he threw a frozen rope all the way across the field to outside of the other hash mark to Henderson, who ran it in.

"Really, our backside corner didn't do anything wrong. When a quarterback rolls that far out on the opposite side of the field, we always coached our backside guy to rotate over toward the middle of the field some. It was just a ridiculous throw by an outstanding quarterback." Then the Oilers went on a terrific drive, and it was during a timeout that Andy Booth felt compelled to remind his head coach who he was and who he was not.

"I remember we'd called time, and Coach Strahm came out on the field to talk to the offense. Coach told me because we'd been throwing so many outcuts [short sideline pass routes], the safeties were creeping up. He told me he'd like me to throw one deep.

"Well, I knew what I could do and what I couldn't do, and I was not a drop-back-throw-it-deep quarterback. I looked at Coach and said, 'Ahh, Coach, Bo's sitting over there on the sidelines.'"

Strahm remembers the moment. "I have to laugh just thinking about it. Here's this kid that had just taken maybe ten or fifteen snaps the entire year heading into the game, doing a terrific job throwing the short routes and running the option and handling the ball beautifully on handoffs to Pearson and Shelton and Yeager, and I'm asking him to transform himself into John Elway in the biggest game of his life.

"Needless to say, I backed off and said, 'Andy, you're right. Let's stick to the short stuff. You keep doing exactly what you're doing!'"

And so, the drive continued with Booth contributing big time, teaming with Robert Shelton on a 14-yard catch-and-run and running the option for 13 yards and a key first down. Then, it was Andy Booth again, on a three-yard keeper for the go-ahead touchdown.

The fourth quarter began less than favorably for the Oilers, as Central Washington scored to knot the game at 21. It was Kitna again who tossed his third TD pass, to his third different receiver, Todd Murray just thirteen ticks into the final stanza.

After Findlay made a rare mistake when Pearson fumbled at his own 24-yard line, it appeared CW would capitalize. However, the Oilers rose up on defense and forced a four-yard loss on a running play and back-to-back incompletions. Marty Greenlee then left a 45-yard field goal short, and the game remained tied.

Despite the Oilers' ensuing drive sputtering, punter Mark Barnes executed a perfect 34-yard coffin-corner punt, knocking the ball out of bounds at Central's two-yard line. It appeared that field position just might make the difference down the stretch. However, the Wildcats' punter Greg Stoller banged a 52-yarder, and when the Oilers were called for a 10-yard penalty for a block in the back, the field leveled again.

Although each team had two more possessions, no one scored. And so the game ended at an irresolute 21-21 and more than a little confusion. Several of the players were unaware that there would not be an overtime played. One of them was Oiler linebacker Ray Long.

"I started to run over to Coach Strahm to see what he wanted to do if we won the coin toss for the overtime. But, then I noticed that the referees were walking off the field. Then Coach Akers told me it was over. I remember thinking, 'We don't need officials to finish this the right way. Let's stay out here and see who's the last man standing!'"

For center Chad Ulm, there were indeed mixed emotions. "It was kind of like one eye flashed with excitement and the other eye had a tear in it. We really didn't know whether to celebrate or not. It was definitely a strange feeling."

For Andy Booth, as unaccustomed to the press's queries as any player on the planet, he may have said it best when Larry Alter of The Courier asked him how he felt. "I don't know what to feel. I've never been here before. I don't know what a win feels like. I don't know what a loss feels like. I don't know what kind of emotion to express."

For first-year assistant John Wauford, there was also a good deal of confusion up in the booth at game's end. "I remember looking around the booth and asking the other assistants what was going on. When we realized it was over, I asked, 'Do we still get a ring?' When the other coaches said yes, I said, 'All right! We'll take it!' But seriously, I do wish there'd have been an overtime system in place."

Columnist Steve Kelley of the Seattle Times bemoaned the lack of closure. He wrote for the next day's edition, "Two seasons that started in August ended in limbo. An afternoon that was too good to end, wasn't over, even when it was over. The NAIA yesterday became the NA-tie-A."

Even Dick Strahm himself had conflicting feelings, telling Kelley after the game, "We're all kind of down in the dumps right now. Probably right now this feels closer to a loss than it does a win. We did what we wanted to do and didn't come away with a victory.

"I think Christmas morning I might say, 'Thank God we're co-champions,' but right now, I can't give you a big smile and a cheer."

On the other sideline, Jon Kitna reacted to the tie. "The NAIA, unlike the NCAA, is more of a feel-good type of conference, and they figure if two teams can finish up in a tie, they'd rather have everyone feel good after the game, but nobody's feeling terrible either, I guess.

"But, having said that, to be honest, I'd like to come back next Saturday and play them again."

Despite such protestations, the results stood, and each school could lay claim to the same NAIA Division II 1995 national championship. However, that was the last time such an occurrence could happen.

Recalls Strahm, "At the winter convention of the NAIA, a vote was taken, and it was agreed that an overtime would be played from that point on so that there would be a clear-cut winner. Each team would get the same number of possessions from the opponent's 25-yard line. However, that didn't help us in the Tacoma Dome.

"I will say this, though. For our team to play so hard all year and our defense to be so dominating, and then to go into a hostile environment with more than 5,000 people rooting against us and hold Kitna to his playoff low [286 yards passing] and win time of possession by almost double [39:04 to 20:56], well, the Oilers ARE national champions! They wear their championship rings as proudly as I wear mine!"

And so it was over. When it came time for post-season awards, The University of Findlay came up as big as it did on the fields of 1995. No fewer than four players were named First-Team NAIA All-Americans, Cal Dietz, Ray Long, Nate Arnold, and Nate Weihrauch.

About Weihrauch, Strahm would say, "Someone might say you can't come from a Division IV high school like Liberty Benton and be a great college football player. Here is one young man who proved that theory wrong."

Looking ahead to 1996, Strahm had a pleasant problem. He had both of his 1,000-yard rushers (Robert Shelton, who gained 1,115 yards and Troy Pearson, who gained 1,011 yards) back, and he also could look for the return of Chris Jaquillard. Additionally, Bo Hurley would be ready to direct the offense.

As for Coach Strahm, he was named by the vote of his fellow coaches for the third time the NAIA National Coach of the Year. Additionally, he finished just behind University of Toledo's Gary Pinkel and just in front of Ohio State's John Cooper as the top college coach in the Buckeye State.

Heading into the off-season, Dick Strahm felt fortunate. He had overcome both open-heart surgery and cancer in the ten years since Frosty Westering's Pac Lutheran sent his team home from the West Coast a 40-29 loser. He had his son Doug back with him as an assistant coach, and, with two national championships in the last four years, his Findlay Oilers were, indeed, national champions again…and again.

What a great trip to Hamburg, Germany, on May 28, 1994! Picture of the Oilers team after a 21 to 14 win over the Hamburg Blue Devils, with a game crowd of over 10,000 fans.

Coach Strahm and the captains of the 1997 national championship team: (first row) Chris Barber, Coach Strahm, Brett Macy; (second row) Bo Hurley, Tom Hansen, and Terrance Auster.

Chapter 16

An Era Draws to a Close

The winter months that preceded the 1996 season provided Coach Dick Strahm a chance to see the previous season in different shades of light. While certainly a tie and a shared national championship with Jon Kitna's Central Washington wasn't a best-case scenario, Strahm also realized every other NAIA Division II team not competing in the Tacoma Dome the previous December most certainly would have traded places with either co-champion.

However, the ultimate competitor that beats inside of men like Strahm also compelled him to think a lot about what needed to be done for his Oilers to be the lone team standing in the post-season of 1996. For Strahm, he had become accustomed to keeping his eye on the post-season prize. After all, he had taken ten different teams to the playoffs by this point in his Oilers coaching tenure.

In order to get where he wanted to be, Strahm knew he needed both good fortune and dedicated efforts from both coaches and players alike.

As far as good fortune, he needed a strong comeback from Bo Hurley after his knee surgery. Recalls Hurley, now a district manager for Ashland Incorporated and living in Centerville, Ohio, "I had surgery in January and started my rehabilitation right away, so I figured I'd be good to go by August. Really, the knee injury was the first major injury I'd ever had in my football career. I knew there'd be some apprehension until I got on the field and took some hits and made some cuts, but I fully intended to be ready for the season."

While a great deal of talent was slated to return from the national championship squad, Strahm also knew there was some rebuilding to be done. Hit particularly hard by graduation was the offensive line, with strong-side guard Jason May being the only returning starter who would return.

Recalls Strahm, "This was a time when I knew I had to rely heavily on my offensive line coaches Jim McIntosh and Curtis Davidson during our spring practice and continuing during our August two-a-days." Between these two Strahm assistants, they had 31 years of experience coaching Oilers football.

The line reconstruction was, indeed, a formidable job, as McIntosh and Davidson had to find two strong-side tackles, a backside guard, a center, and a tight end. It was a talent search that would certainly take both time and patience.

When spring ball arrived, it was a no-brainer that Bo Hurley would be kept out. Just two months from surgery, Hurley had proven himself to be a quarterback equal to the task of running Strahm's wishbone, and, to do that, he needed to be fully recovered. As a sophomore in 1995, he'd accounted for over 1,000 yards in total offense before the injury in the Tacoma Dome.

The consensus on the football staff was that Hurley's best football was ahead of him as soon as his recovery was complete. Spring gave valuable backup Andy Booth, the unlikely title-game hero, a chance to direct the first offense.

For Strahm, the summer would not include any reconfiguring of his coaching staff. Unlike some of Strahm's first Oilers staffs after his arrival in 1975, he now had a stable staff of assistants. There were no departures from the '95 staff of Jim McIntosh, Doug Coate, Curtis Davidson, Mike Schanski, Doug Strahm, Don Akers, Rusty Smith, and Jon Wauford.

Certainly, on reporting day in August, it was a welcome sight to see nine returning defensive starters walk into the Gardner Fitness Center, young men who were so vital to a unit that yielded a paltry 114 points in thirteen games.

NAIA first-team All-American Nate Arnold was back at defensive tackle. *Bob Griese's 1996 College Football Yearbook* projected Arnold to be the Division II NAIA Defensive Player of the Year. In Oilers terminology, he would be the Stud Tackle, certainly an appropriate term for a player as strong as Arnold.

Recalls Strahm, "Nate was simply an outstanding football player. He was 6'1" and 290 pounds and was so explosive off the ball.

"And, you talk about strong? In the weight room, he could do 25 to 30 reps, at 225 pounds. His arms just pumped like pistons."

Arnold, currently living in his hometown of Lucas, Ohio, in a farmhouse once owned by his grandparents and working as a job superintendent in charge of plumbing and pipefitting for Metzger-Gliesinger Mechanical, recalls his best friend, Cal Dietz, as being instrumental in his own dedication to weight training.

"Cal and I came in together as freshmen. I took a medical redshirt year my first year, so I had a final year of eligibility after he graduated. But our last couple of years together, we really pushed each other in the weight room. We reached the point where we were bench pressing over 400 pounds and leg pressing over 900.

"Cal and I just never saw the weight training as work. We thrived on it because we both knew just how much it helped us on the field."

Joining Arnold on the defensive line were returning starters Howard Heston, the defensive end out of Elyria, Ohio; Chris Barber, who would play the Oiler position, out of Detroit Catholic High School; Chris Garner, the tackle from Cincinnati; and the cat-quick nose guard out of Columbus, Ohio, Ray Jackson. Strahm also knew he would be relying on Josh McDaniels (Marion, Ohio) to play in the line's interior.

At linebacker, while the graduation of first-team Division II NAIA All-American Ray Long certainly left a void, the Oilers would be solid with Mike Powers (Marysville, Ohio), who was second to Long in tackles with 148 in '95, and Cincinnatian Steve Adams.

The secondary's only loss to graduation was free safety Larry Williams, and his replacement had already proven himself to be a big-time performer. Junior Bret Macy, who Strahm lured from the tropical breezes of Pompano Beach, Florida, would slide into Williams' vacated slot.

The other three in the defensive backfield were all starters in 1995 on a defense that returned seven interceptions for touchdowns.

Macy's mate at strong safety was senior Nate Weihrauch. Weihrauch was from Liberty-Benton High School, just a few miles from Findlay, and a player Dick Strahm can credit his son Steve for bringing to his attention.

Recalls Dick, "Really, Steve was the one who initially told me about Nate. Steve and Nate were teammates at Liberty Benton High School. When Nate was a senior, Steve told me I just had to pay more attention to him when I came to his games. I started to do just that, and that's when I decided Steve was absolutely right. This young man could play for the Findlay Oilers.

Recalls Steve, "Nate was a year older than I, and everybody on our team really looked up to him. Simply put, he was the most intense competitor I have ever seen on a football field.

While injuries had hampered Weihrauch during the 1995 post-season, he was fully recovered for his senior year.

As Weihrauch, still living in the Findlay area and now working as the athletic director for Findlay High School, recalls, "I was really geared up for 1996. We all felt we had a great chance to repeat as national champs. While expectations were always high at Findlay, in '96, we really had a lot of great athletes."

Returning starters at the corners were Terrance Auster (Dayton, Ohio) and Demetrice Boykin (Naples, Florida). Both had outstanding cover skills.

As long as Hurley was healthy, Strahm felt equally good about his offensive backfield. He had two 1,000-yard rushers returning in three-back Troy Pearson (Detroit, Michigan) and four-back Robert Shelton (Columbus, Ohio). Chris Jaquillard was also champing at the bit to crack the offensive-backfield rotation after sitting out all of 1995.

At the two-back, in addition to Jared Wojtas (Granger, Indiana), Dick Strahm received a great gift in the form of a transfer from Bluffton College. Defiance (Ohio) High School graduate Jamie Smiddy had started as a freshman for the Beavers in '95 at the same school where his older brother Gary had played so capably. During the summer of 1996, Smiddy decided to transfer to Findlay.

Recalls Smiddy, currently living in Williamsburg, Kentucky, and working as an assistant football coach at the University of the Cumberlands, "Although I started for Bluffton in '95, I wanted to come to Findlay for a number of reasons.

"First of all, Bluffton was a non-scholarship school, whereas at Findlay I had the opportunity to pick up some financial aid.

"I suppose my main reason for going to Bluffton out of high school was my older brother had done so well there, but I realized after my freshman year that I wanted to be a part of a really special program, which Findlay had.

"We went 5-5 at Bluffton, which certainly isn't terrible, but there was Findlay coming off a national championship, a program with so many great players and coaches, so I called Coach Coate, who'd given me his card when he was at my high school a couple years before on a recruiting visit."

Beyond those reasons, there was one more that Smiddy felt made Findlay the right choice. "My coach in high school was Jerry Buti, who played for Coach Strahm in the 1970s, so I felt the transition to Findlay would be somewhat easier.

"Listen, even in high school, I knew I wanted to coach football. Coach Buti's style and mentality were all about ball-control offense and tough, physical play. I figured, that came from Coach Strahm, and, of course, I was right.

"I was able to see up close two men who were just great coaches and great men. In my own coaching career, I've taken more than a few bits and pieces from both of them to create my own coaching philosophy. I coach the running backs and also serve as the strength and conditioning coach here at the Cumberlands, and while I certainly wanted to kind of craft my own coaching philosophy when I first started, I'd have been a fool not to have been heavily influenced by both Coach Buti and Coach Strahm."

Now in his sixth year at the school in Williamsburg, Smiddy remembers the adjustment he had to make when arriving in Findlay. "The two-back was pretty wide open. I learned that a really good one [Bill Yeager] had just graduated and the position was really wide open.

"Of course, in Coach Strahm's wishbone, you have to accept your role if you're going to play two-back. While at Bluffton my freshman year I got around ten to fifteen carries a game, I realized at Findlay the two-back did a lot of blocking and that number would probably go down.

"But, I learned to accept the role. Of course, if you're a running back and a competitor, you want the ball, but it really was all about team at Findlay. It didn't take me long during August two-a-days to realize we had such a potent running game and really what I would call an equal running attack with a lot of different backs getting the carries. It was a little humbling at first to not be the featured back, but there are sacrifices you make when you play for a team with so many weapons."

For Dick Strahm, he felt that he was hung up just a bit on the horns of a dilemma. Recalls Strahm, "I wasn't sure during our August pre-season how to bring Bo [Hurley] along. Should I get him ready to start the season and assume everything was good with the knee, or should I go with Andy Booth and bring Bo along more slowly, so he was at full throttle during the second half of the season? That was the question on my mind.

"I was confident Andy could perform well if I chose to bring Bo along more slowly, but I really didn't want to go that route if I didn't have to. When you're fortunate enough in your career to get a Bo Hurley, you certainly don't want to sit him if you don't have to."

But the more Strahm and his assistants looked at the junior signal caller, the more apparent it was that there were few, if any, ill effects from the surgery. And, as Hurley recalls, he had little doubt he was fully recovered.

"Listen, of course, there was some nervousness until I got out there during our first intrasquad scrimmages and saw how the knee held up when I made my plants to throw the ball and when I made my cuts, but after the first few reps, I felt the knee was sound.

"Of course, starting quarterbacks aren't really subjected to contact in preseason, so I still needed to see how I'd react after taking some hits under game conditions. But, I fully expected to be ready for our first game."

The major concern during preseason was rebuilding an offensive line decimated by graduation. Strahm wondered how quickly coaches McIntosh and Davidson could match the rather large pieces needed to create a cohesive unit.

By the time August camp was drawing to a close, the pieces had been found and locked in place. Tom Hansen, the junior out of Toledo, had played tight end the previous season and lettered, but a knee injury that required a brace inhibited his ability to run routes. Additionally, his aggressiveness made him a logical choice to fill the outside tackle position.

Hansen, who currently lives in Findlay and works as a senior engineer for Findlay Telecom, remembers his conversion from tight end to tackle well. "I remember Coach Strahm talked to my dad and told him he was thinking about the move. When my dad said something to me, he said, 'It really didn't matter what I said to Coach Strahm, so you're moving to tackle!'

"Really, the switch was OK because I just wanted to start. I had two years of eligibility left, and it was time for me to start making an impact."

And, make an impact Tom Hansen did! Recalls Strahm, "As soon as I saw Tom coming out of his stance, I knew he'd make a fine offensive tackle. He was such an aggressive young man, and, man, could he ever hit! He took every player who ever lined up against him as his own personal challenge, and he wanted to destroy that force that stood in his way."

Playing beside Hansen at inside tackle would be sophomore Brian Musser, the 6'3," 293-pound native of Clyde, Ohio. In the next two years, Hansen and Musser would work together so effectively that Hansen remembers the symbiotic nature of their relationship. "Listen, offensive linemen have to rely so heavily on each other when it comes to blocking schemes. I truly believe two linemen who are lining up beside one another are about the closest thing to brothers on the football field that you can get.

"With Brian, there was such chemistry that by the end of our second year together in 1997, we didn't even have to call line checks very often. We both just knew what to do when the defensive line shifted on our side. It's really hard to explain to people who never played down in the trenches a foot or so from another player lined up beside him, but Brian and I just knew what adjustments we needed to make without calling anything out."

As far as who is responsible for making Brian and him such an outstanding pair of tackles, Hansen has an immediate response. "Absolutely no doubt about it. It was Coach Mac [McIntosh], the best position coach I ever had. He was a tough guy with a heart of gold. If you screwed up, he let you know about it, but we all knew how much he cared about us. "I suppose in a lot of ways, I could also be talking about Coach Strahm, the man I will always call 'Coach' no matter how many years go by since my playing days. "I guess when you have coaches as special as those two men, you just can't help but become a pretty good football player."

The Oilers also had found themselves another in a long line of outstanding centers. Dan Franks, Brian Musser's high school teammate in Clyde, the player responsible for getting the ball into Hurley's hands and then taking on a blocking assignment. Franks would become a two-year starter, in the process putting his name right beside the great Oilers centers, players like Dave Berger, Chad Ulm, Bill McIntosh, Ryan Sbrissa, and Marty Simon.

Recalls Strahm, "Those Oilers centers over the years had a lot in common. Collectively, they weren't very big, but they were all very strong, in the weight room and on the field. I'll tell you something else. They were also strong academically. Anyone who ever tells you that there's not much thinking to just snapping a ball between your legs just doesn't know much about the game of football or the intricacies and techniques of blocking."

The last pieces of the offensive line were snapped into place when Joey Barlow, the 6'3," 292-pounder out of Westerville, Ohio, and 6'5" Findlay native Darrell Ramsey established themselves at backside guard and tight end respectively by August's end.

In addition to the lanky Ramsey, Hurley would also find excellent pass-catching targets in wide receivers Jason Hamby, a native of Centerville, Ohio, and Ben Dils, out of Baltimore High School in Granville, Ohio.

Handling the place kicking would be Tom Sellers, from Tipp City, Ohio, who was Mr. Automatic in 1995, converting all but one of his 62 point-after-touchdown attempts. The punter, out of Miramar, Florida, would be sophomore Brandon Kittendorf.

Now that the positions were determined, it was time to see if Strahm's Oilers could hang a fourth Division II NAIA national championship skin on the wall in 1996. As most coaches will tell you, winning it all is hard enough. Doing it a second straight time is even harder, but that was the goal as Findlay broke camp and headed into the season.

Strahm remembers a condition so common for early-season games certainly was evident in the September 7 opener on the road in Campbellsville, Kentucky, against the Tigers of Campbellsville University.

"It was just incredibly hot, probably close to 90 degrees and humid, and I think that had a lot to do with our very sluggish first half. I remember we only had a Seller's field goal and a three-point lead at the break.

"Now, once we got acclimated to the conditions, we did much better in the second half offensively. Our head trainer, Vi LeClair, and her staff did a great job keeping our players watered down."

When the sweaty Oilers trudged off the surface of Tiger Stadium, they did so with the season's first shutout, 30-0.

As far as the running attack, the former Toledo Woodward star Chris Jaquillard celebrated his return to football. He captured leading-rusher honors with 98 yards on eight carries and a touchdown.

Hurley showed no ill effects of the knee injury in the previous December's title game by completing 5 of 9 and two TD passes to Hamby.

Defensively, of course, Nate Arnold anchored an outstanding defensive line, and Kyle Doak, the sophomore of out Salem, Ohio, made the opener memorable. The strong safety came off the bench to pick off a pass and run it in for a touchdown.

After an open date, the Oilers engaged the Tiffin University Dragons in the home opener before a large and enthusiastic home crowd. The defense extended their shutout quarter stretch to eight in a 42-0 whitewash. In such games, young performers can be evaluated and one certainly worth keeping an eye on was sophomore free safety Craig Aukerman, who appeared to be a definite up and comer. He recorded his first varsity interception in the win.

Offensively, while Hurley uncharacteristically struggled with accuracy, completing just 7 of 16 throws, three of those were for touchdowns.

On the final Saturday in September when a slight nip in the air warranted a light jacket for a typical spectator, the Oilers again played host, this time to the Geneva College Golden

Tornadoes, a team that blew in from Beaver Falls, Pennsylvania. In a game Strahm remembers as being much closer than the final score might indicate, Findlay prevailed, 35-15.

"We played well in the first half and got a big TD run by Bo on an option [49 yards] and a big interception return by Nate Weihrauch [81 yards] and were up by three scores.

"But, give Geneva credit. They came back and got it to 28-15 with plenty of time on the clock in the fourth quarter."

However, Tom Sellers split the uprights from 29 yards out to end any hopes of a Geneva miracle finish.

Hurley hurt Geneva both with both his arm and his legs, completing five passes for 84 yards and rushing for another 93 yards on 15 carries.

Recalls the Oilers' new two-back, Jamie Smiddy, "I realized after just three games that Bo Hurley was, simply put, 'the man.' Let me tell you something. When he ran the option, no one ever got the pitch. He was going to run it. The coaches knew it. We knew it. Heck, even the opponents knew it. But, knowing it and stopping it are two different things."

On October 5, UF took to the road, traveling to Malone College in Canton, Ohio. The Pioneers' home field was Paul Brown Stadium in Massillon, Ohio, named for the former Massillon High School coach and NFL coaching legend, and the stands spilled over with Malone supporters smelling an upset.

In an extremely physical, low-scoring, every-possession-counts contest, the Oilers prevailed, 13-10. The game was tied at seven at halftime and at ten after three quarters before the rock-steady senior out of Tipp City, Tom Sellers, boomed a 40-yard game-winning field goal to send the visitors scampering off the field winners for the fourth time in as many starts.

Hurley was remarkable, running the option as he gained 153 yards on 22 carries. He also found time to complete eight passes for another 88.

Next up was a home contest on October 12 with the Tigers of Olivet Nazarene University. The team from Bourbonnais, Illinois, hung tough early, down only 14-7 at the intermission, but were dominated in the second half, yielding 21 points and countering with only six.

Statistically, the Oilers' 35-13 win was punctuated by Troy Pearson's 112 yards rushing and two touchdowns and All-American strong safety Nate Weihrauch's two interceptions and the sophomore Aukerman's one.

The Oilers had reached the halfway point of the regular season a perfect 5-0 and remained that way in week six. They made the long trip to Davenport, Iowa, to take on a perennial NAIA power, St. Ambrose.

When all was settled, Findlay proved it could win a shootout, this time 41-31. Hurley was again the quintessential dual threat, this time topping 100 yards in both running (105) and passing (143). Of his ten completions, five went to favorite target Jason Hamby and two were TD tosses to Darrell Ramsey and running back Troy Pearson. Linebacker Steve Adams, out of Cincinnati, recorded a key interception.

In week seven, Findlay returned home to take on Trinity International University, a team out of Deerfield, Illinois, the very team that had given UF its only loss of the 1995 season in the opener.

Recalls Strahm, "Of course, we used that as motivation during our week of practice. I brought it up, I don't know, maybe twenty or thirty times?"

Whether or not that had any impact on the game's result, who knows? All that is known is that the Oilers recorded their third shutout of the campaign, 20-0, in what Strahm remembers as a total team effort.

Then, at 7-0, it was time for the longest bus ride of the year, traveling to Mt. Pleasant, Iowa, to take on Iowa Wesleyan. Recalls Strahm, "We drove to South Bend, Indiana, for an early lunch and then on to Chicago and into Iowa. It really was a grueling ten-hour bus trip one way."

Apparently, after the long bus ride, the Oilers running backs felt the need to stretch their legs, and stretch them they did! In a 42-16 UF win, the Orange and Black ran up 440 yards on the ground. Chris Jaquillard led the way with 112 yards on 11 carries, and Robert Shelton scored twice.

As far as special teams, Craig Aukerman recovered a blocked punt in the end zone for a touchdown. Aukerman, now a linebacker and special team coach for the Miami University Redhawks in Oxford, Ohio, recalls his sophomore season. "I started the season at safety, but we had so many injuries in the secondary, that I was moved to cornerback and worked into a starting role by the second half of the season. To be a sophomore starting on a defending undefeated national championship team was really very special."

The final two weeks of the regular season offered little in the way of challenge for the Oilers.

St. Xavier University from Chicago came into Northwest Ohio and left a 56-14 loser. Hurley was very accurate throwing the ball, hitting on 10 of 12 for 130 yards and two touchdowns. One was a big-time 75-yard touchdown toss to Jason Hamby and another went to Darrell Ramsey.

Then the Oilers' tenth consecutive win came at Jim Wheeler Memorial Stadium in Upland, Indiana, the home of former Hoosier-Buckeye opponent, Taylor University. On that November 16, UF ended their regular season the same way it began it, with a shutout. This time, the Oilers also provided more scoring, as evidenced by the 56-0 final tally.

It was at this game that Dick Strahm witnessed the last interception for a touchdown in his coaching career. Nate Weihrauch returned an interception 73 yards for a touchdown.

Hurley tuned up for the playoffs by remaining ultra-accurate. He completed 10 of 11 passes, meaning he was 20 of 23 in his last two regular season games.

Recalls Hurley, "I think by this point in my career, Coach Strahm started trusting me enough to allow for a more open offense. By no means were we a West Coast, 'chuck-it-early-and-often' offense, but I was getting a lot more opportunities to throw than when I was a sophomore.

"I'd be lying if I said I wasn't happy with the change. In high school [Upper Scioto High School] we spread receivers out on both sides and ran a run-and-shoot [Hurley threw for almost 6,000 yards], and it wasn't unusual for me to throw it thirty times or more every Friday night.

"So, I really was going to try to show Coach Strahm that throwing more wouldn't really be a crime."

For the 10-0 Oilers, they certainly weren't about to sneak up on anybody in the post-season. First of all, they were the top-ranked team in all of Division II in the NAIA. Second, their first opponent had already seen them up close and personal just seven weeks earlier.

On November 23, the Golden Hurricanes of Geneva College again would invade Donnell Stadium with the hope of reversing the outcome of their 31-15 loss of September 28.

Despite his team's 22-game unbeaten streak, Dick Strahm remained cautious heading into the game. "We jumped on them early and then had to hold on [in that first game], but this is a whole new war, a whole new season, and we can't expect that to necessarily happen again. I look for a whale of a football game between two very physical football teams."

After Geneva's regular-season loss to the Oilers, the Hurricanes won six of their last seven, losing only to Malone, 26-25. Geneva's big gun was the 245-pound tailback Willie Murray. Strahm felt there was a key to limiting Murray's effectiveness. "Murray is going to get his yards. What you try to do with [him] is try to get him to run east and west as best you can. If you get him running north and south, at 245 pounds, he's going to run over a lot of people."

On the first playoff Saturday, it was power football, a staple of Strahm's teams over the years that was the deciding factor. In the third quarter alone, the offensive line, with five first-year starters, overwhelmed Geneva, clearing the way for Chris Jaquillard and Troy Pearson time and time again. The Oilers' running game produced 146 yards in that quarter alone and 320 for the game.

Jaquillard grabbed leading-rusher honors with 117 yards on 17 carries, and fullback Pearson chipped in with 85. And of course, the 6'3," 220-pound quarterback out of Alger, Ohio, made his presence known with three rushing touchdowns of his own.

The Oilers defense held Willie Murray to just 87 yards in 24 carries. Defensive game MVP, the linebacker Mike Powers, had ten solo tackles, four assists, a fumble recovery, and a sparkling one-handed interception that had thousands of Oilers fans leaping to their feet.

A key decision just before halftime by Dick Strahm paid off after his All-American defensive tackle Nate Arnold stripped Willie Murray, forcing a fumble deep in Geneva's territory at the ten. Leading just 10-7 at the time, Strahm's offense failed to move the ball, and, on fourth down, Tom Sellers kicked a 33-yard field goal to make it 13-7.

However, Geneva was called for a personal foul, and Strahm decided to do something many coaches would never do. He took the points off the board to try for the touchdown. Hurley then justified his head coach's decision by flipping a TD pass to a wide-open Jason Hamby in the back of the end zone, and the Oilers went into halftime leading 17-7 and feeling somewhat more comfortable.

After the game, Strahm spoke with the sports editor of *The Findlay Courier*, Larry Alter, about the decision. "Don't ever take three points off the scoreboard? Who said that? Vince Lombardi? Woody Hayes? Evidently, Strahm didn't say it!

"The reason I did it was there were 31 seconds left, and we had one timeout. We were going to go half the distance [on the penalty]. We wanted to get down there close enough, and if we didn't score, we could still call time out and kick another field goal."

The win set up another chapter in the most intense rivalry of Dick Strahm's career at Findlay. The Titans of Westminster would again invade Donnell Stadium after the university's unwavering support of Strahm's teams over the years again manifested itself by the school's administrators' submitting the highest bid to guarantee the Oilers would host the game.

Prior to the contest, Strahm spoke without the slightest bit of hyperbole when he said, "If you believe everything is relative, this is Oklahoma and Nebraska, Florida and Florida State, Ohio State and Michigan.

"Our kids know they are playing the best of the best, and they'll be just as excited game day as players from those teams are. The only difference is there won't be 85,000 people in the stands."

Titan coach Gene Nicholson's team was 4-2 at one time before rattling off five consecutive wins, by a combined score of 170-30. Westminster's two losses were by a combined nine points. In other words, a touchdown, an extra point, and a field goal were all that separated them from matching the Oilers' 11-0 mark.

When Nicholson said that his defense, led by two-time NAIA All-American linebacker Craig Mills, was perhaps the best in school history, it was indeed a powerful statement, given the level of success Westminster had achieved. That meant Nicholson felt his defense was even better than the 1988 and '89 teams that were undefeated and won back-to-back national championships.

Certainly, room in the trophy cases at both schools was at a premium. Westminster had won national titles in 1970, '76, '77, '88, '89, and '94 and was a runner-up three other times. The Oilers had national titles in 1979, '92, and '95 in addition to their runner-up in 1978.

For the Oilers to advance to the semifinals, Strahm knew his defense had to slow down Titan tailback Andy Blatt. Blatt had 1,064 yards and 13 touchdowns in just eight games and would enter the contest as the second most prolific touchdown-maker in the history of the NAIA.

On Saturday, December 7, it was the Oilers' Hurley who the Titan coach, Gene Nicholson, felt made the difference in a dominating 28-9 UF win. "With Hurley, Findlay runs a two-phase attack. One phase is to run between the tackles. The other is for Hurley to keep the ball. He made all the big plays. He became the next dimension to their power game. He's the catalyst to why they are where they are now."

The Oilers were heading for the Division II NAIA semifinals, thanks to solid rushing efforts by Bo Hurley (139 yards), Chris Jaquillard (86 yards, 2 TDs), Troy Pearson (77 yards), and an emerging power runner, two-back Jamie Smiddy (51 yards).

Defensively, the Oilers took Andy Blatt right out of the mix, limiting him to just 65 yards on 19 carries.

After the contest, Dick Strahm identified what he saw as the key to the first half. "I thought our football team was mentally ready to play. We made a mistake [a fumbled punt at their own 20-yard line] early. We gave them the ball deep, but they came away four plays later with no points. That may have been the whole difference.

"We beat one of the better teams in the country. In the playoffs, if you can run the football, play great defense, and have good special teams, you're going to be tough to beat. And, right now, the Oilers are doing all three."

Chris Jaquillard commented after the game on the dominating performance of an offensive line short on experience at season's beginning. "It's awesome running behind guys like Tom Hansen, Jason May, and Brian Musser. Basically, you just see the hole and run to daylight."

Again, Findlay won the bid to host the next game, and the opponent would certainly be traveling a long way to get to Donnell. The Western Washington Vikings came into the contest not only with predominately West Coast personnel but also a West Coast offense, the antithesis of the Oilers' ball-control, run-dominating attack.

The Vikings head coach Rob Smith, who had taken his teams to the playoffs four times in the last five years, recognized the challenge the Oilers presented. "I consider Findlay to be the best team in the country. There's a reason for their number-one national ranking. They'll be, by far, the most physical team we've faced. We don't really see that type of football when it's just line up and here we come. This is classic Midwest football."

However, Smith's observation cut both ways. Just as his Vikings weren't accustomed to seeing an offense which relied on power rather than deception, the Oilers were not accustomed to an offense with so many receiver packages and so many footballs flying through the air. Additionally, Findlay had suffered some injuries in the secondary and would be without two key performers, Terrance Auster and Craig Aukerman.

And, on December 14, the Vikings of Western Washington handed Strahm's Oilers their first loss in 24 games, coming away with a 28-21 win on enemy turf.

Bret Macy, currently the general manager for Pompano Motor Company in his home town of Pompano Beach, Florida, remembers all too well the part of the Western Washington attack that was pivotal. "With the losses of Auster and Aukerman, we had some inexperience, and they just went right after it. Western Washington knew the short pass would work, those throws where the quarterback would just take a two- to three-step drop and the ball would be gone. And, that's what we just couldn't find an answer for."

All-American defensive tackle Nate Arnold remembers the final game of 1996 and the problems the West Coast offense presented. "The ball was out of the quarterback's hand so quickly, our defensive line just couldn't get there fast enough to apply enough pressure.

"I was never more frustrated in a football game in my life because I was blocked as well as anybody had my whole career. The whole season just went by so fast. People always say your senior year is like that. Despite the way my Oiler career ended, I have such great memories of my time in Findlay. My junior and senior years, we went 22-2-2 and won a national championship. A lot of guys who played college ball would want to trade places with me.

"And, of course, playing for Coach Strahm was a privilege. The biggest thing he did was take a bunch of immature kids and make them men. He taught me so much about integrity and honesty. Thanks to him, I found out I could be a leader. I was self-sufficient when I left to return to my hometown [Lucas, Ohio]. You might say I came to Findlay a boy, and, thanks to Coach Strahm, left a man."

Bo Hurley remembers the game that ended the '96 season well. "The injuries in our secondary really hurt. Also, I got injured in the second half. I hurt my Achilles' and missed most of the third quarter."

After three quarters, the Oilers were down, 28-13. The gritty Hurley managed to return and, at one point, completed seven straight passes, including a TD toss to split receiver Walter Jackson with 2:48 left on the game clock. After a successful two-point conversion pass from Hurley to Troy Pearson, an onside kick was unsuccessful, and the Vikings ran out the clock.

Strahm hit the nail squarely on the head after the game during his press conference. "The problem was we couldn't get the ball away from them, and that's not typical of us." Western Washington ran 82 plays to Findlay's 68, and the Viking quarterback Darren Erath surgically dissected UF's defense with quick-outs, slants, and pop passes over the middle. He completed 27 of 35 passes for 243 yards and three touchdowns.

The gracious Strahm refused to blame injuries in the secondary and Hurley's ankle woes for the loss. "It's been a great run. It's disappointing obviously. But you have to understand that all year long, for thirteen games, every team we played was going to play the very, very best against us because we've been ranked number one since August. It's been a great motivator for teams that played us.

"I've been in a lot of playoff games, and I know a lot of times you have to be lucky to win. But, that wasn't true today. Western Washington won because they were the better football team."

For the 1996 season, the awards were numerous. Nate Arnold and Nate Weihrauch both were named first-team NAIA All-Americans. Offensively, Jason May also was tabbed a first-team All-American. Troy Pearson was an honorable-mention All-American selection. Bo Hurley, as accomplished in the classroom as on the field, was an NAIA Academic All-American. His record-breaking football season included 2,066 yards in total offense and 30 touchdowns, 13 rushing and 17 passing.

While a senior academically, Hurley would be back for his final year of eligibility. Recalls former UF president Ken Zirkle, "Bo was just the epitome of a student-athlete. He was so good on the field not just because of his physical ability but because he was intellectually gifted. He actually graduated at the end of 1996. In '97, he began work on his MBA [Master of Business Administration]."

After the joy of the holiday season, muted in the Strahm household somewhat by thoughts of the loss, the calendar rolled over into 1997 and, by late February, the Oilers head coach was anxious for spring practice. The weight room at the Phil Gardner Fitness Center was busy with 74 Oilers lettermen, including fourteen starters. No doubt, Strahm had to smile thinking about his senior class. Recalls Dick, "We had twenty-five seniors returning in '97, which is the most I ever had. I had a real feeling that 1997 could be a very special year."

But, before spring practice, Strahm had some matters to address. For one, he had a colonoscopy scheduled for Monday, March 3, a necessary but not very pleasant experience. Little did the football coach realize when he awoke on the Sunday before the procedure that there would be far more serious medical matters he again would be forced to combat.

Recalls Strahm, "I remember I'd just gotten home from church, and it was such a nice day, I decided to walk my customary three miles. Then I would start drinking all the medicine you have to take to flush your lower tract for the procedure. Dr. Slee in Toledo thought I better have the colonoscopy just to make sure everything was clean. It had been just two years before when I had my cancer surgery.

"Well, after drinking the medicine, I became so sick and was vomiting so badly something happened that I would have to say was the toughest thing I've ever had to go through in my life.

"I finally went to bed still feeling very poorly and woke up early in the morning to leave for St. Vincent's Hospital in Toledo. As I got out of bed, I discovered both my right hand and leg were numb.

"My son, Doug, and my wife, Ginger, were taking me to Toledo for the colonoscopy. Once we got there, Doug told Dr. Slee the trouble I was having with my right arm and leg. It just so happened that Dr. Slee had a friend in the hospital that day who was a very well-known neurologist, Dr. Peter Zangara.

"After the exam, Dr. Zangara said that I had suffered a stroke. He thought that when I was vomiting, I must have burst a blood vessel in the back of my head, which triggered the event. So, I was admitted to the hospital.

"For the next five days, I got progressively worse. I couldn't move my right arm or leg at all. I couldn't even do something as simple as touch my belly button with my right hand.

"But, again I was fortunate that God sent me so many good people. At the end of five days and a number of tests, I started some rehab. It was then Dr. Zangara felt there was what he termed 'a window of opportunity' to move me to a hospital that specialized in rehabilitation for stroke victims.

"The doctor mentioned two hospitals he felt were excellent, one in Green Springs, Ohio, and Flower Hospital right there in Toledo. He said I'd be there between four and six weeks. I chose Flower because it was closer to Findlay and also my daughter Gina and her family lived in Toledo.

"I was then taken to Flower Hospital and admitted. While I was in my room, the doctor and nurse came in. I think they knew I had my head down a little bit.

"One of the nurses said to me, 'Let me tell you something, Mr. Strahm. You are kind of lucky.' Believe me, I wasn't feeling very lucky at that point in time, given the fact that I couldn't move my right arm or leg. She continued, 'You should know that stroke is the third-leading cause of death in the country, and you are still alive.'

"So, I acknowledged that good fortune and asked her what was the number-one cause. She told me that it was heart disease. I then asked what was number two, and she told me cancer.

"I figured I'd already whipped number one and number two, so why couldn't I also defeat number three?

"I then asked her if she knew what was the fourth-leading cause. She said automobile wrecks. So, I told her I'd never drive in another car again, only tanks. My family chuckled, shook their heads, and then smiled at me."

Recalls Dick's younger son, Steve, "Here Dad was facing this very scary set of circumstances, and there he was, lying in bed and cracking jokes!"

For Dick Strahm, the next several weeks found him admiring his caregivers more and more. "Once I started my rehabilitation, I realized just how exceptional the nurses at Flower rehab center were. They were caring, loving, helpful, and tough when they needed to be. I could see that they just really wanted me to succeed.

"At first, I couldn't walk. The nurses had to take me to the rehab area in a wheelchair. I was willing to face this stroke head on, no matter how long it would take to get better. I just have always believed that God never has given me anymore than I could handle, so I kept telling myself that I would defeat this thing.

"I remember at first the nurses had to tie me on the stationary bike because I could pump my legs just a little before falling off. Nurses had to stand on either side to stabilize the bike.

"There were two nurses, in particular, who were just outstanding. These ladies made me work. They would get on each side of me with a four-inch band around my waist and walk me down the hallway, helping me learn how to walk again.

"Then I would be on my back, and they would have an elastic band on my right leg, and we would stretch over and over. I worked as hard as I could and kept my eye on the prize, which was, of course, to return to doing what I loved, coaching football. I knew I had to keep a positive attitude and remember that God was right beside me, pushing right along with me.

"I also thought again as I had in the past when I had heart and cancer issues that there is power in prayer, and so many were praying for me.

"During my month at Flower, I was also in group therapy. In one exercise, we relearned how to hold dishes and wash them. Another day, we did food preparation. I remember my job was to cut strawberries. I had to cut the stems off, lay them sideways, and cut them into two pieces. It was so hard holding the knife with my right hand, so when no one was looking, I'd switch the knife over to my other hand.

"I'll tell you, those ladies didn't miss a trick, though. They'd catch me and say, 'Coach, right hand, right hand!'

"In another exercise, I had to flick cotton balls across the table with the fingers of my right hand. I just couldn't believe how hard something that simple was.

"I remember there was a man in our group who had ALS. We took a field trip to the Toledo Art Museum just to get a break from the hospital. My job was to push the wheelchair for the man with Lou Gehrig's. It gave me something to hold on to.

"That trip really showed me how important the simple pleasures are. It was neat just riding in a bus again, looking out the window, seeing other people. Despite the hundreds of bus rides, some of them pretty grueling, I'd taken in football traveling to away games, I was excited to be in that bus. Certainly, there's some irony there."

Finally, Dick Strahm was released from Flower and was able to return to Findlay to continue the physical therapy necessary before he could even think about returning to the sidelines. Someone Strahm remembers as so vital in his recovery then came into his life. Julie Stall is now a Findlay housewife, looking after her husband Jamie and four children, ages ranging from 10 to 2.

However, in 1997, she and Jamie had just moved to Findlay and had yet to start a family. Julie was a physical therapist for the Findlay Rehabilitation Center and was assigned to Dick Strahm's case.

Recalls Stall, "I evaluated Dick and created a treatment plan for his lower extremities to enhance both coordination and balance. We worked in 90-minute sessions three times a week for four months.

"When I saw him for the first time, he was in a wheelchair and looked pretty depressed. But, as our sessions evolved, and he began seeing the progress he was making, his mood got more and more upbeat.

"I remember we did a lot of drills to redevelop the movements he would need to coach. Much of our work was done in the grass, things like sidestepping and back peddling. He was just so determined to get back on the field. When I told Dick I wanted him to work on something at home, there was no doubt in my mind he would do his homework.

Recalls Strahm, "Julie was, pure and simple, a godsend. She was so positive and never gave me any reason to think I couldn't come back. When we weren't outside working, we'd be inside. Julie would have me attempt things like putting five screws in a piece of wood with my right hand. Other times, I'd take a sponge out of a bucket of water and squeeze out the water. As time went by, I was able to squeeze harder and harder."

Strahm also is grateful for so many others who helped him recover. Of course, there was his family, Ginger, Gina, Doug, and Steve.

Recalls Steve, "Dad's resolve to get back to coaching was just amazing. I remember when he first got home from Flower Hospital, it took everything he had just to squeeze a stress ball. But, as all great fighters, he just wouldn't quit and kept getting stronger and stronger, especially working on that treadmill at home."

The treadmill was a gift from Philip J. Gardner, yet another wonderful gesture from the scores of people in the Findlay area who were staunch supporters of the longtime Oilers coach.

Strahm reflects back on what three ingredients were needed to complete the recipe for a successful return from stroke. "Well, you take a lot of kindness and dedication from all of the people at Flower and from Julie Stall and you combine that with the loving support of my family and then you add a whole lot of God's help and mix them all together."

Of course, Strahm shouldn't rule out his own sense of optimism and an indomitable will to overcome adversity. He had beaten back coronary disease and cancer and was absolutely set on doing it again with the stroke.

Despite his timetable to be back on the field for spring practice in April, Strahm wasn't quite ready. He managed to make it back riding in a golf cart to look in on his team on the last practice of the fifteen-day period, but that was about all he was ready for. Recalls Strahm, "That's when you really learn to appreciate your assistant coaches. They really ran things for me as I was continuing my comeback."

The comeback advanced into the summer as the three sessions a week continued with Julie Stall. Strahm again was set on proving that medical adversity was nothing more than just another opponent to game plan for and defeat.

Through intense effort, Strahm once again was mobile and functional, despite having some residual effects from the stroke. His right hand would always be numb, although he re-learned how to write and do other tasks. A limp that altered his stride was caused by what his doctors called a "dropped foot" on his right side. A brace helped, but he couldn't walk more than 120 yards before his hips began to hurt from the strain. Still, that was more than enough to walk the length of a football field.

By August of 1997 Dick Strahm was back on the field taking command of the team he loved. There was certainly an overwhelming sense of optimism in the Oilers pre-season camp. The coaching staff had returned in its entirety. As far as personnel, not only did Findlay have fourteen starters returning but much like Jamie Smiddy's transfer during the summer of 1996, Strahm again welcomed a transfer who would turn out to be an outstanding football player.

This time, it was a player so good, he had started at linebacker for Purdue in the powerful Big Ten. The former Division I starter's path to Findlay was indeed a circuitous one.

Recalls Strahm, "My assistant Don Akers recruited the Cincinnati and Dayton areas and while making a visit to those areas during the summer, he found out about a player named Bart Conley who'd left Purdue after he and his family had a falling out with the coaching staff over the severity and treatment of a shoulder injury he had suffered. It had been two years since Conley had last played, but he was anxious to use his final year of eligibility.

Strahm remembers, "Now, had Bart enrolled in a school for the upcoming season that had a football program, he'd have lost his last year of eligibility. However, as luck would have it, he didn't.

"So, Coach Akers got Bart and his father to come to Findlay for a visit. When they walked in my office for the first time, I looked at this rangy young man who looked more like one of Coach [Ron] Niekamp's forwards here at Findlay. Bart was around 6'3," 225 pounds.

"As I talked to Bart and his dad, I found out he was enrolled in summer school. As far as wanting him, was there ever a doubt? How many times does a former Big Ten starter walk into the coach's office at an NAIA school and say, 'I want to play for you'?

"So, we got his winter and summer grades and his Purdue transcript and turned everything over to our admissions office. Actually, this was so far into the summer that by the time our admissions people told us Bart was cleared to play, we were already about three or four practices into our preseason.

"We got Bart suited up and by the end of the first week of practice, he had learned the defense and had won a first-team position at linebacker. I remember our first scrimmage. We ran a sweep, and Bart was the first guy to get to the corner waiting to see who showed up. Really, he was the missing link for our defense. Now, I had Steve Adams (Cincinnati) and Roger Hamilton (Oak Harbor, Ohio) and Bart playing linebacker, which was just outstanding. Another linebacker who I know would have done well was Brad Eckenrode (Dayton, Ohio), but a serious knee injury finished him for the season."

The defensive line again figured to be strong. While Nate Arnold had graduated, plenty of quality players remained. Chris Barbara returned for his senior year at end. The Oilers had depth at defensive tackle with Brett Jones (Monroeville, Ohio) and Chris Karsnia (Erie, Pennsylvania), Agunanda Brookins (Cincinnati), and Brandon Chaney (Elida, Ohio). Big Josh McDaniels (Marion, Ohio) would hold down the nose guard position.

The secondary was projected to be one of the quickest in all of the NAIA. Cornerbacks Terrance Auster and Demetrice Boykin returned for their senior year. Fellow senior Bret Macy returned at free safety, while strong safety was manned by Craig Aukerman.

Offensively, the line returned Joey Barlow at backside guard, Dan Franks at center, and the twin strong-side tackles, Brian Musser and Tom Hansen. Filling the graduated Jason May's strong-side guard slot would be John Latell (Girard, Ohio). Tight ends would be Matt Leliaert (Osceola, Indiana) and Darrell Ramsey. The offensive line certainly had size, averaging 276 pounds.

Both Jason Hamby and Ben Dils returned to provide excellent wide receivers for Bo Hurly.

The offensive backfield would feature a new look. Jamie Smiddy remembers a welcome change that greeted him heading into his second season as an Oiler. "Since Troy Pearson had graduated, Coach Strahm moved me to three-back, which meant I'd be getting more carries, especially on the 22-2, one of our bread-and-butter plays. I was very pleased with the change, needless to say."

Chris Jaquillard returned for his final season as the four-back and Jared Wojtas (Granger, Indiana) and Ken Keirns (Delphos, Ohio) were set to slide into Smiddy's old two-back position.

Shane Kittendorf returned to punt, and Bret Bahn (Arlington, Ohio) would try to fill the big shoes of placekicker Tom Sellers, who'd graduated the previous spring.

For 1997, the NAIA had undergone a notable change, with Divisions I and II merging. Whichever team was the last standing could truly make the claim that it was the best in all of the NAIA.

As far as the schedule, the Oilers would face more teams that were NCAA Division II schools. This meant UF would be competing against schools that were able to offer many more than the eight scholarships that Dick Strahm had at his disposal.

On September 6, the Oilers, most of whom felt they had left a project unfinished from the year before on the field against Western Washington, opened at home against Campellsville University. Heading into the season, Strahm was certainly aware that his Oilers would be the circled team on every opponent's schedule, given Findlay's number-three national ranking in the preseason.

The opener was anything but easy for UF. At the end of the first quarter, the Oilers actually trailed 13-0. The game remained close throughout before the home team finally prevailed, 28-20. Hurley ran for 82 yards and threw for 155 more and two touchdowns. Both Ramsey and Hamby had four catches, and each caught a TD pass.

After a bye week, the Oilers took to the road and traveled to Erie, Pennsylvania, to take on Mercyhurst College. Recalls the former offensive tackle Tom Hansen, "I'll never forget that game. Mercyhurst had just completed a stadium renovation and on the local television station I heard one of the players being interviewed tell a reporter that he and his mates intended to christen the field with a win over Findlay.

"You talk about bulletin-board material, at least the verbal equivalent of it! When it came time for our Friday night meeting and Coach Strahm stood in front of us, he looked around the room and said, 'Well, I think all of you saw the news. I guess there's nothing more left to say.'

"And, that was it. It was the shortest and most effective pep talk I've ever heard. We went out there the next day and really put a whippin' on them."

The final score was 44-14, as the Oilers posted an astonishing total in yards rushing, with 410. Jaquillard led the way with 102 yards on 17 carries and a pair of touchdowns. Defensively, Roger Hamilton and Craig Aukerman both registered interceptions.

Week three saw Findlay back at Donnell to host the Dragons of Tiffin University. The Oilers won in a rout, 56-14, totaling 600 yards in total offense, 420 of it on the ground. Jaquillard rushed for 92 yards, and Hurley threw touchdown passes to both Darrell Ramsey and Jason Hamby. Defensively, Demetrice Boykin picked off two passes, and senior linebacker Matt Harp (Pickerington, Ohio) grabbed one.

Findlay got its fourth win on the road at Olivet Nazarene University in Kankakee, Illinois, 35-24. Hurley was masterful, rushing for 98 yards and completing 24 of 37 throws for 332 yards. Recalls Hurley, "When I first played for Coach Strahm in '94, if you'd have ever told me Coach would ever let me throw the ball 37 times in one game, I'd have called you a liar!"

The Oilers returned home and ran their record to 5-0 when they pulled away from the stubborn St. Ambrose Fighting Bees and doubled them up, 48-24. Ahead just 27-24 at the end of the third quarter, Findlay got busy on the offensive end with three late touchdowns to salt the game away.

Chris Jaquillard had his finest day ever as an Oiler, rushing for 166 yards on 16 carries. Hurley was 10 of 18 for 170 yards and two more touchdowns, both to Jason Hamby, whose big day included eight catches and 154 receiving yards.

In week six, it was back on the bus, headed for Deerfield, Illinois, to take on Trinity International. The Oilers' defense produced a strong effort, and UF emerged from the contest with a 34-7 victory. Terrance Auster intercepted a pass for the third straight game.

Offensively, this time Bo Hurley made Darrell Ramsey the featured target instead of Hamby. Ramsey caught nine passes for 154 yards and a touchdown. Jamie Smiddy also caught a Hurley TD toss.

On the Saturday before Halloween, Findlay was home to Iowa Wesleyan College and blitzed the visitors, 62-7. Jaquillard again ran wild, rushing for 164 yards on 12 carries. Hurley hit 7 of 10 passes for 181 yards and three TDs. While Ramsey only caught two balls, both were for touchdowns, with the two totaling 129 yards. Bart Conley had two interceptions and Dan Periat (Toledo, Ohio) another.

While few could have imagined a more efficient offensive display than 62 points, the next Saturday in Chicago, Strahm's squad hung 70 on the scoreboard versus St. Xavier University while allowing only eight. Backup running back Bret Swaney (Celina, Ohio) took rushing honors with 104 of UF's 354 yards on the ground. Auster and Aukerman both picked off passes to pace a strong defensive performance.

For a third straight game, Findlay scored over 50 points in week nine when the Oilers overwhelmed Taylor University, 55-7. Two-back Jared Wojtas had 59 yards on an inordinately high number of carries (12) for a back primarily used as a blocker. Hurley continued his remarkable season, completing 15 of 23 for 218 yards and a personal best five touchdown passes. Both Ramsey and Hamby grabbed two.

Defensively, Bret Macy had an interception, one, of course, seen in person by his parents. This wasn't odd recalls Dick Strahm. "Bret's parents flew in for every one of his games both his junior and senior seasons. They were terrific supporters of their son and the Oilers football program."

In week ten, Findlay finished the regular season 10-0 for the second-straight year, beating Tri-State University from Angola, Indiana, 29-15. Jaquillard paced the running attack with 129 yards and Hurley completed 9 of 17 for 109 yards and a score. Macy was the defensive star as the senior co-captain picked off two more passes.

And, so it was on to the playoffs, and the first hurdle was again a rival of epic proportions. The Westminster Titans came to Findlay for the eighteenth game the schools had played since 1983. Findlay was in the midst of a multi-year run that had seen it win 38 of its last 43. In the last eight seasons, the two schools had almost identical records. While Westminster had gone 72-18-2, Findlay had gone 74-15-3.

Perhaps the thing that made Titan head coach Gene Nicholson apprehensive was his team had turned the ball over thirteen times in the final two regular season games.

Despite the fact that these two teams usually played close ball games, the first round of the 1997 NAIA playoffs was all Oilers, all the time. Strahm's team routed the Titans, 40-0, getting 266 yards of total offense from Hurley and three touchdowns from Chris Jaquillard.

Titan coach Gene Nicholson conceded after the game, "They [the Oilers] are just bigger, stronger, and a more mature team. They just overpowered us up front, both offensively and defensively and were more physical than we were at the point of attack."

Bart Conley was all over the field, just as he had been all season long. For the season, he was the Oilers' leading tackler, registering 80, with 14 of them resulting in losses, including three sacks.

Hurley set the offensive tone early when he took off on an option and ran 71 yards for a score to put the hometowners on the scoreboard.

Round two again had an opponent with a familiar ring. The Geneva Golden Tornadoes would be making their third visit to Donnell in the last two years. The last time was, of course, their 38-13 loss in the first round of the 1996 playoffs.

Despite losing twice to the Oilers the previous year and having four regulars out with injuries, Geneva head coach Gene DeMarco welcomed the chance to compete. However, he was also realistic about his team's chances, telling *The Courier* sports editor Larry Alter a few days before the contest, "We know that we will have to play very, very well to have any success against the class program of the entire NAIA. I just hope we can play better than we did the last two times we came to Findlay. Eight turnovers in those two games just isn't the quality of football you need against a team as good as Findlay."

DeMarco continued, "They're different from the Findlay teams of the last couple of years because of their ability to throw. Of the four game tapes we have, Hurley averaged 25 passes. By their throwing, you are really in a pickle. Jason Hamby is one of the best receivers in the NAIA and his ability just adds so much to their offensive package."

As far as the December 6 game, DeMarco proved to be somewhat of a prophet by bringing up the turnovers of his team's previous two losses in Findlay. In the third straight loss to UF, this time by a 28-7 score, the Hurricanes again proved far too generous, giving the Oilers four more turnovers on a snow-covered and wind-swept Donnell Stadium surface.

Findlay controlled the clock with a multi-pronged attack on the ground, featuring Hurley (84 yards), Jaquillard (74), Jamie Smiddy (35) and Jared Wojtas (26).

Defensively, Craig Aukerman and Billy Minter (Youngstown, Ohio) had interceptions, and Agunanda Brookins recovered a fumble, as did Roger Hamilton after a bad snap on a punt attempt.

Following the game, Geneva coach Gene DeMarco graciously commented to *The Courier's* Larry Alter, "We made a statement earlier that we felt this was one of the best small-college football teams we have ever seen. And the way they played today certainly demonstrated that. If anyone is going to beat them, they are going to have to be one great team. I really think this team will win the national championship."

After the game, Bo Hurley was the mouthpiece who articulated the thoughts of so many on the team, especially the seniors. "Last year was a pretty bad feeling losing to Western Washington. This is why I came back to play another year, the opportunity to play for a national title. I know we have to get by one more opponent, but we look at it as unfinished business. Our goal will be to win our next game and get to the championship game."

While the win was nice, the Oilers did suffer a major loss to injury. Hurley's favorite target, wide receiver Jason Hamby, broke his collarbone and would be lost for the remainder of the playoffs.

For Findlay, the next game would again be home, and the opponent would indeed be formidable. Doane College, from Nebraska, was 11-0, and the Tigers were just as intent as the 12-0 Oilers on reaching the NAIA national title game, a game which starting in 1996 would be held in Savannah, Tennessee, for three consecutive years.

For Doane, football tradition stretched back even farther than Findlay's. The Tigers had been playing football for 106 years. Tiger coach Fran Schwenk commented in the week prior to the game, "Eleven wins is a new mark for us, and now we have a new challenge and a new goal. These kids are on a mission."

Strahm had to prepare for a team which utilized speed and quickness in a West Coast style of attack, an attack similar to that of Western Washington the previous year.

On Saturday, December 13, with a trip to the national championship hanging in the balance, the stakes couldn't have been higher. And, the game certainly lived up to anyone's expectations that two teams with a combined record of 23-0 should play so very evenly all the way down to the final ticks of the game clock.

On that mid-December day, Strahm's Oilers trailed 17-9 at the half and again 25-18 with just 6:21 in the fourth before the Black and Orange rallied. With Craig Aukerman pulling double duty by coming in on trips packages (three wide receivers) to compensate for the loss of Jason Hamby, Bo Hurley turned it up a notch, working the package to perfection. He completed seven passes in a row. The final throw was the money toss, a five-yarder for a TD to Aukerman, streaking across the middle to bring the Oilers to 25-24 and 1:58 on the clock.

Then, things really got interesting. As the Oilers lined up to kick the point that would knot the score and potentially send the game to overtime, Doane was flagged for having too many players on the field and for lining up off sides. With the ball now resting a yard and a half away from the goal line, Strahm, the long-time Oilers coach known to be somewhat conservative, decided to roll the dice.

He called time out and gathered his offensive unit around him. Tom Hansen, the big outside strong-side tackle, remembers the moment vividly. "Listen, I don't want anyone to get the idea that Coach Strahm would let a player call such an important play. After all, if we don't score, we lose.

"But just to show you he was the kind of coach who wanted players to feel they were a big part of decisions that needed to be made, Coach looked at me and said, 'What do you think we should do?' I said, 'Run 46 Toss right off my butt, and we'll score. If we can't get a yard and a half, we don't deserve to go to the title game.'

"Coach Strahm looked at Bo and said, 'There's your play.'"

And, with that, the Oilers executed. Chris Jaquillard bulled into the end zone behind the unbalanced right side of the offensive line for the 26-25 Oilers lead.

Recalls Strahm about Hansen's recollection with a laugh, "Well, I did look around the huddle and asked the question, but I was really asking it rhetorically. I knew the play I wanted to run. And, when Tom gave me the same play I was about to call, I was even more sure it was the right call.

"Listen, I believed in my guys on that offensive line, and I believed in Chris Jaquillard. If we didn't get it in, I'd have been a dunce instead of a hero."

Doane got the ball down to the Oilers' 41-yard line on their final possession with 36 seconds and a third and two. On the snap, Craig Aukerman tackled Doane quarterback Matt Reiling for a two-yard loss.

Then, on a fourth-and-four, Reiling again dropped back, looking left. It was Aukerman again, coming on a full strong safety blitz, who drilled Reiling and forced the fumble that pulled the plug on the team from the Cornhusker State.

In addition to the brilliant two-way performance of Aukerman, Bo Hurley was somewhat of a comeback kid. After throwing two interceptions early, remarkably only his second and third of the entire season against 25 touchdown passes, he came off the mat to throw his third touchdown pass of the game to set up the most dramatic 54-inch run in Oilers football history.

For the 13-0 Findlay Oilers, it was on to Savannah, Tennessee, to take on the other semifinal winner, Willamette University, out of Salem, Oregon, in a game already dubbed "The Rumble on the River." given the fact that Savannah sits on the Tennessee River, about 60 miles east of Memphis.

Certainly, Jim Carroll Stadium would have a hometown feel for the Oilers, since 1,940 miles separated Salem, Oregon, and Savannah, Tennessee. Two people who decided to make the drive from Findlay were Julie Stall and her husband, Jamie.

Recalls Strahm's former physical therapist, "I remember we had to make an appearance at a Christmas party. We left early and drove until about eleven, stayed over-night in Kentucky, and then, on Saturday morning, drove in to Savannah. We got there about an hour before the game.

"After my work with Dick, I guess I just became a fan, so Jamie and I started going to the home games. When the team kept winning, I really wanted to see that final game to see if Dick could, kind of, put an exclamation point on his recovery."

For the Oilers, they would be traveling to the city dubbed The Catfish Capital of the World without the services of Jason Hamby, so there was little doubt Craig Aukerman would continue to see action on the offensive side of the football in addition to filling his customary slot at strong safety.

The Oilers' opponent making the long trip from Oregon, the Willamette Bearcats, were making their first visit to the title game. Coach Dan Hawkins, who has since moved up the coaching ladder and is currently the head coach at the University of Colorado, had inherited a 1-8 program just five years earlier. Willamette is the oldest university in the West and, like Findlay's semifinal opponent Doane, had been playing football for over one hundred years.

Certainly, Hawkins had to be able to recruit well to get to the title game. For one thing, his university offered no athletic scholarships and as far as spring practice, he told reporters, "Sure we have spring ball. It's called baseball." In addition to the absence of athletic scholarships and spring football, the entrance requirements were very stringent. All freshmen needed at least a 3.5 GPA in high school and a 1230 on the SAT.

Dick Strahm has a vivid recollection of how event officials really tried to make the atmosphere big time on the bus drive in. "I remember we got a state police escort all the way from Memphis to Savannah. That's 60 miles of lights flashing and sirens, which our players were thrilled by."

For the UF seniors, it would be their second trip to the title game. Certainly, for senior starting defensive end Chris Barbara, his circumstances had changed dramatically since arriving on the Findlay campus in 1993 as a freshman. He came as a quarterback. However, by his sophomore year after a red-shirt year in 1994, he had become an Oiler on defense.

By his final year in 1997, he had switched positions again to defensive end. The co-captain and the rest of his mates were set on bringing the prize back to Findlay.

Findlay, without Hamby, would be playing a team that also had to overcome a significant injury. Bearcat starting quarterback Chuck Pinkerton broke his leg in Willamette's semifinal win over Sioux Falls. Nonetheless, Coach Hawkins was quick to point out that backup Jay Douglass had taken a lot of snaps and was more than equipped to lead the team, especially from a mental standpoint.

Strahm's main concern heading into the game was defending the 13-0 number-two ranked Bearcats' gimmicky offense. Strahm told reporters prior to the game, "Coach Hawkins calls what his offense does the 'Fly Set.' All I know from looking at game tapes is this offense is enough to drive you nuts. It looks like 28 guys are in motion. They'll have a guard, the center, and one wide receiver on one side; everybody else is on the other side of the ball. Then, they'll line up four guys, and a slot comes across as fast as he can come. They'll snap the ball with perfect timing and hand the ball off to the slot, who is going about 100 miles an hour the other direction! And, of course, there are a bunch of variations off that."

So, it was clear that Oilers linebacker Bart Conley and the rest of the defense would certainly be tested. Since the Oilers had only allowed 82.5 yards per game rushing and just six rushing touchdowns in thirteen games, the defense was confident they would be equal to the task. While the defense had given up 16 touchdown passes, they also had 21 interceptions.

Historically, the game would mark the twenty-ninth time that two teams that had finished first and second in the final regular season rankings were to meet in the title game.

Saturday, December 20, arrived, and the weather was just perfect. The temperature was in the upper fifties, and sun drenched both the natural grass of Jim Carroll Stadium and the fans who sat on either side of it.

The game would be televised on the Fox Sports Ohio network with action called by play-by-play announcer Dave Woloshin and color commentator Johnny Majors, the former University of Tennessee All-American tailback and former head coach of the Pitt Panthers and the Tennessee Vols.

It took virtually all four quarters to determine the best team in the entire NAIA on that gorgeous afternoon. When it was settled, it was the Oilers who played an almost mistake-free game to take the crown, 14-7.

The defense, led especially by linebacker Bart Conley and defensive game MVP strong safety Craig Aukerman, contained the motion-oriented offense, breaking down only once in the second corner when it allowed scatback Tim Blair to spin out of Aukerman's hit in his own backfield and scamper 71 yards for a tying touchdown.

Bo Hurley got the Oilers on the board first with a perfect strike to a leaping Aukerman for a touchdown.

Just before halftime, it appeared the Oilers would go up a touchdown after linebacker Steve Adams recovered a Bearcat fumble deep in Willamette's territory at the 14-yard line. However, Chris Jaquillard was stopped short of the goal line on fourth and two, and the teams left the field tied.

Recalls Hurley, "I think the fact that we came up short inspired us offensively. We were determined to get it in the end zone in the third quarter."

And, that's exactly what happened. It was Hurley himself who took off on an option and, behind excellent blocking, turned up field and outraced the Bearcats for 60 yards and the eventual winning touchdown.

Offensive game MVP fullback Jamie Smiddy was an absolute battering ram as he rumbled for a career-best 126 yards. So many of Smiddy's runs were vital in Findlay's possessing the ball and moving the game clock.

The Oilers committed no turnovers to Willamette's three. A Steve Adams interception with less than ten ticks left sealed the victory. All it took was for Bo Hurley to kneel down, and the Oilers' celebration was officially on.

For Strahm, in his twenty-third year, the 14-0 national championship season was his sweetest moment. "What made that year so special is overcoming the stroke. I can't express how big a part of my success as head coach can be attributed to my assistants. That year, they had to do so much, especially with spring ball and recruiting while I was recovering. Any successful head coach, I'm sure, would agree. Really, you're only as good as those you surround yourself with.

"Certainly, the '97 season was special for a lot of reasons, perhaps none bigger than having my son Doug with me on the sidelines for one final great season. He'd gotten a very good offer to go into business not long after the season and would be leaving coaching."

Of all those who were on Strahm's staff, none had a more intimate connection with Oilers post-season football than Jim McIntosh. He not only had matched Strahm by being on the sidelines for all five national championship games but he also has been a part of every playoff game in school history. McIntosh was a senior linebacker for the Oilers in 1964 when By Morgan Sr. took his team to the school's very first playoff game, a game in which McIntosh and his teammates suffered a 32-21 loss to Sam Houston State, Texas.

The Oilers would not taste the playoffs again until Strahm's fourth year at the helm and McIntosh's second year as Strahm's assistant. That meant there were only two years out of Strahm's entire Oilers career that he couldn't have looked over and seen Coach Mac standing beside him.

Recalls McIntosh, "I'd decided even after I retired from education [twenty-four years as a math teacher and another six as an assistant principal] after the '94-'95 school year that I wasn't done coaching. I kind of decided as long as Coach came back, I would, too."

After the game, as Strahm walked across the field heading to, no doubt, a jubilant locker room, he was joined by Julie and Jamie Stall. Recalls Strahm, "How fitting it was that someone I owed so much to was there to walk with me across the field. It's something I don't think I'll ever forget."

When Strahm got to the locker room, a couple of his assistants were being interviewed and getting what amounted to some well-deserved recognition. Third-year coach Jon Wauford talked about the '95 co-national championship and how it compared to the prize that had just been won. "This means a lot more than the first one [in 1995]. The first win, I was just starting to get in the groove with the program. These kids, a lot of them, I've coached now for a couple of years. This one is all ours, and no one can have any of it."

Secondary coach Mike Schanski was quick to point out the contributions of just about everybody. "What a great job. The offense sucked it up when they had to and got a couple of TDs. Defensively, I can't say enough about the kids and the guys like [assistant coaches and student and graduate assistant coaches] Jon Wauford, Don Akers, Doug Strahm, Nate Weihrauch, and Howard Heston, who I worked with.

Curtis Davidson sought to identify what made this national championship so special. "This is my third national championship game, and they always seem to get better. This one is special because of the adversity that Coach went through. The kids wanted to win it for Coach Strahm. This one was special."

The twenty-five seniors would move on, but they have memories that will last a lifetime. The Oilers were 26-1 in the last two years and 42-6-2 in the last four.

Beyond the wins and losses, so many of the Oilers speak in reverential tones about their head coach. Craig Aukerman told the press about Coach Strahm, "His record speaks for itself. Just his overall record and the number of championships he's won just are mind-boggling. He's been through the best times and also the worst. We really feel in our hearts he was the best small-college coach in the country."

Bret Macy recalls Strahm's speech at the team meeting the night before the game. "I remember about two or three minutes into the speech Coach began to tear up. The entire team just leapt to their feet. Let me tell you something. When the man spoke, it was magic. He had such an incredible impact on my life. That's for sure."

Tom Hansen remembers Strahm today as "a helluva fighter." He thinks he knows why Strahm's teams expended such effort. "I think kids just played harder for Coach Strahm than other coaches because he gave them chances. Some of our guys had screwed up somewhere along the line, and Coach gave everyone a chance. I guess you might say players just didn't want to let him down."

After the game, Strahm told the press something about his elation over his fourth national championship in five tries. "I think I can define the word *utopia*. I don't know how I could feel any better than surviving a stroke and feeling great, being 14-0, being a grandfather for the first time last Sunday [Strahm's daughter Gina had given birth to a son, Hunter]. I just don't now how it could get any better than this."

After the national championship game, Dick and Ginger finally were able to think about Christmas, just three days away. After getting his gear unpacked, Dick Strahm decided a trip to the Findlay Mall was in order.

Recalls Strahm, "While shopping, I was so gratified to get so many handshakes and congratulations from people I believe are so very special.

"Then, a little gray-haired lady walked up to me and said, 'Aren't you Coach Strahm?' I thought I was about to receive another congratulations, so I said, 'Yes, ma'am, I sure am.'

"She then said she had my story on her refrigerator. She said, 'Coach, I pray for you every night.' You see, the story she'd put on the fridge was an article on my bouts with cancer and stroke, but said nothing about our national championship.

"That really hit me. She was praying for my health and recovery. I just thought that had to be the most important thing that had been said to me in months.

"I thanked her and hugged her. I don't mind saying when I walked away, there were tears coming down my cheeks. I continued walking down the mall, remembering the prayers from people at the College First Church of God and all the cards I'd received from friends and coaches from all over the country during my recoveries. And, I know these prayers helped pull me through.

"I realized just how fortunate I was to have survived heart attack, cancer, and stroke and to be surrounded by so much love.

"I remember thinking a man couldn't ask for more. I also knew why every morning when I got out of bed, I say, 'Thank you, God, for this day and for allowing me to be a part of it all.'"

As the post-season awards were dispensed over the first few weeks following The Rumble on the River, it was no surprise that the champs were well represented. Strahm was named the Rawlings-NAIA National Coach of the Year for the fourth time in his illustrious career.

As far as the players, not only did Bo Hurley again achieve Academic All-American honors but he also was named the Rawlings-NAIA National Player of the Year. When Hurley departed Findlay, he did so with much of his MBA work done and also nineteen school records. And, he also looks back with no regrets that his stops at Ohio State and University of Cincinnati didn't work out better. "People will sometimes ask me whether I wish I'd have gotten a chance at OSU or UC, and I tell them all the same thing. I tell them I have absolutely no regrets whatsoever. I couldn't have asked for more than what The University of Findlay or Dick Strahm gave me. And, I made so many close friends. Certainly, one of those was my roommate my last year, Craig Aukerman.

"While I hated to see Jason Hamby go down with that injury, what a great job Craig did in the Doane game and the Willamette game."

For Chris Jaquillard, the national championship was sweet redemption. He would go on to graduation in the spring of 1998, fulfilling the promise he made to UF president Ken Zirkle in the summer of 1994. The two would certainly share some private words on graduation day when Zirkle handed Jaquillard his diploma.

As far as NAIA All-Americans, in addition to Hurley's national recognition as player of the year, Tom Hansen was named at offensive tackle, Bart Conley at linebacker, Craig Aukerman at defensive back and Darrell Ramsey at tight end. In addition, Josh McDaniels and Terrance Auster were accorded honorable mention All-American honors at defensive tackle and defensive back, respectively. In a sad footnote, Ramsey would only live another ten years, dying August 19, 2007, of a heart attack suffered while he was playing basketball.

More than a few thought that Dick Strahm would retire. An appreciation dinner and roast was organized in February, and as a token of appreciation, Dick Strahm was presented a check for the total of donations solicited from community members. And just how much did his supporters appreciate the Coach was evident when a check was presented written in the amount of $35,000.

Despite some speculation as to whether Strahm would ride the incredible national championship wave into retirement, the coach fully intended to return for his twenty-fourth season.

Strahm threw himself, as always, headlong into recruiting. Certainly, with the senior-laden team of 1997, there were many holes to fill. Recalls Strahm, "That's one reason I didn't retire. I just didn't want to leave a bare cupboard. Not only were we going to be very young but we also were going to be facing a far more difficult schedule."

The reason for the increased degree of difficulty in scheduling had everything to do with a decision by Findlay's administration, led by President Ken Zirkle. The decision was for The University of Findlay to become an NCAA Division II school, which meant Findlay would be playing several schools that offered many more scholarships than the eight that Strahm had to offer.

While the Oilers would be eligible one more time for the NAIA post-season, getting the eight wins it would probably take against the likes of teams from Grand Valley State University, University of Indianapolis, and Hillsdale College with a green team would indeed be challenging.

Since his prostate cancer surgery in October 1995, Strahm had blood drawn every three months to make sure everything was OK, and, in late March, he drove to Toledo to see Dr. Emmert to take another PSA test.

The phone call that Strahm received from the doctor a couple days later was not encouraging. The PSA number had risen. More X-rays and tests soon followed and an appointment was scheduled to go over the results. When Dick went up to see Dr. Emmert at his office in Sylvania, just outside of Toledo, the doctor told him that he had cancer that had spread to his lymph nodes and along his back. Dr. Emmert said that his opinion was that there had been some cancerous cells left behind from his surgery three years earlier. Dr. Emmert felt the cancer had spread too far for radiation to be a treatment option.

Recalls Strahm, "You talk about going from the top of the mountain to the bottom of the valley in less than four months!

"I went to a second oncologist in Toledo, who wound up saying the same thing that Dr. Emmert had. The cancer had spread too far for radiation to be effective, and the best they could do was put me back on Casodex, a pill, and give me monthly Lupron injections to slow the rate of growth of the cancer.

With great concern, Strahm headed back to Findlay to coach spring ball. Strahm confided to good friends Ann and Larry Hersey that he again had cancer concerns, and it was Ann who gave Dick the name of an oncologist at The Cleveland Clinic. An appointment was made and more X-rays taken for a third opinion.

Recalls Strahm, "I remember they took something like 200 X-rays at the Cleveland Clinic. It would take some time to study every angle of what was happening inside Dick's body. Meanwhile, for the rest of April and most of May Strahm was researching on the Internet, studying as much he could about yet another opponent and thinking of ways to game plan against it.

When he returned to Cleveland for the follow up, the news was still anything but positive as Strahm recalls. "The doctor showed me the X-rays and exactly where the cancer was. It was indeed in the lymph nodes and down my back. Again I was told the tumors were too big and had spread too far for radiation to be effective. I left the Cleveland Clinic that day feeling I had been given a death sentence. I had seen three doctors, and all had said the same thing. With the Casodex and the Lupron injections, they all felt I was looking at around three or four more years to live.

Recalls Strahm, "In early June I drove up to see a dear friend of mine, Mike Cicak. Cicak, who still lives in Toledo and is a very successful entrepreneur who a hand in several businesses in Northwest Ohio, remembers the moment the door to his office swung open. "I knew immediately that something was very wrong. Dick is usually so positive, but he really looked depressed. Then he told me what was going on and what the three different doctors had said.

"You see, I had prostate cancer about a year earlier and made a very thorough study to decide which treatment option would be best. I went to Baltimore to Johns Hopkins. There was a Dr. Patrick Walsh, who has won several national physician-of-the-year awards, who had pioneered a nerve-sparing prostatectomy as a means to treat tumors.

"After I met with Dr. Walsh, it seemed to me to be the best treatment option, but he wanted me to see someone he called one of the top radiologists in the country to also hear about radiation as a treatment option. The man's name was Dr. Arthur Porter, and he practiced in Detroit.

"So I returned home and made the drive up to see Dr. Porter. I was very impressed with what he had to say and the radiation machine he showed me but still felt the nerve-sparing procedure was best for me. He thanked me and said if he could ever help me in the future to certainly contact him.

"I immediately picked up the phone and called Linda Filipczak, who was Dr. Porter's nurse and clinical manager. She told me that while Dr. Porter was not in the office that day, she could meet with Dick to initiate treatment."

After Cicak hung up the phone, he grabbed his keys and shepherded Strahm out the door to his car

In a matter of a couple hours, Dick Strahm was sitting across the table from Linda Filiczak and told her his story. She said she felt Dr. Porter could certainly help and made an appointment for Dick to see him in late June.

Meanwhile, Strahm had an appointment with a fourth oncologist in Toledo to read yet another set of X-rays the Findlay coach had had taken.

Recalls Strahm, "Again, I heard the same thing from this doctor. He told me he felt the cancer had spread too far. He was not optimistic in suggesting chemotherapy, and he felt the Casodex and the Lupron was the best way to go.

Recalls Strahm, "I asked whether three years was about how long he felt I had to live, and he said, 'That's a pretty good guess.'

"After I left, I was so depressed that I called Dr. Porter's office to cancel the appointment. I just didn't feel there was any reason to hope for a different outcome. I was intent on doing some research and contacting some of the largest cancer hospitals in the country. The secretary said that Linda was busy and couldn't come to the phone, so I just told her to cancel the appointment, which she did.

"The next day, I got a call from Linda, and she asked why I canceled. I told her what the fourth doctor had said, and she said that she had seen Dr. Porter perform miracles with his revolutionary radiation treatments. So, I re-made the appointment."

The following week Dick Strahm and his wife, Ginger, drove up the night before the appointment and checked into a motel near the Karmanos Cancer Institute, where Porter kept an office. The appointment was scheduled for 8:30 in the morning, and Strahm certainly wanted to be on time.

Recalls Strahm, "The next morning, I first met with Linda. She drew blood and sent me for more X-rays. When I was done with that, I rejoined Ginger in the waiting room for about an hour's wait while Dr. Porter went over the results of my blood work and my X-rays.

"Linda came out a little over an hour later and said that Dr. Porter would see me. We went into his office, and a short while later, the door opened and here came Dr. Porter with a smile on his face. Up to that point, none of the doctors I'd been seeing ever walked in smiling.

"He said to me, 'You're the coach, so I'm going to draw you a picture of what's going on in you. With that, he whipped out a pen and began drawing on the sheet of paper covering the examination table. He showed me right where the cancer was.

"I really had one question for the doctor who stood before me wearing a bow tie. I said to him, 'Can you get the cancer?' He looked at me and said, "I believe I can.' He then said, 'Coach, let's make a game plan. Right now, the tumors are too big to radiate, but we can get them smaller by taking the Casodex and the Lupron injections the other doctors advised.'

"He told me I was to take the pill each day and take the Lupron injections once a month into the summer and throughout most of the football season. The plan was to stop the Casodex and Lupron at the end of October. Then right after our last game I would start the radiation treatments.

"So, I now had a game plan and finally found a doctor who told me that there was not only hope but a likelihood he could rid me of this insidious disease."

And so, for Dick Strahm, it was settled. That was the treatment option he would select. Despite taking medicine to prepare for the daily doses of radiation he would undergo five days a week for several months, beginning in late November, Strahm was committed to coaching his twenty-fourth season.

When Strahm began taking the Lupron injections, it didn't take long for him to notice there were certainly side effects to the shots. "I think I got about ten to fifteen hot flashes during a typical day. My face would get very flushed, and it felt as if I was overheating. For some reason, Ginger had very little sympathy for me when I had the hot flashes."

In early August Strahm returned to the practice field to fill the considerable holes left by graduation and gear his team up for play against a very challenging schedule, loaded with Division II NCAA teams.

For writers who had known Strahm for years, like Dave Hackenberg, sports writer for the *Toledo Blade*, Strahm's resolve was remarkable. As Hackenberg said while having lunch with Strahm just days before UF's first pre-season practice, "Some 64-year-olds play with their grandkids, raise roses, and eat dinner at 4:00 p.m. Dick Strahm wins national championships."

As far as his coaching staff, everyone remained in place with the exception of Doug Strahm. He was replaced by another who had played for Dick Strahm at Findlay. Chris Garner would coach the defensive line. The graduate and student assistant coaches who changed yearly would be Rich Rausch, Dale Brindese, and Matt Lieliart.

Regarding the shift to NCAA Division II, Strahm scoffed at anyone who felt he was returning for another season just for the opportunity to compete on a new and tougher level of play.

He told Hackenberg, "Why would I want to leave the NAIA? Eight straight years in the playoffs. Three national championships since 1992. You kidding? But I realize the NCAA affiliation is best for The University of Findlay and the overall athletic program in the long run."

Strahm also lamented the league UF would be joining. "Of course, we're jumping into the toughest Division II league [Midwest Intercollegiate Football Conference] in the nation with just a handful of starters back, and we might get our butts kicked.

"I guess it might not make much sense to be coming back and go through this. My wife thinks it's proof the stroke did affect my brain. But, seriously, I'm not worried about how I go out if this turns out to be my final season. Whether we go 10-0 or 3-7, I'm just going to enjoy the season.

"Technically, I still have cancer and will undergo radiation after the season, but I can still call plays. I can still chew some ass when I have to. And, I love being on the sidelines, and I love those young men."

And, so it was on to NCAA Division II football with a team led by seniors such as wide receiver Jason Hamby, running back Jamie Smiddy, defensive end Roger Hamilton, and the man who'd better be in good enough shape to start at cornerback and also come in often as a wide receiver on offense, Craig Aukerman. While as a junior, Aukerman only came in sporadically as a receiver, much more would be asked of him in 1998, since NAIA All-American tight end Darrell Ramsey would miss the entire season with an arthritic knee.

For Strahm and his staff, one of the first orders of business was to decide on a starting quarterback. Both Hurley and his capable backup, Andy Booth, had graduated and moved on.

The player Strahm selected was Trevin Sears, a 6'1," 200-pounder out of Valley View High School in Farmersville, Ohio. As evident by his 45 touchdown passes in high school, Sears could certainly throw the ball. And, throwing to the likes of Hamby and Aukerman was a comforting thought.

In addition to Sears, the backfield would include Ken Keirns (Delphos Ohio); Eric Chinn (Detroit); Laflore Walker (Ft. Wayne, Indiana); Shane Falke (Elida, Ohio), the returning offensive MVP of the title game, Jamie Smiddy, whose running style seemed to match the name of his Ohio hometown, Defiance; and Robert Shelton, back after sitting out the 1997 season.

As far as the offensive line, coaches McIntosh and Davidson would again be faced with a massive rebuilding project, a project which grew larger when it became known that starting tackle Brian Musser decided not to return to Findlay for his final year.

Recalls McIntosh, "The only returning starter was strong-side guard John Latell. The rest of the puzzle, we needed to figure out."

The two coaches did indeed get it figured out in August. Massive 6'7," 380-pound John Haskin (Delphos, Ohio) won the job at inside tackle and 6'5," 270-pound Matt Plas (Vermillion, Ohio) took over at the outside tackle. The center would be 6'2," 260-pound Jason Granger (Celina, Ohio). Rich McCarty (Fremont, Ohio), at 6'1," 280 pounds, would fill the back-side guard slot, and 6'2," 240-pound Ryan Grooms (Toledo, Ohio) was slotted for tight end duty. Defensively, in addition to Roger Hamilton (Oak Harbor, Ohio) at end, returning starter Brett Jones (Monroeville, Ohio) and Brandon Chaney (Elida, Ohio) were set at the tackles. Also rotating in at the tackles would be Chris Karsznia (Erie, Pennsylvania). The nose guard out of Cincinnati would be Bret Hebenstreit. Size was a concern as only Jones was at least 250 pounds, and he was right at that.

The Oiler would be Jon Gillman, out of Germantown, Ohio, and the linebackers would be Terry Joliff (Kenton, Ohio) and freshman Jesse Howard (Springfield, Ohio).

Except for Aukerman, the secondary also would be green. Eric Fegley (Elmore, Ohio) would play free safety. Aukerman's cornerback partner would be Andy Waddle, another freshman out of Springfield, Ohio.

When Shane Kittendorf elected not to return to Findlay, the punting job fell to Chris Merrick, who'd kicked for the University of Toledo Rockets the previous season. Bret Bahn (Arlington, Ohio) returned to handle the place-kicking chores.

In assessing the schedule, Strahm felt at least four or five opponents would have been comparable to an NAIA playoff team of previous years.

The Oilers opened the season carrying a regular season 27-game winning streak into their September 12 home opener versus the Wayne State University Tartars out of Detroit. And on the inaugural Saturday, the Oilers made it 28 in a row with a 39-13 win.

Jason Hamby had a big first game with eight catches for 127 yards, and Trevin Sears' first TD pass of his career. Sears completed 9 of 15 for 140 yards in a very respectable opener.

Jamie Smiddy led the rushing attack with 96 yards on 17 carries while Keirns, Chinn, and Walker produced another 125 combined yards on 28 additional carries.

Defensively, Aukerman had a key interception, returning it 75 yards before being knocked out of bounds at the three.

Strahm thought the Oilers had shown more enthusiasm than he'd seen during the preseason.

The Oilers remained home in week two and ran their record to 2-0 and 29 in a row with a 24-7 win over Ferris State University out of Big Rapids, Michigan. Jamie Smiddy again paced the ground game with 132 yards in 22 carries and two touchdowns. Among Trevin Sears' four completions in eight attempts was one to a freshman out of Ottawa, Ohio, Mark Inkrott, a player who would one day be good enough to play in NFL Europe.

In week three, the Oilers had their first big challenge. Not only was the game on the road but it was against a perennial NCAA Division II power, Grand Valley State, a playoff team the previous year after finishing a 9-1 regular season.

Certainly, the Lakers out of Allendale, Michigan, had a quarterback who would test the Oilers. Jeff Fox had thrown for 2,422 yards and 18 TDs in 1997.

Strahm remembers well the sickening feeling he got when he first saw the Lakers up close. "I was standing just outside our locker room and saw them in the tunnel. They were huge. A lot of the players were jumping up and down and pointing at our locker room door, motioning my guys to come out.

"I'm glad I was the only one out there looking at them. Otherwise, I'm not sure I'd have gotten any of my guys out of the locker room."

As it turned out, Strahm's sinking feeling was well founded. The Oilers' 29-game streak came to an abrupt halt as the Eagles routed the Orange and Black, 50-7.

For Dick Strahm, it was the worst loss since his very first Oilers game way back in 1975, a 56-8 loss to Indiana Central.

Recalls Strahm, "The thing I remember about both those games is we were just physically overwhelmed. Grand Valley was bigger, faster, and stronger. Additionally, it was one of those games where Murphy's Law ruled; what could go wrong, did. We fumbled, we threw interceptions, and we even had a punter go down on one knee to field a low snap on our own five yard line. Boom! First and goal, Grand Valley!"

The next Saturday, the Oilers played more competitively at Key Stadium against the Greyhounds of the University of Indianapolis. The Greyhounds were yet another team that qualified for the playoffs in 1997, and they proved too much for the Oilers, as they dropped them 33-12.

Recalls Strahm, "We just didn't have the horses that Indy had." The lone bright spot may have been the growing improvement of Trevin Sears, who ran for 107 yards and threw for 121 more, including two touchdowns, both to Jason Hamby.

Back home in week five, UF climbed back over the .500 mark with a convincing 34-7 win over Northern Michigan University out of Marquette.

Then it was on the road to take on the Chargers of Hillsdale College in Hillsdale, Michigan, at Frank "Muddy" Waters Stadium. The Oilers lost a tough one, 17-14. Even after all these years, Dick Strahm still remembers the lost opportunity. "We took the opening kickoff all the way down the field to the four-yard line and wound up not scoring. When you wind up losing by three points, you tend to remember those lost opportunities.

"By this point in the season, I had Craig Aukerman playing a lot of wide receiver in addition to corner on defense. By the end of that Hillsdale game, he was running on fumes. We didn't even have him go back to the huddle on offense."

Aukerman remembers how stamina became more and more of an issue his senior year. "That Hillsdale game, I started cramping up. I was in on over one hundred plays, counting offense, defense, and special teams, so Coach just had me take a knee instead of going into the offensive huddle.

"It was actually pretty funny. I remember Trevin would break the huddle and just yell over to me, "Run a post!' There wasn't a whole lot of deception, I guess.

"My junior year, I maybe was only averaging ten or fifteen plays on offense, but in 1998, I was out there a whole lot more, but I never minded.

"It was what Coach Strahm felt gave us our best chance to win, and, as about every guy who ever played for him would tell you, I'd have done anything for Coach Strahm. If he could battle all the health issues he had to confront, I could play both ways. It was the same as if my dad asked me to do something. That's the kind of impact Coach Strahm had on me."

The next week Gene Nicholson brought his Westminster Titans to Donnell for the last time in Dick Strahm's career. And, how sweet it must be for Strahm that, after years of struggling against Westminster, he closed with a flourish, going 6-1-1 over the final eight games against Westminster.

The 1998 game went to the Oilers, 42-28, as Trevin Sears had his finest game of the season, throwing for 261 yards and four touchdowns. While the freshman receiver Inkrott was beginning to assert himself, catching six balls, one for a touchdown, it was the senior Aukerman who continued to amaze Oilers fans by catching five for 76 yards and a touchdown in addition to playing full time on defense.

On Halloween Saturday, the Oilers played host to Northwood University out of Midland, Michigan, and what transpired could only be described as a good old-fashioned shootout. Strahm remembers the game as being one that would belong to whoever had the ball last. "Unfortunately, Northwood did, and UF lost, 49-42.Smiddy rushed for 110 yards on 17 carries, and Sears completed 12 tosses for 126 yards and a touchdown. Craig Aukerman chipped in an interception.

In week nine, Findlay rebounded by beating Mercyhurst College in Erie, Pennsylvania, at Tullio Field. The final was a third consecutive high-scoring affair, with this one going to Strahm's troops, 41-35. Smiddy ran for a solid 130 yards, and Sears threw three touchdown passes, all to the emerging freshman pass-catching star, Mark Inkrott.

While he didn't know it at the time, on the second Saturday in November of 1998, Dick Strahm coached what was to be his final game of football ever. The game was against a strong Ashland University Eagles squad, yet another Division II NCAA playoff team of the year before. In the game at Donnell, Ashland defeated a spirited but overmatched Oilers squad, 43-28.

UF quarterback Sears threw the football a very un-Strahm-like 42 times (23 completions) for 328 yards and three touchdowns, but it wasn't enough. Craig Aukerman picked off the final pass in what can only be described as a brilliant Oilers career as well. Following the season Aukerman would be named an All-American for the second straight year.

For Dick Strahm's first season in a brand new league and playing in Division II of the NCAA, a 5-5 record must be put into perspective. It was a season where a couple breaks could have turned 5-5 into 7-3. Recalls Strahm, "Really, the only game in which we just couldn't compete was the Grand Valley State game. Two of our losses were by a total of ten points."

For Dick Strahm, it was enough football for the time being. He put aside his thoughts as to whether he should return to coach the Oilers in 1999 for another time, and on Monday, just 48 hours after the final game, made the trip to the Barbara Ann Karmonos Cancer Institute in Detroit. The 222-mile round trip that separated Strahm's Findlay home and the institute certainly made for a long day, and in the ten-week period and 39 total radiation treatments, so many would step up to take the wheel for Dick Strahm.

Of course, there was family, but there were also people like Ann Hersey, Dale Gillespie, Jim Dysinger, and Larry Alter. And, needless to say, they are all people who remain in Dick Strahm's heart and memory.

Recalls Strahm about the treatments, "The machine that Dr. Porter used resembled a saddle, and the treatments themselves were about as cutting edge as existed at that time. Certainly, the treatments were tiring, but I was determined to do anything to get rid of the cancer."

As far as a typical day at the Karmonos Center, Strahm remembers well the protocol. "First, I would go into this little locker room, take off my clothes, and put on a blue gown you see all the time in the hospital.

"Once I was done, I went out into the waiting room, which I used to call The Blue Gown Ward because that's where all of us who were undergoing treatment would wait.

"All of us had a number assigned when we checked in, and on the bottom of the TV monitor that's where our numbers would come up when it was time for the treatment. Sometimes the wait would be well over an hour, depending on what day it was. Dr. Porter wanted me to take five doses of radiation a week on most weeks.

"When my number came up, I'd proceed down the hall and into the room where the machine was.

"During my treatment cycle, I had the opportunity to meet a lot of people. There were people who had throat cancer, lung cancer, brain cancer, and stomach cancer.

"Probably, many of them today are no longer with us. Some were in far worse condition than I was. I recall two doctors from Los Angeles, California, also were in the Blue Gown Ward

"I remember one man with both brain and lung cancer. He was going through both chemotherapy and radiation. One morning while we were in the Blue Gown Ward waiting for our number to be called, he said to me, 'The biggest concern I have about this damn cancer is my daughter is getting married this summer. I so much want to walk her down the aisle. I'm going to give it my best shot.' I don't know if he made it or not, but his attitude was the best.

"I remember another man with throat cancer. He had a habit of sitting by his locker complaining and then taking the complaining out into the waiting room. I knew he was hurting, but I also knew there were so many others sitting and waiting who were in far worse shape than he. I talked to Dr. Porter about him, and he said the man was going to be OK, although he was going to suffer some because he had been a three-pack-a-day smoker for many, many years.

"Then, it really began to bother me that he was complaining so much, while others with far more serious types of cancer weren't complaining half as much or not at all.

"The next day, I walked up to him in the locker room and said, 'Can I say something to you, Bob?' He said, 'What's the problem?'

"I said, 'You are complaining so much in front of the people out in that other room, many of whom aren't going to make it. You and I *are* going to make it. We need to be positive with our friends in the Blue Gown Ward.'

"He looked down, mumbled an apology, and then from that moment on, I saw quite a change. He told me a few days later that he'd told his family what I said, and they agreed with me that he needed to cut out all that negativity, for his sake as well as others."

After ten weeks of radiation, Dick Strahm's PSA numbers started to return to normal. Strahm knew who was responsible. "Thank God, for Dr. Porter and Linda Filipczak and also for Mike Cicak. Without Mike's hooking me up with Dr. Porter and Linda Filipczak, well, I just don't think I'd be alive.

"Now, I continue to get my PSA checked at the Blanchard Valley Regional Health Center in Findlay. My oncologist is Dr. Stephen Lutz, a terrific doctor and an even better human being.

"I guess the longer we live, the more we know there is a heaven and a God, and it is He who has sent people into my life when I needed them the most.

"In all my struggles with health issues, I've tried to live the same message I've preached to thousands of players who played for me, and that is that life is ten percent what happens to us and ninety percent how we react to it."

By early February, Strahm had completed his thirty-ninth and final radiation treatment. Despite the time-consuming nature of the treatment, Strahm continued to coordinate his assistant coaches' recruiting assignments and even met with recruits and their parents after he returned 222 miles later from the Karmonos Center. Recalls Strahm, "Whether or not I was going to return, I wanted to prepare as I always had."

When April rolled around, it was still Dick Strahm who stood out on the practice field and put his team through its paces during spring ball.

Then, in early May, Dick Strahm again suffered a setback. This time it was heart pain first and then yet another heart attack. It was back to Cleveland Clinic to have a procedure whereby three stents were inserted to reopen the circumflex artery, which was a vein taken out of Strahm's leg during his open-heart surgery of 1987. There would be more trouble keeping the circumflex artery open and two more heart attacks, first in 2000 and again in 2004. It was the doctors' opinion that the artery simply was not stable enough and had such little elasticity that it would not stay open. It is a condition that Strahm will always have, a condition that may one day trigger a fatal attack but not a condition that will prevent Dick Strahm from rising each morning, thanking the Almighty for what another day may bring with its endless possibilities.

Strahm returned from this latest serious medical issue, and as May came to a close, he was still the head coach. But, it was evident that the radiation treatments, followed so closely by yet another heart surgery, had left him very tired, and his family sensed it.

Recalls Strahm's wife, Ginger, "I really felt Dick had gone about as far as anyone could go. I sat down with him, and we had a long talk. The kids were there, too. We just felt his energy level just wasn't where it had always been.

"The radiation treatments especially really took a lot out of Dick. He couldn't really run or even walk very well after the stroke and then came the radiation and then another heart surgery. However, although the kids and I all felt it was time to step down, the decision had to be Dick's."

Strahm remembers his initial resistance and eventual resignation to the idea that he had indeed gone about as far as he could go. "I still loved football and those sidelines as much as I ever did. But, I just knew my energy level and stamina were not what they needed to be to allow me to continue. So, since I wasn't interested in shortchanging the very program I'd spent almost a quarter century building, I decided to step down."

On June 2, 1999, the 65-year-old Strahm announced his decision to retire as Findlay's head football coach during a news conference filled with reporters, family and friends. The front-page headline of *The Courier* the next day declared, "A Master at Winning: Dick Strahm Bows Out as Oilers' Head Coach." For The University of Findlay, an era had ended.

And, so it was. Strahm's decision was irrevocable. He would accept a position as special assistant to the president and now continues to use his speaking ability, salesmanship, and unlimited supply of charisma working in development for The University of Findlay.

Dr. Jim Houdeshell, the man who originally hired Strahm as Findlay's head football coach, had a chance to observe first-hand the special qualities that made Dick so successful as a coach. According to Houdeshell, traits that set Strahm apart from others were his work ethic, his uncanny ability to relate well with people, and his expectation that his players produce results. "He took the time to visit with players one-on-one," Houdeshell commented. "And, if a player had a bad practice, Dick had the ability to make him feel good and the next day come back stronger than ever."

Dr. Kenneth Zirkle, who during his presidency at The University of Findlay was perhaps the Oilers' number one fan, had the opportunity to witness Strahm's ability over the last 15 years of his coaching career and through three of his championship seasons. Zirkle pointed out several qualities that he thought made Strahm an exceptional coach. "Number one, basic honesty. Dick always exhibited honesty, no matter what the situation. He was always upfront no matter when, no matter what. He was the same with his assistant coaches and the players.

"He treated all players equally. During that era many coaches had a difficult time unifying their teams. He treated everyone equally and wouldn't tolerate behavior based on race. He was consistent and so were his assistant coaches. He was looking for excellence, and it didn't matter what color. And it happened because of Dick.

"Number three. He expected players to give their all. He handled pressure well and helped his players handle it well. One time he gave his players a day off in the middle of the week, telling them that he thought they already knew their plays. He would give those extra incentives that boosted self-confidence.

"He was flexible. For him, classes came first. A lot of people don't know that he pushed that. Some players would need to leave practices early in order to attend classes. Also, he always stressed that players represented all of The University of Findlay wherever they were and whatever the situation."

Dick's brother, Dale, perhaps said it as well as anyone could as he sought to get to the heart of what has made the Dick Strahm story so special. "Here's why I am so proud of my brother. A lot of guys in the coaching profession never really find their niche. They're always seeking the next job, looking for a bigger program, more money, and while this is happening, they don't pay enough attention to the job they currently have.

"Well, what Dick did was he fell in love with Findlay and the university and the people, and while he had an occasional flirtation with a couple of schools over the years, the fact of the matter is, he stayed.

"And, in doing so, he made a difference in so many people's lives in that one small town that both he and the people he touched were enriched beyond measure. I think my brother is perhaps the rarest of breeds in all of college coaching, and that's someone who lived in the moment and gloried in that moment, and, more importantly, stayed put long enough to enjoy the next moment."

Not only did he enjoy the moments, he was one of the most accomplished coaches in small-college football, accumulating a remarkable 183-64-5 record and garnering accolades all along the way – capped with a national championship ring with four diamonds in it.

He cherishes a lifetime of memories on the playing fields of Toledo Libbey, Lakota, Bryan and Warren Western Reserve high schools and on to the University of Toledo, Kansas State University and Findlay College, later to become The University of Findlay. Although he has embarked on the next journey of his life without the sidelines that he loved to walk, he left behind a veritable treasure chest of achievements as well as the deep and abiding warm wishes of the legions of those whose lives he touched.

Strahm's 24-Year Career at The University of Findlay

Four NAIA national football championships – 1979, 1992, 1995 and 1997
National NAIA runner-up in 1978
Four-time NAIA Coach of the Year
Twelve-time NAIA District 22 Coach of the Year
NAIA semifinals – 7 appearances
NAIA playoffs – 12 appearances
NAIA playoff record – 19-7-1
22 winning seasons

Hoosier-Buckeye Collegiate Conference record – 79-29-2,
with 9 conference titles in 15 seasons
27-game regular season winning streak, 1995-97
Mid-States Football Association record – 20-2, with four titles – 1994-97
Coached 38 NAIA All-Americans, 16 NAIA Scholar-Athletes
First NAIA Player of the Year – Bo Hurley, 1997
Collegiate record – 183-64-5
High school coaching record in ten years – 70-19-1
Overall record – 253-83-6

Hall of Fame Inductions

National Football Foundation and College Hall of Fame,
    South Bend, Indiana, 2004
Toledo City League Hall of Fame – 2000
NAIA Hall of Fame, Nashville, Tennesee – 1999
National Football Foundation, Toledo Chapter Hall of Fame – 1998
The University of Findlay Athletic Hall of Fame – 1995
Toledo Libbey High School Hall of Fame – 1995
Hancock Sports Hall of Fame – 1988

Gathered for the Dick Strahm Roast held at the Findlay Country Club in February 1999 were: Jim Ryan, Nick Hillman, Pat Gibson, Kevin Cassidy, Gene Fernandez, Dick Strahm, and Denny Guerra. When they were done Strahm was totally roasted!

Chapter 17

In Strahm's Words

I would like to begin this final chapter by quoting Andrew Carnegie (1835-1919), who was the founder of Carnegie Steel, the company which later became U.S. Steel. He recognized that one's success in life really is largely dictated by those with whom he surrounds himself. As a matter of fact, he wanted the following to be his epitaph: "Here lies a man who was able to hire people much wiser than himself."

I believe that could be my epitaph too, because the success that I had as a head football coach for thirty-four years, both in high school and at The University of Findlay, was so dependent on the players and assistant coaches who surrounded me.

That's the key point I wanted to make in my acceptance speech during my induction into the Rawlings/NAIA Hall of Fame in 1999.

I told the assembled crowd that evening in Nashville, which included so many of the NAIA coaches who voted for me, that while their intention was to honor me, the recognition that was given to me had a much broader application.

The honor also recognized all the young men who ever played for me, especially my four-year people. They can all smile knowing they played such pivotal roles in the successes I've been blessed to have had, especially in Findlay.

There were times during my battles to overcome some pretty serious health issues that my assistants had to step up and take on added duties to keep the program on course.

Speaking of assistant coaches, I have been asked over the years at football clinics and other programs, "Coach, you've had so many great assistant coaches. What makes a good assistant coach?"

As a head coach, I always believed it was my responsibility to make sure my assistants knew what they were doing. I felt they had to be well prepared before they ever walked out on the practice field.

So, before the pre-season practices, I would conduct coaching meetings, and would call on each assistant coach to stand in front of the staff and explain what his coaching duties were.

Coach's loyal friends gather at his retirement announcement: (front, from left) Jim Houdeshell, Dean Pees, Pat Rooney, Rev. Darrell Prichard; (back of Pat Rooney) Cliff Hite.

For example, I'd have the defensive end coach explain what the responsibilities of his defensive ends were in our basic 52-angle defense. I wanted that coach to demonstrate knowledge as to what his defensive end does:

1. If the ball comes to him;
2. If the ball goes away;
3. If the sprint-out pass comes to him;
4. If the sprint-out pass goes away from him;
5. If the tight end blocks down;
6. If the tight end releases
7. If the tight end blocks him one-on-one;
8. How he plays the trap;
9. How he plays the kick-out block.

I felt this was vital because I wanted each of my assistants to demonstrate the kind of knowledge he would be expected to cover when he conducted his own meetings for his position players.

Another important issue for me had to do with the drills my assistants used. I insisted all were shown to me on the board prior to their being used. I also wanted my assistants to be clear in their explanation to me how the drill would help our players execute their positions more effectively. I just felt practice time was so valuable that I wanted to leave nothing to chance.

Now, when it came to our practices, I always made it clear to my assistants that regardless of whether we were doing half-line, seven-on-eleven, or skeleton work, if a player didn't execute his assignment correctly, I expected the position coach to correct the player immediately.

If it happened again, I expected my coach to get in his face. Now, understand, I never allowed any of my coaches to grab a facemask or make any type of physical contact with a player. Those techniques were always outlawed on my practice field. But I did expect some very sharp criticism. I would strongly suggest that the assistant coach get this young man's attention.

However, after practice, I always wanted to see the assistant coach find the player he criticized on the field and either walk off the field with him or meet him in the locker room and have a positive talk with him. Most of my coaches did an outstanding job.

I didn't ever want a player leaving the locker room and going back to his dorm with a sour taste in his mouth about the assistant coach, me, our program, or our school. That way, you wouldn't lose him, something you never want to do. Every player on your team, from your All-American all the way down to the last guy on your bench has the potential to make you a stronger football team.

You coach to *not* lose players. You coach to keep each player involved and make not just the team better, but the player better, too. Over the years, I've seen so many instances where football really was the swing vote that decided which way a young man might go. While I don't know for certain what would have happened to Chris Jaquillard after sitting in a prison in Stryker, Ohio, feeling as low as he had in his whole life, I do know what I saw after Dr. Zirkle allowed him to enroll at The University of Findlay. I do know what he became playing football for the Oilers; and I do know what kind of successful man he has become today.

As far as my assistant coaches, the two best at getting in a player's face at practice and later building that player back up before he left the locker room were Curtis Davidson and Jim McIntosh. They were both with me many, many years (McIntosh, 22 seasons and Davidson, 14), and I saw so often that ability to be equal parts good cop and bad cop.

As long as I saw my assistants were able to do this, there was no need for me to step in. As a coach or really any kind of boss, if all you can ever do is motivate by instilling fear, people will not respect you, and they learn to turn you off. Then, neither you nor the players are really accomplishing anything.

As far as practices themselves, there was something else I felt was very important as far as a head coach and an assistant's relationship.

Now, let's say I've got a young assistant running a drill, and perhaps he's changed it a bit since he told me of its use, and he's running it differently than I would prefer. Well, I'll let him go ahead and run it his way and not step in. But, after practice, I'll talk to him and redirect him by telling him how I want it run in the future.

As a head coach, I never wanted to do anything to undermine the authority of my assistant coaches because I knew how important they were to a team's success. I never wanted to either lose them by making them resentful of me or having my players lose respect for them.

I know back when I was an assistant in Toledo under Jack Murphy, I always remembered how much I appreciated Coach Murphy coming flying down that hill at practice to confront a young defensive lineman who was challenging my authority. By doing so, he sent a message loud and clear to both me and the players.

To the players, the message was, "You will *not* disrespect my coaches!" To me, the message was, "I trust you completely, I respect your coaching ability, and I have your back at all times." It was a good lesson that I was able to use more than once at Findlay.

I was a classroom teacher for many years, and it would be the same thing if I were teaching a social studies lesson and the principal walked in and tried to tell me in front of all the students not to teach the lesson my way but, rather, his way. Be honest. If someone did that to you, you'd resent that person from that point forward.

But, if he waited until after school and called you into his office and explained how he'd like you to teach the lesson in the future so that it could be more effective, you'd probably be a lot more receptive to what the man had to say.

Really, I think there are six qualities that make a good assistant coach. There are probably more, but I see six as critical.

1. **He has to be a hard worker** and, if he's married, he has to have an understanding wife. Thankfully, my wife, Ginger, was all of that and more. To be a good assistant coach, hours spent on football cannot matter. I think a lot of people get out of coaching today because of the hours one must put forth in order to have a successful program. Coaches are going to work Saturdays and Sundays. In college, it would not be unusual to be riding on a bus returning to campus after a game and getting home at midnight or 2:00 or 3:00 a.m. on Sunday morning and working all the next day. An assistant coach must be a very dedicated person who wants to be successful.

2. **A good assistant must be loyal**. As a head coach, I never wanted to hire an assistant who'd had any problems with loyalty issues in his past. Good assistants must be loyal to their head coach, loyal to the institution, loyal to the young men they are coaching, and loyal to the community. I personally do not care to have a coach on my staff who is always whining or complaining about something. He needs to be a total team player with no personal agenda.

3. **Hire an assistant who is willing to learn** and is receptive to new ideas. I never wanted a yes man in my staff meetings. There is nothing wrong with a new coach sitting in a staff meeting and saying he doesn't quite understand something. He is willing to go to clinics, read books, study films, observe other school's spring practices. Learning is a continuous thing.

4. **He must be a good person.** What I mean by a good person is a good family man, reliable, great attitude, loyal, and honorable. When I hire a coach, I expect them to be good members of the community, and to interact with the faculty in a positive way.

5. **He must earn the respect of the players he is coaching**. As an assistant coach, it is not required that all his players like him. But it is imperative that they respect him. They will respect him if he's a good person. They will respect him if he knows football. They will respect him if they learn from him, which leads to number six…

6. **He must be a good teacher**. A lot of coaches can get on the chalkboard and talk X's and O's, but the sign of a good assistant coach is the one who can take his players and teach them how to be better football players. We tell our players we want them to get a little bit better each day. So, it is up to these position coaches to make sure that happens. Not too long ago, one of my former assistants, Dean Pees, now the defensive coordinator of the New England Patriots, told me that he felt every coach, whether high school, college, or pro, would benefit by having been a high school teacher, so they know how to teach. Some of the best assistants I had were also outstanding classroom teachers where they had the ability to make a difference in someone's life.

When you put all six of these qualities together, you are going to find yourself a good assistant coach.

Since I was fortunate enough to win a lot in my coaching career, both in high school and college, people have asked me over the years what makes the difference between winning and losing. **I can identify six key factors why I think my teams won as much as they did.**

1. **Superior personnel**, and I can't stress this enough. Coach Woody Hayes said it best in his book, *You Win with People*. I read that book from front to back many times. I believe that's exactly what happened at The University of Findlay; we won with good people. Recruiting is the name of the game, and my assistants at Findlay knew how to recruit winners. That's a big reason why we won thirteen league championships, 19 of 27 playoff games, and four national championships. We won with superior personnel.

Even at the high school level, the importance of recruiting can't be understated. Of course, I don't mean trying to get players from other schools to come play for you. What I do mean is recruiting your own school. When I was at Lakota and starting a brand new football program, I recruited from door to door and, sometimes from bean field to bean field! Certainly, I also worked the halls in Bryan and Warren as well. I was always looking for someone who could help us.

The type of player I went after had to have three characteristics. I wanted a player who was a good student, someone who had a strong desire to succeed not only on the field but in the classroom. I also wanted a player who was a good person. I talked to a recruit's parents, other coaches who had that young man, his teachers, his principal, really anyone who could give me more insight into the recruit. Of course, the third ingredient I always wanted was athleticism. Since football has so many positions to fill and injuries are so prevalent, I wanted players who were good enough to play more than one place. Some truly outstanding Oilers who played for me, players like Chris Barbara, Bob Sutyak, Cal Dietz, and Tom Hansen, wound up in positions they'd never have dreamed of playing when they came into the program. Having two out of three qualities will not work. A recruit must have all three – that's the young man we want.

2. **Superior conditioning** is the key that separates winning and losing. I guess the old expression, "The harder you work, the harder it is to surrender," is true. I was the conditioning coach, and I sold every team I ever coached on the idea that we would out-condition any opponent we faced. We ran hard during and after every practice; we never walked between drills. Even my coaches and I didn't walk to the next drill.

We wanted the fourth quarter to be ours. That's why when we were done with practices, just about the time we thought we'd run enough perfect 40s, I'd yell, "Fourth quarter!" and we'd run some more. We believed we were going to out-condition our opponents.

Whether we did or not, that didn't make any difference. It was what we put in their minds. It is what they believed. The other teams may have been doing the same thing we were doing, but our players were going to believe they were in better shape. They were going to believe that they were in better shape because we ran harder and longer. Whether we did or not, who knows? But when it came to the fourth quarter in our games, our teams yelled, "Fourth quarter!" because they knew that was the quarter we had been working hard for all week. If we were behind, we believed we could win it in the fourth quarter. Why? Because we worked on it during practice. Through superior conditioning, we worked to be mentally and physically tougher than our opponents in the fourth quarter. Conditioning is really one of the building blocks to positive attitude.

3. **Limiting mistakes** can make the difference between winning and losing. The team that makes the fewest mistakes has the greatest chance of winning. I felt it was essential to get on the blackboard and prove to our players why limiting mistakes was so important by explaining the consequences of turnovers, fumbles lost, interceptions, penalties, and kicking games.

You need to explain this in a way that gets their attention. I think we sometimes assume they know these things. Assume nothing. I know I did this both in high school and college. Take nothing for granted. For example, make sure they understand what the turnover ratio means and why field position is so critical.

I remember one time I was speaking to the team about field position. They looked rather uninterested; so I got on the boards, got excited, and explained the importance of field position. All of a sudden I had everyone's attention.

I recall we made a three-year comparison of our turnovers versus our opponents'. The results showed that our opponents' turnovers doubled over the past three seasons. They made twice as many mistakes. Our winning percentage is vastly going to improve when we win the battle of mistakes. We do a lot of board work on this during two-a-days, so they understand what we are talking about.

That may sound a little elementary, but I believe in two words: *simplicity* and *execution*. I based my total program around those two words.

4. **Superior mental attitude** is critical to winning. I think a team must believe they can win. That's why the last thing I said to my teams at our Friday night meetings was, "Gentlemen, I want each and every one of you to remember one thing: You are going to win tomorrow. Come hell or high water, you are going to get up off the ground and win the fight."

I remember my first year at Findlay when we lost three games by 2, 3, and 3 points. I thought those young men were satisfied because they were playing them close. If the games were tied or they were behind in the fourth quarter, they didn't believe they were going to win, although they wanted to win. We had not started our "the fourth quarter is our quarter" routine yet. There is a big difference in wanting to win and knowing that you're going to win somehow, some way. Everything we did in practice, every drill, every catch, every interception, we got excited about. It's all about winning. Remember, if you believe you're going to win, you're probably correct.

And believe me, we pushed that fourth-quarter run at the end of practice. It was hard, very hard. They mentally must believe that they can win if the game is close in the fourth quarter. Mental preparation is just as important as physical preparation.

5. **Superior teaching** by a coaching staff comprised of men who excel in preparing young players is essential. In my 34 years as a head coach, I was fortunate to have many coaches who were as superior classroom teachers as they were outstanding football teachers. They just loved to teach, and they got excited about the opportunity to teach players how to improve each day. Coaches should be well prepared before they go on the practice field. I expected that there wouldn't be much talking on the practice field. My coaches had two opportunities to talk: 1) to meet with their players before they went on the field and 2) when the coaches were introducing something new or were reviewing from yesterday's practice.

I required all players to be on the field 15 minutes before practices to meet with the position coaches.

6. **Superior placement of players** for the greater good of the team leads to winning more games. I think some coaches have a knack for being able to take certain players and put them in a position to help the team. At The University of Findlay, when we decided to move a player to a different position, I wanted to meet with that young man before he went on the field. I believe you must sell the young man on the move. I would explain that the move would make us a better football team.

We had many young men who agreed to make a change that would improve the team. A few examples are: Ken Agee, a first-team, all-city running back from Cleveland, whom I convinced in 1979 to start at nose-tackle to help us develop a great defense; Cal Dietz who agreed to move from nose-tackle – which he loved – to offensive tackle, becoming an NAIA first-team All-American in 1995; Tony Holland, who switched from tight end to offensive tackle, and Bob Sutyak, who made the transition from quarterback to free-safety in 1992.

There were various young men who put the team first and their personal goals second. Remember the concept: "Big team, Little me," meaning there is no "I" in team. In order to be successful, your team, organization, staff, and family must believe in this concept.

For The University of Findlay to be successful I firmly believed three things had to happen if we were to win consistently.

1. **We had to play great defense**, and we wanted the reputation for playing good defensive football at Findlay. I had very good defensive coaches who totally believed in what we were trying to accomplish. Part of my philosophy was we were going to put some of our best players on defense.

2. **We were going to run the football.** We needed to be a tough-minded and physical offensive football team. We wanted to control the football and the clock. We were going to run an offense that wasn't going to hurt our defense, and we were not going to have a lot of turnovers in our offense. Some of this philosophy changed with Bo Hurley, as he was allowed to throw the ball much more.

3. **The kicking game** has been estimated to be 20 to 25 percent of the total game, and, therefore, it makes sense that 20 to 25 percent of our practice time should be spent on it.

Of course, when it comes to winning, it's all about the post-season in college. Certainly, I have been blessed to win a lot at Findlay in the playoffs. Of course, much of what made us successful during the regular season made us successful in the post-season. **I was questioned by the press one time as to what the reasons were that The University of Findlay football team did so well in the playoffs.** My answer was:

1. **Attitude.** If you believe you're going to be successful, then chances are you will.

2. **Being very positive.** If you have a positive person who always thinks he can win, you can count on him to always do his very best. Even if you're behind in the fourth quarter, this athlete still believes he can win. When a negative thought comes up, he will replace it with a positive one.

3. **Enthusiasm.** I think it is important to be enthusiastic. I know one thing: a person who is enthusiastic is a person with great or intense feelings for a cause. And the cause is to win! Many times we did not come out yelling and screaming and hollering, but as I watched our players warm up, I could see it in their eyes. I could see it in their faces. I could see their hands and their white knuckles. I knew they were intense. I knew they wanted to win.

4. **Assistant coaches.** I think when you get to the playoffs, you need your assistant coaches even more. The head coach is in meetings with the press. He is taking care of all the details of the travel plans – overnight accommodations, who is staying with whom, parents, tickets, and meeting with the president and the athletic director. When you get to the playoffs, your assistant coaches are one of the main reasons a team is going to do very well.

Attitude was vital in the post-season. We coaches preached to our players that while the opponents would obviously get stronger, that never would impact how hard we would play. Our effort would be constant and total, so it really came down to worrying a lot less about what our opponent would do and spending a lot more time on what we planned to do.

I can't stress enough the importance of attitude. I really believe it is the deciding factor in where you finish. I remember a story told by Reverend Robert H. Schuller, the famous televangelist and author who believes so strongly in the power of faith-based positive thinking.

Schuller wrote in his book, *Tough Times Never Last, but Tough People Do!*, about his daughter Carol, who was in a terrible motorcycle accident when she was a junior in high school and lost a leg. After a seven-month hospital stay, she learned to walk with a prosthetic leg and was doing quite well. When she told her dad she intended to play on the softball team her senior year, Dr. Schuller asked his daughter how she intended to play ball if she couldn't run. Her response was a classic example of positive thinking. She said, "I've got that all figured out, Dad! When you hit home runs you don't have to run."

Shortly after her recovery from the accident, she was on a Hawaiian Islands steamship cruise with her parents. She noted all week the curious stares at her artificial leg. So, at the Friday-night amateur talent show, she went on stage and told the audience what had happened to her and about her faith in God. There was one thing about that story that I had to read over and over again – the words were so important regarding attitude. She told the hushed crowd, "It's not how you walk that counts, but who walks with you and who you walk with." What a great attitude she had!

I often posted in the locker room a quote from the noted author and educator Charles Swindoll. I had my players read it, and I have also sent copies to cancer patients I encountered during my own treatments. To me, there is such a profound element of truth in what Swindoll says:

"The longer I live, the more I realize the impact of attitude on life. Attitude, to me, is more important than facts. It is more important than the past, than education, than money, than circumstances, than failures, than successes, than what other people think or say or do. It is more important than appearance, giftedness, or skill. It will make or break a company…a church…a home. The remarkable thing is we have a choice every day regarding the attitude we will embrace for that day. We cannot change our past. We cannot change the fact that people will act in a certain way. We cannot change the inevitable. The only thing we can do is play on the one string we have, and that is our attitude…I am convinced that life is 10 percent what happens to me and 90 percent how I react to it. And so it is with you…we are in charge of our attitudes."

I think the article has a whole lot to say about how we live our lives. A winning attitude has to be learned. It just doesn't happen. Players have to be taught how to win. They have to be instructed how to win. So, the coaches have to be winners. It is hard to teach someone to be a winner if you are not a winner yourself, and I mean in all things that you do. It's *attitude*.

Another posting I used was a famous poem from an anonymous author. I used it to put the point across to my players that they had to be accountable to themselves first and foremost if they really wanted to get better.

The Man in the Glass
When you get what you want in your struggles for self
And the world makes you king for the day,
Just go to a mirror and look at yourself,
And see what that man has to say.
For it isn't your father or mother or wife,
Whose judgment upon you must pass.
The fellow whose verdict counts most in your life
Is the one staring back from the glass.
Some people might think you're a straight-shooting chum,
And call you a wonderful guy.
But the man in the glass says you're only a bum,
If you can't look him straight in the eye.
He's the fellow to please, never mind all the rest,
For he's with you clear to the end.
And you've passed your most difficult and dangerous test,
If the guy in the glass is your friend.
You may fool the whole world down the pathway of years,
And get pats on the back as you pass.
But your final reward will be heartache and tears,
If you've cheated the man in the glass.

During two-a-days I had the opportunity to talk with the team each evening. I would try to give them something to think about. Topics I usually talked to them about year after year after year were:

1. **Be the best you can be.** Be the best you can be right now. Be tough on yourself. It doesn't make any difference what you are as long as you are the best you can be. I believe the most frustrating thing in the world is to go through life knowing that you could have

done a better job. I always want to do the best that I can with the opportunities that God has given me. If I fall a little short, then I'm still further ahead than if I hadn't reached at all. Your talent is a gift from God. What you do with it is your gift back to God. Give life your best shot – you only go through it once.

2. **Attitude.**

3. **MAGIC.** The letters stand for "*Make A Greater Individual Commitment*." If each player made a greater individual commitment to what we wanted to accomplish, then it was going to work like magic.

4. **Three rules to live by.** I believe you should always try to *do what is right*, *do your best*, and *treat others as you wish to be treated*. This applies to your teammates, living in the dorms, the classroom, your workplace, your family, your church. I sincerely believe that if we keep these three rules in mind as we go through life, we will live a better and more fulfilling life.

5. **How to stay focused.**

6. **Great work ethic.**

7. **Never look for the easy way out.**

8. **Always do a little more than you are expected.**

9. **The three Ds: dedication, determination, and desire.**

10. **Do you really want to be a winner?**

11. **Family, faith and trust in God.**

12. **Having class.** If you have class, you don't need much of anything else. If you don't have it, no matter what else you have, it doesn't make much difference.

13. **Make the Big Time where you are.**

During our two-a-days at Findlay, I really made it a personal mission to get our freshmen through. I didn't want them to quit, and I made it my personal business to take them under my wing.

Every day, I made a point to put my arm around them at one time or another, no matter if a young man was one of our top ten freshmen or was in our bottom ten. I felt it was my job to keep them in college. I owed it to them and to their parents.

Regardless of how much any player would eventually contribute to our football team, I just knew how important it was that my young people not quit by walking away from challenges. My belief has always been that if you quit once, it makes it so much easier to quit the next time things get tough and the next and the next.

In trying to help the freshmen, right around the fourth or fifth evening at our team meeting, I would try to use a little humor to open up the lines of communication and to try to keep my youngsters from losing heart and quitting.

I would explain to the team, especially the freshmen, that they could talk with me about any personal problems they might be having.

I told them I was going to go into my office, and I would have three chairs in front of my desk. I wanted any player who was struggling with the decision whether to continue on or quit to come in one at a time and sit in one of the three chairs.

I explained the chair on the left was for anyone who was homesick and wanted to see his family (though usually it was his girlfriend!).

The chair in the middle was for anyone who was contemplating quitting because playing football at Findlay just wasn't what he thought it was going to be.

The chair on the right was reserved for any player who felt he'd simply lost his desire to play. I called that circumstance "losing your stinger."

Well, on those nights I'd get players, mostly freshmen, to come in. For those who sat in the homesick chair, I'd tell them that their families had waited eighteen long years for them to leave the nest. I told them with my tongue firmly planted in my cheek that their moms and dads asked me to tell them not to come home. The locks had been changed.

For those who sat in the middle chair reserved for those who were disillusioned about what they thought football would be like, I again tried to use humor. I'd ask the player just what he expected it to be. I'd say, "Football is blocking, tackling, and running. Which one do you have a problem with?"

For those who sat in the "lost-stinger" chair, I knew I had a tougher sell, but I tried. I tried to get each player to see the big picture and project himself beyond those hot, exhausting days in August to cooler temperatures, the thrill of game day, and practices that were not as tough as the ones in the sweltering heat.

Most of the time I was able to get them to reconsider. I would ask them to try to get through two-a-days. It's an accomplishment they would remember for the rest of their lives. After two-a-days, then it's all downhill.

As I look back over my coaching career, especially my Oilers days, I can't help but think back on my coaching colleague and sometimes rival, Frosty Westering of Pacific Lutheran University. Frosty won more than 300 games and collected three NAIA national championships and one NCAA Division III national championship before he was inducted into the College Football Hall of Fame in 2005.

Frosty presented me with a book he'd written during the weekend of our playoff game in 1995. The name of the book is *Make the Big Time Where You Are,* and I've read the book more than once and thought about how it relates to my own career.

I thought about the Ohio State opportunity back in 1972 when I got down to the final cut for a position on Coach Hayes's staff. I also thought about how close I came to getting the Northern Illinois University head position in 1982.

After reading Coach Westering's book a second time, it really sunk in that it doesn't matter where you are coaching if you're doing the best job you can at the position you have. I finally understood that The University of Findlay *was* my Big Time!

As I told my players many times, "The Big Time for you is right here and right now. It's not in the Big Ten or the Mid-American Conference. Donnell Stadium is your Big Time! The last few years of my career, I quoted often from Frosty's book to my teams:

> "The Big Time is not a place;
> It's a state of mind.
> It's not something you get;
> It's something you become."

I had the opportunity to coach in the Big Eight Conference, which is now the Big Twelve, and the Mid-American Conference. But I spent 24 years at The University of Findlay coaching in the NAIA football conference, going to 27 playoff games. During my years at Findlay, I ran across some outstanding NAIA coaches, and I have no doubt they would have been successful coaches anywhere.

Joe Fusco, from Westminster College in Pennsylvania, was inducted into the College Football Hall of Fame in 2001. When he retired another outstanding coach, Gene Nicholson, took over.

Another coach who comes to mind is Bill Ramseyer who turned Wilmington into a very solid program.

Carlin Carpenter from Bluffton College coached for a couple years at Ohio University before he took the position of head football coach and athletic director at Bluffton College.

There are just so many wonderful coaches and fine men. Ron Findlay was the head football coach at Campbellsville College in Kentucky, and is now retired. Kevin Donley coached at Georgetown, Kentucky, and is now at St. Francis in Fort Wayne, Indiana. Dan Hawkins at Willamette University, who we played for the national championship in 1997, then became the head coach at Boise State University, and he is now at the University of Colorado as head coach. Fred Martinelli of Ashland College was inducted into the College Football Hall of Fame in 2002. Tom Beck, who was the head coach at Illinois Benedictine, Elmhurst College and Grand Valley State University, and Charlie Richard from Baker, Kansas, were both inducted into the College Football Hall of Fame with me in 2004.

I believe these coaches could have been successful coaching anywhere. They truly made the Big Time where they were.

As far as my bouts with heart disease, cancer, and stroke, I know you can't fight them without God. He certainly has been at my side all the way. I think of a couple Bible verses that I've repeated so often when times got tough. "If God is for us, who can be against us?" [Romans 8:31] is about as powerful a rhetorical question as has ever been written. "For nothing is impossible with God" [Luke 1:37] is a verse I have often repeated when the hour was so dark.

I have met so many outstanding people through these various diseases. I believe God has allowed me to meet these people, because in some cases I had to search for them. I have met doctors, nurses, technicians, and therapists who were such great help to me.
In addition, people in my church and various prayer groups have supported me and helped me through these difficult problems. I know that their prayers work and there is no greater proof of that than what I have been able to overcome.

My family, of course, has been my rock. Although it has been difficult for all of them, my wife and my children have been such a big support. My grandchildren, Hunter, Danielle, Dalton, and Zachary, have always been able to put a smile on my face.

Additionally, I owe so much to pastors Darrell Prichard and Larry White. With these men, I have had so many meaningful talks about God, my medical struggles, and world problems. Larry and I talked weekly, and he played a very important part of my life as we walked the walk. How very difficult it was when Larry succumbed to cancer.

However, just when I was dealing with my grief from losing such a powerful presence in my life, Pastor Bill Reist, now the senior pastor at the College Church of God, was sent into my life. He has become a good friend and listener.

Once Pastor Prichard retired, Pastor Will Miller led us in many of our pre-game prayers. They will never be forgotten by the Oilers players and coaches.

After my retirement from coaching, I've continued to deal with health problems. In May 1999, I went back to the Cleveland Clinic because I was having some chest pain. Another heart catheterization revealed that one of the arteries (circumflex) that they had replaced during open heart surgery thirteen years before was about 90 percent plugged. They inserted three stents, but the procedure was not successful.

In 2000, I had another heart attack a week before Father's Day. That landed me in the hospital for six days. Back at the Cleveland Clinic in July 2000, doctors discovered that the circumflex artery in the back of my heart was nearly 100 percent closed, and, because of the weak elasticity of it, they really couldn't do anything to keep it open.

In June of 2004, I suffered another heart attack. My cardiologist in Findlay, Dr. Beekman, sent me by ambulance to Riverside Hospital in Columbus, but, again, there was nothing the doctors could do.

Who intervened each time? God. When I was going through the heart attacks and laying in the ICU, I can't tell you how many times I said the Twenty-third Psalm, one of my favorites. Each time I've had to face these problems, I have continued to recall Bible verses from memory, pounding them into my mind. Following are a few verses that I would like share from which I've been able to draw strength as I went through various health crises.

> **Philippians 4:13** – "For I can do everything with the help of Christ who give me the strength I need."
> **Matthew 21:22** – "If you believe, you will receive whatever you ask for in prayer."
> **Proverbs 3:5** – "Trust in the Lord with all your heart, do not depend on your own understanding."
> **Proverbs 3:6** – "Seek his will in all you do, and he shall direct your paths."
> **Proverbs 16:33** – "We may throw the dice, but the Lord determines how they fall."

It's my personal belief that faith overcomes fear and that God always makes a way when there is no way. When I was in the hospital recovering from cancer surgery, I received a prayer in the mail from someone in Findlay I'd never met. I have said this prayer often and also have shared it with many friends when they faced their own health problems. The prayer is entitled "I Said a Prayer for You Today," although the author is unknown. It is so beautiful and has so much meaning, that I'd like to share it:

> I said a prayer for you today,
> And know God must have heard.
> I felt the answer in my heart,
> Although he spoke no word.

I didn't ask for wealth or fame,
(I knew you wouldn't mind).
I asked Him to send treasures
Of a far more lasting kind.

I asked that He'd be near you
At the start of each new day;
To grant you health and blessings
And friends to share your way.

I asked for happiness for you,
In all things great and small.
But it was for His loving care
I prayed the most of all.

God has given me this great opportunity to live. If I can share what has helped me along the way, especially with those who are battling cancer, heart disease, and stroke, I'm happy to do what I can. I have been able to fight all three of them, although ultimately, health issues forced me to retire from coaching.

Most people have family and friends and church members to help them in times of crisis. But, even if that's not the case, you always have God. He will go with you into battle. He will play the game with you. He will run interference. He will be by your side all four quarters. Trust me when I say that, as I know what I am talking about, and I know what he can do.

Now at the conclusion of this book, this is my fourth quarter. I am now ready to finish the game. I am reminded of the song that Bob Hope used to sing at the end of his shows, "Thanks for the Memories," and then he would end with "Thank you so much." Now seems the appropriate time to thank those most important in my life.

To all the assistant coaches who coached for me: Your time, loyalty, commitment and energy will never be forgotten. Thank you so much.

To all the players who I had the privilege to coach: Your work ethic, loyalty to the program, and willingness to sacrifice and to put the team first is much appreciated. Your blood, sweat, and tears will never be forgotten. Thank you so much.

To the boosters and the people in the communities surrounding Lakota High School, Bryan High School, Warren Western Reserve High School, the University of Toledo, Kansas State University, and, of course, The University of Findlay: Your great support and enthusiasm were always the best. Thank you so much.

To the volunteers in the foster parent program in Findlay: Your effort and willingness to help our football players will never be forgotten. Thank you so much.

To the administrators who I worked for and learned from who made my job so much more enjoyable: Victor Woods, Howard Rogge, John Scharf, Dr. Glen Rasmussen, Dr. Ken Zirkle, Dr. Jim Houdeshell, Dr. DeBow Freed and Martin Terry. Thank you so much.

To the faculty in all the high schools and universities where I have been: Your support was so important. And, especially to the faculty at The University of Findlay, for whom I have so much respect, I will never forget you. Thank you so much.

To my beloved family, words seem inadequate to thank you. My wife, Ginger, went through every emotion of every football game I ever coached. If there was a model coach's wife, it would be Ginger. She was and always will be my first and only choice. We've been together 46 years and still counting.

The three children that Ginger gave me – Douglas, Gina, and Steven – have brought me immeasurable joy in my life. They have been like three guardian angels helping me through all my health crises. They are the best I could ever have hoped for. Doug's wife, Lisa; Gina's husband, Matt; and Steven's fiancée, Traci, have made my family even more special. Thank you so much.

Ginger and I have four grandchildren, and they are truly the "happening" in our lives. Gina and Matt have shared with us Hunter and the twins, Danielle and Dalton. Lisa and Doug have shared with us Zachary. We love them all so very much. Grandchildren definitely make growing older much easier. Thank you so much.

To my only sibling, Dale, who although he is nine years younger, I find it hard to believe any two brothers could be closer. We always have each other's back. Not only do I love Dale, but also his wife, Diane, and their three sons Brian, Bradley, and Bret. For being a part of my life, thank you so much.

To all my buddies, both past and present – the friendships will never fade. The good times we've shared are indeed some of my fondest memories. They will never be forgotten. Thank you so much.

Epilogue

I say this with profound sincerity, Richard Strahm is as engaging a subject as I have ever covered in my writing career.

Dick and I spoke several times a week, met in person several times a month, regularly e-mailed back and forth, and also, on occasion, used the U.S. Postal Service. By the time the book was set to go to print, I'm guessing I spent over a hundred hours talking with the former Findlay Oilers coaching icon.

And, if you factor in dozens of interviews I conducted with former coaches and players and a host of other people so important in Dick Strahm's life, I spent another hundred hours not talking to Dick but talking about Dick.

Sometimes lost to the casual observer of Dick Strahm is his sense of humor, a trait I hope I have been able to bring to the forefront in the narrative. It's a sense of humor that was, perhaps, shrouded somewhat by the vestiges of old-school football and core-value methodologies, but it is a sense of humor I saw so often during our time together.

During the early stages of the project, I went to meet with Dick in Findlay to drive further north to Bowling Green to have a working breakfast with Larry Killgallon, a former player of Dick's at Bryan High School and yet another of what Dick has spent a lifetime collecting, a longtime friend.

On my drive to Findlay, I encountered some traffic driving up Interstate 75 from Lima, my home base, and was eight minutes late when I slid into Dick's front seat in the parking lot of the Koehler Fitness and Recreation Complex on the campus of The University of Findlay.

Before I could apologize for being a tad tardy, I saw the coach's eyes narrow. Then, in a voice that was equal parts growl and grumble, he said, "If you were playing for me, the bus would have already left." Right when I was thinking that I was in trouble, there was a hearty laugh, allowing a nervous writer off the hook. Thank goodness!

Later that morning, Larry Killgallon told me something he remembered some forty years after he played for Coach Richard Strahm. "Coach had this rule. You couldn't swear. He wanted us to be gentlemen."

When I asked him if his coach followed his own rule regarding language, Killgallon paused and said with a wink, "Not so much." He went on to explain, lest there be any misunderstanding. "Now don't get me wrong. Never was there any language demeaning to a player, and never was there any what one might call strong language. But, the coach sprinkled a little salt in when he really needed to make a point, which certainly makes him no different than about any coach I can think of." Admitted Dick, "Something may have slipped from time to time."

When Killgallon told his former coach at Bryan High School that his son was an All-District punter for the Golden Bears of Bryan and was averaging around 45 yards a punt, the coach had a ready response. He started by saying, "Larry, I'm sure your son is a fine punter, but there's a test I'm not sure he's encountered yet that he'll need to pass. I'll put the ball on the one and rush eleven guys at him with his heels on the back line of the end zone, and then I'll tell you what kind of a punter he is."

To some, Strahm's response might seem a bit jaded, but Killgallon understood perfectly and agreed that it really is how a person responds to pressure and adversity that determines the measure of that person.

And, for Dick Strahm, his heels have been almost touching the end line more times than five men do in their lives. From heart attacks to heart catheterizations to open-heart surgery to cancer to stroke and back to cancer and to heart attacks, Strahm has endured.

As for me, I have certainly gotten as much as I gave during the completion of this book. Perhaps the greatest gifts were the dozens of interviews with people whose one common denominator was that somehow, somewhere, they have been impacted by having known Dick Strahm. While all are listed in the works-cited section, I think some deserve another mention because of what they were able to give me.

My sincere thanks to Dave Ebersole, whose comeback from a severe injury in a lawnmower accident was told with such clarity and attention to detail; to Hayden Fry, the longtime Iowa Hawkeye head coach, who provided me details of the induction ceremony for the members of the 2004 class who are now enshrined in the College Football Hall of Fame in South Bend, Indiana; to Joe Novak, the former Northern Illinois University football coach who painted such a vivid picture of the years when he was Dick's assistant at Warren Western Reserve High School; to Chuck Ealey, who never lost a game he started either in high school at Portsmouth Notre Dame or in college as a Toledo Rocket and who allowed me to see the remarkable Toledo Rocket 35-game winning streak over a magical three years.

I also need to tip my cap to Gary Hinkson, the former Toledo Rocket safety who still holds the school record for career interceptions and who gave me such insight intothe two head coaches who presided over the streak of the Rockets, Frank Lauterbur and Jack Murphy; to former New England Patriot All-Pro Steve Grogan, who spoke with such clarity of his days as a starting quarterback for Kansas State at the height of the brilliant Oklahoma and Nebraska teams of the Big Eight during the 1970s; to Dean Pees, the former kid from Ohio's Hardin County, who never forgot that long before he began collecting Super Bowl rings as the defensive coordinator of the New England Patriots, he was given his first college coaching job by Dick Strahm.

Thank you as well to Jim Houdeshell, who has worked full time for The University of Findlay for over fifty years and possesses both the firmest of handshakes and the clearest of recollections of events decades old one could possibly imagine; to Chris Jaquillard, who never once abdicated responsibility in taking ownership of the troubles he encountered and whose life certainly shows that it's not where one starts but where one finishes that matters most. And, thanks to Kevin Cassidy and Scott Garlock, who conveyed to me not only the essence of Dick Strahm's influence on their lives but also the pride they feel in returning as men to become Oilers assistant coaches; and, finally, thanks to Bo Hurley who allowed me to see the special qualities that made him the NAIA National Player of the Year in 1997.

I was also given the chance to see something so special when I attended two reunion dinners for former Oilers players. I remember the hearty hugs shared by successful men who truly believe that the friendships formed in the sweltering August heat on an Oilers practice field and tested again and again all the way through the snow-covered and windswept playoff fields of mid-December are indeed bonds that can never be broken.

I will always remember the booming volume of Jim McIntosh's voice at such gatherings, the historical perspective brought to the table by sports editor Larry Alter, and the undeniable truth about former champions, and that truth is that a championship season becomes more and more special with every new calendar that is tacked on the wall.

I was also gratified that the book experience allowed me to connect to a bigger world. It was just days after I interviewed Dick Strahm's former assistant coach, Steve Mohr, to glean what he could give me about the early Oilers-Strahm years that I flicked on ESPN and saw Coach Mohr of Trinity University talking about his team's last-second miracle 28-24 win over Millsaps College on a hook and *fifteen* laterals. The game-ending play was nominated for an ESPY and was one of the most replayed sports videos of 2007.

And, as I brought this project to a close, I couldn't help but feel grateful to so many, one in particular who was taken from us far, far too soon. Sadly, I can only say posthumously, to Gilbert Hyland, "Thank you for being the conduit that connected Dick Strahm and me initially." It was Gil who played a prominent role in convincing Dick to take a chance on someone who had only written one book prior to this one. While cancer took Gil in the fall of 2006, his sense of commitment to lend a hand in worthwhile projects and his sense of compassion for his fellow men and women are indeed missed each and every day. Gilbert, I wish you were here to see the finished product of what you helped initiate.

Certainly, a big thank you goes to my editor, Charlene Hankinson, whose advice and mechanical acumen in all things linguistic were invaluable to whatever success this book achieves. Despite responsibilities, both in her work for The University of Findlay and in caring for family members in need, she always found time to help me to write with greater clarity.

And, of course, thank you to every former player of Dick Strahm's, each captured in youthful freeze frame. Each of you is a vital part of this narrative.

It goes without saying that the biggest thank you is reserved for someone who worked just as hard as I did in bringing this project to completion, Dick Strahm. It was he who arranged every interview I did and was always just ten telephone numbers away when I needed something from him. It was he who separated all the print research material year by year, made trips to the library to find sources to advance the book, and, perhaps most importantly, allowed me to find a comfort zone necessary to continue throughout a project which always had the potential to overwhelm me. Everything I asked of the old coach, he responded. Beyond any tangible rewards this book brings me, the greatest is certainly gaining the friendship of one of the all-time great human beings.

While there are those who will marvel at Dick Strahm's impressive number of coaching wins in high school and college, especially the 183 Findlay Oilers wins over which he presided, there are three wins I find the most impressive. According to the National Center for Health Statistics, the three leading causes of death are heart disease, cancer, and stroke, and Dick Strahm has defeated all three. Now that's something that inspires awe!

Coach Dick Strahm's Oilers Roll Call

A

ABBOTT, Mike
ABEL, Tom
ADAMS, Eric
ADAMS, Jeff
ADAMS, Steve
ADDISON, Carl
AFFHOLDER, David
AGEE, Ken
AHR, Steve
AKERS, Shawn
ALBRIGHT, Tom
ALGE, Kris
ALLAN, Todd
ALLEN, Jon
ALSTON, Dahl
ALTENBURGER, Brian
AMBROSE, Rich
AMBURGEY, Jim
AMSTUTZ, Brian
ANDERSON, Bob
ANDERSON, Butch
ANDERSON, Mike
ANDERSON, Richy
ANVERSE, Shawn
APPLE, Scott
ARMSTRONG, Curtis
ARMSTRONG, Gray
ARMSTRONG, Mike
ARNOLD, Nate
ASH, Lanny
ASH, Mike
ASHBAUGH, John
AUKERMAN, Craig
AUSTER, Terrance
AUVIL, Todd
AUXIER, Rich
AXE, Scott

B

BAARLAER, Joe
BABCOCK, Joel
BAHN, Bret
BAHSEN, Chad
BAKER, Brent
BAKER, Mark
BAKER, Tim
BALLINGER, Jeff
BALSIZER, Mark

BAME, Bruce
BAME, Jon
BANASZAK, Jason
BANKER, Harold
BARBARA, Chris
BARBER, Steve
BARLOW Joey
BARNES, Mark
BARR, Jeff
BARR, Keith
BARTON, Jeff
BATTON, Scott
BAUMBICK, Ray
BAUMGARDNER, Mike
BAUMLEIN, Alan
BEAL, Tom
BEAMER, Trent
BEAMON, Wes
BEARD, Wilson
BEATTY, Todd
BECKMAN, Matt
BECKMAN, Tim
BEDIAKO, Joe
BELCHER, Marty
BELL, Jim
BELL, Josh
BELLAM, John
BENJAMIN, Gary
BENNETT, Gary
BENNIS, Jeremy
BENSON, Chris
BENSON, Roger
BERG, Kevin
BERGER, Bill
BERGER, Dave
BERGER, Jason
BERNOLA, Sam
BETCHKER, Eric
BETHEL, Richard
BICKERSTAFF, Don
BIHN, Steve
BINGHAM, Robert
BIRR, Andy
BISHOP, Mike
BLAIR, John
BLAKE, James
BLANKENSHIP, Larry
BLASTIOLE, Louie
BLAUSEY, Doug

BLOOMER, Tom
BOALS, James
BOBO, Mike
BOGART, Tim
BOGEDAIN, Ben
BOGNER, Michael
BOLDEN, Nelson
BOLGER, Jeff
BOLTON, Dexter
BONNETTE, Andy
BONNORONT, Doug
BOOTH, Andy
BOOSE, Eric
BOSS, Bruce
BOYD, Justin
BOYER, Brad
BOYER, John
BOYKIN, Demetrice
BOYKIN, Robert
BRANDSTADT, Eric
BRAUNING, Mike
BREGE, Todd
BREITFIELD, Scott
BRENEK, Dave
BRENEK, Joe
BRICKNER, Marty
BRIGHT, Danny
BRINDISE, Dale
BRINKMAN, Rick
BROCKMAN, Dana
BROOKINS, Agunanda
BROYLES, Rick
BROWN, Brian
BROWN, David
BROWN, Doug
BROWN, Greg
BROWN, Jack
BROWN, Jeff
BROWN, Jeffery C.
BROWN, Kelly
BROWN, Mark
BROWN, Nate
BRUNNER, Matt
BRUTON, Richard
BUCHANAN, Jack
BUCK, Brian
BUCKMASTER, John
BUNCH, Matt
BURICH, Eric

BURKS, Richard
BURMAN, Doug
BURTRAW, Jonathan
BUSH, Aaron
BUTI, Jerry
BUTLER, Carl
BUTLER, Tim
BYRD, Charlie
BYRD, Mike

C
CAFFARO, Dave
CAFFIE, Carmen
CAHALL, Chad
CALDWELL, Chris
CALDWELL, Jim
CAMP, Brian
CAMPBELL, Craig
CAMPBELL, Dan
CAMPBELL, Jerry
CAMPBELL, Matt
CARPENTER, Brody
CARRIG, James
CARRUTHERS, Dempsey
CARSWELL, Kevin
CARTER, Steve
CASIMIR, Jim
CASSIDY, Kevin
CAVINEE, Shane
CHANTHAVANE, Adelthsack
CHENEY, Brandon
CHERRY, Ron
CHEW, Doug
CHINN, Eric
CHRISTMAN, Jeff
CHRISTY, Todd
CIAMMAICHELLA, Dick
CLARK, Caleb
CLARK, Todd
CLARK, Travis
CLAYTON, Eric
CLEMONS, Matt
CLYMER, Jason
COATE, Doug
COBB, Chris
COCHRAN, Ben
COCHRAN, Wayne
COFFMAN, Greg
COGAR, Jim
COLATRUGLIO, Tony
COLE, Greg
COLE, Neil

COLE, Terry
COLEMAN, Brent
COLEMAN, John
COLEMAN, Lawrence
COLLETT, Mike
COLLIER, Dan
COLLINS, John
COLOMBO, Thomas
COLTER, Mark
COMER, Travis
COMPTON, Jeff
COMPTON, Mike
CONCEPCION, Noel
CONLEY, Bart
CONLEY, John
CONNESS, Grant
CONRAD, Brian
COOK, Barry
COOK, Chuck
COOK, Mike
COOK, Rod
COOPER, Robert
COOPER, William
CORBIN, Bob
CORGGENS, Ray
CORLEY, Dave
COTTERILL, Chris
COTTERMAN, John
COTTOM, Rich
COTUGNO, John
CRAGER, Craig
CRAGER, Curt
CRAMER, Dave
CREPS, Kevin
CREWES, Jamon
CROLEY, Ryan
CROMER, Paul
CULPEPPER, Datalion
CUMMINGS, Delmond
CUNIFFE, Brent
CUOZZO, Gary
CUPP, Keith
CURTIS, Larry
CUTLIFF, Edward
CUTRELLI, Paul

D
DALES, Doug
DALLY, Bo
DAMSCHRODER, Robert
DANHOFF, Dave
DARR, Roger

DAVID, John
DAVIDSON, Curtis
DAVIS, Robert
DAVIS, Scott
DAVIS, Shane
DAVIS, William
DEAN, Jeff
DEETZ, Ben
DeGARBINO, Leo
DeGEORGE, Dan
DEISER, Greg
DeMARCO, Tony
DENDIU, Troy
DENHAM, John
DENNISON, Shane
DEPRIEST, Ken
DIALS, Brad
DIBLING, Mike
DICKERSON, Stephan
DIETZ, Cal
DILLARD, Lynn
DILLER, Wayne
DILS, Ben
DILTS, Randy
DOAK, Kyle
DOWE, Gerald
DRAPER, Greg
DRAPER, Jim
DROZ, Chris
DUKES, Charles
DUNCAN, Charlie
DUNCAN, Joe
DUNCAN, Thomas
DUPONT, William
DUTY, Jeff

E
EARDLY, Shawn
EASTER, Jamie
EASTON, Bill
ECKENRODE, Brad
EDMONDSON, Albert
EDWARDS, Dan
EDWARDS, David
EDWARDS, Jon
EDWARDS, Kory
EHLINGER, Mike
EISAMAN, Tracy
ELIAS, Matt
ELINGER, Mike
ELKINS, Marcus
ELLIOTT, Don

ELLIOTT, Sherman
ELLIS, Ron
ELLISON, Larry
ENDERS, Ben
ENGLE, Darrell
ENGLE, Roger
ESTES, Gary
EVANS, Jamie
EVANS, Nick
EXLINE, Marty

F
FACKLER, Bruce
FAINE, Adam
FALKE, Shane
FANNON, Mark
FARABEE, Randy
FEASEL, Brad
FEGLEY, Eric
FEJES, Tim
FENNELLY, Joe
FENSTERMAKER, Tony
FERGUSON, John
FERGUSON, Larry
FERNANDEZ, Dennis
FERNANDEZ, Gene
FERNANDEZ, Marcus
FERRENCE, Dave
FEUCHT, Todd
FIEGEL, Ty
FIELDS, Jason
FILIATER, Chad
FINCH, Ben
FITZGERALD, Robert
FLEMING, Ron
FLOWERS, Jason
FORYS, Tom
FOSTER, Brad
FOUGHT, Danny
FOURMAN, Sky
FOUST, Matthew
FOX, Kevin
FRANK, Lee
FRANKLIN, Kerrick
FRANCO, Brad
FRANKS, Dan
FRAZIER, Mike
FREDERICK, Glen
FREDERICK, Steve
FRONZAGLIO, Jerome
FROST, Tim

FRUTH, Dan
FRYZEL, Chris
FULTZ, Shawn
FUNK, Roger

G
GALVAN, Roel
GANGWISCH, Bryan
GARLOCK, Scott
GARNER, Chris
GARRETT, Greg
GARTLAND, Kevin
GATEWOOD, James
GEARHART, Chris
GEBHARDT, Kevin
GEDEON, Brian
GEDEON, Chris
GEDEON, Dave
GETZINGER, Mike
GHOLSTON, Steve
GIBSON, Pat
GIBSON, Tom
GIERHART, Nolan
GILES, Joe
GILLESPIE, Robert
GILLEY, Eric
GILLIG, Trevor
GILLMAN, Jon
GILPIN, David
GIORANDO, Joe
GIRCSIS, Scott
GLASS, Scott
GLOVER, John
GODMAN, Jamie
GOODBURN, John
GOODWIN, Tim
GOODWIN, Tony
GORDON, Brent
GORDON, Jomo
GORZE, Jeff
GRANGER, Jason
GRASSON, Pete
GRAY, Jerome
GREER, Terry
GRIFFIN, Dennis
GRIFFITH, Mike
GRIMES, Duke
GRINNONNEAU, Lee
GROOMS, Ryan
GROSS, Rick
GRUDEN, John

GUERRA, Denny
GUICE, Alphonsa
GUSCHING, Russell
GUSTWILLER, Mike

H
HAAS, Roy
HALE, Chuck
HALEY, Chris
HALEY, Matt
HALL, Alan
HALL, Dennis
HALL, Jeff
HALL, Scott
HAM, Duane
HAMBRICK, Randy
HAMBY, Jason
HAMID, Khaleel
HAMILTON, Kirk
HAMILTON, Roger
HAMLER, Brad
HAMMOND, Tony
HANELY, Bryan
HANKINS, Steve
HANSBRO, Lamont
HANSEN, Tom
HARDER, Adam
HARDWICK, Ernest
HARDY, Greg
HARP, Matt
HARRIS, Alvonta
HARRIS, David
HARRIS, Frank
HARRIS, Keion
HARRISON, Eric
HARTMAN, Mike
HASKIN, Roe
HATFIELD, Rick
HAUNHORST, Dusty
HAUPERT, Brent
HAUSFELD, Randy
HAYNES, Mark
HEADLEE, Bob
HEARD, Chuck
HEATH, William
HEBENSTREIT, Bret
HEILMAN, Randy
HEIN, Shawn
HEINTZELMAN, Steve
HEITKAMP, Bob
HEIZMAN, Scott

HENRY, E'Leon
HEPHNER, Tony
HERRON, Greg
HESTON, Howard
HEY, Jeff
HEYDINGER, Brian
HEYDINGER, Stephen
HICKMAN, Lee
HIGGINS, Darrell
HILL, Andrew
HILL, Brian
HILL, Michael
HILLMAN, Nick
HINTON, Bill
HIRSCHFIELD, Mike
HOANG, Bao
HOBER, Mark
HODGE, Tim
HODGSON, Dave
HOFFMAN, Brian
HOGUE, Sam
HOHL, Michael
HOLLAND, Tony
HOLLEN, Bob
HOLLIS, Melvin
HOLMAN, Jason
HOLTZAPPLE, John
HOLTZHAUER, Chip
HOLTZWORTH, Jason
HOPPE, Matt
HORD, Jason
HORN, Jamie
HORNER, Andre
HOUCK, Lee
HOWARD, Darren
HOWARD, James
HOWARD, Jesse
HOWARD, William
HOWERY, Fred
HUBER, John
HUBER, Sean
HUBANS, Bill
HUBANS, Mike
HUFF, Gary
HUFFMAN, Jeff
HUFFMAN, Jeffery D.
HUFFMAN, Jon
HUGHES, Leon
HUNT, Alan
HUNTER, Reginald
HURLEY, Aaron
HURLEY, Bo

HUSSEIN, Mike
HUSSING, Mike
HUTCHINGS, John
HUTCHINSON, Derek
HUTTON, Rick

I
INKROTT, Mark
INNIGER, Bob

J
JACOBS, John
JACKSON, Ray
JACKSON, Thomas
JACKSON, Todd
JACKSON, Walter
JAMES, Earnest
JAMES, Erik
JAQUILLARD, Chris
JARRETT, Stoney
JEFFERSON, Charles
JEFFERSON, Scott
JENKINS, Bobby
JENNINGS, Delbert
JENNINGS, Steve
JESCO, Steve
JOACHIM, Terry
JOHNSON, Contrell
JOHNSON, Heath
JOHNSON, Kirk
JOHNSON, LaKeith
JOHNSON, Steve
JOHNSON, Tim
JOLLIFF, Terry
JONES, Brett
JONES, Dwight
JONES, Greg
JONES, Lee
JONES, Lenzell
JONES, Luther
JONES, Rick
JONES, Robert
JOSEPH, Dion
JUDD, Todd

K
KAISER, Sam
KAJFASZ, Troy
KARCHNER, Joshua
KARRAS, Alex
KARSZNIA, Chris
KATES, Randy

KAYSER, Joey
KECK, Joshua
KEIRNS, Ken
KEISER, Dustin
KEITH, Joe
KELLAGHER, Bill
KELLEY, Keith
KELLY, Randy
KELSEN, Kevin
KEMP, Steve
KENDALL, Eric
KENNEY, Craig
KIMMEL, Kevin
KINTZ, Mike
KIRK, Dan
KIRK, Mark
KITTENDORF, Brandon
KITTENDORF, Shane
KITTRELL, Dave
KLINE, Floyd
KLINE, Korey
KLOEPFER, James
KLOEPFER, Jerry
KNAPKE, Brad
KNICK, Gordon
KNIGHT, Raynar
KNISELY, Brett
KNOX, LaForest
KOEPKE, Keith
KOHLER, Brad
KONOPKA, Mike
KRAMER, Doug
KRAMER, Hank
KREAIS, Larry
KROUSE, Dustin
KRUGH, Joe
KRUGH, Kerry
KRUPP, Bryon
KRYNZEL, Todd
KUJAWA, Gary
KUNS, Gary
KUSTRIN, Matt
KUTHAN, Mike

L
LABBE, Timothy
LAING, Jeff
LAMBERT, Erin
LAMBERT, Mark
LANCE, Mike
LANE, Avery
LaROCHE, Jason

LaROCHE, Paul
LATELL, John
LATELL, Matt
LAUNDER, Rocky
LAUTH, Paul
LAUTZENHEISER, John
LEACH, Rodney
LEAL, Noe
LEASE, Jeff
LEE, RaShawn
LEGHART, Bob
LEIGHTON, Mike
LEINHAUSER, Mike
LELIAERT, Matt
LENGEN, John
LESTER, Frank
LETANY, Steve
LEUGERS, Darin
LEWIS, James
LEWIS, Marcus
LIEBAS, Matt
LINDEMAN, Bob
LINK, Ron
LITTRELL, Dave
LITWINKO, Mark
LONES, Mark
LONG, Ken
LONG, Ray
LONG, Rod
LONSWAY, Tim
LOPEZ, Fred
LORA, Harold
LOVER, James
LOVETT, Justin
LOWE, Al
LUDWIG, Chris
LUNDIE, James
LYON, Trevis
LYTLE, Kelce

M
MAAG, Denny
MACK, Charlie
MACK, Darin
MACKEY, Kerry
MACON, Bert
MACY, Bret
MAGLICIC, Matt
MAISCH, Jim
MAJORS, Scott
MANDZAK, Tom
MANLEY, Robby

MARHEFKY, Jacob
MARRET, Kyle
MARTIN, Jeff
MARTSOLF, Bruce
MARZULLA, Richard
MASTRO, Todd
MATERNI, Ray
MATHENY, Tom
MATTHEWS, Bob
MAUK, Kyle
MAY, Barry
MAY, Des
MAY, Jason
MAYS, Mario
McADOO, Steve
McALLISTER, Chuck
McBETH, Nathan
McCARTY, Rich
McCLUSKEY, John
McCORD, Jeff
McCORD, Tom
McCRACKEN, Matt
McCRARY, Demar
McCREARY, Charles
McCUTCHEON, Joel
McDANIEL, Doug
McDANIELS, Charles
McDANIELS, Josh
McDONALD, Ed
McDUFFIE, George
McDUFFIE, Tom
McGEE, John
McHUGH, Mike
McINTOSH, Bill
McKEE, Toby
McKINLEY, Bob
McKINNEY, Richard
McLAUGHLIN, Scott
McNEIL, Rick
MEIBERS, Ken
MEINHOLD, Jeff
MENARD, George
MENDENHALL, Chuck
MERCER, Kevin
MERRIMAN, Matt
MESCHER, Jamie
METKER, Kevin
MEYER, Andy
MEYER, Harry
MICHELAKIS, Joe
MIELCAREK, Rick
MIKETA, Richard

MIKESELL, Jeff
MILLER, Bill
MILLER, Chris
MILLER, Darin
MILLER, Dave
MILLER, Emby
MINTER, Billy
MISHOS, John
MITCHELL, Chuck
MITCHELL, Nick
MITCHELL, Todd
MITSCH, Kevin
MOILANEN, Craig
MOLINARO, Frank
MONAK, Rob
MONTGOMERY, Dave
MOORE, Cory
MOORE, John
MOOREFIELD, Joe
MORDENT, Mike
MORGAN, Isaiah
MORGAN, Ryan
MOSS, Jim
MOYER, Randy
MOXLEY, Chad
MUIR, Jamie
MULDROW, Jermaine
MULHOLLEN, Jerry
MULLINS, Chris
MULLINS, Terry
MURPHY, Dennis
MURPHY, Mike
MURPHY, Michael W.
MURPHY, Vincent
MUSSER, Brian
MUTERSBAUGH, Steve
MUTO, Sam
MYERS, Mike

N
NAGY, Jeff
NAGY, Jim
NEALEIGH, Dave
NETHERTON, Bob
NEUMAN, Tim
NEWBURG, Mark
NEWLAND, Karlton
NEWMAN, Kevin
NICHOLS, Kevin
NICHOLS, Kevin
NICOLOSI, Jason
NIEDBALSKI, Allan

NIGHSWANDER, Al
NISWONGER, Mark
NIZZI, Dan
NORDYKE, Terry
NORMAN, Doug
NORWOOD, Jermaine
NOTTKE, Ryan
NOVAK, Jim
NOWARD, Dave
NUNAMAKER, Tom
NYE, Greg

O
O'BRIEN, Jeff
OGG, Scott
OHLER, Tim
OILER, Joe
ORIANS, Doug
ORIANS, Jerrod
ORRELL, Danny
OSWALT, Keith
OUSLEY, Terry
OWENS, Craig

P
PAGE, Curtis
PAGE, Greg
PALLANTE, John
PALMORE, Reginald
PARKE, Brenan
PARKER, Damon
PARKER, Roger
PATRICK, Tony
PATRICK, Trent
PATTERSON, Joe
PEACE, Robert
PEARSON, Troy
PEES, Todd
PELLETIER, Allen
PELLIGRINI, Kenton
PENCE, Mitch
PENN, Gary
PEOPLE, Curtis
PEQUIGNOT, John
PERIAT, Dan
PERKINS, Bobby
PERRINE, Paul
PERT, Bill
PETERSON, Robert
PHILLIP, Greg
PHILLIPS, Harry
PHILLIPS, Larry

PHILLIPS, Mark
PHILLIPS, Nate
PHILMORE, Mark
PICKETT, Victor
PIERCE, Zach
PIGHIN, Brooks
PINA, Rick
PISANELLI, Jon
PITTS, Tony
PLAS, Matt
POOLE, Kedrick
POORE, Tim
POTTER, Chris
POWELL, Marc
POWELL, Steve
POWERS, Mike
POWERS, Tom
PRAHL, Tom
PRICE, Tony
PRICE, Robert
PRICE, Tyrone
PRISBY, Ross
PRITT, Dan
PRUITT, Ron
PRUITT, Steve
PRZYBS, John
PURCELL, Paul
PUTNAM, Aaron
PUTT, Steve

Q
Quatman, Matt
Quick, Jeff
Quinn, Billy

R
RAGLAND, Loren
RAMMEL, Charles
RAMSEY, Darrell
RANDOLPH, Walter
RAY, Andrew
RAY, Jeff
RAY, Ryan
RAYMOND, Don
REARDON, Jerry
REED, Joe
REED, Patrick
REED, Troy
REESE, Olden
REIDLING, Mike
REITZ, Rick
RESNER, Stephen

REYNOLDS, Rick
RICKLE, Chad
RIDDICK, Chris
RIEBESELL, Charles
RIGHTER, Mark
RILES, Jamie
RILEY, Chris
RILEY, Shane
RILEY, Shawn
RINDERLE, Eric
RINEHART, Harold
RISNER, Jeffrey
RISSER, Dan
RITCHIE, Spencer
RITZHAUPT, Sean
RITZLER, Mark
RIVERS, Scott
ROACH, Andre
ROBERDS, Mike
ROBERTS, Andre
ROBERTS, Randy
ROBEY, Jason
ROBINSON, Ron
RODE, Doug
RODENHAUSER, Kevin
RODRIGUEZ, Alex
ROGAN, London
ROGERS, Chuck
ROLAND, Raajih
ROLLINS, James
ROME, Brian
RONCAGLI, Pat
ROSE, Aaron
ROSE, James
ROSS, Bill
ROSS, Charles
ROTAN, Richard
ROTHHAAR, Chris
ROTHHAAR, Mike
ROWE, Tony
RUPPERT, Todd
RUSS, Tim
RUSSELL, Jim
RUSSELL, Kevin
RUSSELL, Tony
RUTZ, Mike
RYAN, Jim
RYMAN, Scott

S
SALEEM, Ron
SALDANA, Jason

SANDERS, Charles
SANTISO, Aaron
SAWYER, Lyle
SBRISSA, Ryan
SCHEY, Doug
SCHICK, Chad
SCHILLING, Dan
SCHLESSMAN, Scott
SCHMITZ, Pete
SCHOCHOW, John
SCHROEDER, Trevor
SCHULTZ, Jason
SCHUMACHER, Paul
SCHUMM, Eric
SCHUTTE, Ed
SCHWERER, Mike
SCOTT, Andy
SCOTT, Brent
SCOTT, Josh
SEARS, Trevin
SEDLACK, Thomas
SEEBURGER, Joe
SELLERS, Tom
SEVERIN, Dennis
SEXTON, Jeff
SEXTON, Robert
SHARISKY, John
SHAW, Chad
SHAW, Jomo
SHEALEY, Lance
SHEETS, Kreg
SHEFFIELD, Alvin
SHELTON, Robert
SHEPHERD, Jerome
SHILLING, Steve
SHILT, Ted
SHIVLEY, Ralph
SHOOP, Nicholas
SHOULTS, Bob
SICLAIR, Mark
SIESEL, Greg
SIGLER, Scott
SILCOTT, Robert
SIMISON, James
SIMON, Marty
SIROTA, Mitchell
SIVIK, Darrell
SIZEMORE, Robert
SKELLIE, Tom
SKLERES, John
SLOAN, Brad
SLOWEK, Jeff

SMIDDY, Jamie
SMILEY, Todd
SMITH, Andy
SMITH, Brandon
SMITH, Charles
SMITH, Chris
SMITH, Craig
SMITH, Doug
SMITH, Duane
SMITH, Eric
SMITH, Jack
SMITH, Keith
SMITH, Kevin
SMITH, Lawrence
SMITH, Mark
SMITH, Mike
SMITH, Milan
SMITH, Rodney
SMITH, Rusty
SMITH, Sam
SMITH, Scott
SMITH, Shawn
SMITH, Tim
SMITH, Todd
SMITH, Tom
SNIPES, James
SNOOK, Timothy
SNYDER, Brad
SNYDER, Brian
SNYDER, Tim
SOMMERS, Dave
SPANGLER, Larry
SPENCER, Joe
SPENCER, Steve
SPENCER, Tracy
SPIKES, Troy
SPRATLEY, Vincent
SPRUNGER, Nate
SPYCHALSKI, Tom
SPYCHALSKI, Craig
STACHECKI, Craig
STANLEY, Todd
STAUNTON, James
STEED, Doug
STEELE, Nick
STEINECKER, Greg
STEINER, Jeff
STENCIL, Bill
STERLING, Matt
STEVENS, Alan
STEWERT, Franklin
STEWERT, Howard

STEWERT, John
STEWERT, Troy
STIERGOFF, Shane
STINE, Rob
STOCKER, Hans
STOCKER, Mike
STOCKSLAGER, William
STOFEL, Jason
STOKES, Eric
STOLTZFUS, Mike
STOLLY, Henry
STOOTS, Jason
STOUGH, Randy
STOUT, Kevin
STOVER, Tim
STRAHM, Doug
STREET, Paul
STRICKLAND, Randy
STRICKLER, Robert
STRUBLE, Erin
STUCKY, Mike
STULTS, Tony
SUDLOW, Joe
SULLIVAN, Jeff
SUTYAK, Bob
SWANEY, Bret

T
TABORN, Richard
TAGLIAPIETRA, Tim
TAVERNEER, Chet
TEAMAN, Andrew
TEMAR, Chris
TESNOW, Dick
TESNOW, Tom
THACKER, Kris
THAMES, Dan
THIEL, Barry
THEISEN, Chris
THEISEN, Derek
THOMAS, Allan
THOMAS, Bill
THOMAS, Willie
THOMPSON, Cameron
THOMPSON, Jon
THOMPSON, Loren
THOMPSON, Ryan
TIPTON, Ron
TOBIAS, Jason
TOOMAN, Duane
TOTH, Greg
TOWNSEND, Roland

TRAINER, Geoff
TRICE, LaRon
TRINA, Paul
TSCHANEN, Matt
TUCKER, George
TUGGLE, Richard
TUMULTY, Joshua
TURK, Ray
TYLER, Durand
TYREE, James

U

ULM, Chad

V

VAIL, Rick
VALLIERES, Paul
VANDENEYNDE, Mike
VAN TRESS, Mark
VARNER, Dan
VELEZ, Raul
VERHOFF, Jeff
VERROCO, Mark
VIGILLE, Curley
VISSOTSKI, Steve
VOGT, Brian
VRANCKEN, Todd

W

WADDLE, Andy
WADDLE, Dan
WAGNER, Doug
WALKER, Balewa
WALKER, Leflore
WALLACE, Derrick
WALSH, Tom
WALTER, Matt
WALTERS, Eric
WARD, Bill
WARD, Jermaine
WARD, John
WARE, Jason
WARNER, Darryn
WARREN, Jim
WARRINGTON, Jacob
WASHINGTON, Brian
WASNICK, Chris
WATKINS, Marty
WATKINS, Terry
WATTS, Mark
WAUFORD, Brian
WEAVER, Wade

WEBB, Heath
WEDDLE, Rick
WEDEMYER, Pete
WEIHRAUCH, Nate
WELSH, Keith
WELLS, Wally
WEST, Darnell
WHITE, Russell
WHITE, Todd
WILLIAMS, Derek
WILLIAMS, Jason
WILLIAMS, Larry
WILLIAMS, Mark
WILLIS, Charles
WILSON, Jim
WILSON, Tim
WILT, Bob
WILT, Jeremy
WIMBERLY, DeMya
WIMES, Michael
WINANS, Jack
WISE, Brian
WISE, Greg
WOJCIECHOWSKI, Ryan
WOJTAS, Jared
WOLFE, Dave
WOLFE, Trevor
WOLFORD, Jeffrey
WOODS, Darryl
WRIGHT, Dana
WRIGHT, Doug
WRIGHT, Mike
WRIGHT, Ron
WUTHRICH, Steve
WYMER, Terry
WYSOCKI, Mark
WYZLIC, Marty

Y

YAJKO, Mark
YANNACEY, Mike
YEAGER, Bill
YEAGER, David
YEAGER, Scott
YODER, Cory
YODER, Dave
YORK, Dan
YOUNG, A.J.
YOUNG, Brian
YOUNG, Chuck
YOUNG, Milt
YOUNG, Patrick

Z

ZAHLER, Scott
ZANDERS, Derrick
ZARBAUGH, Greg
ZEGARELLI, Mike
ZIMAK, Scott
ZIMMER, Doug
ZINSMEISTER, Joe

Works Cited

A

Alter, Larry. "A Master at Winning—Dick Strahm Bows Out as Oilers' Head Coach." *The Courier* 3 June 1999, A1+2.

Alter, Larry. "An Era Ends: Strahm Retiring as UF Coach." *The Courier* 1 June 1999, A1.

Alter, Larry. "4 Oilers All-America First-Team Picks." *The Courier* 18 Jan. 1996, B1.

Alter, Larry. "Ekland, Winter, Reunited." *The Courier* 8 Sept. 1993.

Alter, Larry. "Findlay Shuts Door on Geneva," for the *Pittsburgh Tribune-Review* 7 Dec. 1997, D5.

Alter, Larry. "Georgetown, Findlay Are on a Mission." *The Courier* 20 Nov. 1992, B1+3.

Alter, Larry. "Georgetown Knocks Oilers Out of Playoffs." *The Courier* 6 Dec. 1991, B1+3.

Alter, Larry. "Heitkamp Named All-American." *The Courier* 15 Jan. 1993, B1-2.

Alter, Larry. "Jones Key Figure in Westminster's Attack." *The Courier* 3 Dec. 1993, B1.

Alter, Larry. "Let's Get Ready to 'Rumble on the River.'" *The Courier* 20 Dec. 1997, B1.

Alter, Larry. "'Lightning' Unit Lifts Oilers into Semifinals." *The Courier* 8 Dec. 1997, B1.

Alter, Larry. "Mental Aspect, Kicking Game Important." *The Courier* 17 Dec. 1992, B1.

Alter, Larry. "NAIA Needs Tie-Breaker." *The Courier* 18 Dec. 1995, B1+4.

Alter, Larry. "Next Chapter in Oilers Football Set to Unfold." *The Courier* 4 Sept. 1998, B1.

Alter, Larry. "No. 1-Ranked Oilers Claims NAIA Crown." *The Courier* 22 Dec. 1997, B1+3.

Alter, Larry. "Not Much Changes for Oilers, Titans." *The Courier* 18 Nov. 1994, B1.

Alter, Larry. "Oilers, Benedictine Mirror Each Other." *The Courier* 11 Dec. 1992, B1.

Alter, Larry. "Oilers Defeat Northmen, 21-6." *The Courier* 9 Nov. 1992, B1.

Alter, Larry. "Oilers' Defense Shuts Down Westminster." *The Courier,* 25 Nov. 1991, B1.

Alter, Larry. "Oilers, Doane on a Mission." *The Courier* 12 Dec. 1997, B1.

Alter, Larry. "Oilers Drill Geneva Using Power Game." *The Courier* 25 Nov. 1996, B1.

Alter, Larry. "Oilers Face Huge Challenge." *The Courier* 15 Dec. 1995, B1+3.

Alter, Larry. "Oilers, Geneva Will Be Hotly Contested Game." *The Courier* 5 Dec. 1997, B1.

Alter, Larry. "Oilers Hope to Strike Quick Against Geneva." *The Courier* 21 Nov. 1996, B1.

Alter, Larry. "Oilers Knock off Malone in NAIA Playoffs." *The Courier* 4 Dec. 1995, B1-2.

Alter, Larry. "Oilers Open NCAA Play with Win over Tartars." *The Courier* 14 Sept. 1998, B1+3.

Alter, Larry. "Oilers Post 7th Straight Win." *The Courier* 13 Nov. 1995, B1.

Alter, Larry. "Oilers Rally Past PLU 21-14 in NAIA Playoffs." *The Courier* 20 Nov. 1995, B1-4.

Alter, Larry. "Oilers Roll, 70-8." *The Courier* 3 Nov. 1997, B1.

Alter, Larry. "Oilers Rout Georgetown, Roll into Quarterfinals." *The Courier* 23 Nov. 1992, B1+3.

Alter, Larry. "Oilers Rout Westminster, 40-0." *The Courier* 24 Nov. 1997, B1.

Alter, Larry. "Oilers, Titans in Another Battle." *The Courier* 21 Nov. 1997

Alter, Larry. "Oilers Topple Tiffin, 28-14." *The Courier,* 21 Nov. 1993, B1+3.

Alter, Larry. "Oilers, Westminster Eye Another NAIA Showdown" *The Courier* 4 Dec. 1992, B1.

Alter, Larry. "'One Big Play': What Dick Strahm Wanted, He Got." *The Courier* 22 Dec. 1997, A1+6.

Alter, Larry. Personal interview. 15 Oct. 2007.

Alter, Larry. "PLU's 'Golden Arm' To Test Oilers' No. 1 Defense." *The Courier* 17 Nov. 1995, B1+3.

Alter, Larry. "'Rumble on the River' Is Dream Matchup." *The Courier* 19 Dec. 1997, B1.

Alter, Larry. "Showdown Ends in 21-21 Deadlock." *The Courier* 17 Dec. 1995, B1+4.

Alter, Larry. "63-13 Win Sends Oilers to NAIA Championship." *The Courier* 11 Dec. 1995, B1-2.

Alter, Larry. "Strahm Got to Make 21 New Friends." *The Courier* 17 Aug. 2004, B-1.

Alter, Larry. "Strahm Honored by Peers." *The Courier* 12 Jan. 1999, B-1-2.

Alter, Larry. "Strahm's Playoff Philosophy Fairly Simple." *The Courier* 8 Dec. 1995, B1.

Alter, Larry. "Strahm: 'We Were What You Call Hungry.'" *The Courier* 15 Nov. 1976, B-1.

Alter, Larry. "Tiffin, Oilers to Begin NAIA Playoff Quest." *The Courier* 19 Nov. 1993, B1.

Alter, Larry. "UF Can Win 3rd Crown." *The Courier* 13 Dec. 1995, B1.

Alter, Larry. "UF Football Classic Has Storybook Ending." *The Courier* 15 Dec. 1997, A1.

Alter, Larry. "UF Football Team Roars into Playoffs." *The Courier* 16 Nov. 1992, B1.

Alter, Larry. "UF, Malone College Almost Mirror Images." *The Courier* 24 Nov. 1995, B1-2.

Alter, Larry. "UF Oilers Advance to NAIA Championship." *The Courier* 14 Dec. 1992, B1+5.

Alter, Larry. "UF Oilers Advance to NAIA Semifinals." *The Courier* 7 Dec. 1992, B1+4.

Alter, Larry. "UF Oilers Considered 'Underdogs' in NAIA Final." *The Courier* 19 Dec. 1992, B1.

Alter, Larry. "UF Oilers Knock Off Ferris State." *The Courier* 21 Sept. 1998, B1+3.

Alter, Larry. "UF Oilers, Westminster in Rematch." *The Courier* 1 Dec. 1993, B1.

Alter, Larry. "UF Oilers Win NAIA National Title." *The Courier* 21 Dec. 1992, B1+4.

Alter, Larry. "UF's Doak Has Come All the Way Back." *The Courier* 18 Sept. 1998, B1.

Alter, Larry. "UF's Sprunger Named NAIA Offensive Player of the Week." *The Courier* 13 Oct. 1992, B1.

Alter, Larry. "UF Takes 27-Game Streak into Opener." *The Courier* 11 Sept. 1998, B1-2.

Alter, Larry. "Unbeaten Oilers Thump Another Ranked Team." *The Courier* 12 Oct. 1992, B1-2.

Alter, Larry. "Veteran Squad Returns for Strahm's Oilers." *The Courier* 14 Aug. 1992, B2.

Alter, Larry. "Weihrauch Will Start in Championship Tilt." *The Courier* 16 Dec. 1995, B1+5.

Alter, Larry. "Westminster Knocks Oilers from Playoffs." *The Courier* 21 Nov. 1994, B1-2.

Alter, Larry. "Westminster Sloshes Past Findlay Oilers, 24-0." *The Courier* 21 Nov. 1994, B1-2.

Alter, Larry. "Wright Selected for Senior Bowl." *The Courier* 12 Jan. 1987, A1.

Angelo, Tony. "Reserve Wins 9th, Rout Withrow with Ease, 75-6." *Warren Chronicle Tribune* Nov. 1968.

Angelo, Tony. "Western Reserve Starts Countdown for Football." *Warren Tribune Chronicle* Aug. 1968.

Arnold, Nate. Personal interview. 28 June 2008.

Aukerman, Craig. Personal interview. 28 June 2008.

Aurora 1967. Eds. Nancy Andrews, Deanna Foreman, Barbara Herron. 1st ed. Warren, Ohio: Inter-Collegiate Press Co.

Aurora 1968. Ed. Cheri Peck. 2nd ed. Warren, Ohio: Inter-Collegiate Press Co.

Aurora 1969. Eds. Janet Tricker and Kathi Hostert. 3rd ed. Warren, Ohio: Inter-Collegiate Press Co.

Aurora 1970. Eds. Kathi Hostert and Laurie Pipenur. 4th ed. Warren, Ohio: Inter-Collegiate Press Co.

B

"Battle All the Way for Lakota and Loop Crown." *Fostoria Review Times* 2 Nov. 1960.

"Bears Drop Final Football Contest to Napoleon: Take Third in League." *Bryan Times* 3 Nov. 1962, sec. 1:1+.

Beck, Steve. "Liberty Center Tigers Hand Napoleon First NWOAL Loss of Season, 12-8." *Bryan Times* 16 Oct. 1965, sec. 1:1+.

Beckman, Tim. Personal interview. 23 Feb. 2008.

Beekman, Jerome. Personal interview. 24 Feb. 2008.

"Biography of Dr. Cosgrove." www.clevelandclinic.org.

Blakney, Ray. "Findlay vs. Williamette [*sic*]." *The Courier: Savannah, Tennessee* 18 Dec. 1997, 1D+6.

Bolden, Nelson. Personal interview. 15 Oct. 2007.

Brennan, Christine. "Ealey's 35-game win streak at QB unforgettable." *Buckeye Buzz* 10 Jan. 2003.

"'Brrrrr' Frosty Fingered Bruins Thaw Out; Chill Swanton Bulldogs." *Bryan Times* 26 Oct. 1962.

C

Cassidy, Kevin. Personal interview. 11 March 2007.

"Chamber of Commerce in Ypsilanti, Michigan." www.ypsilantichamber.org.

Chambliss, Gordon. Personal interview. 12 Sept. 2007.

"Chuck Ealey Speaks." www.chuckealeyspeaks.

Cicak, Mike. Personal interview. 25 June 2008.

"CNN-Cold War." www.cnn.com

"College Football Hall of Fame Enshrinement." *South Bend Tribune* 13 Aug. 2004, SS5.

"College Hall of Fame to Induct Five Coaches in 2004." *The Extra Point* May/June 2004, 5+24.

"College Hall of Fame: Tour the Hall." National Football Foundation http://www.collegefootball.org.

"Coach Strahm in Hall of Fame." *The Blade, Toledo Ohio.* 12 May 2004, 2.

Cummins, Mike. "Bears Next–Forget Nap Win, Bryan Looms Ahead." *Defiance Crescent News* 7 Oct. 1964, sec. 1:1+.

Cummins, Mike. "Bears Nudge 'Dogs in Heart Stopper." *Defiance Crescent News* 10 Oct. 1964, sec. 1:1+.

D

Daren, David. "Strahm's Can-Do Attitude Overcomes Obstacles." *NAIA News*, Vol. 48, No. 7, 8.

"Darrell Green.com" http://www.darrellgreen.com.

"Dedication, Richard Strahm." *National Football Foundation Wistert Chapter Hall of Fame Program* 2 March 1998.

"Defibrillate." Answers.com http://www.answers.com.

Dennison, Nathan. "Commemorative Cans Give Strahm a Coke and a Smile." *The Courier* 16 Sept. 1999, A1-2.

Dennison, Nathan J. "Strahm's Influence Touched Many Lives." *The Courier* 3 June 1999.

DePauw University Intercollegiate Athletics. www.depauw.edu.

"Dick Strahm–Beating the Odds." *Sidelines Magazine* Spring, 1998: 12.

Diehl, Bob. "Bryan Bears Blank 'Pelier." *Bryan Times* 11 Oct. 1963.

Diehl, Bob. "Bryan-Defiance Grid Scrap, Prestige Packed Struggle!" *Bryan Times* 5 Oct. 1963.

Diehl, Bob. "Golden Bears Sprint to Big Victory Over Archbold 22-8." *Bryan Times* 4 Oct. 1963.

Division II 23rd Annual Football Championship-University of Findlay Oilers vs. Linfield College Wildcats Program, 19 Dec. 1992.

Dwiggins, Margaret. "Former Coach Takes Heart Health Seriously." *The Courier* 18 Jan. 2007.

E

Ealey, Chuck. Personal interview. 11 Aug. 2007.

Ebersole, Dave. Phone interview. 30 June 2007.

Education in Motion. The University of Findlay 2007-08.

Egbert, Dave. "Champion Oilers Make Queen Ginger Proud." *The Courier*, 10 December 1979, 1.

E-mail from Mark Kelly, 10 July 2007. kellyawards@cityofbryan.net.

E-mail from Paul Helgren. 1 Aug. 2007. PHelgre@UTNet.UToledo.Edu.

F

Fentress, Aaron. "NAIA Champions, Findlay Overpowers Linfield in Final." *The Blade: Toledo, Ohio* 20 Dec. 1992, 1.

Fernandez, Gene. Personal interview. 15 Oct. 2007.

Findlay College 1984 Media Guide, ed. G. Fred Graf.

Findlay College Oilers 1986 Football Media Guide, ed. Gail Billet.

Findlay Football 1998 Media Guide, eds. David Faiella and Troy Berry.

"Findlay National Champs Again." *The Blade: Toledo, Ohio,* E1-2.

Findlay 1989 Football Action Guide, eds. David Faiella and Troy Berry.

Findlay 1995 Football Guide, eds. David Faiella and Troy Berry.

Findlay 1991 Football Guide, ed. David Faiella and contributors Steve Rothsatz and Jessica Morrow.

Findlay 1997 Football Guide, eds. David Faiella and Troy Berry.

Findlay 1996 Football Guide, eds. David Faiella and Troy Berry.

Findlay 1993 Football Guide, ed. David Faiella and contributor Mike Junga.

Findlay 1992 Football Guide, ed. David Faiella and contributors Joe Thomas and Chris Walker.

Findlay vs. Geneva Souvenir Program, 20 Sept. 1986.

Findlay vs. Hamburg Blue Devils Program, 11 Sept. 1993.

Findlay vs. Wilmington Souvenir Program, 9 Nov. 1985.

"Former WC Football Coach Retires after 44 Years." Wilmington College 2004 http://www.wilmington.edu.

Fry, Hayden. Personal interview. 22 March 2007.

Fry, H. and G. Wine. *Hayden Fry: A High Porch Picnic.* Champaign, Illinois: Sports Publication, 1999.

Fryman, John. "Strahm Inducted into Hall of Fame. *Bryan Times* 3 June 2004, 14-15.

G

Gibson, Pat. Personal interview. 15 Oct. 2007.

Gilman, Andrew. "Coach Keeps Winning, on and off the Field." *The Jackson Sun*, 3C.

Gilman, Andrew. "Findlay Brings Experience." *The Jackson Sun*, 2C.

"'Go, Go' Gotshall Gallops to Four TD's as Bruins Bump Locomotives." *Bryan Times* 20 Oct. 1962.

Grant, Denise. "Pandora's Sprunger says 1992 UF Season Was 'All Good.'" *The Pandora Times* 7 Jan. 1993, 1.

Glon, Tim. "Findlay's Defense Faces Challenge in Playoff Opener." *The Lima News* 1991, B1.

Gray, Jerome. Personal interview. 15 Oct. 2007.

Grogan, Steve. Personal interview. 12 Sept. 2007.

Guerra, Dennis. Personal interview. 15 Oct. 2007.

H

Hackenberg, Dave. "A Well-Kept Secret." *The Blade: Toledo, Ohio* 22 Oct. 1979.

Hackenberg, Dave. "Beard's Goals: 'Same as Oilers'." *The Blade: Toledo, Ohio* 7 Dec. 1979.

Hackenberg, Dave. "Bolden Era Enters Final Week." *The Blade: Toledo, Ohio,* 10 Nov. 1980.

Hackenberg, Dave. "Coach Left His Mark on UT Football." *Toledo Blade,* 16 Oct. 2005.

Hackenberg, Dave. "Findlay Cast Returns for Football Encore." *The Blade: Toledo, Ohio,* 26 August 1979 FB 14.

Hackenberg, Dave. "Findlay Cuffs 'Jackets, 21-7, Clinches NAIA Playoff Berth." *The Blade: Toledo, Ohio* 11 Nov. 1979.

Hackenberg, Dave. "Findlay Playoff Demise False." *The Blade: Toledo, Ohio* 8 Nov. 1979.

Hackenberg, Dave. "Findlay Rips Northwestern on Fast Start." *The Blade: Toledo, Ohio* 9 Dec. 1979.

Hackenberg, Dave. "Findlay Routs Jamestown in NAIA Playoff." *The Blade: Toledo, Ohio* 18 Nov. 1979, sec. D8.

Hackenberg, Dave. "Findlay Stops Lutes, 9-0." *The Blade: Toledo, Ohio* 2 Dec. 1979.

Hackenberg, Dave. "Findlay to Host Unbeaten Team in Playoff." *The Blade: Toledo, Ohio* 12 Nov. 1979.

Hackenberg, Dave. "Funk Plants Roots as Star Tackle for Findlay." *The Blade: Toledo, Ohio* 20 Sept. 1979, sec. D: 4.

Hackenberg, Dave. "Gibson Vital Cog in Findlay Success." *The Blade: Toledo, Ohio* 14 Nov. 1979.

Hackenberg, Dave. "Nationally-Ranked Oilers Tackle Bluffton." *The Blade: Toledo, Ohio* 15 Sept. 1979.

Hackenberg, Dave. "Oiler Flanks Well Protected." *The Blade: Toledo, Ohio* 29 Nov. 1979.

Hackenberg, Dave. "Oilers Have Superfan in McMahon." *The Blade: Toledo, Ohio* 28 Nov. 1979.

Hackenberg, Dave. "Strahm Frustrated in Bid to Advance." *The Blade: Toledo, Ohio* 10 Aug. 1980.

Hackenberg, Dave. "Strahm on the Job after Heart Surgery." *The Blade: Toledo, Ohio* Aug. 1987, 20.

Hackenberg, Dave. "Yep, He's Gonna Coach." *The Blade: Toledo, Ohio* 23 Aug. 1998, C1-2.

Hahn, John. "Clark One of Many Heroes." *The Lima News* 20 Dec. 1992, C1+5.

Hahn, John. "Findlay Captures National Title." *The Lima News* 20 Dec. 1992, C1.

Hankinson, Charlene J. "Kenneth Zirkle, Two Decades of Growth." *Findlay Magazine,* Vol. 91, No. 1: 4-8.

Hannen, John. "Oilers Strike It Rich with Strahm." *The Blade: Toledo, Ohio* 9 Dec. 1979.

Hanneman, Dave. "Midwest Versus West Coast in NAIA Semifinals." *The Courier* 12 Dec. 1996, B1.

Hanneman, Dave. "Oilers, Titans Renew NAIA Playoff Rivalry." *The Courier* 5 Dec. 1996, B1.

Hanneman, Dave. "Strahm Headed for Hall of Fame." *The Courier* 12 May 2004, A-1 + A-5.

Hanson, Tom. Personal interview. 28 June 2008.

Hatfield, Rick. Personal interview. 15 Oct. 2007.

Heiman, Mark. "Findlay Oilers Wear Down Hamburg Blue Devils, 28-7." *The Courier* 11 Sept. 1993, B1+4.

Heiman, Mark. "Football Maturing in Germany." *The Courier* 10 Sept. 1993, B1.

Henry, Tom. "Findlay U's Title Drive Good Therapy for Coach." *The Blade: Toledo, Ohio* 18 Dec. 1997, News Section 2, 25-26.

Hiller, Sue and Jimmy Stanton. "Beating the Odds." *The Extra Point* March/April 1998.

Hinkson, Gary. Personal interview. 31 July 2007.

Homan, Jim. "Findlay Preps for Playoffs with Rout." *The Lima News,* 1992.

Holmberg, Nelson P. "Linfield Falls in Title Game." *The Columbian* 20 Dec. 1992, D1.

Horn, Jamie. Personal interview. 23 Feb. 2008.

Houdeshell, Claire. Personal interview. 19 May 2007.

Houdeshell, Jim. Personal interview. 15 Oct. 2007.

Huffman, Nate. "Sprunger Plays Big Role in 21-6 win." *The Pulse* 11 Nov. 1992, 4.

Hurley, Bo. Personal interview. 2 July 2008.

J

Jaquillard, Chris. Personal interview. 13 March 2007.

Junga, Steve. "Jaquillard Scores Clincher; Findlay Reaches Title Game." *The Blade: Toledo, Ohio* 14 Dec. 1997, C1+4.

K

Kagy, Gina. Personal interview. 15 April 2007.

Kelley, Steve. "Central, Findlay left thinking 'tie' should be four-letter word." *The Seattle Times* 17 Dec. 1995, D4.

Killgallon, Larry. Personal interview. 23 June 2007.

L

Langham, Jim. "Work Ethic Has Been a Key for Nate Sprunger." *The Defiance Crescent-News.*

"Late Explosion Stuns Findlay." *The Blade: Toledo, Ohio* 4 Nov. 1979.

Lauterbur, Frank X. Personal interview. 11 Aug. 2007.

Lee, Bill. Personal interview. 21 July 2007.

Lenhart, Chris. "UF Oilers Dominate District 22 Selections." *The Courier* 5 Dec. 1991, B1.

Lesar, Al. "Coach Proves Goals Are Crucial in Any Battle." *South Bend Tribune* 14 Aug. 2004, A1 + A10.

Life Issues Institute. "More Hope for Premies." http://www.lifeissues.org.

Long, Aaron Q. "UF Supporters Greet National Champs." *The Courier* 21 Dec. 1992, A1+14.

M

Macy, Bret. Personal interview. 28 June 2008.

Maag, Dennis. Personal interview. 15 Oct. 2007.

McIntosh, Jim. Personal interview. 15 Oct. 2007.

McLain, Mike. "Football Was West Side Pride, Glory." *Warren Tribune Chronicle* 12 June 1990, A1+.

McLain, Mike. "Raiders Remembered, Reserve's Best Unite to Discuss Good Old Times." *Warren Tribune Chronicle* 5 May 2007, 1A+.

McLaughlin, Scott. Personal interview. 2 May 2008.

Memorial Bergen-Belsen, an Overview, Gedenkstatle Bergen-Belsen.

Miami vs. Toledo, Official Program, 31 Oct. 1970.

Mohr, Steve. Personal interview. 11 March 2007.

Montgomery, John. "Gambles Pay Off as Oilers Win, 26-25." *The Courier* 15 Dec. 1997, B1.

Moorefield, Joe. Personal interview. 24 Feb. 2008. "MSFA Highlights." 27 Oct. 1997.

Murphy, Jack. Personal interview. 11 Aug. 2007.

N

NAIA Rawlings-NAIA Hall of Fame Dinner Program, 10 Jan. 1999.

Newman, Murray. "Raiders Grab 4th at Austintown, 34-0." *Warren Tribune Chronicle* Oct. 1969.

Newman, Murray. "Western Reserve Opens Grid Season Saturday." *Warren Tribune Chronicle* Aug. 1969.

1974 KSU Football Official Program, 14 Sept. 1974.

1964 Pro Football Encyclopedia, ed. B.R. Ampolish. New York: Reese Publishing, 1964.

Nineteenth Annual Toledo Athletic League Hall of Fame Banquet Program, 6 Nov. 2000.

Nolen, John. "Findlay Players, Coach Say Folks Underestimated Them." *The Sunday Oregonian* 20 Dec. 1992, E9.

Novak, Joe. Personal interview. 21 July 2007.

O

Ohio Historical Society. *University of Findlay.* http://www.ohiohistorycentral. org.

"Ohio State Assistant Worked with Florida's Meyer at Bowling Green." *The Tiffin Advertiser-Tribune* 15 Dec. 2006, 3B.

"Oilers Dominate All-MSFA Picks." *The Courier* 29 Nov. 1995, B1.

"Oilers Trim Taylor, 29-7, Near Playoffs." *The Blade: Toledo, Ohio* 28 Oct. 1979.

Olmstead, Dick. "Harding and Reserve Await Home Battles." *Warren Tribune Chronicle* Aug. 1969.

Olmstead, Dick. "Niles Shatters Western Reserve's Record, 23-14." *Warren Tribune Chronicle Oct. 1969.*

Olmstead, Dick. "Raiders Blank Third Foe: Burch Scores 2." *Warren Tribune Chronicle* Sept. 1969.

Olmstead, Dick. "Raiders Grab 7th, 30-6, Over Hoban." *Warren Tribune Chronicle* Oct. 1969.

Olmstead, Dick. "Raiders Roar 38-0, Over Ashtabula Rival." *Warren Tribune Chronicle* Sept. 1969

Olmstead, Dick. "Rambling Raiders Twist Tigers' Tails." *Warren Tribune Chronicle* Sept. 1968.

Olmstead, Dick. "Rampaging Raiders Avenge 1967 Defeat." *Warren Tribune Chronicle* Oct. 1968.

Olmstead, Dick. "Raiders Set Records, Rout Ashtabula, 56-0." *Warren Tribune Chronicle* 8 Sept. 1968.

Olmstead, Dick. "Raiders Seek Second Win Here Saturday." *Warren Tribune Chronicle* 13 Sept. 1968.

Olmstead, Dick. "Western Reserve Halted at Canton McKinley." *Warren Tribune Chronicle* Oct. 1968.

Olmstead, Dick. "Western Reserve Tests Big Panthers." *Warren Tribune Chronicle* Aug. 1968.

Olmstead, Dick. "Western Reserve to Gun for 7th Win at Niles." *Warren Tribune Chronicle* Oct. 1968.

Olmstead, Dick. "Wintersville Here for Saturday Battle." *Warren Tribune Chronicle* 10 Oct. 1969.

"ONU Surprises Findlay with Tie." *The Blade: Toledo, Ohio* 8 Nov. 1979.

P

Pees, Dean. Personal interview. 8 Dec. 2007.

Phillips, James. "Instant Replay, Titans Ousted from Playoffs by Findlay Again." *The Herald: Sharon, Pennsylvania* 6 Dec. 1992, B1-2.

"Pinkel voted tops in Ohio." *The Blade: Toledo, Ohio* 29 Jan. 1996, 17.

Pisanelli, Fred. Personal interview. 25 July 2007.

"Players to Watch." *The Courier: Savannah, Tennessee* 18 Dec. 1997, 1D.

Puskas, Ed. "Strahm Paying Visit to Warren Area." *Warren Tribune Chronicle* 29 April 2007, 1D+.

Putnam, Daniel. *A History of the Michigan State Normal School (Now Normal College) at Ypsilanti, Michigan, 1849-1899.* Ypsilanti, Mich. [The Sharf Tag, Label, and Box Co.], 1899.

R

Ramsey, Duane. "Toledo Making Habit of T-Bowl." *The Collegian* 28 Dec. 1971.

Ramseyer, Bill. Personal interview. 1 Dec. 2007.

"Remembering Softball's Flame-Throwing King." from *All Things Considered,* National Public Radio, www.npr.org.

Richmond, Reed. "Findlay Crushes Hanover to Win Share of Conference Title." *Sports* 15 Nov. 1976, 1-2.

Roach, Dean. "Lakota Coaches Face Problems." *Daily Sentinel Tribune* Sept. 1960.

Roberts, Cliff. Personal interview. 21 July 2007.

S

Saneda, Frank. Personal interview. 30 June 2007.

Sbrissa, Ryan. Personal interview. 23 Feb. 2008.

Schooley, Duane. "Bears Bounce Back to Drop Van Wert, 38-0, Delta Next." *Bryan Times* 18 Sept. 1965.

Schooley, Duane. "Bears Derail Locos." *Bryan Times* 24 Oct. 1964, sec. 1: 1+.

Schooley, Duane. "Bruins Keep in League Race By Murdering Locos, 70-0." *Bryan Times* 23 Oct. 1965, sec. 1:1+.

Schooley, Duane. "Bears Hang On For Victory Over Archbold Blue Streaks.' *Bryan Times* 16 Oct. 1965, sec. 1: 1+.

Schooley, Duane. "Bruins Keep in League Race By Murdering Locos, 70-0." *Bryan Times* 23 Oct. 1965, sec. 1:1+.

Schooley, Duane. "Defense Stars as Bears Grab Fourth Straight Win, 30-14." *Bryan Times* 9 Oct. 1965, sec. 1: 1+.

Schooley, Duane. "Ebersole Scores 3 TDs as Bryan Rally Tops Indians." *Bryan Times* 2 Oct. 1965, sec. 1: 1+.

Schooley, Duane. "Findlay Defense Spurs 7-0 Victory Over St. Ambrose." *The Blade: Toledo, Ohio* 1 Dec. 1985.

Schooley, Duane. "Golden Bears Best Swanton 28-0 for First League Win." *Bryan Times* 12 Sept. 1964, sec. 1: 1+.

Schooley, Duane. "Golden Bears Bounce Back, Rip Delta Panthers, 42-12." *Bryan Times* 26 Sept. 1964, sec. 1: 1+.

Schooley, Duane. "Golden Bears Rip Wauseon Indians 30-0, Defense Stars." *Bryan Times* 3 Oct. 1964, sec. 1: 1+.

Schooley, Duane. "Killgallon, Ebersole Star as Bruins Garner League Win." *Bryan Times* 25 Sept. 1965, sec. 1: 1+.

Schooley, Duane. Personal interview. 30 June 2007.

Schooley, Duane. "Schooley's Scribblings." *Bryan Times* 16 Nov. 1965.

Schooley, Duane. "Tigers Grab Title Share with 24-14 Victory Over Bryan." *Bryan Times* 6 Nov. 1965, sec. 1: 1+.

Schooley,Duane. "Van Wert Jinx Keeps Grip on Bruins; VW Wins 46-20." *Bryan Times* 19 Sept. 1964, sec. 1: 1+.

Schooley, Duane. "Westhoven Leads Napoleon to 34-16 Win Over Bruins." *Bryan Times* 11 Sept. 1965, sec. 1: 1+.

Schudel, Matt. "Eddie Feigner, 81, Unbeatable Softball Pitcher." *The Washington Post* 12 Feb. 2007.

Shanahan, Hal. "Montpelier Bounces Back into Contention–Bryan Big Test for Locomotives." *The Blade: Toledo, Ohio* 16 Oct. 1962.

Shanahan, Hal. "Strahm Strums Happy Tune." *The Blade: Toledo, Ohio* 30 Oct. 1964.

Shanahan, Hal. "Stubborn Bears Defense Keeps Delta in Check." *The Blade: Toledo, Ohio* 22 Sept. 1962.

Simrel, Dan. Personal interview. 6 Aug. 2007.

Smiddy, Jamie. Personal interview. 2 July 2008.

Snyder, Gary. "The Morning After—Taking Things for Granted." *Toledo Times.*

Souply, Ron. Personal interview. 6 Oct. 2007.

Stall, Julie. Personal interview. 26 June 2008.

"Steve Grogan—Official New England Patriot Biography." www.patriots.com.

Stewert, Dottie. "Life Is a Game, but Football Is Serious." *Hot Springs Village Voice* 1 Feb. 2006.

Strahm, Dale. Personal interview. 22 March 2007.

Strahm, Doug. Personal interview. 9 Dec. 2007.

Strahm, Ginger. Personal interview. 10 March 2007.

"Strahm Inducted." *The Courier* 16 Aug. 2004.

"Strahm Named to College Hall of Fame." *For Your Information* 13 Aug. 2004, 1.

Strahm, Steve. Personal interview. 25 Feb. 2008.

"Strahm to Be Honored at UF Game." *The Courier* 9 Sept. 2004, B2.

Swearingen, Jim. "Defeated Niles Hopes to Spoil Raider Spree." *Warren Tribune Chronicle* Oct. 1969.

T

Tagliapietra, Tim. Personal interview. 15 Oct. 2007.

Taylor, Jim. "Hinkson, a Leader of Unbeaten Rockets." *The Blade: Toledo, Ohio* 27 Dec. 1971, 34.

Taylor, Jim. "It's 3 of a Kind for All-Winning TU." *The Blade: Toledo, Ohio* 29 Dec. 1971, 22.

Taylor, Jim. "One Man's Opinion—Tangerine Tie Best for MAC." *The Blade: Toledo, Ohio* 28 Dec. 1971, 29.

Taylor, Jim. "Spiders Likely to Be Trapped in Rocket Web." *The Blade: Toledo, Ohio* 28 Dec. 1971, 29.

Taylor, Jim. "Strahm Upholds TU Defense." *The Blade: Toledo, Ohio* 19 Nov. 1970.

"The Human Side of Dick Strahm." *Rocket Football Magazine* 1971, 20.

The National Football Foundation and College Hall of Fame 2004 Commemorative Program. 13-14 Aug. 2004.

"The Prostate-Specific Antigen (PSA) Test: Questions and Answers." *National Cancer Institute* www.cancer.gov.

The 1973 Kansas State Football Brochure, ed. The Sports Information Office, Kansas State University, Manhattan, Kansas.

The 1969, 1970, 1971 Unbeatable Rockets, A Blade Tribute, December 1971.

The University of Findlay vs. St. Xavier Souvenir Program, 16, Oct. 1993.

The University of Findlay vs. Trinity College, 10 Sept. 1994.

The University of Findlay vs. Westminster College, 16 Sept. 1995.

The University of Findlay vs. Westminster, 18 Sept. 1993.

"The University of Findlay." www.findlay.edu.

The University of Findlay Football Media Guide, The Tradition Continues, ed. David Buck, 2005.

"The University of Findlay—125th Anniversary—History." http://www.findlay.edu.

Timamus, Eddie. "Fry, LeVias to enter Hall of Fame." *USA Today* 13 Aug. 2004, 14c.

"Timeline." http://xroards.virginia.edu.

"Trinity University Welcome." www.trinity.edu.

Tooman, Duane. Personal interview. 15 Oct. 2002.

Trina, Paul Jr. Personal interview. 1 Dec. 2007.

Trina, Paul Sr. Personal interview. 21 July 2007.

"Trina Top Offensive Player in Findlay Rout." *The Blade: Toledo, Ohio* 9 Dec. 1979.

"TU Grid Coach Strahm to Join Kansas State." *The Blade: Toledo, Ohio* 16 Jan. 1973.

U

"UF's Strahm NAIA Coach of the Year." *The Courier* 4 Jan. 1993, B1.

V

Villanova vs. Toledo, Official Program, 18 Sept. 1971.

W

Walker, Teresa. "Carroll Stadium Will Have Donnell Feeling." *The Courier* 20 Dec. 1997, B1.

Weihrauch, Nate. Personal interview. 1 July 2008.

"Welcome to Bryan, at the Top of Ohio." http://www.cityofbryan.com.

"Welcome to the City of Findlay." www.ci.findlay.oh.us.

"Welcome to Manhattan!" www.ci.manhattan.ks.us.

"Welcome to the Village of Bellaire!" www.bellairemichigan.com.

"Western Reserve Awaits Tough Grid Campaign." *Warren Tribune Chronicle* August 1968.

Wheeler, Ken. "Linfield, Findlay Set for Showdown." *The Oregonian* 19 Dec. 1992, E1-2.

Wheeler, Ken. "Playing in the Shadows." *The Oregonian* 19 Dec. 1992, D1+9.

Wilmington College. "Former WC Football Coach Retires after 44 Years." 2003 www.wilmngton.edu.

Wirick, Bill. Personal interview. 12 June 2007.

Wintle, Walter D. "You Can If You Think You Can." *Poems That Live Forever*, comp. Hazel Felleman. USA: Doubleday, 1965, 310.

Wolfrum, Tim. "Strahm Fits Right in with College Greats." *The Lima News* 16, Aug. 2004, D1.

Wright, Branson. "Heitkamp, Oilers Await Major Test in Linfield." *The Lima News* 18 Dec. 1992, B1+4.

Z

Zedlitz, Bob. Personal interview. 20 May 2007.

Zirkle, Kenneth. Personal interview. 23 Feb. 2008.